INVITATIONS

INVITATIONS

Changing as Teachers and Learners K-12

Regie Routman

HEINEMANN
Portsmouth, NH

Heinemann
A division of Reed Elsevier Inc.
361 Hanover Street
Portsmouth, NH 03801-3912
Offices and agents throughout the world

Library of Congress Cataloging-in-Publication Data
Routman, Regie.
    Invitations : changing as teachers and learners, K–12 / Regie
Routman. — Updated, expanded, and rev. resources and Blue pages.
        p.   cm.
    Contains The blue pages by the same author.
    Includes bibliographical references and index.
    ISBN 0-435-08837-8 (alk. paper) : $38.50. — ISBN 0-435-08836-X
(pbk. : alk. paper) : $28.50
    1. Reading—United States—Language experience approach.
I. Routman, Regie.   Blue pages.   II. Title.
LB1050.35.R68 1994
372.4′1—dc20   94-29709
                                                         CIP

Editor: Toby Gordon
Production: Renee Le Verrier and Melissa L. Inglis
Cover design: Jenny Jensen Greenleaf
Cover photo by Kevin G. Reeves:
        WEB reading program: daily book check and independent reading
        in Joan Servis' grade 4 class, January 1991.

Printed in the United States of America on acid free paper
99 98 97 96 95 94 HP 1 2 3 4 5 6 7 8 9

For Frank, Elizabeth, and Peter

Contents

Permissions

We are grateful to the publishers and individuals below for granting permission to reprint material from previously published works.

Page 13: Cambourne's Model of Learning. From *The Whole Story: Natural Learning and the Acquisition of Literacy in the Classroom* by Brian Cambourne. Copyright 1988, Ashton Scholastic Ltd., Auckland, New Zealand. Reprinted by permission.

Page 25: Response to "Boycott the Basals." Reprinted by permission of Richard C. Owen, Publishers, 135 Katonah Ave., Katonah, NY 10503.

Page 64: Jelly on the Plate. From "Jelly on the Plate." Modern Curriculum Press. Reprinted by permission.

Page 142: From *Jamaica's Find* by Juanita Havill. Text copyright © 1986 by Juanita Havill. Illustrations copyright © 1986 by Anne Sibley O'Brien. Reprinted by permission of Houghton Mifflin Co.

Page 254: "Am I Becoming a Good Speller?" Reprinted by permission of R. D. Walshe, for the Primary English Teaching Association, Sydney, Australia.

Page 282: From *Zoo Books 2: Alligators and Crocodiles*; copyright 1986 by Wildlife Education Ltd., 930 West Washington St., San Diego, CA 92103. Reprinted by permission of the publisher.

Page 306: "Evaluation Data Gathering Profile." Adapted from a form developed by R. Anthony, T. Johnson, N. Mickelson, and A. Preece. Reprinted by permission.

Page 322: "Concepts About Print." Adapted from "Concepts of Print" test in *The Early Detection of Reading Difficulties*, 3rd ed., by Marie M. Clay. Copyright 1985. Heinemann, 361 Hanover St., Portsmouth, NH 03801. Reprinted by permission.

Page 113b: From "Champions by Rebel Williams." Reprinted by permission of The Wright Group, 18916 N. Creek Parkway, Suite 107, Bothell, WA 98011.

Page 186b: *Amos & Boris* Teacher's Guide. Reprinted by permission of H. P. Kopplemann, Inc., 140 Van Block Ave., Hartford, CT 06141–0145.

Page 187b: *Journey to Topaz* Teacher's Guide. Reprinted by permission of H. P. Kopplemann, Inc., 140 Van Block Ave., Hartford, CT 06141–0145.

Page 198b: Getting Parents Involved Letter. From the Fall 1988 newsletter of the Whole Language Teachers Association, 16 Concord Rd., Sudbury, MA 01776. Reprinted by permission.

Page 204b: Parents as Allies in Children's Education. Reprinted by permission of Shary Rea, 850–1001–13th Ave., S.W., Calgary, T2R 0L5. Canada.

Page 210b: Book Club Form. Reprinted by permission of Nellie Edge Seminars, Inc., P.O. Box 12399, Salem, OR 97309.

Other credits for works in this book include:

Page 235: Chapter 10, "Integrating Spelling into the Reading-Writing Classroom," is an expanded and revised version of an unpublished manuscript that was co-authored with Linda Cooper and Elaine Weiner.

Page 263: Chapter 11, "Setting Up an In-School Publishing Process," derives largely from the work of Marianne Sopko.

Page 55b: The annotations for "Journals" were co-authored with Dawne Boyer.

Page 170b: Appendix A, "A Folk/Fairy Tale Unit," was co-authored with Joan Servis.

A Note on the Use of Pronouns

To maintain a personal and objective tone, the use of he/she and him/her has been alternated and balanced throughout this book.

A Note on the Use of References in the Body of the Text

When a professional resource or children's book is cited only once in the text, the author, date, and publisher are included along with the resource cited. When that reference information is not provided in the body of the text, consult the index to locate full publishing information. The boldface page number in the index indicates the page where full publishing information is located.

Acknowledgments

I owe a debt of gratitude to so many educators, students, and parents in the Shaker Heights, Ohio, City School District whose voices are woven into this book. Most of all, I am grateful to the many teachers in my school district who have welcomed me into their classrooms each day and have made my own growth and continued learning possible. Although the written words in this text are mine, the ideas have emerged from continuous sharing and working with my colleagues and the children in their classrooms.

I am grateful for the support and trust of the principals in the buildings where I worked from 1987 to 1990—Don Coffee, Rebecca Kimberly, Margaret Lennard, Bernice Stokes, and Larry Svec—as well as Jean Sylak, director of elementary education, and Mark Freeman, superintendent of schools. I am also appreciative of their allowing me the freedom to take risks and find my own way as a teacher supporting other teachers. I am deeply thankful especially to Bernice Stokes for her encouragement, trust, support, and friendship. As the principal in the building where I am based, she has supported me daily and made it possible for me to continue to grow professionally. To Delores Groves, the principal in our grades 5 and 6 building, I am thankful for her ongoing support and friendship.

The writing of this book has been an enormous effort and could not have been completed without the assistance of many people. First, I am greatly indebted to those who thoughtfully and generously took the time to respond to one or more chapter drafts: Richard Allington, Pam Anderson, Bonnie Daniels, Paul Daniels, Dollye Finney, Peggy Gerhart, Margie Glaros, Joseph Grimes, Robin Grimes, Vicki Griminger, Jim Henry, Theo Husband, Rebecca Kimberly, Carol Lyons, Loretta Martin, Bill Newby, Ellen Potter, Mary Pryor, Jeannine Rajewski, Peg Rimedio, Kathy Roskos, Ellen Rubin, Lee Sattelmeyer, Jim Servis, Sam Sexton, Cheri Shapero, Karen Sher, Marcy Silver, Marianne Sopko, Bernice Stokes, Rob Tierney, Elaine Weiner, and Kathy Wolfe. Their feedback contributed significantly to my revision process and made the book clearer, more accurate, and more readable.

Second, the following people took the time to talk with me and share ideas and materials: Cheryl Ames, Patsy Bannon, Julie Beers, Deanne Blackburn, Reg Blue, Ruth Blumenthal, Dawne Boyer, Donna Brittain, Connie Brown, Darla Carlson, Jean Church, Charleen Civiello, Kittye Copeland, Anna Cresswell, Sylvia De-

Marco, Judy Detunca, Marie Dingwall, Jacqueline Douglass, Kay Dunlap, Hilda Edwards, Marilyn Eppich, Nancy Erkkila, Frank Gabbert, Susan Gardner, Bill Goepfert, Onajé Grimes, Sheri Grossman, Dede Hall, Jerry Harste, Tom Hatch, Judy Heiskell, Betty Hess, Ann Hogsett, Karen Horton, Lois Hudson, Bob Justice, Tom Kelly, Barbara Kittrick, Beth Lazerick, Carol Lindow, Susan Long, Susan Mears, Marisa Mercurio, Ella Moore, Dick Needham, Lori Oczkus, Donna Ostberg, Jim Paces, Maria Padovani, Michael Pellegrino, Robyn Platt, Joyce Pope, Debbie Powell, Linda Powers, Billie Price, John Ridley, Kitty Rose, Joyce Russell, Linda Salvadore, Nancy Sargeant, Debbie Schaedlich, Bob Scholl, Susan Scheps, Nancy Schubert, Karan Shelley, Peggy Sherman, Karen Shiba, Karen Smith, Barbara Speer, Brenda Spivey, Tudy Stewart, Sylvia Tallentire, Bob Thomas, Colleen Thompson, Nancy Tuttle, Sally Wilson, Jill Wisneski, Maryann Young, Bonnie Yousif, Deborah Zinn, Donna Zorge.

Some people deserve to be on both lists, but I have simply listed them in their more major role.

Most importantly, I am thankful to the special people in my life who have supported and sustained me through the long, arduous writing process of this book. Andrea Butler read a major portion of the manuscript and gave generously of her time and knowledge. Her honest feedback helped me regain a necessary perspective I had lost and cleared up confusions I was struggling with. I am indebted to her for her warm friendship and kindness as well.

While many teachers generously gave their time and support, several also sustained me throughout the writing process. Their voices and input are major contributions to this book. Holly Burgess continued to offer to read chapters and give honest feedback from the perspective of a high school teacher. Joan Di Dio read and gave valued input to many chapters. For her insights, time, honesty, and ongoing friendship, I am continually grateful.

I am also grateful to Joan Servis, from whom I have learned so much and whose classroom community of learners has been an ongoing source for my own professional development. Joan read and responded to several chapters and was always available to answer my questions. Our friendship as well as our weekly professional sharing continue to be a welcome and necessary part of my own growth.

Linda Cooper read and reread almost the entire manuscript. She tirelessly and generously gave me excellent suggestions and honest feedback. Her daily friendship and support have been a major sustaining influence throughout the writing of this book. Additionally, many of her own teaching ideas are an integral part of this text. I will always be grateful for both her knowledge and her caring ways.

I am also grateful to the secretaries in all the buildings in our district for their unfailing kindness and cooperation, and especially to Beverly Scoby and Linda Mendelsohn, the wonderful secretaries at Mercer School, where I am based. I am thankful, too, for our district library media office, which, under the leadership of Ellen Stepanian, has been constantly helpful in providing me with copies of journal articles, meeting any special requests, and obtaining information I needed. Thanks also to Lois Markt, who was largely responsible for my training and follow-up support as a Reading Recovery teacher.

With *Resources for Teachers* in the blue pages, I was most fortunate to have the help of many talented educators whose considerable input and expertise have greatly enriched this book. Susan Hepler generously shared her extensive knowledge of children's literature, wrote most of the children's literature annotations, and responded to a chapter draft. Our many hours on the phone together and our frequent correspondence discussing book titles, as well as discussing our personal and professional lives, were a highlight in writing this book.

I was also most fortunate to have the talent of Vera Milz, who shared the writing of annotations for the recommended professional books. Without her time and vast knowledge of professional literature, that section would be far less complete.

I am grateful for the title suggestions from Mary Krogness for the grades 7–8 recommended literature, as well as for her support as a fellow teacher and writer. For the recommended literature for grades 9–12, the input and suggestions from Don Gallo—expert in YA literature—have been invaluable. Thanks also to Dana Noble, a talented high school English teacher in our district, for taking time to read and consider most of Don's suggestions along with his own, to thoughtfully write the annotations for the grades 9–12 lists, and to respond to several chapter drafts.

In facilitating the publishing process, I am most appreciative of Philippa Stratton, editor-in-chief at Heinemann, for having respected my voice as an author and for taking so much time to patiently conference with me over the manuscript. The friendship we developed as a result of our time together has been an added pleasure.

Thanks also to Cheryl Kimball, production editor at Heinemann, who supported me through the arduous final stages of the book. Her flexibility, knowledge, support, and humor went a long way in easing tensions.

To the staff at G & H Soho who worked conscientiously to edit the manuscript and produce the book under a tight deadline, I am grateful.

I am also appreciative of the efforts of Leslie Schwarz of Heinemann Services who facilitated my writing process through her friendship and by taking care of so many small details.

Ultimately, I could not have completed this book without the support and love of my special friends and family. I am grateful for the constant friendship and love from Harriet Cooper. My aunt, Gloria Mills, has cheered me on. Susan Neuman— my stepsister, colleague, and friend—has encouraged me in so many ways. Our parents, Mildred and Manny Leventhal, have been constant supporters of my work. And Margaret Marshall has offered her continuous support and pride in my work.

My son, Peter, supported me throughout the process and took the time to read and comment on many chapters. His honesty, gentleness, and encouragement have meant so much to me. My daughter, Elizabeth, helped continuously with the final copyediting process and gave me valuable suggestions in so many areas. I have benefited so much from her writing talents, clear insights, and generous help. Most of all, I am thankful for my husband Frank, who offered his constant love and support and who put up with a wife who was always working and feeling stressed. Without his affection, help, and patience, I could never have written this book and continued teaching at the same time.

Finally, while its inadequacies are mine alone, I believe that this book is truly a collaborative effort, made possible by the generosity, support, and openness of teachers, administrators, librarians, parents, students, and my friends and family. To all of them, I am deeply grateful.

January 1991

Acknowledgments

In verifying and providing information as well as in updating and reviewing resources, the following people were very helpful: Julie Beers, George Cannon, Marlene Cohn, Linda Cooper, Terry Cooper, Mary Costello, Elaine Farge, Barbara Gallagher, Don Gallo, Andrea Goode, Carol Levine, Loretta Martin, Nancy O'Connor, Sara Phillips, Alison Preece, Joan Servis, Jan Shields, Barbara Speer, and Ali Sullo. Special thanks to children's librarian John Philbrook at the San Francisco Public Library for his help and comraderie in locating outstanding multicultural literature.

For all the support I received from Heinemann, I am most appreciative. A special thank you to Mike Gibbons for getting me whatever information I needed so quickly and efficiently. Thanks also to Carolyn Coman, Ray Coutu, Melissa Patten, Leigh Peake, and Sheila Peters for diligently tracking down resources and providing relevant publishing information. A special thank you to Peggy Hansen for her meticulous proofreading and copy editing efforts. A heartfelt thank you to Melissa Inglis, Production Editor, who assumed the complicated task of putting the many separate pieces together with good humor, steadfast dedication, and careful attention to detail. Thanks also to Production Manager Renée LeVerrier for skillfully coordinating and expediting production efforts and to Jenny Greenleaf for her lively cover design. To Toby Gordon, Publishing Director and wonderful facilitator of the entire process, a generous thank you.

Once again, as with the 1991 "blue pages," I am especially grateful to Susan Hepler, Vera Milz, and Dana Noble for their friendship, dedication and first-rate contributions to *The Blue Pages: Resources for Teachers from Invitations*. Collaborating with each of these talented educators has been a pleasure and an enriching personal and professional experience. This updated, expanded, and revised edition could never have been completed without their considerable input and expertise.

Finally, I am especially appreciative of the continuing support, patience, and love from my husband Frank.

July 1994

INVITATIONS

1

Beyond Transitions

Invitations in grade 1:
choosing to read during independent work time

I am a teacher. I don't say "just a teacher" anymore because I feel proud of the job we teachers do and of our ability to have an impact on students' lives as well as on our own.

In the early 1980s, when I was experiencing success using literature and meaning-based strategies to teach reading and writing to all learners—including at-risk students—I thought other teachers could benefit from my story of what had happened in one elementary building. Somehow, I had the notion that perhaps I could write a book for teachers. At the time, the idea seemed outrageous. I had never even had an article published. I did not consider myself a writer, and I was an "unknown." I was—like so many teachers—quietly and diligently working in one classroom, largely isolated from other teachers. Still, something inside me persisted, telling me to at least try. Over the next several years, my book proposal received a series of rejections, but I continued to look for a publisher. While there were wonderful books for teachers on whole language written by educators from New Zealand and Australia, there were no books written by an American teacher. I believed I had a different perspective to offer that would be useful for teachers in the United States.

In the spring of 1988, my book, *Transitions: From Literature to Literacy*, was jointly published by Rigby in Melbourne, Australia, and Heinemann in Portsmouth, New Hampshire. The response to the book has been gratifying. Teachers across the country have read the book, reflected on their teaching, and made changes. Many teachers have written to me sharing their concerns, questions, changes, hopes, and struggles.

When I wrote *Transitions*, I was teaching in an elementary school where the majority of students were part of a minority, lower socio-economic population and where many students were failing to learn to read successfully with traditional methods. In my book, I told the story of what happened in the primary grades in

1

one school when we moved from the basal text and worksheets to a literature approach to reading and writing. That story took a new turn in the fall of 1987 when our district began a reorganization effort as a result of declining enrollment and racial imbalance. At the same time—because of the leadership of parents, teachers, librarians, and administrators—our board of education made a district-wide commitment to move toward more meaning-centered approaches to reading and writing. This approach was to be implemented largely through the use of the best of children's literature. Teachers across our district began working to integrate the language processes—reading, writing, speaking, listening—and move toward what has become known as whole language.

While *Transitions* was written to give support to teachers in beginning the change process, especially as it relates to the use of literature in the classroom, this book, *Invitations: Changing as Teachers and Learners K–12*, begins where *Transitions* left off. It was written to support and encourage teachers in their further transitions in teaching and learning. As a teacher working with teachers and students, I share what I have observed, and I discuss connections, insights, and reflections other teachers and I have made. My hope is that reading the book will promote some self-reflection, risk taking, greater understanding of the principles of language learning, and a closer tie-in between theory and practice. The book is about changing as teachers and learners and is meant to be a series of invitations and possibilities to facilitate literacy in the classroom.

While the book was written to be read from beginning to end, it can easily be read in any order. Each chapter is complete within itself. You could begin with "Evaluation" (Chap. 13), "Integrating Spelling into the Reading-Writing Classroom" (Chap. 10), "Components of Whole Language" (Chap. 3), or whatever topic you are interested in. It is a long book, and I am respectful of the time constraints we teachers have, so use the book to suit your own purposes. The "blue pages" at the end of the book comprise an extensive annotated *Resources for Teachers* section meant to supplement and support the teacher as a professional, especially in the use and selection of children's literature and professional literature.

It was not my intent to write such a long book, and I have wrestled with the length of *Invitations*. In the end, however, I decided not only to include reading and writing topics but also to address the issues we teachers all struggle with, and to do so in depth. If the change process is to be successful, we teachers must lead the way by becoming knowledgeable professionals. I have devoted a chapter to the importance of establishing support networks since most of us work in school districts which do not have strong support systems or ongoing staff development plans. Chapter 14 presents many strategies for working with learning disabled and at-risk students since they are a part of every classroom. An entire chapter is devoted to journal writing so that teachers can implement it and sustain it in a meaningful way. Since so many of us struggle with classroom management, Chapter 15 discusses many specifics for successfully organizing the whole language classroom.

In writing *Transitions*, I tried to stay away from the term "whole language," fearing its overuse and misuse. While I still have those concerns, "whole language" has become such a widespread, accepted term that I now use it as a point of common reference. It is to be hoped that some day there will be no need for special terminology. When I was visiting a school in Auckland, New Zealand, I used the term "whole language" in my conversation with some teachers at lunch, after having spent an exciting morning in whole language classrooms. One New Zealand teacher, never having heard the term, asked, "What's that?" The principal responded, "That's what we do."

Beyond Transitions

Since the fall of 1987, I have been serving as a language arts resource teacher, assisting and supporting teachers in our five k–4 buildings in their transition to whole language. I am in each of these buildings one morning a week where I work with teachers on an invitational basis. In each building, I have organized and facilitated a weekly, before-school language arts support group where teachers meet to share issues and ideas in their teaching and to tie theory and practice together. These voluntary meetings have been invaluable for staff development and for teachers to collaborate and share ideas and concerns (see pp. 465–472).

Each morning I also go into classrooms at the request of teachers. I demonstrate lessons in reading and writing, conference with teachers, coach teachers, and provide and suggest teaching strategies and resource materials. In the afternoons, I am based in one building where I work daily with students, supporting and supplementing their reading-writing program in coordination with the classroom teachers. Rather than pulling students out of the classroom, I work in the second grade rooms (see pp. 144–146).

Recently, my role as a resource teacher has occasionally extended to our grades 5–6 building, our middle school, and our high school. What began in our district as mostly a primary grades focus on whole language has now begun to extend to the secondary level. The transitions have been slow, but the movement to more meaning-based and student-centered approaches is growing steadily.

Because of my daily work with teachers in classrooms in my district and my communication with teachers across the country, I became aware of a need for guidance and support for teachers who had already made the transition and commitment to more meaning-centered approaches. Teachers were asking for more assistance in going further with literature and whole language once they had taken the initial plunge. I also became aware, because of my interaction with secondary teachers in my own district, that the whole language process is the same from kindergarten through twelfth grade and that the elementary model has much to offer secondary teachers. The issues we struggle with in the elementary grades— using literature meaningfully, giving up some control and allowing children more choices, writing for authentic purposes, considering holistic strategies for at-risk students, establishing a collaborative classroom, evaluating, questioning our teaching—are critical issues for the kindergarten teacher as well as the senior high English teacher.

I believe the experiences of teachers and students in our district are representative of many school districts around the country and apply to many teachers and classrooms. Our school district is an "inner-ring suburb" of just under 5,000 kindergarten through grade 12 students, half minority and half nonminority. In terms of economics, families range from poor families on public assistance to extremely wealthy families. We deal with the same problems of student achievement that most diverse districts experience. *Invitations* concerns the issues we all think about and struggle with in our efforts to make our teaching more relevant to our students and ourselves. This book moves beyond transitions in one elementary school to include the continuing transitions of many teachers across a school district.

Reflections

Recently a teacher asked, "How can I know if I am really becoming a whole language teacher?" I could not give her an answer because it's one she'll have to find for herself. The best I can do is share my own and other teachers' experiences and reflect on current research and theories of literacy learning.

Perhaps, more than anything else, whole language is about all learners feeling whole and able and part of a community of learners. It is about belonging and risk taking and feeling successful as teachers and learners. It is about the power of collaboration to break down the isolation of teachers and to establish communities of belonging and learning for all students and teachers.

I recognize that change is difficult and risky for most of us. Whatever we do for the first time, whether it is small-group guided reading, shared writing, integrating spelling, or holistic evaluation, we are bound to bungle it at the start. This is natural behavior for all new, comprehensive processes and procedures, and we need to be forgiving and patient with ourselves. The main thing is to begin, to give it a try. Once you have made that first attempt, you can make modifications. One group of undergraduate students told their professor to go easy with them because they were in the "rough draft stage." Becoming a whole language teacher means being prepared to always be in a draft stage in some areas. However, you can't make revisions and improve at a task until you have first tried it. Don't worry too much about getting it "right." Decide what it is that's important for you to change and have a go at it. Adapt what seems right for you and your students. Go slowly, and add only one new component or procedure at a time. Continue to read, risk, and reflect. Trust your intuition. Slowly your confidence will build and your competence will grow.

I invite you to reflect on your teaching and begin to make meaningful changes. I wish you good luck and a safe, exciting journey.

2

Becoming a Whole Language Teacher

Language arts support group: establishing criteria for schoolwide holistic writing

"What About the Skills? Shouldn't I Be Teaching Them?"

When I saw Maria in the fall of her second year of teaching, the change in her demeanor and outlook was absolutely striking. Full of broad smiles and enthusiasm, Maria Padovani was a teacher who exuded confidence. Her classroom was a joyful, collaborative community where the teacher and learners supported and learned from each other. Every day she and her students were reading, discussing quality literature, and writing for a variety of authentic purposes. Skills were being learned and taught as much as possible in the context of genuine reading and writing experiences.

Maria had not started out that way. Despite the fact that she had received university training in whole language and had done an exceptional job in her field experience and student teaching, a "skill and drill" philosophy dominated her thinking during her first year of teaching. Because almost all of her schooling—from kindergarten through college—had been based on a skills model in traditional classrooms, that model initially prevailed in her first year of teaching.

Although Maria had *seemed* well prepared to teach, what she was prepared with was methodology. She could make up activities to go along with books; she could do journal writing; she could take children through the steps of the writing process; and she could teach a skills lesson—all as long as someone else laid out the framework.

In an effort to become as competent as possible, Maria sought out colleagues for advice and support, worked at school most evenings until 7 P.M., and continued working at home late into the evenings and over weekends. Nonetheless, she continued to feel overwhelmed and inadequate, and she often ended the day in tears. No matter how hard she tried, things didn't seem to come together for her. "I saw what some other teachers were doing, but I had no idea how they were arriving at what to do. I just thought they must be spending hours planning."

That first year Maria felt tremendous pressure to do everything, and to do it well. She was afraid of disappointing people and worried about not measuring up to the standards of her colleagues. She was constantly looking at what others were doing and not giving herself credit for what she was doing well. Whenever she walked down the hall and saw a new bulletin board or walked into another teacher's room and saw "something," she wondered if she should add it to her lesson plans. Initially, too, Maria felt she should go to every workshop that she heard about, whether it was on literature, writing process, spelling, or management.

Most of all, Maria was preoccupied with teaching "skills," and one of the hardest things for her was to decide what skills to teach and how to teach them. She was constantly asking, "Shouldn't I be teaching skills? I see so-and-so doing a lesson on verbs (or capitalization or grammar). Shouldn't I be doing that?" I did not have the answers for Maria, and we struggled together. When she would ask, "Why do you have to teach grammar or punctuation?" I asked her, "Why do you think you have to teach it?"

Maria later said,

> The questions made me go back and reflect, reason out and modify what I was doing. Also, the suggestion to pick out one thing to concentrate on and not try to do everything was helpful. Last year, I chose to focus on making my questioning more meaningful in reading groups. This year my focus will be on integrating the skills into writing.

Maria also noted the positive influence of a whole language summer workshop. After the sessions, she had felt inspired to read many journal articles provided by the workshop as well as several recommended professional books. She noted, "The reading made me question the way I was doing things. I saw how contrived a lot of my teaching was. I began to move toward experience-based writing instead of just assigned writing and to really think about my teaching."

Before Maria could offer children choices in decision making about their own learning, she had to find her own literate voice—slowly and thoughtfully. She had to examine and determine what she believed about how children learn before she could make thoughtful, ongoing decisions about her teaching. Once Maria could combine her strong educational background and experiences with a clear theoretical literacy model, she was on her way to becoming a whole language teacher.

> I realize now that I was missing a clearly defined philosophy. Until you have that and it's your own, you continue to struggle. I integrate a lot of different people's ideas. I think about what Calkins and Graves and others say. I continue to read, explore my thinking, question my ideas, and share with colleagues. Now, however, I have the understanding of the philosophy, and the ideas and activities just come to me.

Maria continues to value the time she invests in professional reading, attending workshops, and participating in our district-level whole language support group. She has been instrumental in helping fellow teachers in a nearby school district begin their own support group and has felt rewarded by being able to help other teachers. She continues to choose one focus for her teaching and learning and accepts the fact that she cannot be an expert at everything. She is still concerned about "skills," but is feeling more confident about integrating skills into her teaching. She often feels she wants to be doing more, but she does give herself credit for what she does well. She also accepts the fact that there will never be enough time to do everything. She is now most concerned with having her children develop a love and appreciation of reading and writing.

"I'm the Only One Having Difficulty"

Walking into Loretta Martin's second grade classroom, one sees children reading books of their own choosing as the mainstay of the reading program, buddy journal writing, spelling as part of the writing program, a child-centered room where children are productively in charge of their own learning, and a relaxed teacher clearly enjoying herself and her students. Loretta is a confident whole language teacher, but she did not start out that way.

When Loretta first began to make changes in her teaching, she felt isolated in her struggles: "Every time I tried something new, there was always some snag. The lesson didn't flow, and the immature kids didn't catch on. I was upset, but I wasn't comfortable sharing my failures. It seemed as though everyone else was talking about their successes."

While she felt good about some of the changes she was making in her teaching, Loretta was also extremely frustrated.

> When you have workbook pages for phonics, spelling, handwriting, and reading and you're trying to add literature, as well as teaching all the other subjects, you feel very stressed. I felt that way for three years. I was so busy getting through all those required skills and workbook pages every morning. The kids were worn out with all the work I gave them.

Loretta knew she wanted to have a whole language classroom, but she was aware that she lacked an understanding of the philosophy. With twenty years teaching experience in grades k–2, Loretta considered herself a traditional teacher but an eclectic one who incorporated many approaches. She was known as an excellent teacher who held high expectations for all her students. She always read aloud to her class and incorporated literature into her basal program, but literature and reading were "entirely separate." Reading was what she did when she used the basal and did skills work. Literature was the pleasurable time, for enjoying books and talking about authors, that came after the reading work.

Loretta began making changes in her teaching about five years ago. She began by adding chart poems in enlarged print and children's books to her reading program. Gradually the excitement of the kids and the support of the parents encouraged her to give up the basal entirely. She credits a supportive principal, the intervention of Mary Krogness—our district writing expert—observations of colleague Elaine Weiner, and an observation of the first grade literature program at Moreland School (see Routman, 1988)* for beginning her transition. "I couldn't get over the comprehension, fluency, and excitement of first graders reading *Ira Sleeps Over* (by Bernard Waber) in late fall," Loretta observed.

The turning point in Loretta's transition to whole language came when she attended a week-long conference—"The Pursuit of Literacy: Creating the Whole Language Classroom"—in Geneseo, New York, in the summer of 1989. She was inspired by speakers Lucy Calkins, Dorothy Strickland, Charles Chew, and Violet

*See index for pages giving full publishing information.

Harris as well as by many teachers she met. At the conference, Loretta was able to share her frustrations and failures with other teachers who were also looking to understand the whole language philosophy. "Until that conference, I thought I was the only one trying new things that didn't work," Loretta commented.

During the conference, she also went to a bookstore and purchased many professional titles.

> I had seen most of these books but knew I didn't have time to read them during the school year. I recognized the covers from seeing them at our language arts support group. I had already read and been very influenced by several books on whole language. I was especially impressed with books about minority children who became successful readers and writers. As a black teacher, the success of black children was really important to me.
>
> I spent a lot of time during the rest of the summer doing professional reading. As I read, I wrote down what I wanted to do in my class—a message board, a daily morning message, reading by choice, abandoning spelling workbooks and phonics pages. That fall I was able to implement lots of changes in my teaching.

Loretta sees one of her biggest changes as focusing on the positive. To her that means not only noticing what kids can do but also what they are doing. In the past she relied on tests to tell her what kids couldn't do and structured much of her teaching around those results. "Now, even when the child has only written a few sentences and I know they can do more, I am accepting of what the child has done. I know they've learned a lot more than what they put on the paper."

Today, Loretta continues to attend conferences, interact with other teachers at those conferences, and share with her colleagues. She is an active participant in our weekly language arts support group meetings, and she has begun to share her knowledge with teachers in other districts. While she has gained many ideas and perspectives from attending workshops, she notes: "It wasn't the workshops that led to major changes in my philosophy and teaching. It was taking the time to do the professional reading and reflect on my teaching."

Understanding Language Learning

Loretta's statement is true for me too. I am largely self-educated in whole language, and most of that education has come from the professional reading I have done and continue to do. While professional workshops and interaction with colleagues have been extremely valuable, it is, most of all, the reading that has caused me to reflect insightfully about my teaching. Professional reading has led me to confirm directions I am heading toward, question present practices, and continue to make changes in my teaching. Looking at the books that have had the greatest effect on my teaching and learning, I see they are all a combination of theory and practice. Those are the books that have enabled me to make the vital connections between the how and the why of teaching-learning and to think, "Aha, so that's why that works."

As a result of putting theory and practice together through my professional reading and more than twenty years of teaching experience, I have come up with my own theory of learning and teaching. My theory is still growing and constantly changing, but it is where I am now. My beliefs are based on my daily interactions with students and teachers in classrooms and on observations I have made. I continually apply my beliefs and connect them to whole-life contexts.

Underpinning my beliefs is my understanding of the necessary conditions for language learning. Here I have been largely influenced by the research and teachings of three educators: Don Holdaway in New Zealand, Brian Cambourne in Australia, and Kenneth Goodman in the United States. Additionally, in formulating my learning theory, I have been greatly influenced by the work of Frank Smith, Jerry Harste, Donald Graves, Marie Clay, Andrea Butler, and Nancie Atwell.

Some major understandings include:

- Literacy acquisition is a natural process.
- The conditions for becoming oral language users are the same as for becoming readers and writers.
- Young children enter school with much knowledge about literacy.
- Becoming a reader and becoming a writer are closely related.
- Optimal literacy environments promote risk taking and trust.
- Becoming literate is a social act and a search for meaning.
- Literacy development is continuous.
- Genuine literacy acts are authentic and meaningful.

Holdaway's Developmental Model

In the 1960s and early 1970s, Don Holdaway, the New Zealand educator responsible for developing shared book experience, theorized that the ways children acquire oral language could be used as a developmental model for all language learning. He found certain conditions to be common all over the world in learning spoken language, and he translated those conditions into a "Developmental Model for Language Learning" (*The Pursuit of Literacy: Early Reading and Writing*, Michael Sampson [ed.], Kendall/Hunt Publishing, 1986). Holdaway's model has had the greatest influence on my teaching. I carry the model in my head, and I try to employ it in every teaching situation. When my teaching breaks down, I go back to the model.

Developmental Model for Language Learning

1. Observation of "demonstrations"   In learning to speak—and to read and write—the child observes competent adults that he admires as genuine users of the literacy act. The act that is modeled is authentic and purposeful. The learner is a spectator with no pressure to perform.

2. Participation   The child is invited to participate and collaborate because he has a need for and genuine interest in learning to talk or mastering a particular skill. The "expert" welcomes the "novice" while explaining, instructing, and demonstrating what to do. The act becomes collaborative, as in a confirming conversation ("Oh, you want juice? Here it is.") or in a shared reading or shared writing.

3. Role playing or practice   The learner is given the opportunity to practice the skill without direction or observation by the demonstrator or teacher. This is the critical trial and error period when the learner independently engages in the literacy act and attempts to self-regulate, self-correct, and self direct his own learning. The competent user or teacher is nearby if needed.

4. Performance   When the learner feels competent, he voluntarily becomes the demonstrator, and the model or teacher becomes the audience. This is the time for the learner to share what has been accomplished—whatever the level of development—and to receive approval and acknowledgment.

Applying the Model in My Life

The model became significant to me when I was learning how to use a word processor. My son Peter, a computer whiz, handed me the Macintosh manual and said, "Mom, anyone can figure out how to operate the Mac by reading the manual." I picked up the manual and tried to pore through it, but I couldn't make sense of it. What may have been clear to someone with a computer background was totally unclear to me. I felt stupid and frustrated. "Peter," I said, "you're going to have to show me." I watched carefully as he demonstrated for me. He sat right next to me and encouraged me to try while he was right there to help me. He slowly took me through the steps I needed to know and showed me over and over again until I had some glimmer of understanding. Probably the most important step was when Peter left the room. Only then could I work out the difficulties and take as much time as I needed. I was embarrassed to have my son see what a slow learner his mother was on the computer. I needed to practice, make mistakes, and get it right on my own, without him looking on. If I got into trouble, I knew Peter was in the next room, and I could call on him. Then, when I felt ready, I proudly called him in to show him what I could do on the word processor. His smile and my pride were big rewards.

Demonstrations need to more than just take place in our teaching. When learning occurs—in any area of the curriculum—the learner engages with the demonstration.

Engagement with Demonstrations

1. Doable by the learner
2. Purposeful for the learner
3. Learner feels safe to take a risk
4. Works best if learner admires the demonstrator
   (Adapted from Cambourne, 1988, pp. 54–55)

Looking at both the developmental model and the conditions for engagement—and applying them to my experience in learning to use a word processing program on the computer—I see that a number of interrelated factors contributed to my success:

1. I had a need for and an interest in learning how to use the computer. I was writing a book while working full time, and I had a publisher's deadline to meet.
2. I had someone I trusted and admired available (but not ever present) to guide me.
3. I had time to practice independently.
4. I was rewarded for my efforts. I was proud of myself; my son was proud of me; I was able to revise my writing more easily and write more efficiently.

Analyzing how I learned to use a word processor made me especially aware that one demonstration is rarely enough. I can remember when I used to think that because I had shown students something once, they should be able to do it. However, most of us need to be shown over and over again, especially in those areas that are difficult for us.

I believe that when students aren't learning, it's because the demonstrations we are giving, or not giving, are not adequate and/or are seen as not meaningful or necessary to the learner. This idea seems especially significant at the secondary level where many students are apathetic or turned off. Students become engaged with teacher demonstrations and begin to take responsibility for their learning only when they have meaningful curricular choices that relate to their interests and their lives.

For some young children, phonics worksheets and workbook pages are not doable even when the teacher explains how to do them. Not doable either is learning a weekly set of spelling words or memorizing long lists of vocabulary words. Whenever we expect students to complete tasks that do not have a meaningful context, we can expect some students to experience great difficulty.

I get very nervous around audiovisual equipment, especially when I am doing a presentation. If the slide projector jams or the microphone doesn't work properly, I am helpless to fix it. I especially worry about the overhead projector malfunctioning because I use many overhead transparencies to support my talks. Recently, just before I was to begin a presentation to a large audience, the audiovisual man came up to me and said, "Sometimes the bulb goes out on this projector, but don't worry, there's a spare. Here's what you do to get it in use." He then proceeded to demonstrate how you slide one lever over, lift another lever up, move something else down, and let the bulb drop into place. When he was on step 2, I was already confused. It was such a simple procedure, but I needed him to show it to me at least two more times. Feeling foolish about needing to be shown again, I was embarrassed to ask him. What went through my mind was that if there was a problem, I would ask someone from the audience to help me. I simply stopped paying attention because replacing the bulb did not seem doable to me, and past experiences with mechanical equipment made me feel insecure about fixing a malfunction myself.

How many students in our classrooms simply stop "tuning in" because they feel the assignments are not doable or relevant to them?

Applying the Model to the Classroom

I believe the conditions that are present for acquiring oral language need to prevail for all literacy instruction across the curriculum. What has particularly impressed me about Holdaway's developmental model is that there is no place in the model for competition, exclusion, criticism, or coercion. The model includes only cooperation, acceptance, approval, and an invitation to join in. Implicit in the model are teachers as real readers and writers; a curriculum and materials that are interesting, meaningful, whole, and relevant to the learners; and a safe, nurturing environment that promotes social interaction and collaboration. "What we're concerned about in whole language is setting up the organizational, intellectual, and social patterns that allow acquisition to occur." (Don Holdaway, address at the annual meeting of the International Reading Association, New Orleans, Louisiana, May 4, 1989).

Cambourne's Model of Literacy Learning

In the 1970s, the Australian researcher Brian Cambourne spent hundreds of hours carefully observing young children who were becoming successful literacy learners. He documented what he saw happening and translated his observations into a set of conditions for learning: immersion, demonstration, expectation, responsibility, use, approximation, response, and engagement. Engagement occurs when the first seven conditions are present. (See Figure 2–1 for an explanation of these conditions; see also Cambourne, 1988.) "Cambourne's conditions," as they are often called, are necessary conditions for all effective language learning. They operate simultaneously in every successful whole language classroom and provide the context for language learning. Cambourne's work helped me understand the importance of engagement with demonstrations.

Goodman's Reading Research

In the mid-1960s, Kenneth Goodman observed first- and third-graders and documented what they did in the process of reading. He noted, among other things, that when the children were asked to read a whole story, they could read words in context that they could not read out of context; they expected print to make sense, and they attempted to read for meaning, as evidenced by the approximations and self-corrections they made. Goodman noted the "miscues" readers made as "something unexpected that the reader does in the process of reading," as opposed to "errors" or mistakes.

Goodman's research showed us that it was not necessary to introduce and drill words out of context, teach phonics in isolation, teach reading in a hierarchy of skills to be mastered, or use contrived reading materials. In relation to understanding the reading process, Goodman's work was revolutionary.

My Learning Theory

My Beliefs about Language Learning for Teachers and Students

Based on the work of notable educator-researchers, on my daily classroom experiences working with children and teachers, and on where I am now in my own teaching-learning process, I hold the following beliefs and attitudes. I see these beliefs as necessary for optimal learning for both students and teachers. Once I had these beliefs and attitudes in place, concerns about the skills and activities fell into proper perspective.

I share my beliefs only as a way for you to think about your own beliefs. Each person's learning theory will be somewhat different, based on individual life experiences, observations of students, interactions with colleagues, professional reading, knowledge, and interpretation of the research and understanding of language learning. There is no one correct set of beliefs. My beliefs and attitudes

Figure 2-1 A Schematic Representation of Brian Cambourne's Model of Learning as It Applies to Literacy Learning

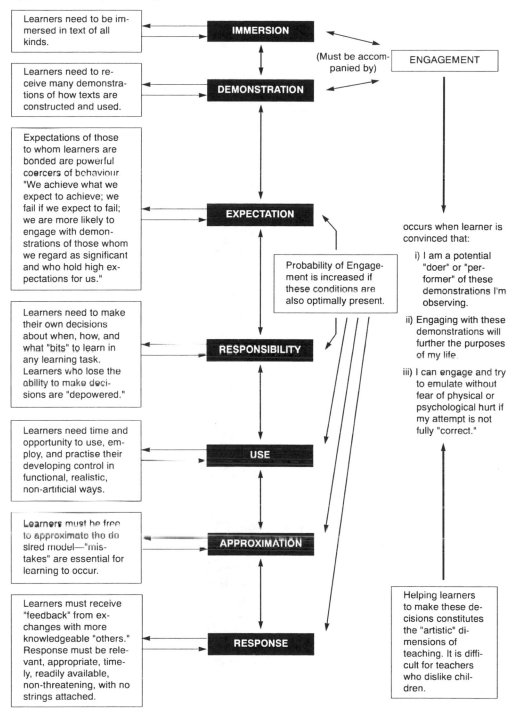

From *The Whole Story: Natural Learning and the Acquisition of Literacy in the Classroom*, by Brian Cambourne, published by Ashton Scholastic Ltd., Auckland, New Zealand, 1988, p. 33. Reproduced with permission.

continue to develop and change, to be integral to all areas of my teaching, and to influence the way I approach children, the curriculum, and learning.

- The developmental level of the learner must be respected.
- All students and teachers can learn.
- Focusing on the strengths must come first when looking at learners.
- We teachers need to demonstrate ourselves as "joyfully literate."
- Learners need many opportunities for "languaging."
- The learning process is highly valued.
- Evaluation is ongoing.
- The goal of education is independence.
- Learning is lifelong and requires thoughtfulness.
- The teacher is a facilitator and colearner.
- Curriculum is negotiated, and learners have choices.
- "Demonstrations" are necessary for learning.
- Sharing is an important part of all learning.
- Sufficient time is needed for optimal learning.
- Collaboration and social interaction foster literacy development.

- *Respect for the developmental level*   I believe that all children enter school at their readiness level and need to be instructed wherever they happen to be in the developmental literacy process. I see this as true for older students, too; we need to instruct them wherever they are in the learning process. When I design a program to fit the student, rather than trying to fit the student into a predesigned program, the student usually learns successfully.

For us teachers, too, respect for the developmental level means welcoming, encouraging, and accepting all teachers—wherever they happen to be in the process of moving toward whole language. I have found that when teachers feel accepted as they are, they are usually open to change. I believe respect for the teacher-learner and student-learner is primary. Our tone of voice, behavior, and attitude must value and kindly regard all learners. The "literacy club" must be open to all, with no special entry requirements.

- *Expectation that learning will occur*   Regardless of the child's language or background of experiences, I believe every child is capable of learning to read and write if he or she is viewed as a learner who possesses fundamental abilities. In two decades of teaching reading, I have *never* worked with a child who failed to learn to read. I expect the child to learn, and I give off that expectation.

Interestingly, when I go into classrooms and do demonstration teaching, I usually don't know the individual children—who are the supposed bright ones and who are the perceived dull ones. Often, following a lesson, teachers will tell me they were surprised by a particular student's participation and comments. This has happened so often that I think the only explanation can be expectation on the part of the teacher. Because I have no prior knowledge of children's abilities, I have the same expectations for them all. The children sense that I expect them to be able to participate, and they do.

Too often we give the message to students and parents that a child cannot learn or that, at best, he will learn at a slow pace. The mother of Onajé, a learning disabled (L.D.) student who became a successful reader, was told by the local Association for Children with Learning Disabilities that "Your son may never learn to read" but not to worry about it because "When he's older he can have access to a secretary and tape recorder." Chapter 1 and L.D. programs, where the usual expectation is for the child to receive services for the entire year (or for a substantial part of his school career), could drastically reduce their numbers if administrators and teachers changed their expectations of what these students can do. One of the powerful messages of Reading Recovery is that the program's high "recovery" rates document that children's learning can be greatly accelerated when we expect it to happen. Just as important, Reading Recovery demonstrates that expectations about "remedial" learners can change.

As teachers, we also need to have high expectations for ourselves as learners. I once heard a well-known publisher say he believed that only 30 percent of teachers were capable of becoming whole language teachers, that the rest of us weren't smart enough. I've thought about that statement for a number of years, and after working with many teachers, I'm convinced he's wrong. It's my opinion that becoming a whole language teacher has as much to do with openness and flexibility as it has to do with intelligence.

• *Focus on the strengths*   One of the hardest shifts for teachers is to focus on the strengths. I think it's almost a cultural phenomenon that we notice what's wrong before we see what's right. When I was visiting schools in Australia several years ago, I hung onto an empty potato chip bag for two days before I decided where to discard it. On the back of the bag was printed, "Please dispose of this thoughtfully." Here we say, "Don't litter." The positive wording, "Please dispose of this thoughtfully," played over and over again in my head and encouraged me to act in a responsible manner.

As a Reading Recovery teacher working with at-risk first-graders, I have had to write a diagnostic summary of each child after an initial evaluation. If the only thing the child could do was write his name, then that's how I was taught to begin the narrative. "The child *can* write his first name." Anecdotal records, individual education plans, and reporting to parent forms need to note the child's strengths before noting the weaknesses.

It is not just focusing on the child's strengths that can be difficult. As teachers, we tend to be very critical of ourselves. We are quick to point out all the things we are not doing. We need literally to pat ourselves on the back for what we are doing well. "Are you reading aloud to kids?" Great. "Are you trying to give students some choice?" Wonderful. "Are you thinking about your teaching?" Bravo! "Have you added literature to your program?" Fantastic! So often we are doing important things and not valuing them. We need to notice and value what we are already doing.

Focusing on the strengths also means focusing on the possibilities, appreciating and valuing students' cultures and getting rid of the "Yes, but . . ." mentality that says, "Whole language might work in your school, but we can't do it here because . . . we have too many students in our class, . . . our kids are too diverse, . . . we don't have funds available for books, . . . there's too much content we have 'to cover,' . . . our parents don't cooperate," and on and on. Focusing on the strengths means getting rid of the excuses. With a positive attitude, a group of kids, paper and pencil, and access to a library, teachers probably have enough going for them to be successful.

• *Display of joyfulness*   Don Holdaway has often said that we must display ourselves as joyfully literate readers and writers if we expect our students to become joyfully literate. I have also heard Frank Smith say that it is our responsibility as educators to make school so interesting that students will want to learn. The only way students will choose to read and write beyond the school setting is if they view reading and writing as enjoyable and purposeful.

Recently some visitors to our school commented that while students in their own classes spent time reading books, students at our school seemed joyful about their reading. They spoke of observing one of our young students walking through the front door enthusiastically reading a book. I think this has happened because our teachers are genuinely excited about books.

• *"Languaging" encouraged*   Language learning is an ongoing, social, active process, and students need many opportunities to interact in reading, writing, listening, and speaking with each other. "Languaging" must be purposeful; language is best learned through its use and not its practice. The actual room arrangement— how desks are clustered and where the teacher is—contributes to the languaging that does or does not take place.

It is not only students who need time to talk together. We teachers also need to be encouraged to interact. We have spent so many years working isolated in our own classrooms that it is a new-found experience to have engaging, professional, and social conversations with our colleagues. This really hit home for me after a visit to Australia.

When I returned from New Zealand and Australia several summers ago, a colleague asked me what impressed me most about the schools. When I responded "morning tea," I surprised myself. I had not realized until then what an impact that event had made on me. Morning tea occurs each morning at about 11 A.M. After teaching for two uninterrupted hours, teachers meet for fifteen minutes in a common area where they drink coffee or tea, have a snack, and talk with each other. While the children are outside for a recess, the teachers have a chance to complain about how certain students drove them crazy that morning, what they did last evening, what was on the news. The point is, they socialize, and they enjoy it. I never saw so many smiling teachers as I did in the several schools I visited in Australia. I thought about what would happen if we made time for morning tea in U.S. schools. Most teachers would stay in their classrooms and grade papers. We continue to work in isolation from one another.

• *Process orientation*   Process orientation refers to noticing and valuing what the student (and the teacher) does in the process of reading, writing, listening, and speaking. For us teachers, this means valuing the process as well as the product, because it is in the process that the learning takes place. While the product is still important, emphasis shifts to how the student arrived or is arriving at the final product or goal. It means expecting students to hand in a final copy with all the drafts and revisions attached. It means record keeping that notes a student's strengths, weaknesses, and needs. Process orientation also means not over-emphasizing correctness. For the young child, a totally error-free paper may not be realistic even in a final copy.

Perhaps, most of all, process orientation means not just tolerating predictions and approximations but celebrating those that show evidence of thinking and learning. Students need to be encouraged to approximate and try out words, meanings, spellings, and conventions. Valuing the process means recognizing and trusting students to learn.

Process orientation applies to us teachers in transition, too. We need to value ourselves in the learning process even if we are not "there" yet. Implicit in process orientation is lots of risk taking, which acknowledges that learning happens gradually over time. Teachers moving toward whole language need to feel safe to take risks, try out, and make mistakes.

• *Ongoing evaluation*   I believe that evaluation, not just of students but of ourselves as teachers, needs to be ongoing. Evaluation focuses on the value of what students and teachers are doing and notes growth over time.

In particular, evaluation is reflective. That is, the learners—both the student and the teacher—develop the ability to observe themselves carefully in the teaching-learning process. (See Chap. 13, "Evaluation," for a complete discussion of the topic.)

• *Independence fostered*   I believe in promoting independence by not doing for learners what they can do for themselves. This is part of the notion behind invented spelling, prediction in reading, and expecting students to take responsibility for tasks such as editing their work, choosing their topics, and establishing classroom rules. The goal of education needs to be independence. Learners read meaningful material and use all the systems of language to work through a challenging text. Independence means that learners are able to examine and monitor their own behaviors in the learning process. Traditional education has made students and teachers dependent on texts and other people for solutions and curriculum.

Dana Noble, a ninth grade teacher moving toward whole language, comments, "I particularly enjoy pushing my students towards independence in their writing, 'putting them in the driver's seat,' as Nancie Atwell calls it, in decisions about what their writing should do or accomplish. After a while, they begin to take pride in their new-found independence."

• *Lifelong, thoughtful learning*   I believe whole language teaching is about students and teachers who can make intelligent choices, think and analyze critically, and choose to go on learning—in all areas of their lives—even when they are not in the classroom or taking formal course work.

A colleague who recently returned from a conference said that *for the first time* she disagreed with some of the points a speaker made. She had been attending conferences for years, taking in everything she heard as "truth." But now she had some knowledge of her own; she had been reading, thinking, and talking to colleagues and making changes in her teaching. She was no longer a passive learner. She had begun to question and analyze. She felt exhilarated at being able to "sift out" what she found to be irrelevant and incorrect for her. We celebrated her new-found "thoughtfulness." Whole language teaching and learning is about becoming an articulate and critical reader, writer, speaker, listener, and thinker. That's not just kid stuff. That's for us teachers too.

● *Teacher as facilitator and colearner*   I moved from teacher-as-director to teacher-as-facilitator several years ago. Only recently, however, did I make the transition to teacher as colearner. I added "colearner" after I was able to give up even more control and share the responsibility for learning and teaching with fellow teachers as well as with students. As a colearner I do more listening and less talking. I am an observer, encourager, participator, and respondent. I am a coach.

● *Negotiation of curriculum: The importance of choice*   For us teachers and students, negotiating the curriculum also means finding our own answers for what should be taught as well as working through problems in our own way. It means deciding what to read and write and being able to make responsible choices and decisions.

While lesson plans and general goals are established and clearly written, I capitalize on the teachable moment and "go with the flow." If something comes up that needs to be taught or an unplanned discussion arises from a topic, plans are altered to fit the needs of the class.

Being able to make choices is an integral part of whole language. Students and teachers must be free to choose their reading books and their writing topics most of the time. In many classrooms, especially where students are in remedial programs or are placed in lower-level tracks, freedom to engage in meaningful literacy acts is still very restricted. Choice implies trust of students and teachers, and this trust does not come easily.

When my own children were at our district high school, there was a required summer reading program. Each summer, students were expected to complete two or three required books that usually comprised about one thousand pages of challenging reading. During the first days of school in the fall, they were tested to be sure they had done the reading. I suggested several times to the English department that they might want to consider having only one required book and letting students choose two others from a list of about a hundred books. I was told, "How will we know if the students have read the books?" It all came down to trust. That required reading hung over my kids all summer like a curse. I could never get them to pick up another book "just for enjoyment" because they felt so bogged down and restricted. Not until after they graduated high school did they become readers—that is, people who choose to read when they have some leisure time.

High school teachers who take the risk of giving students choices express their surprise and delight when they see the results of allowing students—even low-achieving students—to read any book. A group of teachers at our local high school found that when students could choose any book to read independently, nearly all students read and kept a journal with little in-class guidance. They noted that previous assigned reading had never been as successful in getting students to read independently.

Negotiation of the curriculum also means sharing the responsibility for learning with the learners. I no longer feel responsible for providing all the activities or all the questions to go along with a book or unit of study. Students are capable of developing their own questions and projects if enough modeling has been done. Teachers are capable of developing meaningful plans if they have a solid theory and a philosophy of learning.

- *"Demonstrations" taking place*   The word "demonstrations" was coined by philosopher-educator Frank Smith. I have heard him say, "Either you tell the child, 'Great job,' or you say, 'Let me show you how to do that.'" Without a doubt the biggest visible changes in my teaching are reflected in the demonstrations I do—many of them over and over again. I do most of my demonstrations on the overhead projector because it is an easy to use audiovisual machine that helps me grab and sustain the kids' attention.

A fifth grade teacher noted, "I'm not comfortable with modeling. It's real scary for me. But I know that if the kids see me taking risks, they'll begin to take risks too."

I strongly believe that we must go through any process we expect our students to go through and that our students must see us work through the process. One of the biggest differences between elementary and secondary classrooms is in the number of demonstrations taking place. Many high school teachers skip steps 1, 2, and 3 in Holdaway's developmental model and go right to step 4—performance. The assignment is given and the student is expected to do it on her own. The English teacher, or last year's teacher, is supposed already to have taught "that." However, if teachers *in any subject area* expect students to complete an assignment thoughtfully and independently, for example, a research paper, teachers themselves must also be willing to do a research paper and share their own thinking processes, note taking, drafting, revising, preparing final copy, or whatever else they expect of their students.

I demonstrate my mental processes by thinking aloud: I demonstrate I am a writer by writing with and in front of students and teachers and by sharing drafts of my writing. I demonstrate that I am a reader by sharing and discussing books I am reading and by talking through the process I use to figure out unknown words. I demonstrate revision and editing by taking my writing or a student's (with permission) and showing the students what I have done or how to do it. The more complete and relevant my demonstrations, the greater the students' understanding and the more independently they can eventually work.

Demonstrations need not come only from the classroom teacher. Older students can effectively demonstrate for younger ones; students can demonstrate for each other; and teachers can demonstrate for one another.

- *Sharing*   I believe that sharing should be an integral part of every whole language classroom. There may be daily whole class share time where students and teachers set aside time for responding to ideas and concepts expressed in print and oral language. One such time is shared book experience, where the class gathers as a community to read and reread rich literature. There is small-group sharing through reading and writing conferences with peers and with the teacher, book sharing, project sharing, or acting out plays and scenes. Group share time promotes more interesting writing because students hear one another's ideas and writing styles. While the teacher is an important audience, the teacher is only one audience and, very often, not the primary one.

An important part of sharing includes teachers sharing with teachers—by grade levels, across grade levels, throughout the district, across the state and nation. In our school district, teachers from kindergarten through twelfth grade have an opportunity to share in our evening district support group, which meets every six weeks. That has been a stimulating and valuable time for understanding processes and concerns across the grade levels. It also promotes collegiality among teachers who would not ordinarily work together.

In general, I find we teachers need a lot of encouragement to share with our colleagues. We feel self-conscious about spotlighting ourselves, and we assume other teachers already know or do what we do. Yet whole language is possible only when teachers generously share their knowledge and network with each other. It can be too overwhelming to try to work out everything yourself.

• *Valuing time*   For teachers and students, time refers to time for reflection, time for sharing, sustained time for reading and writing, wait time, and time for collaborating.

Whole language does not just happen. It develops slowly over time. I believe we teachers need time for reflective observation of ourselves and our students and for understanding what whole language is all about. We need long chunks of time over vacations and summers to engage in professional reading. Students need frequent and regular time for sustained silent reading, even at the high school level. Students need wait time when reading—time to work out trouble spots and figure out solutions without being interrupted, and they need time to think before responding. Students also need blocks of time for writing. Teachers need the freedom to work out schedules so that meaningful blocks of time can be created, and they need occasional release time during the school day to collaborate with colleagues.

• *Collaboration and social interaction*   Collaboration is closely linked with "languaging" and is one of the greatest benefits of whole language. Becoming a whole language teacher can be a difficult process. The process seems a lot more manageable and possible when ideas of what's working and not working are shared with colleagues and when teachers jointly plan literature and thematic units. Our weekly language arts support groups foster collaboration and sharing (see Chap. 16, "Establishing Support Networks"). Some teachers find that by combining their two classes occasionally they can create a workable opportunity for teacher collaboration. Other teachers find that by getting together after school or during common planning periods collaboration of ideas is possible. With collaboration, students, teachers, administrators, and parents work together. In keeping with the developmental model, competition is absent, and there is a spirit of true cooperation.

Collaboration also means administrators and teachers working together in a democratic fashion, not in a "we-they" manner. In Australia, some principals go back to classroom teaching after five or six years, and they do not consider it a demotion. On the contrary, they seem to welcome the opportunity to work more closely with teachers and students.

I agree with Jerry Harste, who sees collaboration as even more desirable than cooperative learning. He writes, "I discovered what it means to collaborate rather than cooperate. When we cooperate we work towards some mutual goal, but when we collaborate we expect to go out changed in the end, to become a different person" (Watson, Burke, and Harste, 1989, p. 65).

I am a different person than I was years ago when I worked in isolation. Collaborating with teachers and students has changed me and my views of literacy. With genuine collaboration—where there are no fixed rules—there are always surprises and new insights. Collaboration with my colleagues continues to be a joy and a privilege that suppoprts me in finding my own literate voice.

Finding Our Literate Voices

Before I found my own literate voice and could apply my beliefs to teaching, I had to learn to trust myself, allow time for change, and give up some control—all of which I continue to struggle with.

Trusting Ourselves

"First you have to believe in yourself. Then the answers will come as you interact and learn along with your students, your colleagues, the professional books and journals you read, the courses you take, the reflection and self-evaluation in which you engage" (Bird, 1989, p. xi).

I have been in the process of becoming a whole language teacher since the mid-1970s. I continue to question my teaching, read professional articles and books, attend workshops, talk and interact with my colleagues, and try out new ideas. One of the hardest things has been to trust my own intuition, to believe that what I am seeing or doing is valid and appropriate or to be able to decide that what I am doing is not appropriate and needs to be set aside. I think the reason it is so hard for us teachers to trust our own instincts is that we have had years of pre-conditioning and pre-packaging that gave us the message that the plans and answers are in textbooks and manuals. We bought the notion that people and publishers who did not know us or our students somehow knew more about our students and teaching than we did.

Over time, I have slowly learned that the answers are not in the books. The books and the experts can cause us to reflect and give us new ideas, but they cannot be used as prescriptions. The most highly acclaimed book and the most knowledge-able expert are, at best, useful resources. We teachers have to find our own answers and tailor our lessons to our particular group of children and ourselves. This is no easy task. Most of us have received training and methodology in the courses we have taken as opposed to education that promotes thinking and decision making. Frank Smith stated it well when he said: "Many teachers are trained to be ignorant, to rely on the opinions of experts or 'superiors,' rather than on their own judgment" (1983, p. 5). Indeed, we have been well taught that the answers lie outside of ourselves.

Even as I am writing this passage, I am thinking, "What do Ken Goodman, Don Holdaway, and Jerry Harste say about becoming a whole language teacher?" I have to stop myself from reading their thoughts and summarizing their writings and focus on what I think. After all, I am in the classroom every day working with children and teachers. I spend a lot of time reading and reflecting. I am a knowledgeable practitioner. Still, sometimes it is hard to trust myself.

We have to trust ourselves and value and adjust our own thinking even when the suggestions and ideas come from a highly reputable source. This idea really hit home with me when I was demonstrating a lesson for a colleague. She had asked me to do a writing lesson with her intermediate grade class—"something that will get them motivated because they don't like to write." I had just finished reading Don Graves's book, *Investigate Nonfiction* (1989), which is full of inspiring, practical ideas. I seized on his lesson of having the students write a letter to someone in the school community requesting a change in policy or practice. It seemed like a wonderful idea, and certainly the examples he presented spurred me on without question. Instead of adapting the lesson to fit my particular context, I adopted it exactly as Graves presented it.

What I had failed to take into consideration was this particular group of students. Given the opportunity to talk first about possible people they could write to and concerns they could write about, they used the lesson as a gripe session. Even when it was apparent that the lesson was degenerating and students' comments were clearly out of line, I forged ahead. After all, the idea came from a renowned author. This is not to say that the idea was not an excellent one for another group of children, perhaps even for most children, but for these children it was a disaster. It was only after I read through some of the negative letters that resulted—letters that would have caused an uproar if we had sent them—that I finally let go of the idea. Because I failed to trust myself to adapt an idea to my specific context, I was unable to redirect the lesson.

"First you have to trust yourself."

Allowing Time for Change

I believe that the transition to whole language is at least a five- to ten-year process. When I say that publicly, teachers breathe a sigh of relief and administrators gasp.

I think we need to be honest about exactly how difficult the transition is. So many teachers read about how whole language classrooms are supposed to look and function, and then they worry that they're not measuring up. They wonder what's wrong with them because they are still struggling and full of self-doubts. Let me say it loudly and clearly. I don't know any teachers who are not struggling, and I don't know any teachers who have it "all together." I struggle daily as I work in classrooms with teachers. Some days I even feel like an imposter. When a lesson goes badly, I feel inadequate. However, it is in the struggle that the learning takes place. I may feel better when a lesson goes well, but there's no doubt that I have learned the most from the failures. It is the failures that make me re-examine, change focus, and add a different dimension.

A high school English teacher with fourteen years of experience expressed his uneasiness about moving toward whole language: "It's a lot easier to do things the way I've always done them. I used to know what to expect. My plans were in order, and there were few surprises. Now I sometimes feel inadequate and unsure of what direction I'm going. The whole process is very unsettling, and yet, I know it's right."

It's not easy to struggle, but we need to know it is a normal and important part of the process for us all. Researcher Brian Cambourne has stated:

It seems that any learning associated with creating meaning through any medium typically involves some kind of struggle before the full potential of that medium is under control—art, music and mime, as well as print. Furthermore, there appears to be something genuinely pleasurable derived from the struggle which is experienced in these situations. Remove the struggle and you remove the pleasure. (1988, p. 5)

In my struggle to make literature-group discussion time more meaningful, I believe it has taken me more than ten years to ask the really important questions to go along with the books. Having milked the basal for skills for many years and having been conditioned to listen for right answers, I have found it difficult to use the literature *just* for pleasure and appreciation and to make connections with our lives. It has also been difficult to learn to redirect discussions so that the students— not the teacher—have ownership of the meaning making. This does not mean I was not a good reading teacher before; I was. However, I am a better teacher now because I am guiding students to construct and validate their own meanings.

I think there is another message that needs to come across. I am in and out of classrooms every day, and I have yet to see a "pure" whole language classroom, whatever that may be. I do not see every subject tied together by theme and children's needs, and I have rarely seen a totally integrated program. The totally integrated classroom takes many, many years to achieve. Even then, I'm not sure it is always possible.

I used to feel I didn't measure up because I wasn't integrating everything. Andrea Butler helped me some years ago by reassuring me that I was a whole language teacher. Now I believe that if I am integrating the language processes in meaningful, authentic ways, that's whole language. The ideal integration—across the total curriculum—is still a goal, but I'm not a failure because I'm not there yet.

I am privileged to work daily with a group of public school teachers whom I consider unusually dedicated and talented. Most of us work way beyond contract hours, and we take time to reflect on our teaching. We are all struggling to weave in demands of the curriculum and required objectives along with trying to become whole language teachers. In addition, we are adjusting and juggling schedules for children leaving and entering classrooms throughout the day for various special services. We are dealing with a diverse and challenging population in school and are leading busy private lives and taking care of our families outside of school. We need to give ourselves credit for all that we are doing well and for the growth we are striving for in our teaching. If we are integrating reading, writing, speaking, and listening in a natural, meaningful way—even part of the time—we are whole language teaching.

Teachers, parents, and administrators need to be realistic about how long meaningful change (not just cosmetic change) really takes. There's often an expectation that if a district or school makes a commitment to whole language, everything should be in place in one year. I have never seen that happen. Typically, I notice that teachers feel comfortable adding one new component to their program each year—perhaps shared book experience the first year, journal writing the next year, an independent reading program the following year, shared decision making about rules and curriculum the next year, and integrating spelling after four or five years. The thoughtful, slow change that is occurring may not always be visible, but it is change of the highest order—stemming from a greater understanding of the philosophy and of the literacy model of learning and teaching.

Finally, I believe we need to be kind to ourselves and accept and acknowledge that the kind of deep change we want to make takes time, lots of time. We need to go slowly, let ourselves make mistakes, and, most of all, give ourselves credit for what we are doing well and for the risks we are taking.

Giving Up Control

Giving up some control has been my most difficult transition in becoming a whole language teacher. To gradually move from directing a classroom, where no one speaks without a raised hand and being called upon, to being a colearner in a cooperative environment where students freely express their opinions was unsettling at first. To slowly change from an environment where all comments are directed to the teacher to a more flexible setting where students have some choices and respond to one another, as well as to the teacher, has not happened easily.

Initially, the kids don't really believe we teachers want them to make choices. They have had years of conditioning: in writing for the teacher, in answering to and for the teacher, and in looking for the "right answer" they think the teacher holds and wants from them. To write and think for themselves is a totally new experience for many of them, and at first they do not believe this is really the desired goal. At the secondary level, where quiet classrooms with lecture formats have been the norm for a long time, trying to move to a more democratic setting can initially be unnerving for both teachers and students.

Part of giving up control has been adjusting to a different model—an interactive, collaborative model of teaching and learning instead of the traditional, transmission model which has us teachers as the source of all knowledge. High school teacher Holly Burgess comments, "My big fear was I wouldn't be a real teacher if I wasn't teacher centered and directive. It's so hard to get away from that after being tied to that model for so many years. When I get nervous or apprehensive, I still retreat to structure."

Some teachers fear that giving up control means giving up on discipline, but I do not see that as the case. I see giving up control as referring to giving more ownership and choice to students and trusting students to be responsible. It may take a while, but teachers report being pleased with the results when they begin to let go. High school English teacher Dana Noble comments:

> I conducted a writing workshop based upon the Atwell model and found that a pair of students seemed always to be talking and laughing, generally very excitedly when they should have been writing (as I often reminded them). However, when they completed pieces I found evidence of their positive influence on each other. I had (and still have) trouble giving up control.

Mary Pryor, a second grade teacher, noted that she had changed her procedures for her annual autobiography project. In the past, she had sent home written directions for writing the final page, "About the Author," and students received help from their parents. This year she modeled what an author page looks like and gave the responsibility to the students to do in class. She was delighted with how well the children did. In addition, she had previously done all the final proofreading herself. This year she modeled some proofreading expectations and was pleased to see how much the children were able to do themselves.

Joan Servis, a fourth grade teacher, has her students work in groups to write reports on prairie wildlife to go along with their literature study of *Sarah, Plain and Tall* by Patricia McLachlan. She had always set up the format for the reports, but this year she let the children choose their own formats. She states, "Ninety percent of the students came up with a better format than mine."

I found that when I began to give up some control and became less directive, not only were my professional relationships enriched. Improved relationships extended outside the classroom. For myself, when I finally stopped having all the answers, I became a more effective parent and developed a healthier relationship with my children. Now when a problem is presented I am not so quick to give solutions. Rather, I am more likely to ask, "What do you think?" and then listen to what my family has to say.

Giving up control also includes giving up being controlled by materials. It refers to taking more responsibility for the materials we teachers are using and how we are using them. As long as publishers' programs are determining how and what we teach, the materials—and not the teacher and students—are controlling instruction.

"The Basal Is Not the Enemy"

"Materials in the hands of a teacher who holds a skills model are skills materials. Materials in the hands of a teacher who holds a whole language model are whole language materials."

That highly significant statement was made by Paul Crowley at the annual meeting of the International Reading Association in May 1989. While quality literature and materials are necessary for excellent instruction, the materials we employ are only as strong as our theory of language learning. It is the way we teachers combine theory and practice that determines the effectiveness of our materials.

In some school districts, whole language has erroneously become synonymous with giving up the basal. It has become common to hear teachers say, "We're doing whole language. We're using literature." I recently overheard a teacher say, "I teach reading in the morning. I *do* literature in the afternoon." While this teacher saw herself as a whole language teacher because she was using literature, her statement indicates that her theoretical beliefs have not changed. She still views reading as the basal and skills work—and literature as something "extra," to be done after the reading work is out of the way. She is clearly giving her students the message—whether she states it or not—that reading is getting the skills.

It is not unusual to see classrooms with no basals but where books of literature are read whole class, round-robin style. Seatwork consists of packets of vocabulary words to look up and lots of questions to answer in written form for each chapter. Even though literature is being used, children have few actual choices during reading time. Using literature, reading Big Books, and doing journal writing are not enough. Unless we also know why we are doing what we are doing, the way we do these activities may be no different from the skills-based, fragmented, teacher-directed basals we have set aside. Conversely, it *is* possible to take a basal story and use it meaningfully.

Undoubtedly, we need to examine basals closely and continue to put pressure on publishers to make them better. The teachers' manuals and workbooks need to be used judiciously—if at all. If they are used, attention needs to shift to the enrichment section, with little or no focus on the segmented, required skills. When basals are used, I believe they must be heavily supplemented with authentic books, self-selected reading of all types, and genuine oral and written responses. At the same time, we also need to be looking very carefully at whole language materials—if there is such a thing. Some whole language companies are producing so many materials that it's beginning to be difficult to distinguish them from the basal companies. One company goes so far as to say, "If it's not from _____, it may not be whole language." Teachers need to be knowledgeable enough about language learning to choose how to use all materials appropriately.

Educators need to guard against the common tendency to pit whole language against basal texts and to set up whole language as an orthodoxy. We must take great care not to give the message that there is only one right way to be a whole language teacher. Perhaps, most importantly, we cannot ignore the very practical issue that many teachers do not have the option of giving up the basal textbook. Basals are still mandated by many, indeed probably most, boards of education.

In talking with teachers around the country, I worry that the whole language movement may be promoting exclusiveness. To imply that one can be a whole language teacher only if no basals are used or only if certain specific procedures are followed is dangerous because this places far too much emphasis on materials and methods. When I first gave up basals and workbooks, I spent years as a "basal basher" with minimal tolerance for basal users and publishers. As a literature "purist," I spent a lot of time pointing out the bad features of basal texts. Over the past several years, however, I've come to realize that the basal is not the enemy. The basal text is, at best or worst—like any material—a resource. In the hands of a knowledgeable professional, it can be used holistically and intelligently, particularly if the worksheets are set aside. Becoming a whole language teacher is not conditional on the materials the teacher is using; it is conditional on the teacher's theory of how children learn. It is the literacy model the teacher holds that determines the type of instruction that actually goes on in the classroom.

Whole language is not just about giving up the basal. Rather, it is about having teachers and students decide together what is worth knowing and how to come to know it. It is about setting up a learning environment that is purposeful, authentic, and based on both the children's and teachers' needs and desires to know.

One strength of whole language is that the teacher is a decision maker. To tell teachers they cannot use basals or any other commercial material is as directive as the school district that mandates their use. I don't like being told I must do something in order to gain acceptance. I prefer to look at the evidence and make my own decisions and choices based on careful evaluation, reasoning, and sound judgment. That is, after all, what we are hoping children in our whole language classrooms will be able to do.

Transition to whole language is a very slow process. Most teachers seem to need to hang on to their basals for a while as they gradually move toward a literature and meaning-centered approach. We need to be supportive, accepting, and encouraging of all teachers who are choosing and attempting to move toward whole language. We need to remember that becoming a whole language teacher-learner is a humbling experience; the process is ongoing, probably for life.

Stages in Becoming a Whole Language Teacher

In examining my own behaviors in moving toward whole language, I see myself as going through the following stages:

1. I can't do this. It's too hard, and I don't know enough.
2. Maybe if I find out about it, it's possible.
3. I'll do exactly what the experts say.
4. I'll adapt the experts' work to my own contexts.
5. I trust myself as an observer-teacher-learner-evaluator.

Like many of us, I started off feeling overwhelmed and inadequate, and becoming a whole language teacher seemed out of reach. Part of that feeling stemmed from defensiveness and a reluctance to change. Gradually, because of curiosity and wanting to grow as a teacher, I moved to stage 2, where I took the time to explore—mostly through professional reading and attending conferences. Listening to educators at conferences and interacting with teachers in process made whole language seem like a possibility. At that stage, however, whole language seemed possible only if I could get all the activities in place.

Looking back, I see that initial preoccupation with activities as normal. For myself and others, becoming a whole language teacher seemed so initially overwhelming that we looked to get the materials and activities in place for some comfort and security. One teacher described herself as having spent an exhausting year "scrambling for activities." After a year of attending our district support group—where much time had been spent talking about learning theory she realized that she had changed her activities while holding on firmly to a traditional philosophy. She excitedly announced her insight at our final spring meeting and said she was now ready to begin to do some professional reading and think about why she was doing what she was doing.

As I continued to attend conferences, read professionally, reflect on my teaching, share ideas of what was working and not working with colleagues, and observe children, I slowly began to feel that meaningful change was possible for me. I came to realize that the process is not about activities and covering curriculum but about ongoing thinking and analysis of educational philosophy and teaching methods.

I have spent the longest time at stage 3. Jerry Harste has called a similar stage "adopting a guru." After I read Donald Graves, I taught the writing process exactly as he wrote about it. When I read Frank Smith, Ken Goodman, Nancie Atwell, Marie Clay, and many other experts, I did not question anything they said; I simply adopted their stances. I did not yet have the confidence or well-developed theory base to take my own stand, and I had not yet become a kidwatcher.

Gradually, after many years of teaching, reflecting, observing, and collaborating, I began to feel confident about my own beliefs about literacy learning. While I am still highly influenced by many great educators, I have begun to adapt what I read to my own learning-teaching contexts. Because I can articulate my own learning theory, I can apply my theory to what I read and observe and make thoughtful decisions about my teaching.

The last stage builds on stage 4 and is where I want to be. It makes me a part of a community of learners that recognizes that for all of us—even the "experts"— beliefs grow and change. I am now as influenced by my fellow teachers as I am by the great educators. Because of my observations and ongoing evaluation of myself and students, I am better able to trust my beliefs and adjust and apply them to new contexts. I recognize that I will always be a learner. I welcome the fact that I will be in the process of "becoming" all the years that I remain a teacher.

Resources

The following resources have been particularly helpful in furthering understanding about whole language and in developing a personal philosophy. They have also proved useful and thought provoking in group discussion. See also "Themed Journals" (pp. 27b–29b) for complete journals devoted to whole language. For a complete listing of recommended resources see *Resources for Teachers* (blue pages in this book and in Routman, 1988).

Cambourne, Brian. 1988. *The Whole Story: Natural Learning and the Acquisition of Literacy in the Classroom.* Richmond Hill, Ontario, Canada: Scholastic-TAB Publications Ltd.

    For teachers ready to take the time to understand the theory behind whole language, this text (201 pp.) offers detailed insight into the language learning process. The in-depth discussion of Cambourne's eight conditions of learning is thought provoking and applicable to the classroom.

Cazden, Courtney. 1992. *Whole Language Plus: Essays on Literacy in the United States and New Zealand.* New York: Teachers College Press. See annotation, p. 8b.

Church, Susan. February 1994. "Is Whole Language Really Warm and Fuzzy?" *The Reading Teacher,* pp. 362–370. See annotation, p. 43b.

Cochrane, Orin (ed.). 1992. *Questions and Answers About Whole Language.* Katonah, NY: Richard C. Owen Publishers. See annotation, p. 10b.

Cochrane, Orin and Ethel Buchanan (eds.). 1993. *Teachers' Stories: Starting the Year with Whole Language.* Winnipeg: Whole Language Consultants. See annotation, p. 10b.

Corderio, Pat. 1992. *Whole Learning: Whole Language and Content in the Upper Elementary Grades.* Katonah, NY: Richard C. Owen Publishers. See annotation, p. 10b.

Crafton, Linda K. 1994. *Challenges of Holistic Teaching: Answering the Tough Questions.* Norwood, MA: Christopher-Gordon. See annotation, p. 10b.

Crafton, Linda K. 1991. *Whole Language: Getting Started . . . Moving Forward.* Katonah, NY: Richard C. Owen Publishers. See annotation, p. 11b.

Dolyniuk, Peterette. 1992. "Do Nothing to Destroy the Joy." See Appendix K, pp. 213–214b.

Edelsky, Carole, Bess Altwerger, and Barbara Flores. 1991. *Whole Language: What's the Difference?* Portsmouth, NH: Heinemann. See annotation, p. 13b.

Forester, Anne D. and Margaret Reinhard. 1989. *The Learner's Way.* Winnipeg, Canada: Peguis. See annotation, p. 15b.

Forester, Anne D. and Margaret Reinhard. 1991. *On the Move: Teaching the Learners' Way in Grades 4–7.* Winnipeg, Canada: Peguis. See annotation, p. 16b.

Fox, Mem. 1993. *Radical Reflections: Passionate Opinions on Teaching, Learning, and Living.* San Diego, CA: Harcourt Brace & Company. See annotation, p. 16b.

Freeman, Yvonne S. and David E. Freeman. 1992. *Whole Language for Second Language Learners.* Portsmouth, NH: Heinemann. See annotation, p. 16b.

Garan, Elaine M. March 1994. "Who's in Control? Is There Enough 'Empowerment' to Go Around?" *Language Arts,* pp. 192–199. See annotation, p. 45b.

Goodman, Ken. 1986. *What's Whole in Whole Language?* Portsmouth, NH: Heinemann.

   This excellent, short guide (79 pp.) for teachers and parents explains what whole language is all about. Ways to make language learning easy are given; the learning theory behind whole language teaching is discussed; principles of whole language instruction and learning are listed; implementation objectives and specifics are concisely noted.

Harp, Bill (ed.). 1993. *Bringing Children to Literacy: Classrooms at Work.* Norwood, MA: Christopher-Gordon. See annotation, p. 19b.

Heald-Taylor, Gail. 1989. *The Administrator's Guide to Whole Language.* Katonah, NY: Richard C. Owen. See annotation, p. 20b.

Holdaway, Don. Winter 1989. "The Big Questions Behind Whole Language," *Teachers Networking: The Whole Language Newsletter.* Katonah, NY: Richard C. Owen Publishers.

   This is a wonderful article for understanding the theory behind whole language. Holdaway explains what is meant by natural language learning, how it operates, and what the implications are for educational practice.

Holdaway, Don. 1979. *The Foundations of Literacy.* Portsmouth, NH: Heinemann.

   This classic text (232 pp.) by the originator of shared book experience is a must reading and rereading for anyone wishing to understand the roots and rudiments of whole language. Holdaway gives many examples of how to induce the development of literacy strategies that respect the developmental learning model.

Mills, Heidi and Jean Anne Clyde (eds.). 1990. *Portraits of Whole Language Classrooms: Learning for All Ages.* Portsmouth, NH: Heinemann. See annotation, p. 26b.

Newman, Judith. 1991. *Interwoven Conversations: Learning and Teaching through Critical Reflection.* Portsmouth, NH: Heinemann. See annotation, p. 28b.

Newman, Judith (ed.). 1985. *Whole Language: Theory in Use:* Portsmouth, NH: Heinemann.

   Canadian teachers share their experiences for teaching and understanding reading and writing. Particularly useful for increasing theoretical understanding are the articles by Judith Newman: "Insights from Recent Reading and Writing Research and Their Implications for Developing Whole Language Curriculum," "Using Children's Books to Teach Reading," and "What About Reading?"

Pace, Glenellen. January 1991. "When Teachers Use Literature for Literacy Instruction. Ways that Constrain, Ways that Free." *Language Arts,* pp. 12–25. See annotation, p. 48b.

Raines, Shirley C. and Robert J. Canady. 1990. *The Whole Language Kindergarten.* New York: Teachers College Press. See annotation, p. 31b.

Robb, Laura. 1994. *Whole Language, Whole Learners: Creating a Literature-Centered Classroom.* New York: William Morrow. See annotation, p. 32b.

Smith, Frank. 1983. *Essays into Literacy.* Portsmouth, NH: Heinemann.

   This is a book you will want to own or have in your school library. Smith gives us lots to think about concerning how we are teaching reading and writing and how we should be teaching. This is an absolutely terrific book for understanding learning theory and for helping form one's own philosophy of learning and teaching.

Smith, Frank. 1988. *Joining the Literacy Club.* Portsmouth, NH: Heinemann.

   Smith's second collection of literacy essays discusses the teacher's role as critical in facilitating all students' entrance into reading and writing clubs. By "literacy club" Smith means the social nature of literacy learning and children's natural desire to be part of the community of learners. This inspiring, thought-provoking reading contains lots of specifics for fostering club membership.

Strickland, Kathleen and James. 1993. *Uncovering the Curriculum: Whole Language in Secondary and Postsecondary Classrooms.* Portsmouth, NH: Heinemann. See annotation, p. 36b.

Vacca, Richard T. and Timothy V. Rasinski. 1992. *Case Studies in Whole Language.* Orlando, FL: Harcourt Brace & Company. See annotation, p. 39b.

Walmsley, Sean A. and Ellen L. Adams. April 1993. "Realities of Whole Language." *Language Arts,* pp. 272–280. See annotation, p. 50b.

Watson, Dorothy. November 1989. "Defining and Describing Whole Language." *The Elementary School Journal,* pp. 129–141.

   Watson describes whole language and includes the content of the classroom and the beliefs whole language teachers support. This article comes as close as you will get to giving a satisfactory working definition of whole language. Excellent for discussion.

Watson, Dorothy, Carolyn Burke, and Jerome Harste. 1989. *Whole Language: Inquiring Voices*. Richmond Hill, Ontario, Canada: Scholastic-TAB Publications Ltd. See annotation, p. 40b.

Weaver, Constance. 1990. *Understanding Whole Language: From Principles to Practice*. Portsmouth, NH: Heinemann. See annotation, p. 40b.

Weaver, Constance and Linda Henke. 1992. *Supporting Whole Language: Stories of Teachers and Institutional Change*. Portsmouth, NH: Heinemann. See annotation, p. 41b.

3

Components of Whole Language

Sustained silent reading

The purpose of this chapter is to present possibilities and raise awareness of what constitutes a balanced literacy program. Components of a whole language program as organized by the teacher and students are discussed and include:

- Reading aloud
- Writing aloud
- Shared reading
- Shared writing
- Guided reading
- Guided writing
- Independent reading
- Independent writing

This chapter is meant to encourage teachers of all grade levels and subject areas to look at their teaching and think about incorporating and integrating the various components in ways that both suit their purposes and respect a whole language view of teaching and learning. For clarification and organization, the balanced reading and writing programs are delineated. In actuality, however, there is little or no separation between reading and writing. And while literature is viewed as the mainstay of the literacy program, literature is meant to include fiction and nonfiction and to encompass the content areas. Implicit in the various approaches to reading and writing described here are many opportunities for speaking, listening, sharing, and evaluating.

A Balanced Reading Program

A balanced reading program includes the following components:

- Reading aloud
- Shared reading

31

- Guided reading
- Independent reading
- Language opportunities to respond critically and thoughtfully

Each of these components or approaches is part of the ongoing reading program through the grades. While most of them can be integrated into a daily program, there is much room for flexibility. Shared reading, guided reading, and/or independent reading are sometimes missing from the reading program. By discussing these various approaches in depth, options and opportunities may seem possible and desirable. (For an excellent description of the above approaches to reading, especially for kindergarten and grade 1, see Mooney, 1990.)

A Balanced Writing Program

- Writing aloud
- Shared writing
- Guided writing
- Independent writing
- Language opportunities to respond critically and thoughtfully

Each of the above approaches—in natural combination—make up part of the daily writing program. These approaches, which include demonstrations by teachers, offer lots of opportunities for student choice, involvement and response, and teacher guidance. The examples presented are meant to encourage a wide range of possibilities.

A Balanced Reading Program

Reading Aloud

Reading aloud is seen as the single most influential factor in young children's success in learning to read. Additionally, reading aloud improves listening skills, builds vocabulary, aids reading comprehension, and has a positive impact on students' attitudes toward reading. It is the easiest component to incorporate into any language program at any grade level. Reading aloud is cost effective, requires little preparation, and results in few discipline problems. Nonetheless, it is sometimes neglected just because it is so easy and pleasurable. I can remember for years feeling uncomfortable about spending daily time reading aloud—the children and I were enjoying it so much. It took me a long time to accept that one doesn't have to suffer, do hard work, or require written responses for an activity to be worthwhile.

In kindergarten and grade 1, much of what we read aloud may be repeated readings of favorite books and poems. Teachers find when they place the read-alouds in the classroom library, children often choose these books to read. Reading aloud should take place daily at all grade levels, including junior high and high school. With limited time periods at the secondary level, the read-aloud may be a poem, excerpt, or short story used as a read-aloud or shared reading. The read-aloud is completed in just a few minutes at the beginning of the period and helps set the tone for the class. One middle grade teacher begins each afternoon with a poetry read-aloud, with each student being responsible for a week of poetry reading. The teacher has lots of poetry books in the room all year, from the library and classroom collection, and students choose favorite poems and practice reading them before presenting them to the class.

Frank Smith tells us that everything we need to know about reading and writing we can learn from authors. I believe this strongly, along with Nancie Atwell's notion that we have to make students "insiders," able to see the way the author has chosen to put the text together. Reading aloud is a powerful technique for promoting story enjoyment and literature appreciation and for noting what authors do in the writing process so that students can make similar choices for themselves.

Shared Reading

I define shared reading as any rewarding reading situation in which a learner—or group of learners—sees the text, observes an expert (usually the teacher) reading it with fluency and expression, and is invited to read along. The learner is in the role of receiving support, and the teacher-expert accepts and encourages all efforts and approximations the learner (the novice) makes. Each reading situation is a relaxed, social one, with emphasis on enjoyment and appreciation of the stories, songs, rhymes, chants, raps, and poems. The literature is carefully chosen for its high quality of language and illustrations and often includes rereadings of favorite stories and poems. Following shared reading, students have opportunities to reread the literature independently. When enlarged texts are used, little books of the same title are always available.

While shared reading has traditionally been associated with beginning reading in the primary grades and the use of delightful stories, poems, and songs in enlarged print (especially predictable Big Books with rhyme, rhythm, and repetition), shared reading is appropriate and desirable for children of *all* grades, even through high school. Some secondary foreign language teachers have successfully used Big Books and shared reading as a way to reinforce language and add motivation and interest. Second language learners (ESL students) pick up rhymes and sight vocabulary and develop reading fluency from nursery rhymes and predictable books with repetitive patterns. In addition to enlarged print in Big Books and on charts, regular-size print can be made visible to all students by using transparencies of several prechosen pages on the overhead projector. As in all shared reading experiences, the emphasis is on enjoying and appreciating the text.

Shared reading is one way of immersing students in rich, literary-level language without worrying about grade level or reading performance. For young children who have had limited exposure to the language of storybooks, shared reading and discussion of stories provide a framework for literature and language. For reluctant and struggling readers of all ages, shared reading offers a nonthreatening approach to reading that strengthens skills and enjoyment. High-frequency words and the conventions of print, seen over and over again, are learned naturally without boring drill. Poems that are reread for pleasure provide a way for students to build reading fluency and confidence as well as develop an appreciation of poetry.

A variation on the technique of shared reading that works well is to introduce nursery rhymes or poetry orally first. Once students become accustomed to hearing the language, reading the text visually follows easily and naturally. Listening to the language first works well for beginning readers as well as for older, reluctant readers.

Shared book approaches may include:

1. Teacher reading
2. Student reading
3. Paired reading
4. Tape recorder

Teacher Reading

In a shared reading experience, the teacher gathers the students together—often on the floor in front of her—and invites students to read along with their eyes or aloud with the teacher. Some of us have a designated carpeted area; others ask students to move desks to create such an area. A rug can be rolled out or individual carpet squares can be used; even the plain wooden or linoleum floor will work. Students sit together in a relaxed, informal manner. An engaging Big Book, a chart poem, an overhead transparency, or a copy of the selection or book is available for each student to hold or see, and students join in on an invitational basis. With older students, where shared reading is likely to occur with the use of the overhead projector or individual copies of the text, shared reading works fine with students seated at their desks. Usually the selection is read first by the teacher. On the next reading—or even on the first reading—many students will attempt to participate orally or will follow the text with their eyes. In kindergarten and grade 1 especially, to promote one-to-one matching and letter-sound links, the teacher points to each word at the same time the word is spoken.

The introduction of a book is always carefully done to invite predictions and excite the imagination. Before reading, the teacher will point to the title and author, front and back covers, book jacket, and table of contents and ask the children what they think the book will be about. The teacher may go through the pictures and ask children to predict what is going to happen. Some typical questions might be: "What do you think the focus of the book might be?" "What do you think the author is trying to tell us about . . . ?" All responses are valued and accepted. This is a time for encouraging oral language and having children listen to one another. Enough wait time is given for children to formulate their responses. Guided questioning continues throughout the story to maintain student attention, involvement, and participation. Typical questions are: "What do you think will happen next?" "What might _____ do to solve the problem?"

Shared reading is an effective way to vary the daily read-aloud book or assigned silent reading. Instead of reading an entire chapter from a book, the teacher may combine reading aloud with shared reading and/or silent reading. Or the teacher might begin a chapter with several pages of overhead transparencies (that have been made by reproducing the text). The children see the print and are invited to read along, silently with their eyes or aloud. Cloze procedures (explained on p. 141), where the teacher pauses and invites students to fill in the words orally, may also be used as long as the emphasis is on group enjoyment and participation. The chapter might then be completed by having students read aloud or silently or by combining these approaches.

Shared book experience is always a joyous time, with each child treated as a reader with no pressure to perform. We welcome children's predictions and interpretations. A sense of community builds as teacher and students share favorite literature. It is important to keep this time just for reading, responding, and sharing. Shared reading is never the time to go over assignments or seatwork.

Student Reading

A student may volunteer or be selected by the teacher to do a shared reading. Poetry works particularly well here. A student has practiced a poem of choice over and over until he feels he can read it smoothly and with expression. Copies of the poem are distributed, or the poem is put on the overhead projector, and the rest of the class follows along visually and joins in.

In Linda Powers' second grade class, students lead the daily shared poetry sessions. Usually two or three poems are read in about five to seven minutes. While the sessions begin early in the school year, with the teacher reading the poems on the overhead projector while moving a line marker down the page, our students happily take over the job after several weeks. Putting students in charge creates ongoing enthusiasm for reading poetry in the classroom. Students are always on the lookout for favorite, new poems to add to the classroom collection. The classroom notebook, where the poems are kept, is also available for student reading throughout the day. Adding new poems to the notebook—as well as locating old favorites—has also been a natural way to teach alphabetizing.

Paired Reading

Shared reading may also be paired reading, with one person reading and another following along. This technique is a powerful one for supporting less able readers. Usually a more competent reader is paired with a less competent one. For example, a teacher might read with one student or a student might read with another student. The more able reader (the expert) reads the text aloud while the less able reader (the novice) follows along. The less able reader, with no pressure or expectation to read, follows the text visually and enjoys the story.

Some of us are beginning to use this technique regularly as a way to promote heterogeneous grouping and give all students access to literature. The student who is unable to read all the words of the text independently can now join a reading-group discussion of a book that he is able to comprehend orally but may not be able to read silently. Paired reading can take place with students in the same class or with an older student reading with a younger one (see pp. 477–478).

Paired reading is also an enjoyable way for two students to complete a reading assignment or share a story. The students might go into the hall or to a designated spot and take turns reading: One reads and the other follows along, with the students supporting each other as necessary.

Tape Recorder

Many of our primary grade classrooms use cassette tapes to accompany favorite picture books. At listening posts, students follow along visually with the commercial or teacher-volunteer–made recordings. While the focus is on reading for pleasure, repeated listening and rereading of favorite stories aids fluency, development of sight word vocabularly, and story comprehension. The tape recorder is also a powerful and nonthreatening tool for struggling middle grade or older students. By having a volunteer tape book chapters, students can follow the text at their own pace to get phrasing, fluency, and meaning.

Some teachers find time to tape a single page of a text for a poor reader. Especially if the child is already familiar with the text, listening, looking, and following along without pressure builds fluency as well as self-esteem. Often, voluntarily rereading a page the student already comprehends helps the individual to become a better reader.

Reading that students cannot accomplish silently on their own may be accomplished with the support of a tape. Students may be encouraged to follow along a short section repeatedly and then be prepared to read the section orally the next day in reading group. Hearing themselves able to read more fluently is a tremendous confidence booster for students.

Strategies for Shared Reading

Shared reading leads quite naturally into innovations on books, dramatic or musical interpretations, and meaningful literature extensions that often utilize the visual arts and relate meaningfully to the text. Shared reading is also a natural way to teach skills and specific features of print. However, caution is necessary. In all cases, the text should be read and reread several times purely for enjoyment. We have observed that students request to read and love to reread favorite stories. Then, on the third, fourth, or fifth reading some teaching strategies can be utilized. Andrea Butler recommends making not more than one or two teaching points in a shared reading session. On a first reading, I often do not even use the pointer. I might slide my finger or the pointer along loosely, but at this time I am not concerned about one-to-one matching and specific words. I simply want to share a piece of literature I love and have the children savor the language, imagery, and story.

On subsequent occasions, I might do some work with specific features of the text. Repeated exposure of students to rhyming words in books and poems—with occasional use of an oral cloze procedure—makes the use of isolated rhyming worksheets unnecessary. Sometimes, I pause when I get to a particular word or phrase and let the children fill in the expected language. Some teachers use Post-it™ notes to mask (block out) high-frequency words or conventions of text so that children fill in the missing text.

Shared reading is also an excellent time to help children discover features of text—letters, phonemes, punctuation, and high-frequency words as well as do innovations on text. I use a sliding mask (see Appendix E) to highlight features of the text and naturally blend word parts in context. Specific procedures, rationales, and many examples of using Big Books and shared language experiences are provided in depth in *The Foundations of Literacy* by Don Holdaway (1979, pp. 64–80 and 126–146). (For procedures and ideas for shared reading for older children, see Adrian Peetoom, *Shared Reading: Safe Risks with Whole Books* [Richmond Hill, Ontario, Canada: Scholastic-TAB Publications, 1986, 32 pp.])

Figure 3-1   Creating Songs for a Shared Reading Experience

Tune: "Oh, the Preacher Went Down to the Cellar to Pray"
Lyrics: Joan Di Dio

The second graders went down (echo)
To the classroom to read (echo)
They picked out their WEB books
And were HAPPY indeed!
  (We're gonna read and read . . . and read some <u>more</u>!)
           } Repeat, higher

Now, Amelia Bedelia (echo)
Is one of the friends (echo)
We meet in our reading
So the fun never ends!
  (We're gonna read and read . . . and <u>read</u> some more!)
           } Repeat, higher

We're reading Beverly Cleary (echo)
Who can't be beat!
And then, of course,
There's the great Bill Peet!
  (We're gonna read and read . . . and <u>read</u> some more!)
           } Repeat, higher

Now, the <u>Little's</u> series
Is so much fun!
Their world is so tiny
But they get things done!
  (We're gonna read and read . . . and <u>read</u> some more!)
           } Repeat, higher

We're gonna read <u>some</u> WEB books fast
We're gonna read <u>some</u> WEB books slow
But they're ALL gonna help us grow.

Don't forget the <u>JOURNALS</u>!

Oh, we write in our Journals (echo)
Almost every day
"Cause a second grader
Has SO MUCH to say!
           } Repeat, higher

Refrain:
  Yes, we write in our Journals
  About how we feel.
  Sometimes it's "made-up"
  And sometimes it's real!
  We're WRITERS, now
  In second grade!

A Specific Example: Reading a Poem

I like to use the overhead projector and an oral cloze procedure with favorite poems from my childhood or favorite poems the children choose. Using two 5 by 7 inch index cards, I employ the bottom card to cover the text completely and move down the page one line at a time; I use the top card to expose the text gradually, word by word, as the card moves to the right across each line. With rhyming words, we need show only the beginning consonant, digraph, or blend for students to complete the rhyming couplet. An example of an old favorite is the following:

> I had a nickel and I walked around the block.
> I walked right into a baker shop.
> I took two doughnuts right out of the grease;
> I handed the lady my five-cent piece.
> She looked at the nickel and she looked at me,
> And said, "This money's no good to me.
> There's a hole in the nickel, and it goes right through"
> Says I, "There's a hole in the doughnut, too."
> (From *A Rocket in My Pocket*, Holt, 1988)

Despite the fact that my grown children have warned me not to sing in public, I sing everything that has a tune to it or that the music teacher will set to music. Children love to sing, and following the words along on the overhead, in the text, or on individual printed sheets makes the reading/singing fun and easy. One primary teacher used the daily literature as a springboard for a song that became a class hit (see Figure 3–1). For older, reluctant readers, favorite songs and raps with acceptable lyrics can be used for a shared reading experience. Children enjoy adding their own sound effects and dramatic movements to the songs.

Guided Reading

> In guided reading the teacher and a group of children, or sometimes an individual child, talk and think and question their way through a book of which they each have a copy. The teacher shows the children what questions to ask of themselves as readers, and of the author through the text, so that each child can discover the author's meaning on the first reading. Guided reading is dependent on the teacher being aware of each child's competencies, interests, and experiences; being able to determine the supports and challenges offered by a book; and accepting the role of supporting learning rather than directing learning (Mooney, 1990, p. 11).

Guided reading is the heart of the instructional reading program. Here we meet with students to think critically about a book. Selections that have been assigned for silent reading are discussed, with the children responding to the text in open-ended and personal ways. Most of the time with the group is spent in discussion, in appreciating and enjoying the language of literature, and in sharing personal and group insights. Often there is oral reading, but not round-robin reading with emphasis on getting the words right. This is oral reading for pleasure, for emphasizing particular descriptive passages or settings, for backing up a statement in discussion, and for noting strategies that children are employing. Even at the secondary level, students request and seem to need to read aloud. There will be teachable moments—for example, stopping to examine a concept or a feature of the text—and specific teaching for strategies as the need arises. During this time, vocabulary, as it relates to the text and children's lives, is discussed in the context of the book. Relating a book to children's lives, to other books, and to other authors are worthwhile connections the teacher guides. (See Chap. 6, "Responding to Literature," for detailed information on literature response logs, asking important questions, literature discussion groups, and various responses to literature.) While guided reading as discussed here refers to literature in the reading program, guided reading also needs to extend to texts and informational books across the curriculum.

While I believe strongly that small groups should be heterogeneous (see Chap. 4, "Grouping for Success: Taking a Close Look at Ability Grouping") and grouped according to interests and not abilities, for me the exception is first grade, especially early in the school year. To try to meet all students' needs, I find that small groups based according to ability that meet for fifteen to twenty minutes a day to develop specific strategies and reading fluency are appropriate. For the teacher it can be extremely frustrating to have small-group, literature sessions that include students who do not yet have one-to-one matching (of spoken word to printed word) along with students who are already reading or on the verge of reading. Even in first grade, however, the majority of reading time is heterogeneous, whole-class shared reading. And, once children are reading fluently and have moved to independent silent reading, most of the small-group reading time can be spent on discussion, and mixed ability groups are desirable. This can happen toward the end of the school year.

Although there may be some short-term ability grouping in first grade, all books in the classroom reading center or library are available for all students to choose to read independently. Additionally, it is always advantageous to invite small groups of interested children to "read" and enjoy a book together.

I see guided reading in kindergarten as being invitational and an opportunity to explore books and print. Students who have enjoyed a shared reading of a Big Book may choose to "read" it with the teacher or with the teacher and a small group.

Whole-Class Guided Reading

In whole-class guided reading, all students read and discuss the same book at the same time. Each student has a personal copy of the book, and the teacher guides the literature discussion. While this is often a transitional stage for many teachers, there are benefits in whole-class reading.

I have observed that as teachers have moved into literature and away from the basal text, whole-class reading seems to be the norm. Most of us initially feel overwhelmed at the thought of reading all the new titles, planning activities without the aid of a teacher's manual, and managing three reading groups and the accompanying independent work assignments. Whole-class reading makes reading instruction time manageable. At times, and in moderation, whole-class reading is an excellent way to get to know the children, observe strategies and attitudes, and build a reading community. I have always liked starting off the year with each student having a copy of the same book. It is an opportunity for me to model good questioning techniques, encourage open-ended responses, observe the students' reading abilities and attitudes, and promote the enjoyment of the literature in a relaxed, congenial setting.

In time, however, I believe there should be opportunities for small groups to meet so that all of the children's voices are heard. I have found it impossible to have an entire class of twenty-five children involved in a discussion. The same seven or eight children tend to dominate, and you never get to know all of the children as readers. The only way to involve all children in meaningful discussion and to observe the strategies they are using is to meet in small groups of about six to nine students or to meet with individual children.

In my own district, the first year we moved into literature-based reading I was surprised to find most teachers doing whole-class reading most of the time. It took me a while to understand the dynamics. It was not that teachers were taking the easy way out—far from it. They were working harder than ever. Teachers simply did not yet have the confidence, the management techniques, and all the activities they felt they needed to break into small groups. Reading and teaching just one book without the aid of a detailed teacher's manual was initially very time consuming and emotionally demanding. It was the working together in the buildings—in our weekly support groups and with each other—that gradually encouraged most teachers to move into small, guided reading groups. The impetus for change also came from the frustration teachers had experienced when it came time to write report cards as they found they could not give specifics about individual students' reading.

For most of us, the transition to two, three, or four guided reading groups has taken at least several years. This is important to keep in mind because it would be easy to just look on the surface and judge ongoing whole-class reading as a lack of effort on the part of teachers. In rare cases this may be true. However, for almost all teachers I have worked with, whole-class guided reading is the beginning of the transition from the basal to literature.

Even with whole-class reading, the format may be varied. A reading period may begin with the teacher reading aloud while students follow along visually in their own copies. The teacher can take this opportunity to "think aloud" and make thought processes and strategies visible to students. For example, the teacher can think aloud about how the meaning of a word is inferred from text and background experiences. Students may then be asked to read some pages silently for a specific purpose. A page of text can also be put onto a transparency and placed on the overhead projector. Part of the page may be read as a shared reading and part may be read silently. Students may be asked to read to answer a specific question or to note the author's purpose. Students who read quickly and finish early may be told, "Find the line that tells us . . . " or "Find the sentence that lets us know . . . ." The transparency may also be used with a sliding mask (Appendix E) to note specific vocabulary or do word analysis. Within whole-class reading and discussion there may also be paired reading or individual silent reading of text, followed by whole-class discussion.

Small-Group Guided Reading

In the small-group guided reading session, most of the time is devoted to high-level discussion, with the teacher and students reacting to all or part of a book. (This topic is discussed in detail in Chap. 5, "Responding to Literature: Early Transitions" and Chap. 6, "Responding to Literature: Later Transitions.") In first grade, the guided reading lesson is geared mostly to developing fluency, confidence, and early reading strategies and to promoting independence. In secondary classes, guided reading allows all students to develop insights into theme, style, divergent opinions, higher-order thinking, and various forms of literature.

Guided reading groups may also be the place to do direct and indirect teaching of vocabulary, phonics, and word-attack skills. As the need arises, we develop strategy lessons for particular skills. Many of these lessons will occur on the spot. Small-group guided reading sessions are also used with struggling readers to teach and reinforce strategies. For example, students who are successfully contributing to a heterogeneous discussion group because they have received support reading the text (usually through a paired reading) may be called together at another time during the day to practice reading portions of the text and receive guided reading at their instructional level. (See "Teaching for Strategies," pp. 138–144, for specific examples of small-group strategy lessons.)

Individualized Guided Reading

Some teachers are very successful in combining an individualized reading program with whole-class shared reading experiences. The program is individualized in that students self-select fiction and nonfiction books, self-pace their reading and performance, and conference with the teacher. In place of small-group instruction with the same book that the teacher may have selected, in an individualized guided reading program the teacher either meets individually with students or guides small-group discussions with students who share reactions to different books they have read or are reading. In conferencing one-to-one, the teacher may ask the child to do some oral reading, retell a story, or answer some questions to assess comprehension. On-the-spot teaching of needed strategies will take place. (See David Hornsby, Deborah Sukarna, and Jo-Ann Parry, *Read On: A Conference Approach to Reading*, [Portsmouth, NH: Heinemann, 1988] for suggestions and procedures.)

While an individualized reading program is terrific for placing important emphasis on self-selected reading and children's interests, my personal bias is that small-group guided reading—discussing the same book—is necessary to reach the high level of critical thinking and interaction that can evolve only from in-depth discussion of a book that a group of students are reading or have read. And without teacher guidance and encouragement, some worthwhile books might never be picked up and come to be appreciated by the students on their own. Additionally, a totally individualized approach can be difficult to manage. Finding the time to meet regularly and in depth with every student can be a real challenge to any teacher.

Depending on a particular group of students and their needs, the combination of approaches will vary. There is no one right way or best way. As long as your reading program is balanced, with a variety of reading-writing-listening-speaking possibilities that include guidance, choice, and response, there are many options.

Independent Reading

Opportunities for students to read self-selected books is an indispensable part of a balanced reading program. In independent reading students are in charge of their own reading—by choosing their own books, by doing their own reading, and by taking responsibility to work through the challenges of the text. "The teacher's role changes from one of initiating, modeling, and guiding to one of providing and then observing, acknowledging, and responding" (Mooney, 1990, pp. 72–73).

The importance of voluntary reading cannot be overstated. In a study of fifth-graders' activities outside school, it was found that "time spent reading books was the best predictor of a child's growth as a reader from the second to the fifth grade" (Richard C. Anderson, Paul T. Wilson, and Linda G. Fielding, "Growth in Reading and How Children Spend Their Time Outside of School," *Reading Research Quarterly*, Summer 1988, p. 297).

Since there is no question that reading achievement is positively influenced by the amount of time spent reading books, we must provide time in school—even at the secondary level—for students to read books of their own choosing. According to the research study just cited, even ten minutes a day of independent reading can increase reading proficiency.

Providing a wide selection of all types of fiction and nonfiction books through school and classroom libraries is essential. Our available books include both familiar books and new titles and are representative of children's interests and reading abilities. Books are changed and added to as needed to promote high interest and meet the demands of the curriculum. Guiding students to select books and gain familiarity with authors is necessary, especially at the start. When I bring lots of books into the classroom library, I take time to do brief "book talks." I tell just enough about the book to whet students' appetites and give them some guidance in self-selection. Even when I have not read the book, by looking at the synopsis of the book on the jacket flaps or back cover, I can give some useful information. For introducing students to books, having students "sell" their favorite books to classmates also works well.

Setting aside time for reading, with us teachers as reading models, must be a priority in all classrooms. For some students, school is the only place where quiet reading time and the possibility of developing the reading habit is conceivable. Outside of school, video games, video cassette recorders, movies, music, telephone calls, and television often preempt what could be time for reading.

In some classrooms, individualized reading of self-selected books may be the mainstay of the reading program. In others, it is a small but vital part of the total reading program—often taking place after lunch or at the end of the day, when students and teachers find pleasure in a favorite book. While quiet is desirable for voluntary reading time, silence is not necessary unless the teacher and students prefer it. Young children—for example, kindergartners—enjoy reading a book together, talking about a book, or dramatizing a story during their voluntary reading time. Some teachers call this sustained shared reading time.

Many teachers find it works well to begin with five to ten minutes a day of SSR (sustained silent reading), RR (recreational reading), DIRT (daily independent reading time), DEAR (drop everything and read), or whatever the teacher chooses to call this time. Then, depending on the ages of the students, in-class time when the teacher and students read quietly can last up to twenty to thirty minutes or more daily.

Quiet reading time of self-selected books is also a desirable and appropriate alternative to workbooks and skills sheets. We no longer need to feel guilty that students are "just reading." Reading is probably the most worthwhile activity students can be doing. As a part of independent work time, many teachers now encourage and expect students to read.

WEB Reading: A Home-School Independent Reading Program

In addition to daily time set aside for in-class reading, we also expect students to read voluntarily outside of school. Until children can read independently, the expectation is for parents to read to and with their children. What we call WEB (Wonderfully Exciting Books) reading is part of our balanced reading program. WEB helps create a community of readers. Students recommend books to each other and share book information and responses in daily interactions and interviews. Most of our students seem to get "hooked" on reading through daily expectations for independent reading. Our goal is for books to become a relevant and pleasurable part of every child's life.

With a voluntary reading program, it is important not to stress the number of books read because books vary in length and difficulty. However, when beginning WEB for the first time, some teachers like to keep a tally of the books each student reads. When a student reads ten books or a multiple of ten, a special incentive may be added as a motivation to continue to read. Eventually, the reward for reading should simply be enjoyment of the book itself.

Selecting Books

Students select books from multiple sources: the classroom library, the school library, the public library, the home, the bookstore, a friend, or any other available source. Finding out what children are interested in, helping them choose books at library time, and introducing them to books by an appealing author may help them with the selection process. Students are encouraged to select any book they like, and affirming their selections creates a climate of encouragement and trust. "Book talks" or sharing a Big Book, with little books available, greatly increases the choices for many young readers. Besides the teachers' introduction of books, students are also motivated by their peers to read books they might never have selected on their own. Some teachers note that about half the books students choose to read have been recommended by other students.

While students are free to choose what they like, they are also guided to read a wide variety of literature and to choose books at their independent reading level. Independent level means that students recognize 95 percent of the words used in a selection and comprehend 90 percent of the content. This is the easy reading level, where students read without teacher or parent help. Reading lots of books at this level promotes comprehension, vocabulary development, fluency, and overall reading facility.

Some students will choose books that go beyond their independent level—because they heard the story and loved it, because a friend read it, or just because they want to try it. I no longer tell a child, "This book is too hard for you." I may jot a note to the parent saying that the child will need help reading the book or will need to have it read aloud, and I may suggest to the child that he read it with a parent or sibling. Children often surprise us. A book that seems too hard may sometimes be read by the child if motivation and engagement are high enough.

At the same time, when children consistently read books that are too hard for them, they will not be able to tell much about the book. These students need to learn how to select appropriate books for themselves. Learning how to do that may first mean choosing some difficult, inappropriate books. Though we need to offer guidance, we also need to let students go through the selection process—and make mistakes—so they can learn to choose appropriately for themselves.

In selecting books, it is common, and beneficial for young students to choose to reread a favorite story. Not only do young children enjoy rereading stories; they actually have a need to do so. Rereading a story aids fluency, comprehension, and familiarity with the language and structure of the story. Older children, like adults, occasionally like to reread a book, and they should be allowed to do so.

At times, students will need to be encouraged to raise the quality of their reading. However, like adult readers, they must be allowed to read light, unsubstantial material for a time if that is what interests them. Above all, we want them to choose to read.

The parents of a group of third grade girls "hooked" for months on dime store novels became exasperated by the poor quality of the books their daughters were reading. In their desire to lead their children to some notable authors, the mothers finally asked the teacher, "What are some authors you would recommend?" The teacher sent home a list of authors such as Roald Dahl, Judy Blume, and Beverly Cleary with a list of the books they had written. The parents' involvement eventually led the students to respected authors.

See Appendix D, "Using the Goldilocks Strategy to Choose Books" to guide you and your students in book selection.

WEB Procedures

Students are expected to read twenty to thirty minutes each evening, to be responsible for bringing their books to and from school daily, keeping a record of their daily reading (as soon as they are able) and of books completed, and being prepared to be interviewed while reading and/or upon completing each book.

Parent involvement is an integral component for a successful WEB program. A letter is sent to parents at the start of the school year (later, for first grade) explaining WEB reading and inviting parents' cooperation (see Appendix J3). When necessary, parents are asked to become involved to encourage students to take more responsibility for completing independent reading. In addition, our principal lets teachers, parents, and students know that daily WEB reading is a school expectation for all students.

In the early grades, WEB reading is a significant part of children's learning to read successfully. Many of the books children choose will come from the classroom library and will be books heard and read during shared book experience. In addition to pleasurable reading, daily practice on familiar books builds sight vocabulary, fluency, and confidence. (For more information on WEB reading in the primary grades, see Routman, 1988).

In the intermediate grades, on the first day of school or in early fall the children are introduced to the daily routine of logging in their self-selected independent reading. In Joan Servis' fourth grade class, WEB takes place for approximately the first twenty minutes of each morning throughout the school year. The students enter the room, hang up coats, unpack book bags, and open their literature response logs. They use the last section of the log to record their daily book reading.

Figure 3-2   Sample of a Daily Record of a Fourth-grader

	Reading Log	
11/1	This Island Is't Big Enough For the Four of Us !	P. 77
11/2	"	P.108
11/3	"	Finished
11/6	The Return of the Indian	P.71
11/7	"	P.110
11/9	"	P.144
11/10	"	P.170
11/13	"	Finished
11/14	Almost Starring Skinnybones	P.60
11/15		Finished
	Emily and the Green Circle	P.28
11/16	"	P.100
11/17	"	P.141
11/20	"	Finished
	The Story of Helen Keller	P.62
11/21	"	P.93
11/22	"	Finished
11/27	The Kid in the Red Jacket	Finished
	Betsy — Tacy	P.67
11/28		Finished
	The Borrowers	P.8
11/29	"	P.27
11/30	"	P.55
12/1	"	P.76
12/4	Forgot book at home	

A separate recording log or folder could also work well. Students write down the date, name of the current book, and page number where they stopped reading at home (see Figure 3–2 for a typical student's record). If they have completed the book, they write "finished" and sign up on the chalkboard for an oral interview by the teacher or a peer who has also read the book. Students then read silently or select a new book from the classroom book spinner or school library. (The latter works if the school librarian has some available time when students can come to the library for book selection.)

Monitoring independent reading   Teachers try to make time to check WEB reading daily or at least several times weekly. In the early grades this means meeting with students one-to-one, listening to them read, and/or checking comprehension. As students get older and more fluent, the daily check may be only a quick look to see that they are keeping track of their daily reading in their logs. Often this check is done first thing in the morning while students are settling in and doing independent reading or at the end of the day or class period.

Fourth grade teacher Joan Servis uses an interview process to check understanding and appreciation of the book read. The interview follows a demonstrated format (see Figure 3–3). Each child has a copy of the WEB format in a separate WEB pocket folder (which also holds books completed each month). At the beginning of the school year, the teacher demonstrates, whole class, how to interview a student about a completed book. After several demonstrations, the teacher encourages several students to demonstrate peer interviews. When the class seems familiar with the process, all students may volunteer to interview independently during WEB time.

After successfully completing an interview, the student puts a check after her name on the board and records the book title on a monthly book list in her WEB folder (see Figure 3–4 for a typical monthly list). This list of completed books, collected monthly, is very helpful in evaluation of students' progress. The teacher can see at a glance the amount of reading a student has done, the level of difficulty of the books read, the genre of the books, and whether a student needs help in selecting books. Students also look at their book lists to note the authors and types of books they are reading. In addition to keeping a record of books read, some students and teachers keep a list of "Books I Want to Read."

Monitoring independent reading in reading group   Some teachers prefer to do the WEB check as part of the guided reading group. This is time well spent. While one student is briefly talking about a book, others are listening. In this way, many students have learned about—and been influenced to read—books they would not otherwise know about.

Students come to group with their WEB books. The teacher does a quick check and writes on the student's record card what page she is on. Some teachers keep a file box (with a 4 by 6 inch card for each student) at the reading table. If there has been a problem or a particular observation, it is briefly noted on the card. For example, the teacher might suggest the student reread a section for better under-

Figure 3-3   WEB Interview (Created by Joan and Jim Servis)

FICTION

1. Name of book
2. Name of author
3. Illustrator's name (show examples of work)
4. Why do you think you picked this book?
5. Describe the setting
6. Tell about the problem, but don't give away the secret of how it was solved!
7. Would you recommend this book? Why or why not?

NONFICTION

1. Name of book
2. Name of illustrator or photographer
3. What is the book about?
4. What did you learn?
5. Would you recommend this book? Why or why not?

Figure 3-4   A Monthly Record of a Fourth-grader

Dina   September

1. The Diamond Champs - Matt Christopher
2. Thank You Jackie Robinson - Barbra Cohen
3. Song of the Trees - Mildred Taylor
4. The Dog that Stole Football Plays - Matt Christopher
5. Johny No Hit - Matt Christopher
6. How to Fight a Girl - John Robbins
7. Four in the Family - Enid Blyton
8. The Great Quarterback Switch - Matt Christopher

standing. Or if the student isn't enjoying a book, a new one may be selected. If a new book is being signed out, the title is noted. With the occasional student who continually chooses another book, an interview may be necessary to determine the student's interests and concerns and to give guidance in book selection.

In a reading group of seven or eight students, WEB check takes about ten minutes. For some students, the check is merely noting where they are in the book. For others, the check will involve asking a question or two. (See "Open-ended Questions," p. 107, pp. 117–119, and Figure 3–5 for suggested questions that have worked well.) It is not necessary for the teacher to have read a book to be able to determine if the student has understood it. By asking open-ended questions while looking through the book and listening to the student, the teacher can get a feel for the student's understanding, engagement with the text, and enjoyment level.

I have found that it takes teachers at least a year to incorporate this kind of quick WEB check without feeling rushed. Students tend to want to talk a lot about a book they are enjoying, and teachers are reluctant to cut them short. However, the purpose of this brief check is to acknowledge interest in the reading the student has

Figure 3-5   Some Suggested Questions for Checking WEB Books

1. Why did you choose this book?
2. Would you recommend it? Why or why not?
3. What was the most interesting part?
4. Why do you think the author wrote this story?
5. Did anything strike you about the author's style or the way the author put words together?
6. Did you learn something new?
7. Are you like any of the characters in the book? How or how not?
8. What was your favorite part?
9. What was the problem in this story?
10. If you could change one part of this book, what would it be? Why would you change this part?
11. Will you read another book by this author? Why or why not?

done and to check that the book is on a level the student can easily read and understand. Once I feel confident about that, I may gently interrupt the student by saying, "That's great. I can tell you're really enjoying the book," and I move on to the next student.

Asking questions   One of the guiding principles that has helped me the most in asking worthwhile questions with WEB books is, "Are these the kinds of questions I would ask my friends if we were having a discussion about a book we had read or a movie we had seen?" I have never yet asked a friend to give me the main idea for a particular chapter and the supporting details to go with it. Nor have I ever tested friends on their factual understanding of the book. Rather, we share insights about characters, talk about why certain passages or sections were memorable or boring, share emotional reactions, try to make connections to our own lives, and clear up confusions we might have had while reading. We need to be asking questions in school that allow for those kinds of connections, and we need to listen to the varied responses of our students.

Mike Pellegrino, a new third grade teacher, says he found the open-ended questions especially helpful in eliciting more interesting and insightful responses. At first, he was asking literal questions and questions the students answered by just reciting the story. "I didn't get any insight into the students' thinking. Now we're getting more deeply into the books." He admits to being surprised by how easily students were able to answer open-ended questions. He has especially liked the following questions—and the thoughtful responses they have evoked.

"Is this story like any other story you have read? Why?"

"Think about the characters in the story. Are any of them the same type of character that you have met in other stories?"

We also want to ask questions that make students aware of what authors do so that they can think about doing similar things in their own writing. In checking Michael, a second-grader who had read the first few chapters of *Ramona the Pest* by Beverly Cleary, I learned he had paid careful attention to the text.

ROUTMAN: Did anything strike you about the way the author puts words to-
                        gether?
MICHAEL: Sometimes she writes the words over and over again, like on page
                        10, "This is a great, a great day, a great day!"
ROUTMAN: Why do you think the author does that?
MICHAEL: To make the book interesting and sound like singing.

The Teacher as a reading model   One of the most important parts of WEB, or any independent reading program, is that students see their teacher as a reading model who reads in the classroom at the same time they read. That means not just observing the teacher read but also hearing talk about the books the teacher is reading. When I demonstrate the WEB check for a teacher, I also demonstrate myself as a reader. I bring in the books I am presently reading and talk briefly about them to the students. Students are always fascinated to learn about what the teacher is reading. I briefly mention something about why I chose the book and what I am getting out of it. If the book is a mystery, I might tell them that it was hard for me to stop reading the night before. Just as students' reading needs to be balanced with different genres and authors, I try to balance my reading to include adult fiction and nonfiction along with children's books and professional books.

Attitudes of teachers and students   Fourth grade teacher Joan Servis says WEB is the favorite classroom activity of most of her students. Some comments from her students have included, "It's so much better than SSR because you get to talk with someone about your books" and "WEB has made me become a lifelong reader." It has not been unusual for entering new students who are poor readers to become proficient readers through daily WEB. An accompanying boost in self-esteem is also noticeable.

While initially it can seem overwhelming to be adding WEB reading to an already full program, the benefits are worth the effort. Third grade teacher Karen Horton tried WEB reading for the first time two years ago and notes that it has taken her most of that time to feel comfortable and confident with the management of the process. She has this to say:

> Having some suggested questions to start with was really helpful. It gave me a place to begin. Then I could go from there, add my own questions and make the procedure my own. I've seen tremendous value with WEB reading. It helps kids become readers and teaches them the use of leisure time. Overall, I am very pleased with the way students have learned to remember to bring their books back and forth between school and home and to talk about their books.

Finally, our own reading attitudes are critical to the success of the independent reading program. Merely putting books in the room and expecting children to read is not enough. Unless we take a personal and sincere interest in what children are reading and display ourselves as joyful and excited about reading, many children will not actively participate. Additionally, we have to be careful not to turn independent reading into a tedious, required program. While we want to encourage, we don't want to push so hard that we turn students off to reading. There is a difference between mandating reading and having high expectations that it will occur. The latter, gently and firmly fostered by a caring teacher, can make all the difference.

Evaluating Books

Students enjoy rating and evaluating the books they have read. Thinking about what makes an excellent book helps make students critical readers and writers. Some teachers have student include their ratings with their record of books read. To help students determine what makes a good book, a whole-class shared writing works well. (See pp. 59–66 for a discussion of shared writing.)

The following "What Makes a Book a 10?" is the first draft from a grade 3 class:

Beginning	Keeps reader interested
	Introduces main characters and setting
Ending	Reader wishes there was a sequel or wants to read the series
	Reader feels satisfied
	Reader wants to read more books by that author

Whole Book	Should be on reader's level or below
	Print should not be too small for reader
	Story should be exciting in some way
	Story should have an interesting plot
Characters	Should be very interesting
	Should have a problem of some kind
	Should be well described so you feel you know them
Setting	Should be so well described that reader can picture it
Pictures	Should go along with the story
	Reader should be able to feel what the picture means

Teachers enjoy working with their own students to write classroom guidelines. Based on students' knowledge of literature, responses will vary.

Critic's corner   Another way to evaluate books was suggested by a fourth-grader in Joan Servis' class. The student was inspired by "Critic's Corner" on "The Today Show," where Gene Shalit discusses and evaluates movies.

"Critic's Corner" occurs weekly and is an opportunity for a student to recommend a book to the class. The student sits in the author's chair and tells the class about the book, stressing why she recommends it. The children may ask questions or make comments. Often other students affirm the "critic's" choice, telling the class that they read and liked the book also. "Critic's Corner" often promotes a book that will then make the rounds of the entire class.

"Critic's Corner": student evaluating a book read independently

A Balanced Writing Program

While various approaches to writing are discussed here individually, in reality, these approaches are intertwined and interdependent. In a balanced writing program, writers regularly interact with and overlap all of these approaches.

Writing Aloud

Writing aloud is a powerful modeling technique at any grade level for getting students' attention and demonstrating various aspects of writing. Writing aloud occurs when the teacher writes in front of students and also verbalizes what he is thinking and writing. As children observe the teacher in the act of writing, the teacher makes explicit what he is doing—the thinking, the format, layout, spacing, handwriting, spelling, punctuation, discussion of vocabulary. Writing on large chart paper, the overhead projector, or the chalkboard, the teacher verbalizes his thought processes as well as the actual transcriptions as he is doing them, and students relate the spoken word to the written word.

For older students, even at the high school level, writing aloud offers students a framework of what a good essay, short story, or report might look like before the student is assigned to write one. Writing aloud increases students' interest and motivation in writing as well as the quality of student writing. Writing aloud demonstrations can take many formats, and several are demonstrated on succeeding pages.

Writing a "Morning Message"

I first saw this approach demonstrated by second grade teacher Loretta Martin, who picked up the idea of "Morning Message" at a whole language conference. The teacher writes a message to the students about what will be happening that day in terms of activities and schedule or about what has happened or will be happening in the teacher's life. Some teachers use writing aloud in place of a daily schedule written on the chalkboard. "Morning Message" is an excellent way to connect news of the classroom or news about the teacher to reading and writing. See Figure 3–6 for a substitute's message and a teacher's message.

The teacher thinks aloud while writing the message on the overhead projector. Students read along with their eyes and may also read aloud along with the teacher. After the message is written, the teacher takes a few minutes to ask children questions and familiarize them with conventions of writing. I might ask,

Why did I capitalize . . . ?
Why did I begin a new paragraph here?
Why did I use a comma . . . ?
What do you notice about . . . ?

Instead of the teacher explaining and giving the answers, students are asked to think and figure out the reasons for the conventions used.

I have demonstrated "Morning Message" for many teachers. They are always amazed at how students become totally engaged and how much can be written and

Figure 3-6 "Morning Messages"

Oct. 5, 19☐

Good Morning
I am here for Mrs.
Martin. She is in another
state today-New York. Sh
is attending a conference
with 2,000 other teachers.
She will be gone today and
tomorrow.
    You have gym this
afternoon, so don't forget
to change your shoes.
    Have a good day ☺ /

November 29, 1989
Nov. 29, 1989

Good morning,
    Thanksgiving is a special
time for families. I know that
many of you will celebrate
this *holiday* with your families,
in town or out of town and
even out of the state of
Ohio.   city   state
    I will go to Chicago, Illinois
to visit with my mother and
her family. My mother has
twelve brothers and sisters! There
will be lots of good food,
children, adults music, and
probably not enough chairs!

talked about in a very short time. The whole activity takes about five to seven minutes and is a fine and enjoyable way to reinforce skills—spelling, punctuation, grammar, paragraphing, capitalization, or any parts of writing you want to bring to the children's attention. Because I believe it is important to write in our best form and demonstrate what competent writers do, I do not deliberately make errors for children.

Second grade teacher Loretta Martin comments, "I feel writing aloud with my students clearly puts so many of the conventions we want to teach children in the proper context of written language without teaching skills in isolation."

One teacher who had said, "This sounds great, but I can't see it happening on any kind of regular basis with our tight schedules" was surprised how easy "Morning Message" was to implement and how little time it took once she tried it.

Writing a Draft from an Assigned Topic

In moving toward a more democratic (student-has-ownership) style of teaching, many of us initially have difficulty allowing students to self-select most of their writing topics. One way to get involved in the writing process and engage students who say they do not like to write is to choose a topic that everyone knows a lot about and can relate to. For students who are unpracticed and lacking confidence in writing, writing a draft that is short and focused can serve to loosen them up and help them gain confidence with the written mode. However, even when the topic is assigned, lots of leeway for meaningful student choice is provided. Later, more choice can be given, with several topics assigned and students having the option of choosing one.

Beginning with a whole-class brainstorming session seems to help get some students started. In that way all students have something to write about. See Figure 3–7, "A Bad Day," for one example of an assigned topic and the preliminary brainstorming. Unless there is an authentic reason to do so, most of these drafts do not go to final copy because the purpose here is to focus on writing interesting content. At a later date, some students may choose to develop a piece into more final form.

Figure 3–7   Brainstorming an Assigned Topic

A Bad Day
1. hair didn't look right
2. breaking something
3. being awakerd early
4. being blamed (framed)
5. a death of a family member (pet)
6. forgetting homework
7. having a substitute
8. being embarrassed
9. visiting the doctor
10. "F" on test
11. a broken wrist
12. missing the bus
13. tardiness
14. detentions
15. invaded by insects
16. raining on a picknic
17. falling in the mud
18. losing a friend
19. getting sick
20. missing recess

From Joan Rivitz's grade 4 class, January 1990.

Being an Expert

One writing topic that has proved successful across the grade levels—even for reluctant writers—is writing about being an expert at something. The idea for this topic came from second grade teacher Elaine Weiner, who heard it suggested at a whole language conference she attended. This is a particular favorite because the writing focuses on the strengths of students. As teachers and students learn about one another's unknown talents and gain appreciation for individual aptitudes, a sense of community builds.

This is also a good topic to take to final copy because it is often short and focused. We often use students' completed and illustrated pieces to put together a class book of "experts," which is shared with parents at open house. We sometimes use the copying machine to enlarge pieces and make a Big Book of expert writing. The book is always a classroom favorite. Students enjoy reading about one another's areas of expertise. The entire writing project takes several weeks from start to finish.

Brainstorming and drafting   With our expert writing, I begin by brainstorming (on the overhead projector) some things that I am an expert at. My list changes regularly, depending on what I've been doing. I want to show students that being an expert does not have to refer to something major. A recent list of mine follows:

> Putting a meal together quickly
> Cleaning a bathtub
> Loving my dog Tobi
> Making jam
> Killing flies
> Teaching reading and writing
> Keeping Frank's socks together
> Taking care of plants
> Shopping for clothes on sale
> Making turkey gravy
> Losing my gloves and my glasses
> Writing letters

Students then brainstorm their own lists, and those that would like to share do so. See Figure 3–8 for two "expert" lists from fourth-graders.

Next, I select one of my own expert areas to write about and brainstorm what I might want to include in my paper. Depending on the ages of the students, I might do a semantic mapping where categories are kept together, but usually I just jot down possibilities (see Figure 3–9).

I also write down three areas I will include—and that students are to include—in the piece of writing:

- How I became an expert
- What I do that shows I'm an expert
- How I feel about it

Figure 3-8   Two "Expert" Lists from Fourth-graders

1. (playing basketball)
2. making things out of foil
3. making poem and my own card
4. (trashing my room)
5. playing tick ball
6. (getiny mad quick)
7. dancing
8. staying up late and geting up at 7.00
9. cooking...
10. playing with the cat
11. playing the recorder
12. playing the clarinet
13. (drawing) ✓
14. checkers
15. roler skating
16. bowling
17. riding my bike
18. reading book

1. taking a long time
2. making friendship bracelets
3. drawing
4. keeping my room messy
5. talking on the phone
6. watching T.V.
7. swimming
8. skating
9. cooking
10. fighting with my brother

Figure 3-9   Possibilities for One "Expert" Topic

Killing flie's

glass + paper method
problem in my house
fly swatter
wrist action
mess on wall
average number per day
exterminator
wet towel
describe flies
my feelings

Listing what's required helps students organize their writing and provides a framework for those not used to choosing their own topics. Students' writing will often include three paragraphs, one for each of the areas listed.

I begin by writing my first draft in front of the students on the overhead projector. I think aloud, reread what I've written, and discuss possibilities. Then I ask students to choose which expert area they want to write about and to brainstorm their own possibilities. After checking these ideas to be sure students have enough information—and conferencing with them when necessary—students begin to write their drafts.

Modeling Response. After the first drafts are completed, I model the response process aloud in the following manner:

1. I ask for a volunteer to read his piece.
2. For the first reading, I just listen and try to get the overall feel and message.
3. On the second reading, I listen more critically and take notes.
4. I take my notes on the overhead projector so students can see my thinking and the comments I am making. Because this must be done quickly, I write down just enough to jog my memory so I can give constructive feedback. I divide my response paper (the overhead transparency) into two parts, one for noting what I liked and the other for noting questions, confusions, and suggestions.
5. I begin by making specific, positive comments such as "I liked the words you used to describe . . . ." "I like the way you told how . . . ." With questions or confusions, I word my comments carefully: "I wondered why . . . ." "I was confused when . . . ." "You might want to think about . . . ." From the start, it is important to demonstrate that general comments such as "I liked your story" are not helpful to the writer.

I try to demonstrate specificity by noting particular words or ideas that grabbed my attention or specific places where clarity is needed. Being a helpful responder requires very concentrated listening; it is a difficult task which must be carefully modeled before one can expect students to try it. It takes us teachers a while to feel secure and knowledgeable with the response process. Teachers that try it find they become more skilled with time and practice.

With each suggestion or question raised, the writer is guided to use a colored pencil or marker and write a note to herself—something that will signal her to look carefully at part of the writing for possible revision. Time is not taken now for the writer to defend or explain ideas. The writer merely makes notes for later consideration. Students will tend to want to "answer" the questions that have been posed to them. To save time, we are firm about having them just write the question and consider changes later.

I now call for a second volunteer, and I model the process once more. This time students and the classroom teacher also participate. I coach students to make positive, useful comments. I give feedback from my notes, again taken on the overhead projector in front of the class. Many demonstrations will need to take place before students become skilled responders. I also place my draft on the overhead, read it, and take questions and comments from students. They see me write notes to myself that may determine later revisions. More important, students see that their comments and suggestions are taken seriously. Figure 3–10 is an example of the beginning of a draft.

After drafts have been revised, some students volunteer to show how and what comments affected their revisions. They read aloud and explain to the class the actual changes they made. I also share my changes. Finally, with permission, I reproduce several revised drafts, make tansparencies, and model the editing process on the overhead projector (see pp. 177–179 for editing demonstrations).

Because peer response is difficult to do well, I believe it works best when teachers guide the process. As much as possible, students need to see and hear over and over again the kinds of comments that are helpful to a writer. Until students are well practiced in skillfully responding to drafts, merely putting students in groups to respond to one another is not useful in the revision process.

In modeling the response process, an effective approach is for two teachers to combine their classes and respond to each other's drafts. Students are very interested in the kinds of comments made and in their teachers' reactions. English teacher Dana Noble noted, "My students were very concerned about my feelings when a teacher suggested changes for my choice of words until I said I welcomed it!" Authentic teacher demonstrations, where teachers verbalize their thinking aloud, encourage students to model similar responses with their peers.

Figure 3-10   Demonstration of an Early "Expert" Writing Draft

Narrowing the focus of a draft   One topic that has worked well is to write about something that is or has been difficult to do. Again, I begin by brainstorming, but here I also try to narrow the focus. When students choose football, math, or babysitting as areas that are difficult for them, I ask them to choose one small aspect of their topic and tell about it in detail. In my demonstration, I have talked about how hard writing is for me and have narrowed my focus to one aspect that is especially trying for me—getting started. Following is a recent rough draft as I wrote it on the overhead projector in front of a group of fourth-graders.

> I wake up thinking about how I will begin. My stomach feels tight and uneasy. I get into the shower and try to put the beginning sentences together, but they do not come. I eat breakfast, read the newspaper for longer than usual, get dressed slowly, make the bed, clean up a bit. I look at the clock. 8:30 A.M. I've been up since 7:00 A.M. It is time to get to work.

Figures 3–11 and 3–12   *Draft by a Fourth-grader about Something That Is—or Has Been—Difficult to Do*

Figure 3-12

Reluctantly, I drag myself over to the computer, sit down and turn it on. I flex my fingers up and down, in readiness to use the keys. I move papers out of the way, adjust the chair to just the right position. It is time to start.

The blank screen is in front of me, gray and empty and beckoning. I stare at it for what seems like a long time. How to begin. The words do not come. I move my hands together, squirm around on the chair and stare at the screen again. The room is silent. I look out the window and watch a bird starting to build a nest. I must begin!

I place my fingers over the keys. The silence continues as my fingers gently rest on the keyboard. And then the gentle clicking noise begins. My fingers are moving across the keys, and words start to slowly pour forth onto the screen. It does not matter that the words will have to be changed and rewritten. I have done the hardest part—just getting started.

Figures 3–11 and 3–12 are examples of drafts written by two fourth grade reluctant writers following the writing-aloud demonstration. The first talks about an agonizing wait before being sent onto the basketball court by the coach, and the second describes pressure to perform in a baseball game. These were significant pieces of writing because they came from students who rarely invested in their writing.

Shared Writing

Frank Smith has said, "The most direct and relevant way to demonstrate to a child the power of writing is to write with the child." Shared writing, where the teacher and students compose collaboratively, with the teacher acting as a scribe and expert to her group of apprentices, is appropriate for older as well as younger students. Shared writing goes beyond language experience in which the teacher takes dictation from the child's language. In shared writing, the writing is a negotiated process with meanings, choices of words, and topics discussed and decided jointly by students and teacher.

As in shared reading, in shared writing the teacher's role is an enabling, supportive one that encourages and invites students to participate and enjoy writing experiences they might not be able to do on their own. Shared writing is a relaxed, social time where the teacher and students are gathered together informally, sometimes on a rug or in a designated floor space, as in shared reading.

Shared writing often develops naturally as a response to shared reading. Younger students who have become familiar with favorite texts often opt to create their own innovations and stories with guidance from the teacher. Eventually some of these new texts become enlarged, illustrated texts for shared reading and wall stories posted around the room before they are bound into Big Books. As is usually the case with stories the children create, they choose to read these stories over and over again. We may also suggest topics for shared writing as a way to show children various possibilities.

With the teacher collaborating with students and acting as a scribe—and not expecting students to create texts on their own—children learn that writing opportunities are available to them. Because children are focusing on the composing-thinking process without the additional task of transcribing, shared writing frees their imagination and helps them gain confidence in writing independently.

The language we teachers use in the shared writing context is critical for a genuine, participatory experience. For example, instead of saying, "I don't feel that sentence fits," I might say, "What do you think about . . . ? Does that fit?" to make the process more democratic. Or instead of saying, "Let's put this in dialogue," I might try, "What do you think about using dialogue here?" While teacher input is important, we don't want to take over. The teacher's voice should guide rather than dominate.

Shared writing may take many forms:

Wall stories and Big Books

Stories, essays, and poems

Original story endings

Retellings

Class journal entries

Class observations of pets, plants, and science experiments

Shared experiences, such as field trips and special visitors

Class rules and charts

Weekly newsletters to parents

News of the day

Curriculum-related writing

Reports

Information books

Evaluations of books and activities.

Advantages of Shared Writing

Because shared writing is a powerful approach for promoting development and enjoyment of writing—yet one that is seldom employed, especially with older students—its many advantages are listed with the hope that more teachers will give shared writing a try and realize its benefits:

- Reinforces and supports the reading process
- Makes it possible for all students to participate
- Encourages close examination of texts, words, and options of authors
- Demonstrates the conventions of writing—spelling, punctuation, and grammar
- Provides reading texts that are relevant and interesting to the children
- Focuses on composing and leaves writing (transcribing) to the teacher
- Helps students see possibilities they might not see on their own
- Recognizes the child who may have a wealth of verbal story material but be unable to write it down
- Gives both teacher and students confidence in their writing ability
- Gives the reluctant-to-write teacher a supportive environment

Many teachers are terrified to write. For most of us, our education in writing focused on the editorial aspects rather than on the creative, composing parts. We were trained to write correctly and for the teacher. For teachers who don't like to write or who are fearful of writing, shared writing is a nonthreatening way to become personally involved in the writing process. The support teachers receive from their students is often enough of a boost to give most teachers confidence to begin writing themselves.

During the first week of school, shared writing can be used to establish the rules and procedures for the classroom. Rather than having the teacher post the rules ahead of time, children enjoy working them out with the teacher. With the teacher acting as scribe, students are actively involved with the teacher in the decision making process. When students have some ownership of classroom expectations, they tend to act more responsibly in respecting the rules. The final, revised charts may be written out by the children so that the reading material on the walls is by the children.

A Shared Writing Lesson in Grade 1

Shared writing is a powerful way to demonstrate to children that their own observations, along with guidance and self-questioning, can markedly improve the quality of writing. I was invited into a first grade classroom where the teacher was frustrated by the boring quality of the daily journal entries. Most of the children were writing short, simple entries like "I went to my friend's house. We played together. I had fun. Then I went home." I suggested we write together about something the class knew a lot about, such as a recent shared experience. Several children wanted to write about the class pet, the rabbit that lived in a cage at the front of the classroom. Working through the story together provided natural opportunities for elaborating on the text and demonstrating how much the children knew about their subject. What follows is the shared writing experience—the thinking, composing, and scribing about the class rabbit. (*T* stands for teacher—me—and *S* stands for a student responding.)

T: How should we begin? Can someone start off our story?

S: We have a rabbit in our classroom.

T: (*Writing slowly and orally stretching out the sounds of the words*) "W-e h-a-v-e a r-a-b-b-i-t i-n o-u-r cl-a-ss-r-oo-m."
(*Silence*)

T: What does the rabbit look like?

S: She is brown all over.

T: Yes, she is brown, but take a good look at her. Is she brown everywhere?

S: No, her tail is white.

T: How about if we say, "She is brown all over except for her tail, which is white."

S: We need to tell that her bottom is light brown.

T: Good. Let's add it here. "She is brown all over except for her tail, which is white, and her bottom, which is light brown." Anything else?

S: She likes to nibble things.

T: What does she like to nibble?

S: She likes carrots, paper, crayons.

T: "She likes to nibble things likes carrots, paper, and crayons." Oh, I put an *s* after that second *like*; that shouldn't be there. I'll just cross it out. That's what writers do when they make a mistake. They just cross it out. What else can you tell me about your rabbit?

S: She has brown eyes.

T: Where do you think we should we put that?
(*Silence*)

T: Can someone find the part that tells what the rabbit looks like?

S: Where we say "She is brown all over . . ."

T: Yes, that's right. How about if we put, "She has brown eyes" right after that so we keep the parts about what the rabbit looks like all together? (*Puts in a caret and writes and verbalizes, "She has brown eyes"*) This is what writers do when they need to stick something in. They make kind of an arrow like this; it's called a caret.

S: (*Calling out*) She has *small* brown eyes.

T: O.K. How should we add that in?

S: Put a caret after *has* and write in *small*.

T: Yes, that's right.

S: The rabbit has pointed ears, too.

T: Where do you think we should add that?

S: We could say, "She has small brown eyes *and* pointed ears."

T: I like the way you combined two related things into one sentence.

s: I want to add, "She has *long*, pointed ears. Use a caret and put in *long*.

T: That's great. You really understand how to use that caret. When you are writing on your own, and you get an idea you think belongs before something you have already written, just use the caret and write it in. Anything else about your rabbit?

s: She has a lot of accidents. Once she peed on the carpet. (*T writes it down while verbalizing*)

s: When she stands up, she looks fat.

T: (*Writes it down while verbalizing*) Anything else you want to say about your rabbit?

s: When she yawns, we can see her teeth.

T: (*Writing and verbalizing*) "When she yawns, we can see her teeth." What does your rabbit do all day?

s: Sometimes she knocks over her food bowl.

T: What happens then?

s: We have to clean it up.

T: (*Writing and verbalizing*) "Sometimes she knocks over her food bowl, and we have to clean it up."

T: Why does she knock over her food bowl?

s: Because she's mad.

T: What is she mad about?

s: She's mad because we won't let her out.

T: How about if we write, "She does that when she's mad because we won't let her out."

The completed text appeared as follows, and children eagerly read and reread it:

> We have a rabbit in our classroom. She is brown all over except for her tail, which is white, and her bottom, which is light brown. She has small brown eyes and long pointed ears. She likes to nibble things like carrots, paper, and crayons. She has lots of accidents. Once she peed on the carpet. When she stands up, she looks fat. When she yawns, we can see her teeth. Sometimes she knocks over her food bowl, and we have to clean it up. She does that when she's mad because we won't let her out.

The first grade teacher reported enthusiastically that there was an immediate improvement in the quality of the children's daily journal writing, especially a noticeable addition of descriptive detail. Shortly thereafter the first grade teacher felt confident enough to do her first shared writing, an account of a class field trip to the art museum.

A Shared Poetry Writing Lesson in the Primary Grades

Inspired by a lesson I saw in an Australian classroom, the poem "Jelly on the Plate" from *Jelly on the Plate: An Anthology of Poems*, collected by June Factor (Modern Cirriculum Press, 1987) became a model for children writing their own patterned poetry in a second grade class (see Figure 3–13). We began by repeatedly enjoying

Figure 3-13   Patterned Poetry Model

Jelly on the plate,
Jelly on the plate,
Wibble wobble, *wibble* wobble,
Jelly on the plate.

Paper on the floor,
Paper on the floor,
Pick it up, pick it up,
Paper on the floor.

Piggy in the house,
Piggy in the house,
Kick him out, kick him out,
Piggy in the house.

Traditional

the rhythm of the poem together in shared reading and discussing the illustrator's choices to go along with the poem. We then talked about how the poem was written—the style, format, rhythm. In a shared writing draft, I recorded everything the children discovered about how the poem was put together. Notice all the information they garnered about how the poem was constructed without the teacher telling them. If they failed to notice something, I prodded them with a question like, "Do you notice anything about line . . .?" or "What does the poet do to show . . .?" Our draft follows exactly as we wrote it:

2 beats per line

Commas at end of lines 1, 2, 3 and in middle of line 3

Line 4 ends with a period.

Every line starts with a capital.

Line 3 is different—uses action words and different print

All 4 lines are on the same basic idea

On line 3, words are repeated

Lines 1, 2, and 4 are the same: A, A, B, A

First word of lines 1, 2, and 4: 2 syllables

Last word of lines 1, 2, and 4: 1 syllable

Using Holdaway's developmental model (pp. 9–10) and the illustrations on the page that the poet did not include, I demonstrated—with student participation on an invitational basis—how other verses might be written. On large chart paper I wrote:

> Lego on the floor,
> Lego on the floor,
> Build it up, build it up
> Lego on the floor.
>
> Monkey in the tree,
> Monkey in the tree,
> Swing on down, swing on down,
> Monkey in the tree.

For the next stage, the practice phase, students broke into groups of four and wrote original verses using the illustrations on the poem and the guidelines on our draft. Classroom teacher Mary Pryor and I walked around and gave guidance as necessary. These verses were then shared with the whole class. Figure 3–14 is an example of one group's work.

The following week, when I was back in the classroom, we chanted the poem "Jelly on the Plate" several times again; and, looking at the illustrations carefully, we talked about in what room of the house the action of the poem might have taken place. The students speculated it could be a playroom, child's bedroom, kitchen, or den. I then told them that they were to choose a room in their house to write their own poem and illustrations for. First they were to take a careful look at that room and note everything in it. I modeled first by choosing my kitchen and coming up with the following list:

cookbooks, jelly, window, flowers, refrigerator, dishes, silverware, platters, crack in ceiling, cups, napkins, pepper mill, towels, coffee, glass jars, pots, pans, hanging plants, turkey, stove, cupboards

Figure 3-14   A Group-written Verse

Then, in front of the students, I wrote three verses to go along with some of the items. One verse follows:

> Pepper in the mill,
> Pepper in the mill,
> Twist it hard, twist it hard,
> Pepper in the mill.

After students carefully observed and wrote down what was in the room they had selected, they were ready to work individually on drafting verses to go along with room items. Before showing their verses to either Mary Pryor or me, they were expected to use the original poem and the chart we had written to check their poems carefully for form, punctuation, capitalization, choice of words, and so on. We expected students to correct whatever they could on their own by using our classroom chart.

Next, students were given large chart paper to use as a "sloppy copy" to lay out in pencil their poems and illustrations. Once those had been revised and edited, they worked on large chart paper to write the final copy of their poems in their best handwriting and with carefully done, colorful illustrations. Individual pages were then spiral-bound into a class Big Book, which became a year-long class favorite for rereading and enjoying.

The entire project took place over several weeks and was a great success. We noted especially that low-ability students felt a particular pride and joy in their work. I emphatically believe that the amount of demonstrating, opportunities for participation, and practice that students received *before* they were expected to work on their own was vital for the high level of achievement that resulted.

Guided Writing

As in guided reading, the teacher's role in guided writing is to guide students, respond to them, and extend their thinking in the process of composing text. Also, as in guided reading, where the student holds the book and does the reading, in guided writing the student holds the pen and does the writing. By contrast, in writing aloud and shared writing, the teacher does the writing.

The teacher's role in guided writing is one of facilitator, helping students discover what they want to say and how to say it meaningfully with clarity, coherence, interest, style, form, and individual voice. Teachers are supportive rather than directive, suggestive rather than prescriptive. Ownership of the writing always remains with the student. Our role is to empower writers to discover their own meanings.

Guided writing is the heart of the writing program. It takes place when students have time to write and the teacher is available for guidance. It may occur during whole class, small group, or one-to-one as part of writing workshop, story writing, journal writing, content area writing, letter writing, report writing, or any other form of authentic writing. Guided writing, like guided reading, occurs after students have had many opportunities to see writing demonstrated aloud and in shared contexts. Also, as in guided reading, there are opportunities for choice, decision making, and peer response and for making connections to students' lives.

Demonstrations in selecting topics, drafting, responding, revising, editing, and other minilessons that have been done by the teacher in writing aloud and in shared writing are now incorporated independently by students—with teacher and peer guidance—into their own writing. Mechanics or skills are taught strategically, as the need arises, in the context of the genuine writing situation.

My own insights on the teaching of writing—especially the rationale and procedures for conferencing, response groups, revision, and editing in guided writing—have been heavily influenced by the work of Nancie Atwell, Donald Graves, Lucy Calkins, and Jan Turbill. Their major works are excellent resources for establishing authentic teaching-learning-writing processes in the classroom. (See Jan Turbill, *No Better Way to Teach Writing!* [1982]; Nancie Atwell, *In the Middle* [1987]; Donald Graves, *Writing: Teachers and Children at Work* [1983]; and Lucy Calkins, *The Art of Teaching Writing* [1986]. For secondary teachers, add Tom Romano, *Clearing the Way* [1987] and Steven Zemelman and Harvey Daniels, *A Community of Writers* [1988]. All of the books were published by Heinemann, Portsmouth, NH.) These sources give clear guidelines and procedures for revision, editing, conferencing, classroom management, minilessons, publishing, and lots more. (For examples of guided writing, see Chap. 8, "Authentic Contexts for Writing.") See also the "blue pages" for additional resources.

As with all language learning, the role of guidance in writing is to lead the learner toward independence: ". . . every conference trains writers for the most important conferences of all. Those are the conferences writers must hold with themselves during the writing process" (Murray, 1989, p. 124).

Independent Writing

The purpose of independent writing—like that of independent reading—is to build fluency, establish the writing habit, make personal connections, explore meanings, promote critical thinking, and use writing as a natural, pleasurable, self-chosen activity. In independent writing, the student has opportunities, many of which are student initiated, to write without teacher intervention or evaluation. The student takes responsibility for working out the challenges in the writing process. Writing experiences may include, but are not limited to, journal writing, responding in a log, and freewriting. (See Chap. 9 for information on journal writing and Chap. 6 for information on literature response logs.)

Writing to Learn

"Writing to learn," often done in a learning log or curriculum-related journal, can be a form of independent writing. "Writing to learn may be defined as short, spontaneous, unedited, exploratory, personal writing that's used not to affect an audience but to channel, crystalize, record, direct, or guide a person's thinking." (Zemelman and Daniels, 1988, p. 103; see pp. 103–113 for specific examples of writing to learn in the classroom.)

I see writing to learn as one of the most powerful techniques available for developing critical thinking. While I have heard and used the terms "writing as a thinking process" and "writing to learn," their meaning became clear to me only in the process of writing this book. While I began with an outline and general idea of what I wanted to say and accomplish, I had no idea how a chapter would turn out—or even what it would finally include—until I struggled my way through it. It was in the process of writing that I cleared up confusions, worked through problem areas, organized my thinking, checked references and notes, and synthesized my thoughts. It was through writing that I learned what I wanted to say. The actual process of writing forced me to think about concepts and come to some understanding and conclusions. It was not just that I wrote what I already knew. In the process of writing and thinking, I learned what I knew, what I didn't know, and what I needed to know. In using writing as a vehicle for thinking, I was able to clarify and extend my knowledge. Even more than that, when I was finished, I found I actually knew more—and felt smarter—because of the hard thinking and learning the writing had forced me to do.

Based on my own experience, I am convinced that we must provide many opportunities for writing as a thinking process across the curriculum—in mathematics, art, music, science, social studies, foreign languages, and more. (For specific procedures on how this can be done, see *Resources for Teachers*, especially Atwell, 1990; Murray, 1989 and 1990; Zemelman and Daniels, 1988; and the index entry "Learning logs.")

Figure 3-15   *A Fifth-grader's Freewriting*

Freewriting

Freewriting allows and encourages students to write without interruption in any form they choose. For a short, timed period, students write as quickly as they can without worrying about spelling, grammar, and correctness. For students who have been used to writing everything for the teacher and worrying about correctness, freewriting can help develop confidence and fluency in writing. Once students relax with it, they enjoy and value freewriting (see Figure 3–15 for a fifth-grader's comments). Focused freewriting can be used for "freeing up" students' prior knowledge and is a valuable strategy in the content areas. (See Bayer, 1990, for suggested procedures.)

Reflections

While the various approaches to reading and writing have been separated for purposes of clarity and demonstration, this separation is artificial. In reality, reading and writing are connected and flow together.

In our whole language classrooms, reading and writing topics are relevant to students' lives, interests, and the school curriculum. Conferencing, responding, revising, demonstrating, and encouraging are ongoing with students and their reading-writing processes. The classroom environment encourages collaboration, risk taking, responsibility, and reflection and provides time and space to read and write.

I have found it takes most of us many years to achieve balanced reading and writing programs. We need to allow ourselves time to try out and incorporate the various approaches/components while recognizing the importance of moving toward an integrated and balanced literacy program.

In looking at the various approaches to reading and writing, it is the degree of teacher intervention, support and choice that determines the type of approach being employed. While we need to begin reading and writing with lots of teacher demonstrating and scaffolding (reading and writing aloud and shared reading and writing), gradually students take more ownership and responsibility for their own learning processes (guided and independent reading and writing) as teachers guide students toward independence.

Grouping for Success

Taking a Close Look at Ability Grouping

Students collaborating and taking responsibility for their own learning

When Elliott was invited to be part of a mixed-ability reading group in second grade, the experience dramatically changed his view of himself and his life in school. As a very poor reader in the first grade, Elliott's instruction had focused on skills and structured readers. Now, for the first time, he had the opportunity to read a whole book, the same wonderful book his classmates were reading.

At the end of second grade, I interviewed Elliott:

ROUTMAN: What was reading like for you in first grade?

ELLIOTT: I had a lot of trouble with big words. All reading was very hard for me.

ROUTMAN: What was different about reading this year?

ELLIOTT: I was part of a reading group.

ROUTMAN: How did you feel when your teacher first put you in *Charlotte's Web*?

ELLIOTT: I felt very happy. I'd never been in a very hard book before. I could read some hard words but not all.

ROUTMAN: Were you worried about not being able to read hard words?

ELLIOTT: Mrs. P. says, "Go back. Does that make sense?" If I couldn't figure it out, she would tell me.

ROUTMAN: What was it like discussing a book?

ELLIOTT: Answering questions was really hard for me at first. But it's not hard for me now. I like to tell what I think.

ROUTMAN: How did you feel being in the *Charlotte's Web* group?

ELLIOTT: I felt like a person who would never get as far as *Charlotte's Web*, so I was really surprised when I got that book. I thought I would never get finished with the book when I saw all those chapters. Sometimes

I could do the reading by myself and that made me happy. I was amazed when I could do some reading all by myself.

ROUTMAN: That surprised you?

ELLIOTT: Yes. It made me anxious to go on by myself.

ROUTMAN: Did it make you feel smarter?

ELLIOTT: Yes, because it was a very hard book, and I felt smarter for having read all those hard words.

ROUTMAN: Do you feel you can read hard books now?

ELLIOTT: Yes, if I get some help on the hard words.

ROUTMAN: How do you feel about reading?

ELLIOTT: I think that I'm getting better at reading, and I'm starting to like it better. I feel better about school because I can learn, and I'm getting smarter.

Elliott is a literate person. He became a reader, writer, and thinker when he was viewed as a capable learner. He was fortunate to be in a classroom with a teacher who was questioning traditional grouping practices and attempting to move away from a subskills approach to reading. His teacher was in transition, reflecting on her teaching and adjusting her theory and practice based on her professional reading, interaction with colleagues, and observation of her students.

Elliott is typical of the large population of learners who have traditionally had separate, segmented, and less challenging instruction—often because of their cultural and economic backgrounds, perceived deficits, and language differences. His experience illustrates the far-reaching potential for literacy when we begin to examine and change our teaching to include equal expectations for all students. As Elliott's story demonstrates, whole language and the best of children's literature are not just for some students. *All* students and teachers that I have worked with and observed learn more easily and feel more confident when they are engaged in meaningful enterprises and are part of a collaborative community.

The practice of grouping students by ability, especially for reading and math in the elementary grades and for all major subject areas in secondary schools, is common. Once they are in a lower track, however, students receive separate and unequal instruction, are treated differently, and are unlikely to move to a higher group (see Bloome, 1989; Braddock and McPartland, 1990; Gamoran, 1992; Goodlad and Oakes, 1988; Slavin, 1988; Wheelock, 1992). Because ability grouping is pervasive in classrooms, we need to examine its effects carefully and explore possible alternatives.

Transitions

All the years I was a classroom teacher I grouped children by the level of their ability in reading and math, especially as was determined by a standardized test. Homogeneous (ability) grouping was the norm, and, frankly, I never thought much about it. In teacher training, even on the graduate level, I don't recall being exposed to any research that was against ability grouping, and I certainly didn't believe I could be harming children by segregating them by ability. I was a caring teacher who believed ability grouping aided achievement. The thought that I might be contributing to impairing the attitudes and self-esteem of students placed in the lowest reading group never entered my mind.

My positive attitudes about ability grouping were also influenced by the fact that, years ago, my own children were in the top reading groups in the elementary grades and in the advanced tracks at the high school. I admit, although not proudly, that I believed that the "highest-ability" and "lowest-ability" students were best served in homogeneous groups. Although I often felt a twinge of conscience when I saw so few minority students honored for high achievement at awards ceremonies and graduations, I wasn't ready to see grouping as a possible culprit.

I began to have doubts about ability grouping in the late 1970s when I began to take a serious look at what was happening to students who failed to learn to read successfully. I was working in an elementary school as a reading specialist with mostly minority students, and I saw firsthand the damaged self-concepts of these children after only one year of failing to learn to read as well as their peers. I saw the methods and materials being used with these students as the main cause of their failure. The basal textbooks, worksheets, and isolated skills approach were to blame. I sought to teach reading and writing in more meaningful ways and began to teach small groups of remedial students with children's literature. The positive results and far-reaching effects of that endeavor are related in *Transitions: From Literature to Literacy* (Routman, 1988).

However, it was not until the mid-1980s that my views began to change. Our district reorganized as a result of racial imbalance and declining enrollment. Four elementary schools closed, with the remaining five buildings housing all kindergarten through grade 4 students. (A separate building housed all fifth- and sixth-graders.) Mercer School was located in the highest socioeconomic area of the district and had a predominantly (over 90 percent) white population. Moreland School, located in the lowest socioeconomic area of the district, had close to a 90 percent black and transient population. The majority of students from Moreland School, where I had been teaching for twelve years, were bused across the district to Mercer School where I was assigned.

In order to avoid potentially explosive relations between the school and the community, some teachers began to re-examine their grouping policies. After the reorganization, if teachers at Mercer School had continued to organize their reading groups as they had always done—homogeneously by ability—the "highest" groups would have contained almost all white children and the "lowest" groups almost all black children. While there were black children reading at the highest levels, they were few in number. This was not a black-white issue but rather a socioeconomic one; nevertheless, the groupings would have appeared racist. In addition, sensitivity was needed because the Moreland community already felt slighted by the closing of a well-loved school.

When several teachers first decided to group heterogeneously, an amazing thing happened. Children who had been predicted by standardized test scores to have difficulty reading did better than anticipated. By incorporating shared reading, paired reading, and the use of tape recorders for assigned silent reading—and by including all children in group discussions of their assigned books—many of the children began to "read" books that were above their test levels.

The children proved that when reading is viewed as constructing meaning from text rather than just decoding words, then most students of average intelligence become capable readers. When vocabulary is discussed in the context of the story, students see the relevance of word meanings and are enabled to read the text more efficiently. That is, when the focus of reading and group time is discussing a book and reacting personally to it, most students—even if they have needed assistance with reading the words—can participate on a high level. The children also showed that when the teacher is gentle, caring, and has high expectations for all students, every student has the opportunity to become a capable reader.

Students' Attitudes

In the spring of 1989, I interviewed some former Moreland School students who had been among the first in our district to be immersed in a reading-writing classroom in first grade. As fifth- and sixth-graders now, I was curious about their attitudes toward reading and writing. The main results of these interviews are given in "Taking a Look at Teacher and Student Attitudes," (pp. 365–370). Here I address the unexpected and unsolicited information that came out about grouping. The insights of these young people are cause for reflection.

> Jolene was a proficient reader who made sense out of print despite her difficulty using phonics cues. On our standardized reading test, she scored in the 99th percentile in reading comprehension in the fall of second grade. She was reading challenging chapter books that she understood, and she loved to read. However, in December of second grade, Jolene moved and was placed in a classroom with a phonics-based teacher. Because of her inability to complete phonics worksheets, she was put in the lowest reading group, and she received daily pull-out support from the school's reading specialist. (Jolene is discussed in Routman, 1988, pp. 209–210.)

JOLENE: In second grade, I was put in the lowest reading group. I didn't feel good about myself. I had higher expectations for myself. I knew I was smart. The teacher just didn't know I was smart. In third grade, I transferred to a new school, and it was hard to adjust. I tried to tell the teacher I was a good reader, but she wouldn't listen to me. She kept me in the lowest group. That made me feel bad. All my friends were in higher groups. In fourth grade, my teacher knew all kids had ability. She really encouraged all the kids.

My mother was my biggest influence. She taught me that I could do and be whatever I wanted. I think I'm in the medium reading group now. That doesn't phase me because I know I'm good.

I think grouping is unnecessary. It makes kids feel bad, like they can't be as good as the next person. I think there shouldn't be any grouping.

Jamaar had been one of our best readers in first grade. However, he often exasperated his teachers because he did not work up to his potential, and he failed to get assignments done. I was surprised by his spontaneous and candid comments about grouping.

JAMAAR: I don't think grouping is fair, because if a person can't read fluently, the teacher puts them in a lower group. If they can read
semi-good, they should be in the top group. Kids in low groups
feel bad. The teacher puts that group down because they can't
read good. He doesn't work with that group much, or explain the
book. He just assigns worksheets and makes them read books on
their own and never checks the worksheets. He spends a lot of
time with you if you're in the top group or the middle group.

If I were a teacher and a kid couldn't read, I'd help them. I
wouldn't put kids in groups.

Nicky had always been a serious, hard-working student. In sixth grade, she was still a top student and in the highest reading group.

NICKY: I think grouping is childish. People in the low group feel bad, like
they don't know as much. If I were a teacher, I would do away
with grouping.

Hard to Reach Students: What Can Happen When the Grouping Structure Is Changed

Mario entered third grade at Mercer School as a virtual nonreader. He was streetwise, socially adept, and totally uninterested in school. He was moody, his behavior was disruptive, and he had difficulty completing assignments. Although he appeared to have at least average intelligence based on his fine verbal and social skills, school seemed to have no rele-vance in his life. At home he was "boss," with few limits set. It was not unusual for him to rest with his head on his desk, or even to fall asleep in class, because he had been up past midnight watching videos.

In first grade Mario had been in the Reading Recovery program, and in second grade he had the services of the Chapter 1 program. He had caring teachers, but he was failing to learn to read and write. He found academic demands overwhelming and school very boring. He had always been in the lowest reading group, and he knew it.

Mario's third grade teacher grouped him for reading with other students—but not by ability. The first book read was *The Comeback Dog* by Jane Resh Thomas, and it was done whole class. After that, Mario was placed in the group reading *Mr. Popper's Penguins* by Richard and Flo-rence Atwater (Little, Brown, 1938). He could not read most of the words but he could enjoy and appreciate the story. For silent reading assignments, he was paired with a strong reader who read to him while he followed along in his personal copy of the book. Occasionally, Mario would attempt to read a paragraph or so to his partner. After initially just listening during group discussion, he eventually began to participate. His comments and perceptions were accepted and encouraged. Mario also began to take risks and make predictions based on what had been read and discussed. After a while, his whole demeanor changed. During reading time, he was most often on task, eager to respond, and smiling. Unexpectedly, his actual reading skills began to improve. His Chapter 1 teacher reported being very surprised when Mario volunteered to read a paragraph from *Mr. Popper's Penguins*. Sensitized to the language and the author's style, having heard the passage already read by a peer, and having met success as part of a reading group, he felt confident enough to try it himself.

I had been Mario's Reading Recovery teacher. Initially confident of his potential for success, he had been one of my most frustrating students in many years of teaching. In spite of intensive instruction, frequent communication with his parents, and genuine caring, I had failed to reach Mario. When his third grade teacher enthusiastically described his participation in reading group, I reverted to my traditional background and put her on the defensive by asking, "What are you doing about the skills?" The truth of the matter was that by immersing him in quality literature and including him in the reading community, she was doing more about the skills than any of his previous teachers had done. As he became involved and accepted in the reading process, Mario began to see himself as a reader and could begin to see the relevance of using and needing reading skills.

This is not to say that Mario became a good reader in the traditional sense; he was still severely reading disabled. By the spring of third grade he received one-to-one reading support from the learning disabilities teacher. In addition, he remained part of his classroom reading group. However, it was through the pleasurable act of reading and group acceptance that Mario acquired the desire to read and the confidence in himself to try. Without that desire and effort, there could be no chance for success. After that, it was not just Mario's reading that was positively affected. The acceptance and respect he received from his reading group spilled over into other academic areas. He began to see himself as a valued and participating member of the community of learners in his class.

As a first-grader, Elliott (whose interview begins this chapter) had barely functioned in the lowest reading group, where he spent most of his time on skills sheets and "sounding out." By the end of the school year, he was lacking in self-confidence and was not a risk taker. He saw himself as a very poor reader. While the better readers in his class were involved in delightful children's books along with the basal, the poor readers had only the basal and its accompanying structured activities. Elliott's first grade teacher believed, as many teachers do, that literature was all right for the good readers, but the poor readers needed the basal text to learn how to read.

In second grade, Elliott was placed with a teacher who had decided—for the first time—to use literature (and no basals or worksheets) with all of the students, not just the good readers. It was a big risk for her but one that would have a permanent, powerful effect on both herself and the children.

She began the year with homogeneous grouping, finding the challenge of using only literature initially overwhelming. The four poorest readers began with *Frog and Toad* books by Arnold Lobel, and they remained with this series for several months. All of the group discussion, skills work, silent reading, oral reading, repeated readings, and written assignments came from these books.

In February, the teacher decided to try mixed-ability grouping. She was determined that Elliott and all her students should have the opportunity to read the most challenging book in the literature collection for second grade, *Charlotte's Web* by E. B. White. She invited me into her classroom weekly to provide support, to demonstrate lessons, and to answer questions and dispel doubts. It was not only the children who benefited; as teachers, we grew professionally. For each of us, these times represented a positive learning experience as we shared ideas and concerns, closely observed students without at the same time having to teach, and took the time to carefully examine the teaching and learning that seemed to be taking place.

The emphasis in the guided reading group was on story enjoyment and responding to the text with skills being taught in the context of the literature as the need arose. Because the text was too difficult for Elliott to read on his own, before he came to reading group he was either paired with a student who read the text to him as he followed along or was asked to follow along with a tape the teacher had made. The tape recorder proved especially beneficial because he could reread a chapter at his own pace.

At his teacher's request, I sat next to Elliott in reading group for many weeks. She was worried that he might not be doing well enough. Was he getting the meaning and developing the skills? Did I think he was over his head? Initially Elliott was over his head. He had never participated in a group focused on high-level discussion, and his answers to questions seemed confused and off the mark. But after several months of daily group discussion, he began to respond meaningfully, and it became apparent to us that he was a capable child. Eventually, Elliott was also able to complete reading assignments independently and answer written questions in his reading spiral notebook.

When Elliott was initially handed *Charlotte's Web*, he was wide-eyed and incredulous. Each week as I observed him in his guided reading group, his growing confidence and pleasure as a reader and member of the class community of readers became more and more evident. I doubt that he would have had the same chance for success and confidence building if he had remained in the lowest reading group. Looking back, what I remember most vividly about Elliott is the smile on his face while he was participating in reading group. Like Wilbur in *Charlotte's Web*, he was absolutely radiant.

What Does the Research Say About Organizing Classes by Ability?

In summarizing the research on the achievement effects of grouping at the elementary and secondary levels, Robert Slavin, who has done a comprehensive analysis of the data available on ability grouping, states that "every means of grouping students by ability or performance level has drawbacks that may be serious enough to offset any advantages" (1989, p. 68). Other important findings are as follows:

- Studies of whole classes grouped by ability, special education, and gifted students show "no benefits for ability-grouped class assignment or special education assignment and only inconsistent and flawed evidence in favor of special programs for the gifted" (Slavin, 1989, p. 71).
- Within-class grouping by performance level for one or two subjects, if students are heterogeneously grouped the rest of the day, may aid achievement in those subjects. (Research in this area has been mostly limited to mathematics achievement in the upper elementary grades.)
- Self-contained classes in the upper elementary and middle grades are favored over departmentalization—where students are taught a major subject by another classroom teacher. (Research here is limited.)

At the elementary level, where ability grouping in reading is standard practice, Hilda Borko and Margaret Eisenhart studied reading groups in four second grade classrooms in a small town/rural public school. They concluded that the reading groups function as social and linguistic communities that can promote or hamper school success: "the content of reading instruction, student conceptions of reading, rules for participation in literacy events, and teacher expectations and evaluations differ across ability groups" (Borko and Eisenhart, in Bloome, 1989, p. 120).

Taking Another Look at Ability Grouping

If we are to be knowledgeable, conscientious professionals, we need to carefully re-examine the homogeneous grouping practices that are widespread in the United States. Ability grouping, especially as it has been applied to reading in the elementary grades, needs to be changed. Although some teachers are grouping heterogeneously and encouraging cooperative learning groups, based on my interaction with teachers in our school district and across the country, this seems to be the exception and not the norm.

Since the best-known studies of ability grouping at the elementary school level have not demonstrated higher student achievement for either high-track or low-track students, teachers need to re-examine their grouping practices. At the high school level, where almost all schools have some tracking, results are less clear—partly because so little research exists. At the very least, educators at the secondary level need to be looking at less tracking. Alternatives to tracking that include cooperative learning techniques have proved effective for both high- and low-ability students at all levels. Well-known researchers strongly suggest consideration of thoughtful and workable alternatives to tracking to provide quality education for all students (see Braddock and McPartland, 1990, and Goodlad and Oakes, 1988).

Other teachers and I have found that when students are grouped heterogeneously in a cooperative learning environment that respects and values all students, it is not only the lower-ability students who benefit. Gifted students can sometimes explain something in a way that is easier for students to understand than if the teacher explains it. With peer tutoring and cooperative learning, the gifted student has to evaluate what students already know, rethink and reorganize concepts, and demonstrate and explain ideas clearly. In doing so effectively, gifted students clarify and extend their own thinking. Additionally, we have noticed that providing opportunities for all students to work together creates a classroom community of learners and promotes the self-esteem of all students.

Given that the research about the questionable benefits and possible harmful effects of ability grouping has been around for at least fifty years, why do most teachers ignore the results of that research? Looking at my own teaching practice, I think I failed to take the research seriously because:

1. I believed all children in my classroom were being taught well.
2. I had no university training that presented the relevant research.
3. My administrators supported and encouraged ability grouping.
4. There was no parental pressure to move toward heterogeneous grouping, especially from parents whose children were in high-ability tracks.
5. Initially I did not really believe the research—or I chose to ignore it—even when I read it. Only after much soul searching, observation of children, and rereading of relevant research was I able to make a philosophical shift that translated into teaching practice.

While most of the research on ability grouping deals with achievement, the long-range psychological effects on students cannot be ignored. Based on my own experiences, I see this as perhaps the area in which most of the damage occurs. What has become especially clear to me, as I continue to struggle with the issue of homogeneous grouping in a context beyond reading in the elementary grades, is that students in low-ability tracks feel alienated and suffer feelings of low self-esteem. I believe the damage to their self-concepts may be irreparable and lifelong. In addition, I have observed that these students, as compared with students placed in high-ability groups, often have lower standards set by their teachers academically as well as behaviorally. The material they are given to read is often less interesting; the questions they are asked are less demanding; the wait time they are given for responding to questions is shorter; and they are interrupted and corrected more often when reading orally. All of these practices on the part of teachers contribute negatively to students' feelings of self-worth and competence. If our job is to teach and develop whole students, not just teach academic subjects, then we must begin to structure our classes more heterogeneously and treat all students intelligently and with respect.

5

Responding to Literature

Early Transitions

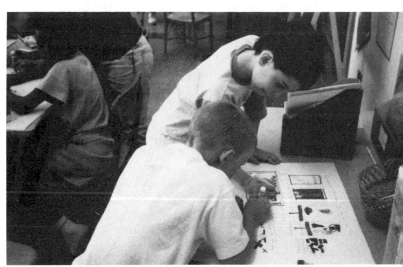

A literature extension in grade 2

Moving into Literature: The First Years

In the fall of 1987, after a district-wide reading committee composed of teachers, administrators, and librarians had been meeting and planning for one year, our district made a long-range commitment to move toward a literature approach to reading and a process approach to writing. A holistic language arts philosophy for kindergarten through grade 12, written by the committee, was adopted by the board of education; and in place of new basal texts, multiple copies of quality children's literature were purchased for kindergarten through grade 6.

Learning to Use the Core Books

We began with about six core books for each elementary grade. These core titles were carefully selected by the reading committee with input from the grade-level teachers. Enough copies were purchased for the books to be used whole class and for each teacher to have a personal copy as a teacher's edition. The core books would serve as the mainstay of the reading program, with questions, activities, and discussion centered around them. While many supplemental titles also became a part of the literature collection in each elementary building, it was the core books that teachers were expected to introduce children to.

How the core books were used was decided (and is still decided) by individual teachers. Books were read whole class, aloud, with small groups, independently, or with any combination of these approaches. There was no mandate that these books had to be "covered." If a teacher did not like a title or didn't have time to get to it, the book might simply be available in the room for children to choose to read independently.

At the same time, the teacher could continue to use the basal text and workbooks. The use of workbooks, however, was highly discouraged by principals, and

79

after two years no new reading workbooks were purchased. Many teachers chose to use a combination approach for several years.

To facilitate the transition to literature and whole language that first year, we were granted release time by grade levels for two half days. The first in-service focused on understanding the theory and research underpinning whole language. The second concentrated on the use of the core books. Without teachers' manuals we were very concerned about management, and we wanted questions, and especially activities, in place. Under the leadership of Rebecca Thomas, a knowledgeable librarian and authority on children's literature, teachers worked together by grade level developing folders of meaningful suggestions and activities to go along with our literature collection, especially the core books.

Teachers made visual brainstorming maps, or webs, to highlight key areas for discussion. For example, second grade teachers created "Bill Peet: Getting to Know an Author/Illustrator." The web included suggestions for activities, such as taking a close look at Bill Peet characters and their characteristics, personification and imagery, ecology and math tie-ins, and suggested extension activities. Looking back at the folders several years later, I see that we probably had too many activities for some books, but we had made a good start, and we needed the security that putting ideas in writing provided.

Besides the webs, the folders that have been developed for our core books contain information that individual teachers and librarians have contributed over the years. These include excerpts about the book from other resources, ideas from other sources for questions and extensions, information about the author, and activities that teachers and librarians have developed and used successfully. Every elementary school teacher in our district has at least one folder for each book in our core collection. The folders have also been helpful to new teachers and teachers who have changed grades in getting started with unfamiliar books. However, not everything in these folders is excellent. It has been up to the teacher to be knowledgeable enough to pick and choose what is appropriate.

Beyond activities to go along with the books, in some buildings teachers used the weekly language arts support groups to work through a core book together. For example, in one building we read and discussed *Danny the Champion of the World* by Roald Dahl. We decided a week ahead of time what chapters we would focus on at the next meeting. Teachers then read the chapters and wrote in the margins of their copies questions, activities, and vocabulary to highlight. Some teachers also noted particular pages that would be good for reinforcing certain skills—for example, a page with lots of contractions, possessives, or compound words.

When we came together as a group we talked about what we thought was important, what were good questions for particular chapters, and what activities we might use to introduce the book or tie the whole book together. We added to and changed what we had done on our own by writing in additional suggestions/questions in our personal copies. We discovered that by working together and learning from each other we could come up with a very good book guide. The group was also an effective way to build confidence in our abilities to plan approaches on our own.

Many of our teachers now write what used to go into a separate book guide or folder in their personal teacher's editions of a core book. The space above the opening of each chapter, the margins, and the space at the end of the chapter all provide room for writing in important questions for discussion. The inside back cover may be used to list "Related Activities." Having the guide in the book makes it handy for the classroom teacher or substitute.

Beginning Transitions in Using Literature Meaningfully

Despite the fact that we had the literature, folders of activities, and some in-service, many of us still had difficulty deciding what questions and activities, and how many, were appropriate to go along with the books. It was common initially to "basalize" the literature by asking too many questions and requiring too many written responses, too much vocabulary study, and too many activities. Considering our past training, that was almost to be expected. Certainly, I am among those who at one time "killed" a good book by dissecting it for every possible skill and activity. It was not unusual to hear a teacher say, "After months on that book, the kids hated it and so did I."

After being wedded to the basal for so many years, I think it is part of the normal process of change to teach literature poorly before teaching it wisely. The change from the basal, with all its teacher-directed activities and manual instructions, to literature where there is no manual and the teacher and children choose the stories, questions, and activities can be overwhelming. Not used to making decisions and giving children choices, many of us did what we had always done. In planning for instruction, we created guides and worksheets every bit as burdensome as the basals we had just set aside. Only with the gradual development of our beliefs about language learning has our confidence developed in using literature thoughtfully.

In the first few years, most core books were read and discussed whole class. Many teachers felt they couldn't manage the new literature approach and also worry about independent seatwork. At the same time, when there was grouping, it was usually homogeneous, ability grouping. That has gradually changed.

After three years of using a literature approach to reading, more and more teachers are beginning to use small-group discussion, and increasing numbers of teachers are using heterogeneous, mixed-ability grouping. Some teachers have begun by having all students in the class read the same book. However, instead of one large class discussion, they divide the class into three or four groups. Initially, using one book has allowed teachers time to work out the management of having a literature discussion group while the rest of the class is working independently. Gradually, with confidence and time, many have moved to having several books going at one time. The books may or may not be related by author or theme.

At the same time, many teachers are now beginning to worry less about focusing on activities and are spending more time on developing critical thinking and encouraging children's personal responses to literature. As our knowledge and understanding of whole language has grown, we find that book-related activities present themselves naturally to us and the students. What has become the larger challenge is to ask the really important questions and to encourage the kinds of responses to literature that promote and integrate reading, writing, discussion, listening, and thinking on the very highest levels.

Chapter 6, "Responding to Literature: Later Transitions," addresses these concerns and describes the efforts some of our teachers are making. (For more information on early transitions into literature by some teachers in our school district, see Routman, 1988.)

While our district moved directly from the basal to literature, based on my experience, that is not typical. Recognizing that most school districts seem to begin their transition process to a literature approach by maintaining the use of a basal text, what follows is the story of a school district that used a basal approach but supplemented it with more meaningful activities and trade book literature.

With the hope of promoting more thoughtful responses to literature, the rest of this chapter examines how to use a basal story more holistically, demonstrates how to make a meaningful book guide, and provides examples of worthwhile literature extension activities.

Looking at a Basal Story and Using It Holistically

A local school district recently decided to "move into whole language" based on the decision of a reading/study committee composed of teachers and administrators. Multiple copies of trade books were purchased for guided reading. At the same time, the district adopted a new basal series. Funds were available for both purchases because of an anticipated reduction in the use of basal workbooks. As contradictory as it sounds, I know of several school districts that have followed a similar course. A group of teachers and administrators make the decision to move toward whole language but don't want to rattle the school community and the board of education. One assistant superintendent told me, "We weren't prepared to do away with the basal. The basal offered a comfort level that most of the staff and community still needed, and we wanted to take everyone with us."

As facilitator for a whole language institute for the teachers and administrators, I suggested that we look at the new basal text to see how it could best be utilized. I asked the reading specialist to select what she considered to be one of the best stories, and she picked "Keep the Lights Burning, Abbie" from the grade 2, first semester basal. The story, based on a real-life event that took place in 1856, centered on a young girl, Abbie Burgess, who kept the lighthouse lamps lit during a fierce storm while her father went to get needed supplies. The nine-page story was adapted from the forty-page book by Peter and Connie Roop (Carolrhoda Books, 1985).

At the time I read the story, I had no idea it was an adapted version. Nowhere in the basal is there even a hint that "Keep the Lights Burning, Abbie" is not an original story. The acknowledgments section says, "Reprinted by permission . . . ." Not only does the adapted version lack the mood, detail, setting, and language of the original, but most of the charming watercolor illustrations by Peter Hanson are missing. Also missing is the informative page "A Note from the Authors," which gives background on lighthouses as well as factual information about Abbie Burgess.

Additionally, wonderful classics such as *Daniel's Duck* by Clyde Robert Bulla (Harper & Row, 1979), *Frog and Toad Together* by Arnold Lobel, and *Dandelion* by Dan Freeman (Viking, 1964), which our first-graders read in original book form—are needlessly adapted in these second grade basals. While the newer basals are much improved, with many stories by notable authors, there are still far too many adapted versions—not just of the text, but of the illustrations.

With the basal, besides being aware of adaptations, it is also important to realize that students spend only about ten minutes a day actually reading the text if the teacher's manual is followed. Therefore, it is imperative that teachers become selective and critical of the basal selections they do use. Furthermore, the basal must be supplemented by authentic literature with lots of time available for reading and discussion. If children are to become readers, they must spend most of their reading time reading. Additionally, teachers need to become judicious in selecting what is worthwhile from the text and the teacher's manual and to make sure that the questions and activities employed are worth the children's time and attention. This can make the difference in whether or not students come to enjoy and value reading.

In order for teachers to feel they could use the required basal in a more meaningful way, all participating teachers in the workshop were asked to read "Keep the Lights Burning, Abbie" and take a critical look at the accompanying teacher's guide and workbook pages. I was amazed and upset to find that the teacher's guide "lesson organizer" for that story is twenty-six pages long and includes sixteen possible worksheets! It took me well over an hour to study the guide, far longer than the time it took to read the story, and I remember feeling what a waste of a teacher's time it was and how insulting such manuals are to teachers' intelligence. The focus was on unimportant skills in isolation and not on meaning.

While some of the questions the teacher was directed to ask were good, there were far too many of them, sometimes as many as three or four for one page of text. There were fill-in-the-blank worksheets available for "teaching" characterization, comprehension, using new words, filling in correct words, vocabulary, critical words in the story, time lines, unstressed vowel sounds, words with r-controlled vowels, reality and fantasy, main idea/details, keeping a log, and capitalization. The worksheets did not require any real thinking and were not worth the time they would take to complete. All of the skills could be taught meaningfully in the context of reading and discussing the story.

At the top of the worksheet on "teaching characterization" this advice was given: "Remember: To understand a character in a story think about what the character says and does. Also think about how the character speaks and acts." Sentence 1 stated, "Makiko's friend Carmen laughed a lot. She always had a smile on her face. Carmen was _____ (surprised, naughty, or happy)." (Student Workbook, "Garden Gates," Morristown, NJ: Silver Burdett & Ginn, 1989, p. 30.) The simplistic worksheet used names that were not in the story and was really a cloze exercise that could be answered through the context of the sentences. Surely this cannot seriously be called "teaching characterization." The way for students to understand characterization is to talk about the actual characters in the story!

As is often true in basal teacher guides, the suggestions in "more ideas for selection follow-up" are the best. Yet this is the section most teachers skip because it's extra and not required. This section includes open-ended questions, a suggestion to reread the story as a play, and ideas for role playing and keeping a log. Unfortunately, more practice skill sheets were also included. With the assistant superintendent in attendance, I urged teachers to skip the worksheets and most of the teacher's manual and develop their own questions and activities. We would first do that together by trying to develop a meaningful guide.

Developing a Guide for Literature

Once teachers have had practice in making and using guides for literature, they can develop their own framework for a good guide. It is important to know what makes a meaningful guide, not only for doing it yourself but for being able to look at commercial guides and deciding whether or not they are worth your, and the children's, time. Now that teaching with literature is big business, commercial publishers have responded with slick, seductive packages to lure unsuspecting teachers. Unfortunately, most of these guides are poorly prepared. They include too many questions and activities, as well as isolated vocabulary study, and go off in unrelated directions. Additionally, they usually cost too much money.

In moving into a literature approach, the first guides that teachers create are often just as poor. Based on the training many of us have had, this is a natural transition, and we should not be too hard on ourselves. In a sincere effort to cover all the important concepts and skills, initially we do too much. I know many well-meaning teachers who have worked hours creating literature packets for their students. They use these as management tools for conducting the reading group and for assigning seatwork. In addition to skills activities, multiple choice questions, and vocabulary words to look up, these all-inclusive organizers often contain every conceivable kind of extension activity related to every aspect of the curriculum. I have seen teachers take E. B. White's *Charlotte's Web* and have students do research reports on spiders as well as read about and study pigs and farms and then create math problems to go along with them all. One teacher even brought a live pig into her classroom. While none of these extension activities are inherently bad, they take children away from the book's potential impact on the reader. As far as good literature is concerned, we could do well to heed the maxim "less is more" where questions and activities are concerned.

We were fortunate in our district to have Susan Hepler, a well-known literature consultant and an expert in constructing literature guides, available to teachers for a recent, full-day summer in-service. Although I was not able to attend, colleagues shared their notes, and at a later date, Susan responded personally to my questions about making a guide. Susan has provided the most useful information to teachers on guide making that I have come across (see Hepler, 1988).

The following suggestions and format for making a teacher's guide for a book are adapted from Susan Hepler's work. In making a worthwhile guide, keep in mind that questions and activities should enhance readers' enjoyment of the book and bring them back to the text for reexamination. Time spent with a book should be worth the effort, actively involve the reader, and be true to the book's intention.

Since making book guides takes thoughtful time, titles should be chosen that are quality literature. (See "Recommended Literature by Grade Level, K–12," in the *Resources for Teachers* section for suggestions by grade level and Appendixes B and C for specific examples of excellent guides for a picture book and a chapter book.) A book guide is not meant to be used as a rigid formula. Rather, it should be a flexible framework for the teacher for using a book holistically, for promoting critical thinking, for enjoying a story, and for allowing readers to examine their own feelings.

Framework for a Meaningful Book Guide

Summary

Include author/illustrator credits.

Give a brief summary of about two sentences.

If relevant, mention something about the plot, characters, artwork, theme.

Initiating Activities

Book introduction; keep brief.

Have students make predictions regarding setting, characters, and possible content from available information—book jacket, chapter titles, opening pictures, dedication.

Thinking Critically

Picture books: 6–8 questions

Chapter books: 3–5 important questions per chapter or reading chunk

No more than 30 questions for a chapter book

Ask questions that stay with the book, relate to the artwork, or deal with understanding the characters, major themes, or the book's impact on the reader.

Phrase questions that invite many responses.

> What are some ways . . . ?
> What clues does the author give to . . . ?

Phrase questions that ask for evidence.

> How can you tell . . . ?
> How do you know . . . ?
> Why do you think . . . ?

Related Activities

For complete book: 4–6 activities

Allow students some choice and collaboration. Out of the 4–6 activities (some short, some long term) students select (or the teacher assigns) 1–3 activities.

Activities should lead students back to the book and require some work in depth: examining plot, character change, author's style.

Most activities should include a written component in a suggested format: diary, newspaper article, explanation, description, poem.

An activity may include extending critical thinking through discussion based on reacting to the book as a whole.

Some activities should include illustrations. Well-done artistic interpretation is valid, enjoyed by students, and is a change of pace from writing.

Some activities may take students beyond the book by involving other books by the same author or on the same theme or by making connections to their lives.

As a clarification, the answers to the questions included in the book guide are not meant to be written out by students; they are for teachers to use in guiding discussion before, during, and after reading. However, a response to a question might be written if it is part of the related activities at the conclusion of the book. The number of questions and activities depend on the length and depth of the book, how much time is being spent on it, whether discussion is whole class, small group, or one-to-one with the teacher, and whether discussion is taking place as the book is being read or after the book has been read through in its entirety. For the latter, there would be far fewer questions, and they would be more global; for example, "What is friendship?" "What is courage?" "What have you learned about . . . ?"

Creating a Book Guide

After discussing the framework for a meaningful book guide, teachers and administrators in the aforementioned summer institute worked together as a whole group. We created the following guide in about fifteen minutes. (Since everyone had read the story, to save time we omitted the summary.) For teachers who had never done this before, their questions and activities were more meaningful than the basal teacher's guide and took 75 percent less time to prepare than to read the instructions in the teacher's manual.

Book Guide for "Keep the Lights Burning, Abbie"

Initiating Activities

1. Look at the title and pictures and predict. How is the girl dressed? Where do you think this story takes place? What do you think it is about?
2. What do we know about lighthouses? Provide necessary background information. (For example, Gail Gibbons' *Beacons of Light: Lighthouses* [Morrow, 1990] would work well here.)

Thinking Critically

How do we know that Abbie is responsible?

How do we know Abbie was brave?

How did Abby react when the storm came?

What makes this story seem real to you?

Why was it important that Abbie keep the lights burning?

Related Activities

Write a journal entry as if you were Abbie. How would you have felt?

Compare the basal story with the original book.

Discuss how you think Abbie changed as a result of this experience.

For teachers creating guides for the first time the hardest part is to avoid the tendency to overkill. Initially teachers found it difficult to believe that the guide was long enough and involved enough. One teacher said, "I would have been inclined to have students create a journal showing a week out of Abbie's life" (instead of a day). While the activity was a good one, it would probably have added days to the time spent on only a nine-page story. Without the usual amount of written products it takes time to feel that reading instruction and comprehension have truly taken place.

Following the guide we produced as a whole group, teachers met in small groups by grade level and constructed guides for some of the picture books and chapter books that had just been purchased for the district. Each group's draft of its guide was written on an overhead transparency and shared with the entire audience. Typed copies of all guides were later distributed to all in attendance. Many teachers commented on how valuable and doable the guides seemed and how much they appreciated the opportunity to work with their colleagues.

As I talked with teachers a year later, many remarked that one of the direct results of the workshop was the realization that the basal could be used differently. Teachers who in the past had felt "skills driven" and compelled to do every workbook page now felt knowledgeable and confident enough to choose the stories and workbook pages they saw as worthwhile. The comfort level of most of the teachers seemed high. With few exceptions, teachers were choosing to use a combination of the basal text and trade book literature and were incorporating more meaningful strategies in their teaching. Several teachers mentioned that the guides constructed at the workshop had been extremely useful. Additionally, both teachers and administrators emphasized that the use of workbooks had been substantially reduced in all the buildings. Clearly, teachers were focusing more and more on the meaning and enjoyment of stories while gaining confidence that students were learning the skills. High scores on basal unit skills tests and students choosing to read constantly confirmed this.

Literature Extension Activities

To assist the creating of meaningful book guides and responses to literature, the following section presents various activities that can be used to extend and enhance the understanding and enjoyment of literature in the classroom without resorting to worksheets. A worthwhile literature extension activity

- grows naturally out of the literature
- encourages students to thoughtfully re-examine the text
- demonstrates something the reader has gained from the book

Activities can be done individually, with a partner, in a small or large group, or whole class. The majority of activities should be explained and in some cases demonstrated by the teacher before students are asked to work independently. Taking the time to explain and demonstrate the assignment raises the child's confidence level and increases his chances of doing a successful job. Students should also understand the purpose of doing the activity, and there should be ample time for sharing and displaying completed projects.

The activities and strategies that follow are presented with a strong caution. In no way are they meant to be all inclusive or used as a "recipe." They are merely suggestions that have proved successful over time. They include ideas for dramatic, artistic, and written responses. Activities that are overused, or always assigned without choice, can become boring and meaningless for students. Too much response can turn students off to a book and to reading and writing. Indeed, we need also to recognize the importance of continued silent reading, or silence, as a response. You don't always have to do something with a book in order to enjoy and appreciate it.

The most important caution, however, involves understanding educational theory about how children learn and our role as teachers. Merely incorporating different activities without an accompanying change in beliefs will result in no real, meaningful change. Always we need to be connecting learning with the activity by asking:

- What is my purpose in selecting this activity or strategy?
- How does it fit with my beliefs about learning and teaching?
- How will this activity enhance the students' appreciation and knowledge of the literature?

While we all admire creative teachers who come up with great ideas that children enjoy, we need to be sure that we know the purposes behind those ideas. Students, too, should be able to tell why they are doing a particular activity.

The main response to literature in the classroom should always center around personal enjoyment, discussion, and activities that help connect the literature to the students' lives. Above all, we want the students to continue to choose to read and write. If the literature and related activities are well chosen, not only will comprehension be extended but students' lives will be enriched.

Tried and True Enterprises

Frank Smith (1988, p. 70) prefers the term "enterprises" to "activities," which he sees as an overused term. Many of the most worthwhile enterprises arise from collaboration, from teachers planning together and students working together without pressure and restrictions. (Besides the list that follows, see "Writing for Authentic Purposes," pp. 170–171, "Literacy Extension Activities," pp. 35b–39b, and Routman, 1988.) The enterprises on the following pages are not listed in order of significance.

- Rewrite or retell the book or story as a play, short story, picture book, folktale, soap opera, parody, or television script.
- Write an introduction, epilogue, different ending, or an additional chapter.
- Design a bookmark, book jacket, or front and/or back cover.
- Make a poster that advertises the book, depicts favorite scenes, or describes a "wanted" character.
- Keep a diary from the point of view of one of the characters.
- Write an original dialogue between two characters.
- Make a diorama, mural, or filmstrip depicting scenes or major settings from the book.
- Act out a favorite scene, perhaps with simple puppets (such as "lunch bag puppets") or as a pantomine.
- Write a letter to the author or book character with questions and suggestions.
- Advertise the book through a commercial, Reader's Theater, or radio show.

- Dress up as a character and discuss/justify your behavior and actions.
- Illustrate the settings of the book as a visual map, travel brochure, photo album, or poster.
- Make a comparison chart of several versions of a tale, different illustrations in similar versions, or various books by the same author.
- Make a Big Book, picture book, or wordless book from a chapter book.
- Using a folded paper booklet or sheet divided into eight sections, illustrate the major happenings of the book in sequence, and include with each picture several sentences that sum up the event.
- Make a class graph of favorite characters, books, or authors.
- Create a dictionary for specialized language or facts learned from the book.
- Find and read original reviews of the book. Give a summary report. Write your own review.
- Research information about the author.
- Create an enterprise that demonstrates your enjoyment, appreciation, and understanding of the book.

Making an Eight-Page Book from One Sheet of Paper

This is a fantastic, favorite resource that students are able to put together on their own from grade 1 upward. Using any size piece of paper, and cutting and folding according to the directions below, an eight-page book is created without staples or tape. The standard 8½ by 11 inch sheet is most useful because it is plentiful in most schools as copy paper. Also, when this standard size book is opened and flattened, it can be copied on the Xerox machine—allowing for multiple copies of text for reading, writing, and illustrating.

Teachers and students alike love these eight-page books. We have used them for note taking on field trips, making picture books from chapter books, collecting true facts from a novel, creating individual vocabulary booklets or skills booklets (for homonyms, compound words, synonyms from books), sequencing main story events, summarizing, and illustrating favorite sections of a book. The possibilities are endless. Directions and samples follow.

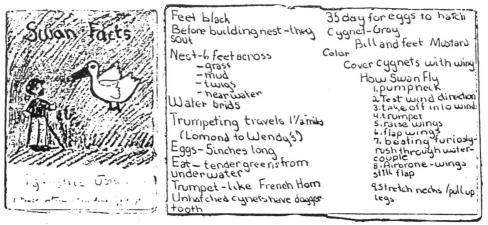

Cover and two pages from a third-grader's book of "Swan Facts," as found in *Trumpet of the Swan* by E. B. White.

MAKING AN EIGHT-PAGE BOOK FROM ONE SHEET OF 8½" BY 11-INCH PAPER

8½"

11"

Fold in half

Fold in half again

Then fold over

Open sheet of paper
Cut paper with scissors
to center of fold

Open sheet and fold
over to form a diamond

Push in sides to form..............8-PAGE BOOK!

Flip Booklets

Flip books are easy to put together, and young children enjoy them. They can be used to depict events, feelings, personal histories, scenes from a book, or anything you can think of. Using 8½ by 11 inch paper, two or more sheets of paper are folded and then stapled on the common fold with a long-arm stapler. Directions and a sample follow.

Fold three sheets of 8½ x 11" paper
this way:

Based on an idea by beginning first-graders after hearing/reading *The Fat Cat* by Jack Kent (Scholastic, 1971).

Creating Take-offs on Favorite Stories

Many books for young children work naturally as springboards for writing. The stories naturally suggest themselves as writing models, and children use the basic structures to create original texts. This is very different from restrictive, patterned writing, which is sometimes overused. (See Wason-Ellan, 1988, "Using Literary Patterns: Who's in Control of the Authorship?")

Following are some texts that have worked well. (For additional titles, see "Books Which Invite Writers to Write"— "Recommended Literature," blue pages, and Routman, 1988, p. 76.) Excerpts from first-graders' take-offs are included.

Gelman, Rita Golden. *Why Can't I Fly?* (Scholastic, 1986)
Heller, Ruth. *Chickens Aren't the Only Ones* (Grosset & Dunlop, 1981)
Kellogg, Steven. *Can I Keep Him?* (Dial, 1971)
Wells, Rosemary. *Noisy Nora* (Dial, 1973)
West, Colin. *Have You Seen the Crocodile?* (Harper & Row, 1986)
Viorst, Judith. *The Tenth Good Thing About Barney* (Atheneum, 1971)

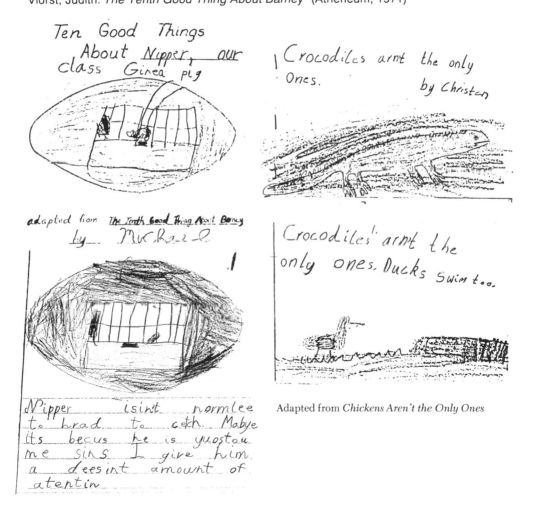

Ten Good Things About Nipper, our class Ginea pig

adapted from *The Tenth Good Thing About Barney* by Michael

Nipper isint normlee to brad to cdth. Mabye its becus he is yuostou me sins I give him a deesint amount of atentin

Crocodiles arnt the only Ones. by Christen

Crocodiles' arnt the only ones. Ducks Swim too.

Adapted from *Chickens Aren't the Only Ones*

Picture Mapping

Picture mapping sequences the major events of a story without words. Students who prefer drawing to writing especially favor this activity. Small groups enjoy working together and re-examining the text and illustrations to decide whether an event is a main idea or a detail. Usually not more than ten to twelve pictures are included in a picture map.

Intermediate grade students have had great fun doing circular picture maps of William Steig picture books because a number of his stories begin and end in the same setting. Note the picture map below of *Brave Irene* by William Steig (Farrar, Straus and Giroux, 1986), done whole class. Picture maps done in small groups or individually yield different interpretations. As long as students can support their decisions from the text, all reasonable responses are accepted.

Venn Diagram

The Venn diagram is a visual device for comparison that uses two concentric circles. Concepts in common are denoted in the space created in the intersection of the two circles. The diagram can be used to compare two books, two versions of a fairy tale or fable, two different mediums for a story—a book and a videotape—or two characters. Phrases are used to note characteristics of a story or character. For very young children, pictures may be used instead of words. The Venn diagram may be used from kindergarten through high school—whole class, small group, paired students, or individually for older students. Because it is so visual, it is easy for students to grasp.

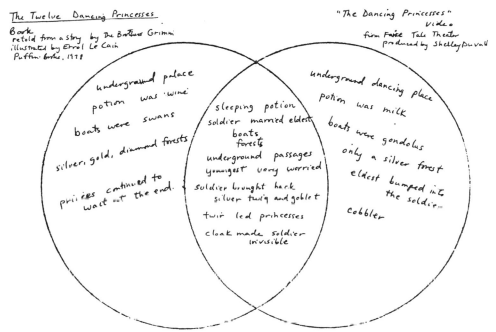

The Twelve Dancing Princesses
Book
retold from a story by The Brothers Grimm
illustrated by Errol Le Cain
Puffin Books, 1978

"The Dancing Princesses"
Video
from Faire Tale Theater
produced by Shelley Duvall

underground palace
potion was 'wine'
boats were swans
silver, gold, diamond forests
princes continued to wait at the end.

sleeping potion
soldier married eldest
boats
forests
underground passages
youngest very worried
soldier brought back silver twig and goblet
twin led princesses
cloak made soldier invisible

underground dancing place
potion was milk
boats were gondolas
only a silver forest
eldest bumped into the soldier...
cobbler

By Karen Horton's third grade class, 1989–1990.

Storymapping

Various formats may be used for storymapping. The purpose is for students to recognize and analyze the structure and elements of a story by noting the setting, characters, problem or conflict, events, and resolution. Storymapping helps students internalize the structure of stories; it is useful for aiding understanding of new stories and writing original stories.

Many of these elements will be viewed differently by the reader, depending upon one's point of view and personal interaction with the text. Note the storymaps of several first-graders for *There's a Nightmare in My Closet* by Mercer Mayer (Dial, 1986). All responses are different; all interpretations are valid.

THERES A NighTMaRe in My closeT
Book Title

setting: In his room

characters: The BOY and The nightmare

problem: Th A Boy GeTs sKard.

Event 1 — he was mad BuT hot To mad

Event 2 — The nTehnTMARe GeTs In Bed

Event 3 — The monSTer CrISe

resolution: That The Boy Let the monSTer InhTS Bed

THERE'S A Nightmare In My Room
Book Title

setting: House

characters: a little boy and his dad and monsters.

problem: There are monsters in his room.

Event 1 — Monsters berknedid in bed room.

Event 2 — Get rid of them.

Event 3 — look for the monsters avry were.

resolution: find monsters thay were bad gis.

Good woRk Michael ★

There es a Nightmar in my Closet
Book Title

setting: Bedroom

characters: A Boy and his Nietmer

problem: The nietmer gets woond id

Event 1 — The Boy hs. chirin uV a Nietrmer

Event 2 — He gets reday to shoot.

Event 3 — The Monstre KrISe.

resolution:

The Niet mer maexs freneeds Wit the Boy

Reproducing Photographs from a Shared Experience

A delightful remembrance of a field trip, classroom visitor, or any shared class experience can be captured by taking pictures of the event. On the school copying machine the teacher reproduces the color or black and white photographs. The photos may be selected and sequenced by the teacher and made into individual booklets or a class Big Book. Students write and read their own text. The photos help students focus and recall main events and details.

The example below shows books produced by first-graders (near the end of the school year) after a visit by a doll maker. Working in small groups with teacher guidance, the students wrote rough drafts, revised them, and produced their own final copies for the first time.

Mrs Eady Visited us. she took us to The rug. And she had Some doll Skin And she was holding the Skin up.

Guess What they're doing? They're Stuffing a lot of Cotton. Mrs. Pope And I Like The way Terry And Terry's mom Work.

Now Beth is Stuffing The head So The head will Look Real. Jerome is Not Going to Eat That. Is He? No!

Pages 1–3 from "The Making of Elizabeth, a Doll" by Raquel. Idea developed by Joyce Pope.

Reader's Theatre

I first learned about Reader's Theatre when I heard Lynn Rhodes describe it at a national IRA conference. I have been using it and demonstrating it to teachers and children ever since.

Reader's Theatre involves creating a script from a narrative text and performing it for an audience. Students work cooperatively to write a dialogue, rehearse it, and read it to the class. Props are minimal. Interest and involvement are high.

We have used Reader's Theatre to dramatize and retell one scene or chapter of a book, to highlight the personality of particular characters, or to advertise and promote a favorite book read independently. After the script is written, the writer or writers choose students to practice and read the character parts.

Below is a Reader's Theatre from *More Stories Julian Tells* by Ann Cameron, as written by a group of third-graders after I modeled and talked through a scene from the book on the overhead projector.

Robert, Amanda, Alison

characters: Gloria, Julian narrator   pp. 25-27

narrator: It was seven-o-clock at night and Julain was waiting for Gloria to call.
(the phone rang) it was Gloria.

Julain: hello Gloria

Gloria: look out your window

Julain: I don't see anything unusal.

Gloria: Whatch the wall across from the window.

narrator: Julain watched a yellow circle of light on the wall

Julain: It lookes like the sun

Gloria: It is the sun. look out your window again

Julain: Your right Gloria you win.

narrator: The End

Creating Simple Story Frames

Kindergarten and first grade children can demonstrate their comprehension of a story by illustrating and/or briefly noting their characters, setting, problem, and solution in a picturebook story. Such open-ended frames allow differing points of view and encourage students to think about the problems or events that they feel are most important. Note three first-graders' responses to three different story frames.

Story	Problem	Solution
Mouse Sou...	The weasel caught the mouse and the mouse was going to be mouse soup	the mous tricked the weasel.
Tikki Tikki Tembo	Tikki fell in the well and he was in there a long time.	the. Old man Got tikki out of the well.

Story	Characters	Setting
If you give a mouse a cookie	boy / mouse	House
The Carrotseed	mem dad boy Big Brotke	otside Lauree Elen e-h

Name LAUREN
Date ...
Title THE TROLLEY RIDE

• I drew the story in order

Idea developed by Peg Rimedio.

Writing Feature News Articles from Book Events

A feature story, with a headline, is written about a main event in a book. The feature is written as if it had been found on the front page of the newspaper where the event takes place. Students will first need to be familiar with how feature newspaper articles and headlines are constructed.

Then, taking on the role of news reporter and putting themselves at the scene of the event, the students need to tell succinctly what happened. The first sentence should reflect the headline, and quotations should be from eyewitnesses to the event. Students will need to reread the text for key events and phrases. This activity could also take the format of a nightly news show, with students reading their headlines and stories. Another variation could be to pull facts from an actual newspaper article and turn it into a story.

Below are some headlines and feature stories from Patsy Bannon's third grade class based on *Trumpet of the Swan* by E. B. White (Harper & Row, 1970).

LOMOND WAVE

U.F.S. TAKES VALUABLE TRUMPET

By Tori Skubic (L.W.)

Billings, Montana - A valuable musical instrument was stolen by an unidentified flying swan.

The swan rammed right into the window of a music store. The swan broke the glass and cut himself. Luckily, the swan was the only one injured.

The swan caused $900.00 in damage. The police want to arrest the thief. The police are looking for the trumpet and the swan.

WHITE BIRD ROBS MUSIC STORE

By Sharon Moffie (L.W.)

Billings, Montana - A huge white bird flew into a music store and stole a very valuable trumpet.

The bird was injured by crashing into the store's window, but no one else got hurt. A saleslady fainted when she saw the bird.

The police came and tried to arrest the robber.

There was $900 worth of damage done to the store. The owner tried to shoot the bird, but missed.

The bird flew away with the trumpet.

GIANT BIRD BOMBS MUSIC STORE

By John Pope (L.W.)

Billings, Montana - A giant swan robbed Mallard's Musical Instrument Store yesterday. The music store was robbed of a valuable trumpet.

The swan flew through the glass window of the store! The swan was injured by the broken glass. No one else was hurt. A salesgirl fainted!

One eyewitness said, "It was a terrifying experience!"

The manager fired at the bird two times, but missed. The police came, but the bird escaped. The owner complained that $900 worth of damage was done to his store.

Creating Comic Strips

Students of all ages enjoy turning a scene, event, chapter, or book into a comic strip. Students like to study actual comic strips first for format and use of color. Many teachers find the "bubbles" help students understand the use of conversation and quotation marks.

Below is a comic strip done by a third-grader from a scene in *Nora and Mr. Mind-Your-Own-Business* by Joanna Hurwitz (Morrow, 1977).

Idea developed by Patsy Bannon.

Making a Photo Album

Students enjoy putting together a photo album or scrapbook of important events, scenes, and characters from a story. This can be used to highlight settings, characters, or main events. Each snapshot or photo is captioned with a description. Corners to hold the photos in place are made with black Magic Marker in the shape of small triangles.

Below is one page of illustrated photos by a third-grader based on *Danny the Champion of the World* by Roald Dahl.

Idea developed by Sylvia Tallentire.

6

Responding to Literature

Later Transitions

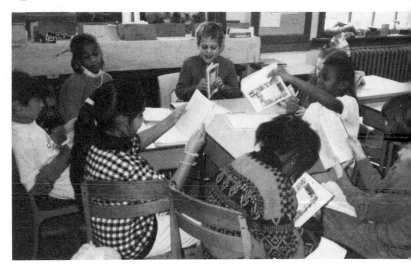

Heterogeneous literature discussion group: fourth-graders leading their own discussion of Every Living Thing *(Rylant, 1985)*

Three to five years after moving from the basal to literature, some of us have begun to make a further transition to a more collaborative response to literature. Teachers are ready to ask fewer- but even better—questions, plan fewer activities, and encourage more student ownership and participation. One way to achieve this is through the use of literature response logs and literature discussion groups.

This chapter elaborates on using literature response logs, asking important questions, and facilitating discussion groups as a means for promoting high-level thinking and reasoning from the primary grades through high school. The formats given here are meant only to serve as flexible guides for many possibilities in responding to literature. Various uses of the formats are examined in detail because they have been a very successful vehicle for some teachers and students. You will want to adapt their use, choose your own formats, use certain components, try out what appeals to you, and add your own unique experiences and expertise.

Literature Response Logs

A literature response log is a journal for recording reactions to literature. It has also been called a reading response log, literature log, reading log, or reading journal. It is an excellent tool for connecting reading to writing, for extending the meaning of the text, and for giving readers ownership of their literary experience. Responding in writing to a question, impression, mood, or reaction generated by the reading seems to promote critical thinking. The response may be intellectual or emotional, personal or general, or a combination. In any case, the literature response usually goes beyond mere summarizing and factual recall.

Written responses may be in the form of responses to open-ended questions, freewriting, vocabulary words, or illustrations. Responses may also include dialogue journals—personal, written interactions between the student and the teacher or between two students.

Students' written responses can be used as a springboard and reference point for group discussion. Additionally, the literature response log can be an effective evaluation instrument. The teacher, student, and parents have ongoing, visible evidence of the student's reactions, interpretations, and thinking regarding a particular book. Finally, the literature response log is a meaningful alternative to answering traditional comprehension questions and writing lengthy, mandatory book reports.

Literature logs can be used from the end of grade 1 all the way through high school. For first-graders, I have found students most receptive to the log when they are at the point where they can read silently and their invented spelling has progressed to the stage where it is easily readable. High school students, used to directed reading assignments, will need lots of oral and written modeling by the teacher before they can honestly express their interpretations and reactions to books. Initially, they begin by thinking and asking, "What does the teacher want?" and "What is the purpose of all this?"

For the literature response log, we have used a spiral notebook, a three-ring notebook, or a booklet put together for the specific book being read. To make a booklet I simply fold sheets of mimeograph paper together and staple them at the centerfold with a long-arm stapler. Paper can be lined, unlined, or a combination of both. A different-color sheet can be included for the cover, which students design. Students are expected to date each entry and write legibly.

What we and the students look for in the reading response log is a reflective response to the literature. It is important that the focus remain on the content of the response and not on the mechanics. There is no red penciling in the log. Comments—written or oral—that the teacher or students make should relate to the content of the message. Care always needs to be taken that not too much writing is assigned or expected. We want students to continue to enjoy to read. Some days no written response is expected. Students just read and enjoy the literature. The response may be simply a personal appreciation of the literature.

As a management tool, literature response logs offer built-in independent work while the teacher meets with other reading groups or students. The students who are not in a reading/literature group read silently and respond to literature in their logs and through other activities the teacher and students have agreed upon. As opposed to worksheets, which encourage "right answer" responses and rarely expand thinking, the literature response log encourages the widest possible range of responses. The student is encouraged to interact with the text and use her own experiences and the book to interpret and construct meaning from what she reads. The student is always encouraged to go back to the text to support her response. The exception to re-examining the text would be responding to a read-aloud book or asking students to write a reaction or response following the reading.

High school teachers who use a response log format, either for guided reading or independent reading, report that they never see evidence of "Cliffs Notes." One high school teacher commented, "I have had some trouble teaching students the value of logs, but there is never a doubt about whether they've done the reading." The only way to respond personally and thoughtfully to a text is to read it.

Ways to Use the Literature Response Log

My favorite way to use the literature response log is as part of the guided reading program. The whole class, or small groups of students (up to eight), read a book and meet to discuss their impressions after reading silently. (See pp. 38–41 for discussion of guided reading and pp. 122–132 for literature discussion groups.) One advantage of the literature response log is that it encourages students to assume responsibility for the discussion. While the teacher is present to guide the discussion and model questions and responses, students do most of the talking. Instead of the teacher dominating the discussion, with comments directed mostly to the teacher, students talk with each other. Students refer to their entries as a reference to back up specific points they make. Because they have already thought about a question that has been posed, their confidence level rises, and they are often more likely to participate in the discussion. Many of us have noticed that the discussions are livelier, and students have better recall of what they have read. Often the silent reading has taken place the previous day, and the log jogs students' memories. One third-grader said, "I remember the chapter better because I can look at my notes."

At the end of the discussion time, typically about ten to fifteen minutes, I write the next silent reading assignment and requested response on a small, portable chalkboard. (If a different book is being used with each group, several small boards may be used and set aside for easy reference.) While I usually have ready an idea for a general question, I am just as likely to choose a question or issue that has arisen from the discussion that has just taken place. Students copy the response question into their logs and know exactly what is expected of them. In that way, when the teacher is with another group—that day or the following day—students are ready to work independently. Students, teachers, and parents also have a clear record of questions and responses.

For most of us who have been used to asking many questions, asking one or two questions may initially not seem substantial or engaging enough for independent work. However, the type and substance of the questions are quite different—as this chapter demonstrates—and teachers that move to this format are quickly convinced of its benefits. (In addition, students have other options for independent work. See "Classroom Management and Organization," pp. 437–442.)

The literature response log can also be used as a dialogue journal (Atwell, 1987) without group discussion. A written transaction occurs between two students or between a student and the teacher. In that case, it is recommended that the teacher also keep a reading log so students have the teacher's response as a written model. Students, or student and teacher, exchange logs, react to each other's perceptions, and write thoughtful comments to each other. The paired exchanges could vary daily or weekly. The teacher would first need to model what is expected in a thoughtful response. See Figure 6–1 for an example of a student's response to another student and Figures 6–10 and 6–11 for examples of a high school teacher's responses to a student's log. '

There is no one right way or best way to use the literature response log. Vary the way you use the log with students and adopt what works well for you and your students. Keep in mind that we first need to show students, by thinking aloud and writing in front of the students, how he or she would respond to a question or give a

Figure 6-1   Literature Response Log by a Ninth Grade Student

personal reaction to what has been read. One demonstration is rarely sufficient. We demonstrate again and again until students have a clear sense of expectations and possibilities. Using Don Holdaway's developmental model, I begin by giving a demonstration myself and then inviting students to participate.

Even with demonstrations, students need time to get used to the new format. Those who tend to rush through assignments may do the bare minimum and not give thoughtful responses at first. Also, students who are not used to putting ideas into their own words may also have difficulty at first. Because participation in follow-up group discussion is often based on the log, students—who all enjoy being part of a lively discussion—do not take long before they are completing their logs satisfactorily.

We have found it works well for us or the students to choose only one question or format for a particular day's response. Initially, teachers find it difficult to believe that comprehension is being adequately addressed. As teachers, we have been used to requiring lengthy responses, book reports, summaries, large numbers of vocabulary words to be looked up, and/or answers to many specific questions.

However, when teachers and students look at larger issues from literary and personal perspectives, the important details, major happenings, and themes do emerge.

The goal is not to come to common agreement but rather to share various viewpoints and interpretations. The teacher's viewpoint is also shared, but it is only one opinion in the group and is not considered more important or more valid than the ideas of the students. The teacher's role is to guide the discussion but not dominate it. The following are some strategies you can demonstrate for students in using the literature response log. They are not listed in order of significance.

- *__Respond to an open-ended question.__* The question that you or the students select should reflect the overall theme or feeling of the chapter or reading chunk of several chapters. The question should be genuine; that is, one right answer is not already in the teacher's head. (See "Asking Important Questions," pp. 117–119.) A good question may elicit some surprising and varied responses. One question is usually enough. We do not want students to be overburdened with writing. If you choose your question carefully, the key points of the chapter will come out in the discussion. The question is merely the vehicle to get the thinking going. It may call for prediction before reading, a reaction after reading, and/or a response during reading.

Teachers used to asking a lot of questions, many of which have been at the literal level, need time, trust, and the ability to risk to realize that all of the important facts surface when an important question is asked. In fact, by being asked inferential and critical questions, the reader is focused on higher-level thinking, and the literal level takes care of itself.

Some examples of questions that work well are:

What else do you learn about a particular main character?

How does the character feel about . . . ?

What is (a particular character) concerned about?

Describe the relationship between . . . .

What has the author done to build suspense in this chapter?

What do you predict will happen in the next chapter?

What does the author do to make you want to continue reading?

What do you think is most important about what you just read?

Was there anything about what you just read that surprised you?

What do you think the author is trying to tell us about . . . ?

What do you hope to find out in this chapter? What did you find out?

What do you think the focus of the next chapter will be?

What do you think it means when . . . ?

What would happen if . . . ?

Again, we teachers will need to demonstrate how to respond meaningfully before expecting students to do so. Older students—especially at the secondary level—find it less threatening to talk about events in the story, as they have always done. After many years of focusing on plot, they need time and repeated demonstrations before they can begin to respond more thoughtfully and personally.

In their response logs, students are encouraged to make deductions based on the text as well as to prove their points referring to the text and applying their own knowledge and experiences. If the purpose of the log is to support students' ideas in literature discussion groups, they need only write down key words and phrases. This is also a good example of purposeful note taking. If the log is not being used with discussion groups, expecting complete sentences is appropriate.

Joan Servis, a fourth grade teacher who uses literature circles effectively, uses the same question or prompt for all students even if students are reading different books. One question may serve for one chapter, several related chapters, a picture book, or a short story. Joan has her students prove their points and concepts by noting page numbers and specific quotes to support their thinking and inferences. Hers is a terrific technique—one I have used repeatedly with great success.

Here is an example of a prompt and demonstration for Chapters 1 and 2 of *Danny the Champion of the World* by Roald Dahl. Note that complete sentences are not expected here. The purpose is to expand thinking, have students read the text carefully, and use their notes as a catalyst for discussion.

> What do you learn about Danny's father? Prove your conclusions by jotting down a key phrase or insight from the text and the page it is on.
>> Poor—did not own much, p. 3
>> Loved Danny—lavished his love for Danny's mother (who died) on Danny, p. 4
>> Mechanic—owned a filling station, p. 5
>> Storyteller—made up a different story every night, p. 9
>> Not educated—"I doubt he had read twenty books in his life," p. 9
>> Could be trusted—"was an eye-smiler," p. 9

Notice that the characteristics at the left are gleaned from the text—but not necessarily stated in the text. The student has to infer traits about the character through the author's language. When the student comes to group discussion, he will refer to his notes to jog his memory and make his points. Figures 6–2 and 6–3 are examples of fourth grade students' responses to a question shortly after the literature response logs were introduced and modeled.

You will be able to tell by the level of the discussion if the question was a high-level one. The broader the question, the better will be the group discussion. With a probing, comprehensive question all the important points of the chapter will

Figure 6-2   Response to **Sarah, Plain and Tall** *from a Fourth-grader*

From *Sarah, Plain and Tall* by Patricia MacLachlan

Figure 6-3   *Response to* **The Lion, the Witch and the Wardrobe**

4-9-90

what does C.S. Lewis do to set the scene
for the book?

<u>Introduced Characters</u>

Peter, Susan, Edmund, Lucy P.1+
professor "odd looking". P.2
"That old chap will let us do   unexpected
anything we like" house full of   places. p.4.
p.2
"Brothers + Sisters argue p2 .
"on come off it said Edmund" p.2
"setting the tone" made Lucy
feel .... creepy p.3
" characters are adventuresome

Peter was trying to get them
to go around the house, p.3
                              england
"takes place during war" Dangerous pl
Professor is strange in taste.
"They came into a room full of
armour" p.4
"Professor is rich"
"Exploring the house" p.4
"old wardrobe"
Two mothballs fell" p.5

From *The Lion, the Witch and the Wardrobe* by C. S. Lewis.

surface. A limited question will elicit a limited response. Students and teachers need at least several months to get comfortable with the questioning.

(For further examples of open ended questions that work well, see the next section, "Asking Important Questions.")

● *Reflect on your personal reactions while reading.*   Based on life experiences and points of view, a piece of literature affects individuals differently. One use of the log, often employed for responses to books read independently or in an individualized reading program, is for the reader simply to write down what was going through her mind while reading. The written response can be done while reading or after the reading is completed.

Some suggested prompts include:

As you are in the process of reading, write down some thoughts that are going through your head.

Were you reminded of something in your own life as you were reading?

What were you thinking or wondering about as you read this chapter?

What was your overall reaction to what you just read?

What questions came to your mind as you were reading?

I modeled my in-process reading-thinking for a group of second-graders who had read *Stone Soup* by Marcia Brown (Scribner, 1975), a story about a group of hungry soldiers who "trick" some unwilling villagers into feeding them. I quickly jotted down phrases on Post-its to recall my immediate impressions while reading. Then, using the overhead projector, I thought out loud as I wrote:

> I was surprised that such a greedy group of villagers could be tricked so easily. I think people are like that. If they believe they will get something good for themselves, they'll believe anything. However, the peasants were not only greedy. They were curious. No harm was done. Everyone wound up eating a great meal.

When writing in front of the students, I point out that personal responses can often begin with: "I was surprised by . . .", "I noticed that . . .", "I wondered why . . .", "I didn't understand when. . . ." Familiarity with possible beginnings often helps them get started.

• *Choose several unknown vocabulary words.*   Students at all grade levels can be asked to choose several vocabulary words from the chapter (or several chapters) that they would like to know the meaning of and to write down what they think the words mean. Students are encouraged to choose words they might encounter again. This procedure needs to be modeled because students often have trouble choosing words they don't know. Once students become familiar with the procedure, it is enough for them just to write "vocabulary" in their log, but initially I give the following prompt, which they write in their log:

> Choose three words (or another small number) that you would like to know the meaning of. For each word, write the line number and page number it is found on, how it is used (partial or complete quote), and what you think the word means.

Then, when we meet for reading discussion, students refer to the specific lines, page numbers, and contexts so other students can participate in talk about the words' meanings. Very often a word can be determined by the context. When it cannot, this is the ideal time to use the dictionary. While the teacher can also choose words to highlight, it is not only the teacher's words that will be discussed.

With the teaching of vocabulary, it is unrealistic to expect students to look up, memorize, or understand the meanings of fifty to a hundred words or more per book. Several words per chapter usually means twenty to forty words per book, which may still be too much. Use your discretion based on your students' needs and ages. Just because students have looked up and even tested well on a large number of words does not mean they have learned those words. Vocabulary that is truly learned can be meaningfully applied to new reading, writing, speaking, and listening contexts.

A further recommendation is to post the important words that arise (those the student is likely to come across and use again) on a chart and to use and refer to those words over and over again in classroom conversation. In that way, students come to "own" the words, and they begin to appear in their own conversations and writing.

If I were to give a vocabulary test when the students have finished the book, I would ask them to choose a specified number of words from our list and use each word in a sentence that demonstrates the meaning is understood. I would not expect all students to be responsible for the same words or to have learned all the words. Imagine us as adults being expected to learn the same set of words from a novel we have read. Our individual needs and prior knowledge of vocabulary are too diverse to expect that a common list of words would emerge.

Another way to highlight vocabulary and lead into a discussion on the author's use of words is to give prompts such as the following:

> As you are reading, note the way the author uses descriptive words and phrases. Choose some that appeal to you (with page numbers) that you might choose to use in your own writing.
>
> What are some of the words the author uses that give insight into a character's personality?
>
> What particular words that the author used gave you a vivid picture of the setting?

- *Illustrate a part of the text.* It is important to allow time for artistic interpretation as another way to respond to text. Most students, even older ones, relish the chance to draw as a change of pace. In addition, students who are not proficient readers and writers may enjoy the opportunity for artistic expression. Some response prompts include:

> Draw a favorite part of the story.
>
> Based on the author's description, draw a particular character.
>
> Design another cover for this book.
>
> Draw the setting as described by the author.
>
> Select a scene and draw how you picture it.
>
> Assume the role of illustrator for the chapter(s) you just read.

When I introduce *Danny the Champion of the World* by Roald Dahl, to third- or fourth-graders, I read the first few pages aloud and ask students to form a picture in their minds. Then I give each child a reproduced copy of the setting as Dahl wrote it. As I reread the description aloud, I ask the students to underline the parts they could consider putting into their illustrations. First, I do a demonstration and show them the parts I would underline. Often I do this on the overhead projector, inviting student participation. Below is one paragraph from the ten-paragraph description (pp. 5–7).

> The filling station itself had only two pumps. There was a wooden shed behind the pumps that served as an office. There was nothing in the office except an old table and a cash register to put the money into. It was one of those where you pressed a button and a bell rang and the drawer shot out with a terrific bang. I used to love that (p.5).

This is an excellent activity because it directs students' attention back to the text in a careful, critical manner. It is much harder to do than it appears. Students have to re-examine the text, think about spatial placement, layout, detail, color, size, perspective, and what is important to include. (See Figure 6–4 for one student's interpretation.) In this particular book, I show students the illustrator's interpreta-

Figure 6-4 *A Student's Interpretation of the Introductory Setting in* Danny the Champion of the World

Figures 6-5 and 6-6 *Second-graders' Responses to* Fantastic Mr. Fox

Figure 6-6

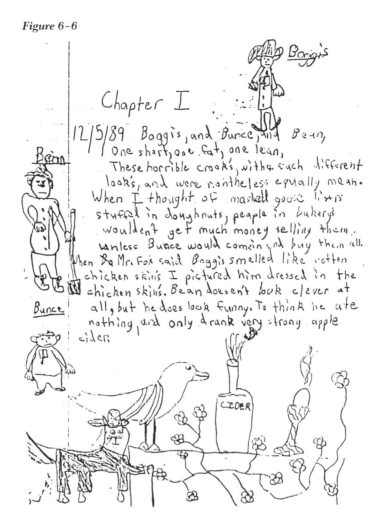

tion after they have completed their drawing. In rereading, one group of students noticed that "the square brick building to the right of the office" was pictured in the book with wood siding, an error on the part of the book illustrator

- *Examine the author's style and motives.*

  Why do you think the author put in the minor characters . . . ?

  What is the format of this book? Is it effective?

  What clues does the author give . . . ?

  How does the author use humor (or . . .)?

  Why do you think the book ended the way it did?

  Is the author's style of writing and organization like any other you have encountered? Explain.

- *Freewrite.* Have the students write anything they would like to about the book so far. See Figures 6–5 and 6–6 for two second-graders' responses to *Fantastic Mr.*

Fox by Roald Dahl (Knopf, 1970). To encourage students to respond personally in freewriting, you may want to demonstrate how some sentences might begin with "I":

I noticed . . .
I was confused . . .
I was wondering . . .
I disagree . . .

● *Imagine another point of view.*

If you were the main character, what would you do and why?
Write a letter to the main character.
Write a letter to the author of the book with any questions you have.
Write a diary entry from the point of view of a particular character.

● *Make up one or more questions for discussion.*   Even primary grade students can be expected to formulate their own high-level, open-ended questions once the teacher has done lots of modeling. Students come to reading discussion with their question(s) written in their reading logs. After the group responds to some of these questions, discussion can focus on which questions worked well and why. One third-grader who asked a factual question commented, "My question wasn't that good because it only had one right answer. There wasn't really anything to talk about."

● *Respond to a final question when the book is completed.*   While there is nothing wrong with an occasional teacher-made test, having students draw their own conclusions after the book has been read and discussed is more meaningful in terms of learning. Because students have been active participants in group discussion, they will be able to write thoughtful responses. Older students can respond to questions they create themselves.

After small groups of fourth-graders had completed *A Taste of Blackberries* by Doris Buchanan Smith, a first-person story of a boy's coming to grips with his best friend's death, I asked them to respond to one of the following questions as a final evaluation:

Who is the main character? Why do you think so?
Why do you think this book is called *A Taste of Blackberries*?
What is your reaction to this book?

See Figures 6–7 through 6–9 for sample responses. Notice that even when two students choose the same question, their responses vary. Both extend and confirm the meaning of the book. Both are valid and can be used in evaluating students' appreciation and understanding of the text.

Other concluding questions that work well are:

How does this book fit with others we have read?
Why do you think the author wrote this book?
What character in the book are you most like or most unlike? Explain.

Figures 6-7, 6-8, and 6-9   Fourth-graders' Responses to **A Taste of Blackberries**

- Jett M.

Why do you think the book is called A Taste of Blackberries I think it is called that because at the begining they were going to pick the berries but they weren't ripe but at the end the narrator picked the blackberries for Jamie because he was dead and I was thinking about Jamie and wondering if he remembered the taste of Blackberries because it was sweet and sour like a taste of life or Death

Figure 6-8

Brooke B   2-2-90

1) Why did you think this book is called A taste of Blackberries?

I think this book is called A Taste of Blackberries because it is life saying a taste of life. A taste of life means something has to go like Jamie dieing and something has to go right, life finally getting over Jamies death. And also At the beginning of this book it starts out in a blackberry patch and they are tasting blackberries.

Figure 6–9

Joby 2·2·90   A Taste of Blackberries

① Tell your reaction to the book?

② My reaction to A Taste of Blackberries was phenominal. The book was very touching. It deals with things that 3 + 4th graders should be able to handle - such as your best friends death. Death is a very serious matter. I think this book handled it, so that young people would understand these unfourtunate mishaps.

With practice and experience, students respond in their literature response logs with intelligence and insight. As they become accustomed to sharing their interpretations, their confidence grows and the quality of group discussion improves. High school teachers note that open-ended questions help students go beyond the usual summarizing of plot.

Teachers also note a carryover to other areas. A third grade teacher said that when students were talking about books read independently, they began backing up their points with quotes from the text. One fourth grade teacher noted that her students were more thoughtful in their responses to social studies questions once they were used to responding in their literature logs. Other teachers note carryover to the content areas, especially in note taking. Jotting down key phrases in the logs on a daily basis is good practice for picking out important points in other texts. (For using response logs across the curriculum, see *Resources for Teachers*, Atwell, 1990, and "Journal Articles," pp. 233–234.)

The literature response log can serve as a reading record of the student's thinking and learning. Teachers find that students' responses not only become longer with time, they also become more thoughtful and insightful. Perhaps the greatest value of the literature response log is that the student comes to realize that what he has to say is valid and important.

Adjusting to the use of logs can be easier for students than teachers. Linda Cooper says that originally she didn't like the responsibility for having to think up a good question: "I hated it at first because it was hard for me. But the kids' enthusiasm kept me going. I saw how much they liked it and how it helped discussion. Their notes jogged their minds, and they could remember a lot better what they had read."

Elementary grade students are practically unanimous in their enjoyment of using the logs. They like the fact that the logs are for them and that they'll all get a chance to talk. They also like the idea that the teacher checks the log only to see that it's done or to respond personally but not to make corrections. That students enjoy and benefit from the logs is apparent by the following typical comments by intermediate grade students:

EVAN: I like using it because all my thoughts are together in one place.

RHONDA: It helps get the discussion going.

AMY: I like it for organization. Everything is easy to find.

TASHA: It refreshes your memory. My notes help me think better.

ISAAC: I like it when someone is talking and I can look at my notes and think of something to add.

Asking Important Questions

In order to provide optimum guidance to students in responding critically to literature, we need to be able to ask the kinds of questions that promote thinking on the very highest levels. This is no easy task. Years of directive questioning in teachers' manuals that put a high priority on factual questions and simple answers makes the transition to higher-level questioning difficult. Most of us have spent years assessing comprehension and listening for the right answers. It takes a long time, as well as the ability to risk and trust ourselves and our students, to ask open-ended questions and questions that facilitate comprehension. Broad-based open-ended questions encourage a variety of responses and are probably the highest-level questions we can ask. They encourage thinking on many levels, value students' background knowledge and experiences, and allow readers to go beyond the text in making meaning.

Open-Ended Questions

Among the best open-ended questions are prediction questions, with readers describing what they think will happen in the story or predicting an answer *before* they read. Then they confirm, adjust, or disprove their predictions before reading on. Even very young children can predict based on prior knowledge, past experiences, and what they see on the cover and in the illustrations. Older children can predict from all these factors as well as from what they already know about literature and authors. Prediction questions work equally well with nonfiction and often stimulate children's interest in a topic.

The following open-ended questions have proved to be particularly helpful for teachers from the primary grades through high school, both for questioning and as models for creating thoughtful questions. Some questions are particularly effective when a book is read and discussed chapter by chapter. Others seem better suited to a whole book when students read straight through for confidence and fluency.

1. Where and when does the story take place? How do you know? If the story took place somewhere else or in a different time, how would it be changed?

2. What incident, problem, conflict, or situation does the author use to get the story started?

3. What does the author do to create suspense, to make you want to read on to find out what happens?

4. Trace the main events of the story. Could you change their order or leave any of them out? Why or why not?

5. Think of a different ending to the story. How would the rest of the story have to be changed to fit the new ending?

6. Did the story end the way you expected it to? What clues did the author offer to prepare you to expect this ending? Did you recognize these clues as important to the story as you were first reading it?

7. Who is the main character of the story? What kind of person is the character? How do you know?

8. Are there any characters who changed in some way during the story? If they changed, how are they different? What changed them? Did it seem believable?

9. Some characters play small but important roles in a story. Name such a character. Why is this character necessary for the story?

10. Who is the teller of the story? How would the story change if someone else in the book or an outside narrator told the story?

11. Does the story as a whole create a certain mood or feeling. What is the mood? How is it created?

12. Did you have strong feelings as you read the story? What makes you think of them as you read the story?

13. What are the main ideas behind the story? What makes you think of them as you read the story?

14. Is this story like any other story you have read or watched? Why?

15. Think about the characters in the story. Are any of them the same type of character that you have met in other stories?

16. What idea or ideas does this story make you think about? How does the author get you to think about this?

17. Do any particular feelings come across in this story? Does the story actually make you think about what it's like to feel that way? How does the author do this?

18. Is there any character that you know more about than any of the others? Who is this character, and what kind of person is he or she? How does the author reveal the character to you? What words would you use to describe the main character's feeling in this book?

19. Are there characters other than the main character who are important to the story? Who are they? Why are they important?

20. Is there anything that seems to make this particular author's work unique and different? If so, what?

21. Did you notice any particular patterns in the form of this book? If you are reading this book in more than one sitting, are there natural points at which to break off your reading? If so, what are these?

22. Were there any clues that the author built into the story that helped you to anticipate the outcome? If so, what were they? Did you think these clues were important when you read them?

23. Does the story language seem natural for the intent of the story and for the various speakers?

24. Every writer creates a make-believe work and peoples it with characters. Even where the world is far different from your own, how does the author make the story seem possible or probable?

25. What questions would you ask if the author were here? Which would be the most important question? How do you think the author might answer it? (From Harste, Short, and Burke, 1988, pp. 300–301)

Open-Ended Questions for Nonfiction

Dorsey Hammond of Oakland University, Rochester, Michigan, suggests five basic questions to ask with informational articles. Students first brainstorm what they already know about the subject, predict possibilities, and raise questions about what they want to find out. Then they read the selection.

1. Did we find the answer to our questions?
2. What questions do we still need to find out about?
3. What else did you learn that you didn't know?
4. What was the most surprising or interesting thing you learned?
5. What have you learned by reading this that you didn't know before?

Teachers, of course, add their own questions to these basic questions.

Using Open-Ended Questions as a Model

High school teacher Dana Noble used the following questions to go along with *Night* by Elie Wiesel for his ninth and tenth grade students. Students responded first in their literature response logs and then in follow-up group discussions. He found the questions helped students go beyond the usual summarizing of the plot and into thinking about the book in depth. See Figures 6-10 and 6-11 for two entirely different responses to the same prompt and for the teacher's response.

Reading 1, pp. 1–20.   May 24

Who is the teller of the story? What kind of person is he? Make as many judgments as you can and cite evidence for your inferences.

Reading 2, pp. 21–43.   May 25

Some characters play small but important roles in a story. Name such a character from this reading. What does this character add to the story and why? Jot down page numbers for specific evidence.

Figures 6-10 and 6-11   High School Students' Responses to a Common Prompt and Their Teacher's Responses to Their Logs

> Andrew P
> journal #4
> 6/1/90

> The Jews in the camp have two serious problems. They are, should they pray to god and the selection. On page 17 and 18, Elie and the rest are trying to decide if they should pray. Elie says to himself, "Why should I pray to god when we are in this death camp?" Most people decide to pray because they want to show god that they can worship him even in that hell hole.
> The selection process was horrible for the prisoners. Prisoners were examined by doctors to see if they were fit enough to work. Those who weren't were taken to the crematories. There was absolutely nothing for the prisoners to do except pass. Elie and his father both passed the physical, but some do not, they will eventually be killed. I can't understand how anyone could be that cruel.

> Andy,   6/1
>   It is incredible. I suppose we have to look at ourselves. Could we do the same under similar conditions?
>   Watch the movie "Mississippi Burning" and see how Southern whites treated blacks — as recently as the 1960's!
>   Dn

Reading 3, pp 45–62.   May 29

Did you have strong feelings as you read this chapter? What did the author do to make you feel strongly? Support your responses by citing, quoting, and so on.

Reading 4, pp. 63–80.   May 31

What serious problems do characters have, and how successful do you think they are at solving them? Quote lines that show the enormity of the problem.

Reading 5, pp. 81–98.   June 1

What idea or ideas do these chapters make you think about? How does the author get you to think about them?

Figure 6-11

Adam

One problem that Eli faced is his anger. His anger towards the G(german) army and towards God. He said, "what are you, my God?" This disturbed me. It shows him loosing faith and once you loose faith you die in there. Another problem that a character is facing is Eli's father. Eli is also suffering in this. Eli's father said, "I'm asking this of you .... Do as your father says". Elis father was going to give Eli his fork and spoon. Eli would not take it for he didn't want his father to give up hope,

adam,
   I feel for Elie also in his loss of faith, but I disagree that "once you lose faith you die." My thoughts are that Elie was so angry in his loss of faith that anger kept him alive.
   Notice how tenacious Elie and his father are at surviving the horrors that follow.
                              Dn

Reading 6, pp. 99–109.   June 4

Are there any characters who changed in some way during the story? If they changed, how are they different? What changed them? Did the change seem believable?

Guiding Students to Construct Their Own Questions

Embracing Frank Smith's suggestion of teacher collaboration (Smith, 1988), fourth grade teacher Nancy Schubert and I modeled creating questions for Chapters 1–6 of *The Lion, the Witch and the Wardrobe* by C. S. Lewis. We talked in front of the students as we attempted to come up with open-ended questions. We stressed that we were formulating questions that did not have a right answer but had a wide possibility of answers. We came up with the following:

1. How is the professor different from most grownups?
2. Why do we feel better after the conversation with the professor?
3. Do you know anyone like Edmund?
4. Why do you think C. S. Lewis put him in the story?
5. How could the Queen have found out the Faun betrayed her?

Students then worked in groups of four discussing and writing their own questions for these chapters. Nancy and I walked around providing guidance as necessary. Each group was asked to come to a consensus on its one best question and share it with the class. Interest for this activity was very high, and we were surprised at how well students were able to create questions on their first attempt. Their selected best questions were as follows:

1. Why didn't Lucy know it was snow on the ground when she first came into Narnia?
2. Do you think there are many passages to Narnia? Why or why not?
3. Do you think Lucy would have believed Edmund if the adventure had first happened to him? Why or why not?
4. Why do you think Lucy went with Mr. Tumnus?
5. How do you think the Queen felt when she took Edmund? Describe.
6. Why do you think time stopped while Lucy was in the wardrobe?

Important questions go beyond the text but bring the reader back to the text. Significant questions do more than just ask recall of what was read; they make students think about what they read—before, during, and after reading. If students are to become actively literate adults, they need to be asking their own questions as they are reading, writing, thinking, and discussing.

Literature Discussion Groups

The literature discussion group, as described here, goes hand in hand with the literature response log and refers to heterogeneous, small-group, student-directed, and teacher-guided discussion that occurs as a book is being read. This section focuses on procedures and formats that have worked well for a small group of teachers who have made, or are making, this kind of transition to responding to literature. However, these ideas and procedures may also be used with another format and adapted for whole-class or homogeneous small-group discussion, as well as for group discussion that does not occur until students have read the entire book. What is presented here is not *the* way, it is but one way. As with all whole language teaching, flexibility, choice, and ownership are primary. It is up to you and the students to decide what will work best for you.

Jerome Harste urges us to use the notion of conversation and voice as criteria for determining whether or not our educational programs are effective. He notes that "schools are real good at silencing kids" and that, as teachers, we must constantly be asking ourselves:

"Have I heard each student's voice?"

"Have I put in place a structure where conversation can continue?"

(Presentation to teachers, Shaker Heights, Ohio, City School District, May 14, 1990)

A literature discussion group gives every student an opportunity to speak and be heard. The teacher is a member of the small group but not its president. Students take ownership of the learning process and often go beyond what is expected. Talk moves past prediction, central story, and plot happenings to critical analysis. Reflective questioning and responding, as described earlier in this chapter, encourage the highest levels of critical thinking and evaluation. Using textual references, prior experiences, and background knowledge, students state their opinions, make inferences, draw conclusions, analyze character motivation, and synthesize ideas in new ways. Students justify their opinions with evidence from the text, and the discussions are often quite lively. It has not been unusual, even with eight-year-olds, to have the students leave the group still talking about a book.

Allowing Time for Change

A genuine literature discussion, where the focus is on inquiry, does not just happen because the teacher moves from the basal to literature. Most of us have been entrenched for years, closely following teachers' manuals and asking lots of short answer-type questions. Students have been trained to sit passively, waiting for instructions, and to respond with the "right" answer. Once a student realizes her point of view is sincerely wanted, valued, and respected, she views school differently. We found that once we were able to give up some control in leading a discussion, the discussion flowed better, and more students were eager to participate.

Moving from leading the discussion to assuming a less central role has been a big adjustment for most of us. As teachers used to directing, we have needed time to adjust to a more democratic discussion format. Students have needed time, too. Students who have not had experience with in-depth interaction with a book over time may need months before they feel comfortable participating in discussions. One teacher said, "I realize now that it was the participation of the students which had to come first. We could get to the meat of the question later. But it was very tense for me at first." It is important to allow ourselves and our students lots of time for change and give ourselves credit for taking a risk and trying a new format.

It is not unusual for discussions to be superficial at first. Years of constant questioning have kept students in a subservient position, and some—often those who have a hard time sharing their feelings—are intimidated by the new process. Students who have never really been asked to think deeply about an issue also need lots of time and modeling before they begin to express their views.

Importance of Parent Education

As with any change we make in teaching, parents need to be informed—not only so they know what's going on in the classroom but also so they will foster high-level questioning and discussions at home.

A student was having a conversation with her mother about a question that had been posed for several chapters and said, "On page 52, it says . . .". Her mother responded, "I don't care about the page. Just tell me the answer."

Changes in Teacher Language and Behavior

• *Make your points with statements rather than questions.*   Acting as an equal member of the group, the teacher can still bring out salient points, share a favorite part of a story, and express her opinion, but this is done conversationally rather than with questions. When we ask questions, it not only directs the response to ourselves but implies we are looking for a particular answer. For example, rather than interrogating students with questions like "Do you think . . . ?" or "How do you feel about . . . ?" which direct students' comments back to the teacher, comments might begin like the following: "I'm not sure what you mean by that"; "I think that . . ."; "I was thinking about the way the author . . ."; "I was surprised to learn . . .". The teacher can also challenge students: "Prove your point"; "Stay on the topic."

Without being chief director, the teacher offers what he thinks by making clarifying statements or redirecting discussion. This invites students to agree, disagree, or take off from the teacher's comments. Eventually such modeling will pay off, and students will lead the discussion on their own even when the teacher is not present.

• *Allow for periods of silence.*   Allowing for wait time and reflection is difficult at first. Initially, the silence hangs heavy, and teachers are apt to jump in and say something like, "What do you think about . . . ?" Instead, teachers might try allowing for silences up to about ten seconds and then saying something like, "This is your discussion. It's up to you to carry it on." After a while students get the message that they're in charge.

Organization and Procedures

Getting Started

Grouping   Our literature discussion groups are usually heterogeneously grouped, with five to eight students in a group. Three groups of seven to eight students each has been the most common arrangement in our classes. We have found that more than eight in a group does not allow for interactive discussion by all students. However, if the class size is large, the groups may have to be larger. A group of ten will still allow more voices to be heard than a whole-class discussion where, typically, the same students tend to dominate. Occasionally whole-class grouping occurs with a core book when there are enough copies for each student.

In the beginning, teachers like to choose the heterogeneous groups to ensure a balanced mix of students. As new books are discussed, it's a good idea to change the group makeup to promote optimal and varied peer interaction. Some teachers have found that it works just as well for students to choose the group they will be in. If three groups are to be formed, the teacher can give a short talk about each book, telling just enough to get students interested. (Books may be related by theme or author, but they don't have to be. See *Resources for Teachers*, "Recommended Literature by Grade Level, K–12," for excellent book choices.) The books are then available for perusal, and students sign up for their first, second, and third choices. We have found that students almost always get their first or second choice.

Seating arrangement   Students sit anywhere around the reading table or designated floor areas. The teacher sits among them as a contributing member of the group rather than at the head of the table as the dominant leader. With a kidney-shaped table, it works well if you place several chairs at the center for students and take a seat off to the side where you can still see the entire class. The physical location of the teacher has a dramatic effect on the discussion. Having the teacher seated off to the side represents a subtle change, but it sends the message to the students that a democratic community of readers and thinkers is gathering, not an autocracy where all the decision-making power rests with the top person. Moving off center makes it easier for the teacher to be an equal voice in the conversation. With this arrangement, students also tend not to direct all comments to the teacher.

One teacher found it took her a month to move away from the center of the table. After sitting at the helm for fifteen years, it was difficult to give up her space.

Using the books   Each student needs to have a personal copy of the book. If you do not have multiple copies in your school, your school or public librarian may be able to borrow copies from other libraries.

The teacher also needs a personal copy of the book. As previously noted, in our district, each teacher receives a copy of each core book, to be used as a teacher's edition. Teachers write in questions to ask students to respond to in their logs, underline important vocabulary to be noted, and make any other comments they may want to bring out in discussion. This edition also serves as a guide for the substitute teacher.

Establishing procedures for independent work time   So that the discussion group can function without interruption and with the teacher's total involvement as a participant and observer, students not in the group need to know exactly what is expected of them.

For some teachers who have done almost all literature and discussion whole class, I have often been asked to demonstrate how the management works. I explain to the students that the teacher will be meeting with a literature discussion group and will not be available to students working at their seats. I let the students know that we, as a class, need to establish some guidelines for acceptable behaviors. I put the responsibility on them to try and elicit their responses. I let them know that we will be writing a first draft and that revisions will probably be necessary after we see how our rules are working. I might begin, "What should you do if you have a question and need some help?" I write their responses on the overhead or large chart paper. If a rule seems out of line, I might say, "Does everyone agree with that? Will that work?" I also ask the teacher if she is comfortable with the rule. She may state it another way or give additional feedback.

The end result should be a set of rules that is comfortable for both you and the students. We try out the rules and make modifications as necessary. If there is a problem one day, I might say something like, "I had difficulty hearing everyone today during discussion group. I need your help. What do you think we need to change so things work better tomorrow?"

Even though establishing procedures with the class is more time-consuming than just stating the rules, the time is well spent. Because students create the rules, they take them seriously. Once a satisfactory working set is agreed upon, a final draft is made, and the rules are posted. The rules should be brief and stated positively. The following is a draft written by Julie Beer's third grade class. The original draft stayed as written.

Independent Work Time Rules

- Whisper.
- Stay in one area away from other people.
- Do your work.
- Leave room only if positively necessary.
- Be considerate to people in reading group.

Time allowance for discussion   You will find that with practice and experience, you can easily meet with three groups in an hour. Everything important that needs to be said in a discussion comes out in ten to twenty minutes. Fifteen minutes has been about average for our groups. Depending on the length of the book, a discussion group can last anywhere from a day to several weeks to as long as six weeks. Most teachers try to meet with groups daily. Some meet with groups three days a week. In classes where teachers are combining group discussion time with checking of WEB books (pp. 45–48), each group time will need to be about ten minutes longer.

Students not in group   While one group is involved in discussion other groups are reading, responding in their logs, and working on book-related activities. (For specifics, see "Literature Extension Activities," in Chap. 5, and Chap. 15, "Classroom Management and Organization.") Students not in group work independently for thirty to forty-five minutes.

Procedures

Reading the book—allowing time in class   Nancie Atwell's *In the Middle* (1987) legitimized reading in class and freed many teachers, especially at the secondary level, to allow and value time for reading in school. For reluctant readers especially, the results can be dramatic. High school English teacher Holly Burgess comments, "It's been so wonderful to look up and see them reading. It's such a surprise. I don't know why, but it is."

Having students do their silent reading assignment in class is the first order of business once discussion groups start to meet. Rather than assign the whole book at one time, we assign chapters, individually or in small chunks. With discussion taking place while students are reading, confusions can be cleared up. If discussion takes place only after the book is completed, memory of comprehension—rather than comprehension as it is occurring or just occurred—tends to be the focus.

While the teacher is meeting with one group, other groups are reading and responding in their logs and/or completing assigned or self-selected activities. Even if the teacher is working with the whole class, it is still important to value time for silent reading. This is especially difficult for secondary teachers who may have students for only thirty-five to forty-five minutes. Nonetheless, giving this time pays off. A struggling tenth-grader wrote in her log: "If I didn't have to stop reading for my classes, I wouldn't stop. That says something because I never read. I used to hate reading. I'm beginning to enjoy it."

Some middle school and secondary teachers who use literature discussion groups have found a workable plan is to allow Mondays and Tuesdays for reading and responding to logs, Wednesdays and Thursdays for discussion group meetings, and one day for "catch-up." (See Figure 15–7 in Chap. 15, "Classroom Management and Organization," for a high school teacher's plan.)

Students who cannot read the text easily will need to be paired with a better reader or provided a tape to follow along. The purpose of literature discussion group is to talk about the book. Opportunities to work on word-attack skills and reading fluency will happen at another time. As long as the student can listen to the story and understand it—even if he can't read all the words—he can participate effectively in group and should be given the opportunity.

What Happens in a Literature Discussion Group?

• *Being prepared*   Students come to group with their reading and log assignments completed, and the teacher makes a quick check to see that they are prepared. Anyone who is unprepared is sent back to his seat to complete the reading and log. I say something like, "I'm sorry you can't join us today. Please come to group when you've completed your work." This is a very effective management technique. Students do not like to be left out of the group and miss the animated discussion. Teachers who have been pessimistic about the effectiveness of this method express surprise at how well it works. After missing group for just a few times, it is rare for a student not to take responsibility for being prepared.

• *Setting rules for discussion*   Some teachers like to have a student leader pose the question or begin the day's discussion. Others find a leader unnecessary. As in a normal conversation between adults, students do not raise their hands. This practice takes a bit of time for students to get used to, but once they do, they are completely comfortable. If they want to make a point, we encourage them to politely let the speaker finish his remarks and then intervene with comments such as:

> Excuse me . . .
> I'd like to add . . .
> I disagree . . .
> I agree because . . .
> I don't understand what you mean . . .
> I'm confused . . .
> I'd like to expand on that . . .

Some teachers post these phrases on a chart in view of the group so students have easy reference for discussion language. Of course, this practice needs to be modeled first by the teacher. In the beginning, to elicit these kinds of comments, the teacher might comment on a student's use of language and procedures. I might say, "I like the way Ned made his point. He started out by saying what he disagreed with and then backed it up with evidence."

Having a student-led group where students talk with one another without first getting a signal from the teacher sounds questionable to some teachers at first. They wonder if the group will be chaotic. Quite the contrary. Once students are practiced in a more democratic format, they relish the change. Engagement is high, and off-task behavior is rare. Believing that students can manage a group without hand raising requires a teacher willing to take a risk, to trust, and to allow time for change.

● *Using the log in discussion*   Students have their logs open and refer to them—to confirm or disprove—when someone else is commenting. The question that has been posed serves as the catalyst for discussion.

● *Reading orally*   Students or teachers may choose to read a section from the book to back up a point or highlight the author's use of language. The only time we take the time to reread a section, either silently or orally, is when it is obvious from the discussion that comprehension has not occurred.

A Literature Discussion in Grade 3

Third-graders, new to open-ended questions, literature response logs, and leading their own discussion, were discussing Chapter 8 in *The Comeback Dog* by Jane Resh Thomas. Daniel, a nine-year-old boy who has been having difficulty coping with the loss of his dog "Lady," has mixed feelings about a stray dog he's been caring for that has now disappeared. The question for the students was, "How was Daniel feeling?" Part of the discussion follows. Notice that it begins with students not connecting to each other, but gradually they get into the discussion.

MATT: Here, on page 55, it says "He pressed his face against the glass . . . until his eyes hurt." I think Daniel was spending a lot of time watching for the dog.

SARAH: I think Daniel is being pushy. The dog is probably not ready to be close to Daniel.

DAVID: I think he was kind of worried, because when he was studying, his mind kept wandering to "Lady." On page 56 it says, "But he couldn't concentrate. His thoughts returned to 'Lady.' "

MATT: I agree. He was distracted.

QUENTIN: Yeah. He woke up in the middle of the night. (*Using his log*) "She was gone, and good riddance. He would forget her." He was glad the dog was gone.

ANDREA: I disagree. Daniel was angry and disappointed. Rather than show his disappointment, he got angry. I felt like that whey my dog ran away.

DAVID: His feelings are really mixed up. He wants her and he doesn't want her at the same time.

Beneficial Outcomes

● *Listening skills improve.*   In the past, when students addressed most of their comments to the teacher, not all other students listened carefully. Now, because students are no longer looking at and to the teacher for answers and approval, they not only listen better to each other but they come to value listening to each other.

• *Comprehension improves.*   It has been interesting to observe students come to discussion without a strong understanding of what has been read. Initially they seem lost; yet, as the discussion continues, they begin to make connections. By talking, listening, and having other students fill in gaps, what has not been understood becomes clear. Third grade teacher Peg Gerhart notes, "I can tell when students are confused, and I can see the confusion clear up. As discussion continues, a light bulb goes on."

Parents also notice a difference in their children's understanding of text. One mother said, "My youngest son has a different orientation toward books. My older children read but not with the same critical analysis."

• *At-risk and low-ability students succeed.*   One of the greatest results of heterogeneous literature discussion groups has been increased participation by and improved self-esteem of at-risk and low-ability students. With demonstrations and practice, learning disabled and other at-risk students are able to answer questions in their logs, even if their responses are mostly literal at first. We also notice that these students are more likely to initiate conversation with the log-discussion format. This seems particularly significant for students who in the past were most often relegated to phonics and skills work. In discussion, as long as students can back up their opinions with evidence, they are viewed as being correct.

Third grade teacher Marilyn Eppich states,

> Jeffrey sometimes has a hard time making connections. He reads on a very low level. I paired him with a better student for reading. During discussion, I have been surprised by his level of understanding and by the fact that he has not been tentative making comments. He takes a firm stand
>
> Also, he's not a writer, so this process, where he only has to write a little, has been good for him. Also his writing is hard for me to read, but here, the writing is not for me. It has to make sense only for him.

It has also been interesting to note that visitors often assume from the quality of the literature discussion that the group is a high-ability one. Not only are they surprised to learn that the group is mixed ability—they often have trouble telling the "highs" from the "lows."

• *Social relationships change.*   Because the groups are mixed ability and everyone's voice is given equal weight and respect, we notice that low-achieving students are afforded new respect by their peers. Also, through the use of the logs and follow-up discussion, students realize that individuals differ in what they perceive from the same piece of literature and that it is normal and healthy for people to have different points of view.

• *Students take ownership.*   We notice that students do not easily back away from what they believe. One day a group of third-graders was discussing *Danny the Champion of the World* by Roald Dahl. The log question had been, "Describe the keeper." Diane, a former Reading Recovery student, said the keeper was "nice." She was challenged by every member of the group, who gave reasons to support the keeper's nasty, mean disposition. Diane disagreed and offered, "The keeper was nice because he didn't use his gun or chase them." From her vantage point, she backed up her view and refused to concede. We quietly cheered her independent thinking.

• *Students are more honest.*   We have noticed that students tend to be quite candid when they are talking with one another and not focusing on what the teacher thinks about their responses.

• *Teachers come to trust students more.*   We have noticed that even when the question we pose isn't as good as it could be, everything that is significant about the reading comes out in discussion. This has happened so consistently that teachers give up constantly worrying about covering everything and begin to trust the students to uncover what is significant to them and to the text.

• *The teacher has time for critical observation.*   As an equal participant in the discussion, rather than the director, the teacher can really see what students are learning. Once students have moved to leading the discussion, the teacher can sit on the fringes as a teacher-researcher, observer, and evaluator. What needs to be taught and demonstrated becomes apparent.

• *Substitute teachers find the format very workable.*   Several substitutes have commented on how impressed they have been with the level of discussion and the students' ability to carry on independently. Because students are used to leading their own discussions, the substitute teacher can sit in with the group without having to manage and direct it.

Literature Discussion Group: What's Different? A Summary

• Heterogeneous grouping
• Students lead discussion
• Teacher participates as one voice
• Teacher sits among students (not at center)
• No hand raising
• Students talk mostly to each other
• Silences in discussion are okay
• May be no consensus
• Most of the time spent on discussion (very little oral reading)

Evaluation

Students' attitudes.   One of the greatest benefits of utilizing literature discussion groups is the attitude of the students. Even struggling readers enjoy the opportunity to voice their opinions and have them count.

I asked third-graders who had been using literature response logs and discussion groups for the first time to comment on how they liked or disliked this new approach compared with their past experience where reading of literature was assigned and they then came to a teacher-led reading group (which often was whole class) with just their books. Here are some of their comments regarding discussion:

JAMISON: Discussion is just like a conversation. It's better because you can say what you really think. As long as you have the proof, no one can dispute you.

ROBERT: I like it because you get to talk to other people.

JULIE: It's a lot more interesting. You get to talk more.

CLIFF: I like it better because you can give your opinion without raising your hand.

BRIA: It's better because there's less independent work to do at your seat.

ANDREW: I like it because you can have your ideas, and you don't have to agree with someone else's, even the teacher's.

VALERIE: I like that we get to have a longer discussion and that it's okay to say when you don't understand things or disagree with someone.

RHONDA: You have to think a lot about what you believe.

JAMES: I like it because you don't have any right or wrong answers.

Teachers' attitudes   Teachers report feeling a sense of exhilaration they have never felt before in a reading group. There are magical moments, difficult to recapture, and spontaneous comments and surprises.

Above all, the importance of genuine conversation is affirmed. Peg Gerhart, who has been an elementary teacher for nine years, sums it up well when she says the process has "made me revalue how important conversation is in the interaction between teacher and student and for student growth and development."

Peg has been moving gradually to a more meaningful literature approach. She says she began comfortably with literature using "basalized packages" and whole-class teaching. When she had difficulty writing specific comments on report cards, she realized she was not aware of the reading strategies students were using. "I'm a risk taker, and I knew I had to change," she said.

I modeled for Peg once a week for a number of weeks, gave her time to work out the kinks on her own, coached her, and gave her feedback. After several months she had this to say:

> The biggest and most difficult thing for me has been giving up control. It was very tense for me at first. It really bothered me when we weren't on the question. I bit my tongue, and then I saw something else emerging. Kids who didn't talk were talking. I was absolutely amazed by some of the responses. The level of discussion was so high. It surprised me, even shocked me. Students I thought would have been silent came up with high-level ideas. I could see thinking going on I had never seen before. I was pleasantly shocked. That's what convinced me.

Peg sees herself continuing to change and refine the discussion process. She believes teachers have to be open to suggestions and new ideas but also need to accept, "This is where I am right now." She is finding comments on report cards easier to write now because she knows her students better.

Marilyn Eppich, a third grade teacher, tried literature discussion groups and was delighted at how well they worked and how much they increased her enjoyment of teaching reading. She comments: "I can really sit back now and listen instead of always thinking about what my next question should be. That's why I'm enjoying it so much. I'm also getting to know the kids better as well as listening to their responses. Teachers don't take time to listen enough."

Self-Evaluation

Self-evaluation, for teachers and students, is an effective way to improve the quality of discussions. Notice to whom students are looking at and talking to during discussion. If students are still focusing on the teacher, the teacher's voice is still the dominant one. See if you can get a colleague to observe you during discussion group and give feedback. We have found it also works well to tape record discussions occasionally. Students enjoy evaluating how the discussion went—what was good about it and what could be improved. It's also a good way for the teacher to note her interactions, tone, comments, and conversation.

The teacher can also ask students for feedback. Linda Cooper gave the following questionnaire to her students to fill out after several months of using literature response logs and discussion groups:

1. What do you like about the way we are doing discussion now as compared to before?
2. What do you think we should change?

What Happens in the Long Run: Further Transitions

Ideally, another step in the process of moving away from teacher-directed classrooms toward more empowerment for students is literature discussion groups that function independently and simultaneously without direct teacher involvement. This step can occur only after both students and the teacher are comfortable with the discussion groups. Based on my experience, making the transition takes many years of teaching with literature. Understanding and practicing a philosophy consistent with language learning are required, as well as excellent management techniques, before discussion groups can function without teacher involvement. Teachers and students will first need to have a great deal of experience with self-management, collaboration, and responsibility in a democratic classroom.

Even then, independent groups are not common. Therefore, teachers need not feel inadequate if they continue to be part of the literature groups. In fact, as long as the teacher is only one member of the group and her voice does not dominate, I personally find it advisable to have the teacher's opinion and reactions part of the discussion. It is our job to guide the children in making connections and discoveries they might not make on their own and to continue to model good questioning and response techniques.

If the transition does occur, teachers can choose which group to join on a particular day and occasionally use student self-evaluation forms to check on how the other groups managed. Or teachers can use that time to carefully observe how a group interacts and take anecdotal records on particular students' contributions. With practice and sufficient modeling, students become quite capable of choosing their own questions (they can receive a set of selected questions to choose from or write their own questions) and even deciding how much should be read for the next meeting. (For further information, see "Literature Circles" in Harste, Short, and Burke, 1988.)

The format of the literature discussion groups can be carried across the curriculum. Students can meet in groups and discuss their findings from their research/readings/thinking in social studies, science, and mathematics.

Reflections

The way students are asked to respond to literature in school influences their development as readers, writers, and thinkers as well as their enjoyment of literature. Through discussion and identification with characters and themes, students come to understand the consequences of human behavior and see connections to their own lives. Readers become familiar with genres, authors, characters, places, new concepts, and literary language and use some of these insights in their own writing. Perhaps most significant, literature has the power to help develop students as critical readers, writers, and thinkers. As adults, these are the people who read with questions in mind, substantiate their opinions, take an intelligent stand on an issue, read the newspaper analytically, question politicians' jargon, and act as thoughtful citizens. If we are to educate students thoughtfully for the future, literature can be the vehicle for thinking on the most critical levels.

7

Teaching for Strategies

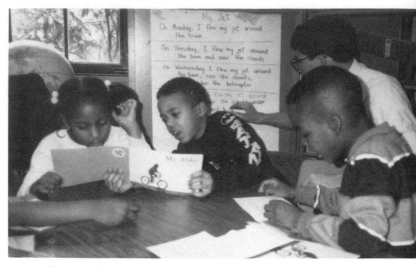

Putting theory into practice:
first grade teacher Jim Henry doing a
shared writing lesson in reading group

"I wonder if the kids are really learning anything."

Teachers who make the transition from the basal to literature worry a lot about whether or not skills are being taught. Additionally, many teachers feel nervous that they are not teaching enough. I have found this to be a common feeling among beginning whole language teachers. We teachers feel guilty spending reading time reading, discussing, and enjoying the literature. We have spent years teaching reading using lots of skills sheets. Without worksheets, where you can "see" skills work, it's hard for teachers to trust that the skills are in the books and that learning is truly occurring. Many of us devise activities to be sure skills teaching occurs.

Understanding the Difference between Skills and Strategies

Because it is important to bring skills teaching to the strategic level, we need to understand the difference between skills and strategies. While skills teaching is a necessary part of all good instruction, it is our beliefs about learning combined with our approach, method, context, and timing that determine whether or not we are teaching skills so that they later become useful strategies for the learner.

In discrete skills teaching, the teacher—or the publisher of a program—decides what the learner needs, and the skill is directly taught, often in a predetermined sequence, and then practiced in isolation. The skill, whether it includes word attack, alphabetizing, sequencing, or vocabulary acquisition, is directly taught with an emphasis on practice and automatic, correct responses. The teacher or program controls how much practice or exercises students need. Application of the skill to new, meaningful contexts rarely occurs.

In teaching for strategies, however, skills are taught in a broader context because the learner demonstrates a need for specific skills in the instructional/learning setting, perhaps in a guided reading group. The skill is taught because the learner genuinely needs to use it—or the teacher anticipates the learner's upcoming need to use the skill. The teacher guides the student to self-determine the generalization and think through possibilities in authentic contexts. While the teacher may question and suggest, it is the learner who is encouraged to make deductions and consciously apply what is learned from one context to another. Don Holdaway notes, "The major difference, then, between 'skills teaching' and 'strategy teaching' concerns the presence or absence of self-direction on the part of the learner" (1979, p. 136).

In other words, a skill—no matter how well it has been taught—cannot be considered a strategy until the learner can use it purposefully and independently. Application of a skill to another context is far more likely to occur when the skill has been taught in a meaningful context that considers the needs of the learners. I have observed that teachers begin to focus on strategies when they begin to change the climate of their classrooms from teacher dominated to student centered and when they come to view reading and other language processes as constructive and interactive.

Applying the distinction between skill and strategy to the teaching of sight words, phonics, and vocabulary, we see clearly that merely teaching the skills in isolation and practicing on worksheets has no relation to meaningful teaching. While we may believe that a skill has been covered, until the learner can discover how to utilize the skill in varied reading and writing contexts, skills teaching is largely a waste of time. *The learner must know how and when to apply the skill; that is what elevates the skill to the strategy level.*

It has taken me many years to become convinced that all the skills are in the literature and that the literature itself can be used as a vehicle to teach skills strategically. Most of us initially need to see concrete evidence of skills teaching, and we use the literature to teach and practice the skills we believe children need. Even then, we must be careful that skills work does not interfere with enjoyment of the story and that our focus on skills results from a genuine need for meaning.

I have observed that after about five years or more, teachers seem to move away from practicing specific skills in literature to promoting strategies in the ongoing context of genuine reading and writing, as the need arises. By becoming careful observers of our students and practicing ongoing evaluation, we can determine what strategies students are using and not using. We need to give ourselves time for this transition. As our own learning theory develops, and as we begin to take ownership of our teaching and rely less on directed instructional programs, we have less of a need for a predetermined skills agenda.

Making the Transition

All the skills required in a district's course of study—such as using grapho-phonics cues, making generalizations, finding the main idea, understanding figurative language—can be developed in the context of the literature. We don't really need separate practice exercises. However, transitional activities may give us confidence and peace of mind until we are convinced that skills are being learned through everyday authentic reading and writing activities.

While courses of study designate concepts and skills to be taught, there is usually latitude in how concepts are to be taught. Even when there is a required text, the text can often be used as a resource and reference instead of as the total curriculum.

The following are examples of activities that may be used to promote high-level skills teaching for teachers who feel the need to teach skills directly but who want to do so more meaningfully. Many of these activities can be used for independent work—in place of worksheets—while meeting with a reading group.

Quotation Marks

- Have students write conversations with each other. Model the activity first through oral language, and write down what the speaker says.

- Reproduce a page of familiar conversational text from a book being read. Using white-out liquid, remove quotation marks. Make a transparency, and model—with student participation—how and where quotation marks would go. Then have students work together, or independently, to put quotation marks on another page they have already read where the quotation marks have been whited out and the page reproduced for students. Students self-check with the original text.

- Select several pages of familiar text that has lots of conversation. Students take the part of the characters and speak their parts. This will first need to be demonstrated.

Homonyms

- Students are guided to notice homonyms in literature and their own writing. A class chart is begun, and as new homonym pairs are discovered they are added to the chart.

- Individual homonym booklets can be made using literal pictures.

- Linda Cooper grows a homonym "pair" tree in her room. When students come across homonym pairs in their reading and writing, they write and illustrate the words on a double-folded paper shaped like a pear. The "pair-pears" are attached to the tree (see Figure 7–1).

- Have students write comic strips with "bubbles" and then take the message in the bubble and write it using quotation marks. Demonstrate the activity first.

Compound Words

- Students make individual compound word booklets from words they come across in their reading. See Figure 7–2 for a page from a third-grader's book.

Overused Words

- Have each student make a thesaurus to encourage the use of interesting, vibrant language in writing. For example, students can keep a record of words authors use for such overused words as "happy," "nice," "said," "walked," "mad." Words come from independent reading and group reading and are referred to in writing. William Steig and Roald Dahl are two authors that give elementary students a wealth of interesting, alternative words.

Figure 7-1   Homonym "Pair-Pears"

Figure 7-2   Pages from a Third-grader's Compound Word Book

Figure 7–3   Illustrating Idiomatic Expressions

Contractions, Possessives

- Select a short, familiar passage and have students note the contractions. Some teachers like students to make their own contraction booklets, noting contractions and what they mean as they come across them in their reading.

Figurative Language

- Students note figurative language as they come across it in their reading and illustrate the idiomatic expressions (see Figure 7–3).

The skills just listed are being applied at the strategy level when students are using them appropriately and independently in new, meaningful contexts. For example, the student who uses quotation marks or homonymns correctly in a story she is writing is indicating that she understands how and when the skill is used.

Using a Picture Book to Teach for Strategies in the Primary Grades

Selecting the Book

Working with a small group of struggling second grade readers, I demonstrated for the classroom teacher how literature could be used to teach skills strategically. I selected the picture book *Jamaica's Find* by Juanita Havill (Houghton Mifflin, 1986), the story of a young black girl who finds a stuffed dog at the park and wrestles with whether or not to keep it. The book was carefully chosen for its appeal to children, its potential for interesting, meaningful discussion, its natural and predictable language and the good match between illustrations and text. It was also a book the students had never heard or seen, and I believed the readability level was just about right for these children. That is, they would be able to read the book with about 90 percent accuracy.

While it is important for young children to have lots of practice reading familiar, easy books, they must also be regularly introduced to books on their level that they have never seen before. In that way the teacher can note what strategies the reader is using and not using and give appropriate guidance.

Introducing the Book

Talking through the book together before reading it gives reluctant readers familiarity and control of language patterns and vocabulary, a motivating interest in the story, and a feeling of "I can read this." The introduction should be short—not more than five to seven minutes—and be carefully planned by the teacher so the language children need to know to read the story is included. As children become more independent readers, the introduction will become even shorter—perhaps just a sentence about the book.

For this lesson each child received a copy of *Jamaica's Find*, and we predicted what the story might be about by looking at the cover. After accepting the students' responses, I gave a short summary of the book to give them a framework for reading. "Yes, you are right. This is a story about a girl about your age who finds something that doesn't belong to her, and she has to decide what to do about it." Then, before we began reading, I went through the book page by page and talked about the pictures, being careful to put any unfamiliar or difficult words in their ears. Hearing unfamiliar language before being asked to read it builds in potential for success. Vocabulary is never introduced in isolation.

At the same time, we used this time to discuss possible solutions for Jamaica's dilemma. "What do you think she should do?" "What's another possibility?" "What might happen if she does that?" "How is her problem solved?"

Reading the Book

Whether meeting with one student or a group of students, most of reading time is spent reading the story. By giving each child an opportunity to read, or reread a page or two of the story, the teacher can carefully observe reading behaviors.

- Does the child have one-to-one matching of spoken word to printed word?
- What strategies is the child using (picture cues, visual cues [grapho-phonics], sentence structure, sentence context, rereading, memory for text)?
- What does the child do when in trouble (stop and wait for the teacher; "sound it out," reread to predict, check, or self-correct)?
- What strategies does the child need to be using?

As the children are reading the book, I take the opportunity to teach for strategies as the need arises. I keep a small chalkboard and chalk with me at the reading table as well as a slide (see Appendix E). The following are examples of teaching points made in the process of students reading.

Jason began on the first page (p. 5), which read, "When Jamaica arrived at the park, there was no one there. It was almost supper time, but she still had a few minutes to play."

JASON: "When Jamaica . . ." (*silence, looks to teacher*)

ROUTMAN: Skip that word and read to the end of the sentence.

JASON: "When Jamaica . . . at the park, no one was there."

ROUTMAN: What would make sense? Where is she?

JASON: "When Jamaica *arrived* (*reads it easily*) at the park, there was no one there. It was almost *super* time, but she still had a few . . .

ROUTMAN: Keep going.

JASON: . . . to play."

ROUTMAN: It's the end of the day. Is it *super* time? Does that make sense? Think about what would make sense.

JASON: "It was almost *supper* time, but she still had a few *minutes* (*reads it easily*) to play."

ROUTMAN: Good for you. I like the way you looked at how the word began and put in what made sense.

I did not interrupt Jason when he misread "supper" for "super." If I had told him to "sound it out," he still couldn't have read it. By letting him read to the end of the sentence, he had a chance to self-correct through the meaning of the sentence.

Meredith had trouble with the word "stains" in a sentence that described the stuffed dog Jamaica found as being covered with grass stains. Using the small chalkboard, I wrote the word "rain," which I thought she might know. She read it easily. I wanted to point out that a pattern she already knew—"ai"—could be applied to a new context. I wrote "stain" and asked, "How does it *start*?" (emphasizing the "st" to put the sound in her ear). She then read the word "stain."

Julia got stumped on "returned" in the sentence, " 'But, Jamaica, you should have returned the dog, too,' said her mother" (p. 15). Using the slide (Appendix E), I moved next to her and exposed just the "re" and asked her to read that. She did. Then I moved the slide to show the next letter, "t," and asked her to start the sentence again. She read "returned" without difficulty.

Teacher Language to Encourage Independence

Some teacher prompts that help get the child thinking, predicting, sampling text, confirming, and self-correcting include:

- Look at the picture to help yourself.
- Get your mouth ready to say it.
- Look at how the word begins.
- Does that make sense?
- Does that sound right? Does it fit?
- Does that look right to you?
- Start that sentence again.
- Skip that word and go on. Now, what do you think it is?
- Where have you seen that word before?
- Think about a word you know that has the same sound in it.
- Put in a word that makes sense, and go on.
- Is that right? Check that again.
- If that word was . . . , what would you expect to see at the beginning? at the end? What do you see here?
- What can you do to help yourself?

I always want to give the child the message that it is her job to do the reading work and that she can do it. It is also very important to verify for the child what she knows and make her aware of the strategies she is using. By praising and encouraging all attempts and noting what the child has done well, we build self-esteem and encourage the repeated use of the desired strategies. On subsequent rereadings—which are done for pleasure and to build confidence, fluency, sight vocabulary, and practice in using meaningful strategies—improvement is noticeable.

Such comments as the following may be helpful:

- I like the way you tried to help yourself.

- Good for you. I saw you checking the word with the picture to see if you were right.

- I like the way you worked out the hard part.

- I noticed you tried . . . when you had trouble. Good for you. That's what good readers do.

Incorporating Skills Work

As part of a rereading, I will sometimes do some skills work. When the story is well chosen and of high interest to the children, they enjoy repeated readings. However, I do not incorporate the skills work until children are fairly fluent with the story. Enjoyment and understanding of the story always come first, and any skills work is only a small—and meaningful—part of reading time. Care is taken not to "basalize" the literature and extract it for isolated skills.

Cloze exercises, where the student uses meaningful context to complete or fill in the part of a word or whole word that is missing from a text (see Figure 7–4), are a particularly worthwhile skills activity. The student uses thinking and meaning ("What would I expect to see?") to bring "closure" to the missing parts of the text. It is always a good idea to have students read the entire passage first so they see the value of reading ahead when they can't figure out a word. We want students to learn that the context can help them make predictions.

I wanted to firm up the children's use of consonant blends because facility with blends can help them make predictions. If the reader can begin the word by making the sound of the consonant blend, then, by using the context of the sentence, she should be able to figure out the word even if she cannot read the word in isolation. I reproduced page 8 of *Jamaica's Find* and whited out parts of ten words while exposing the consonant blend. While the general rule in constructing cloze exercises is not to omit more than one out of every ten words, I use common sense and the meaning of the passage as a guide. If the passage seems readable omitting words that are less than ten words apart, I am comfortable doing so (see Figure 7–4).

The first time I give such an exercise, we work it through together as a group. After that, children work in pairs to figure out the missing words. I rarely have them do this kind of exercise independently because I want them to problem solve, and working with a partner facilitates problem solving. The exercise may be redone independently as a follow-up activity if a child needs more practice.

This kind of cloze exercise is an excellent practice lesson for showing students how being able to read just the beginning of a word in meaningful context is often

Figure 7-4   Cloze Exercise

Then she climbed up the st____There was a red sock hat on the

ladder st__. Jamaica took it for a ride. She slid down so fast that

she fell in the sand and lay fl__on her back.

When she rolled over to get up, she saw a st____dog beside

her. It was a cuddly gray dog, worn from hugging. All over it

were faded food and gr____stains. Its button nose must have fallen

off. There was a round white sp__in its place. Two bl__ears hung

from its head.

enough to figure out the whole word. I also find that this type of exercise helps children's spelling. Children self-check their papers with the book. When they proofread, they are expected to correct their answers. If they write in a word that is different than the author's but does not change the meaning, the word is acceptable. That reinforces another strategy—when you can't read a word, put in a word that makes sense and go on. However, caution is needed here. We must be careful observers of children's substitutions to be sure children are not just guessing but are actually putting in meaningful alternatives. When children substitute words that don't make sense, comprehension is lost.

Teaching Sight Vocabulary Meaningfully: A Small-group Guided Reading Lesson in Grade 1

While some children will learn to read naturally through immersion in daily reading and writing activities, most children benefit from some guided instruction. Even at the beginning of first grade, literature can be used to teach sight vocabulary, promote fluency, and develop reading strategies.

After a story has been read in reading group, some high-frequency words can be put on index cards. A student having difficulty identifying a word can be helped to find ways to help herself. She can be asked to go back to the text and find the page that contains the word. Using pictures and the story context, and matching the word on the index card to the word on the page, the student is guided to read the word. The student is always encouraged to use the meaning of the original text to help figure out the word. Teaching words in isolation, without connection to context, is not a part of meaningful reading instruction.

First grade teacher Jim Henry used the book *My Bike* (by Craig Martin) to build sight vocabulary and fluency. As in the previous lesson, the book was introduced first and then read. After the book—with its cumulative, repetitive structure about a boy who rode his bike "around the trees, over the bridge, under the branches, through the puddle, up the bank, and down the hill" before he crashed—had been read several times with a group of struggling first-graders, Jim used the text to build sight vocabulary in a meaningful way. The words "up," "down," "over," "under," "around," and "through" were written on 4 by 6 inch file cards to reinforce careful attending to text. While students might be reading the words in context through the story pattern and pictures, having to examine each word by itself forced them to attend to specific letters in the word.

While children were expected to read the words, they were not expected to do so without the support of the text. They went back to the text to find the word that fit—through context, pictures, configuration, and teacher guidance. When Rick was unsure of "through," Jim asked, "Do you know where to find it in your book?" Richard flipped through the pages, read it in context, and then read it on the card. When Caleb read "up" for "under," he sensed it was incorrect. On his own, he checked his book and used the picture of the bike "under" the tree to self-correct. When Sarah read "under" for "around," Jim asked, "could that be 'under?' What would you expect to see at the end of 'under'?" Sarah went back to the text and self-corrected.

To further reinforce vocabulary and make the reading-writing connection, Jim and the children wrote an innovation on the text. High-frequency words were written and read in a new context. Students had to go back to the text to figure out the pattern of the book and check for vocabulary to be included. Questions such as, "How will the next line begin?" "What word could go here?" and "How should we write that?" put the responsibility on the children. Jim verbalized the sounds in sequence as he wrote. After the story was written and read on a chart, individual booklets were reproduced for each child. Putting in illustrations to match the new text became meaningful independent work.

The shared writing, which the students called *My Jet*, followed the pattern of *My Bike* and included:

> On Monday, I flew my jet
>   around the town.
> On Tuesday, I flew my jet
>   around the town,
>   and over the clouds.

The cumulative structure continued to build for each day of the week and concluded with:

> On Saturday, I flew my jet
>   around the town,
>   over the clouds,
>   under the helicopter,
>   through the sky,
>   up the mountain,
>   and down to the airport.
> On Sunday, I crashed!

Demonstrating How to Figure Out an Unknown Word

I use silent reading of a passage read whole class or in small groups to demonstrate how good readers substitute meaningful words and go on reading when they can't read a word. I find that some students have never been shown how to do this.

After the whole class or group has read a page silently, I ask, "Did anyone have trouble with a word while reading?" (See pp. 398–399 for a discussion of this strategy.) Robert raised his hand and spelled "distributed." I wrote it on the overhead transparency. I told him, "Read the sentence, and when you get to that word put in something that makes sense." He read, "All the drawings and papers that had been hanging around the room were taken down and 'passed out' to the various artists and writers in the class" (from Joanna Hurwitz, *Class Clown*, Morrow, 1987, p. 91). After complimenting Robert on his meaningful substitution, we did some word analysis with the word on the overhead projector.

Relating the Known to the Unknown

I often show students how familiar patterns and little words they already know can be applied to figuring out new words. Using a small chalkboard at the reading table, I write a word I think the student knows and use it to guide him in reading the unknown word. Some examples follow, with the easier word being noted first. I often underline the known pattern in the new word.

it, sit,
and, land, stand
out, shouted, about
at, that

Giving Verbal Support for Structural Words

Beginning readers often have difficulty with words such as "they," "what," "that," and "when," especially if the word is the first one in a sentence. If "they" is the first word, I might say, "What did *they* do?" Other prompts might be, "*What* happened?" or "What do you think *that* is?" Stressing and emphasizing the structural word, and putting the language in the child's ear, is often enough to get the child going on her own.

See also Appendix P, "Reading Strategies for Unknown Words."

Changing the Pull-out Model: Applying Strategy Lessons to a Supportive Reading Program in the Classroom

In the fall of 1990, after four years of working as a Reading Recovery teacher, I elected—with the support and collaboration of my principal Bernice Stokes—to go into second grade classrooms and work closely with the classroom teachers to support reading-writing strategies. Believing strongly that the traditional pull-out program was not working for many at-risk children, my principal and I discussed alternative possibilities. We believed second grade was a critical year for reading success. Based on my many years experience as a reading specialist, I had found that if students were not successful readers by the end of second grade, it was unlikely that most of them would become confident, proficient readers at a later date.

While I am viewed as a resource teacher interacting with all students, most of my daily time in each second grade classroom is spent working with a small, targeted group of about five students who have been identified through teacher observation and standardized test scores as needing additional reading-writing support. While these students are included in reading and discussing the same core book literature as the other students in the class each morning I give further support to those who are unable to read the text easily and need to learn to apply strategies to their reading. Additionally, the classroom teacher and I work closely together and use similar holistic approaches in the teaching of reading.

We begin most afternoon sessions with a five- to ten-minute whole-class shared poetry reading or with "book talks," where students volunteer to talk about a favorite WEB book and why they recommend it. Then I meet with the small targeted group of students (plus several others who may choose to join us) for twenty to twenty-five minutes. The two major areas we have focused on during our guided reading time have been gaining confidence with reading and understanding the core books and receiving guidance at the students' instructional levels.

• *Reading the core books* Sometimes we read ahead several pages and discuss what is happening in the story so that students feel more confident and participate more readily in the next day's class reading and discussion. Most often, because the text is above the students' oral and silent level (but at their listening-comprehension level), I employ an oral cloze technique where I read and students follow along in their personal copies using a line marker. I pause on a word I expect them to be able to read by using the meaning of the story and the beginning consonants of digraphs and by making connections to other words they already know.

At times, I tape several favorite paragraphs of text that have been read and discussed in class. Using the listening center and headphones, students use part of their independent morning work time to listen and follow along over and over again. This technique has been terrific for building confidence as well as fluency. Students later enjoy showing off their increased reading ability when they come to group.

After students feel comfortable with a portion of a favorite text they have practiced with the tape, I make a cloze exercise out of it, as in Figure 7–4. Students complete the words in writing, then check the book to see if they are correct. Incorrect spellings are self-corrected, and students are then asked to turn over their papers and write several words they have just completed in the cloze exercise. The success rate and enthusiasm are high.

• *Guidance at students' instructional level* Using a predictable book and the strategies discussed in this chapter, I spend much of our time teaching for strategies while building confidence and fluency. As part of a balanced reading program, it is critical for all students to be guided in reading text at their instructional level where they recognize ninety out of one hundred words with solid comprehension.

• *Writing as a response to reading* Occasionally we do an innovation on the text or shared writing. Students' writing becomes their reading material, and engagement and interest are high.

• *Monitoring independent reading* I do a WEB reading check (as discussed on pp. 44–48) at least several days a week. Here I am checking for fluency, comprehension, and appropriateness of books.

Working daily in the classroom with another teacher and students has been a privilege. I have enjoyed the daily collegiality and communication, the opportunity to get to know all the children, and the increased potential for children's reading-writing success when two teachers collaborate. However, I am aware that welcoming another teacher into the classroom is no easy matter, and I am appreciative of teachers' risk taking and flexibility.

Second grade teacher Linda Powers, who joins our small guided reading group when she can, notes:

> Initially I was apprehensive about having another teacher in the classroom daily. I worried about getting off schedule and being forced into a time slot. However, this disadvantage is outweighed manyfold by the benefits I see the children deriving. I see kids building confidence early in the school year. Reading ahead in the core book gives them an advantage which allows them to participate readily in discussion. The look of pleasure and pride on Tamika's face when she was able to read a passage in *The Velveteen Rabbit* (by Margery Williams) [Doubleday, 1969] with a high level of accuracy and the self-knowledge that she was doing an excellent job made me realize this was worthwhile.
>
> I never thought I would find it fun to have another teacher in my classroom, but I have enjoyed the collaboration, and we're sure having a good time together.

Self-Evaluation Checks in Teaching for Strategies

Because most of us have had training that emphasizes discrete skills teaching, heightened awareness is necessary to move toward teaching for strategies in reading.

- Is your language fostering meaning-based strategies and independence when a student can't read a word, or are you relying only on, "Look at the letters" and "What sounds do those letters make?"
- Are you using engaging books with predictable text that support the reader, or are your texts dull and sequentially based for skills?
- Are you guiding students to apply strategies, or are you teaching for mastery of skills?
- Are you giving students sufficient wait time and encouragement to figure out words and meanings on their own, or are you quick to supply the answer?
- Do other students know it is the reader's job to do the work and that they need to give the reader quiet wait time, or do students call out words?
- After students have one-to-one matching and some confidence as readers, are you introducing students to unfamiliar text to note what strategies they have under control, or are students reading only books they have already heard?
- Are you asking important questions that follow naturally from the text and encourage more than one possibility, or are you looking for only one "right" answer?
- Is vocabulary taught in context during and after reading, or are you introducing words in isolation before reading?
- Are follow-up activities leading to further enjoyment and engagement with the text or are they merely keeping students busy while others are in group?

Phonics in Perspective

"Phonics is the rock upon which the house of reading is built."

A first grade teacher told me that recently, and I could relate well to her thinking. That was my position for at least the first fifteen years I was a teacher. I have been able to modify my thinking and my teaching only after much professional reading, reflecting, and observing of children—especially as a Reading Recovery teacher.

Phonics continues to be an emotional and political issue, and it does not seem likely that educators will ever come to a consensus. While most teachers feel very strongly about their particular approach to teaching phonics, phonics is also an area many teachers feel guilty, uncomfortable, and defensive about. Few primary teachers actually talk about how they teach phonics, and most of them teach it behind closed doors.

The question is no longer *if* phonics should be taught but rather *how* phonics should be taught meaningfully. Successful readers view reading as an interactive, meaning-getting process, and grapho-phonics is one of the necessary cueing systems they utilize (see Figure 7–5). Proficient readers function with an interdependence between the three cueing systems: semantics, syntax, and grapho-phonics. Semantic cues (context: what makes sense) and syntactic cues (structure and grammar: what sounds right grammatically) are strategies the reader needs to be using *already* in order for phonics (letter-sound relationships: what looks right visually and sounds right phonetically) to make sense. Phonics proficiency by itself cannot elicit comprehension of text. While phonics is integral to the reading process, it is subordinate to semantics and syntax (see Figure 7–5). See also Appendix O.

Figure 7-5   The Three Cueing Systems

The reading process can be viewed diagrammatically:

Any one area cannot exist in isolation from the others if comprehension is to be maximized.

Part of the reason some children have difficulty learning to read is that we have overattended to one cueing system, and most often it has been grapho-phonics. In addition to depriving children of more meaningful strategies, overattention to phonics takes away from time that might be better spent on reading authentic texts. Parents, too, have generally overvalued the role of phonics in reading. One mother said, "When I told my child to sound out the word and he couldn't do it, he began to get frustrated, and I backed off. I didn't know what else to do to help him figure it out." We need to teach parents higher-level strategies that go beyond phonics (see Appendix J2, "Ways to Help Your Child with Reading at Home").

Through critical attention to relevant research and careful observation of children in the reading-writing process, we teachers can intelligently decide how to teach phonics. For our answers, we need to look to the child and carefully observe daily reading and writing behaviors. We also need to examine the most relevant research and draw meaningful conclusions. (For a listing of significant research, see Manning, Manning, and Kamii, 1988; Turner, 1989; and Weaver, 1990, pp. 109–141.) Finally, we need to apply how children learn all language processes to the acquisition and teaching of phonics.

Issues in Teaching Phonics: In Isolation or in Context?

"I loved phonics because I came to school already reading. It wasn't a puzzle I had to figure out. I could never understand why the kids who couldn't read as well as me had so much trouble with phonics" (Holly Burgess, English teacher, conversation, fall 1990).

For many teachers, beginning reading is still equated with teaching phonics, and phonics is taught systematically and sequentially, in isolation, as a separate subject. One problem with teaching phonics in isolation is that most young children have no idea how the sounds they are connecting with letters relate to reading. For a reader who is already struggling, having to rely heavily on the least important of the three necessary cueing systems adds a further handicap. The sound of a letter is useful only in the context of a word that is already embedded in a meaningful sentence. Also, because there are so many exceptions to phonics rules, the reader often needs to see the word in a broader context to determine its pronunciation. Furthermore, and most important, in order for children to see the purpose of letter-sound relationships, phonics skills must develop from authentic language experiences.

I was in a kindergarten class recently where the teacher was flashing individual letters, and the children were doing a fine job of making the sounds (in isolation) to go along with the letters. However, when I introduced and read a Big Book to the children and asked them to find a word that began with one of the letters they had studied, they were unable to make the transfer to a real reading situation. What they had learned was an isolated skill, not a strategy. They did not know how or when to apply what had been taught. They could parrot a response but were unable to make any meaningful literacy connections.

When we give young children phonics worksheets or flash letters and words in isolation, we are asking them to go from letter to sound—an unnatural and complicated task where some children have no success. Children naturally go from sound to letter, from the oral mode to the written mode, when writing and using invented spelling. Going from sound to letter respects the principle that learning proceeds from the known to the unknown. When children start with real words and what they know, they can better hold the sound and connect it to a letter in their minds.

I prefer to teach phonics strategically, in the meaningful context of the predictable stories children read and write every day. In the context of written language, phonics instruction facilitates meaning making and independence. Most of reading time is spent on reading and most of writing time is spent writing on self-selected topics, so that children develop much phonetic awareness naturally as they try to make sense of texts. However, because I am aware that some children do not just "pick up" phonics, I also guide students to discover and apply phonics generalizations by using the literature and the children's needs to determine the phonics I teach.

It has taken me well over ten years to feel completely comfortable with this approach. One thing that eased my further transition was holding onto the spelling workbooks for a while after I had long given up phonics worksheets. Knowing that the skills were still being covered relieved my conscience and helped my comfort level. Like many teachers, I did not believe children would really learn to read without a heavy dose of phonics first.

Contexts for Teaching Phonics Strategically

In meaningful phonics teaching, connections of sounds and letters are always made in real-life contexts. Beyond the book or story, we lead children to make connections in other contexts—signs, labels, charts, calendars, poems, and children's names.

Even with a natural approach to phonics, it is perfectly acceptable to call attention to sounds and words that we know students will need for reading and writing. In choosing Big Books to read, we are sensitive to the phonics and rhyming words that can be highlighted. For example, I have noticed that the Frank Asch books, some of which are available as Big Books, contain many examples of words with consonant digraphs. *Happy Birthday, Moon* (Prentice Hall, 1982) and *Mooncake* (Prentice Hall, 1983) have lots of words with "th" and "wh."

Rather than telling students what the sounds and letters are, however, I have found that an inquiry method that has the children "discover" the sounds and rules works best for engaging students in meaningful phonetic associations. I might say, for example, "What do you notice about the words . . .?" I see several words that begin with 'th.' Who can point to one?" "Can you find any other words with the same sound?" This approach is in direct contrast to that of most commercial phonics programs which tell students the rule or generalization and then present practice examples as skills in isolation rather than in the context of meaningful, continuous text.

Opportunities for ongoing phonics teaching and evaluation arise daily in the following contexts, all of which are discussed in this text:

- Shared reading
    Big Books, stories
        cloze exercises, masking (see Appendix E), blending in context

Poems
highlighting sounds on a poem chart; for example, mun<u>ch</u>, lun<u>ch</u>
Reading and rereading
- Shared writing
- Writing aloud
- Self-selected writing
journals, stories
- Guided reading
strategies for reading
using cloze technique—powerful for group phonics connections
using known words to work out unknown

Within these contexts, there is nothing wrong with direct, explicit teaching of phonics as long as it is done strategically. Words can be taken out of context as long as they are put back into context. Don Holdaway has developed two techniques that work well. One is the use of a sliding mask to highlight and blend words and word parts; the other is the use of a "flag" to highlight a word by taking it out of context and then putting it back into context. (See Appendix E.) The key is to remember that when a word is taken out of context to study it or break it apart, it always goes back into the context of the sentence before moving on. (See Chap. 9, "Personal Journal Writing," and Chap. 10, "Integrating Spelling into the Reading-Writing Classroom," for more information on teaching phonics meaningfully.)

Phonics Charts

Making enlarged phonics charts is perfectly appropriate in the whole language classroom. The order of sounds taught and the words used as examples are determined by the teacher and children, as the need arises in the context of reading and writing. This is very different from the use of traditional phonics charts that emphasize rules and use a prescribed sequence and fixed set of words.

For example, after *Who's in the Shed?* (Parkes, 1986) had been enjoyed over and over again during shared book experience in a first grade class, I demonstrated for the teacher how the "sh" sound could be reinforced through the book. I asked the children, "Who can find a word that begins with 'sh' [I made the sound] on this page?"

So the sheep had a peep
through a hole in the shed.
What did she see?

A child was then invited to come up and point to a word. As the child pointed to "sheep" and read it, I used the sliding mask to blend the word parts and highlight the "sh" and the whole word. I then wrote the word on our new "sh" chart, stretching out the sounds and verbalizing as I wrote it. In the same manner, children found "shed" and "she" on that page and subsequent pages, and those words were added to our chart. I then asked if anyone's name should be added to our chart, and "Josh" and "Shelia" raised their hands. We talked about whether the "sh" was at the beginning or end of the names. Nicky volunteered that *New Blue Shoes* by Eve Rice (Macmillan, 1975) had "shoes" to add to our chart. Rosa pointed out the word "should" from one of the week's chart poems. Later in the day *Noisy Nora* by Rosemary Wells was reread, and the children discovered other words to add to our chart—"hush," "shouted," "shrub," "trash," "crash."

It has worked well to tell children, "When you find a word as you are reading, come up and put it here on the chart." Limiting the words to books helps keep the spelling on the charts fairly accurate (we also tell children to write in pencil) and keeps the children from calling out scores of words. Children easily and excitedly work together to fill up our charts, and they develop increasing phonetic awareness and knowledge in the process (see Figure 7–6).

During the first week of school in one first grade classroom, we were focusing on "t" after having read and enjoyed several Big Books together. Children searched the room for "t" words and found "August" on the calendar, "today" on the bulletin board, "Mrs. Routman" on the chalkboard, and "t" words on titles of books. We discussed where to put the words on the chart—on the left words that begin with "t," on the right words that end with "t," and in the middle words that have "t" in the middle. One eager little girl brought me a book called *Trucks* and pointed to the "t." With encouragement ("Look at the picture. What could that word be? It begins with the 't' sound.") she read the title and was delighted with herself.

Figure 7-6   A Phonics Chart in First Grade

Phonics charts are posted in the room for children to add to and refer to. Separate sheets can be hole-punched and put together into a Big Book. I like to keep all the pages together for easy referral and organization in a large, spiral-bound chart tablet (24 by 16 inches). In the kindergarten classroom, phonics charts may be made with pictures from magazines with the word written next to each picture.

Personal Phonics Booklets

Some kindergarten and first grade teachers also have students keep their own sound and letter books in which students draw or paste in pictures to represent sounds for letters. (See Figure 7-7 for a page from a kindergartner's personal phonics book done during the second month of school.) Sometimes these books are also used to practice handwriting after the teacher has demonstrated the formation of the letter(s). One first grade teacher has students write optional "tongue twisters" (see Figure 7-8).

Some first grade teachers have students keep lists of words that students notice from their reading to go along with particular letter-sound combinations. Students can always read these words *before* they examine them phonetically. These booklets serve as personal phonics charts. See Figure 7-9 for a student's page from Joyce Pope's first grade class. Notice that the words come from the context of the classroom—"honey" and "hungry" from the familiar storybook *The Hungry Giant* (The Wright Group, 1980), "wishy," "washy," and "lovely" from *Mrs. Wishy-*

Figure 7-7   *A Page from a Kindergartner's Personal Phonics Booklet*

Figure 7-8   Phonics "Tongue Twister"

NAME Christen   fr

TONGUE TWISTER

TRY WRITING YOUR OWN TONGUE TWISTER.

Freddy the frog went to
Frank's house to have french
fries whith his friend.

Idea developed by Jim Henry.

Figure 7-9   Page from a First-grader's Personal Phonics Booklet

2-28-90

y=ē

honey
hungry   Lovely
mommy   Library
wishy   February
washy   trolley
candy   noisy
country   puppy
Lady   sunny
hairy   foggy
Krissy   rainy
Lindsay

Washy; "Krissy" and "Lindsay" from children's names in the class; and "rainy," "sunny," and "February" from the calendar bulletin board.

Such individual phonics books are appropriate as long as they are a very minor part of the total reading program and students have some ownership over what goes into them. I have noticed that teachers tend to move away from these booklets once they are convinced that children are learning phonics in the normal course of daily reading and writing. One teacher said, "I did the booklets because *I* needed to see the evidence that phonics was being taught."

Teaching Short Vowels: Getting Perspective

The appropriateness of teaching short vowels to very young children needs to be re-examined. Reading the following partial paragraph, which begins like a story, helps provide some clarity. If you get stuck while reading, you should keep going, read for meaning, and put in what makes sense.

> -nc- -p-n - t-m- th-r- w-s - h-nds-m- y--ng w-lf n-m-d
> L-b-. L-b- l-v-d w-th h-s m-th-r -nd f-th-r -t th- -dg- -f
> a d--p, d-rk w--ds. -v-r- d-- L-b- w-nt t- h-nt -t th-
> n-rth -dg- -f th- w--ds, n--r th-e l-ttl- v-ll-g- -f C-l--s . . .
> (Weaver, 1988, p. 80).

I have used the preceding exercise repeatedly to convince kindergarten and first grade teachers that children can read quite well without knowing short vowels. Many teachers have told me that being able to read this paragraph with all the vowels missing forced them to examine their heavy emphasis on vowel sounds. The importance of beginning consonants, then ending consonants, and finally medial consonants is clear. Notice how important the "th" digraph is for reading about 20 percent of the words. Notice also that being unsure of the name of the village didn't affect the meaning at all.

Try an exercise like this with parents at open house to explain why vowel worksheets will not be used and coming home. Take any meaningful paragraph, delete the vowels, and you obtain the same result.

The teaching of short vowels to young children has largely gone unquestioned. It has been prescribed for years by commercial programs, most of which place emphasis on vowel sounds and their associated letters. Parents, based on their own education, expect phonics to be taught. And teachers feel they must cover all the sounds because of the perceived expectations of the next year's teachers and state and local testing requirements.

However, if teachers observe children's daily writing, they quickly notice that short vowels do not appear regularly in the writing of most kindergarten children and beginning first graders. The message that children are giving us is that they are not yet developmentally ready for short vowels. Most students are not ready to apply these sounds in reading and writing until the end of first grade. In our failure to heed that message, many young children have been labeled poor readers based on their inability to hear sounds in words—especially vowels—on worksheets. Additionally, emphasis on short vowels puts undue stress on second language learners (ESL students), who characteristically have difficulty identifying and hearing the different vowel sounds in words.

The blame for overemphasis on phonics cannot be laid entirely at the publishers' doorsteps. Educators have ignored the research, bought the programs, and insisted on lots of phonics exercises for very young children. John Ridley, Editor-in-Chief of the Elementary School Division of Houghton Mifflin Company in Boston, noted, "We have recognized the appropriate handling of phonics for a long time but there has been resistance through a range of pressures to have phonics taught earlier and earlier despite research to the contrary" (conversation, August 1990).

Recently there appears to be a shift in the marketplace. Teachers seem to be finally resisting the wholesale marketing of phonics through workbooks and drill sheets. Publishers have begun to respond with programs that attempt to teach phonics through the context of poems and stories.

Phonics: A Suggested Teaching Order

By being attentive to children's daily reading and, especially, their daily writing (as in their journals), teachers can easily note what phonics generalizations children have mastered and what they are ready to be introduced to. While there is no predetermined order for teaching letter-sound relationships, the following suggested sequence may be helpful when the teacher is trying to decide where to place emphasis first in the early grades. This order is based on my own observations working with young children.

- Beginning consonants
- Ending consonants
- Consonant digraphs ("sh," "th," "ch," "wh")
- Medial consonants
- Consonant blends
- Long vowels
- Short vowels

Instruction should always have meaning for the child and not just follow a prescribed sequence. After the lesson on "t" the first week in first grade, a number of children had questions about "th." Many saw the first letter "t" in "th" and wanted to add it to our "t" chart. We had just read *The Trolley Ride* (Rigby Education, 1987), in which the word "then" appears six times. Some children could already read "the" in several contexts. One student brought over a book called *Things That Go* by Anne Rockwell (Dutton, 1986). Because the children asked for it, it was appropriate and timely to move directly to "th." A discussion of whether "t" and "th" sound the same followed, and one student noted " 'th' makes a different sound." We began a "th" chart on the spot. "Brother," "mother," and "father" were added to the chart during our journal writing time. At least half a dozen students immediately referred to one of those family words and wrote it correctly in their journal entries. Even more noted "the" and incorporated it into their journal entries.

In determining what letter-sound relationships to highlight, we need to be constantly observant of children's needs and be flexible in our teaching. For example, word endings, especially "-ing," are often needed early in writing and should be taught as the need arises. It will also be necessary to do repeated demonstrations, individually and in small groups.

Demonstrations of how we are teaching phonics need to occur with parents, too. For parents to understand the meaningful teaching of phonics, we need to educate them about the current research and how we are applying it to the classroom. When parents see that phonics is still being taught and are shown the how and why, they are very supportive.

Making the Transition to More Meaningful Phonics Teaching

Kindergarten Teachers' Changes

Most kindergarten teachers in our district moved away from commercial phonics programs several years ago to the use of a "sound of the week" program, which immerses children in art, cooking, writing, and related activities to learn particular sounds in a prescribed sequence. Some kindergarten teachers have made a further transition to where the sounds that are covered for a particular week emerge naturally from daily classroom experiences. Daily reading of Big Books as well as daily writing are used to develop letter-sound awareness. A class-generated story or sentence can be the impetus for focusing on particular sounds. Teachers keep a record of what sounds have been introduced so they are sure none are overlooked.

Making the transition from "sound of the week" phonics to teaching phonics in the context of daily reading and writing is not easy. Kindergarten teacher Kathy Wolfe says,

> It was really difficult to make this change. I felt real guilty for a long time, but I was finding teaching a "letter of the week" was no longer relevant. It was an activity in isolation while I was trying very hard to teach everything in context. I saw that the children were learning their letters and sounds through all our reading and writing so I began to feel it must be okay to teach this way. Before, when I was teaching a letter, if a student wasn't ready for it, he wasn't learning it anyway. Now, I see when children need a letter, they try to figure it out through self-discovery, seeing me model, asking a friend, or looking at print around the room. I think I can finally relate teaching phonics to the way children learn to talk. I trust that it will happen.

As an example of teaching a sound in context through discovery and inquiry, a lesson that developed in a kindergarten class follows. While the teacher had decided that the day's rereadings of Big Books would be useful for focusing on the "g" sound, the children discovered the sound-letter associations. In reading through *One Cold Wet Night* (Melser and Cowley, The Wright Group, 1987), the repeated phrase "One cold wet night the farmer got out of bed and said, I'm going to be warm tonight" was used to highlight the "g" letter-sound association. "Who can find a word that begins with the "g" sound?" When a student came up and pointed to "got," I used the slide to mask the word and blend the word parts smoothly. "Say it with me: g--o--t." Before I could go on, Craig offered, "I see another word," and he was invited to come up and point to his word, "going." Other students commented that the "g" was also at the end of the word. Then a discussion about "tonight" followed after several children noticed the letter "g" in the word. They could tell that the "g" sound was not in the word. I noted, "Sometimes a letter you can see makes no sound." Because they seemed satisfied with that explanation, I made no further remarks.

Next, the children reread *Sing a Song* (Melser and Cowley, The Wright Group, 1987), which included the refrain, "Sing, sing, sing a song, Sing a song together." "Where do we find the "g" sound here?" They discovered "g" at the end of "sing" and "song" and in the middle of "together." One of the children noticed "go" on a chart poem and got up to point it out. When I asked if anyone's last name started with "g," Robin Griffith and Sam Gates raised their hands. We started a "g" chart which the teacher and children added to as new words were discovered through reading and writing.

First Grade Teachers' Struggles

Most of us seem to find the transition from prescribed phonics in isolation to teaching meaningful phonics in the context of literature very difficult and slow going. It may be reassuring to know that most teachers are struggling with making phonics teaching more relevant and applicable to reading and writing. I believe it is critical to remember that before we can change our teaching, we have to carefully re-examine our beliefs in the light of current research and learning theory.

Susan Mears has been a first grade teacher for eight years. In talking about phonics, she describes herself as "struggling awfully" despite the fact that she had done much reading and thinking about phonics teaching:

> I did more phonics in context this year, noting beginning and ending sounds and digraphs in chart poems and Big Books. The kids really liked the big charts we made where they could add their own words, but I am still struggling to find a balance in teaching phonics. I find myself feeling pressure from some of the second grade teachers who expect kids to arrive with solid word attack skills. Also, I feel guilty for not giving spelling tests. When I'm teaching all the phonics sounds, I feel as though I'm teaching spelling too. I still teach phonics separately even though I don't see kids transferring the skills. I notice that every time I pull a sound out of context, two or three kids give me an example of a word that doesn't fit the rule at all. I'm still not comfortable with the way I handle phonics.

Colleen Thompson has been teaching first grade for two years. After a series of workshops on whole language, she began to question the traditional workbook approach to phonics teaching:

> I have continued to teach phonics lessons through the workbooks, but I now see that the kids don't transfer that phonics to their reading. I had five kids who learned to read who never did catch on to phonics. I still use the workbooks, but I'm trying to use context more. If I can feel comfortable teaching phonics in context, I'd rather go that way. I saw this year that all the sounds are in the literature books. This next year I plan to spend most of reading time reading. I see I have to work with the parents too. They use only "sounding out" when working with their kids. If the child can't read the word in isolation, parents think the child is not reading and has just used memorization. I need to make them aware of the other cueing systems.

Promoting Vocabulary Development

Vocabulary development is best promoted through wide reading where new words are learned incidentally (Nagy, 1988; Herman and Dole, 1989). Therefore, we need to encourage extensive reading—reading aloud to students, guided reading with students, and independent reading by students—and teach strategies for inferring meanings of words through context. We also need to share this information with parents so they can promote vocabulary development at home.

Most vocabulary is not acquired through direct instruction and memorization. Students do not "own" a word just because they have looked it up in the dictionary or used it in a sentence. Unless they can generalize a word's meaning to apply it to a new context, vocabulary work has remained at the skills level, and transfer of learning will be slight.

In *Teaching Vocabulary to Improve Reading Comprehension*, William Nagy (1988) demonstrates the futility of having students look up unknown words in the dictionary. He lists a series of words followed by their definitions in *Webster's Third New International Dictionary* (1961) and challenges the reader to use each word correctly in a sentence. Without some prior knowledge of the word, it is very difficult to use the word correctly. "Definitions do not teach you how to *use* a new word" and "definitions do not effectively convey new concepts" (p. 6). Dictionary definitions can be utilized only if the student already understands related concepts.

We teachers can best promote vocabulary development within the context of literature when the meaning of the text can be used to determine word meaning. We can guide students to use what they know and what the author presents to construct word meanings strategically at the concept level. Vocabulary is developed during or after reading when semantic relationships can be made. The only time I introduce a word before reading is if understanding a particular word is critical for comprehending the passage. This is more likely to occur with reading in the content areas than in the literature/reading program.

In guiding students to utilize the context, we need to demonstrate how this is done. In reading *Charlotte's Web* by E. B. White, I showed a group of second-graders how the author helps the reader with word meanings. In the beginning of Chapter VII, "Bad News," White begins by discussing flies as a nuisance. "The cows hated them. The horses detested them. The sheep loathed them." I think out loud and show how "hated" can be used to infer similar meaning for "detested" and "loathed." White then goes on to say that Charlotte "always put her victim to sleep before eating it. . . . 'I always give them an anaesthetic so they won't feel pain. It's a little service I throw in'" (p. 48). I verbalize how the previous text lets the reader know that "victim" means a fly and that the meaning of "anaesthetic" can be figured out even if you can't read the word.

Students need to know they can make meaningful substitutions and continue reading. It is also important to point out that the author's choice of words affects the mood, interest, quality, and tone of the writing so that young writers will begin to think about choosing their own written words carefully.

Dictionaries are consulted when the need arises—when the definition of a word that is needed for understanding cannot be inferred. This is what many adults do. When I am reading, I rarely stop to look up a word in the dictionary. I try to glean the meaning, substitute a word or phrase that makes sense, and go on. Only when the word is necessary for understanding a major concept—or when I have come across a word many times before and am curious about its meaning—do I look it up. We need to apply the same real-life use to the classroom.

Because of the high correlation between vocabulary and reading comprehension (Nagy, 1988; Herman and Dole, 1989) and because students enjoy learning new words, knowledge of vocabulary is important. However, since drill and practice exercises account for little actual vocabulary development, I believe that most time for vocabulary acquisiton should be related to applying acquisition strategies to independent reading. Self-selection should be a major part of how vocabulary is studied; that is; students should choose most of the words they want to learn. With a full-length chapter book, focusing on several words per chapter or about twenty words per book is sufficient. Students can keep personal vocabulary notebooks. Because the words have importance for students, there is greater likelihood of recall. (See Chap. 6, in "Responding to Literature: Later Transitions," pp. 110–111, for suggestions for vocabulary instruction; see also Nagy, 1988, for procedures for vocabulary acquisition from kindergarten through college.)

8

Authentic Contexts for Writing

Choosing to co-author a true book about sharks: grade 1

Becoming a Writer

A colleague asked me, "What teacher influenced you in your writing?"

"I don't know. I can't remember any teacher that way," I replied.

"Surely, there must have been someone," she persisted.

No one had ever asked me that question before, and I realized I had never thought about it. Surely, there *must* have been someone. Thinking back through my school career, I could only remember writing for the teacher, diagraming sentences, being concerned about "getting it right." I was not much of a reader initially, so it couldn't have been the influence of the great authors. I read in school and completed assignments, but I didn't become an avid reader until well into high school. It was then that my mother's influence—gently nudging me to read books she had loved as well as seeing her constantly reading—finally rubbed off.

But writing? That was something else. If not a teacher, then who? Then it came to me. My grandmother. My grandmother who had completed only sixth grade because she had to work to help support the family. Living and working, not schooling, were her education. Grandma had a way with words, a cackling sense of humor, and a stubborn streak that drove much of her family crazy, but to me she was wonderful. While I was growing up, and all through my teenage years, we spent many hours visiting together. Some evenings she told me stories for hours, and the way she put words together fascinated me. Many stories she wrote down, and read to me. I can still see her reaching up into her crowded bedroom closet and pulling down a large, faded cardboard box filled with her written memories. At the time, I did not realize that she was a born storyteller or that I was her private audience. I only knew that her words, her voice, her raw emotions captivated me. She embellished stories and poems of the old country, of hardship, of a failed romance, of her children, of marriage, of getting old.

After a while, Grandma would usually stop and say, "And now you have to hear a real author." And she would select a passage from *Gone with the Wind, The*

Good Earth, or some classic she loved and read to me. "Listen to the words, and feel them" she would say. "They are beautiful." I still remember Margaret Mitchell's descriptions of the devastated South during the Civil War. Being read aloud to as a teenager had a powerful effect on me. I began to appreciate the depth, beauty, and possibilities of language.

When my grandmother was in her late seventies, she enrolled in a writing class at the local high school. Always desirous of more education, she wanted to become a "writer." I don't think she, or any of her family, acknowledged she was already a "real author." I have only recently realized the extent of Grandma's influence on my own desire and ability to write.

The Importance of Being a Writing Model

I sincerely believe that we should not ask children to go through any process we have not experienced ourselves. Our students must have writing models if they are to become writers, and we teachers need to be those models. Generally, we have come to believe this about reading. Almost every teacher I know reads with and to children every day—during read-aloud time, sustained silent reading, and guided reading. Not so with writing.

Most of us don't write with children or share our own writing. In fact, many of us don't like to write and are afraid to write. We have been conditioned by our own traditional schooling to view writing as an assignment by and for the teacher. Though we meticulously lead children through the steps of the writing process, we have never been through the process ourselves. Yet just as we would never consider taking music, art, or athletic lessons from a teacher who talked about the subject but had never actually done it, we cannot be teachers of writing until we demonstrate the craft ourselves. We must become genuine users and risk takers before we can expect the same of our students. This is not an easy task. Writing is tough work, even for those who do it regularly.

There are many ways to begin to become a writing model. One way is to share a copy of a letter or note written for a real purpose. Another way is to try a shared writing after a common class experience such as a field trip. Or two classes can be combined, with one teacher writing in front of the children and the other teacher providing support. I believe it's okay to tell the students we've never written in front of a class before and are feeling very anxious. We don't need to worry about botching the job. Children will respect and learn from a process if they know the teacher is sincere and cares about them. If the fear of writing before the class is too great to actually do it, try inviting a writer into the classroom. The individual need not be a famous author. He or she could be a parent, the principal, a colleague—anyone who makes writing a real part of daily life. Students must know adults who write and who are willing to demonstrate their thinking-writing-revising-editing processes for them.

Being a Writer Means Being Vulnerable

When my book *Transitions* was published, I was terrified. I didn't know that I was going to feel that way, but as the book was about to be unveiled (at the International Reading Association annual meeting in Toronto in May 1988), I felt as though I were being undressed in public. The writing of the book had been a very private undertaking, the reading of it would be a public one. All my inadequacies would be on view for everyone to see. I remember feeling sick to my stomach and wanting to go into hiding. My principal and good friend Delores Groves, who had come to Toronto to celebrate and be part of a symposium on whole language with me, chided me for the way I was dressed. I had on all dark colors, no jewelry, and little make-up. She encouraged me to "brighten up," and she was right. Looking back, I think I wanted to become invisible.

> Readers peer into the writer's very soul. They judge the depth of sensitivity, the clearness of thinking, the soundness of values, and the range and sophistication of verbal skill. If beauty and truth embody the writer's spirit, they will be revealed. So, too, will shallowness and ineptitude (Romano, 1987, p. 41).

In workshops for teachers, I have always stressed the importance of teachers writing—and writing in front of their students. I had always shared drafts of my own writing on the overhead projector, but I had never demonstrated writing in front of my peers. It took me seven years to get up the courage to do that!

While giving a presentation to teachers and administrators at the K–8 writing conference in October 1989 in Columbus, Ohio, I talked about journal writing and how to make it come alive for students. I listed some topics that I could write about: needing a haircut and perm, making jam, raking leaves, driving to Columbus, being nervous about my presentation. I didn't know I was actually going to write in public until I did it. As I began composing on the overhead projector, the room became silent. I felt apprehensive because I had no idea what I was going to write or how it would come out. The audience seemed as surprised as I was by my public act of writing. This is what I wrote:

> Late last night some friends came up to my room, and we were sharing pictures from our lives. As it got later and later, I started to get really nervous because I needed some quiet time to organize my thoughts for the next day's presentation.
>
> I had trouble sleeping. I kept waking and looking at the clock and wondering when it would be 6:00 A.M.
>
> My stomach was doing flip-flops all morning—through breakfast and through Lucy Calkins' keynote talk. But once I started talking, my nervousness disappeared, and I began to relax.

My handwriting was as illegible as usual, I had several cross outs, my content was sparse, but at least it was a genuine attempt, and teachers appreciated that. Several teachers told me it was the first time they had ever seen another teacher write. One teacher later wrote to me and said seeing me write had given her the courage to begin to write in front of her students.

My own feelings of vulnerability have helped me be empathetic to students— and teachers—who share their writing and have sensitized me to the need to set up a classroom writing climate that is supportive and encouraging. We all need to feel that our writing and best efforts are valued if we are going to take the risk of sharing writing and accepting responses.

Teachers Writing Together: Taking a Risk

Some of us have found that writing in front of students becomes possible if we first go through the process with our colleagues. In one building, where our weekly language arts support groups had begun focusing on the writing process, teachers were honestly talking about the fact that they did not write themselves. Based on an idea by Harste, Short, and Burke (1988), I read *The Relatives Came* by Cynthia Rylant (Bradbury, 1985) as a springboard for triggering personal, family memories. After listening to the story, principal Larry Svec and about twelve teachers began to write a draft of a fond family memory. Because I wanted the writing to have a real purpose, I suggested that the written memory might be given to the actual person as a gift.

We took about six weeks of our regular support group meetings to write our drafts, meet in small response groups to give feedback, write final copies, and share finished pieces. Several teachers commented about how vulnerable they felt sharing their writing with peers. One teacher said she was surprised at her own sensitivity to a minor suggestion that was made after several very positive comments had been offered. "It made me realize how careful we have to be with students. I had no idea I would feel so defensive about my writing."

Third grade teacher Lee Sattelmeyer took the initiative to word-process completed pieces and, working with school secretary Judy Kalan, put together a book called *Musing: Reflections upon Our Life* and gave a copy to all who participated. The morning we received the bound books at our support group meeting, everyone sat captivated, reading privately. The response went beyond respectful silence. A community had been created. We knew each other better, trusted each other more, and felt closer as friends and colleagues. Several teachers said it was the first time they had ever written and shared publicly and that the experience would make it easier to demonstrate themselves as writers to their students.

Setting up the Classroom Environment for Writing

The climate of the classroom, both emotional and physical, contributes to students' willingness and eagerness to write. We need to examine and be able to articulate our own beliefs about writing before we can foster an environment that meaningfully engages students in the writing process. For me, Nancie Atwell has said it best:

A Framework of Beliefs about Writing

1. Writers need regular chunks of time.
2. Writers need their own topics.
3. Writers need response.
4. Writers learn mechanics in context.
5. Children need to know adults who write.
6. Writers need to read.
7. Writing teachers need to take responsibility for their knowledge and teaching. (Atwell, 1987, pp. 17–18)

I add two additional beliefs about writing:

1. Writers need to feel safe to take a risk.
2. Writers need a genuine purpose for writing.

Making the Writing Process Real
Genuinely Engaging in the Writing Process

In many writing classrooms, writing is not natural. Instead, writing is a mechanistic process that has all the how's without the why's. Many of us have bought into "process writing" without the necessary personal conviction to make it significant for students. It is not unusual to walk into a classroom today and see the steps of the writing process posted on the wall in sequential order. Certainly I remember starting that way. I took students through the steps as if following a recipe. On Monday we did prewriting or rehearsing. On Tuesday we did the first draft. Wednesday we revised. Thursday we edited. Friday we published. While this description is a bit exaggerated, I—like many other teachers—believed that I could teach the writing process by taking students through sequential steps. Only when I became a writer myself and began to write with students and colleagues could I see that "doing writing process" was not valid.

<u>My writing process</u>   When I began to write regularly, I became very aware that writers don't go through an ordered or exact process. I never get up in the morning thinking, "Today I will be prewriting." My prewriting or rehearsing goes on constantly. I prefer the inclusive term "percolating" for the ongoing, thinking, reconsidering process that takes place throughout the writing process. (see Romano, 1987, pp. 55–58). Even after I have written drafts and made revisions, I am still percolating. My percolating goes on when I am driving, swimming, eating, walking, trying to sleep, sitting at the word processor about to write, taking a shower, listening to colleagues, cooking dinner. For Romano, "percolating" is "anything done in relation to the piece of writing aside from producing a draft or revising one." That could include outlining, brainstorming, jotting notes. For me, percolating is mostly a mental process, the thinking that goes on before I write.

Once I begin to write, the percolating stops and the writing takes over. Writer Madeleine L'Engle says, "Don't think. Write. We think before we write a story, and afterward, but during the writing we listen. It is an act of focused attention, which is very different from conscious thinking." (In "How They Feel about God," by Madeleine L'Engle [a review of *Writer's Revealed* by Rosemary Hartill], *New York Times Book Review*, November 5, 1989.)

I never go neatly through steps; I meander back and forth through stages. I percolate, write a draft, revise, percolate, rewrite the draft, percolate, begin a new draft, revise a previous draft some more, and so on. I don't follow any sequential steps. I let the writing—and what I think I might want to say—lead me. As much as possible, we need to allow students the same time and latitude to find what works for them.

We also need to allow students the opportunity to set a piece of writing aside. Again and again, while writing this book, I experienced writer's block and was unable to continue writing a chapter or section. By moving to a different topic, I found I could often come back to a previous draft more easily at a later date. This is not to say we should not give students due dates, but we can build in flexibility as much as possible.

Perhaps hardest of all, we need to create uninterrupted blocks of time. I cannot write anything meaningful in a half hour. I need long, quiet periods of time. While this may not be possible in the classroom, we can look at our schedules and try to put writing at the center of the curriculum, at least part of the time. Based on my own writing experiences, I now believe that writing *is* thinking and that through writing we learn to write and think more clearly. I believe writing must become central to our teaching and integral to all subject areas across the curriculum.

Valuing Revision

Revision is at the heart of the writing process and is fundamental to almost all good writing. Students can understand revision and the need for it when revision is demonstrated as a genuine part of what good writers do. On the other hand, when it is presented as "step three" in the writing process, students rarely take it seriously.

Donald Murray calls revision "central to the act of discovery" (1990, p. 171). Revision means, literally, looking again at a piece of writing and *re*-visioning it. It is for me both the most challenging and joyful part of the writing process. Early revisions on a quickly written draft are the hardest because the writing has no clear form or direction yet. Final revisions are when I have the most fun: playing with individual sections and words and seeing the promise of the piece as a unified whole.

Revision requires careful attention and thinking and refers to any changes the writer makes in an attempt to improve clarity, organization, wording, fluency, and understanding. Revision includes changing one word for another, but it is much more. Words, sentences, and whole paragraphs may be added, deleted, or moved around. The writing is reshaped, molded, and polished.

When I go into classrooms to assist with children's writing, I try first to demonstrate myself as a writer. I bring in my chapter drafts to pass out. I tell students that when I write a draft I get my thoughts down quickly, not concerning myself with getting things right. This is the time for exploration, and I usually have no idea how a draft will turn out. I am rarely satisifed with a first draft, but it is a beginning.

For a particular chapter, I do at least five or more drafts, and I share these with students and let them draw their own conclusions. When I ask students what they have noticed about the drafts, I find it interesting that students are always surprised by the number of "errors." They view any marks on the paper—the changes, crossouts, rewordings, rearrangings—as "mistakes" (see Figure 8–1). I explain to them that this is how writers work, that no one gets it right the first time, that writing is difficult, creative, time-consuming, and tiring work, but worth it, because the finished piece brings a wonderful sense of creative accomplishment.

I always let students know how tough revision is ahead of time, and I find my honesty does not scare them off—quite the contrary. Like the pilot warning passengers that they are about to experience turbulence, letting students know that revision will be challenging helps prepare them for the work ahead.

I also talk to students about the role of response in revision and how that works

Figure 8-1   Partial "Messy" Chapter Draft by the Author

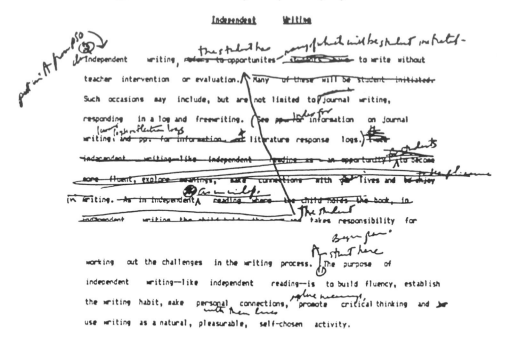

for me. I let students know that because my audience is teachers, I always have each chapter draft read by at least three to five colleagues. I sincerely want and need to know what seems unclear or confusing, missing, needing reorganization. I want to know whether my tone is invitational, whether the content is relevant, whether the information is clear. I also want to hear—and need to hear first—what has been helpful and clearly written. Because writing is such hard work, the writer always needs supportive messages along with suggestions for changes.

I explain that as only one writer-reader, I cannot possibly be sure whether my writing is clear and complete. I then show students two actual chapter drafts that I gave to teachers for reactions. The first one has no comments on it except "very good." The second is filled with comments—reader reactions, suggestions, confusions, new learnings. I ask students which response has been helpful to me as the writer, and they are quick to comment on the usefulness of the second one.

I also let students know that because I respect my reader-responders, I take every comment and suggestion seriously, and I make more than 90 percent of all changes suggested. Students see the necessity for the revision process, and they do "buy into" it. I have found that they are not "turned off" with honest talk about the difficulty and necessity of revision. On the contrary, they appreciate the honesty and realistic expectations and come through the task admirably.

While teachers may not have extensive drafts to share with students, most of us have something we write that requires revision—letters to parents, handouts to explain the curriculum, a note to a favorite person on a special occasion. When you find yourself writing something that requires going back and making changes, save it, and share it with your students.

Looking at Writing Errors as a Necessary Part of Learning

When a new student who has come from a school in which correctness and form in writing have been emphasized above meaning and exploration, enters a reading-writing classroom, the student's writing may be correct but it is also usually dull and lifeless (see Figure 9–10 in Chap. 9). Overemphasis on correctness produces unimaginative writing.

Connie Weaver said it best in a significant article entitled "Welcoming Errors as Signs of Growth" when she noted "growth and error go hand in hand" (*Language Arts*, May 1982, pp. 438–444). She cited research which showed that as writers risked new forms, they made more errors until the form came under control. For example, Weaver noted that while sixth-graders were found to have more "sentence sense" errors than fourth graders, the sixth-graders were experimenting with more complicated constructions, especially the use of subordinate clauses.

We need to notice the kinds of errors students are making and to not see them all as negative. Especially important is the recognition that as students get older and try out new, more sophisticated forms, they may temporarily make more errors as they develop insights. The amount of writing may also decrease temporarily while students are struggling to get things right. This is very much akin to the young child trying out a more sophisticated form of speech. Before getting the correct form under control, the child needs lots of time to practice and exaggerate—and needs to be encouraged and congratulated for risk taking. We need to encourage students to experiment with form while continuing to guide them in proofreading their work.

Donald Murray observes,

> Many teachers complain that their students can't write sentences. I complain that many of my students write sentences. Too early. Following form, forgetting meaning. Following language toward correctness. For its own sake . . .
>
> We don't know enough about how to write badly—and why. Syntax often breaks down when we approach a new and interesting meaning . . . (1989, p. 39).
>
> All writing is experimental. We don't know what works until we try it. Failure is normal and instructive. From failures we see ways to achieve success (1989, p. 123).

I believe we need to give students lots of opportunities for experimentation and practice without concern for grading. Only a very small percentage of writing should be evaluated, the rest should be for students to try out alternative forms, styles, and genres.

Using Published Authors for Demonstrations

Often the best way for students to write successfully in a particular genre is to immerse themselves in the literature of that genre. For example, students need to examine and appreciate models of quality fiction before they can be expected to write fiction themselves.

When reading aloud or working with a reading group, I often stop and note the way the author has created a mood, setting, or character description in a work of fiction. I may reproduce a page or paragraph and share it on the overhead projector, highlighting key words and phrases the author has used. I want to make students what Nancie Atwell calls "insiders," privy to what authors do, so students may think about similar possibilities for their own writing. Even young children can take note of what authors do and begin to apply it to their own writing.

When a second grade class was getting ready to write stories for an upcoming "Young Authors' Conference," we focused on how good stories begin. We looked at the "leads" in books we had already read and discussed—*Charlotte's Web* by E. B. White, *Sam, Bangs and Moonshine* by Evaline Ness, *Wump World* by Bill Peet, and *One Morning in Maine* by Robert McCloskey (Viking, 1952). In particular, we noted that the author made the setting descriptive and clear right at the beginning. A number of students were able to use these demonstrations to create their own interesting leads (see Figure 8–2 for two examples of first attempts). Student examples of quality writing were also used as demonstrations for other students.

I have come to believe that literature provides the best models of language. Through reading, thinking about, discussing, and interpreting great literature, students come to learn most of what they need to know about language—especially if the teacher takes the time to note the demonstrations the literature provides (for example, the leads, the conventions, the vocabulary). *The way to become a writer is through becoming an insightful reader.* That insight comes directly from Frank

Figure 8-2   Two Second Grade Students' First Attempts at Writing Leads

Smith's article, "Reading Like a Writer" in *Joining the Literacy Club* (originally published in *Language Arts*, May 1983, pp. 558–567). A favorite quote that I often reread from this article follows:

> To read like a writer we engage with the author in what the author is writing. We anticipate what the author will say, so that the author is in effect writing on our behalf, not showing how something is done but doing it with us. This is identical to the spoken language situation where adults help children say what they want to say or would like and expect to be able to say. The author becomes an unwitting collaborator. Everything the learner would want to spell the author spells. Everything the learner would want to punctuate the author punctuates. Every nuance of expression, every relevant syntactic device, every turn of phrase, the author and learner write together. Bit by bit, one thing at a time, but enormous numbers of things over the passage of time, the learner learns through *reading* like a writer to *write* like a writer (p. 25).

Setting Up the Environment for Writing

I have a small room in my house where I write. All my tools and equipment are there—word processor and printer, comfortable chair, books, pens, pencils, Post-its, wire baskets to hold papers, file cabinets, drafts, loose notes, dictionary, writing notebooks, stapler, scissors, tape, white-out liquid, paper clips, rubber bands, blank paper, wastebasket, blank file folders, folders organized by topics and work samples, paintings, pictures of my family, clock, light, coffee cup.

When I begin writing, the room is neat and organized, but once I am "in process" there are papers and piles on every available surface, including the entire floor. Eventually, I encroach on surfaces in adjoining rooms, and drafts and papers take over the dining room table, kitchen table, chairs and ledges. I am by nature a fairly neat person, but not when I write. Writing is "messy." I become disorganized in order to find my organization. I need to see all the parts so I can rearrange, discard, add, reshuffle, rethink, and rework to create a meaningful whole. My writing room becomes orderly again only after I have worked through the writing challenges. I cannot put away my tools until I have satisfactorily used them.

I mention all this to sensitize us as teachers to the needs of writers. While clearly it is not possible for each student to have his own room in school, the traditional fixed space of the desk could be expanded. For example, for students who work well independently, long tables could be set up in the hall just outside the classroom to give writers more space and freedom. Children could be allowed to spread out on the floor in class. They might even be allowed to leave their "messy work" where it is if there will be another opportunity later in the day to write. Post-its, paper, pens, tape, and so on, could be readily available for student use.

Just as important, we can attempt to arrange classrooms to be as comfortable as possible for students and teachers to write (see Figures 15–1 and 15–2 in Chap. 15). Students should know where to find writing supplies and what areas of the room they may use when they write. It works well to have several areas for conferencing. A few desks pushed together can serve as well for a conference area as a larger table.

We could take a lesson from our kindergarten teachers, many of whom have created authentic spaces for writing. Children write all over the room—at the writing center, in the play area, with the teacher, with a friend, spread out on the floor, at big tables. Another lesson we can take from kindergarten is the importance of talk in learning to write. Young writers need and enjoy collaborating, and they use their talk to expand and clarify ideas. We need to make all classrooms more user friendly for writers.

Demonstrating the Use of Writers' Tools

Before students become immersed in the writing process, take some time to show how writers work. Let students see drafts with cross outs, arrows, carets, and individual cues to the writer (such as letter codes) to move a section. Many elementary teachers have found it works well to have students write on only one side of the sheet and skip every other line. This practice makes cutting and pasting and adding and deleting easier later on. We let students know that writers don't just recopy and that a messy draft is normal. We actually demonstrate how cutting and pasting is done with scissors and tape and show how colored pens or pencils may be used in the editing process.

I always show students a messy draft (see Figure 8–1). Showing a draft by a colleague or an author would also work well. In "The Author's Eye" series, Roald Dahl and Katherine Paterson (1988) share their thoughts, jottings, and writing drafts, and students can see the thinking-revising process.

Writing for Authentic Purposes

Relevant Writing

The writing that goes on in classrooms must be relevant to students if they are to become engaged in and value the process. Practicing writing through exercises, skill sheets, and isolated activities does not produce good writers and, in fact, is not real writing. Our focus must be on writing for real purposes.

This section gives examples of some of the forms of writing we use in our daily lives. As such, I believe they are appropriate forms of writing (and reading) for the classroom and can be used as guides for authentic writing. The forms or genres listed are not in any particular order and are not meant to be all inclusive. Notice that basal stories, worksheets, book reports, and the five-paragraph essay are not listed; these forms exist only in schools.

This list may prove useful for generating ideas for meaningful independent work, providing optional opportunities for writing-publishing and for encouraging communicating-thinking-learning-writing in a variety of genres. In all cases, the writing should connect with reading, the curriculum, other children, varied audiences, and real purposes.

In most cases, we will need first to demonstrate the particular form or genre by immersing students in many reading-writing examples. For example, before expecting students to write directions, book blurbs, an author page, a newspaper article, or a report, we must first expose them to many pieces of quality writing in that genre so that they become familiar with the format, style, language, and conventions.

Specific examples of letter writing, story writing, and journal writing are discussed and demonstrated following the list of possible writing forms. Because personal journal writing—where students write about their own experiences—is such a powerful vehicle for getting started successfully with authentic writing, the next chapter examines in detail the rationale, benefits, and procedures of this form, especially as it applies to the elementary grades.

Books
Stories
Reviews (of books, movies, restaurants, products)
Author page (for books)
Directions
Notices
Newspaper articles
Reports
Interviews
"How to" manuals
Advice columns
Surveys
Questionnaires
Evaluations
Instructions
Essays
Advertisements
Memos
Poems
Diaries
Scripts/plays
Comic strips
Rules
Proposals
Invitations
Journals
Crossword puzzles

Dedications
Brochures
Newsletters
Anthologies
Yearbooks
Book blurbs
Thank you notes
Greeting cards
Summaries
Recipes
Lists (for shopping, gifts, parties, trips, things to do)
Calendars
Messages
Bulletins
Posters
Signs
Charts
Letters
Postcards
Conversations
Want ads
Announcements
Song lyrics
Magazine articles
Guides
Assignments
Commercials

Writing Letters

I write letters all the time. I probably write fifteen to twenty letters a week—to friends, to family, to colleagues, to teachers who write to me, to my publisher. I prefer writing and receiving letters to talking on the telephone. After a long day at work interacting with lots of people, I welcome the solitude and peaceful reflection letter writing affords. I enjoy the opportunity to put down on paper thoughts and feelings that may be awkward to express over the phone. And while I usually word process letters that have a professional or business audience, I always write by hand when I want to be personal, despite my poor handwriting. I also enjoy saving and savoring letters I receive and rereading them at a later date. I treasure special letters from my husband, my children, my father, my aunt, my principal, my good friends, and my colleagues.

Letter writing is a necessary life skill. If we are to communicate effectively, we must be able to organize our thoughts on paper. For giving and receiving information, we all rely on letters to some extent. Currently, with fax machines in most offices, the letter or memo—often handwritten for quick transport—is being employed on a regular basis.

As teachers, we must demonstrate our own writing processes for students before we can expect them to take the process seriously and invest their full energy in it. Recently I wrote a letter to *The New York Times* in response to a short article I had read in the "Hers" section of the Sunday magazine section. I brought in my rough drafts and my revisions and used a third grade class as an audience for feedback on the clarity of the piece. Later I showed the children the final, finished copy with the changes I had made. Students are always amazed to learn that teachers have to work at writing, that most people do not get a written message right the first time, and that their insights can be helpful to adult writers.

Another time third grade teacher Lee Sattelmeyer, who uses letter writing across the curriculum, and I were reviewing a draft of a letter he had composed for the school's upcoming open house for parents. The letter, which was largely a philosophical statement, was to be an important cover sheet focusing on the year's curriculum (see Figure 16–4 in Chap. 16). As we were talking, I realized that this was the kind of activity students need to witness. They need to see and hear our thinking, our exchange of ideas, and our actual changes. They need to know that the final, perfectly typed version they would take home to their parents had gone through a long thinking process that began as a draft. Lee and I moved our initial private conversation over planning time into the classroom and made it an authentic demonstration for the children. While we worked out the confusions and inconsistencies of the piece in front of them, they witnessed our struggle to clarify the writing and our eventual satisfaction with its improvement.

When I am invited into a classroom by a teacher who wants to become involved in process writing or who is concerned about the poor writing of her students, I often begin with letter writing for a real purpose. Part of the reason letter writing works so well in the classroom is that it is short and focused. The amount of drafting, revising, and editing is limited because letters are rarely more than a page or two in length. As such, students are willing to invest time in the entire process. Some letters, of course, such as thank you notes to another class that need to be sent right away, are sent as first drafts, and some teachers stamp these "unedited."

Writing a Letter of Appreciation

In one fourth grade class, the teacher, Debbie Schaedlich, and I decided to have the children write letters of appreciation to a person in the school or community. We discussed the idea that most of us write or call to complain when something goes wrong, but we take for granted a job done well. We asked the children to think about thanking someone for something that had never been acknowledged. We began by brainstorming possible people we could write to, and we came up with this partial list: mailman, custodian, teacher, neighbor, coach, principal, librarian, school secretary, school nurse, parent-teacher association, policeman, mayor.

Figure 8–3   *Draft of a Letter to the School Custodians*

March 20, 1989

Dear Custodial Staff,

I can't tell you how pleasant it was to walk into the building last Monday! Things really sparkled, and it really lifted my spirits considerably. The floors really shined, the hallways were cleared, and I liked the smell of the wax and soap. For one Monday morning I felt really happy to be here. I know you had to come and work over the weekend after working all week. Once again, I really appreciate all of your hard work.

Sincerely,
Mrs. Schaedlich

Debbie began by writing a draft of her letter on the overhead projector. While the children looked on, she wrote and thought aloud of possible people she could write to and then decided to write to the school custodians. Her draft is shown in Figure 8–3. Because the teacher modeled the process and the children could engage meaningfully in the task, they wanted to complete the assignment, and they wanted to do it well (see Figures 8–4 and 8–5). They saw that there was a reason to have clear sentences, proper punctuation and grammar, and legible handwriting. All the letters were stamped and mailed after they had been revised and taken to final copy. A number of the students received personal replies to their letters, demonstrating to them the power of letter writing.

Forms of Letter Writing

Letter writing can take many forms: letters to pen pals (students in other schools or younger students writing to older students in the same school), parents, students who are sick, classmates who have moved; notifications of and invitations to

Figures 8-4 and 8-5   Fourth-graders' Letters of Appreciation

April 11, 1989

Dear Little Caesers,

Thank you for giving us two pizzas for the price of one. There are mounds of cheese, and lots of toppings on both pizzas. Plus, there is a very short wait when you pick up the pizza. The pizza tastes great! I was wondering where you get that great taste? You should have more restaurants in Shaker Hts.

Sincerely,

Sam R.

Figure 8-5

4/11/89

Dear PTA,

I'm sorry I didn't get around to telling you how much I appreciated the ballet troupe you sponsored. It was great. I felt like I might be a dancer when I grow up. In March I got real excited because the ballet was coming to Fernway. My favorite part was when the dancers did those big short kicks. Well anyways the ballet was very good.

Yours truly,
Mark S.

174

classroom and school-wide events; and, of course, letters to favorite authors. We have checked with librarians for a list of authors (and their addresses) who generally respond to children, and we have also written to them in care of their publishers. Our students have recently received replies from Norman Bridwell, Joanna Hurwitz, Bill Peet, and Steven Kellogg.

Taking the time to write a personal letter demonstrates caring and personal interest. Second grade teacher Elaine Weiner writes letters to all of her students several weeks before school begins. She introduces herself, tells something about her summer, and says how much she is looking forward to meeting the student. Each year several parents comment on the impact the letters had on them and their children.

Writing a business letter   As an authentic way for students to learn to write business letters, Lee Sattelmeyer uses writing a business letter as part of his social studies unit on the community. After studying and discussing the various parts of their local community, students are asked to choose a person or institution they want to know more about and write a letter of inquiry. Several students, who previously had done little writing, put great efforts into their letters: Their questions and interest were genuine. Most students received replies and were delighted. See Figures 8–6 and 8–7 for a typical letter and a response.

Figure 8–6   An Information-Seeking Letter

Mike Andrikanich
Lomond Elementary
17917 Lomond Blvd.
Shaker Hts, OH 44122
December 9, 1987

Heinen's Supermarket
17021 Chagrin Blvd
Shaker Hts Ohio 44120

Dear Heinen's supermarket,
    My name is Mike Andrikanich. I'm a student at Lomond school in shaker Heights. I'm in third grade.
    My class is studying communities. I would like to know how you got the name Heinens. How does your business affect our community?
    I would like to know how long you have been in Shaker and why you wanted to work in Shaker Heights. How many people work at Heinen's? Thank you for spending time reading this letter.

                    Sincerely,
                    Mike Andrikanich

Figure 8-7   Response to a Student's Letter

December 22, 1989

Mr. Mike Andrikanich
Lomond Elementary School
17917 Lomond Blvd.
Shaker Heights, Ohio 44122

Dear Mike,

My grandfather, Joseph Heinen, started Heinen's as a butcher shop over 55 years ago. His first store was right down the street from where our present store is today.

Our present store is much different from his store, but the purpose is the same - to serve the community with the finest foods at a reasonable cost. Over sixty people work full and part-time to achieve that aim.

We intend to serve Shaker Heights in the years to come and hopefully in another few years we will be able to do it from a new store.

Sincerely,

Jeff Heinen

Jeffrey Heinen

JH/bjm

One form of business letter that has been very effective for engaging students in writing is the informal business letter to obtain information. Some fourth grade students who were interested in the possibility of getting published wrote to sources that publish student writing. They received a sheet listing the name and address of and general information about reputable sources that publish children's work. (For sources, see Seminoff, 1990, and Stoll, 1990.) Out of a genuine need to find out what publishers want, each child selected a source to write to. Students are always more motivated to write when they know there is a chance for publication. In this case, the act of letter writing helped students realize that publication was within the realm of possibility. (See Appendix G for publishers' guidelines for students.)

We began by brainstorming possible topics and questions to include in the letters. See Figure 8–8 for a whole-class brainstorming. Then each student drafted a letter using the business letter format laid out in the language text. Using peer response groups—after many whole-class demonstrations—students revised their letters.

Figure 8-8   Fourth Grade Class Brainstorming Session

Business letter that's friendly
What kinds of things you publish
    nonfiction, fiction, poetry - all
        kinds? bibliography
are you interested in 4th gr. writing?
any particular kind of story?
illustrations - who makes them? Drawings? photographs?
    necessary?
audience - for little kids, what grades?
    age of author
format - typed or handwritten
    length - would take 2 p. story
    story - lots of detail?
        table of contents
        setting
        description
        dialogue
can we choose the kind of print we want?
If you don't like my story, will you send it back?
Will you make changes in my story?
    suggestions for my writing?
Can you send in more than 1 piece of writing?
If accepted, how long till published?
    deadline to get story in?
    dedication allowed?
    title?
Can there be more than 1 author in a story?

Revising. With the students' permission, several fourth-graders' drafts were photocopied, made into transparencies, and shared with the whole class on the overhead projector. First, I modeled my thinking processes aloud (as described in "Modeling Response," pp. 56–57). About a half dozen teacher demonstrations of the response process were given before students met in peer groups to conference with each other. The peer group conferencing was effective for this situation because the format and guidelines were limited enough for students to deal with.

Editing. The responsibility for editing was put on the students. First, we did a whole-class shared writing of what they needed to look for in the editing process. With some teacher probing, we came up with a comprehensive list (see Figure 8–9). Because students came up with the items, as opposed to being told them by the

Figure 8-9   Editing Checklist from a Whole-Class Shared Writing

EDITING

1. Check for misspelled words.
   a. Circle them.
   b. Try to spell those words correctly.
      Ask someone.
      Look up in the dictionary.
      Sound it out.
      Try writing it another way until it "looks" right.

2. Check for punctuation. Reread.
   Use a comma
         after your greeting.
         after your closing.
         between two sentences, before "and" or "but."
         between words in a series.
   Use a period (.), question mark (?), or exclamation mark (!) at the
         end of a sentence.

3. Check for capitalization.
   The first letter of the first word in greeting or closing
   Titles (magazine, book)

4. Indent the first line of every paragraph.

5. Check your format.
   In the business letter, the heading and closing are lined up under each other on the
         right side.
   The publication title and greeting are lined up on the left.
   Skip a line
         after the heading, greeting.
         between body of letter and closing.

6. Check for abbreviations.
   Write out each word completely—streets, numbers, months, states.

7. Neatness
   Spacing
   Best handwriting
   Legibility

8. Clarity
   Stick to the subject.
   Check to be sure you have used the best wording.
   Be sure everything makes sense.

9. Have a friend check your paper before you give it to senior editor (teacher).

teacher, they became more engaged in the editing process and took greater responsibility for their papers. The editing chart remained posted in the classroom for reference, and the classroom teacher and I were firm about not making corrections for students that they could make themselves. Students were also referred to the language arts textbook as a resource for checking format and conventions for letter writing.

Students who have become accustomed to having the teacher find and correct errors do not initially take the editing task seriously. Many students quickly brought their self-edited letters to us as "complete" when there were many editorial conventions that still needed correcting. We gently put the responsibility back on them with questions and comments such as "Take a look at number 2 on our editing chart. Do you have commas where they need to be?" Or, "You need to check the language arts textbook for the correct format of a letter. Notice how the heading is set up." Or, "I still see some misspelled words that I know you can find. Take another, more careful look."

After students have been sent back to proofread a few times, they get the message that it is their job to do the work. One technique that has worked beautifully is to put a Post-it note on the paper with a comment such as "Check the first paragraph for spelling and punctuation," or to note correctly the misspelled words on the Post-its. Teachers are amazed that when they are consistent about refusing to do the work for students, the students eventually assume accountability for the task and are capable of doing much more than had previously been thought. (See Figure 8–10 for an example of a student's draft of his letter.) Having students take ownership for the editing process takes time. In my experience, even with teacher demonstrations, students need at least several months to take responsibility for a process their teachers have traditionally assumed.

For teachers used to taking most of the responsibility for making corrections, shifting the responsibility to the students is not an easy transition. One third grade teacher noted,

> Slowly, I'm becoming more comfortable with giving the editing process over to the students, but it's been very painful. I'm so used to doing most of the work, and trusting them to do it has been unbelievably hard for me. Initially, it seems easier if I just make the corrections, but I see now that they just keep depending on me to do it, and in the long run that's not effective for their learning.

Once teachers do shift the responsibility, they feel freed. Fourth grade teacher Nancy Schubert comments, "I used to spend my evenings with a red pencil. Now that the kids do most of the work, I have some time to read professional books and children's books in the evenings."

Teachers' expectations for editing will vary depending on the age of the students and the writing purposes. However, for all grade levels we need to be careful not to emphasize editing too soon in the writing process. Before dealing with editing, we want to guide students to write interesting, clear content that reflects personal voice and imagination.

Writing Stories

Children, like all writers, write best about what they know. Writing fictional stories seems to work most successfully when children have been immersed in

Figure 8-10   A Student Takes Ownership of the Editing Process

literature and language and can utilize authors for demonstrations of quality writing.

I worked with Brenda Spivey's fourth grade students, who were writing stories for an upcoming "Young Authors' Conference." Before the students began writing, we talked about how writers write from experience. The kinds of stories the children later wrote dealt with real problems for their age group—moving to a new house, making new friends, fighting with a sibling, getting braces, having problems with a teacher.

Planning for Writing Stories

I talked with students first about how authors usually have some general plan for their stories before they begin to write. Some of us have found that having students create a visual plan before they begin to write works particularly well. A terrific idea for "picturing" the character was developed by fourth grade teacher Joan Servis. The technique is excellent for getting students to think and plan for character development. Students are asked to visualize their main character by drawing a picture of him or her, making brief notes about the character, and perhaps even drawing the character in a setting (see Figure 8–11).

Brenda first created her own character on large chart paper and talked aloud as she demonstrated in front of her students. Then students talked about the kinds of characters they could create. Representing the character physically seems to help students get to know a character— his or her attributes, features, personality traits, motivations. Brenda and I also noted that because students knew one another's

Figure 8-11   Visualizing the Main Character

characters through the pictures and brief accompanying notes, subsequent suggestions to peers for revisions were specific and helpful.

After students' main character(s) were discussed and shared with the teacher and peers for feedback, students were expected to complete a storymap before they began writing. Again Brenda demonstrated first by creating her own storymap.

The storymapping was an important next step because it forced students to think through the main problem in the story, the main happenings, and how the story might conclude (see Figures 8–12 and 8–13 for examples). We and the students found that taking the time to plan out the characters and story encouraged more thoughtful, better organized, and more interesting story writing. As a result of conferencing with students one-to-one before they began writing, stories had better focus and development. Storymapping eliminated boring, episodic stories that rambled with no solid plot or resolution.

After the students drafted chapters, they read them to their peers and the teacher in whole-group and small-group conferences. Responding to a student's writing was modeled first by the teacher. The piece was read in its entirety; then, during a second reading, notes were taken to give feedback to the writer (described on p. 56).

While peers can be used in the response process, my personal bias is that the

Figures 8–12 and 8–13   Storymapping, in Planning for Story Writing

Figure 8–13

SAN FRANCISCO

Sarah Kim
Age 10
is Korean-American
has 2 brothers
Parents born in Seoul Korea
born in San Francisco, California
now lives in Cleveland, Ohio
ice skates
plays piano and flute
favorite food is pizza
has black hair and brown eyes

Story Mapping
Grace Lee   April 17, 1990
                Sarah
Problem: is having trouble
making friends after moving.

1. Intro.

2. People make fun of her.

3. make friends with new girl
who is like her.

4. People understand her
better.

Resolution: Makes new friends.

183

teacher is needed to guide the questions and comments. I have found the most effective response groups to be four to eight students sitting around a table with the teacher. Students note first what they think is best about the writing and then offer suggestions for improvement. The teacher demonstrates and guides the process. "It is a fallacy to think that kids can ask the kinds of questions that can evoke exciting thinking," says Mary Krogness.

Students' Observations after Revising Stories

After demonstrating revision with my own writing and with students' writing and assisting students to put revision into practice with their stories for a "Young Authors' Conference," I asked Brenda Spivey's fourth-graders if they would choose to revise in future writings. Remarkably, every student answered "yes," in spite of the fact that revision had taken lots of time and was hard work. One student said, "I'd want to make my story so good that everyone would want to read it, and you have to revise to write like that."

Here are some other typical comments:

SHARON: Revising really helped me see where I needed to make changes. It helped me cut out some parts that didn't matter or belong.

ANDREA: Without revising, the story is just not done. I didn't feel good about my story until I got some response. Revising was kind of hard, but it helped make my story better.

ADAM: Now that we've done all this revision and I understand the process, I'd probably give a new story to more than one person to read.

MARK: My story didn't sound good at first. I was jumping around all over the place. The comments I got from classmates really helped me fix up my story and make it better.

Because revision is often a difficult concept for students to grasp and apply, I wanted to hear how students defined revision after they had been immersed in the process. Some responses included:

- Suggesting things to people to make the story better.
- Getting new ideas about what you might change.
- Helping someone make a story more understandable.
- Making your story better by having others look it over so readers will understand it.

Several students went on to comment that recently when reading books they found themselves thinking about changes authors should have made. I found that insight remarkable! At nine and ten years of age they were now reading like writers, critically noticing authors' use of language:

- When I got mixed up in one chapter, I was thinking what the author could have done to make it clearer.
- Parts of my book were confusing, and I was thinking the writer needed to do a better job explaining.

Using books they were reading independently during sustained silent reading, other students had spontaneously begun using Post-its to mark specific passages that were particularly well written—or not well written—to read aloud to the class. The revision process had come full circle: We had started with writing, and the students took the process into reading, where they began thinking about how authors shape their words.

Evaluation: Teachers' Attitudes

When a teacher moves from being writing director to writing facilitator, students' writing improves and teachers' enjoyment of the process increases.

Brenda Spivey comments:

> The most important thing for me was that it took away my role as goddess of writing. Before, I was in charge of doing it all. Students would write ten to fifteen pages of boring stories, and then it was my job to revise and edit those awful stories. Now, finally, I don't have to have total control. I gave that job back to the students. I'm still involved in every story, but more as a guide and facilitator. My old attitude of "the teacher will fix it for you" is gone. Giving students ownership of the process has been very significant. The quality of writing is a lot better, and it's been a relief not to have everything fall on me.

Dana Noble, a high school English teacher who recently began to move away from his traditional mode toward implementing reading-writing workshop (Atwell, 1987), comments:

> I've felt more successful this year than I have in years. Students' writing has far exceeded what I expected. In the past, I gave writing assignments, allowed some time in class for students to start writing, and assigned the rest as homework. Final copies were turned in and graded. Until this year, I hardly looked at a draft.
>
> This year, kids do all their writing in class. That caused me a lot of stress at first. I couldn't stand seeing them not be productive. At first, I was listening only to the noise in the room and was failing to listen to what was being said. It seemed as though some kids were just "messing around," but when I finally looked at their work, I couldn't believe the improvement. It hit me that I didn't teach that. I've not taught topic sentence and paragraph this year, and I think the writing is more lively. Something really happened when I gave kids time and freedom to write and respond in class.
>
> Also, allowing kids choice has had tremendous impact on their writing. For the first time, I've had important pieces due where every child has turned in assignments. That never happened before. I've allowed students to choose their own format for writing and to collaborate in writing, and the quality of writing is the best I've ever received. The kids seem more aware of audience, too. Another change is that I no longer write on their final copies. I make my comments on Post-its or in pencil.
>
> Also, for the first time, I've started every piece of writing that I've expected them to do. That has helped me a lot with realistic expectations. I've discovered how hard it is to finish things. In the past, I've been strict about having kids meet deadlines. Now I see they need more time, and I give it to them.
>
> I went through a period of feeling, "Am I really teaching anything?" If it

wasn't quiet and orderly and the teacher directing the discussion, it was hard for me to believe anything worthwhile was going on. I still have to stop myself and just listen to what the kids are really saying. I still worry that some teachers look at me and think that I'm weakening the curriculum.

Reflections on Whole Language: Two Teachers' Letter Writing

High school English teacher Holly Burgess began corresponding with me in November 1989 after I presented a workshop on whole language to secondary teachers. Then she and I met to discuss changes she was ready to make in her teaching, including sharing more responsibility with students. At the same time, Holly began reading *In the Middle* by Nancie Atwell and *Clearing the Way* by Tom Romano, and she began to incorporate reading-writing workshop into her daily classes.

Since my full-time teaching at the elementary level left me little time to interact with high school teachers, our correspondence afforded us an opportunity to share and reflect on daily happenings and changes. The following are excerpts from some very long letters over the course of a year. Holly's letters are in regular type and mine are in italics.

November 1, 1989

Thanks for your time and encouragement yesterday (and candy bar!) Now for today's report:

Listening dialogue [discussing what good listeners do] with students went well first period! They covered all the important points and I didn't pass out the hand-out on listening. (Return to control . . . I couldn't resist r-e-a-d-i-n-g it to them. What a waste! What a lesson to me!)

. . . anyway, asked students to sustain a 15-minute write on whatever was on their minds most this A.M., talked about focus, writing what was foremost. Without exception, all were writing for 25 minutes and only one had stopped by the time the bell rang. Ready for some listening partners and "visioning-re-visioning" tomorrow.

November 2

See some real s-l-o-w down with the re-visioning stage. Students appear to think that they are done at this point, doing the sharing as an exercise in isolation, that a re-visioning is really a re-copying. Will do a modeling tomorrow with my writing and with the class as my listening partners for questions and feedback. . . . Is it merely the control issue that boxes me into thinking there is not much "productive" time? . . . I'm a teeter-totter!—weighed down at one end with time on task and on the other with providing a climate free and open enough to allow for the "dead" time that is part of creativity.

November 3

Congratulations on the successful listening dialogue. At least you realized it was a waste of time reading your hand-out to them. I find I learn best when a lesson bombs, so it's never a waste. Really, it's an opportunity for growth. Just the fact that you're examining your own teaching is highly commendable.

Perhaps the re-visioning would be more successful if the students knew and wanted publication. It's important they're revisioning for a genuine purpose—letters that will actually be sent, pieces that will be put into a class booklet, etc. I know this is very hard, but the authentic use part is powerful and motivating.

November 3

. . . I want to believe in the process, but am amazed at my "need" for immediate gratification of self as a teacher that is somehow, probably mistakenly, more "actual" in quiz scores, test grades, you know, all that "measurable" stuff.

November 6

About first period . . . some students were eager to get folders and get writing, more were interested in listening partners. Had a group of three who chased me away. One of my best story-tellers is at least started. He doesn't focus well in the classroom, but has more than once entertained with his descriptive exploits. I will have to review the process again tomorrow. Many are asking questions like, "What do I do now?" or "Do I have to copy it over?" I feel afloat, or better yet, poised on the high dive and I don't swim real well! One student asked if it was okay to write some poetry. It's all real tentative, or perhaps I'm real tentative.

9th period. . . . Students need constant reassurance that whatever they write is okay. I am made uncomfortable by the judgment that English form and fear of it has severely crippled their *believing* themselves to be writers. Need help with the publishing piece. Some threatened to not write at all if I was going to MAKE them publish, even for a class publication.

November 10

It has been an exhausting week! Would like to *see* a real, live model of writing-reading workshop. Seems like "stuff" and "management" and too small a room and my own hang-ups, history and up-tightness keep getting in the way. . . . I thought I had been working on this "letting go" process for years. Now I have discovered how little letting go I'm willing to do.

Perhaps we can meet again soon.

November 14

I have just finished reading the responses to The Learning Tree *by Gordon Parks (Harper & Row, 1963), and I am incredulous! Your students have connected their lives with literature at the very highest level—to help them make sense of their own lives. They write honestly and passionately. They expose their vulnerabilities; you are to be congratulated. They couldn't write so genuinely without the risk taking, caring environment you have obviously created and fostered. Without exception, each piece went right to my core being. These kids are struggling to make sense of their complicated, and often tragic, lives. I see that as the highest level of literacy and education—finding relevance in school to the real world. . . .*

I liked that you didn't "mark" on their writing and left it intact. You could use Post-its to comment on parts that especially grabbed you or to ask questions you have.

You're on the right track. The kids need to know how powerful their writing is because it's authentic and on topics that are highly important to them. Pat yourself on the back for all your small successes and new risks you are taking. Give yourself time. Change that is real and long lasting happens slowly, as you well know.

November 15 (first period)

Started class by ''modeling.'' . . . When I wouldn't talk, but would just write, they eventually got the message. When Farris asked me if I was sure I was all right, Coop said, ''Aren't you going to get the 'status of the class''' —and that was just after introducing the term two days ago. Discovered that I am just as impatient with re-visioning as my students are! There always seems to be something better or easier to do or ''more important'' than taking another look at a piece of my own writing.

It was soooo good to get your letter this A.M.! Thanks for all the affirmation. There is just so much to do and I keep getting in my own way. I'm usually ''relatively'' well organized, but since this (whatever this is?!) has started I feel scattered and disorganized! The teaching of a skill from the actual writing is wonderful, so why do I judge that it's not enough? What is clearly enough, though, is the positive way some kids are responding to class, whether they are reading the book of their choice, writing, or listening to a friend re-visioning. . . .

November 21

. . . I was absolutely knocked out by your students' writing—authentic, powerful, rich, unbelievable! I love the way you took the prose and helped the kids put it in poetry form. I can see why the kids were thrilled. Typing it, too, makes the writing seem more important. . . . I'm so impressed your kids feel safe enough with you to write this honestly. (I'm sure much of it could be published.) . . . [See Figure 8–14 for an example.]

You're taking so many risks; I really admire your gutsiness and intelligence. You're doing it in a highly professional way—really thinking about your teaching and learning and not just trying a new ''activity.''

November 27

. . . I resisted the impulse to PLAN little ditties for my substitute and gave her only the ''freedom'' that I had tried to establish. Although she reported that ''some'' refused to work for her, it seems that they were the same ''some'' that generally refuse to work, read, write, cooperate, etc. In other words, the students kept their commitment to the experience.

November 29

. . . Taught a mini-lesson on good leads that seemed to go okay.

I get lost in Atwell's sheets of accountability. See the need for more of it, but at the moment it is a piece that I am unable to keep up with. . . . Have enclosed a poem by one of my seniors. This is a girl who didn't think she could write. Also had another senior ask me if there was a limit to the length of his story. Made me laugh. I've been remiss about my own writing these last two weeks, and although I clearly see the difference it makes to students, I just can't seem to get started again. . . .

November 30

How wonderful that you submitted the student writing to a possible place for publication. Give yourself credit for everything you are doing. Try to stop bashing

Figures 8–14, 8–15, and 8–16   Poems by High School Juniors

In the ninth grade people said I looked like a Hawaiian.
They cracked their jokes.
No harm done.
In the tenth grade people called me a Mexican.
They cracked their jokes.
My eleventh grade year, people called me a China-man or a Jap.
They crack their jokes.
Maybe a tiny bit of harm done.

My first step-mother was from Thailand.
She's the one who took care of me.
My father and her are divorced,
But I still visit her.
I feel comfortable calling her "Mom,"
But the wife my father has now, I call her "Doris."
It's not like I don't like her or anything like that,
But she's not the one who raised me.
She's still a cool lady.

Racism.
My father is an Afro-American,
My mother (my real one) is from Egypt.
My father has had many racial conflicts...
Two white friends wanted to ride their bikes with my father.
They rode and they had fun (I guess) and
Some men stopped them and asked,
"Why are you riding around with a nigger?"
They tried to get away,
But a man threw a rock causing
My father's white friend to fall off.
The men then beat him up.

To this day my father wonders why
He didn't go back and save his white friend.

Another example.
When my father was in the Air Force (he still is).
He was shipped to Thailand,
Where he met my step-mother.
He was at a party with some of the Thai ladies.
They asked him where his tail was.
They believed that all Black men grew tails at night.

I've been through a lot of racist comments in my life,
But I'm not going to let them stop me from shining.
It's like the Bible said,
"We are a split image of God"
And that's the way it is.

> Joseph Dee Crawford,
> Junior

yourself for what you're not *doing. Whole language focuses on the strengths, not the deficits—ours too, not just the kids'. You've taken some huge risks with some wonderful results. It all takes time. . . .*

As far as Atwell and anything else you're reading, just because it's in a book and by a "guru" doesn't mean it will work for you or is right for you. Make adjustments based on what you believe. Trust your intuition.

December 4

Plodding along on this end. Can't seem to get a re-write together to model for them. I hear myself using their excuses! How difficult it is being a *student-*teacher and having a life too!

Have included some new writing of my junior, level 2 Humanities kids. Aren't they wonderful?

December 6

. . . I love your kids' writing—absolutely splendid, heart-wrenching stuff. Wonderful you're getting it typed. Good to hear you say they are "wonderful." They are! [See Figures 8–15 and 8–16 for examples of poems.]

January 11, 1990

. . . My seniors have "completed" this writing project unit, and although some of the pieces of writing are quite good, their commitment to task has been less so. The bind of judging good writing against or with a look to quantify chafes. And individual knowledge of students' limitations makes me feel highly subjective about the grades. I will have a writing conference (well, actually, an overview conference) with each student next week for decision-making about the grade for the unit. I had hoped to have built-in high grades and am feeling a tug downward about my unmet expectations, which probably shouldn't impinge as much on their grades as on my own! . . .

I need to put some requests in writing for next school year regarding writing/reading approach and changes that I want to make—would like to have you *see* my room and discuss some housekeeping. For me this needs to "happen" before the more important changes of my own efforts, commitment. With fifteen long-legged seniors moving round the room, conferencing with others, areas of quiet or not-so-quiet tested my patience and concentration. I am more keenly aware of my limitations as well as huge areas I wish to change (areas of geography as well as soul-searching!). . . .

January 12

. . . I'm most eager to come over to see your room and your kids and see you! . . . It's wonderful you're thinking about changes for next year already. . . .

Your debate with yourself about grading and quantity of writing is a struggle. Have you thought about having kids evaluate themselves before you meet with *them? Put in writing the criteria you use for grading, and ask them to give themselves a grade and give supportive comments for that grade. I think you'll be surprised. It's been my experience that the kids grade themselves tougher than we do. It could make grading easier for you.*

I'm feeling unusually stressed—trying to write every day after work when I'm really too exhausted. Can't remember if I told you I'm writing a follow-up to Transitions *for Heinemann—contract deadline late September—very exciting but masochistic too. Writing is so hard—especially without adequate time. . . .*

Figure 8–15

Leave me alone

I'm not at home.
I'm not on the phone.
Please—
just leave me alone.

I'm not here.
I'm not there.
I'm somewhere.

I'm fine.
Believe this is true—
Don't call me.
I'll call you.

Orlando Makupson 12-89

Figure 8 16

Life

Born, buck-naked, out of my mother's womb
A man, cooped in a rubber room.

Times changin', time flies.
Caterpillars turn into butterflies.

A kitten grows up to be a tiger.
I grow up to be a writer.

Children grow through puberty
and they reach maturity.

Brian Cunningham   12 80

February 23

. . . I read and modeled with them [11th-graders] an excerpt from Claude Brown's *Manchild in the Promised Land* (Macmillan, 1965), and they were able to find many points in the "story" to wonder about, reflect on, connect with in a personal way. But even more wonderful are the requests over the next two days by five! Count them! Five! adolescent boys to READ *Manchild*. I had two copies of my own to lend, one actually borrowed from library and I will have two of the school's copies next week. They are openly talking about how "live" it is and if you were the least bit "liberal" in the sixties . . . it's still pretty "bold" today! This is basically an I-hate-to-read group.

Am trying to begin (God, how tentative could one possibly sound!) a combined Atwellian concept with a more traditional approach. Haven't thought it through yet and would like to get some feedback from you. I would like to teach—or whatever term works—*A Gathering of Old Men* by Ernest Gaines (Knopf, 1983) to my seniors with a dining room table kind of approach. I don't know if it is possible to do with an old, traditional all-class kind of read, but I have some sanity reasons to want more control with these groups, one of which is graying my hair and brain daily! . . .

March 3

. . . What a joy to read about your students requesting to read. BRAVO! You're doing a lot right if that's happening.

Let's talk about what you're trying—"Atwell plus traditional approach." We can talk by phone or meet after school any day.

So glad you did come to our Monday night district support group. Believe me, you're in the worst stage now. Getting started is the hardest part. It's going to get easier.

. . . One of the most exciting things about moving toward whole language is the reality that it's so hard that you can't do it without collegial support. Teachers, instead of being isolated, wind up collaborating more.

March 6

I can meet you any day after school but Monday or Tuesday. Would like to talk about *Gathering Old Men* approach with you. . . . . The current plan is that we are having SSR on M, W, F (with the exception of the first 15 min. of M and F for journal writing). Tues. and Thurs. are discussion days. Any student who may be behind the general outline of pages to be read may read during this time with no penalty and join the discussion when caught up in reading. One of the already assigned journal entries for a week will be a "literary letter" to me or to another student. Students are encouraged to keep a sheet beside them while reading to jot down any questions. It is my hope that discussion will help lead to questioning. Have one excellent reader who is half-finished with the book (in 3 days) and is sharing with me some of the humor—which is often missed by my students.

No tests or quizzes. . . .

May 3

. . . Thanks for sharing your American Family unit. I like the relevance to students' lives and your communication to parents, too. A couple of thoughts that may be too late for you to do anything with:

1. I hope you also do a family history and demonstrate the possibilities, for example, writing a family story yourself.

2. I think it's important to give students choice, perhaps choosing three out of four parts to do.

3. At completion of unit, perhaps do an evaluation of the project with students. What parts did they like? Suggestions for improvement/change? It will give you an even better format for next year, and allow collaboration with students.

. . .Ha! you laughed about my writing struggles. I've been totally unproductive. I can't believe how little I get done each evening and weekend. I'm feeling really tired. . . .

June 13

>   I devoured "'I Have Never Read Five Books Before in My Life': Reading and Writing Naturally in High School"!!! (in *Portraits of Whole Language Classrooms* [Mills and Clyde, 1990]. I can *see* some of my students writing these same words—and the nonwords, too! . . . think the article is the best synopsis of what I am attempting and have passed it along. . . .

>   Am thinking of beginning the juniors next year with the standby—*The Learning Tree*—it goes well with my students. Help me think of "creative Atwellian approaches"! Haven't decided what to do with my seniors. Since many of them will be students known to me, maybe I won't have too much trouble establishing myself. . . .

>   I am—for the first time ever!—excited about next year in June!

August 31, 1990 (first week of new school year)

>   It has been a good opening! I've included a list of student comments regarding writing. I think their comments are GREAT! . . . My two senior classes have self-selected books and are reading daily. Have begun with reading/writing workshops and am still working out the "structure." . . . I suspect that I am a little slower at jumping in than some, but I think it will help me in the long run to move very slowly. Kids seem very responsive to "ideas" so far, and I am thoroughly enjoying some of the YA fiction. . . . Call when you can.

September 12

>   . . . Classes are going by so well. I am successfully battling the once-in-a-while fear about no tests, quizzes, grades, etc.—at least until it's time for progress and grade cards

>   My biggest fault is that I talk too much and have asked kids to help remind me that whatever I am saying, I have probably spent too much time trying to say it! They are beginning to be glad to oblige. . . .

What comes through in Holly's letters are her struggles to let go of control, her ever-increasing belief in her students and in the reading-writing workshop process, her efforts to incorporate more teacher demonstrating and to give students more choice and flexibility, her desire to create a more workable room environment, and her growth as a teacher moving toward whole language. With the start of a new school year, Holly's voice is more confident and her trust in students greater. She begins by having students self-select books to read the first week of school. She is no longer the same teacher who stated that she "felt like a failure seeing kids so unhappy and so unengaged with school."

I did not really "help" Holly. I provided support, affirmation, and active listening for her risk taking, but she found, and is finding, her own way. Our letter writing served as a way for her to work through some of her dilemmas and confusions and to make personal reflections on her teaching. Teachers in process, at any level, often find that writing down their thoughts serves to clarify the struggle and give them a useful perspective.

Reflections

I no longer believe that writing can be taught. The best we can do as teachers is nurture writing, encourage it, sustain it, and give it time, space, freedom, and room in which to grow. As much as possible, writing purposes, contexts, and audiences must be authentic if we want students to engage in the process. Students must understand and value why they are writing so they see a need for clarity, voice, organization, and even completion.

Perhaps most important, we must be writing models ourselves and also give our students great writing models through literature. Our greatest challenge is becoming risk takers and writers ourselves by making our own writing and thinking visible to our students. For most of us, the shift to valuing writing and making it an integral part of our daily teaching and curriculum is a slow, gradual process. We need to congratulate ourselves whenever we share our own writing with students and whenever we make sincere attempts to write in front of the class or with the class. Until we demonstrate and value the craft ourselves, many students will fail to take writing seriously or to see writing as a tool for thinking and learning.

9

Personal Journal Writing

And one more thing. I am doing good in school.
(Tara's journal, fall of second grade)

Journal writing in the kindergarten

A Look at One Student: Tara

Although Tara was considered one of the lowest-functioning children in first grade at the start of the year, she found her voice and grew as a reader and writer when she had lots of opportunities to write about what was important to her. She was fortunate to be in a classroom where she was immersed in the rich language of stories and had daily opportunities for authentic writing. While most of the writing Tara and other students engaged in happened to take place in a journal, the discussion of personal journal writing—the focus of this chapter—applies to all authentic writing.

The power and benefits of personal journal writing, as well as the impact of literature on writing, are evident when one looks at samples from Tara's journal in first grade (see Figures 9–1 and 9–2). She has moved from random strings of letters (which she stayed with for an entire month) to complete stories and from limited, invented spelling and mechanics to increasing use of conventional mechanics and spelling. Her sense of story has blossomed. Tara has not been formally taught any of these skills, but she has been engaged in authentic language activities in a whole language classroom.

Her confidence at the beginning of second grade is evident in her letter to her parents telling them about open house (see Figure 9–3).

> Mom and Dad,
>
> When you come to open house, I want you to see my dinosaur. And I want you to see my dinosaur hats. And I want you to read my writing journal. And I want you to see my clay dinosaur. And one more thing. I am doing good in school.
>
> From your daughter,
> Tara

Figures 9-1 and 9-2   Samples from Tara's Journal, First Grade

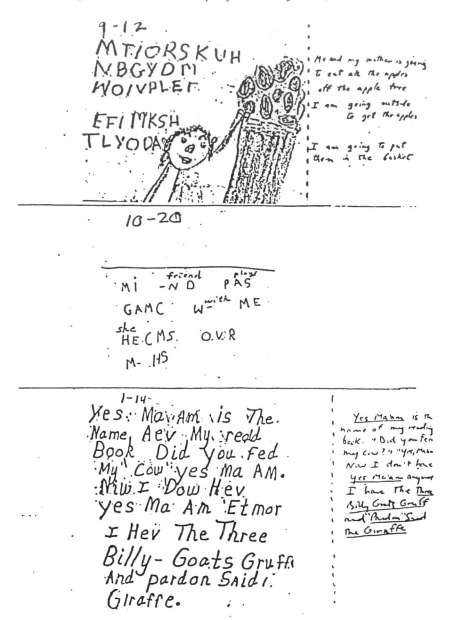

It would be easy to look at Tara's letter (page 198) and see only a child with poor spelling, poor mechanics and poor phonics skills. Fortunately, her second grade teacher saw the strengths in Tara's expressive language in spite of the fact that she still qualified for Chapter 1 because of poor performance on skills subtests of standardized tests. (See Figure 9–4 for a poem Tara wrote and Figure 9–5 for her last entry in second grade before she moved to another school district.)

Tara's second grade teacher described her as above average for content and free expression in writing. Her personal journal writing had helped make that possible.

Figure 9-2

wigglytooth

I Have a Wele. Tof it. Hivt Kam Out Eit Evre Day. I Weglt To See if At Kim Out Eit But At Not Bied To Kam Out I G I Hivf To Wit for a let Logr. I jus Cai't Wat To it. Kum Out Cus I jus Hate to Git it Out.

the hungry hepopolmis. one day a hepopolmis was woikn don the set. il was hungry it ate a red house and a blue and a white. house and a yellou house and thas all. ave the house's he ate then he ate some red. and gray cors but he was sill hungry but he cud fid.

(story continued for several days)

Tara's journal entries included personal stories, stories with literary influences, retellings of stories, poems, letters, and reflections. The journal became a safe and valued place where she could explore language, feelings, and life's happenings in a variety of forms.

Benefits of Journal Writing

For teachers moving toward whole language, journal writing is a component that can be easily implemented wherever teachers happen to be in the transition process. Journals provide a nonthreatening place to explore learnings, feelings, happenings, and language through writing. They also provide opportunities to discover experiences and feelings teachers and students have in common. Teachers who use journal writing have found that when they are sensitive and respectful of students' attitudes, life stories, and learning processes, the children come to value and enjoy journal writing, and journals become an integral part of the curriculum.

I see the power of personal writing as connecting what is significant in children's lives with what goes on in school. Personal journal writing can be a means of validating each child, of saying to each child that what goes on in your life is important, that what you think and feel is relevant, and that everyday events are the things writers write about. Children are full of stories, regardless of their backgrounds, but many of them don't know they have stories to tell. An encouraging teacher can help bring out children's stories and celebrate them. In doing so, we

Figures 9-3, 9-4, and 9-5   Samples from Tara's Journal, Second Grade

Oct. 6
Mom and Dad,
Wen you Came to opne
houuse. I wot you to See
my dase. and I Wot you
to See my dinrsirue
hots and I wot yoo to
redea my widenu gon. and
I wot you to see my
  Caye dinr rue and one
More thege I Im duwene goit
in school. from your drdrea
Tara

Figure 9-4

Nov. 5 .
Blow wind
I See the wind blowin
away I Can see the
wind goin away yes I
Can.. Oh no the wind is
push me away do not
blow me away ok wind .
ok . siad the wind

Figure 9-5

April. 12.

If you ever have a bad dream what will you do. will you hide under your bed or talk to mom or dad about it or dream of something asl. what just what will you do how about read a book.

will you saty up all night no go in eat something or go in snugo up whit your tedebear. how about hide in the cose but something will get you in there

affirm our students, build their self-esteem, and encourage them as writers. Students and teachers also grow to know and respect one another, and a sense of community builds.

When teachers also become part of the journal writing process, our students get to know us better, and we and they see that we are all connected by our humanness. I believe the benefits of personal journal writing are significant for both students and teachers.

• *Promotes fluency in writing*   Teachers note an ease of expression and a greater facility with written language. Dan Kirby (1988) calls the journal "the most consistently effective tool for establishing fluency I have found."

• *Promotes fluency in reading*   The very first reading that some of our young students do is their own writing. When that writing is transcribed, students read it easily because it is their own language, the most predictable text of all.

• *Encourages risk taking*   Knowing they will not be corrected or graded, students write freely, exploring spellings, conventions, language and feelings.

• *Provides opportunities for reflection*   Journals encourage thinking about life and learning. Peter Stillman says, "Think of your journal as being a net for catching shining particles from the day" (Fulwiler, 1987, p. 80).

• *Validates personal experiences and feelings*   Small incidents and life events are viewed as important and relevant to the child's life in and out of school. What the child cares about and values is respected. Writing brings students in closer touch with themselves.

• *Provides a safe, private place to write*   Especially for older students, journals are a place to write for themselves. Sharing is always an option, not a requirement.

• *Promotes thinking and makes it visible*   Having to write thoughts—and learning processes—down forces the learner to recall, re-examine, and organize information. The teacher also sees what has been valued and understood or what the student is confused about.

• *Promotes development of written language conventions*   Teachers note that the sheer quantity of writing in a reading-writing classroom positively influences the correct use of capitalization, punctuation, and grammar. Many children also add chapter headings, titles, page numbers, and indexes; use dialogue; and continue a story from one day to the next without being formally taught.

• *Provides a vehicle for evaluation*   Students can look back through their journals as a way to evaluate their own writing. They can be guided to note their progress in all aspects of writing. Teachers can use journals as one way to check the child's phonics and spelling skills in addition to writing content and style.

• *Provides a record*   Years later, students can look back at their journals and see what was important to them and what they were thinking about at a particular stage in their lives.

Setting the Tone: Introducing Journal Writing

The way journal writing is introduced often determines how receptive students will be to it. By allowing sufficient time for oral brainstorming of possible topics, demonstrating the process by writing ourselves, and placing no value judgments on what students have written and where they may be in the writing process, we set the tone for a positive learning experience.

Without careful introduction, we may turn students off to writing. One upper elementary grade teacher expressed her frustration with the writing of Darius, a new student. Darius had written almost two sentences about playing football, but he had stopped when he couldn't spell "touchdown." It was important to give him the message that he could write.

I stooped down next to Darius so we were at eye level, and I asked him to read me what he had written. Then I asked him some questions about playing football. It was obvious from his smile and easy conversational tone that he was interested in the subject. I asked him if he could write down what he had told me, and he frowned.

ROUTMAN: Did you get a chance to do writing like this—where *you* could decide what to write about—at your old school?

DARIUS: No. The teacher told us what to write.

ROUTMAN: What kind of writing did you do?

DARIUS: Mostly filling in workbook pages or worksheets or copying from the board.

ROUTMAN: Well, in your journal you can write about what you're interested in. You don't need to worry about perfect spelling. Just do the best you can. I see you're stuck on this word; just put down the sounds you hear and go on. Also, your handwriting is beautiful, but in your journal, just think about getting your thoughts down, and try to write a little faster. You don't need to be so concerned about your handwriting.

I stayed next to Darius for a few minutes to encourage him to write down some of the things he had told me. When he hesitated on a word, I reminded him to spell the word as best he could and go on. Based on what he did write and on our conversation, he appeared to be a capable child. His reluctance to write was based on his previous school experiences, not on his lack of ability. It would take time, probably many months, but with demonstration, acceptance, and encouragement Darius would be able to write freely and comfortably in his journal.

With new students, and even with students used to journal writing, allowing enough time to talk about possible topics and demonstrating the journal writing process are critical. It is equally important to be sensitive and accepting, especially when journal writing is first introduced. Students not used to taking risks and selecting their own topics feel especially vulnerable. The teacher who appears disappointed with the first results may be setting the tone for the year by turning students off to writing. Our comments and body language strongly influence not only the quality of our students' writing but also their attitudes toward writing.

Getting Ideas for Topics: The Importance of Demonstrations

Many teachers that incorporate journal writing complain that students' entries quickly become stale and boring. However, teachers find that when they demonstrate through oral sharing and their own writing, the quality of the writing improves dramatically.

As with all demonstrations, once is rarely enough: Usually a demonstration will need to take place many times before more students can apply the concept. If only a few students apply what has been demonstrated, the demonstration has been successful. While demonstrations do not need to take place daily, they do need to occur regularly, as an authentic response to learning-teaching needs.

Valuing Everyday Experiences

When I go into classrooms and demonstrate journal writing, I begin by talking about things I could write about. They are ordinary things but they are important to me: my dog Tobi having fleas, my house needing cleaning, the waffles my husband cooked for breakfast, how I didn't want to get out of bed when the alarm went off, talking by phone with my dear friend Harriet, how worried I am about my aunt who is sick, how I feel about my new haircut. My list of topics is always different, depending on what is going on in my life. I stress that the topics are all things I know and care about and that the students too have things in their lives that they know a lot about.

Talking about what I could write about is the closest I come to being a story-teller. I notice that children are fascinated by the stories in our lives, and I tell mine with gusto. In talking about the waffles my husband made from scratch, I tell about waking up and smelling fresh-brewed coffee—a clue that this would be a lucky day when I wouldn't have to cook breakfast. I talk about how my husband has perfected his recipe and technique after several years. I describe the color and texture of the waffles, the butter melting into the small waffle squares, the delicious taste of hot, pure maple syrup, and my feelings of guilt about eating something so fattening first thing in the morning.

With very young children, my stories and demonstrations are shorter and less involved, but the topics are the same. Illustrations are also included because to know what they want to say young children often need to draw before they write. I want students to see and feel that telling and writing life stories are what writers do, that being a writer doesn't have to mean being a famous author or writing about an exciting place. Most of us haven't taken exciting trips, but we can make writing about ordinary events exciting. Perhaps, above all, I want them to feel that what goes on in their lives is significant. I try to inspire confidence by validating and encouraging what they know and feel and by accepting their best efforts.

Note the difference in Nathan's journal entries at the beginning of second grade when he was self-selecting his own topics but when no demonstrations were taking place. In the first entry, he writes a few sentences about his teacher. The next day, after a demonstration and oral sharing, he realizes he has a story to tell (see Figures 9-6 and 9-7).

I find that after I have demonstrated where my ideas come from and allowed time for oral discussion, children do not have difficulty generating topics. Students prefer and need to select their own topics. One fourth-grader who had previously been assigned topics told me, "I hated that. We had to write on things like 'What did you do over your vacation?' I had absolutely no interest in that."

Figure 9-6   Nathan's Journal Entry Before Demonstration

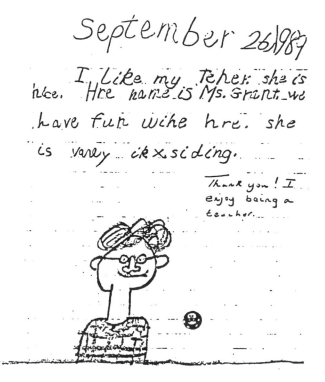

Figure 9-7 Nathan's Journal Entry after Demonstration

The demonstration serves to reinforce the idea that everyday topics are valid. In the spring of the year, in a kindergarten class that was doing journal writing for the first time, I talked about what I could write about—cleaning out my basement, making cookies, having to carry my dog downstairs, being tired—and wound up writing, "I was so tired this morning, I could hardly get out of bed." Following the demonstration, many students wrote about being tired. Other topics they wrote about were eating oatmeal for breakfast, being awakened by a dog barking, having an early Christmas because Grandpa would be away, swinging from a tree in the backyard, getting a new toothbrush.

See Appendix L for "Questions to Think About in Choosing a Writing Topic."

Encouraging Students to Find a Meaningful Topic

I tell students they may write about anything, but I make videos, movies, and television shows off limits unless the experience has had a personal significance for the student. This rule eliminates boring recounting of events. I also encourage students to write about events that have already taken place. When students write about something that is about to happen, they tend to have less to say than when they have already had the experience. Additionally, when I find students writing repetitive accounts about the same topic day after day, I guide them toward a new topic.

Even with demonstrating, there may still be children who have difficulty coming up with topics. Jim Henry, a first grade teacher, notes,

> This past year, after I noticed that students were experiencing difficulty thinking of topics, I looked for opportunities throughout the day to help them generate ideas, and there were many. When the students arrived in the morning excited about something that had happened that morning or the night before I commented, "That would be a great thing to put in your journal!" I commented the same way to students during shared reading experiences when a story or poem prompted reflections on personal experiences.

When journal writing is introduced, and sporadically throughout the year, Jim takes the time to have students share what they are writing about. He then lists the topics that others have written about on the board to serve as an idea stimulator for those having difficulty finding a topic.

Very young children also need to be encouraged that what has happened to them is worthy of writing about. Note the following exchange with a kindergarten student who had begun to write:

KARESA: This isn't so good, but I'm trying my best.

ROUTMAN: What are you going to write about?

KARESA: I am picking apples.

ROUTMAN: Did you really pick apples?

KARESA: No.

ROUTMAN: Why don't you write about something you really did? How about when you made applesauce this morning? What could you say?

KARESA: The applesauce was mushy and icky.

What difference in language when the story was genuine! Karesa was very proud of herself, as exhibited by her big smile.

There is a marked difference in children's writing when topics are assigned and when children can choose their own. See Figures 9–8 and 9–9 for two third-graders' journal entries on two consecutive school days. The first entries, on an assigned topic, are limited and boring. The second entries, done the following day after a demonstration, are more interesting and have a personal voice.

New students who are not used to journal writing and selecting their own topics will need lots of time to take ownership of their writing. The kinds of writing and demonstrations that took place in a previous school are easily detectable by examining a child's writing. When I asked a first-grader who entered midyear if she got to write in first grade, she said "yes." When I asked what kind of writing she got to do, she replied, "handwriting." Her handwriting was fine, but her content was limited and boring (see Figure 9–10). Even at the first grade level, such students may take months before they feel free enough to write in their journals. Figure 9–11 is a journal entry by a first-grader in the same class who has been journal writing daily since September.

Figures 9–8 and 9–9   Third-graders' Journal Entries on Consecutive Days

When nothing seems to work   For students who still have difficulty coming up with a topic, I suggest techniques that have worked for me:

- *Look around the room and outside the window. Something you see may trigger a thought or memory.*

    When I look up at the ceiling, it reminds me of the time the plaster crashed down from our bathroom ceiling in the middle of the night. Looking outside at the trees makes me think about all the leaves that need to be raked in my yard. (See Figure 9–12 for a fourth-grader's entry after he noticed a styrofoam plate on the teacher's desk.)

- *Think back to a special memory—a birthday, holiday, or family outing—and put yourself in the event. How were you feeling? What do you see happening?*

    Oral sharing of some of these memories, before journal writing, often gets students thinking about their own special memories.

- *If all else fails, begin writing, "I can't think of anything to write about" and keep writing about that.*

Figure 9-9

> 11-7-89
>
> If I was president every-
> body can have all the
> Nintenda games and live in
> manchints.

> Nov, 10, 1984
> One time I was going over
> my grandmother house and I
> had a dog. 5 years ago my
> dog was not there so I said
> where is my dog and she
> said we gave the dog away
> so I went in the the room
> and start crying and I was
> so mad I was yeling at
> my grandmother and I did not
> forgive her for a year and
> I start messing with her dog
> and I said what did he
> do so she said he bit the
> groad and I was jumping on
> the chair I was so I was
> about to run away. now that was
> painful.

Sometimes students begin writing by writing that they have nothing to write about, which helps trigger an idea. For young children, a prompt on the board such as, "I like _____" or "I wish _____" may encourage them to finish the thought.

Every once in a while a student will be unable to write, and I accept that. I have days when getting words down on paper is so difficult I just wind up cogitating. We need to allow students the same reality.

Finding a Focus

Once students are writing fairly fluently (unencumbered by letter formation and spelling), which for some may be as early as mid-first grade, I encourage them to:

Figure 9-10   First-grader with No Experience Choosing Her Own Writing Topics

Figure 9-11   First-grader with Journal Writing Experience

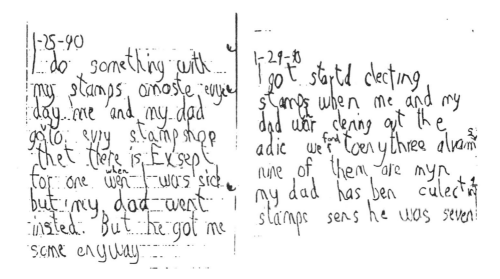

- Choose a topic that is important to them.
- Focus on one aspect of the topic.
- Tell what happened.
- Include how they feel about what happened.

I demonstrate these points orally first and then in writing.

Figure 9-12   Fourth-grader's Journal Entry Inspired by a Styrofoam Plate on Teacher's Desk

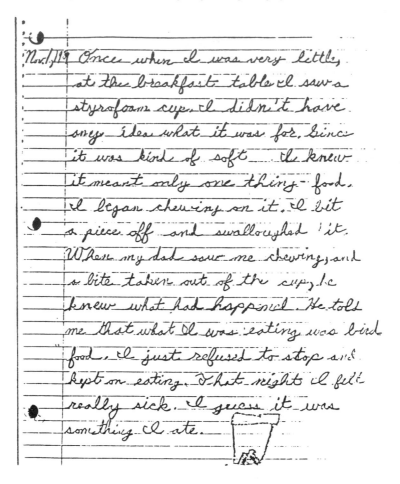

Getting students to focus brings out description and detail that do not come out when they just recount what happened in sequence. For example, when I write about my dog, Tobi, I tell about *one* aspect of my pet: his problem with fleas, his difficulty getting up and down stairs now that he is old, his playfulness, or the way he sleeps. I try to get students to do the same. That focus helps to move them away from telling everything they know about a topic and the tedious mode of "This happened, and then this happened."

Writing in front of students   As I write in front of the children, usually on the overhead projector but sometimes on the chalkboard or chart paper, I verbalize my thinking. Often I have not decided what to write about until I am actually about to begin. Sometimes I change my mind at the last minute, and I let the students know that writers do this. I try to make my thinking visible, and I let students know I have no idea how the writing will turn out. Often I find my focus *as* I am writing. One day, for example, I started off thinking I would write about neighbors (who had moved away) and having an afternoon visit with their year-old daughter. I didn't know until I had begun writing that I would wind up focusing on how the baby reminded me of my daughter Elizabeth at the same age. I let students know that a writer often doesn't know what she's going to say until she says it, a concept I grasped from the writings of Donald Murray and my own experience as a writer.

As I demonstrate, students often see me change my mind about something and cross out words. I tell them that writers cross out because it's quicker than erasing and leaves a record of their first thoughts. I try to discourage erasing and the notion of having a "clean" paper so students will grasp the idea that drafts are normal.

I point out to students grade 2 and above how quickly I can fill a page. I have them note that I write a whole page in five minutes; therefore, in twenty minutes they can certainly do the same. Even though quantity is not the goal, some students need to be shown that it is not difficult to write a whole page and more when a writer has a topic he knows a lot about and a topic that is important to him.

A brainstorming strategy   A strategy that works very well for getting students to focus on small happenings and feelings within larger contexts is brainstorming. Beginning by demonstrating myself, I list all the possible subtopics I can think of to go with my topic (see Figure 9–13). Then I choose the subtopic I want to write about today and try to tell as much as I can about it in an interesting way.

This brainstorming technique is a primary form of outlining that encourages students to group together like information. I have used this technique successfully as early as mid-first grade. Repeated demonstrations are necessary, and the strategy works best with small groups of students.

When students try this guided brainstorming, what happens is that things they might never have thought to include become part of their story. Additionally, when a student is asked to pick only one of many writing options, he tends to do a more thorough job. Figures 9–14 through 9–16 give examples of brainstormings by first-graders and some follow-up writing. Notice in "Going to Grandma's House" the last item that came out on the student writer's brainstorming was "crowded car."

Figure 9–13   Brainstorming Subtopics on the Topic "My Dog"

Tobi

✓ how we got him
what he does all day
what he looks like
his problems
    old age
    arthritis
    stairs
sleeping habits
    blanket
    dreams
what he eats
    begs for food
    change in dog food

Figures 9-14, 9-15, and 9-16   First-graders' Brainstormings on a Topic

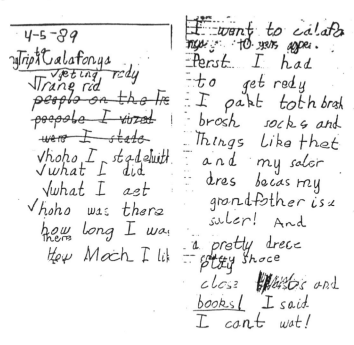

11-14-88

Christmas
√tran Riding.
get Presents.
deckoraf tree
wotch TV.
dad and bruThr
have dinre.
go to Chrche
goto bed.
get up.
open Prethn
cusuns.
Big teste.

Figure 9-15

4-5-89
my Trip to Calafonya
√geting redy
√Trane rid
people on the Tre
poepole I vizet
were I state
√hoho I stadewith.
√what I did
√what I aet
√hoho was there
how long I was there
Hoy Mach I lik

I wont to calafa nya to yers ago.
Ferst I had to get redy
I pakt toth brsh brosh socks and Things Like thet and my salor dres becas my grandfother is a suler! And a pretly drece pretty shoce close coats and books I said
I cant wat!

This would probably not have come out without the brainstorming. Yet it adds an interesting dimension to the story and is what the student chose to write about first. I suggest to students that they check or cross out their subtopics as they write about them. Often students use their subtopics as a table of contents for the beginning of a chapter book on their topic.

Figure 9-16

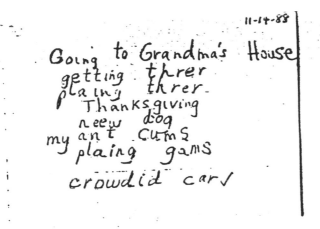

11-14-88

Going to Grandma's House
getting threr
plaing threr.
Thanksgiving
neew dog
my ant cums
plaing gams
crowdid car ✓

weñ we go house to grandma
we get up vere rly:
we poot the Soqcksis in
the car we get in the
car my Babeay Sistr
SiSts in a booSt Set
then we get in to the car
we are vere Squesht

Translation

When We Go to Grandma's House
  We get up very early. We put the suitcases in the car. We get
in the car. My baby sister sits in a booster seat. Then we get into
the car. We are very squished.

The Teacher as a Writing Model

Just as we demonstrate ourselves as readers, we also want to demonstrate ourselves
as writers. In kindergarten and early first grade, these demonstrations take place
mostly in small-group and whole-class settings, with the teacher writing in front of
the children. However, once students can write without teacher intervention, it
works well if teachers write at least several times a week in their own journals at the
same time the students are writing. First grade teacher Jim Henry found that
writing with students—which he felt comfortable doing about mid-year—revital-
ized his journal writing program. Children seemed more excited about their own
writing and enjoyed finding out what their teacher had written.

  Also, just as teachers do not mark papers during sustained silent reading, so too journal writing is best used only for writing if we want students to get the message that this kind of writing is a valued activity. Some teachers enjoy using their own journal writing as an opportunity to reflect on their teaching.

Besides serving as a model for students, teachers' writing and sharing allow students to get to know their teachers as people. Walking into one classroom, I discovered the teacher writing her journal entry with tears in her eyes. Her son had just turned sixteen, and she was writing about her sense of loss and her worry about her son as a new driver.

Teachers' Observations

Karen Horton, a third grade teacher, noticed immediate improvement in the quality and quantity of her students' writing after several demonstrations.

> Before that, I was getting a lot of listing and enumerating. They weren't really saying much of anything. I was amazed at how many kids wrote a whole page and more after seeing journal writing demonstrated. There was a noticeable improvement in the content of the writing, and kids showed a lot more confidence. They felt they had something to say.
>
> Journal writing is a wonderful vehicle for sharing feelings. I feel so much more in touch with the kids' lives now. Sometimes you don't get a chance to talk about things in the classroom, but they can write about it and I know what they are thinking and how they are feeling.

After a teacher demonstration, fourth grade teacher Nancy Schubert says her students were begging to have journal writing "like we did last week" (when they could choose their own topics). Nancy had moved from always assigning topics to letting students choose their own topics. She noticed a dramatic difference in student interest in writing. Nancy notes, "I know now you don't need to give starters or topics or start with a discussion of world or school events. The whole concept of 'real' is very important to the kids. Once in a while, I still assign a topic, mostly, I think, as a test to see if choosing their own topics really produces better writing."

Students' Observations

Here are some second-graders' comments after journal writing was demonstrated:

- I had to work hard to think of what I wanted to write about but then I just wrote. I didn't think.
- Usually I try to write a whole story. It was easier because I just wrote about a small part.
- I didn't know I would get ideas by looking around the room. I have another idea for tomorrow.

When I asked a group of third-graders if their writing surprised them in any way, one girl whose teacher described her writing as mostly lists of what happened said, "I didn't know I could write so much on one thing. It's easier when you focus on one thing you know and care about."

Taking Time for Oral Sharing
Sharing to Get Journal Writing Started

Taking time for oral sharing promotes language development, inspires confidence, and gives reluctant writers possible topics from which to choose. Oral language is used as a tool for learning and is integral to successful journal writing. While some students are talking about what they might write about, others are developing and practicing good listening skills and getting ideas for their own writing. The oral language time also allows the teacher the opportunity to probe and guide the student to awareness of what he already knows but may not know he knows. It is a time for hearing the personal stories of our students. The time for talk also encourages very young children to move way from common, boring topics such as rainbows, hearts, and butterflies.

After my oral sharing, I always take lots of time—ten to twenty minutes—to go around the class and ask, "Who knows what he or she could write about?" When the student says, "My dog," I probe, "What about your dog? What are you going to say?" I try to get them to note small, but significant, incidents and events and to express complete thoughts so they can get them down on paper later.

I remember Jordan, a first-grader described by his teacher as "very slow" and a child who "hardly writes anything in his journal." In our oral sharing, a number of students had talked about their pets. I gently probed, "Jordan, do you have any kind of pet?" I learned he had a goldfish that had just died. By asking him genuine questions ("How did your fish die?" "How did you take care of your goldfish?" "Did you clean its bowl?" "What did you feed it?" "How did you get your goldfish?") and engaging him in conversation, a story emerged. With guidance, Jordan proudly wrote for several days about his goldfish, and that story became his first published book. Without the oral sharing, I don't believe he would have "found" his story.

Initially, some teachers feel guilty about taking time for oral language, but oral language is critical and gives students a framework for writing. Teachers who do take the time note that the quality of student writing is much improved. Kindergarten teacher Kathy Wolfe always takes lots of time for oral sharing before journal writing, and she notes that the students' writing is lively and interesting and that everyone has something to write about.

The following were some orally stated topics—with focuses—from a fourth grade class in early fall after an oral demonstration:

LISA: going to a wedding; choosing and wearing pink and green bridesmaid's dress

NATALIE: cleaning up "junky" room—lollypop wrappers on floor, old pieces of cheese sticking to the sheet, excitement of finding a friend's phone number buried

TOMMY: worry about cat; eyes don't look right, not eating, not sure what's wrong

KARL: dog died; passing a pet shop; went in and saw two golden retrievers

ABBY: starting dancing class, nervous about how it will go

NATASHA: choosing seats at a movie and buying popcorn

Figure 9-17   Validating a Students' Experiences through Journal Writing

Natasha was a "low-ability" student with poor self-esteem, and her journal entry validated an important experience in her life. It was the first time she had ever chosen the seats at the movie theater, and she was elated. Journal writing gave her a vehicle to bring that experience into school and share it with her peers (see Figure 9–17).

Billy was a struggling student in the same class who chose not to share orally. Note how he is able to use his journal entry to talk about a difficult event in his life (see Figure 9–18).

Figure 9-18   Using Journal Writing to "Talk" about a Difficult Experience

page 2

Oct. 11-89

Last Month we were eating dinner I finished my dinner and I whent to wach tv. then My dad said come back here he said son this is hard to tell you but you Now when I said I did'nt have a job thats changed now and I got a job in the same copany for more money I

I said sow then I walked awox wait there one more thing I hove to tell you he said since I got that job we have to move I said to wear he said My boss gove me a choic chicago or california he said I those california I say why da we have to move he said

page 3

I already told because of my job then I walked off

Sharing after Journal Writing

Sharing time is important because it validates and gives children an audience. It is the "show-off" stage, the important last step in the developmental model (pp. 9–10). Almost all young children enjoy the opportunity to "read" their journal entries and talk about their illustrations. With older children, journals are often best treated as private places.

Sharing seems to work best when it is voluntary. In classrooms in which students have had to read their entries aloud, some children develop an aversion to journal writing. One fourth-grader stated, "Last year, we had to read our journals out loud, and I hated that. This year we have an option, and that makes me feel a lot better."

Journal Writing in the Kindergarten

Journal writing can begin the first week in kindergarten if writing is viewed as any marks on paper that have meaning for the child. That could include drawings, squiggles, lines, mock letters (made-up letters), random letters, or anything the child puts on paper that makes sense to her. "During kindergarten, the most typical forms of writing used in connected discourse (such as stories or letters) continue to be scribbling, drawing, and nonphonetic letter strings, with fewer children using phonetic (or invented) spelling, and conventional orthography (dictionary spelling)" (Strickland and Morrow, 1989, p. 72).

Journal writing takes place in all our kindergartens, and our teachers have been largely influenced by the leadership and guidance of kindergarten teacher Jeanette Throne (See "Journal Articles" in *Resources for Teachers*). Writing in the kindergarten extends beyond journal writing into natural contexts, play areas, and writing centers. Children's strong, early foundation in writing continues to have an impact on their writing development and their attitudes toward writing.

Getting Started

When I demonstrate journal writing in the kindergarten early in the school year, I demonstrate many forms of writing while telling them they are already writers (see Figure 9–19):

- Picture writing
- Scribble writing
- Random letters
- Invented spelling—beginning consonants to represent words
- Conventional writing

I do not give more weight to one form than to another. As in other grades, I begin by discussing what I could write about. I start by drawing a picture and telling students that many of them probably draw better than I do. I am careful to refer to drawing as a form of writing and a way of telling my story. I will then "read" my picture. Then I scribble—write my story while I verbalize it—and say, "Some kindergarten children know how to write something like this. How many of you can write like this?" Most hands go up, and I congratulate them for being writers. Next, as I write a random stream of letters, perhaps with some mock letters included, I again slowly verbalize my story and say, "Some kindergarten children write like this. How many of you can do this?" Again many hands go up, and children are complimented for being writers.

Invented spelling is demonstrated next. I might say, "Some children write letters for the sounds they hear in their stories. See if you can help me write my story, 'I cooked scrambled eggs for breakfast.'" I slowly stretch out the sounds in each word, and I accept whatever letters they give me. Then, I ask them to read with me as I point to each "letter-word." Finally, I write the conventional form of my sentence, saying, "This is what my story looks like when I write it. It took me many years to learn how to write like this." I invite them to read it with me.

Before the children begin to write themselves, there will be lots of oral sharing of possible topics. Then, whatever writing form the child chooses, from the start she

Figure 9-19   Demonstrating Journal Writing in the Kindergarten

will be treated as a writer and a reader. We must take great care to see that all children's expressions find acceptance in school.

After the child has finished writing, I say, "Read your story to me. Use your reading finger." The child moves his finger along (perhaps with teacher guidance) and "reads" the story. One little girl was following along her scribble writing with her finger, reading, "We played freeze tag. It was so. . . ." Her finger ran out at "so," and then she said, "Oh, I forgot 'fun.'" She happily added another scribble and went back to reread her complete story. She clearly understood that print contains a message.

While the teacher or parent volunteer writes down the child's story at the bottom of the page (lightly in pencil so the child's writing marks predominate), this is not traditional dictation because children cannot write. This is dictation of a story the child has written. Having children write for themselves from the beginning eliminates the need for traditional dictation. However, some teachers find it worthwhile to continue to incorporate dictation for the depth of oral storytelling that can result. Dictation allows for extensive language in spite of limited sound-knowledge or limited experience with the structure of stories. Occasionally there are children who may not view scribble writing and stringing letters together as writing. Always, respect for the child is primary, and for these children the teacher would serve as scribe for their dictated stories.

Scribble Writing

"Encourage children who are scribbling to write and scribble every day" (Hayes, 1990).

Just as babbling is a natural and expected behavior in learning to talk, scribbling is a beginning stage of writing development that enables emerging writers to explore language. Writing that may mean nothing to the teacher may be filled with meaning for the child. I see scribble writing as a way of freeing children who are not yet ready or interested in forming letters or connecting sounds with letters. Scribble writing allows all children to write from the start of school and to see themselves as writers. With scribble writing as an option, kindergarten children no longer say, "I can't write."

Several years ago I would never have demonstrated scribble writing, mock letters, or random letters. In my old way of thinking writing meant starting with letter formation, and therefore many students believed they could not write. As soon as I started demonstrating scribble writing, almost without exception every child wrote and believed he could write.

I have come to believe that when children are immersed in a print-rich, authentic literacy environment with daily opportunities for language exploration—including reading and writing independently and with guidance—they will move toward invented spelling and conventional spelling when they are ready. It takes a lot of trust to believe this will happen and to accept that children's writing is purposeful for them, even when we feel they can do more. However, as long as children are seeing lots of letter formation and conventional print through teacher demonstrations and through text, they will develop and progress as writers. In the long run, a child's exploration of shapes and lines probably aids letter knowledge and form. Although we may encourage and gently guide students to move to another stage when we think they are ready, essentially we must trust students to let it happen.

For some children, scribble writing seems to make it easier to concentrate on the story they are telling without worrying about sounds and letters. At times, it also seems to be a vehicle for supporting the very verbal child who has much to say. A case in point was Jonathan, a kindergarten student who stayed with scribble writing until mid-year. Jonathan was in Karen Sher's reading-writing classroom with lots of daily opportunities to read and write. Journal writing took place, whole class, once a week with the assistance of a parent volunteer. In terms of average writing development, Jonathan does not seem to have lost any ground by having been allowed to move at his own pace (see Figures 9–20 through 9–22). Karen reflects:

> My year with Jonathan was my first exploration with scribble writing. There were moments when I began to doubt that Jonathan would move to the "next stage." I'm so glad I resisted the urge (and *my* need) to push him, although gentle, positive encouragement *was* given when appropriate. Jonathan had extraordinary ability to express himself through art. I feel that giving him the freedom to fully explore his talent helped to make him feel confident and comfortable with written symbols he freely used by the end of his kindergarten year.

In relation to writing, children's tears are now rare—even the first week of school. When the tears do come, they are usually from a child who is not a risk taker and who won't put anything down unless it's right. One little girl who cried and said she couldn't write finally wrote "The" for the first word in her story and was upset because she couldn't spell the rest correctly. Once these children realize

Figures 9–20, 9–21, and 9–22   Development of a Kindergarten Writer Who Remained with
Scribble Writing Until Mid-year

This was me and my mom and my
dad and my father on the airplane 9·12·87
eating good food.

9–12–87

This is A corvette that's going across a bridge
and the sun's looking at it.

Figure 9–21

that they should do the best they can and not worry, they relax and begin to incorporate invented spelling.

Some kindergarten teachers are uncomfortable demonstrating scribble writing, thinking that it will encourage an early form of writing that may delay movement to the invented spelling stage. Also, some children stay with scribble writing for

Figure 9-22

4-10-90

WeN I
WOS.
At SCoL
MY MOM
BOt me
FIS.

When I was at
school my mom
bought me fish

AT HOM MY
MOM GAYV
me A MONNY
BAYK aNd Lt
WOS KLYr

5/1/90 at home my mom gave me a
money bank and it was clear.

quite some time. This can be unnerving for the teacher who is wondering whether
more conventional writing will ever happen. However, children's daily writing is
not always logical or sequential; at times, children may move back and forth
between stages. Some of us have found that it has taken the vantage point of
looking back over a whole year of writing progress to feel comfortable with scribble
writing and also to feel confident that children are developing as writers. As with

all forms of language learning, there is no best way or one right way; it is up to the teacher to decide what she is comfortable with.

Finally, parents need to be kept well informed about the writing program. Teachers that take the time to communicate with parents about their children's writing stages find that parents are reassured and supportive.

Organization and Management

Scheduling

Many teachers try to schedule journal writing daily for ten to twenty minutes or more. Some teachers schedule journal writing first thing each morning, or at the beginning of a period, feeling that it helps build a sense of community. Others prefer it at the end of the morning or day. Some teachers like having journal writing right before reading groups and independent work time, so that children who want more time can have the option to continue journal writing.

A consistently scheduled time with the teacher helps children expect journal writing, value it, and look forward to it. Even though students should also have options to write in their journals at other times, a scheduled time allows for oral discussion, minilessons and demonstrations, and teacher time to conference individually with students. A scheduled time also gives the teacher time to sit down and write with a group of students, which seems to encourage their own writing. By contrast, when journal writing is only assigned as seatwork while the teacher is involved with other activities, students do not take journal writing seriously or give their best efforts.

My recommendation is to schedule journal writing as often as you are comfortable with it in kindergarten, daily in grades 1 and 2, and at least several times weekly from grade 3 up. Many teachers feel that increasing curriculum demands through the grades makes it difficult to find time for personal journal writing. However, the incorporation of other types of journals—learning logs, reflection logs—makes journal writing a tool for learning across the curriculum and makes it possible to schedule it on a daily basis.

In scheduling journal writing, flexibility is important. If journal time seems to be becoming routine or forced and the children are not enthusiastic about it, think about including it only as an optional activity or setting it aside altogether for several weeks or months.

Supplies Needed

- Journals—may be spiral-bound notebooks, lined or unlined. Most teachers seem to prefer some type of bound book, but a three-ring notebook with dividers also works well, especially if learning logs are being used in several content areas.

   With a machine that spiral binds, using mimeograph paper and sturdy paper for front and back covers, blank books can be made for kindergarten and beginning first-graders. Most of our first grade teachers use lined spirals, but we tell the children to ignore the lines, and they do.

- Crayons or colored pencils—for illustrations (Magic Markers "bleed" through).

- Date stamp—or students may write in the date. Even some of our very young children write the number of the month, a dash, and the date. Writing the number of the month instead of the name saves time. Dating each entry is important for noting progress and keeping an organized, ongoing record.
- Pencils and pens

Choosing a Topic

Some teachers find doing a whole-class brainstorming of possible topics works well after the teacher has demonstrated what he might write about. Others have students do individual brainstormings and keep these in their journals for reference. Figure 9–23 gives a third-grader's personal brainstorming after a whole-class brainstorming of topics.

Some first grade teachers send home a sheet called "Topics for My Journal" at the beginning of the year, which the parent fills out with the child. Some topics that may be included are "Family," "Friends," "Hobbies," "Pets," "Special Places," "Holidays," "Favorite Activities," "Important Memories." The completed sheet is stapled into the front of the journal and is referred to by the teacher and student when the student has trouble choosing a writing topic.

If a student is still having difficulty getting ideas, you may want to suggest to the parent that possible topics to write about be a subject of meal-time discussion.

Figure 9-23   A Third-grader's Personal Brainstorming for Writing Topics

Prompting the parent to say to the child, "You could write about that in your journal" is often enough to get the child going on her own.

Illustrating

Young children often need to draw pictures before they attempt words. After children are writing easily, often by mid-first grade, they are gently encouraged to spend most of their time writing and to save their illustrations for their published books and projects as well as for independent work time. For children who are more comfortable just writing a story, we don't insist on pictures.

Using Dashes and Cross Outs

When I demonstrate writing for young children, I tell them, "If you're not sure what comes next, just put a 'dash,' like this (—), and go on." This practice frees children who stop writing because they "can't spell." I also show how writers cross out when they make a mistake or change their minds. Crossing out is faster than erasing and leaves a record of the writer's first intentions.

Encouraging Invented Spelling

The primary purpose of invented spelling is to free children to write. In a class of twenty-five or more students, the child is able to continue writing and does not have to stop and wait for the teacher. If the child asks me how to spell a word, I say, "Do the best you can" or "What sounds do you hear?" or "How can you help yourself?" When he asks, "Is this right?" I might say, "That's just fine for now." If the children are continuing to ask the teacher to spell words, they are still getting the message that the teacher will spell for them.

When I demonstrate invented spelling (or what is now also being called developmental spelling), I do not deliberately misspell. I ask the children to help me write the words, and I accept and congratulate them on their approximations. In that way, I observe and accept the developmental level of students, and I remain authentic with my own writing. I then write the sentence or paragraph conventionally (under or next to the invented spelling version), and I point out the parts of their words that are conventionally spelled. As I am writing I might say, "Good for you. Look. You got the first and last letters."

The language the teacher uses in demonstrations is very important. When I do my writing after the invented spelling, I always tell the children that it took me many years to write like this. While I am sharing the correct model, I am at the same time giving the message that I don't expect the children to write like adults. This takes away overemphasis on correctness and helps make students comfortable with using invented spelling.

Fostering Independence in Writing

It's a good idea to discuss what writers can do when they can't spell a word:

- Sound it out—stretch out the sounds.
- Ask a friend.

- Use print resources—books, charts, print in room.
- Use a dash.

It also works well to demonstrate for young children how they might use a familiar book, poem, or chart to find a word. I might say, "If you are using the word 'today,' where can you find it?" (calendar board). "If you need the word 'my,' where can you look?" (poem or chart or teacher's modeled writing on the chalkboard). To promote writing fluency, it works best if the child does not stop to look up a word in the dictionary.

For an important, difficult word that a child requests and that I know will be written repeatedly, I will sometimes write the correct spelling. For example, if the child is about to write a story about his pet rabbit, I might say, "You will be using 'rabbit' a lot in your story. This is how you write it."

Making Print Resources Readily Available

A variety of print resources in the classroom encourages children to move toward conventional spelling and independence in writing.

- *Alphabet strips and picture charts*   Young children need to see the letters right in front of them for reference. It is not sufficient just to have the alphabet posted high up on a bulletin board because many children do not yet have the eye-hand coordination to copy letters from far away. Some teachers adhere alphabet strips to each child's desk; others staple a copy of the alphabet, showing upper and lower case letters, inside the front cover of the journal. Many of us also make individual alphabets with picture cues (see Figure 9–24) for each child.

- *Environmental print*   Labels, signs, calendars, children's names, and messages

Figure 9-24   A Resource for K-1 Students: Alphabet with Picture Cues
Compiled by Karen Smith.

that children see over and over again in context in the classroom and at home have a powerful impact on children's writing and reading.

One kindergarten student who was just starting to use beginning consonants to represent words wrote "off" correctly. When asked how he knew the word, he said, "I saw it in my refrigerator. My mommy told me what it said." A first-grader who spelled "Australia" correctly told me, "I can spell it because 'Australia' is on my stamps in my stamp collection."

• *Family words*   Early in first grade, sometimes even the first week of school, we begin an enlarged chart of "Family Words." Words such as "mother," "father," "cousin," "grandpa," and "aunt" get added as children ask for them.

• *Content and theme words*   See "Wall Charts," page 247.

• *High-frequency words*   In kindergarten and early first grade, putting a reference card of most frequently used words at each writing table facilitates writing and gives support to emerging writers. This idea was shared by a visiting teacher from New Zealand, and it works well. By observing the words children need and are using and making them readily available, young writers are aided in the writing process. I start with only four words on one side of a card, add four more words on the reverse, and later move to a card with six or eight spaces (see Figure 9–25). Some teachers start by putting on the board one word that many students seem to be using. When there are four (or more) words on the board that children can read, a guide card is made. The short, high-frequency word list may also be clipped into each child's journal.

Words that children ask for and use over and over again can be put into a personal words section at the back of the journal. I will often say to a student, "You are using this word a lot. I will put it here for you so you can find it when you need it."

Figure 9-25   For Beginning Writers: Reference Card with Frequently Used Words

Encouraging Collaboration

Especially with young children, opportunities for quiet talking seem to promote writing development. Desks clustered in small groups allow for natural sharing ("What are you writing about?") and help with spelling ("How do you spell _____ ?"). Having some children who are strong writing models in each group offers support to peers.

Keeping Track of Skills

Some teachers like to keep a checklist in the journal of skills the child *is* using. For example, when the teacher notices that "I" is used correctly, when sentences are beginning with capitals, or when punctuation is appearing, it is noted and dated on the checklist. This practice is fine as long as the checklist is used by the teacher and student to note behaviors that are occurring naturally. We need to use caution here, however, as overemphasis of mechanics will take away from the primary purposes and benefits of journal writing.

Taking Time for Minilessons

Some teachers like to begin the journal writing period with an occasional minilesson. The lesson might be a demonstration in spacing of words, in finding a focus in writing, in utilizing print resources in the classroom, or in anything the teacher notices from looking through journals that students might benefit from.

Minilessons also occur as we quickly conference with students one-to-one during journal writing time. For a student having difficulty with spelling, some comments might include, "What do you hear at the beginning? Does it start like any word you know? Stretch it out slowly with me. What do you hear in the middle? at the end? What can you do to help yourself?"

Utilizing volunteers

Many kindergarten and first grade teachers find it valuable to have a parent volunteer present one or more mornings a week to respond to every child. Especially if journal writing is done whole class, this practice facilitates getting around to everyone.

Implicit in the use of volunteers is preliminary training by the teacher. Parent volunteers need to understand and value the theory behind invented spelling and to observe how the teacher interacts with students when conferencing. Without both the theory and the practice, parents can send the wrong message to students. I observed one parent focusing on capitalization and punctuation with a beginning first-grader, taking his pencil and "correcting" his "errors."

Setting Up Centers

Many kindergarten teachers schedule journal writing time with students once a week. They meet with a small group around a table while the other students are working at learning centers, for example, painting, pasting, completing a project, listening to tapes, or whatever the teacher has set up. Each day students rotate to a new center.

Responding to Journals

One technique that works beautifully for many of us in grade 1 and above (but no one remembers where the idea first came from) is to make four 3 by 5 inch cards carrying the following messages:

- Collect all journals (teacher checks journals and responds).
- Read entry to partner.
- Share entry with class (about three students are selected).
- Put journals away.

A student is chosen to pick one card. Students love this activity and the anticipation of which journal response will be used for the day.

Providing Time for Sharing

Young children especially love sharing their stories. Sharing should be optional and nonthreatening. In kindergarten, some teachers schedule a sharing time later in the day—either individually, small group, or whole class—and encourage students to "Read me your story."

Communicating with Parents

The purpose of journal writing needs to be clearly articulated to parents. Without understanding the importance of approximation and invented spelling as well as the developmental stages of writing, parents may think teachers are not doing their job if they see that spelling and grammatical mistakes have not been corrected. A letter to parents may be helpful. Also, because journals usually stay in school, some teachers find it works well—especially in the early grades—to reproduce one page a month from the child's journal and send it home. In that way, the parent sees the child's progress. At the same time, this could also be used as an opportunity for self-evaluation—ask the child to "choose the entry that best represents your writing this month." (See Appendix J1 and J11.)

Teacher Expectations

While journals are not evaluated, teachers have expectations of students:

- Entries are required. Though journals are not graded, the completion of a required number of entries may be figured as part of an overall grade.
- While beautiful penmanship is not a goal, handwriting is expected to be legible.
- Invented spelling is welcomed for words the student is not expected to know how to spell. High-frequency words, however, are expected to be spelled correctly, especially by older students.
- At times, with teacher guidance, the student needs to move to a new topic, for example, when the student writes about the same subject day after day.
- Students are always expected to do their best-quality work.

Utilizing Various Types of Journals

While the personal journal has been the focus of this chapter, there are many types of journals and various ways to use them. Some teachers use or combine one or more of the following types:

Personal. Most often this is a first person diary format, but it is not limited to this. Some students mix diary entries with stories. Young students enjoy using the structure of familiar stories to create original ones.

Dialogue. The teacher and student, or student and student, respond to the journal through written conversation. Comments are often brief, informal, private, and direct.

End-of-the-day. A quiet wrap-up before school is over. Kindergarten teachers Sue Fitzpatrick and Karen Sher find that ideas are easily generated at the end of the day. Or teachers can suggest, "Write about the best part of your afternoon."

Reflection. Students reflect on what they learned, what they still have questions about, and what they want to know more about in a particular subject or area.

Learning log. The student communicates how and what he has understood about a concept or unit of study. Students describe their learning processes—that is, "writing to learn." Some content area teachers take five to ten minutes at the beginning or end of a period for students to respond in their learning logs. Learning logs may be used in mathematics, science, music, art, foreign languages, or any subject area.

Writer's notebook. Students keep a record of favorite phrases and words they come across in reading that they might want to use in their own writing. They jot down ideas, thoughts, images, anecdotes, observations, and memories for future topics. (I keep an ongoing writer's notebook and often show it to students.)

Poetry. Students copy favorite poems, write their own poetry, and keep ideas and images for poems (see McClure, 1990).

Class. Observations about a class pet, plant, activity, or trip are kept in a common log and may be entered as a shared writing entry or as individual entries. With younger students log entries are often done in enlarged print.

Responding to Journals

Teacher's journal responses should be genuine and personal. A response may be brief, based on a quick look, or as involved as a personal, written response. Sometimes response means making brief contact with each student. With young children, I like to carry a small chair from student to student so I am at eye level. I might ask, "How's the writing going? Could you read me what you've written?" I am careful to leave the ownership and the writing with the child. I have also found that when walking around conferring with students it works well to focus on one or two students. While a "stop and go" conference will be fine for many, some students will need additional guidance and encouragement.

When I cannot read a child's invented spelling, with extreme care and the child's approval, I very lightly pencil in the words, either just above the child's writing or in the space below it. The advantages of penciling in the words are long term; when the child, teacher, or parent goes back to the early writing, the message is clear. The child also has a model for a word that may be used again. Often, when students are ready, they refer to and use the conventionally spelled word in their new journal entries.

Responding to Teachable Moments

While I believe we must be very sensitive about making any critical comments on children's writing, I also believe that we should take advantage of teachable moments when they arise. If a child we are conferencing with seems ready to deal with a confusion, standard spelling, or editorial convention, then we should teach the skill at that moment. Experience has taught me that it is best to focus on one letter or convention at a time to avoid confusing the child. At the same time, we need to keep in mind that just because we introduce a convention once, the child may not be ready to pick up on it. We may need to point out the convention over and over again.

I was invited by a first grade teacher to assist with journal writing in the classroom the first week of school in September. The teacher had introduced and demonstrated journal writing the previous day. With two of us in the room, we could easily get around and respond to each child's writing.

"Tell me about your story," I said to Brandon, as I pulled my chair up next to him. With great enthusiasm, Brandon proceeded to tell me about his pictures of Batman, Robin, and the Joker. He had not written any scribbles, letters, or words. He told me he did not know how to write. I asked him if he knew how Batman started.

"B"; he called out the letter name without hesitation.

"That's right. Put it here," I told him. He looked at the alphabet strip of upper and lower case letters on his desk and then wrote the letter "D" next to his picture of Batman.

"What else do you hear?" I prompted as I stretched out the sounds for him and said "B--a--t. . . ."

"T," he called.

"Good. Put it here," I said, pointing next to the "D." "Now, what else do you hear?" I stretched out the word again, stopping on the "m" and prolonging it: "B--a--t--mmm----a--n."

Brandon said "m," and wrote "M." We continued the procedure.

I said "Batman" again, emphasizing the "n," and he wrote "N."

As Brandon and I were going through this procedure, I was thinking about whether to say anything about his writing "D" for "B." It was early in the school year, and I was wrestling with my strong feelings of accepting all writing so the child would not feel "corrected" in any way. However, I was also feeling that this confusion could probably be cleared up easily in the present writing context, especially since I knew Brandon could write his name, which began with "B." In the past, I probably would have left things alone. Now, I decided to seize the teaching-learning opportunity.

"Brandon," I said, "Can you point to the letter 'B' on your alphabet strip?" He pointed to "D." "This is the 'B' here," I said, pointing to it. "Point to it here with me, and say it with me, 'B.' Now let's write it down here on your paper for practice. Good. Now write it again."

Brandon quickly seized the moment and said, "Should I change this?" ("D"), and he started to erase the "D" and replace it with "B."

"Brandon, you can erase it, but do you know what writers do all the time when they want to make a change? They just cross out. Now, what is the letter you have just written?"

"B."

"Good. That will be easy for you to remember, because your name starts with 'B,' just like 'Batman.' What a good job you have done! Now, read this word with me." I point to "BTMN," and we both say "Batman."

In our brief interaction, Brandon saw that he actually knew how to write letters to go along with the verbal labels for his pictures. He also cleared up an important letter confusion. Hopefully, by focusing on just the "B" at this time and not comparing it with the "D," Brandon will remember to write the letter "B" for the sound of "B."

Responding in Writing

While students enjoy teachers' written responses to their journal entries and the responses provide reading-writing models, this practice is very time consuming for the teacher. Except for very young students, it's not necessary to read every entry. Many teachers try to work out a system where they respond in writing occasionally. Some teachers collect all journals every few weeks, skim the entries, carefully read one or two that spark their interest, and respond in writing to one or more entries. Here it is important to make the response fit the student's writing. A written response on one journal should not be so general that it can easily transfer to another journal. For example, instead of "interesting" or "I like this," I might write, "This reminded me of when I . . .," or, "It sounds as though you were feeling . . ."

Implicit in written response is no correcting, no red penciling, no grading. Some teachers even feel that any writing on the child's work is unacceptable. They use Post-its to make comments. These may also be used on journal entries in the early grades to transcribe the young child's invented spelling. To respect children's privacy, we tell them if there is an entry they would not like the teacher to read to fold over or fold and staple the page.

Very important, too, is the tone of the response. I believe the main purpose of responding to journals is to give an interested, honest reaction to the message. Any questions or comments should be genuine and come from the teacher's need to know. Questions such as "What else happened?" should be asked only if we really want answers and not just to have the student make the writing "longer." Ownership must remain with the child. While teachers sometimes incorporate correct spelling and grammar in their written responses based on errors the student made, this is never the primary purpose of responding to student journals.

Responding through Publishing

Many of our first-graders use their journals to house all their writing. Teachers recognize children's efforts by making their writing public. Parent volunteers "publish" children's writing, and the published books become part of the classroom library. (See Chap. 11, "Setting Up an In-School Publishing Process.")

Students' Attitudes and Learnings

When journal writing is done well, the writing serves the students' purposes and is valued by the teacher. It then becomes an activity children relish. However, students dislike journal writing when the activity is abused.

A teacher filling in for a first grade teacher on medical leave stated that the students "hated journal writing." That surprised me, because first-graders usually love the opportunities to write their own stories. When I went into the classroom, I asked some of the students how they felt. Sure enough, they hated journal writing. Here were some of their reasons:

- We have to write a long time.
- We have to write a whole page.
- We're not allowed to talk.
- We're not allowed to draw pictures anymore.
- It's hard to think of ideas.

In this classroom, journal writing had been assigned as part of seatwork during reading. There was no oral discussion ahead of time and no teacher demonstrations. Little time had been allocated for sharing, and the expectation was that at least a full page would be filled.

By contrast, in Kathy Wolfe's kindergarten class, journal writing takes place with enthusiasm every day. Kathy greets each child in the morning and talks about what he or she might write about. Children write in a weekly journal that goes home every Friday. Once a week, journal writing is done in a spiral-bound book. There are teacher demonstrations, and several parent volunteers help to ensure that every child has a miniconference and a response to the journal.

After the first year of daily journal writing, we asked Kathy's students to tell us "What We Have Learned about What Good Writers Do." These were their responses in the order the children gave them:

1. Good writers use their imagination.
2. Good writers take their time.
3. Good writers used their brains to think.
4. Good writers read over their stories before they show them to someone.
5. Good writers use lots of detail.
6. Good writers take time to work on their pictures.
7. Good writers always make sure their pictures go with their stories.
8. Good writers check for mistakes.
9. If they need a word, they look around the room, ask a friend, look in their journal or dictionary, or sound it out. They don't worry if they can't spell it.

I think the insights of these young writers are remarkable and apply across the grades. Students involved regularly in personal journal writing—where there is oral sharing, demonstrations, self-selection of topics, collaboration, time to think and write, and respect for the writer—come to value and understand the craft of writing.

Resources

The following limited number of journal articles and sections from texts have proved useful for incorporating journal writing into the classroom. Because writing in the kindergarten is feasible and desirable—yet is often seen as difficult to implement—a number of the resources address writing at that level.

Atwell, Nancie. 1987. "Procedures for Dialogue Journals." In *In the Middle: Writing, Reading and Learning with Adolescents*. Portsmouth, NH: Heinemann, pp. 192–194.

> *Procedures and purposes for dialogue journals, as well as lots of examples, are presented. (See index entry for additional page references.)*

Bode, Barbara A. April 1989. "Dialogue Journal Writing," *The Reading Teacher*, pp. 568–571.

> *The rationale and procedures for using dialogue journals to empower students and teachers— with specific examples from a first and sixth grade classroom—are presented.*

Bromley, Karen. 1993. *Journaling: Engagements in Reading, Writing, and Thinking*. New York: Scholastic Professional Books. See annotation, p. 62b.

Farris, Pamela J. Summer 1989. "Story Time and Story Journals: Linking Literature and Writing." *The New Advocate*, pp. 179–185. See annotation, p. 44b.

Fulwiler, Toby (ed.). 1987. *The Journal Book*. Portsmouth, NH: Heinemann-Boynton/Cook.

> *Over forty educators from the elementary grades through college explore the use of journals— especially the learning log—across the curriculum. Most of the articles in this scholarly text relate to secondary and college levels. "Mathematics Journals: Fourth Grade," by Barbara Schubert (pp. 348–358), is a useful source for elementary teachers ready to use "writing to learn" in mathematics. "The Power of Responding in Dialogue Journals," by Jana Staton (pp. 47–63), gives the rationale and specific procedures for using dialogue journals in the elementary school.*

Furnas, Alfreda. 1985. "Watch Me." In *Breaking Ground: Teachers Relate Reading and Writing in the Elementary School*, Jane Hansen, Thomas Newkirk, and Donald Graves (eds.). Portsmouth, NH: Heinemann, pp. 37–44.

> *Using the overhead projector, a kindergarten teacher demonstrates her own writing process and gets many of her students participating and, eventually, writing and reading independently. Very practical for kindergarten teachers who want their children to write but are unsure how to begin.*

Gordon, Christine J. and Dorothy Macinnis. January 1993. "Using Journals as a Window on Students' Thinking in Mathematics." *Language Arts*, pp. 37–43.

> *The use of dialogue journals in intermediate grade mathematics classrooms is described as a way to gain insights into students' thinking processes.*

Harste, Jerome C., and Kathy G. Short, with Carolyn Burke. 1988. "Journal Writing." In *Creating Classrooms for Authors*. Portsmouth, NH: Heinemann, pp. 153–160 and 280–285.

> *Rationale and procedures for journal writing are clearly presented, with varied and workable options for teachers.*

Hayes, Lynda Fender. March 1990. "From Scribbling to Writing: Smoothing the Way," *Young Children*, pp. 62–68.

> *A kindergarten teacher interweaves the research on young children's natural progression as writers with lots of meaningful and varied writing activities. Kindergarten teachers will find this a particularly supportive and valuable article for promoting all kinds of writing in the classroom.*

Hilliker, Judith. 1988. "Labelling to Beginning Narrative: Four Kindergarten Children Learn to Write." In *Understanding Writing: Ways of Observing, Learning, and Teaching*, 2nd ed. Thomas Newkirk and Nancie Atwell (eds.). Portsmouth, NH: Heinemann, pp. 14–22.

> *A teacher-researcher examines the development of four kindergarten writers. Supportive for understanding processes children go through.*

Hipple, Marjorie. L. March 1985. "Journal Writing in Kindergarten," *Language Arts*, pp. 255–261.

> *A kindergarten teacher describes the functions, procedures, and observations of journal writing in her classroom.*

Kirby, Dan. 1988. "The 'J.'" In *Inside Out: Developmental Strategies for Teaching Writing*. Portsmouth, NH: Heinemann-Boynton/Cook, pp. 45–57.

> *An English teacher describes why the journal works well and gives suggestions for using four different types of journals: the writer's notebook, the class journal, the project journal, and the*

diary. Included are suggestions for teacher responding. Intermediate through secondary teachers will find this article helpful and specific.

Sowers, Susan. 1985. "The Story and the 'All About' Book." In *Breaking Ground: Teachers Relate Reading and Writing in the Elementary School*, Jane Hansen, Thomas Newkirk, and Donald Graves (eds.). Portsmouth, NH: Heinemann, pp. 73–82.

   Before they get into narrative writing, Sowers notes that first-graders prefer to write "all about" books—"a listlike collection of facts, features and attributes of its subject." Helpful for understanding the content and form beginnning writers use.

Staton, Jana. February 1988. "ERIC/RCS Report: Dialogue Journals," *Language Arts*, pp. 198–201.

   This report by a researcher on the use of dialogue journals defines a dialogue journal and gives the benefits of its use. Many references to sources of information on dialogue journals are included.

Unia, Sumitra. 1985. "From Sunny Days to Green Onions: On Journal Writing." In *Whole Language: Theory in Use*, Judith Newman (ed.). Portsmouth, NH: Heinemann, pp. 65–72.

   An elementary teacher reflects on her experiences and personal growth in beginning to implement journal writing. Honest and inspiring.

Zemelman, Steven, and Harvey Daniels. 1988. "Journal Writing." In *A Community of Writers: Teaching Writing in the Junior and Senior High School*. Portsmouth, NH: Heinemann, pp. 99–102.

   Gives logistics and possibilities for journal writing for older students.

10

Integrating Spelling into the Reading-Writing Classroom

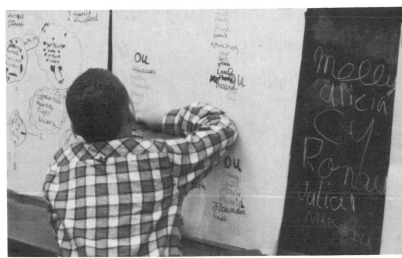

Grade 2: adding a word to the spelling chart

Implementing a Nontraditional Approach to Spelling

"What makes someone a good speller?"

"I think someone is a good speller if they write a lot and read a lot in school and at home" wrote Ben, a second-grader, on his end-of-the-year "spelling interview."

Ben was one of twenty-one second-graders and twenty-six third-graders participating in a new spelling program at our school, where most teachers were still using a traditional spelling approach.

Elaine Weiner, a second grade teacher, and I had been sharing concerns for several years about having to use a spelling text that teaches words in isolation without any meaningful integration of spelling into the language processes. Elaine's interest in making a change grew as we shared and discussed professional articles and books related to current spelling research and practice. Gradually, Elaine began to reshape her philosophy about the teaching of spelling. She felt the need for a spelling program that would reflect the whole language climate of her reading-writing classroom.

In the fall of 1988, when the spelling workbooks had not yet arrived, I approached Linda Cooper, a respected third grade teacher with a strong whole language background. We discussed the possibility of the three of us instituting a new spelling program. Elaine, Linda, and I then met to discuss the teaching of spelling as an integrated part of the reading-writing process. To us that meant that most of the words children would learn to spell would be chosen by them from their daily writing.

This was the first of weekly meetings that continued throughout the school year. At the first meeting we focused on management techniques, the use of spelling lists versus no lists, setting up our program, and documenting children's progress through daily writing. We continued to meet regularly to work out changes in the program, evaluate progress, and keep a log of our observations and reflections. In addition, this spelling support group provided a forum for the sharing of successes.

concerns, frustrations, and anecdotes. Our regular meetings promoted confidence, collegiality, and risk taking.

After establishing a general plan, we asked our principal, Dr. Bernice Stokes, for permission to implement a spelling program that was philosophically consistent with the way children learn. Dr. Stokes readily agreed, partly because of her own frustration with her daughter's failure to transfer spelling words from weekly tests to daily writing and partly because of her respect for us as teachers. She made it clear that our program should include ongoing assessment in the two classrooms as well as pre- and post-testing with the three other classes at both the second and third grade levels. The hope was that the post-tests would indicate that children in our programs were learning to spell at least as well as children using the traditional spelling programs.

Assessment of our informal integrated spelling program, which began in early October, involved four second grade and four third grade classes. Using twenty-five words from the district spelling curriculum and an additional twenty-five high-frequency words selected by the three of us, we set out to informally measure overall growth from October to June. The mean results from the four classes at each grade level on the October pre-tests were within five to seven percentage points. The grade 2 children spelled from 62 to 69 percent of the words correctly and the grade 3 children from 76 to 81 percent, indicating that the spelling abilities of the classes at each grade level were comparable.

Elaine and Linda gave their classes two more tests of high-frequency words during the school year to assess student growth. The results indicated that their students were mastering high-frequency words as a result of their immersion in a reading-writing classroom. Three times during the school year, Elaine and Linda also prepared paragraphs for proofreading. One score was given for the percentage of misspelled words circled and another score for the percentage of standard spellings written. An informal evaluation noted that students' proofreading abilities were developing.

In June, a post-test was administered to each of the eight classes in the second and third grades to informally measure the year's growth. The mean results among all the classes was again within 7 percentage points, with the range from 77 to 84 percent in both grades. It appeared that there was no advantage to teaching spelling with a traditional spelling text.

Elaine Weiner and Linda Cooper noted that most of the words students misspelled came from the district spelling curriculum lists. Students in their classes did significantly better on the high-frequency words, indicating that words that are seen and written often are learned better. The post-test results—including the better scores on high-frequency words—were also consistent the following year in another building for two teachers who used an integrated spelling approach.

Ongoing evaluation by Linda and Elaine involved keeping anecdotal records of students' writing, conferencing with students using the contents of their spelling and writing folders, giving proofreading exercises, and checking on high-frequency words.

At the end of the school year, the children in the informal, integrated program were administered a "spelling interview" questionnaire to determine their attitudes and what they had discovered about learning to spell (see Figure 10–1). Almost every child answered "yes" to the question, "Are you a good speller?"

Figure 10-1   Spelling Interview

MERCER ELEMENTARY SCHOOL

SPELLING INTERVIEW

NAME *Ben Petro* GRADE *2* DATE *June 13.*

1. Are you a good speller? *yes*
   Why do you think so? *Because I read alot of Books And. I spell in school.*

   What makes someone a good speller? *I think someone is a good speller. If they write alot and reads alot in schol and at home.*

2. What do you do when you don't know how to spell a word? *I look it up in our spelling book or Put in my have a go sheet.*

3. What have you learned about spelling this year? *If you don't know how to spell something you sound it out and you can use a file Box to help you and you can look in the dictionary to help you.*

4. What do you think about your spelling progress this year as compared to last year when you had workbooks and weekly tests? *I learn more with a Have a go sheet. Then a book. And it is funner to.*

5. If someone was having trouble spelling a word, how could/would you help that person? *I Sound the word out for them so the could write it*

6. Do you have any suggestions for improving our new spelling program? *I think they should use all the second graders at the same time and at the end of the school year see how much they improve*

When asked, "What makes someone a good speller?" a number of children responded, "A good speller reads a lot." To the question, "What do you do when you don't know how to spell a word?" a student responded, "I imagine what the word looks like in my mind, and if in writing it, it looks wrong, I try again." Several students responded, "You either look it up in the dictionary, look in your file box, or ask the person next to you."

To the question, "What have you learned about spelling this year?" these were typical student responses:

- To try again if I don't get it right the first time.
- I've learned you don't have to use a spelling workbook to learn to spell.
- I've learned how to correct my own mistakes in spelling.
- You can learn how to spell a lot of words if you really want to.

After the success of our integrated spelling program, four more teachers in other buildings in our district—a second grade teacher, a third grade teacher, and two fourth grade teachers—opted to integrate spelling into the language arts after they secured permission from their principals. At the same time, a small number of first grade teachers in our district continued to incorporate an integrated approach to spelling.

The remainder of this chapter examines a whole language view of spelling and recounts how a group of teachers in our district have translated the approach into classroom practice and evaluation. I believe, based on personal experience working with and observing learning disabled students, that the principles and strategies discussed here are as applicable to at-risk populations as they are to regular education students.

Understanding a Whole Language View of Spelling

A whole language view of spelling focuses on taking risks, teaching and applying spelling strategies, and recognizing and correcting misspellings when students edit or proofread their written work. This viewpoint recognizes first and foremost that spelling is learned and taught in the context of writing and that spelling competence, like all language competence, develops gradually over time.

The following principles apply:

Spelling Principles

1. Spelling should facilitate communication of written language, not limit it.
2. Spelling is developmental.
3. The need for standard spelling should be kept in proper perspective.
4. There should be no special spelling curriculum or regular lesson sequences. (From Kenneth Goodman, Brooks Smith, Robert Meredith, and Yetta Goodman, [Richard C. Owen, 1987], *Language and Thinking in School: A Whole-Language Curriculum*, pp. 300–301)

Spelling Stages

A whole language view of spelling, which is based on research, recognizes that children go through predictable stages in developing spelling strategies but that they go through these stages at their own rate. Invented spelling is not just tolerated; it is accepted and welcomed as a normal part of the process of becoming a competent speller. This view is very different from the traditional approach to spelling which expects perfect spelling from young children and which has all students in a classroom memorize the same predetermined list of words each week.

If one acknowledges the research that clearly demonstrates the stages all children go through in learning to spell, then the question becomes not whether to teach spelling as an integrated, developmental part of the language arts but how to accomplish this goal most effectively. Briefly stated, and based largely on the research of Richard Gentry (1982), the developmental stages learners go through in learning to spell include:

1. Prephonemic spelling Children scribble, form letters, and string letters together but without the awareness that letters represent phonemes or speech sounds. Children do, however, create meaningful messages through their exploration. Prephonemic spelling is typical of preschoolers and beginning kindergartners.

2. Early phonemic spelling There is a limited attempt to represent phonemes with letters, for example, using one or two letters for a word ("m" for "my" and "nt" for "night"). Early phonemic spelling is typical of many kindergarten and beginning first grade children.

3. Phonetic (or letter-name) spelling The child uses letters for phonemes—for example, "lik" for "like" and "brthr" for "brother." The child represents most phonemes, understands the concept of a word but is not quite reading yet. This is where we find many of our ending kindergartners and beginning first-graders.

4. Transitional spelling In this stage, children are internalizing much information about spelling patterns, and the words they write look like English words. For example, the child may write "skool" for "school" and "happe" for "happy." Rules are employed, but not always correctly. With reading and writing practice, children integrate more spelling rules and patterns. This stage usually includes first through third grade children.

5. Standard spelling At this stage, children spell most words correctly. We have found this stage occurs by the middle to the end of third grade or in fourth grade. Children are now ready to learn to spell homonyms, contractions, and irregular spellings, as well as to begin to internalize the rules that govern more difficult vowel and consonant combinations, word endings, and prefixes and suffixes. (We have chosen to use the term "standard spelling" instead of "correct spelling." Even when children have not reached the highest level, they are inventing spelling that is "correct" for their developmental level.)

Because many educators have not read the research on how spelling develops, they continue to employ and support spelling practices that are at odds with current research and theory concerning how children learn to spell. Before we can begin to move away from sequential, highly structured spelling programs, a secure knowledge base of how all language—including spelling—is learned is necessary. As educators, we also need to understand and be able to articulate that philosophy to ourselves, our administrators, our students, and the parents of our students. Even more important, we must already have established reading-writing classrooms in which children are reading and writing meaningful texts each day. Until that time, it is probably best to stay with the commercial spelling programs. (See "Resources" at the end of this chapter, especially Wilde, 1990, for help in putting research into practice.)

Components of an Integrated Spelling Program

The spelling program we developed and continue to modify is based on the principles just discussed, past teaching experiences, careful observation of students, and the current research we read and discuss. Our goal is to produce independent writers who are competent spellers. We believe that the best way to achieve this is to immerse students in a variety of meaningful daily reading and writing experiences.

While the implementation process has been slightly different for each teacher involved, we all continue to share the same philosophy: "Standard spelling is the consequence of writing and reading, not the access to it. . . . standard spelling is of little consequence if you do not write. Writing comes first!" (Bean and Bouffler, 1988, p. 47).

Children in our classrooms learn to spell the words they need, want, and are ready for through a variety of spelling strategies and resources.

Choosing Spelling Words

Words children work on for spelling mastery come from the following sources:

1. Words children misspell
2. Words children ask for
3. Words the teacher knows children need
4. Words relevant to a topic or theme

Emphasizing Spelling Strategies

In traditional programs, emphasis is on memorizing lists of words through repetition and drill. Since all the words for the week usually fit the same pattern or rule, it is not uncommon for students to do well on weekly tests and remain poor spellers. Because they are taught rules and not strategies, often students can spell the words only within the controlled workbook or testing framework. This is true as early as first grade. One insightful first-grader proclaimed, "You memorize the pattern, but you really don't know how to spell the words."

In an integrated approach, emphasis shifts to teaching students to utilize spelling strategies and to think about and apply what they have learned in the process of writing. Such an approach recognizes that the spelling of most words will occur in the normal context of reading and writing. Visual memory, sound-symbol relationships, and morphemic (base word) knowledge are developed implicitly and explicitly in teaching the following strategies:

1. Discovering the Rules

Whenever the teacher notices similar spelling errors being made by a number of students, a minilesson (a five- to ten-minute strategy-teaching session) is used to help students form generalizations about spelling rules. As an example, when children do not drop the "e" when adding "ing" to words such as "come," "write," and "have," the invented spellings ("comeing," "writeing," and "haveing") can be written on a transparency. Using an overhead projector, the teacher highlights the problem area and guides the students toward self-correction. Because students have encountered words in print over and over again when reading, they can usually offer the standard spellings and generate the rule. Specific spelling patterns, grapho-phonic generalizations, prefixes, suffixes, and root words are discussed at this time.

At times, words that fit a specific pattern are written on the overhead. Students are invited to come up one at a time and write another word that fits the pattern. Then the rule is generated by the class. Often a chart is made and kept hanging all week so that students can continue to add words that fit the pattern. Rules that work most consistently are the rules for suffixes (see Figure 10–2).

It has been interesting to note that children will also discover a rule before the rule is introduced in the basal spelling program. For example, "tion" in Figure 10–2 is not introduced until grade 4, yet this suffix regularly comes up in grade 2.

2. Recognizing the Limited Utility of Rules

While commercial spelling programs emphasize spelling rules and look for words to fit the pattern, many English words do not fit a rule. Frank Smith notes, "The 'rules' of spelling can be numbered in the hundreds and still carry only a fifty percent probability of being correct for any particular word" (1988, p. 18). When we discover a rule, we also note the exceptions.

3. Applying the Known to the Unknown

We use this strategy a lot with students. Through wide reading and writing students automatically write many words in standard spelling. Often when a student is working through a word on his Have-a-Go sheet (discussed in the next

Figure 10–2   Suffix Rules for -ion Words as Generated by Fourth-graders

tion   or   sion   words

fiction   television
attention   vision
protection   division
concentration   revision.
addition
station
question
subtraction
multiplication
caption
caution
prediction
production
fraction

Words that end with —ion are mostly "tion" but sometimes "sion."

section), we might say something like, "You already know how to spell the word _____. This word ends the same way." It is important to show students how to make connections so they can eventually do this on their own.

For example, when a grade 3 student spelled "anyd" for "annoyed," I slowly pronounced the word and asked, "What word do you know that has the 'oy' sound?" When he did not respond, I asked, "Do you know 'boy' and 'toy'?" The student then attempted to write the word and wrote "anoyd." After I asked, "What do you know about words that have the 'd' sound at the end, like 'stopped' and 'walked'?" he was able to write his second attempt as "anoyed." Lastly, I put a caret in "an‸oyed" and asked, "What missing letter could go here? Think about other words you know." Not only was the student able to write the word correctly, but because he had worked through the problem areas he would probably not misspell it again.

4. Proofreading

Proofreading in spelling (which is most often used when a child is ready to edit a piece of writing that is ready to go to final copy) includes two separate activities:

1. Examination—identifying as many misspelled words as possible
   We have our students circle these words with a colored pencil.
2. Production—correctly spelling as many of the misspelled words as possible
   We expect students to correctly spell at least three to five of the words.

When a piece of writing is being brought to final copy, the child takes a colored pencil and finds and corrects as many misspelled words as possible. The teacher then serves as the final editor and uses a different-colored pencil or marker to identify the misspelled words the student cannot find and correct. The Have-a-Go sheet is often used with the student as a worksheet in moving from the invented spelling to standard spelling.

Systematic attention needs to be given to proofreading so students develop responsibility for this necessary lifelong skill. We have found that students are more effective proofreaders if there is a lapse of time between writing and proofreading. I have also found that it works well to suggest that students look for misspellings by reading one word at a time from right to left, starting with the last word in the last line of their writing. In that way, they are focusing only on individual words and not on content.

Initially, placing the responsibility on students to find and correct spelling errors may seem burdensome to the teacher. Because teachers, especially at the secondary level, have traditionally found and corrected all errors, students may not take the activity seriously. However, no real learning takes place if the teacher continues to make most corrections. In fact, students tend to repeat the errors in subsequent writing. It is important to remain firm and not to accept papers until students have done their own proofreading and/or checked their papers with a peer. (This expectation does not apply in first grade.) Teachers find that when they expect students to assume responsibility for proofreading and when they have given enough demonstrations, students can do much more than teachers had previously thought they could. (See Figure 10–3 for an example of the work of a third grade L. D. student.) However, once students have done their best proofreading, the teacher avoids unnecessary frustration by spelling the remaining words "for free."

Figure 10-3   A Third Grade L.D. Student Assumes Responsibility for Proofreading

5. Using the Dictionary

We teach the use of the dictionary as the need arises, when the meaning of a word needed for reading is not clear from the context or when students desire specific information or want to expand their vocabulary. If the dictionary is referred to often and meaningfully, and the teacher demonstrates how to use it, students will readily learn about guide words, diacritical marks, accents, pronunciations, variant spellings, and multiple meanings. We have a variety of dictionaries available, including an excellent unabridged dictionary such as *Webster's Third International*. Instead of one set of dictionaries for all children in the classroom, several different sets, with fewer copies of each, will stimulate more interest and provide more information. Also, if a computer with a spelling checker is available, children can be taught how to use it.

Dictionary use can also be combined with vocabulary study and etymology (origin/derivation of words). Older students enjoy searching for the derivatives of a base word and reading word meanings in the dictionary. Some teachers use a challenge word of the day or week and invite students to find and discuss variations. For example, for the base word "cycle," a group of fourth-graders came up with "bicycle," "tricycle," "recycle," "cyclical," "cyclic," "cycling," "cyclist."

Resources for Developing Spelling Strategies

We use the following resources to develop strategies in a print-rich environment that provides students with lots of opportunities for reading, writing, and collaboration.

• <u>*Have-a-Go sheets*</u>   The Have-a-Go sheet, adapted from Australia (Jo-Ann Parry and David Hornsby, *Write On: A Conference Approach to Writing* [Heinemann, 1988], p. 61), is based on the idea that children, like adults, can usually identify a misspelled word even if they cannot spell it correctly. Children choose misspelled words from their daily writing and attempt to "have-a-go" at standard spellings. The teacher then conferences with the student to guide thinking processes and confirm or help with the final, standard spelling. (See Figure 10–4 for a low-ability second-grader's Have-a-Go sheet.) This is the technique I use the most when I am unsure of a spelling: I write the word several different ways to see which spelling *looks* right.

Teachers that try Have-a-Go sheets are quickly convinced of their effectiveness. Fourth grade teacher Brenda Spivey says,

> After having had the Have-a-Go sheet explained to me for the first time, I enthusiastically tried it out on my class. I was amazed to find out that it really does work. One little girl, a very poor speller, having used the sheet and spelled a word herself, had a look on her face that could only say, "At last I can spell!" The change in this child alone convinced me that there are methods of teaching spelling that work, unlike the weekly test method. I'm convinced that Have-a-Go teaches children to use a tried and true method that adults have always used!

• <u>*Peer help*</u>   When students don't know how to spell a word and have tried several sources, they will often ask a peer, "How do you spell _____?" Students quickly learn who the good spellers are and seek them out.

Figure 10–4   Low-Ability Second-grader's Have-a-Go sheet

If another adult is nearby, this is the technique I use most often if I am still unsure of a word after having written it several ways. We need to encourage collaboration as an important spelling strategy.

• *Minilessons*   Minilessons involve direct instruction through demonstration as well as provide opportunities for student participation and practice. They are often done whole class, usually at the end of a weekly time set aside for spelling and usually involving the overhead projector. The lessons are based on the needs of the children and on the belief that students don't just "pick up" all the skills they need. Minilessons also occur one-to-one when the teacher conferences with a child. It helps to keep in mind that only about 25 percent of the children may actually apply the skill that is taught to their own writing. A minilesson will probably need to be demonstrated over and over again. As in all language learning, children will acquire the skill when they are ready.

A typical minilesson involves calling the children's attention to a problem some of the students are experiencing. For example, in conferencing one-to-one with a class of fourth-graders, I noticed many were having difficulty knowing when to double the final consonant before adding "ing" or "ed." I wrote some words on the overhead projector (see Figure 10–5, top) and asked them to give me a rule. I wrote down what they told me, "Before 'ing,' double the consonant." I then challenged

Figures 10–5 and 10–6   Working with the Class on a Double Consonant Rule and Testing Its Validity

swiming
swimming

entertaining
hopping   hoping

Before ing, double the consonant

moping
mopping
timing

hatting
paintting
playing
spotted
spotting

Figure 10–6

If the vowel says its name, don't double the consonant.

prying   moping
              entertaining
              playing
              waited

stayed
frying
straying
tieing

them by writing other words (see Figure 10–5, bottom) and asking, "Are you correct?"

There was heated discussion, and an L. D. student who had spelling difficulties gave the rule, "If the vowel says its name, don't double the consonant." I then asked for, and they gave me, words to test out the validity of the rule (see Figure 10–6). Next, I wrote, with input from the students, several words with doubled consonants before the ending and challenged them to make another generalization. They took about fifteen minutes to come up with the detailed rule (see Figure 10–7). Then a student simplified it all by saying, "When the vowel is short we double."

Finally, I called out words orally one at a time and challenged the students to apply what we had been discussing and to spell the words (see Figure 10–8). There was some hesitation as each student who volunteered gave me the desired spelling, but every student spelled his or her word correctly. Usually a minilesson lasts five to ten minutes, but this one had lasted forty-five minutes! It was time well spent. Attention had never wavered, and a difficult concept had been internalized for most of the students.

A minilesson may also be used to talk about words the teacher feels students should know how to spell. For example, Linda Cooper tells her third grade students that she expects the following often misspelled words to be spelled correctly at all times: "said," "what," "when," "too," "color." Students add these words to their file boxes and are expected to refer to them as needed. First grade teacher Peg Rimedio posts a "Words to Remember" list to call attention to words students are using over and over again in their daily writing.

Marcy Silver, a third grade teacher who has just completed her first year with an integrated spelling program, comments:

> While most of the minilessons came from the context of the students' writing, I also checked the spelling workbook to be sure all the skills were covered. Once in a while, I put in a lesson I just thought they should have. The kids love the minilessons. Hands are flying in the air. Kids gather around to write on the charts. There is lots of excitement.

Figure 10-7   The Final Detailed Double Consonant Rule

Figure 10-8 Applying the Class's Double Consonant Rule

chim ing
tipp ing
wet ting
stay ing
tap ing
strapped
stubbed
batting
debat ing
bait ing
skat ing

• *Personal dictionary* Once the child has discovered the standard spelling of a word (usually after it has been worked through on the Have-a-Go sheet), the word is recorded on a 3 by 5 inch card and filed alphabetically in the student's individual file box. Alphabetizing is also taught here as students are expected to file cards in order. Children add the words they want to spell and that teachers expect them to spell. High-frequency words are also recorded in the file box so they are easily accessible. Students frequently use the file box as a reference in their daily writing. There is a lot of excitement as students use their individual file boxes as personal word banks.

Some teachers prefer to have students keep an "I Can Spell" list in the back of their journals. Having a booklet to which pages can be added in alphabetical order would also work well. Each student may also make a personal thesaurus.

• *Wall charts* Wall charts are used to group words around a theme: key vocabulary from a story, common words that need to be spelled correctly, content words, family words, holiday words, and so on. Lists and charts are also compiled to go along with the seasons, months, and topics of study and interest. In addition to wall charts, words from a theme chart may be typed in large print and put into a report cover for reference. Such lists are especially useful in the primary grades where students do not yet have a large core of words they can spell.

In a first grade room, it would not be unusual to see a variety of lists posted in enlarged print. For example, in February one teacher had lists posted for the following: family words (to aid journal writing), winter words, February words, and guinea pig words (for the class pet), as well as various phonics charts. These lists had all been generated with and by the children.

Additionally, in a minilesson as a rule is generated, a chart is started with the rule stated at the top (see Figure 10–9). The children then supply as many words as they can to fit the rule. The chart is then posted, and children are encouraged to continue adding words they find in their reading. After a period of time, usually a week or two, the teacher and the children review the chart and make needed corrections.

Figure 10-9   Creating a Chart Using a Class-generated Rule

Double consonants at the end of a word.

Spelling Big Books   After a chart is taken down from the wall and corrections have been made, a final alphabetized copy is prepared as a page for the class Spelling Big Book. These pages are usually completed in large, legible print by parent volunteers. Often they highlight the repeated pattern in each word in another color so that it stands out to the students. The Spelling Big Book includes a table of contents and serves as a reference for children to use in their daily writing. Because of the different needs of each group of children, a new Spelling Big Book is created each year.

Other spelling references   A variety of visual references is available to students in the classroom, including commercial dictionaries, thesauruses, textbooks, encyclopedias, trade books, magazines, newspapers, spelling reference books, posters, charts, and topic reference books (for example, for seasons, months, holidays, or events). Our students also have consumable spelling resources for daily personal use. (See pp. 261–262 for a description and ordering information.) In addition, books corresponding to a theme or topic are developed by the class for easy reference. For example, a special presidential election book was compiled that listed words such as "Democrat," "Republican," "politician," "registration," and "majority."

Spelling games   Spelling games—commercial, computer, teacher made, and student made—are available and used regularly. These games aid students in developing standard spellings in an informal setting.

Conferencing   As children are involved in their daily reading and writing activities, the teacher—at times with my help as the language arts resource teacher and/or a parent volunteer—confers with individual students. Usually the teacher guides students on their Have-a-Go sheets. Students select misspelled words from their journals, writing folders, or any other piece of writing they are working on and bring them to standard spelling with the help of the teacher.

Often the teacher intervenes after a first attempt at standard spelling. She points out which parts of the word are correct and which still need to be worked on. She may guide the child to the standard spelling by pointing out previously mentioned strategies. More and more, conferencing is occurring as part of the writing process, when there is a need to bring a piece to final copy and standard spelling is expected.

Organizing and Managing an Integrated Spelling Program

The key to management in spelling is making the environment safe for risk taking. Children develop the confidence and desire to solve their own spelling problems without worrying about getting a word right for the teacher or on a formal weekly test. Children recognize that their best attempts are not just tolerated but are genuinely accepted, encouraged, and congratulated.

The Need for Effective Parent Communication

Parents are initially uneasy about a more relaxed view of spelling. Based on their own schooling and experiences with their other children, they expect and rarely question the traditional approach to spelling with its workbook pages to complete, words to study, and weekly tests. Many parents have welcomed the Thursday night spelling drills for the next day's test as a sure way of participating in their child's education. Furthermore, parents are not generally aware of the research supporting a developmental view of spelling.

In addition, some parents get the message that spelling doesn't matter when teachers talk about accepting invented spellings. One parent told me, "We're producing educated people who can't spell." Her older child, a fifth-grader, was still misspelling words like "they" and "friend" in her journal, and the parent was now understandably quite skeptical about invented spelling. While it is acceptable for older children to use invented spelling in rough drafts, we need to expect high-frequency words to be spelled correctly while at the same time we encourage invented spelling for the more difficult words. We have to be very careful to give the message that standard spelling is important and is expected. (See Appendix J12.)

Whenever there is a change in programs, parents must be well informed. A third grade teacher who had not informed all parents of her new spelling program found out just how critical the need is for parental education. A student in her class brought home her spelling book with her Have-a-Go sheets. Her mother erased all the student's attempts and made her write all the words correctly. The student returned to school quite upset.

Sharing our new spelling program with parents continues to be a high priority. Letters go home explaining that the spelling text will not be used and explaining the philosophy and research supporting the new approach (see Appendix J4$_1$ and J4$_2$). Teachers discuss the spelling program during curriculum night (open house) and explain the transition that will occur from invented spellings to standard spellings.

Current research and children's work samples from previous years are used to support teachers' statements and to allay parents' anxieties about invented spelling. Usually teachers share writing samples from an average student from September to June so parents have an idea of what to expect and what is considered typical.

It has been my experience that if the teacher is knowledgeable about spelling development and current research—as well as comfortable with a holistic view of spelling—parents respond positively. In one of our weekly language arts support group meetings that focused on spelling, two first grade teachers shared parents' reactions to invented spelling. One teacher said that the parents of her students were delighted with her spelling program while the other teacher reported that many of her parents had concerns about spelling development. I looked at the two teachers and smiled to myself. One was totally comfortable with invented spelling and one was not. The parents were merely reflecting the messages the teachers had been sending, consciously or not.

Keeping Your Administrators Well Informed

Administrators are busy people who do not appreciate learning about a new program after it has been implemented. One principal was quite embarrassed when she learned from a parent that no spelling workbooks were being used in her child's class.

Consult your administrator before making any major changes in your spelling program. Discuss what you plan to do and share copies of articles and books that support a holistic view of spelling (see pp. 260–261). Invite your principal into your classroom regularly and let him or her know how things are progressing. Let your principal know what spelling lessons have been taught through minilessons. (See Figure 10–10 for a third grade teacher's first semester record, which she duplicated for her administrator.) In that way, when a parent questions the new program or asks how spelling is being addressed, the principal can answer specifically.

Organizing for Success

• *Setting aside time for Spelling*   In getting started, we have found it helpful to designate a consistent, weekly time of forty-five minutes to an hour when children find words from their daily writing to work through on their Have-a-Go sheets. Usually students circle five or more words that they know are misspelled and transfer them to their Have-a-Go sheets. Some teachers choose to do this activity in the editing stage of the writing process when pieces are being brought to final copy. Other teachers prefer to have children choose one new word each day and add it alphabetically to their file boxes. In any case, this is the time when the teacher is available for guidance and instruction.

• *The importance of demonstration*   Before students use the Have-a-Go sheet (or peer conferencing or peer testing), Don Holdaway's developmental model for language learning is employed. Demonstrations will need to take place repeatedly until students understand and can apply the procedures.

To begin with, students are asked to find a word in their writing that they know is misspelled but that they would like to be able to spell correctly. When doing a demonstration, I place a blank transparency of a Have-a-Go sheet (Appendix I) on

Figure 10-10   A Third Grade Teacher's First Semester Spelling Record

Spelling Lessons

Week of
9/5   words spelled w/ oa
ci rated by kids:
    oats   oat   goat
    oasis   ,   boat   soap
    float   coat
    roach   coach
9/11   tion
9/18   end in double cons.   ll, ss
9/25   Past tense formed w/ ed
10/2   ing
10/5 - no spelling
10/16 plurals using s or es
10/23 words spelled w/ igh
10/30 Alphabetic order - file box
11/13 Past tense of final y words
            (ed or ied)
11/27
    Words spelled with ou

    could
    would
    tough
12/4   Contractions
12/11 Compound words
    air plane
    air port
1/7   Words spelled with silent e
            mile, race, hose, prize

1/15   Plurals of vowel + y words   toys   keys
                                    cowboys plays

the overhead projector. A volunteer says a word with its invented spelling. Then we talk through and work through various attempts to spell the word correctly. (See Figure 10–11 for a demonstration that took place at the beginning of second grade.)

First, I slowly pronounce the word, stretching out each syllable. Sometimes the correct pronunciation—especially for a student who has difficulty hearing sounds in words—may be enough for the student to find and correct the error(s). Then I ask the student, "Which part looks right to you?" I will often put a check over the letters that are correct. Next, I ask, "Which part looks wrong to you?" Teachers are always amazed that even poor spellers and L. D. students can often identify the part of the word that looks wrong even if they cannot spell the word. I usually circle that part and ask the student to make a first attempt. After the first attempt, I continue to guide the student with prompts such as the following:

Figure 10-11   Talking through the Spelling of Words: Demonstrating Have-a-Go

- Does it look right now?
- What else could you try?
- What other letters could you use there to make that same sound?
- What do you know about words that have the _____ (for example, "er") sound at the end?
- How else could you spell that?
- You're missing a letter here. (Put in a caret.) What do you think it could be?
- Do you know how to spell _____? This word has a part that's the same.
- Take a look at the wall chart we worked on the other day. Your word is similar.
- What can you do to help yourself?

I verbalize some approaches that can be used if the student doesn't come up with strategies. Finally, I write the standard spelling in the last column, telling the student to look at the word carefully, "especially the tricky part that gave you trouble" and to come up to the overhead projector and write the word. Because the students have been actively involved in working through the trouble spot, even the poor spellers almost always write their word correctly.

• *Utilizing parent volunteers*   Especially the first year, we have found it essential to have several parent volunteers come in weekly to assist with the editing and proofreading processes and the Have-a-Go activity sheets. Parents have also been helpful in transferring spelling words from wall charts to the class Spelling Big Book. If volunteers are not available, students from higher grades may be used. As the teaching of spelling becomes more and more a natural part of all writing the need for volunteer help will lessen, although this may take several years to occur.

Welcoming parents into the classroom on a regular basis is also good for public relations. One first grade mother who helped weekly with journal writing was openly skeptical about invented spelling. She became convinced only after she *saw* her child, and all children in the classroom, internalizing spelling generalizations and making major spelling gains. This parent, who was active and vocal in the Parent-Teacher Association, shared her positive views with the community.

• _Keeping track of skills_   Teachers that move from a traditional spelling program to an integrated one initially find it useful to list all of the skills lessons covered in the spelling workbook program and to check these off as they are taught. Not only does this give the teacher some needed security; as already noted, the results can be shared with parents and administrators.

Many teachers are beginning to keep anecdotal records that note a student's growth in spelling as part of growth in writing. (See Chap. 13, "Evaluation.")

• _Materials needed_

Spelling organizer. Every student has a spelling organizer that serves as a record of the words she has chosen to learn to spell. This bound booklet takes the place of the traditional workbook and includes at the front a self-check list for learning new spellings, a cumulative record of about twelve to fifteen Have-a-Go sheets with Can You Spell It? sheets on the reverse side, and sheets for periodic peer testing (see Figure 10–12).

With the Have-a-Go sheets, we have found that two attempts at conventional spelling are usually sufficient. Three attempts, which we tried last year, did not work well for second-graders. However, upper grade teachers found that some students liked and needed three or more attempts.

Linda Cooper, who designed our original spelling organizer, now uses a simple pocket folder with Am I Becoming a Good Speller? on one side and Have-a-Go sheets, stapled cumulatively and handed out one at a time as needed, on the other side. As with any management tool, teachers need to make adjustments to suit their own needs.

File boxes. Each student also has a file box that holds 3 by 5 inch cards with alphabetical dividers. These supplies are purchased with student money from the annual supply fee. Some teachers save money and have students make their own dividers. Elaine Weiner has her students purchase their index cards and alphabetical dividers in the class store, thereby integrating math and language.

In first grade, Peg Rimedio uses index cards in an envelope stapled to the inside back cover of the writing journal. After words are mastered and listed on the "I Can Spell" sheet, they are taken home. New cards come from the teacher as she sees the need for specific words or as children request them.

Dictionaries. Each child has a copy of a compact personal dictionary and access to complete commercial dictionaries (see pp. 261–262).

Chart paper. We use large, sturdy chart paper (24 by 35 inches). We punch holes at the top or sides for ring binders so that pages may be added and moved as needed for the Spelling Big Book.

Figure 10-12   Pages from the Spelling Organizer

DATE	INVENTED SPELLING	1ST ATTEMPT	2ND ATTEMPT	3RD ATTEMPT	STANDARD SPELLING

CAN YOU SPELL IT ?

PEER TESTING

DATE	WORDS	DATE	WORDS

Am I Becoming a Good Speller?   Very likely you are if you can say...

I *care* about spelling

I will need spelling all the time I am in school. My parents want me to be a good speller. When I leave school, people will expect me to spell well.

I *write* often

The more I write, the more I am practicing spelling. I may not stop to check a spelling as I write my first draft, but I always check when I revise the draft.

I *proof-read* my writing

I finally proof-read any writing I will pass to readers. In doing this, I inspect every letter and all punctuation. Sometimes I also get a partner to check my "proofing."

I *read* every day

Reading leaves impressions of spelling in my mind. It also adds to the number of words I may use. While reading, I sometimes pause to notice spellings.

I *explore* words

For example, I notice letter patterns like *tion*, *ough*, *qu*. And prefixes (like *dis-*) and suffixes (like *-less*). And meaning stems, as in *paragraph*, *biography*, *telegraphic*.

I *check* to be sure

Sometimes while writing I ask for the spelling of a word. But I know that the final way to settle a doubt about a spelling is to consult a dictionary.

I *learn* new spellings

1 Look at the new word and say it softly.
2 Cover it and try to "see" it in the mind.
3 Write it from memory.
4 Check (and if incorrect, repeat the four steps).

There are many other spelling ideas worth trying, such as...

• Keep adding to a personal list of "Words I Have Learned to Spell."
• Find and play spelling and language games that you enjoy.
• Keep improving your handwriting, because that will help your spelling.
• Try out every spelling idea your teacher shows you and make a habit of any idea that works well for you, e.g., working with a partner.

R. D. Walshe, for The Primary English Teaching Association, Sydney Australia. Reproduced with permission.

Post-it notes. Some teachers like students to add words to the spelling chart on Post-its. In that way, words that are found not to fit the rule or pattern may simply be removed. Post-its are also great for alphabetizing practice. Students work together to put the remaining Post-its words in alphabetical order before a final chart is made.

Colored pencils and pens for editing and proofreading.

What Happens during Spelling Time

• <u>*Choosing words to learn to spell*</u>   Some teachers have children choose words from their journals, while others, who prefer not to use journals at all for this purpose, ask students to select words from other writing. Usually teachers ask students to circle the misspelled words before transferring them to their Have-a-Go sheets.

Students are encouraged to choose "important" words they will need to use again and not words that they will rarely use. Students become quite proficient in choosing appropriate words. We have also noticed that, overall, they choose much harder words than those in the basal spelling program.

We usually expect students to find at least five misspelled words, although sometimes they will choose more. Every once in a while we have a natural speller who has few misspelled words. We can utilize that talent by having the student help his or her classmates in the same way we do.

• *Having-a-Go*   Students put the date in the left-hand margin on their Have-a-Go sheets and work through at least five words. They are encouraged to use all appropriate strategies and available resources to arrive at the standard spelling of a word. Usually we tell the students to make only one attempt on each word and then wait for a conference. In the meantime, students work on drafts and revisions of writing in progress.

• *Conferencing*   Conferencing occurs with the teacher, a peer, or a parent volunteer. After a child has worked through the first or several attempts to spell a word correctly, he is guided in finding the trouble spots. The conference is essentially a one-to-one minilesson. Teachers also take the time to check file boxes and spelling organizers to be sure words are being added and spelled correctly.

• *Can You Spell It? sheets*   After the word has been worked through to standard spelling, the child looks at it carefully and writes it on the Can You Spell It? sheet (on the reverse side of the Have-a-Go). This may take place as part of the conference, and I might say something like: "Now, carefully look at the tricky part. That's right. It's just those two letters that gave you trouble. Good. Now write the word here on your Can You Spell It? sheet." The child then writes the word. "Now check yourself. Did you get it right? . . . Good."

The student now takes a 3 by 5 inch card and adds the word alphabetically to her file box. If the child misspells the word, she is referred to her Am I Becoming a Good Speller? folder and is reminded to go through the four steps for learning new spellings:

1. Look at the new word and say it softly.
2. Cover it and try to "see" it in the mind.
3. Write it from memory.
4. Check (if incorrect, repeat the four steps).

• *Minilesson*   The minilesson, as discussed earlier in this chapter, takes place regularly as needs arise.

• *Peer testing*   While some teachers believe all testing is unnecessary, others opt for peer testing, either when students feel they are ready or on a weekly basis. First grade teacher Peg Rimedio does voluntary testing of students' individual words with the help of fourth grade volunteers. Every Friday Elaine Weiner's second-graders test each other on the words they worked through that week. There is no grading of tests by the teacher. However, any word that is missed automatically goes on the next week's Have-a-Go sheet. Elaine says her students' enthusiasm for peer testing is evident. Many students voluntarily copy down their words and take them home to study. Elaine checks first to be sure they are written correctly.

Teachers note that students who are tested on their own words get almost all the words right. It has also been interesting to note that even the poorest spellers know when they've misspelled a word.

Spelling in Kindergarten and First Grade

First grade teacher Peg Rimedio, a former kindergarten teacher, suggests the following.

Kindergarten   Informally noticing beginning and ending sounds in poems, charts, and stories is all the teacher needs to do at this level. As in grades 1 and 2, students can be asked to predict how a word begins or ends as the teacher is writing an experience chart, journal entry, or group story.

Grade 1

1. Have lots of words around the room for reference.
2. Introduce Have-a-Go sheets, the dictionary, and the editing process in a relaxed, informal way. Emphasize exposure and exploration rather than marking what is correct or incorrect. Don't expect mastery.
3. Call spelling activities (noting word parts, rules, and patterns) "spelling" so that children and parents know they are doing spelling.
4. Explore alternatives to traditional spelling tests that put young children under unnecessary pressure. A procedure could be worked out for voluntary tests so that kids can see what they have mastered if they want to.

Evaluation

Teacher Observations from the First Year of an Integrated Spelling Program

From the time our informal, integrated spelling program was introduced, we teachers noticed that the students were enthusiastic and positive. As they were reading, children became aware of how words are spelled. Occasionally, a child would remark, "Oh, so that's how you spell that word." Students readily added words to the classroom spelling charts as they became aware of words that fit a particular pattern.

It was interesting to see students challenge themselves by choosing to learn to spell words that were more difficult than their teachers might have chosen. (See Figure 10–4 for a second-grader's Have-a-Go sheet in early fall.) Students also came to see the need for proofreading. One third-grader commented, "I finished my story. I'm taking it home to go over it." A majority of the students also enjoyed making classroom spelling games. This led to the unexpected bonus of learning cooperation and collaboration as the children worked in small groups.

Parents were amazed at the growth in their children's spellings. In fact, the initial fear about having to defend this new program never materialized. Positive comments were made to teachers informally and at parent-teacher conferences. Many parents verbalized that they liked the spelling program. "It's more meaningful and a better way for children to learn how to spell" was a typical comment.

There were some unexpected outcomes. Elaine Weiner and Linda Cooper had made a list of the specific objectives introduced in the spelling workbook and district curriculum guide. They were surprised and pleased to find that the children had already discovered about 20 percent of the rules in just the first two months of school. Another surprise was the frequency of invented spellings that was still occurring in rough drafts. We thought standard spelling might occur with greater frequency. Children, however, found and standardized spellings more easily and with greater frequency while proofreading.

Finally, we came to appreciate spelling as a developmental process and felt it was probably unrealistic to expect mastery of certain words in one year, even if the words had been introduced. For instance "too," "two," and "to" remained a difficult concept for second-graders, as did "their," "they're," and "there" for third-graders.

Meaningful Evaluation of Spelling

We believe that evaluation of spelling should be a natural part of the writing process. There are many meaningful ways students, teachers, and parents can note spelling progress without resorting to whole-class testing. Daily writing, including journals, stories, narratives, content pieces, and poetry, can all be used for evidence of spelling growth. Personal spelling records such as dictionaries, Words I Can Spell booklets, and file boxes are all ways for children to record words they are now spelling.

Developing proofreading skills is also an excellent way to build spelling abilities. Even as early as second grade, teachers may reasonably expect students to bring a piece of writing to final copy about once a month and get as close as possible to standard spelling.

To note changes in student attitudes and strategies being used, spelling inventories and interviews may be scheduled at the beginning and end of the school year (see Figure 10–1). An interview may even be done whole class. In Ellen Rubin's second grade during the last week of school in June 1990, I asked the children to tell me what good spellers do. I posed the question orally and then randomly called on students who volunteered. On the overhead projector, I wrote their responses exactly as the students gave them to me and in the order stated:

What Strategies Do Good Spellers Use to Get Standard Spelling?

1. Give the word as many attempts as you need.
2. You have to read the word a lot. You have to see the word a lot in stories.
3. Try to memorize words that you need most.
4. The long words are the easy words, and the short words are the hard words because you can't sound out the short words. You can sound out "paleontologist" easier than "were" or "right."
5. Try writing the word until it looks right to you.
6. You can sound it out.
7. You can look the word up in the dictionary.
8. Ask a friend.

9. Good spellers learn to spell the words they use over and over again in their stories.
10. Good spellers read a lot about what they want to spell. If I'm interested in space and I want to spell "Jupiter," I'd read about it.
11. You could look in your spelling box.
12. You could look for the word on the class spelling charts.
13. You could look it up in your "little dictionary"—personal dictionary.
14. You can use the thesaurus—"word bank."
15. Look for the word on "News of the Day"—newspaper.

This was Ellen's first year implementing an integrated spelling approach, and she and I were both delighted and amazed with the responses. We were very impressed with the reading-writing connection the children made and with the focus on meaning and real-life practicality of their responses. For example, it is often easier to spell a long word you can sound out, as Craig mentioned in (4), but we had no idea Craig not only understood this concept but could apply it. Also, the last statements referred to using charts or the dictionary. Just as adults often use the dictionary as a last resort, the students recognized other strategies as being more useful. Finding a word in the dictionary is difficult unless one already knows the correct spelling of at least the first three letters.

Rethinking the Use of Traditional Spelling Tests

We need to look carefully at the widely accepted practice of requiring weekly spelling tests. Not only do they put unnecessary pressure on young students especially, they take up a lot of time in the home that might be better spent on worthwhile literacy activities. I am amazed at how much time parents tell me they work with their children, helping them study for spelling tests. Even with a first-grader, the parents may spend as much as an hour or more drilling words for the Friday test. I think the reason spelling tests are accepted without question is that parents are familiar with the process from their own schooling, and they think the tests are contributing to their child's progress. Testing also makes grading easy, since all a teacher needs to do to arrive at a student's grade is average the weekly test percentages. We need to rethink whether the time and effort that is being put into spelling tests should be invested in an activity that is of questionable value. If testing is seen as necessary, peer testing of individual students' self-selected words, as described earlier in this chapter, is a more viable alternative.

We also need to question the validity of standardized spelling tests where, typically, the student is asked to choose the correctly spelled word from among four choices. Such tests are really proofreading tests. Unless a child can also write the word, the test is not totally valid as a measure of spelling ability.

Students can be devastated by the pressure and effects of weekly testing. Thomas, a bright fourth-grader, spoke with me about his experiences with spelling tests. In first grade, Thomas had been in Karen Shiba's class where spelling was taught incidentally through immersion in reading and writing activities. He had felt positive about himself as an independent writer despite his poor grapho-phonics abilities. While Thomas' invented spelling was a challenge to read, his journal from September to June showed consistent evidence of steady progress in spelling.

In second and third grades, Thomas was in classrooms that put a high priority on doing well on weekly spelling tests. He told me, "I had headaches and stomach aches a lot. I was always thinking about spelling pretests and spelling tests, and it made me sick. I always did real bad on my spelling tests. I hated them. I still think they're a waste of time and unfair. I could do excellent in the workbook and still mess up on the test."

In fourth grade, Thomas began to relax about spelling. He still struggled but noted, "Spelling will probably always be hard for me. This year I'm doing well in spelling. It's easier for me. My teacher doesn't think spelling tests are that important." No doubt his teacher's relaxed attitude helped his own.

Nora, a first-grader who felt very pressured by weekly spelling tests, told her mother—who also happened to be a first grade teacher—"You should do spelling stuff but you shouldn't have tests because the kids who don't get 100 percent feel bad." Nora also told her mother, who did not give spelling tests, "I think you're real smart because you give kids free choice. Because if kids can choose [the words] they want to do it. But if they have to do it, they don't want to do it." Her statements are evidence of a young child's sensitivity to the need for choice while recognizing the importance of doing "spelling stuff."

Reflections

We are all still in the process of developing and reassessing the teaching and learning of spelling in the classroom. Those of us who have tried an integrated spelling program have all completed the first year with the belief that its implementation has been consistent and relevant for our reading-writing classrooms. We believe our children are spelling at least as well as those using a traditional program, and we know they are greater risk takers. We see our children learning and applying phonics generalizations in their daily reading and writing. And we continue to note that our best spellers are usually our best readers and writers, while the majority of our poor spellers also struggle with reading and writing.

We continue regularly to discuss issues, concerns, research, and professional articles having to do with spelling and to spend much time discussing theory and how to put it into practice. Professional reading continues to provide a needed framework as well as a challenge to continue to improve our spelling instruction. We are presently focusing on developing better techniques in classroom management and evaluation.

We have come to believe that spelling methods and materials are secondary to immersion in authentic reading and writing activities. Eventually, we expect that spelling will be totally integrated into our teaching. We will know that has happened when we stop referring to spelling separately and begin teaching all spelling as needs occur in daily reading and writing.

Resources

The following resources are particularly helpful for formulating theory and practice in the teaching of spelling. A number of the articles and books have been discussed in our weekly language arts support groups as we focused on spelling in depth.

Bean, Wendy, and Chrystine Bouffler. 1988. *Spell by Writing.* Portsmouth, NH: Heinemann.

   This text (92 pp.) remains my favorite, as well as the favorite of several of my colleagues, on the teaching of spelling. For the teacher who already understands and accepts the theory behind teaching spelling as a part of writing, this book is invaluable. Lots of detailed "strategy lesson plans" for helping children develop as writers are clearly presented.

Bloodgood, Janet W. November 1991. "A New Approach to Spelling Instruction in Language Arts Programs." *The Elementary School Journal,* pp. 203–211. See annotation, p. 83b.

Bolton, Faye and Diane Snowball. 1993. *Ideas for Spelling.* Portsmouth, NH: Heinemann. See annotation, p. 83b.

Bolton, Faye and Diane Snowball. 1993. *Teaching Spelling: A Practical Resource.* Portsmouth, NH: Heinemann. See annotation, p. 83b.

Booth, David (ed.). 1991. *Spelling Links: Reflections on Spelling and its Place in the Curriculum.* Markham, Ontario: Pembroke Publishers Limited, and Bothell, WA: The Wright Group. See annotation, p. 84b.

Buchanan, Ethel. 1989. *Spelling for Whole Language Classrooms.* Katonah, NY: Richard C. Owen.

   For teachers who have a well-developed theory base for developmental spelling, this spiral-bound handbook (154 pp.) focuses in depth on the stages of spelling development and gives detailed procedures for analyzing misspellings.

Cunningham, Patricia M. and James W. Cunningham. October 1992. "Making Words: Enhancing the Invented Spelling-Decoding Connection." *The Reading Teacher,* pp. 106–115. See annotation, p. 84b.

Gentry, Richard. November 1982. "An Analysis of Developmental Spelling in GYNS AT WORK," *The Reading Teacher,* pp. 192–200.

   Using Glenda Bissex's case study of her son's language development, Gentry details five stages of spelling development and gives guidelines for helping children acquire spelling competence. Gentry believes teachers need to identify and understand these stages in order to teach spelling appropriately.

Gentry, Richard. 1987. *Spel . . . is a Four-Letter Word.* Portsmouth, NH: Heinemann.

   This is a good starting place for teachers and parents. This short (54 pp.), easy to read guide offers the author's personal experience as well as research on learning to spell. Myths about spelling are cleared up; invented spelling is explained; and strategies for teaching spelling are presented.

Gentry, Richard and Jean W. Gillet. 1993. *Teaching Kids to Spell.* Portsmouth, NH: Heinemann. See annotation, p. 84b.

Harp, Bill. March 1988. "When the Principal Asks 'Why Are Your Kids Giving Each Other Spelling Tests?'" *The Reading Teacher,* pp. 702–704.

   This short piece gives a clear rationale for peer testing in an individualized spelling program. Share this with administrators and parents.

Parry, Jo-Ann, and David Hornsby. 1988. "Spelling in the Writing Classroom." In *Write On: A Conference Approach to Writing.* Portsmouth, NH: Heinemann, pp. 57–66.

   This is a highly practical chapter that includes the spelling stages learners go through, the necessary conditions for learning to spell, and lots of terrific ideas for teaching strategies and setting up classroom spelling procedures. Visual representations of activities are very helpful.

Phenix, Jo and Doreen Scott-Dunne. 1991. *Spelling Instruction that Makes Sense.* Markham, Ontario: Pembroke Publishers Limited, and Bothell, WA: The Wright Group. See annotation, p. 85b.

Powell, Debbie and David Hornsby. 1993. *Learning Phonics and Spelling in a Whole Language Classroom.* New York: Scholastic. See annotation, p. 85b.

Routman, Regie. May/June 1993. "The Uses and Abuses of Invented Spelling." *Instructor,* pp. 35–39. See annotation, p. 85b.

Scott, Ruth. 1993. *Spelling: Sharing the Secrets*. Toronto, Ontario: Gage Educational Publishing Company. See annotation, p. 85b.

Sowers, Susan. 1988. "Six Questions Teachers Ask About Invented Spelling." In *Understanding Writing: Ways of Observing, Learning, and Teaching*, 2nd ed. Thomas Newkirk and Nancie Atwell (eds.) Portsmouth, NH: Heinemann, pp. 62–79.

> *Sowers aptly answers the following questions: (1) "What is invented spelling?" (2) "Why should children be permitted to be inventive spellers?" (3) "Other than being 'wrong' instead of right, how does invented spelling differ from standard spelling?" (4) "Are there stages in invented spelling?" (5) "Does invented spelling get better on its own?" (6) "How do you decide what spelling skills to teach an inventive speller?" This informative piece, particularly helpful for understanding invented spelling, includes important information on communicating with parents.*

Tarasoff, Mary. 1992. *A Guide to Children's Spelling Development*. Victoria, B.C.: Active Learning Institute. (U.S. distributor: Peguis Publishing, Winnipeg, Manitoba.) See annotation, p. 85b.

Temple, Charles, Ruth Nathan, Frances Temple, and Nancy Burris. 1993. *The Beginnings of Writing*, 3rd ed. Boston: Allyn and Bacon.

> *This excellent text (287 pp.) examines children's writing, ages four to eight, and has complete chapters on invented spelling, learning standard spelling, and making progress in spelling, and several chapters on writing in different modes. Preschool through grade 3 teachers will find this text very informative.*

Templeton, Shane. November 1991. "Teaching and Learning the English Spelling System: Reconceptualizing Method and Purpose." *The Elementary School Journal*, pp. 185–201. See annotation, p. 86b.

White, Thomas G., Joanne Sowell, and Alice Yanagihara. January 1989. "Teaching Elementary Students to Use Word-Part Clues," *The Reading Teacher*, pp. 302–307.

> *Applicable for students in grade 3 and above, this is a valuable article for actively involving students in using and understanding prefixes and suffixes. Two tables—"The most common prefixes in printed school English for grades 3–9" and "English suffixes ranked by frequency of occurrence"—are especially useful to the teacher. Possible prefix and suffix lessons are included.*

Wilde, Sandra. 1989. "Looking at Invented Spelling: A Kidwatcher's Guide to Spelling. Parts I and II." In *The Whole Language Evaluation Book*, Kenneth Goodman, Yetta Goodman, and Wendy Hood (eds.). Portsmouth, NH: Heinemann, pp. 213–236.

> *Wilde discusses and analyzes four major principles in holistic spelling evaluation: (1) evaluating through natural writing instead of tests; (2) evaluating analytically rather than just in terms of right or wrong; (3) evaluating by looking at strategies employed instead of looking at words in isolation; (4) evaluating as a knowledgeable professional and not just a scorer of tests. Very useful for teachers ready to analyze invented spellings and observe the spelling strategies children use.*

Wilde, Sandra. January 1990. "A Proposal for a New Spelling Curriculum," *The Elementary School Journal*, pp. 275–289.

> *Wilde examines recent research on children's invented spelling, critiques the traditional textbook model of teaching spelling that has ignored the research, and argues for classroom spelling practice that is consistent with how children learn all language—gradually and with lots of practice in meaningful contexts. Teachers and administrators will receive strong theoretical and practical support as well as learn many specific strategies for developing a spelling curriculum that is part of the reading-writing process. An outstanding, comprehensive monograph.*

Wilde, Sandra. 1991. *You Can Read This! Spelling and Punctuation for Whole Language Classrooms, k-6*. Portsmouth, NH: Heinemann. See annotation, p. 86b.

Zutell, Jerry. October 1978. "Some Psycholinguistic Perspectives on Children's Spelling," *Language Arts*, pp. 844–850.

> *This classic, often referred to article reaffirms that the research supporting invented spellings and its implications for teaching has been around for a long time. This is a superb article for gaining a clear understanding of how children learn to spell, for a review of the early spelling research, and for practical applications for school and home.*

Consumable Resources for Students

Teachers of integrated spelling programs have found it useful for each elementary student to have a personal spelling dictionary. These short references are easier to use than a regular dictionary, and they contain space for students to add their own words alphabetically. Our teachers purchase these inexpensive handbooks out of the annual student supply fee. The spelling booklets are collected at the end of the year and are passed on to the next grade's teacher.

Holloway, Judy (compiler). 1989. *Writing Dictionary.* Scarborough, Ontario, Canada: Ginn Publishing Canada Inc. ($2.25) (In U.S., order through Steck-Vaughn Co., Austin, Texas.)

> *First grade teachers and special education teachers have found this dictionary invaluable. Our teacher of developmentally handicapped students says, "All the words my students need are here and easy to find because there are so few words on each page." This terrific resource has delightful visuals and lots of space for beginning writers to add their own words.*

Hurray, Gregory. 1987. *A Spelling Dictionary for Beginning Writers.* Cambridge, MA: Educators Publishing Service. ($2.80, 6 or more)

> *Second grade teachers especially love this easy-to-use resource with its large, clear type for beginning writers (also applicable for grades 1 and 3). An extensive "Word Bank" at the end includes a mini-thesaurus of common words such as "big," "good," and "said" as well as lists of theme words that include the calendar, numbers, colors, clothes, school, and family.*

Sitton, Rebecca, and Robert Forest. 1987. *The Quick-Word Handbook for Everyday Writers.* North Billerica, MA: Curriculum Associates. ($.89)

> *This is a handy resource for elementary students in grades 3 and above. About one thousand high-utility words are included along with a list of abbreviations, states, numbers, months, and days and a list of homophones and sentences delineating homophone pairs.*

11

Setting Up an In-School Publishing Process

A parent volunteer publishing a book with a first grade student

Publishing children's written work in a final copy, printed edition that is shared publicly is a powerful tool for motivating and engaging students in continued reading and writing. However, because publishing in the classroom can be so time consuming, the use of parent volunteers can facilitate and expedite the process. This chapter describes a school-wide publishing effort that has worked well in our district. While the model described might not meet your needs or work for your school or district, my hope is that you can use it to determine your own available resources and possibilities. Perhaps with the support of your Parent-Teacher Association and the school administrator, you may see ways to get the publishing process going in your own classroom or school on a scale you are comfortable with.

A District Publishing Program

Every teacher in every first grade classroom is involved in our district-wide effort to celebrate children's writing and to connect children's writing to reading through publishing. Whether through journal writing, story writing, or writing workshop, children have frequent and regular opportunities to write on self-selected topics. While participation in our organized publishing program is voluntary, any initial reluctance disappeared once teachers have seen the power of publishing.

Since the fall of 1987, we have been extremely fortunate to have Marianne Sopko as the parent volunteer coordinator for publishing in our elementary schools. This volunteer position, which Marianne created, grew out of her involvement in publishing in her son Mike's first grade classroom where she worked closely with me and with first grade teacher Karen Shiba. She was so impressed with what publishing did for the children's self-esteem, as well as for their reading and writing development, that she initiated a district-wide publishing effort. (See Routman, 1988, pp. 110–118 and 194–197, for earlier information on book publishing.)

Our book publishing program places special emphasis on first grade, where the most help is needed and where the power of publishing is most dramatic. For some children publishing promotes a leap into literacy because their own writing may be the first successful reading they do. Additionally, the many books that are published in a school year become a treasured part of the classroom book collection.

For older children publishing remains powerful as a motivation for writing. Many teachers report that the children's published books are the most popular ones in the classroom. Publishing also legitimizes the need for revisions and conventions—correct spelling, grammar, clarity, format—and gives a needed purpose for doing one's best work. Once you "go public," the writing has to be in its best form. There's no question that publishing authentic writing for an audience increases students' willingness to revise.

The Role of Parents

Parents make publishing easy and possible for the classroom teacher by assuming the labor-intensive aspects of the job. In first grade, parents make the book covers and take the stories the children have written in invented spellings—in their journals, notebooks, or writing folders—and transcribe them into standard English with conventional spellings. In some kindergarten classes, parents type stories from the children's journals and take dictation. Always, great caution is taken through training parents and gently reminding them that ownership belongs with the child. Parents are encouraged not to teach or intrude but rather to encourage, support, and guide.

In second through sixth grades, parents make or teach children to make wallpaper book covers. Once teachers learn how to make the books, they take over in guiding students. Many parents also serve as final editors-typists of children's books. Occasionally, after the teacher has carefully demonstrated for them, parents are used in facilitating the revision process.

For the efficient management of the publishing process, each of our elementary buildings has a parent coordinator who oversees the running of the program. The coordinator is responsible for training parent volunteers for publishing, serving as a liaison with teachers and making sure supplies and book covers are maintained and available. We have found the system works best if coordinators are first grade parents. Because their own children directly benefit from the process, the parents recognize the value of publishing and invest their time and effort in it. Marianne Sopko has served as the overall supervising coordinator who trains and coaches each of the building coordinators and meets with them regularly as needed. Past coordinators train incoming ones with support from Marianne.

Even with all of these supports, establishing a comfortable working relationship between teachers and parents takes time, sensitivity, and honest communication on the part of everyone involved. One year, in one building, some well-meaning but overzealous parents organized themselves before teachers were ready. A flyer went out the first week of school asking teachers how many volunteers they wanted and how they wanted them to be used. When teachers showed little immediate interest in getting started with publishing, some of the parents became upset. The teachers, however, were not yet ready to implement a program. They needed the first six weeks of school to establish their routines and get to know their students. Once teachers communicated their needs, the parents understood and respected the teachers' requests.

The Role of Teachers

Asking for Help

For some teachers, it was difficult initially to ask for parent help, perhaps because of their own staunch independence or because they feared parents invading the classroom. However, once teachers give it a try, they find allowing parents to help with publishing is not nearly as disruptive as they had imagined, and they welcome assistance with the editing process. Having parents take care of the mechanical processes of actually making and editing the books frees teachers. Because the parents have been chosen by the teachers and then specially trained by the coordinator, it is uncommon for a parent not to work out to a teacher's satisfaction.

When teachers take the time to be very specific about what they want parents to do, they are particularly pleased with the results. Third grade teacher Donna Brittain gives her parent volunteers a complete set of typed guidelines when her students are publishing their own poetry books.

Record Keeping

It is up to the teacher to keep a record of who has published, completed illustrations to go along with the text, and shared completed books with the class. It is very easy in first grade to overlook a child who has difficulty getting writing down on the page. I was upset one year to learn that one of my Reading Recovery students had published only one book by April. These are the children who especially need the publishing process to foster their literacy skills. Their own language, the most predictable text of all, needs to be used to support their reading development and to build confidence in their abilities. It is necessary, even if it requires that the parent volunteer mostly take dictation, for reluctant learners to have an equal chance. Keeping a class chart and checking off publication dates facilitates an equitable publishing process.

Our first-graders publish an average of six to eight books over a school year. Initially, any or all of their writing may go to publication, but as the year progresses, students are encouraged to choose only their best or favorite pieces. In second grade and above, where much of the transcribing is done by the children, several books per child, per school year, is average. One of these may be a book for the local Young Authors' Conference.

Word Processing

Computers have added a new dimension to children's desire to write. While word processing is available to all students in our district, every fifth- and sixth-grader takes a semester course under the leadership of our computer expert Adrianne Geszler. Students' word processing expertise has aided the publishing process; it is easier and faster for them to do revisions with printed text. Students enjoy the difference in the "feel" of composition produced by word processing versus that done by hand. And students with poor handwriting or learning disabled students who have difficulty reading their own writing find that seeing the piece in type can facilitate the writing process. Finally, when children's rough drafts have been typed exactly as they were written onto a word processing program and printed out double- or triple-spaced, it is much easier for them to see what needs to be edited.

However, word processing is not a panacea. Just because a piece was written on the computer does not guarantee its quality. Unless the writing process is clearly established in the classroom and students understand the teacher's expectations for revision and editing, a story composed on a word processor can be dull or poorly written. Students will not automatically revise just because the word processor is available; they first have to value revision as a strategy. As with all communication and language processes in the classroom, using technology depends largely on the teacher's philosophy and beliefs.

For the last several years, our teachers and students have especially enjoyed the easy workability and large print of "The Children's Writing and Publishing Center" by Learning Company in Menlo, California. However, recognizing how quickly computer programs become obsolete, teachers would do well to check with Learning Company as well as with Sunburst in Pleasantville, New York, and Scholastic Inc. in New York City for reputable word processing programs.

Setting Up the Publishing Program

Space Requirements

Storage space with shelving to house supplies and some designated table space on which to work are necessary. We house all publishing supplies in a corner of our WEB (see p. 452). A round table in our WEB is used for publishing, and supplies are within easy reach. In most of our buildings, tables and chairs are set up in the halls just outside the classrooms for parents and students to work together.

Supplies Needed

Funds for purchasing book publishing supplies are now a part of our school district's annual budget, and our district warehouse now stocks chipboard and rubber cement. As necessary, supplies are replenished by the parent volunteer coordinator. Teachers and parents are welcome to use all supplies but are requested to return items promptly when they are no longer using them. The following supplies are recommended for setting up a publishing program:

- **Wallpaper** (for book covers). A local wallpaper store may be willing to contribute discontinued wallpaper books. It is much easier to work with flat sheets than with rolls, and you get lots of variety. Remove the pages with a razor blade.
- **Chipboard** (for backing the book covers). This cardboard is purchased in quantity at a local paper supply company. One thousand 8 1/2 by 14 inch pieces cost about $25. Each piece, when cut to size, yields a book. To save time and ensure accuracy, we have whole boxes cut at a printer's for about $15.
- **Tape** (for securing the chipboard before pasting). Any cellophane or masking tape works, but Scotch Magic tape is the easiest to use. If you're doing a lot of books, heavy tape dispensers, which permit one-hand use, speed up the process.
- **Rubber cement** (for pasting the covers). There is no subsititute for rubber cement. A quart of rubber cement will do about one hundred books. (Gallon cans are the most economical and can be used with smaller dispensers.)

Empty cans are returned for refilling. Elmer's glue may be used for the margins that are folded down over the cardboard, but we have found through experimentation that rubber cement works best for getting a smooth result on the front and inside covers.

- **Construction paper** (for the inside covers). A heavier weight (#80) produces a nicer result. Look for the best price, variety of colors, and quality of paper.
- **Labels for book titles** (for the title and author). We use mostly C-Line badges with colored borders (red, blue, green, and gold). If you buy in quantity, you may be able to get a discount. Any self-stick blank label affixed to the front cover will work.
- **Long-arm staplers** (for binding). For books using folded sheets, a long-arm stapler that allows sheets to be stapled at the centerfold is a must.
- **Mimeograph paper** (for book pages). Paper is cut to size by volunteers. With 8 1/2 by 11 inch paper there will be one cut; with legal size paper (11 by 14 inch) there will be two 6 1/2 by 11 inch cuts. (See directions for making wallpaper books.)
- **Paper cutter** (for cutting book pages to size).
- **Erasable pens** (for transcribing by hand).
- **Brass paper fasteners (brads)** (for assembling books of single pages). Look for #3 or #4.
- **Punches** (for making holes in cover and pages). "Ticket" punch size works best; a small hole is more desirable for securing the pages with brads.
- **Dictionary** (for checking spelling).
- **Sets of directions for book publishing** (for making book covers). Directions (see the next section, "Making the Book Covers") are posted on a wall near the supplies. Individual copies of directions are also available for parents to take when they are making book covers at home.

Estimated Costs

If wallpaper and labor are donated and mimeograph paper is used from the school's supply, the cost per book is about 15 cents.

Chipboard	2.5 cents/book
Cutting cost	1.5 cents/book
Rubber cement	4 cents/book
Construction paper	2.5 cents/book
Tape	2 cents/book
Labels for cover	2.5 cents/book

Additionally, you will need to plan on start-up costs of about $150. That amount will buy several half-pint- or pint-size dispensers for the rubber cement (which can be replenished from a gallon can), several heavy tape dispensers, several long-arm staplers, brass paper fasteners, punches, and erasable pens. A heavy-duty stapler that can secure up to one hundred pages may be needed for older grades.

Making the Book Covers

We begin each school year with a large supply (several hundred) of book covers on hand. Many parents are willing to take supplies home and make book covers over the summer. In addition, requests to parents for making book covers occur building- and district-wide during the school year as needed. (See Appendix J6 and J7 for sample flyers that were sent to parents.)

We have found that two types of wallpaper book covers work especially well:

1. Folded sheets of paper are stapled into the centerfold of the book. This type is used for first grade publishing (and sometimes in second grade) where the parent editor hand prints the child's story.

2. Single sheets of paper are secured by staples or brass paper fasteners. This kind of fastener is used if children write out their own books (a page can easily be replaced) or if pages are word processed or typed.

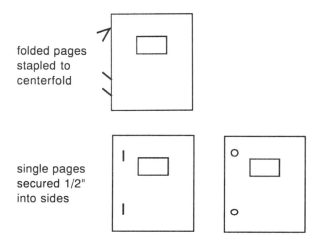

See end of chapter for directions for making the two types of book covers.

Training Parents

Teachers are encouraged to identify parents whom they think would work well with students in the publishing process. These need to be parents who value and understand invented spelling, who recognize the importance of keeping the writing ownership with the child, and who are sensitive and professional about the information they learn about and from children. However, some teachers are comfortable using any parents who want to participate. While several parents per classroom is ideal, having even one parent involved can have an impact on the publishing effort. The parents are asked to come in once a week for at least an hour throughout the school year.

Because of the large number of parents working full-time, some years it is particularly difficult to get parent volunteers. Even working parents, however, can make book covers, and they do (see Appendix J6). If getting volunteers proves difficult, you might try recruiting senior citizens, parents without school-age children, or older students.

Marianne Sopko models the publishing process for each building coordinator. She follows Holdaway's developmental model by demonstrating first, inviting parents to try the process while she coaches, and then giving parents time to practice on their own. She begins by bringing in a child the teacher has indentified as ready to publish. (Some teachers write on the board the names of the children who are ready to publish. In this way, the volunteer knows exactly who to take and in what order.)

First, the child is asked to read his writing. Then, questions—as needed for clarification—are asked. Some regrouping of material may be suggested, but the final decision concerning reorganization is the child's. The child selects a book cover, gives his story a title if one is not already in place, and watches while his journal entries or other written pieces are transcribed into book form. The child is then encouraged to read the book. This is especially important for making the beginning reading-writing connection.

After the child returns to class, Marianne discusses the process and answers questions from the observing parent. If the parent feels ready, the parent publishes the next child's writing while Marianne observes and coaches. It takes Marianne a full hour and a half to cover the key elements and mechanics of publishing, publish one child, and observe the parent publish one child.

The coordinators then train the parent volunteers in their respective buildings, and/or former volunteers are used to train new parents. Even without such a coordinated volunteer program, teachers could train their own volunteers to support the publishing process in the classroom.

Teacher Leadership and Administrative Support in Getting Started

Modeled on the publishing process in our district, two teachers in a neighboring school district wrote a proposal to establish publishing centers at their elementary schools. Both teachers felt the program—which was piloted in two buildings—was successful largely because of the strong support of the assistant superintendent of schools and the two school principals.

Funds were appropriated for paying Marianne Sopko as a consultant, for teachers to be released to observe the publishing process in another school district, and for the purchase of necessary supplies. The principals helped identify parent volunteer coordinators who would be knowledgeable, reliable, supportive, and nonthreatening to teachers and other parents. The principals were also helpful in suggesting the names of parent volunteers who could be expected to work well with teachers and children.

In addition to administrative support, this new publishing effort was successful because two teachers were willing to commit time without pay to meet with the parent coordinator, order supplies, discuss future directions, spend time with the principals, and do professional reading and whatever else was necessary to get the publishing effort organized for the two schools.

Evaluation

Once a publishing program is operative, it's a good idea to take an objective look at how well the program is working: How many books are being published? What is the quality of the books? Are book covers and supplies usually on hand? What are the teacher's and children's attitudes toward the process and products?

Publishing Center Evaluation Form

1. Did you use the services of the publishing center this year?

   Yes _____　　No_____

   If not, are there any changes which would make the program more useful to you?

2 What was the most helpful or valuable aspect of the program?

3. What, if any, problems did you encounter? (scheduling, availability of volunteers, volunteer-student relationships, book format, other)

4. Were the volunteers adequately trained? Would you suggest additional training in any areas?

5. What suggestions do you have to improve the program?

6. Do you plan to use the center next year?　Yes_____　　No_____
   In order to have enough book covers ready by September, we would like to know *about* how many books you think you will publish per student._____

Name (optional) _____

(form developed by Nancy Erkkila and Donna Ostberg)

At the end of the first year of setting up a publishing center, one school system gave the above written evaluation to all participating teachers and administrators. Directions and changes for the following year were based largely on information received from the surveys.

Reflections

We were unusually fortunate in our district to have a parent volunteer spearhead a district-wide publishing effort in the elementary grades. Teachers in other districts who have taken the leadership to work with their administrators and parents have also been successful in setting up publishing centers in their own buildings or classrooms.

It is not only the children's excitement at having their writing published that is significant about the publishing process. Once parent volunteers feel comfortable and confident with their role in the process, many say it is the most gratifying work they have ever done in their child's school. As they witness how important publishing is to students, they come to place a very high value on it. Additionally, they see firsthand the literacy development and potential of all children, and they come to appreciate the power of writing for reading and thinking. Welcoming parents into the school for publishing makes them an integral and vital part of the school community.

HOW TO MAKE WALLPAPER BOOKS
FOR FOLDED PAGES

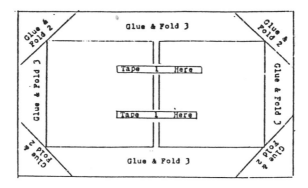

Suggested Dimensions:

Cardboard: 6½" x 7½"
Wallpaper: At least 15" x 9"
Construction paper: 6½" x 12"

1. Tape cardboard to wrong side of wallpaper, leaving
    about 3/8" gap between cardboad pieces at center.

2. Glue and fold wallpaper corners to cardboard.

3. Glue and fold wallpaper sides to cardboard.

4. Glue construction paper lining to wallpaper sides.

5. Cut paper for book to fit dimensions of construction paper lining and staple to centerfold with long-arm stapler.

   -Standard 8½" X 11" paper cut to 6½" X 11" works well.

How To Make Wallpaper Books for Typed Single Pages

Dimensions:
Cardboard: 6½" x 7¼"
Wallpaper: at least 16" x 9"
Construction paper: 13¾" x 6¾"

1. Tape cardboard to wrong side of wallpaper, leaving about 1½" gap between cardboard pieces at center.

2. Glue outer edges of wallpaper and cardboard and fold wallpaper corners to cardboard.

3. Fold wallpaper sides to cardboard.

4. Glue construction paper lining to wallpaper sides.

5. Cut sheets of paper 6¾" x 6¾" to fit the book. This permits typing individual pages which is much easier than typing folded sheets.

When text and illustrations are finished, insert pages into fold of book cover. Staple on outside binding close to where the cardboard interfacing lies <u>or</u> punch holes through binding and pages and secure with brass paper fasteners.

If the book has many pages, you may need to use a heavy duty stapler

TYPING LAYOUT FOR WALLPAPER BOOKS

Left margin needs to be 1 1/4 inches
Top, right, and bottom margins look good at 3/4"
Double space

To keep the process simpler, I recommend typing on only one side of the page--if typing on both sides of the page, BOTH RIGHT AND LEFT MARGINS NEED TO BE 1 1/4 INCHES.

OPTION SETTINGS FOR WORD PROCESSING ON "APPLEWORKS"

IF USING PIN FEED COMPUTER PAPER, enter the following options before typing:

Left Margin (LM): 1.2
Right Margin (RM): 2.2
Top Margin (TM): .6
Bottom Margin (BM): 5.0
Double space (DS)

When the typing is finished, the sheets can be sent back to school to be cut to size to fit the book: 6 1/2" wide by 6 3/4" long.

IF USING SINGLE SHEETS THAT ARE INDIVIDUALLY FED into the printer, use the same options, but add:

Pause Each Page (PE)

As you print, the computer will pause at the end of each page. This allows you to insert the next blank sheet of paper. Then press "Return" and the printer will proceed with the second page.

Top Margin 3/4" (Appleworks .6)

CAN CATS PREDICT EARTHQUAKES?

The answer is yes, but we still don't know how. Many cat owners claim that their cats have saved their lives. Before an earthquake, a cat will act strangely, by starting to hiss and growl, or it may carry its babies to safety.

Typewriter: Left Margin 1¼"

Right Margin 3/4"

WHY DO WE SAY,

"YOU LET THE CAT OUT OF THE BAG?"

(Appleworks: LM: 1.2)

(Appleworks: RM 2.2)

We often say this phrase when somebody gives a secret away. It started back in the eighteenth century when market salesmen would try to cheat people by putting cats in the bags

Bottom Margin: 3/4"
(Appleworks: BM 5.0)

sample page

<———— 6¾" ————>

12

Integration

*Teachers must function
more like orchestra
conductors than like
lecturers: getting things
started and keeping them
moving along, providing
information and pointing
to resources, coordinating
a diverse but harmonious
buzz of activity.*
(Goodlad and Oakes,
1988, p. 19)

*Note taking in grade 3:
collaboration during the practice phase*

What Is Integration?

Integration is implicit in whole language teaching. Integration, or integrated language arts, is an approach to learning and a way of thinking that respects the interrelationship of the language processes—reading, writing, speaking, and listening—as integral to meaningful teaching in any area. Integration refers to integration of the language arts as well as integration of the language arts across the curriculum. Before the latter can be successfully accomplished, the former needs to be firmly in place. Integration also means that major concepts and larger understandings are being developed in social contexts and that related activities are in harmony with and important to the major concepts.

My convictions about what is meant by integrated teaching and learning were confirmed and extended at an IRA conference where I heard Debbie Powell and Dick Needham of the University of Northern Colorado do an excellent presentation: "Authentic Reading, Writing and Content Learning in an Integrated Curriculum" (symposium at the annual meeting of the International Reading Association, Atlanta, Georgia, May 1990). They stressed that topics of study should be based on the "big understandings" you are trying to get across from your curriculum and that these topics be of critical importance to what children need to learn. The "big understandings," or major concepts to be developed, then become the root of unit planning. "Planning begins with substantive content and then integrates the processes (reading, writing, math, science, art, and so on) as tools for the acquisition, organization, evaluation, and application of knowledge." (Needham, IRA, 1990).

Integration, which can occur on a variety of levels, may take place with the study of just one book or one major concept in mathematics—as long as reading, writing, speaking, and listening are interrelated and are consistent with a whole

276

language philosophy. It has taken many of us at least three to five years to feel we are successfully integrating the language arts through literature. Integration across the curriculum is an area some of us are just beginning to explore. I have yet to be in a classroom that is totally integrated—that is, where language, concepts and content are interconnected across the entire curriculum all day every day. That kind of integration is rare and takes many years to achieve.

I believe literature is the best vehicle to achieve integration of the language arts. One piece of literature or one literature thematic unit can invite comparison, encourage synthesis and analysis of the author's and/or the illustrator's styles, expand vocabulary and thinking, and have an impact on student writing. Quality literature can be a vehicle for meaningful units such as the following:

- Books with similar themes
- Books by one author
- Books by one illustrator
- Books in the same genre (for example, mysteries, biographies, poetry, short stories)
- Books with similar characters
- Versions of folk/fairy tales (see "A Folk/Fairy Tale Unit for Grades 3–6" in Appendix A)

Misconceptions about Thematic Units

Somehow, it has become common to equate thematic units with whole language. Many teachers believe that if they are using thematic units, they are "doing" whole language. Not necessarily. Unfortunately, many of the thematic units teachers buy and create are nothing more than suggested activities clustered around a central focus or topic. The units incorporate some elements of math, science, social studies, art, and music, but there is often little or no development of important ideas. This is correlation, not integration. With integration, the relationships among the disciplines or subject areas are meaningful and natural. Concepts identified are not only related to the topic or subject but are important to them. With correlation, the connections are superficial and forced, and there is no important concept development.

Superficial units or themes that focus on such topics as the circus, cars, bears, animals, monsters, dragons, mice, pigs, and kites are commonly used in the elementary grades and are good examples of correlations. Teachers gather together all the books they can find on a subject and plan lots of activities around the topic. Frequently the activities are creative and interesting. However, while these activities may be fun for kids, often the units lack substance and are not based on major concepts. We need to begin asking ourselves whether such units are worth the enormous teacher preparation and class time that they require and whether they effectively foster the development of important concepts and skills. I believe that we need to be investing most of our time in conscious, deliberate, thoughtful topics and themes that go beyond the literal level.

A case in point is a thematic unit on bears, which is often utilized in the early grades. Teachers and students read lots of books about bears, write stories about bears, make bear cookies, draw bear pictures, and so on—all very entertaining and delightful. However, such a unit is not designed to develop important concepts and provide opportunities for transfer of skills. Even when pretend and real bears are compared, we need to ask, how relevant is this to the child's life? We need always to be asking ourselves, "What are the educational objectives and goals of this unit?"

It is possible to take a theme like bears and make meaningful connections to the curriculum and children's lives. In developing themes, primary consideration must be given to developing attitudes, oral language, perspectives to be covered, opportunities for social interaction, and the interrelationship of important concepts. Loretta Martin, a second grade teacher, recently did a thematic unit on bears. The major concepts that she was consciously developing included "Bears are not the gentle creatures we think they are" and "Bears are a family unit with definite nurturing patterns." After brainstorming what they knew and wanted to find out about bears as a whole class, students chose the topic they wanted to learn about and worked in groups. Students chose to investigate such topics as habitat, body skeleton, food, and bears as an endangered species. Students read, wrote, researched, and used the library to locate information. Each group eventually gave an optional oral presentation to the class or conferenced with the teacher about what they had learned.

Second grade teacher Elaine Weiner took the study of trees and tied it to students' lives. The major concepts she wanted to develop were "We cannot live on earth without trees" and "Trees provide shade, beauty, paper, homes for animals, and more." Students observed trees at the school throughout the year and noted changes, growth, and animal life in and around trees through the seasons. The class also identified all the trees on school property. Each student then adopted one tree and kept a year-long observational record. With the help of parents, students also counted and identified the trees in their own yards. The class then did a tally and prepared a group graph that included over ninety different kinds of trees found in students' yards. Students read books and poems about trees and did bark and leaf rubbings of some of the school's trees. A parent who is an arborist also shared what he does in his work.

A thematic unit is an integrated unit only when the topic or theme is meaningful, relevant to the curriculum and students' lives, consistent with whole language principles, and authentic in the interrelationship of the language processes. When planning thematic units, interdisciplinary connections across the different subject areas are not necessary for integration to be occurring. "The only reason to include some other discipline is if it somehow extends and enriches the learning or is beneficial to the student" (Andrea Butler, conversation, September 1990).

Planning for Integration

In planning for integrated instruction, we need to be asking ourselves several important questions. Even if we feel tied to a single text in a subject area, we need to be asking these questions—or others like them—to make our unit of study as meaningful as possible.

- What important concepts do I want students to learn?
- Why should students learn these concepts? Are they intellectually rich and important? Do they foster critical and creative thinking?
- What learning experiences will help develop these conceptual understandings?

- What skills and strategies am I helping to develop?
- Am I setting up a climate that encourages inquiry and choice?
- Am I putting in place alternative evaluation procedures? (See Chap. 13, "Evaluation.")
- What student attitudes am I fostering?

The following informal guidelines may be helpful in developing a framework for an integrated language unit in literature or the content areas. It would be easy to follow the guidelines and create a superficial unit; integration will occur only if whole language principles of language learning are respected and adopted.

Informal Guidelines

In planning an integrated unit, some teachers prefer to do most of the planning themselves. Planning may also be done collaboratively with students to ensure that they have a voice in the curriculum-making process.

- *Planning the unit*

    Select an important topic or theme that is both developmentally appropriate and important to the curriculum and to children's needs and interests.
    Brainstorm possibilities.
        Webbing, mapping, illustrating, listing ideas, jotting down concepts
            Organize information into categories.
            Find out and verify what students already know about the topic.
            Separate known information from "What we want to find out."
    Decide major understandings and concepts to be developed. While this is largely the teacher's responsibility, try to include questions students want to explore.
    Determine activities that will help develop conceptual understandings.
    Determine experiences and activities that can be used to help promote problem-solving strategies.
    Gather resources—quality literature and resources from home, school, and community to be used for observation, exploration, researching, reading, and writing. Consult the school librarian, media specialist, and art and music teachers.
    If students will be expected to do factual writing, plan for students to become familiar with this genre.
    Inform parents of the unit study.
    If applicable, arrange speakers, send out letters of inquiry, and arrange field trips.
    Organize the classroom and set up centers, for example, book and resource areas.

- *Implementation*

    Be sure students understand why the topic is being studied.
    Teach note-taking, report-writing, and research skills if they will be needed.

(For specific information on report writing, see Collerson, 1988, and Graves, 1989, 1990.)

Provide time for reading appropriate resources with questions in mind that were determined in the planning stage.

Add new information to categories from brainstorming. Correct misconceptions.

Include individual, partner, small-group, and whole-class activities.

Promote opportunities for collaboration, choice, and creation of varied formats.

Provide teacher guidance and minilessons as needed (using the developmental model for language learning, pp. 9–10).

Encourage the unplanned learnings—the questions and discoveries that occur as a result of immersion in an engaging topic.

Maintain a climate of inquiry: investigating, collecting data, gathering information, problem solving, revising, rethinking.

• *Evaluation*

Organize new information with what is already known. Allow students some choice: oral presentation, debate, written report, published writing, graph, drama, mural, dance, song.

Provide time for sharing, reporting, speaking, and listening.

Discuss and evaluate new learning; relate old to new.

Balance teacher evaluation, peer group evaluation, and self-evaluation (See Chap. 13, "Evaluation.")

Incorporating the Fine Arts

Music teacher Nancy Tuttle and art teacher Jill Wisneski believe that the major concepts that are part of their courses of study can be meaningfully integrated into classroom teaching. Both believe that communication between specialists and teachers is the key when planning for successful integration of disciplines. Both teachers use their disciplines to extend and enrich responses to literature and to take students to another level of understanding. Promoting and valuing oral language, thinking, creating, collaborating, and problem solving are central to concept development in the music and art areas.

For example, Nancy uses some of the core books in our literature study (after they have been read by the students and discussed with the classroom teacher) to guide students to write their own music. Working together as a whole class, students paraphrase the key points of the text, work through a melody, and produce a song with lyrics. Nancy believes that the "rhythm of music is the rhythm of speech" and that the "phrasing of music parallels punctuation." When primary teachers bring her Big Books, she enriches the reading experience by focusing on the rhythm and cadence of the language.

Jill finds that a child's awareness of line, shape, color, and form can be expanded through connecting art to classroom study and the child's life. For example, when a group of fourth-graders read *James and the Giant Peach* by Roald Dahl (Knopf, 1961), she helped students enrich and extend the text by having them create characters from the book out of clay. Students learned how to use clay properly and skillfully while exploring shape, texture, and character interpretation. In addition, students learn to talk about and critique art while connecting with the visual history of art. This experience helps them in their own decision-making processes while at the same time they create their own art.

Another example of successful integration occurs regularly when first grade teacher Donna Zorge and music teacher Carol Spero collaborate. Carol writes original music to go along with favorite Big Books. Donna and the children create dramatic movements to accompany the songs. Both teachers note the children's confidence, joy, and reading fluency when they can sing the text and follow it along visually.

Integration in the Content Areas

Just as basal texts dominate reading instruction, content area texts dominate the major subject areas. Typically, we have taught social studies by saying, "Take out your social studies book and open to page _____." Then there follows a whole-class, round-robin reading, with the teacher stopping occasionally to ask questions and lead the discussion. Often students are expected to complete end-of-chapter questions designed to assess their understanding of the text. Because such exercises are boring and fail to engage many students, comprehension often suffers.

In contrast, when teachers actively involve students and plan for integration—even when they are relying on one text—student learning and engagement are quite different. Some teachers believe the best place to start with meaningful thematic units is in the content areas. Pappas, Kiefer, and Levstik (1990, p. 331) recommend beginning with expanding the content of social studies or science.

Note Taking

Before students can be successful in the research process, they need to be able to take notes effectively. Note taking is a necessary lifelong skill that students need to have demonstrated over and over again throughout the school year. Using Holdaway's developmental model for learning—demonstration, participation, practice, and sharing—we carefully go through the process in various contexts, taking notes from texts, interviews, news articles, oral presentations, films, videos.

Third grade teacher Julie Beers and I demonstrated note taking before her students were to begin animal research reports. Using a selection on alligators and crocodiles from *Zoo Books* (Wildlife Education, Ltd., 1986), we reproduced the text of the first page and made a transparency. We left the other half page blank to demonstrate note taking on the overhead projector. As we slowly read the passage aloud, we highlighted key phrases and important information by underlining them in yellow magic marker. We verbalized our thinking processes as we worked, and then we showed students how to make the key phrases into notes (see Figure 12–1).

After we had demonstrated the process several times and invited students to participate in choosing the words we should write down, the students broke into small groups. Each group was given a copy of part of a *Zoo Books* article on

Figure 12-1   Note-taking Demonstration

From *Zoo Books 2: Alligators and Crocodiles*, (San Diego: Wildlife Education Ltd., 1986). Text reprinted with permission.

Alligators and crocodiles have fascinated people for centuries. Many "tall tales" have been told about these giant reptiles with the long tails. They are the original models for many dragons, "serpents," and other fairy tale monsters.

The true story of alligators and crocodiles is even more fascinating. The name "crocodile" was first used about 2,000 years ago by Greek adventurers who were traveling in Egypt. The huge crocodiles reminded them of a tiny lizard called "krokodeilos" that lived back in their Greek villages. So the world's biggest reptile got its name from one of the world's smallest. Alligators got their name in a similar way. Spanish adventurers exploring the coast of Florida gave them the name "el legarto," which means "the lizard."

There is one other animal very closely related to alligators and crocodiles. It is called a *gharial* (GAIR-ee-ul). This word comes from India, where gharials live. It was a name first used for *jars* that were long and thin. In the case of this animal, however, it is the *jaws* that are extremely long and thin.

Together, alligators, crocodiles, and gharials make up the group of animals known as *crocodilians* (CROCK-UH-DILL-EE-UNS). Crocodilians are the world's largest *reptiles*. A reptile is a cold-blooded animal that has scaly skin, lays eggs, and breathes with lungs. Crocodilians continue to grow throughout their lives. Some males grow to be more than 15 feet long (4.6 kilometers). And they may weigh over 500 pounds (227 kilograms). Females are usually smaller than the males.

There are also "dwarf" species of alligators and crocodiles which seldom get longer than 4 or 5 feet (1.2 to 1.5 meters). And, of course, others can grow to gigantic sizes. A Saltwater crocodile captured near the coast of India was reported to be 27½ feet long (8.4 meters) and weighed over a thousand pounds (450 kilograms).

No one knows exactly how old this crocodile was. But we do know that crocodilians can live a long time. An alligator in a zoo once lived for 56 years. But some scientists think that crocodiles living in the wild can live to be over a hundred years old.

This young crocodile is trying to capture a frog, but doesn't seem to have the "hang" of it yet. But like all crocodilians, when it grows up, it will be an excellent hunter.

CROCODILES

original models for fairy tale monsters

name first used 2000 years ago

world's largest reptile

part of a group of animals known as crocodilians.
cold blooded, scaly skin, lays eggs, breathes with lungs

some males more than 15' long may weigh over 500 lbs.
females usually smaller

dwarf- up to 4'-5'

can live in wild over 100 years

elephants and a blank transparency. Students were told to place the blank transparency over the article and underline key phrases and important points, as we had done, and then to write their notes on the right side of the page (see Figure 12–2). Groups then came up to the overhead projector with their transparency and placed it over a transparency of the article they had just read. They then shared their notes and received feedback and guidance from us and from other students. Finally, after

Figure 12-2   Two Students' Note-taking Exercise

By Amanda
and Nate

we felt students understood the process, they began to apply taking notes to their individual research reports.

We initially had some problems with the process. We found that four students in a small group were too many to work together well. A better plan was for students to work in pairs, with one acting as scribe and the other giving oral suggestions and feedback. Another problem surfaced when we asked students to read through an entire section before beginning to take notes. We found that they largely ignored that request and took notes as they were reading. When we examined our own note-taking processes, we realized that's what we do as adults.

Examining our own processes as adults has helped us make decisions for teaching. For example, some teachers recommend that students take notes after they have read and closed the book as a way to avoid copying. However, as adults we don't do that, so we allow students to take notes with their books open.

Teachers find that demonstrating note taking pays big dividends. Students become proficient at using and applying this skill in all the content areas. The key to success is repeated demonstrations and reteaching throughout the year with various genres and contexts. Also, when demonstrating and practicing, using a short article seems to work best. Fifth grade teacher Jim Servis finds occasionally collecting students' notes is an excellent check. Using the same content handout, students take notes and turn them in. Jim hands the notes back a week later and asks students to write a cohesive paragraph from their notes. Students quickly see firsthand whether their notes are valid and how important it is to take meaningful notes.

An Integrated Social Studies Unit

The unit "Getting to Know Your State" was developed by fourth grade teacher Joan Servis in response to a required part of the social studies curriculum. The thematic unit is integrated with the language arts and takes place over a four-week period. Because it is important for students to know why a unit of study is being undertaken, they discussed the topic and listed the reasons it is important for them to know about their state (see Figure 12–3). Depending on the topic of study, we may need to make explicit why a unit is being studied or has been studied. Students may not be able to articulate the why's until a unit has concluded.

As we are writing and organizing integrated units, we need to stop and reflect on the important, global concepts we want to develop. Both teachers and students should be able to articulate these concepts.

Larger Understandings/Major Concepts/Desired Outcomes

1. Various factors affect our lives in Ohio, for example, natural resources, climate, pollution, and unemployment.
2. We can better understand our world and work to make it better if we have a better understanding of the factors that influence life in Ohio.

Figure 12–3   Understanding the Reasons for a Unit of Study

3. Finding out about our state necessitates the use of real-life skills—telephoning, letter writing, interviewing, researching. It is important to do these well to obtain necessary information.

Process / Procedures

1. Web/brainstorm the topic   A web is a kind of visual brainstorm and outline that helps to generate ideas and link them to a central focus (Charlotte Huck, Susan Hepler, and Janet Hickman, *Children's Literature in the Elementary School*, 5th ed. [Harcourt Brace, 1993], p. 741).

Figure 12–4 is an example of a brainstorming map made by a recent class. Each year the map is somewhat different. Many of us have found that webbing works best when done with teacher guidance. While such visual maps look easy to read, a lot of information is omitted, and the reader is expected to fill in the gaps. Because most students have difficulty doing this on their own, webs should be done collaboratively and talked about so that students make connections.

2. Select the topic and prioritize   On a card, students list their first, second, and

Figure 12-4   Whole-Class Brainstorming for Social Studies Unit "Getting to Know Your State"

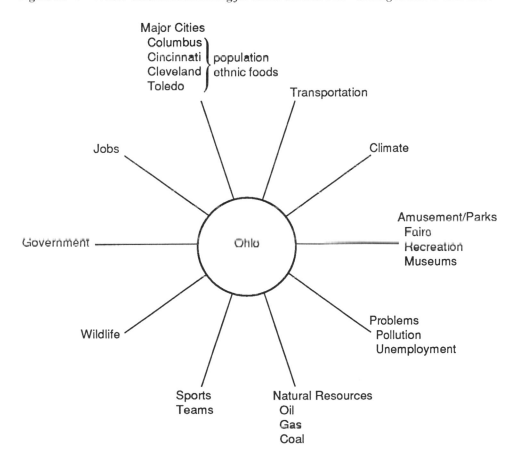

third choices of topics they wish to research. Just about everyone gets their first or second choices.

3. Divide into groups   Up to four students in a group seems to work best for cooperative work. Joan divided her class of twenty-four students into six groups, with four in each of the following topic groups:

- Wildlife
- Amusement parks/recreation/tourist sights
- Problems (present/future)
- Major cities/population
- Climate/jobs
- Government

4. Groups write their own questions to research for their topic of study   For the first few years Joan implemented this unit, she developed the questions and the format for research and study. In a further transition, students now choose their own questions and format. Students also determine the division of labor and how the information they gather will be organized.

5. Conference over questions for study   After each group formulates the questions to answer about their topic, they meet with another group to get its reactions to the substance of the questions. Revisions, additions, and deletions are then made. Finally, questions are turned in to the teacher for final feedback and revision. Conferencing may be necessary to resolve needed changes.

6. Group establishes format   Using the questions they have generated, the group members create a format and decide who will do what and what resources will be needed. Joan checks and okays each format, gives needed suggestions, and assists the groups in gathering what they need—informational books and phone numbers for obtaining information about their state, travel information, and so on.

7. Students take notes on their topics   Students use various resources to find answers to their questions, and they help one another as they are working. Notes are checked by Joan for relevance and proper form. (See "Note Taking" earlier in this chapter.)

8. Students write rough drafts   Notes are organized into cohesive paragraphs. The writing process stops here for this particular project.

9. Groups present information to the whole class   Upon completion of rough drafts, each group decides how it will share its information with the class. Students rehearse their presentations joyfully. Costumes and props are carried in from home, and students get very excited about their performance. Joan advises, "Educate and entertain. Don't bore us." Some past presentations have included radio shows, food festivals, plays, travelogues, quiz shows, questionnaires with audience involvement. Students take notes on one another's presentations.

10. Presentations are evaluated orally   Students begin with positive feedback that includes what they liked and what they learned. At least two positive statements are expected to be made before a suggestion for improvement may be given. The teacher participates as one voice.

11. Group interactions and content learned are evaluated   Students are evaluated on group interaction and presentation and are also asked to complete a teacher-made essay test on the unit. Figures 12–5 and 12–6 are examples of students' self-evaluations. (See also p. 321 for the form students use to evaluate the unit.)

Figures 12–5 and 12–6   Fourth-graders' Self-evaluations of Group Work

Self-Evaluation

_____ SS _____ Discussion Group

Name Lindsay _____   Date 5/21

Book/topic _____ Ohio

1. What did I do well today (and/or improve on) during group discussion?

I got a lot of roles on problems of Cleveland just by my own knolage.

I also tried to organized my group and get them working. I looked at a book called Undiscovered Ohio, but the only information they had on Cleveland, Columbus and Cinncinati was on the Cleveland Metroparks. So I used my knrilage.

2. What do I still need to improve on during group discussion?

I am going to call 1-800-Buckeye and I will make sure everyone gets alot of information!! Also I will try to make sure that none of us goof off at any time, like someone I won't mention names did.

Self-Evaluation

_____ SS _____ Discussion Group

Name Adam _____   Date 5/21

Book/topic Ohio

1. What did I do well today (and/or improve on) during group discussion?

I helped Ginaywu do our government format. I didn't work very hard because I didn't have any information about Ohio's governor. I went to the Library and didn't Know what book I should get. So I didn't get any notes.

2. What do I still need to improve on during group discussion?

I need to improve not talking to much and getting down to buisness instead of not doing anything.

Figure 12-6

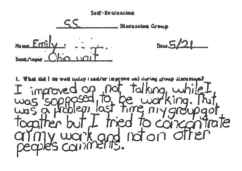

Self-Evaluation
SS. _____ Discussion Group
Name Emily ___ Date 5/21
Book/Topic Ohio unit

1. What did I do well today (and/or improve on) during group discussion?
I improved on not talking while I was supposed to be working. That was a problem last time my group got together but I tried to concentrate on my work and not on other peoples comments.

2. What do I still need to improve on during group discussion?
I still need to improve on trying to find information in my book I keeped on day dreaming and my mind would run away from me.

Self-Evaluation
SS _____ Discussion Group
Name Faisal ___ Date 5/21/90
Book/Topic OHIO/Story

1. What did I do well today (and/or improve on) during group discussion?
I got down alot of places in my city of ohio. We used a map and on it, told us places in certain cities. I got about 26 places in my city. The city I have is cincinnati. People in my group (some of them) called 1-800-Buckeye for information.

2. What do I still need to improve on during group discussion?

Outcomes

One positive outcome of collaborative group work is that students help one another and work cooperatively to improve group dynamics. Even though each group has an area of specialization within the topic, students learn that if groups work together, they obtain more complete information and more thorough and balanced coverage of a topic.

Students also come to realize that they have the power to affect change in their own lives. For example, members of the group researching "Problems" began to talk about the need for recycling waste. At the conclusion of an end-of-the-unit party, students independently collected soda pop cans for recycling. Some students also began to urge their parents to begin recycling cans at home.

Moving toward More Meaningful Mathematics Instruction

Most teachers find that while they may be able to make natural mathematical connections to topics and themes, for the most part mathematics needs to be taught as a separate subject area. However, integration of math still takes place as long as the language processes are being used in a meaningful way and mathematical activities are relevant and supportive of the major concepts being developed.

With mathematics, teachers are beginning to see the value of providing students with interesting and relevant problems to think about, concrete materials to work with, and opportunities to find relationships among mathematical concepts. Holistic professional resources are becoming available in mathematics, and it is no longer unheard of to hear students describing the strategies and thinking processes they used to arrive at a solution. Many of the exciting changes that are coming about in mathematics teaching are the result of the issuance of the *Curriculum and Evaluation Standards for School Mathematics* (k–12) by the National Council of Teachers of Mathematics (1989), an impressive document which views mathematics as a means of communication and as a language system.

We need to familiarize ourselves with *Standards* and look at math the way we view reading and writing—as a language process that children learn developmentally with much modeling, exploration, and feedback. The conditions of language learning (see p. 13 and Figure 2–1) apply for mathematical learning as well. Additionally, mathematics needs to become relevant to children's lives by counting and manipulating real objects, measuring, estimating, graphing, classifying, and problem solving across the curriculum. Cooperative learning groups, teacher demonstrations, child-initiated problem solving, risk taking, and written and oral sharing need to be as much a part of the math curriculum as they are a part of the total language program.

Many teachers who no longer use workbooks in reading hang on to supplemental math workbooks and concentrate most of their instruction on computation practice and drill, including word problems that have no relevance to children's lives. While students do learn to compute, it's at the expense of mathematical processes that require reasoning and thinking.

I believe part of the reason the change to more meaningful math teaching has been slow in coming is that teachers in transition to whole language have focused most of their efforts on the language arts. Realistically, there isn't time or energy to revamp everything at one time. Also, most of us don't have the stamina for sweeping change; we all need the security of something familiar. Implicit in this further transition is time for the teacher to be a learner and time for students to learn at their own pace. Additionally, the resources available on teaching mathematics meaningfully—professional literature and staff development opportunities—have been very limited compared with those available in the language arts. Because little information is available for the teacher ready to make math a meaningful part of the curriculum, at the end of this chapter I have listed some recent journal articles and professional books that have proved to be useful resources.

In looking at the need for change, Beth Lazerick, a secular studies principal of a k–6 building whose doctoral studies focused on math education, states: "Kids have been rewarded in math for getting the right answer, not for developing strategies for arriving at the right answer." She believes kids also hang onto their crutches (for example, their fingers as counters) because they continue to be rewarded for their correct answers. Instead, Beth recommends having students do predicting, sampling, and exploring—and then describing how they got their answers. One suggestion she makes is having children write about and solve real-life math problems. Intermediate grade students might look at their family's actual grocery receipts and determine how much was spent on junk food, vegetables, and so on. Primary grade students could sort, estimate, and count the number of items in the many collections most of them have. In most cases, teachers will first need staff development opportunities in order to become comfortable in implementing these kinds of problem-solving activities in their mathematics programs.

Writing in Mathematics

One of the most exciting possibilities and new realities in current math teaching is the idea of students using writing to reflect on their reasoning processes. Writing provides students a way to extend and deepen their understanding of concepts. It gives them an opportunity to reflect on what they have been doing and to formulate and rethink their ideas. When students commit their thoughts to writing, they extend and cement their learning experiences. The teacher also benefits. When a student describes what she comprehends, the information contributes to the teacher's picture of what the student knows and understands and helps in making instructional decisions. Teachers who allow students to choose how they will demonstrate and interpret mathematical understandings are often surprised and delighted by the variety of responses.

Teachers can also use writing in math as part of the ongoing assessment process. Journals, portfolios, teacher observation, anecdotal records, and self-evaluation have as much a place in math evaluation as they do in other language processes. Having students write about the strategies they used to work through a problem and discuss what they learned makes students aware of their own learning. See Figures 12–7 and 12–8 for two fifth-graders' math journal entries done in math consultant Betty Hess's class.

The Need for Change

Conventional mathematics teaching has not immersed children in a rich math environment or encouraged exploration and responsibility. For the most part, math has been a hierarchical skills-driven program with lots of practice exercises from a commercial publisher. In many cases, math has been more about memorizing facts than understanding processes. A process approach to math starts where the child is, provides many opportunities for real-life, open-ended problem solving, and guides learners to construct their own understandings. Conferencing with other students, talking, listening, writing and reading, and explaining and sharing with peers are integral parts of the program. Finally, students begin to understand the role that mathematics plays in their world.

Figures 12–7 and 12–8   Two Fifth-graders' Math Journal Entries

April 5, 1990

Dear Mrs. Hess,

I finally learned Pi! I have been hearing about it for a while. The concept is actually simple once you see it, not complicated like I thought.

I am very glad you didn't teach us lots of formulas for us to copy and memorize. I really understand the relationships between the circumference, diameter etc. because of the way you taught us. I agree that method 5 and 6 on the sheet you gave us are the least. Number 2 was O.K. but it didn't give me a picture in my mind, and I thought 1 was tedious and pretty senseless. Basically I liked this unit a lot.

(The numbers refer to the possible ways to find Pi)

Figure 12–8

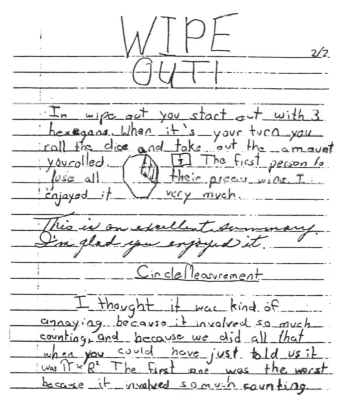

2/2

WIPE
OUT!

In wipe out you start out with 3 hexagons. When it's your turn you roll the dice and take out the amount you rolled. The first person to lose all their pieces wins. I enjoyed it very much.

This is an excellent summary. I'm glad you enjoyed it.

Circle Measurement

I thought it was kind of annoying because it involved so much counting, and because we did all that when you could have just told us it was $\pi \times R^2$. The first one was the worst because it involved so much counting.

Constraints to Successful Integrated Language Programs

While meaningful integration is an admirable and worthy educational goal, we also need to be realistic about how difficult integration is to achieve. This section considers some of the factors that work against successful integrated language programs.

Theoretical Understandings

Before integration can take place, we need an understanding of the theory underlying children's language acquisition, an in-depth knowledge of the literature and resources being used, and an understanding of the curriculum. Without this knowledge of theory and practice, teachers are likely to "basalize" units with only superficial interdisciplinary connections. With a large majority of teachers acting as scripted technicians managing preset commercial programs, we are still a long way from being curriculum decision makers. Ongoing staff development efforts need to include helping teachers to understand integration and develop meaningful integrated language units.

Time

We need to work with our administrators to create uninterrupted blocks of instructional time in daily schedules. On the elementary level, self-contained classrooms—with no switching rooms for various subjects—promote flexibility and offer opportunities for integration. Many teachers find the only way they can tie language arts and reading to the content areas and have time for both is through integration, made possible by large blocks of uninterrupted time.

Additionally, teachers must have release time to plan with colleagues, research topics, write and adjust curriculum, and gather resources. It is unrealistic to expect individual teachers to devote hours of planning on their own time. While common planning time across grade levels is a start, it is not sufficient. Teachers cannot be expected to implement an integrated curriculum without several hours a month of release time for planning. While I noticed that some administrators in Australia were willing to make such a time commitment, I have rarely seen it here in the states.

In one district teachers were expected to meet by grade levels after school every few months to share ideas and plan and write units. One angry teacher commented that because release time had not been provided, many teachers would continue to do "whatever is easier."

Administrative Support

An integrated curriculum requires a fully committed administrator who values and understands the approach and is willing to give teachers time and funds to develop it. Teachers cannot get a budget for curriculum development and the purchase of resources and equipment without administrative support.

Resources

Beyond collections of fiction, there is a need for in-class libraries with quality literature of all types. Nonfiction materials especially—magazines, newspapers, encyclopedias, information books—do not presently exist in most classrooms. There is also a need for flexible, open library times for students—not standard practice in many school libraries.

Curriculum Requirements

Teachers and administrators are constrained by course objectives and state guidelines. Some of these are necessary to ensure that important concepts are developed in logical sequence at particular grade levels. However, many districts further constrain themselves by adopting basal texts and social studies and science textbooks using publishers' guidelines as a total program. These texts should be used as one of many resources—to be referred to, not adhered to.

Reflections

An integrated language curriculum focuses on important concepts through topic and theme development in a manner that is not contrived. Students come to understand their world better through engaging in relevant school experiences. While interdisciplinary integration is a desired long-range goal, we need to begin by working toward integration in smaller areas; we might begin with literature study and then add social studies, science, and math. We need to integrate the language arts and the visual arts—reading, writing, speaking, listening, art, music, drama, dance—into the various subject areas instead of trying to bring every subject into the language arts. The language arts can then be the medium for integrating the subject areas. Finally, as in all difficult transitions, we need to move slowly and allow ourselves time for continuous risk taking, reflection, and rethinking.

Resources for Improving and Supporting Mathematics Instruction

For full information and annotations for the following titles, see *Resources for Teachers*, "Mathematics Books and Resources."

Apelman, Maja and Julie King. 1993. *Exploring Everyday Math: Ideas for Students, Teachers, and Parents*. Portsmouth, NH: Heinemann. See annotation, p. 86b.

Baker, Ann and Johnny Baker. 1991. *Counting on a Small Planet: Activities for Environmental Mathematics*. Portsmouth, NH: Heinemann. See annotation, p. 86b.

Baker, Ann and Johnny Baker. 1990. *Mathematics in Process*. Portsmouth, NH: Heinemann. See annotation, p. 86b.

Baker, Ann and Johnny Baker. 1991. *Maths in the Mind: A Process Approach to Mental Strategies*. Portsmouth, NH: Heinemann. See annotation, p. 86b.

Baker, Dave, Cheryl Semple and Tony Stead. 1990. *How Big Is the Moon? Whole Maths in Action*. Portsmouth, NH: Heinemann. See annotation, p. 87b.

Braddon, Kathryn L., Nancy J. Hall and Dale Taylor. 1993. *Math Through Children's Literature: Making the NCTM Standards Come Alive*. Englewood, CO: Teacher Ideas Press/Libraries Unlimited. See annotation, p. 87b.

Burk, Donna, Allyn Snider, and Paula Symonds. 1992–1993. *Math Excursions Series*. Portsmouth, NH: Heinemann. See annotation, p. 87b.

Burns, Marilyn. 1992. *About Teaching Mathematics: A K-8 Resource*. Sausalito, CA: Math Solutions Publications. Distributed by Heinemann. See annotation, p. 87b.

Burns, Marilyn. January 1988. "Beyond 'the Right Answer' . . . Helping Your Students Make Sense Out of MATH," *Learning*, pp. 31–36.

    Using writing and cooperative learning, Burns details four strategies for promoting thinking and reasoning. Immediate, practical applications to the classroom.

Burns, Marilyn. 1987–1990. *A Collection of Math Lessons*. Sausalito, CA: Math Solutions Publications. Distributed by Heinemann. See annotation, p. 87b.

Burns, Marilyn. 1992. *Math and Literature (K-3)*. Sausalito, CA: Math Solutions Publications. Distributed by Heinemann. See annotation, p. 88b.

Charles, Linda Holden, and Micaelia Randolph Brummett. 1989. *Connections: Linking Manipulatives to Mathematics (Grades 1–6)*. Sunnyvale, CA: Creative Publications. See annotation, p. 88b.

Davison, David M., and Daniel L. Pearce. April 1988. "Using Writing Activities to Reinforce Mathematics Instruction," *Arithmetic Teacher*, pp. 42–45.

    The authors discuss and define five categories of mathematical writing activities: direct use of language, linguistic translation, summarizing, applied use of language, and creative use of language. Activities described have application in classrooms at all grade levels.

Griffiths, Rachel and Margaret Clyne. 1990. *Books You Can Count On: Linking Mathematics and Literature*. Portsmouth, NH: Heinemann. See annotation, p. 88b.

Kamii, Constance. 1985, 1989. *Young Children Reinvent Arithmetic: Implications of Piaget's Theory*. New York: Teachers College Press. See annotation, p. 88b.

Lilburn, Pat and Pam Rawson. 1994. *Let's Talk Math: Encouraging Children to Explore Ideas*. Portsmouth, NH: Heinemann. See annotation, p. 88b.

National Council of Teachers of Mathematics. 1906 Association Drive, Reston, VA 22091–1593. (ph. 703–620–9840). See annotation, p. 88b.

National Council of Teachers of Mathematics. 1989. *Curriculum and Evaluation Standards for School Mathematics*. Reston, VA: NCTM. See annotation, p. 89b.

National Council of Teachers of Mathematics. 1991. *Professional Standards for Teaching Mathematics*. Reston, VA: NCTM. See annotation, p. 89b.

Ohanian, Susan. 1992. *Garbage Pizza, Patchwork Quilts, and Math Magic: Stories about Teachers Who Love to Teach and Children Who Love to Learn*. New York: W.H. Freeman. Distributed by Heinemann. See annotation, p. 89b.

Richards, Leah. January 1990. "'Measuring Things in Words': Language for Learning Mathematics," *Language Arts*, pp. 14–25.

    An Australian teacher (of eleven-year-olds) describes how she uses language to develop children's knowledge and confidence in mathematics. Using math themes and subsequent investigations, she sets out the plans, strategies, and evaluation techniques. Samples of children's writing are also given.

Rowan, Thomas and Barbara Bourne. 1994. *Thinking Like Mathematicians: Putting the K-4 NCTM Standards into Practice*. Portsmouth, NH: Heinemann. See annotation, p. 89b.

Welchman-Tischler, Rosamond. 1992. *How to Use Children's Literature to Teach Mathematics*. Reston, VA: National Council of Teachers of Mathematics. See annotation, p. 90b.

Whitin, David J., Heidi Mills, and Timothy O'Keefe. 1990. *Living and Learning Mathematics: Stories and Strategies for Supporting Mathematical Literacy*. Portsmouth, NH: Heinemann. See annotation, p. 90b.

Whitin, David J. and Sandra Wilde. 1992. *Read Any Good Math Lately? Children's Books for Mathematical Learning, K-6*. Portsmouth, NH: Heinemann. See annotation, p. 90b.

13

Evaluation

The most fundamental goal of all educational evaluation is optimal instruction for all children and evaluation practices are only legitimate to the extent that they serve this goal.
(Johnston, 1987, p. 744)

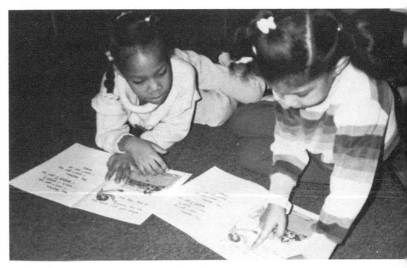

Giving students time to work things out on their own: reading in the kindergarten

Evaluation is a critical issue all teachers struggle with. In an attempt to help clarify some current issues and give theoretical and practical direction to teachers, this chapter examines the effects of standardized testing and considers definitions, beliefs, components, and contexts of meaningful evaluation. This chapter also takes a look at portfolio assessment, confronts report cards and grading systems, offers various means for self-evaluation, and concludes with annotated resource articles that inform the evaluation process. Because standardized testing still dominates assessment, I begin with the effects of standardized testing and attempt to put this issue into perspective.

Effects of Standardized Testing

While eating breakfast one morning, I was reading an article in *The New York Times* entitled "How Two Brooklyn Schools Can Be So Alike and Yet So Different" by Joseph Burger (July 24, 1990). I was struck by the fact that tests still drive all aspects of education. The article described two public schools in poor, black neighborhoods. In one school, over 80 percent of the students read at or above the national average for their grade *based on standardized test scores*; at the other school, less than 40 percent did. The reporter credited the difference to a principal with a strong personal leadership style as well as to a year-long emphasis on test preparation. Teachers at the higher-scoring school were required to have two daily reading lessons: One involved using the basal text and workbooks and the other focused on preparing for reading tests. The principal was quoted as saying: "I would prefer if we could find a different way of evaluating children's progress. But given the reality, I have no choice. Schools are looked at this way. I'm not certain that the instrument is testing what we want to test, but I don't know what instrument would be better."

I did a rough calculation. Based on 180 school days and one hour a day allocated to reading, at least ninety instructional hours were being devoted to passing a fragmented test that would do little to inform the teacher or students of meaningful progress in reading. Yet the results of such tests are used routinely all over the country to judge the effectiveness of schools, to place students in special programs, to track students, to pass or retain students, to decide whether or not certain programs should continue to be funded, to evaluate teachers, and to plan curriculums.

I felt totally disheartened when I finished the article. I believed the students were good test takers, but I was not convinced that the school was producing readers. The article made no mention of anything associated with real reading— reading and discussing authentic literature, reading aloud, choosing books, thinking about books, and finding delight in reading. Reading was defined here in terms of "standard readers," workbooks, and test scores.

Preoccupation with test scores not only robs our students but also harms our teaching. I remember a third grade teacher whose students always had the highest test scores. Not only did she teach to the test but her curriculum was skills-driven, dominated by workbooks, worksheets, and boring drill. When the students went on to fourth grade, where the teacher taught to the students, the test scores always dropped. It looked as though the students lost ground that next year, and the fourth grade teacher felt bad. She believed she was a good teacher, but she knew she was being judged by the students' test scores.

The "worst case scenario" occurred some years ago and involved a teacher who actually changed responses in student test booklets so her class would score well. However, the scores looked so good for a class with many low achievers that it became obvious something was amiss. Something is very wrong when teachers feel driven to go to such extraordinary, and even illegal, lengths to see that their students score well.

As long as we continue to equate reading progress with high test scores, we have little hope of raising a generation of readers: students who are able to read and reason, who are able to relate and apply ideas to their lives and different situations, and who choose to read for pleasure.

Standardized Test Scores: A Look at One Student

Even when we say the tests are not important, we want our students to score well because we teachers are often judged by the results. Recently my principal called me into her office while looking at the standardized test results she had just received. "Did you work with this child?" she asked me. I could tell from the tone of her voice that the news was not good. Doris, a third-grader who had been one of my Reading Recovery students in first grade, had scored in the third stanine in total reading. "Doris is a good reader," I insisted. "Something is wrong with the test. I want to see the test booklet." While I was convinced Doris was a capable reader, nonetheless, I felt quite defensive. Somehow, Doris should have done better.

I spoke with Doris's classroom teacher Linda Cooper, who also saw Doris as a competent reader. We decided to measure Doris's reading by observing her reading processes on an unfamiliar but meaningful text. Doris was asked to read pages 15–17 of *Mr. Popper's Penguins* by Richard and Florence Atwater (Little, Brown,

1938), a lengthy chapter book that is at least at a third grade level. After a brief oral introduction, I asked Doris to read the text. Her accuracy rate was 93 percent, indicating the book was at her instructional level. More significant to us was the definite indication that Doris understood what she was reading. When I asked her, "What was it that *Mrs.* Popper wanted?" Doris responded, "She wanted a clean house!" I had meant to ask her, "What was it that *Mr.* Popper wanted?"—an easier question. Doris, however, had no trouble answering any of the questions or briefly retelling the story. Linda and I felt vindicated: Obviously Doris was a very capable reader.

Because we were puzzled by her low scores on the standardized reading test, Linda and I looked through the test booklet with Doris. We wanted to see if she could give us any insights into how and why she had responded to certain questions as she had. Several factors became apparent. Because Doris thoughtfully used her own background experiences to make sense when reading—as we did in class when reading and discussing a book—she sometimes marked an answer that was correct for her but not for the test makers. For example, in the "Word Reading" section, Doris was supposed to fill in a little circle under the word in each line that goes with the picture. In a picture of a girl in pajamas, sleeping in a bed with a quilt, instead of filling in the circle under "pajamas," Doris filled in the circle under "patches"—"because it's just like my quilt with patches all over," she explained. Following a short "Reading Comprehension" paragraph where a question asks what happened to a mother and son who didn't know which road to take while driving, Doris marked they had gotten "stuck" instead of "lost"—"because when I'm lost I always feel stuck."

The other factor that became apparent was that Doris had been penalized because she was unpracticed with worksheets and word-study skills subtests, which do not measure reading in context. That is, when Doris had to perform a task without the aid of context—the surrounding authentic text, illustrations, and learning setting that help give meaning to a word or groups of words—she was at a clear disadvantage. In many cases where she made an error, she simply did not understand the test format. While we would never spend a whole year preparing for the test, it was obvious that our students would need to have some test taking preparation in—"reading-test-reading" (Reardon, 1990)—if they were to have a fair chance at succeeding in test taking.

Now, about a month before our fall testing, our principal, Bernice Stokes, makes sure students become familiar with test formats. Students receive guidance and practice in analyzing and interpreting the phrasing and structure of the test questions as well as in ruling out unlikely responses and guessing intelligently. One useful strategy on the reading comprehension section is to have students read the questions first. The short, connected paragraphs in this section measure test-taking skills more than they do reading comprehension. Students who have learned how to answer test questions can often do well on this section without ever reading the passage given in the test.

Phonics in Isolation: Looking Beyond the Test Scores

Performance on a subtest can give an inaccurate message about a student's learning abilities and needs. Rather than providing information that could be useful for instructional decision making, the results are neither credible nor reliable. When the results are interpreted literally, low scores on subtests are responsible for placing and maintaining students in adjunct skills-based instructional programs. The message for students and their parents is that mastering a discrete set of skills is of primary importance in becoming a good reader. We need to keep in mind that skills are valuable only to the extent that they can be strategically applied to an authentic reading context.

Doris's lowest standardized test score, a year below grade level, was on the "Word Study Skills" subtest. Here the student was asked to mark one out of three words that had the same sound as the underlined letter(s) in the first word. For example, in the line: "good   tool   found   put," the correct response is "put." (Doris marked "tool.") What is being evaluated here is certainly not reading or even decoding. Never having done an activity like this before, Doris was confused by the directions. Additionally, one reason she wound up in Reading Recovery in the first place was because she had difficulty hearing sounds in words. Doris did well with phonics when she could integrate phonics with semantics and syntax in the context of a meaningful text. Yet her low score on the "decontextualized" subtest pulled her overall reading score way down.

Doris's mother, with whom we had a close working relationship, was upset about her daughter's low score on the subtest and insisted Doris be "pulled out" to work with the Chapter 1 teacher on "phonics skills." She knew Doris was a competent reader, but the test score made her question her own beliefs. Even when we showed her how well Doris had read the passage in *Mr. Popper's Penguins* and talked with her at length about what it means to be a good reader, she still wanted her daughter "to have the phonics she needs." We talked with Doris's mother about the message being "pulled out" for reading help would convey to Doris, and we asked her to trust us. Finally, she gave in.

At the end of the school year Doris's mother said,

> I didn't understand that the test really didn't measure what Doris could do. I'm so glad I listened to you. Doris reads beautifully, and she has no trouble at all with phonics when she has a meaningful sentence or paragraph. She can then figure out almost all the words or put in something that makes sense.

Parents, based on their own education and the way reading has been taught for so many years, overvalue word-study skills tests in isolation. We need to educate parents about the place of phonics in reading, about the unimportance of isolated subtests, and about the failure of standardized tests to assess phonics knowledge accurately. In my own district, since the fall 1990, we have been using a new basis for norming, one that allows a total reading score minus the phonics-structural analysis subtests. At least that's an improvement.

Another reason parents seem to place so much importance on test scores has to do with the amount of time schools devote to standardized testing. At our fall parent conferences, parents traditionally spend quite a lot of time listening to teachers explain how to read the print-outs of the students' standardized test scores. The sheer amount of time we spend on this activity sends the message that "this is important." Since parents perceive test scores as indicators of academic success, we need to educate them about other more legitimate criteria. We need to spend most of our evaluation time on observational measures and to share those with parents as the most valid evaluation indicators of their children's achievement. When teachers have shared portfolios—with multiple samples of student's work in various contexts—parents quickly move away from their preoccupation with test data (Rob Tierney, conversation, August 1990).

What Happens to Test Scores with Whole Language?

There's no question that children like Doris—competent readers who integrate strategies in context but who perform poorly on the various subtests—are handicapped on standardized tests. Nonetheless, most of our students' scores on standardized tests have not been adversely affected by whole language approach to reading instruction. Our director of testing reports that the reading scores in our five k–4 buildings have remained consistent over the past five years.

However, this is not always the case. I have heard stories of lowered test scores during the first years of transition to whole language. Nonetheless, as far as I know, there is no evidence that over the long term students in whole language programs perform less well on standardized tests. In fact, over the long haul, they probably do better, especially if they have had some instruction and practice in test taking.

What is required is that administrators and board of education members have an understanding of whole language and a long-range commitment that goes beyond immediate test results. They must also be willing to consider other indicators as valid measures of success. Norm Smith, a principal of a whole language school in California, commented, "Without the understanding of the Board of Education and their willingness to allow time for the results to show on the tests, a great program might have been stopped in its second or third year." He reported that a longitudinal study showed that "after nearly five years in the program, the overall positive results of whole language are starting to show on tests." At the same time, he acknowledged the immediate success of whole language, as reflected by increased student attendance, a more positive school atmosphere, increased parent involvement, more proficiency in English by students making the transition from Spanish to English, and more positive student and parent attitudes (Bird, Lois Bridges. 1989. *Becoming a Whole Language School: The Fair Oaks Story*. Katonah, NY: Richard C. Owen, pp. 118–120.)

I believe that daily reading and writing with real literature—and instruction that derives from children's interests and needs in the reading-writing process—is the best preparation for testing regardless of the types of tests we are using. Even when a district has a course of study for teaching discrete skills, if teachers teach the skills by immersing students in holistic, meaningful literacy events, the students will do well—as long as they have guidance and practice in "reading-test-reading." The reverse is not true: Teaching discrete skills may yield temporary high scores on isolated subtests, but these results do not necessarily transfer to comprehending meaningful text.

Standardized Testing in Perspective

One needs to look beyond standardized test scores to gather a balanced profile of a student. Testing that relies on one data base from one setting—rather than multiple indicators that look at the student over time—cannot be used to guide the learner

Standardized tests tell administrators, teachers, and parents how a child compares with his peers, but the tests give very little information that is useful instructionally and no information on learning processes over time. A further hazard is that standardized tests are often relied on more for information about students' deficits than for information about their strengths.

Standardized tests, with their multiple choice question format, do not allow the reader to intepret the text based on personal background knowledge and experiences. The right answers have already been locked in by the test makers. Even with improved standardized tests—such as those in place in Michigan and Illinois, which attempt to move away from a skills-based approach to reading to a more interactive, strategic one—the tests can be used only as one assessment measure. While these states and others are working to improve test formats to include more prediction and inferential questions, the questions and answers remain the test maker's, and none are open ended. While the format and questions are better, they are still used in unnatural settings and require limited input from the learner. Nor do the results reflect the student's learning process over time. The same is true for timed essay tests that expect students, under pressure, to write a perfect final copy in one sitting. Such requirements ignore writing as an evolving, reflective, revising, and editing process.

Perhaps most important, we cannot ignore the very real, lifelong damage to student self-esteem that stems from overemphasis on the results of standardized tests. Most standardized and readiness tests do not consider the language differences among different sociocultural groups, so that many children are placed at an unfair disadvantage. It is well known that Chapter 1 and special education programs have a disproportionate number of minority students, and standardized tests have played a major factor in these placements.

Since there seems to be little likelihood that we as a society will be doing away with standardized tests in the near future, it is imperative we monitor *how* such tests are used and interpreted. As responsible educators, we must begin to use other data to provide more reliable evidence for measuring a student's progress or determining a student's placement in a program. As teachers and educators, we must help parents put tests into a proper perspective. We need to invite parents to join us in actively trying to reduce the emphasis on standardized tests.

Perhaps, most important, we teachers must become evaluation experts so we can trust and rely on our own knowledge to best serve students. When we have a good student who scores poorly on a test, we must convince administrators, parents, and the student that the problem is with the testing instrument and not with the test taker. Teachers can do even more: They can try to reduce the focus on basal book tests and teacher-made tests, which are given even more emphasis than standardized tests.

We must also communicate to administrators, parents, and board of education members the recommendation of many respected educators and of the National Association for the Education of Young Children to end standardized testing (including readiness testing) in grades k–2 (Bredkamp and Shepard, 1989; Kamii, 1990). We can work to improve the attitudes surrounding testing in our own school districts. At the very least, we can advocate testing only in the fall of the year so teachers do not wind up teaching to the test. We can find out when and how often state testing is required. Some teachers have been surprised to learn that their school district is actually doing some optional standardized testing. Some states do not require standardized testing until grade 3, yet their school districts begin testing in the earlier grades. Teachers and administrators who have taken the time to check with their state departments of education for the "standard" requirements in assessment often find there is latitude for district choice.

A few states have already begun to replace standardized testing in grades k–2 with informal, classroom-based evaluation. We no longer test in first grade; in our district the Reading Recovery teachers administer a diagnostic survey (Clay, 1985) to first-graders about whom teachers want more information. At this time, some primary teachers in our district are actively involved in an effort to do away with standardized testing in grade 2.

What Is Evaluation and Why Is It So Difficult?

While teachers may be beginning to feel more comfortable and confident with whole language teaching, just to mention the word "evaluation," and you can feel the tension. Teachers feel inadequate, frustrated, and even terrified about handling evaluation fairly and competently. Most of us have had little training or guidance in assessment and evaluation procedures, and our confidence in relying on ourselves to assess students' progress is shaky, at best. Even when teachers feel ready— both theoretically and practically—to move toward more holistic evaluation, just managing the time and logistics for ongoing evaluation can be overwhelming. Additionally, the whole issue of trust plays a major role in the evaluation process. Administrators, parents, community members, and politicians need to value and respect informed teacher judgment, and teachers first need to learn to trust and value their own observations.

"What about evaluation?" is probably the question asked most often by teachers who have begun to move from a transmission, lecture style of teaching to a more democratic, interactive style. There are no easy answers, and the issue is even more difficult for teachers who have to give grades. Like moving from the basal to literature, where most of us have needed lots of time to teach the literature well, we need to give ourselves lots of time for this further transition to more meaningful evaluation in our teaching. The process is a slow, evolving one that requires lots of risk taking and continuous self-examination. Because evaluation is such a difficult area for most of us, at the end of this chapter I have included an annotated list of journal articles and books on evaluation that have proved to be particularly useful to teachers.

Before meaningful evaluation can become an integrated, ongoing, natural part of teaching, we teachers need to have certain conditions in place:

- A thorough knowledge of developmental learning processes and curriculum
- An examination and clear articulation of one's beliefs and goals about evaluation
- Knowledge and experience of how to collect, record, interpret, and analyze multiple sources of data
- Flexibility and willingness to try out and value multiple evaluation procedures to gain a complete picture of the learner
- A strong commitment to understand and implement a meaningful approach to evaluation

Before we can start incorporating meaningful evaluation methods—most of which are based on observation of students and include things like anecdotal records, interviews, learning logs, and running records—we first need to understand and value why this type of evaluation is integral to the teaching-learning process. We need to guard against simply putting procedures into place without understanding the theory behind them. Otherwise, evaluation becomes very much like the basalization of literature that occurs when only the materials change: Merely putting new procedures and activities into place will not result in meaningful teaching.

Another very real constraint to meaningful evaluation is management. Finding the time to add observational procedures to an already packed day is difficult. Management of evaluation procedures is one of the major reasons more teachers are not actively involved in the evaluation process. It's been my experience that, unless a collaborative classroom is formed, teachers do not have time in their daily schedules to make observations and record and analyze them. Until students and teachers share the responsibilities for teaching and learning, the evaluation task appears overwhelming.

Teachers need blocks of time when students can work independently on worthwhile enterprises without direct teacher supervision so they can take time to observe, conference, interview, and meet one-to-one with students. For that to happen, teachers need to have classrooms in which students are largely monitoring their own learning processes. In other words, they have to already have whole language classrooms. Holistic evaluation is a final step—it happens *after* the management, theory, and knowledge base are in place. That's why it's so difficult. To try to simply fit it in before that doesn't work.

Nonetheless, teachers find that when they begin to observe learners in broader contexts—as will be discussed later in this chapter—they start to initiate more holistic evaluation procedures. For example, teachers report that when they give sustained attention to a child's reading, they can do better analysis and teaching.

Defining Assessment and Evaluation

While the terms "assessment" and "evaluation" are often used interchangeably, they are not exactly the same. The distinction became apparent to me when I participated in a preconvention institute at IRA ("Literacy Assessment: Setting an Agenda for the 90's," International Reading Association annual meeting, Atlanta, May 1990). As I now understand it, assessment is only the beginning of the evaluation process.

"Assessment" refers to data collection and the gathering of evidence. "Evaluation" implies bringing meaning to that data through interpretation, analysis, and reflection and includes the kinds of instructional decisions that are made by careful examination of the evidence. I prefer to use the term "evaluation" in a broader context, to designate both the collection of data and the interpretation and application of it. While the evaluation process depends on assessment, assessment is only the first step in the evaluation process. Data, by itself—without observational components and interpretation—has no meaningful place in instruction or informed teaching. You can't make a value judgment about test scores; they are merely raw data. It's the interpretation of that data which brings one to the evaluation level.

For example, interpreting and analyzing Doris's standardized test scores *along with* observational measures of her reading process enabled us to evaluate her reading and not just assess it. We could not make informed instructional decisions by relying solely on Doris's test scores; we needed information from other meaningful contexts in order to plan a sound instructional program.

Very often assessment takes place apart from teaching, although ideally it needs to be an integral part of instruction. "Assessment should be constructed so good instruction is the best preparation" (Karen Wixon at assessment preconvention institute, IRA, 1990). In other words, assessment procedures should go hand in hand with good teaching. For example, when Doris's reading was assessed through a regularly occurring, genuine reading event—reading literature—she needed no special preparation to do well. Educators need to keep Wixon's statement in mind before they accord so much weight to standardized tests. Assessment needs to be meaningful, multimodal, and ongoing and must occur in authentic contexts.

Authentic assessment is at the heart of the evaluation process:

> Authentic assessment isn't a single method. It includes performance tests, such as conversations in a foreign language; observations, open-ended questions where students tackle a problem but there's no single right answer; exhibitions in which students choose their own ways to demonstrate what they have learned; interviews, giving students a chance to reflect on their achievement; and portfolios, collections of student work. The list is limited only by the criterion of authenticity, is this what we want students to know and be able to do? (Ruth Mitchell, in *Portfolio, The Newsletter of Arts PROPEL*, December 13, 1989).

While the holistic evaluation process begins with assessment and the collecting and recording of data, unless we use the data to inform and guide instruction, we are not evaluating; we are merely amassing bits and pieces of information. Before we can become expert evaluators, we have to be excellent observers, or "kid-watchers," as Yetta Goodman calls it. Through kidwatching teachers begin to develop a stronger and more clearly articulated theory base.

The difficult part is that good observation, the most critical component in evaluation, is only as good as the teacher's knowledge base. Before we can become expert observers, we have to be expert learners. We have to be able to observe and value strengths more than deficits. We have to know what to look for: What are the developmental markers we are seeing or not seeing? We have to be expert listeners: What does the student really mean? We have to be able to recognize an individual student's learning patterns and use them to take the child further. We also have to know how to set up the learning environment to maximize student development. Most of all, we need to value observation as integral to evaluation and be willing to risk adding it to our literacy programs. None of this is easy, and most of us take many years to make our evaluation processes more consistent with our beliefs about learning.

How assessment procedures and information are used is what raises the assessment process to the level of evaluation. If data collection is being used only for accountability, for grading and reporting to parents—as it usually is—meaningful evaluation is not taking place. Instead, what is taking place is simply accountability and data reporting. The goal of evaluation, like the goal of teaching, is to make the learner self-monitoring, self-regulating, and independent. The highest goal in evaluation is to have students and teachers able to reflectively appraise their own work and set new directions for teaching and learning. Ideally, self-evaluation becomes the major evaluation mode.

Traditionally, the teacher has been "in charge" of appraising and setting new directions. Shifting this responsibility to the child can seem like a radical and scary departure from what we have been taught to believe and practice. As with any profound change, we need to start slowly and gradually, take the time to understand the theory and beliefs that support the change, and allow time and latitude to make mistakes. In an attempt to ease the transition to more meaningful evaluation, the remainder of this chapter will examine beliefs, components, and issues in evaluation; demonstrate various observational strategies; and discuss the rationale and procedures for self-evaluation.

Beliefs about Evaluation for Students and Teachers

The word "evaluation" derives from "value." Before evaluation procedures can be changed and improved, we need to be able to identify what we value and state our literacy goals. A clear understanding of our beliefs and goals—along with what we want to do and why we want to do it—precedes putting evaluation practices into place.

Your beliefs and goals will be somewhat different from mine, based on your own philosophy, background, and experiences. I present my list only as a way to begin thinking about what evaluation means to you. In the struggle to work through what evaluation means, it's often a good idea to try to put your beliefs and goals in writing and then try to apply them in your classroom.

These beliefs are as important for teacher-learners as they are for student-learners.

My Beliefs	*My Goals*
Evaluation needs to:	Evaluation procedures should:
• Be consistent with theory	• Be based on daily authentic language experiences; be consistent with what we know about language learning
• Be multifaceted	• Include process and product, informal and formal measures, observational data, work samples, conferences, interviews, reading-writing strategies
• Emphasize informal/observational methods	• Highly value and utilize anecdotal records, retellings, reading and writing logs and journals, writing samples, tape recordings, running records
• Be an integral, ongoing part of the teaching-learning process, not separate from it	• Inform teaching by being a natural part of daily classroom happenings

My Beliefs

- Respect and trust teacher judgment
- Report to students, parents, and selves

- Have expectations clearly defined

- Focus on the learner's strengths

- Assess interests and attitudes

- Encourage risk taking and approximation

- Collect, record, analyze, and share data
- Guide the learner

- Be noncompetitive

- Be diagnostic and descriptive
  note growth
  note strengths and weaknesses
  note directions for teaching and future learning
- Promote self-evaluation and self-monitoring

- Place the final responsibility with the learner

My Goals

- Value teachers' observational data
- Give useful, clear information that indicates progress and notes needed new directions

- Explain evaluation criteria to students and parents at the beginning of the term or project
- State first what the learner can do well; avoid negative statements

- Incorporate interest and attitude interviews and surveys and include results in setting instructional goals
- Value invented spelling and attempts at self-correction; view errors as natural part of the learning process

- Include record keeping by students and teachers
- Set directions for teaching and lead to growth for the learner

- View the child in comparison with self—not others; reduce emphasis on grades and standardized tests
- Incorporate narrative; report to students, parents, and ourselves in a way that promotes social interaction, reflection, and growth

- Involve learners in assessing strengths and weaknesses and in setting goals; promote independence
- Eventually enable learners to assess their own learning, develop their own evaluation criteria, and make intelligent decisions for directions in future learning

Components of Evaluation

I see evaluation as involving five components. For evaluation to be meaningful, these components must occur interactively within a naturalistic framework. That is, the observation, activity, test, or task must be relevant, authentic, and part of the teaching-learning process by informing the learner and furthering instruction.

Figure 13-1   Data Gathering Profile

**EVALUATION
DATA GATHERING PROFILE
contexts**

OBSERVATION

anecdotal records
interviews, probes
conversations
response groups for writing
retellings
participation in mini-lessons
shared reading experiences
shared writing experiences
passage reading in books
running records/miscue analysis
audio tapes, video tapes
note-taking samples
one-to-one writing samples
drafts, revisions, sketches
oral presentations
problem-solving groups
whole-class evaluations
responses through performing arts
reading environmental print (K)
dramatic play
learning centers

responses to open-ended questions
literature response logs
learning/reflection logs
writing journals
self-evaluations
completed enterprises/projects/activi-
    ties/assignments/reports/research/
    graphs/charts/illustrations
student-created questions/tests
notebooks
writing folders
reading records of books read
vocabulary records
writing samples (plays, poems, letters,
    stories, published pieces)
responses through visual arts
portfolios

OBSERVATION OF PROCESS   OBSERVATION OF PRODUCT
CLIMATE OF INQUIRY
CONTEXTUALIZED MEASURES   DECONTEXTUALIZED MEASURES

MEASUREMENT

inventories, checklists
teacher-made tests
proofreading exercises
cloze exercises
informal reading inventories
interest/attitude surveys
unit or book tests
dictations
holistic writing assessments
informal reading/writing evaluations

standardized achievement tests
minimum competency tests
school, district, or state tests
norm-referenced tests
criterion-referenced tests
writing vocabulary (Clay, 1985) (K–2)
letter, letter-sound, and word tests
    (K–2)
spelling tests, vocabulary tests
diagnostic tests/surveys
worksheets

Adapted from a form developed by R. Anthony, T. Johnson, N. Mickelson, and A. Preece, shared at Pre-convention Institute, "Evaluation: A Perspective for Change." World Congress on Reading, International Reading Association, Brisbane, Australia, July 1988.

● *Observations of both process and product and collection of data*

> Consider multiple sources of data from varying learning contexts.
> See "Data Gathering Profile," Figure 13–1, for guidance.

The "Data Gathering Profile" is worth examining carefully both as a way of looking at what is meant by balanced evaluation procedures and as a check on yourself. For example, note that the evaluation profile is divided into four quadrants. The two lower quadrants are composed of more traditional assessment measures. While these are important and valid, we want to be sure that *most* of the data we are using for informed evaluation comes from observational contexts, especially process. You may want to keep the profile handy to use as a self-check list of what you are already doing, to monitor your own evaluation procedures, and to see what other kinds of evidence you might want to consider gathering. Adjust the profile to fit your particular teaching situation.

● *Recording of observations and data*

> See the "Data Gathering Profile," Figure 13–1, especially anecdotal records.

● *Interpretation and analysis of observations and data*

> Requires theory and knowledge about literacy learning
> > miscue analysis, running records
> > interviews, probes (example of Doris), use of videotapes

● *Reporting of information*

> Reporting to parents   report cards, narratives, conferences, records
> Reporting at district, local, and state levels—test results
> Communicating to others—achievement, process
> Reporting to self; self-evaluation

● *Application to teaching/learning*

> How teaching is informed and new instructional directions set lead to staff development and continuous self-evaluation; without this step, learner has not been served

Evaluation: Putting Theory into Practice

No single behavior, strategy, activity, or task can provide a comprehensive picture of student learning. Only a variety of measures, examined carefully over a period of time, can give an accurate and complete picture of a student's progress, strengths, and needs. Besides the "Data Gathering Profile" (Figure 13–1), Andrea Butler shared with me a questioning framework that has served me well in deciding the kinds of evaluation measures to utilize. "What do I want to know?" and "How am I going to find it out?" are two questions that can help the evaluation process. See Figure 13–2 for examples of how this framework may be utilized.

Figure 13-2   A Framework for Guiding the Evaluation Process

EVALUATION

What do I want to know?	How am I going to find it out?		
	Informal	*Ongoing*	*Formal*
Oral reading	One-to-one observation Paired reading	Shared reading Guided reading in group	Tape recordings Running records
Spelling	Have-a-Go sheets Free writing Pretests	Writing samples Journal writing	Proofreading exercises/para-graphs Weekly tests Dictations
Reading comprehension	Books child chooses Retellings	Contributions in group discussion Reading response logs Evidence provided to support view-points	Written tests Standardized tests Cloze exercises
Reading-writing attitudes	Books chooses Amount of reading/writing Interview (oral)	Writing journal, writing folder Responses in dis-cussion/conferences Participation in shared reading and shared writing	Interview /written survey Reading records of books read
How student views self as a reader/writer	Attitude survey—oral Books/topics chooses WEB reading	Choices for portfolio Reflection log Questions asked in conferences Oral and written responses to text	Self-evaluations rubrics narratives report cards

Focusing on procedures and contexts that I and other teachers have used suc-cessfully, this section discusses various components from the "Data Gathering Profile," especially those that involve teacher evaluation. Most of these are infor-mal measures. However, just because observation is informal does not mean that it is not highly informed and accurate. Quite the contrary. Teacher observation and judgment, especially of process, are the most valid means to collect and analyze data on children's learning.

Observational Strategies and Informal Evaluation

The following pages highlight some observational processes from the "Data Gathering Profile." The analysis and application of information that needs to accompany meaningful observation of students and recording of data take years of informed practice as well as a solid knowledge of theory and the language processes. Give yourself lots of time to make mistakes, take risks, and try out new procedures. Go slowly. Add one or more contexts from the profile as you feel ready.

At the same time, keep in mind that the "Data Gathering Profile" should not be used as a menu or list of assessment activities but as part of a larger literacy framework. We need always to have an expanded view of literacy assessment—viewing and guiding students to be effective decision makers and active meaning makers who employ reading and writing for a variety of meaningful purposes.

Anecdotal Records

Anecdotal records are dated, informal observational notations that describe language development as well as social development in terms of the learner's attitudes, strengths, weaknesses, needs, progress, learning styles, skills, strategies used, or anything else that seems significant at the time of observation. These records are usually brief comments that are very specific to what the child is doing and needs to be doing. They provide documented, accumulated information over time and offer an expanded view of the student's development of literacy.

Anecdotal records may be taken in a variety of settings, for example: journal writing, dramatic play, oral reading, literature discussion groups, spelling, independent work, and writing. The contexts are limited only by your particular needs

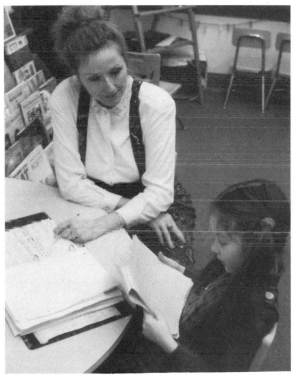

Second grade teacher Ellen Rubin
taking anecdotal records
during a writing conference

and time constraints. While the setting for record taking can be whole class, small group, or individual, most often anecdotal records are taken on individual students, either in a one-to-one setting with the teacher or by the teacher observing the child or the child's work in a particular context. (See Figures 13–3 through 13–7 for variations of anecdotal records. Most of these examples represent first efforts by teachers.)

Figure 13–3   A Kindergarten Teacher's Anecdotal Records of Student's Reading Behaviors

Figure 13-4   A Grade 1 Teacher's Anecdotal Records of Students' Independent Work

strengths   needs

Taylor

10/13
I like Book   ending periods, -er   ēē
   short vowels   beg cap.   CVe   ch   -ing

Plane Rittle
Shawberry Book -great innovation

10/20
On Halloween

-extended on story; sc-; good sight word periods - putting hyphens between words
sense of plural; beg./ende conven.   ow; capitals at beg.
ă ĭ

Journal 10-20

   ch | tr

Witch book 10/25 good effort 'illus.   -ed (using -d) , periods
-great plot development

      Blank book
The Indian Book
   -innovation from beg. pattern
blank book _ Haunted House   -confusion over hard/soft g.
   -good use of written expression "but..."

Figure 13-5   Anecdotal Notes on Third Grade Students' Journal Entries

Allen :

9-6-88   Journal

Very expressive - connected ideas . writes confidently
Getting the idea of paragraphing. Needs to reread for
punctuation + capitals in some places.

Keith   Journal

9-6-88   good effort + detail - story about his dog + how he fetches
                 ï   omits
                 — , He ^ endings + some verb tense difficulty
                 I

311

Figure 13-6   A Third Grade Teacher's Anecdotal Notes on One Student's Reading

Name: Nathan

READING RECORD   (grade 3)

Attitude -
12/6 Enjoyed the book - rate (9¾) told why he did not
rate it a ten. Boring part. Excited about Chester Cricket.

1/6 Rated (8) liked ending but some parts he didn't understand.

1-9 Excited about book - willing to talk about it.
Difficult to get him to stop!

Selection of Books-
12/6 Wild Timothy
Chester Cricket's New Home

1-9 The Secret Garden

Reading Strategies/Comprehension-
12/6 Told about new book - Chester Cricket - described where
he lives. Good details - big ladies - oversized!
Forgot name of boy.

1-9 Told about characters - good detail. Gets the
main ideas and predicts well. - "I think he is like
a doctor.

I have modeled taking anecdotal records for kindergarten teachers who have never gone through the process before and want to learn. With the teacher looking on, I invite the child, or the teacher invites the child, to choose a favorite book to read. I then observe the child "reading" the book and note what the child is doing (see Figure 13–8). I also give positive feedback to the child, telling him what I notice he can do. For early childhood teachers just beginning this process, the checklist of print concepts (Figure 13–13) may be helpful for building an awareness of important behaviors to observe and assess.

Beginning to take anecdotal records is difficult and requires taking a risk. At first, your records may not be particularly informative, but you will improve with practice and your observational skills and use of specific language to match the task will improve. As an ongoing record of students' process and progress, the records will serve you, the students, the parents, and your administrator well. Probably the hardest aspect of taking anecdotal records is finding time in an already full

Figure 13-7   A Third Grade Teacher's Anecdotal Notes on One Student's Writing

WRITING RECORD   *(grade 3)*

Attitude-
10/89 Willing to write. Enjoys writing stories and poems.
3/9 Excellent use of gesslature - detailed
Conversation when writing.

Clarity of Expression-
10/89 Easy to understand. Clear to the reader.
3/9 Clear

Revision and Editing (willingness to change)
10/89 Willing to go back and change around. Needs to spend more time editing in marking pen. Tends to erase.

Mechanics (spelling, captials, periods)
10/5/89 Makes paragraphs when needed.
3/9 Mechanics is improving, knows when to add punctuation + capitals. Spelling improving.

schedule. In addition, there is the confidence factor for us as teachers. We haven't had much training or encouragement in keeping informal records, nor have we seen them be highly regarded. Valuing informal observational data means trusting teacher judgment.

Despite the constraints of time and effort, taking anecdotal records pays important dividends. The records are useful for conferences with the student, parents, or administrator, serve as benchmarks for noting student progress and setting instructional goals, and become objective sources of factual documentation and of specific information for writing narratives on report forms. Anecdotal records can also be used to promote reflection on student growth by the students, parents, teachers, and administrators. Finally, since only the employment of multiple evaluation measures can assure a representative picture of the student, anecdotal records are a way to observe and note process and product in various contexts.

Figure 13-8　Observational Notes of Kindergartners' Reading of a Favorite Book

Noah

chose Obadiah. pointed to title + title page + read it.
  attempt at 1:1 - pretty close
  looking at text - making sense in retelling - very close to text
  knew finger should come out at end of line - moved finger
    to end when he finished reading a line.
  ready to work on 1:1 matching for greater accuracy.
p. 16 - did perfect 1:1 when asked to reread. + given some modeling
  could locate some specific words: "pot" two times
  could find "black" by going back to begin. of line.

Keindre   3-5-90

Lazy Mary - reads title, holds book correctly, reads left to right
  looking at text.   p 3   memorized
                p 4
                p 5   "
                p 7   ',
  has 1:1 matching pretty well - did some s/c when text
didn't fit.
  ? - could identify it
  p 9 - looked at text - had 1:1 matching.
1:1 matching became more accurate as went through book
went back to begin. of text when text didn't fit
  could point to "Mary", "will" several times when asked
actually reading text.
heading to do crisp 1:1 matching

Marcy Silver, a third grade teacher who has taken records for two years, says,

> My anecdotal records have been especially useful during parent conferences. I can be very specific about each child, and the parents feel good because it's obvious I know their child. For example, I might have noted the child's attitudes and facial gestures when he was talking about a particular book. I'd never remember that weeks later if I hadn't written it down. I've also used the anecdotal records to conference with students and to write comments on report cards. After two years, it's going a lot more smoothly. It's definitely been worth the effort.

Organizing for Taking Anecdotal Records To find the time to take anecdotal records, you need to make the process an integral part of your teaching. This is difficult to do unless your classroom is organized collaboratively, with students managing their own behaviors, and you have blocks of time when you are not directly teaching or supervising. Attempting to take observational notes while teaching does not work and serves only to frustrate the teacher. For your first attempts, try involving your students in an activity that you feel confident they can complete independently. Then, call up several students, one at a time, and have them read to you. Use the sample anecdotal records provided in this chapter as a starting framework. With time and experience, you will develop your own style and comfort level and become familiar with the vocabulary that describes language learning.

Many opportunities exist within the normal routines of the classroom when anecdotal records may be taken. When young students are involved in dramatic play, writing at the writing center, or looking at books, the teacher can take five minutes to focus on several students and jot down some notes. When students have assumed a leadership role in a literature discussion group, the teacher can occasionally become an observer and note taker. When you are conferencing with a student, you can jot down relevant comments about what you are noticing or conferencing about. Some teachers who check their students' independent reading daily occasionally use that time to note observations about reading attitudes and strategies used. Once in a while, you can ask several students to join you at a table during sustained silent reading and note what they do in the process of reading. Or instead of scheduling reading groups five days a week, take one day—for example, Friday—to meet with students one-to-one to listen to them read and then make anecdotal comments. Finally, if you have a collaborative classroom where you have provided opportunities for children to work together, you will be able to be a teacher researcher and observer and note the problem-solving strategies students are using and then base instruction on your observations. At the highest level, your anecdotal records can become the basis for self-evaluation, where you begin to note patterns and behaviors that inform your teaching.

For keeping anecdotal records, some teachers use a three-ring binder with dividers, allocating several pages for each student—perhaps one for reading, one for math, and one for writing. Others prefer a spiral-bound notebook with a tab inserted for each student in the class. Some teachers color code their tabs for the five days of the week and divide their class into five groups. On the day they are taking anecdotal records, they focus on the five or six students in a particular color. In that way, you would make observational comments about each student at least several times a month.

One management system that works very well is to use a clipboard while sitting down with the students or while walking around observing. The teacher makes brief notes on an index card or Post-it and adds the comments to the notebook later. An efficient method that many of our teachers favor is to clip a strip of adhesive mailing or package labels to a clipboard and write comments directly on the labels. At the end of the day, the rectangular label is pasted on the child's page. (See Figure 13–9 for a kindergarten teacher's observational comments done on mailing labels that have not yet been pasted onto students' individual records—from "Booklook" setting where students choose books to read independently or with peers.)

Figure 13-9   A Kindergarten Teacher's Observational Notes on Mailing Labels for Pasting onto Student Records

In taking anecdotal records, it is important for all comments to begin positively with something the child *is* doing. This is a difficult adjustment, for most of us tend to begin with what the child is not doing. Focusing on strengths first is important for several reasons. Eventually noticing strengths first becomes a state of mind. Taking a positive view of all children is part of whole language philosophy and all good teaching. In addition, I believe students and parents are entitled to hear about the child's positive behaviors.

Even a young child should be able to take a look at her section in the anecdotal notebook and feel comfortable. This is not to say we don't list the needs and deficits; we do, but *after* we have noted what the child is doing well. A good check is to see if you feel comfortable sharing your records with the student and with her parents. If you don't, you may want to think about your attitudes toward observation. We need to treat our students as we would want to be treated. I know I would be upset if my principal refused to show me her observational notes about my teaching because they are negatively worded.

Before you decide to add anecdotal records to your routines, it's important to look at where you are in your teaching. While lots of talk turns on the need to take anecdotal records, few teachers actually keep such records. In our district, after three years of moving toward whole language, some teachers are just beginning to attempt that additional record keeping. Most teachers seem to need about five years to feel ready to handle and value this additional but crucial responsibility. The exceptions are our kindergarten teachers, many of whom have been taking and utilizing observational notes for years.

While the taking of anecdotal records is of vital importance to the total evaluation process, give yourself time to make this transition. Find the system and time arrangement that work best for you. There is no one right way. As you begin to make taking anecdotal records a part of your teaching, eventually, the task will no longer seem like an extra incumbrance, and you will feel as though you know your students a lot better. Start small, perhaps with one area such as reading or writing. At the same time, you may want to include beginning and ending year interviews or attitude surveys along with anecdotal notes on each child. Keep in mind that your records may be short and infrequent. Some teachers find that taking records as infrequently as several times a quarter (twice in nine weeks) is sufficient help to be worth the effort.

Interviews and Surveys

One-to-one interviews are an ideal way to get to know your students. I prefer interviews to written surveys because students often feel limited by the questions and the space on the page. They tend to respond minimally in writing, and I never feel I have learned much about the student. With a personal interview, you can probe a response and elicit information that reflects attitudes, strategies, preferences, and level of confidence—all in just a few minutes. I think it's worth taking some time at the beginning of school to interview each of your students. If you take just several students a day for five to ten minutes each, you can get through your entire class in two weeks. The specific information you gain will save time later because you will be better prepared to set relevant instructional goals.

You'll probably want to design your own form, survey, or questionnaire based on your and your students' needs. Use the "Reading Survey" (Figure 13–10), "Writing Survey" (Figure 13–11), "Spelling Interview" (Appendix H), and "Writing Interview" (Figure 13–12) as guides.

Here are some additional questions you may want to include. All of these would be too many. Choose those that suit your purposes.

- Where do you read at home?
- How much television do you watch? What are your favorite programs?
- Does anyone read to you at home? Were you read to when you were little?
- Do you sign out books from the public library?
- Name the last book that you read.

- Does anything about reading cause you trouble?
- Who in your family likes to spend time reading?
- Do you like to write stories?
- How do you get your ideas for writing?
- Are you a good listener? Why do you think so?
- How do you feel about speaking in front of others?
- What do you like to do in your free time?
- What is the best present you ever received?
- What is something you think you do very well?
- What is something you think you need to work on?
- What is something you hope to learn this year at school?
- Is there anything you would like me to know that would help you have a good year at school?

Figure 13-10   Reading Survey

READING SURVEY

Name_____   Date_____

1. How do you feel about reading?

2. Do you have a favorite author? Explain.

3. What kinds of books do you like to read?

4. What was your last favorite book? Explain.

5. Do you think it's important to be a good reader? Explain.

6. What do you do when you come to a word you can't read?

Figure 13-11   Writing Survey
Developed by Karen Horton.

Writing Survey

:) I love to write   :| It's OK   :(I hate to write

1. I like to write with

2. My favorite kind of paper is

3. My favorite place to write is

4. My favorite time to write is

5. When I write, I like to have _____ with me

6. I like to write
   a. alone   c. when it's quiet
   b. with others   d. when it's noisy

7. _____ would make it easier for me to write in the classroom.

Inspired by Frank Smith's *Joining the Literacy Club*, fourth grade teacher Joan Di Dio designed a "Literacy Express" membership form to make all her entering students immediate members of the "Literacy Club." Her purpose is for all students to feel that if they have read or written anything at all (which, of course, everyone has), they are already members of the club. The requirements are deliberately kept simple so no one can be excluded. The membership application has blank, lined spaces for "I. Books You've Read" (or "That Have Been Read to You") and "II. *Any* Kinds of Writing You've Ever Done." The idea and form could even be adapted to kindergarten by changing the two headings above to "Books You Like," which could include favorite stories children have heard read aloud, and

Figure 13-12   Writing Interview

WRITING INTERVIEW (grade 2 student)

June 1989

Name *Jari*

1. Are you a good writer? *YES* Why do you think so?
Becase I time I stak to
my writee my story abot
(Because I think I stick to what my story is about.)

2. How did you learn to write?
i practise and practise

3. How do you choose what to write about?
i read storys and go
too classmates if i need
too
(I read stories and go to classmates if I need to.)

4. What do you do to make your writing better?
read it over.

5. If you knew someone who was having trouble writing, what advice would you give that person?
Jest with a story if
you haff any problems
ask me.
(Just with a story, if you have any problems ask me.)

6. What don't you like about writing?
sometimes my hand
gets tired.

7. When you've written a lot of stories, how do you choose the one you want to publish?
i colo are best sory
(I choose my best story)

8. What do you think other writers do about their writing problems?
tink a little
(Think a little)

9. What would you like to do better as a writer?
right more storys

10. What have you enjoyed most about Writing Workshop this school year?
poblising storys
(publishing stories)

"Writing You Like to Do," with available blank space to affirm that marks on paper that have meaning to the child make the child a writer and club member.

Older students can design their own interview forms as a way for the teacher to get to know them. Students can also interview each other. Important questions for an interview form could also come from a shared writing experience. Completed forms may be posted or bound into a book and read as a way for all students to get to know their classmates.

One-to-one interviews, or written interview surveys the child completes, are also useful at the end of the year for noting changes in attitudes and what the child has learned. After two years of being immersed in a literature program, almost all the children in a third grade class responded positively to the question, "Do you like to read?" on a written interview form. The only exceptions were the students who were new to the school. Note in Figure 13–12 a second-grader's "Writing Interview" after a year of daily "writing workshop" (Calkins, *The Art of Teaching Writing*, Heinemann, 1986).

Interviews or surveys can also be used in the content areas to find out student attitudes toward the content, what students have learned, and their suggestions for improving a unit or course. A sample content interview, based on the work of Rogers (1989), follows:

Content Interview

1. What are the most important things you have learned in _____ (science, health, math, social studies) during this _____ (year, semester, quarter, class)?
2. How did you feel about this course (unit, class) and the way it was set up?
3. What did you like best about the unit?
4. What did you like least about the unit?
5. Do you have any suggestions for how this unit should be taught to next year's class?

Conferences

Conferences are a powerful evaluation tool. By following the lead of the student—and not imposing a teacher agenda—conferences enable us to get to know students as learners and to guide them in making literacy connections. Many teachers are starting to use the conferences they are already having with students as a time to make anecdotal observations. In addition to ongoing writing conferences, we have ongoing reading conferences related to independent reading (see WEB, pp. 43–49).

Checklists

Lots of teachers use checklists effectively and wisely. While on the whole I prefer narratives and anecdotal records, there are times when checklists work well. I like to use a checklist, combined with narrative and observational comments, for checking early literacy behaviors—letter-sound knowledge, basic sight words, and print concepts. See Figure 13–13 for "Concepts About Print," adapted from Marie Clay's "Concepts about Print" (1993a). The form can easily be used as a straight checklist by adding vertical lines across the page and writing students' names across the top.

Note the procedures for using the "Concepts About Print" checklist. A real book with simple text and matching pictures would be used to check for understanding of concepts. Under "Letter and Word Knowledge," when checking for understanding the difference between one letter and two letters, one word and two words, and a first and last letter of a word, Clay recommends giving the child two index cards. Choose a page with only one line of print and show the child how to hold one card in each hand, lay them side by side, covering the line of text, and then slide the cards back and forth to expose the print. Once the child can do this, ask him to show you the desired number of letters and words. These are important concepts for checking whether the child understands the difference between a letter and a word. (See Clay, *An Observation Survey*, 1993, pp. 47–52, for specific language the examiner uses for checking some of these concepts.)

I also like checklists when they help put students in charge of their own learning, for example, having students check for specific skills before completing and handing in an assignment. (See Figure 13–14, "Proofreader's Checklist.")

The problem I have with most checklists for teachers is that you wind up spending most of your time focusing on the list to be checked rather than on the

Figure 13-13   Concepts About Print Form

Concepts About Print

Book Handling _____

front of book, cover _____

title _____

turns pages left to right _____

notices pictures _____

points to print when reading (telling) _____

holds book correctly _____

Directionality
understands top/bottom
points top left to begin
beginning to have one-to-one matching
    of spoken word to printed word
moves finger left to right and word for
    word, down the page (return sweep)
reads (turns) pages in order

Letter and Word Knowledge
can locate one letter and then two letters
can locate one word and then two words
can locate a first letter and a last letter
can point to a specific word when prompted
can identify a capital letter and then the same
    lower case letter

Higher Level Concepts
understands use of "."
understands use of "?"
understands use of " "
uses beginning letter sounds
uses final consonant sounds
relies on pictures to tell the story
relies on memory for text
uses structural cues

Adapted from "Concepts of Print" test in *An Observation Survey of Early Literacy Achievement* by Marie M. Clay (Portsmouth, NH: Heinemann, 1993).

child. By looking for progress on a skills checklist, you can easily miss observing the learning that is occurring. The other problem is that when checklists are devised by someone else, they never quite fit the teacher's and student's needs. My personal advice, based on experience, is to use checklists sparingly and then to devise your own forms based on your children and your needs. Use these and other forms (such as those included in "Resources" at the end of this chapter) as models, but adapt them to suit your purposes and the students' needs.

Figure 13-14 Proofreader's Checklist

Proofreader's Checklist

Name_____ Date_____

Before you consider your paper complete, check to see that you have done the following:

_____ Each sentence begins with a capital letter.

_____ "I" is always capitalized.

_____ Each sentence ends with correct punctuation ("." "?" or "!").

_____ The names of people and important places are capitalized.

_____ Speech marks (") are used to show when someone is talking.

_____ Each new paragraph is indented

_____ I have checked and corrected my spelling to the best of my ability.

_____ I have checked to see that my story makes sense.

_____ My handwriting is clear and legible.

Is there anything else you did in checking over your paper? Note it in the space below.

_____

_____

_____

Retellings

Asking students to give an oral or written retelling of what they have read is an effective strategy for evaluating comprehension and is a viable alternative to teacher follow-up questions. Children are in charge of telling in their own words what they have understood, and the setting is relaxed and informal. Retelling is known to help with oral language skills of students and to improve reading comprehension in less proficient readers (Koskinen and others, 1988).

Retelling literally means asking the child, "Tell me about what you've just read." Some teachers may phrase a request for a retelling as, "Retell this story as if you were telling it to someone who had never read (or heard) it before." I always use the retelling strategy when I am doing an informal reading evaluation with a child. It's a quick and efficient way to assess whether the child has grasped the overall meaning of the text. As they are becoming familiar with the process, some teachers like to use a tape recorder so they don't miss any part of the child's responses.

The teacher can guide the retelling process if the child is having difficulty with such comments as, "Tell me what you remember," "How did the story begin?" or "What happened next?". If these strategies fail, specific story questions may be asked. Poor readers, who lack confidence, benefit greatly from the teacher's probing. Guided questioning forces them to rethink the passage, and their retellings often improve substantially.

The retelling strategy is also an effective way to assess long-range comprehension. For example, one month after a content area study, students can be asked to retell in writing the important concepts they remember. (For other ways of retelling, for example, using picture mapping and sequencing activities, see "Literature Extension Activities," pp. 94–101. See also Koskinen and others, 1988.)

Diagnostic Tests / Surveys

Clay's *Observation Survey of Early Literacy Achievement* (1993a), which is used for selecting children for the Reading Recovery program, can easily be adapted in part for end-of-the-year kindergarten and for grade 1 classes. Parts of the survey may also be useful for grade 2 or for entering new students. The "Letter Identification" test asks children to identify fifty-four different characters and includes upper and lower case letters. The "Word Test" asks children to read down a list of twenty basic sight vocabulary words and checks knowledge of high-frequency words. The "Concepts About Print Test" checks important book and print-related concepts. (See Figure 13–13 for a workable adaptation.)

The "Writing Vocabulary Test" asks the child to write down all the words he knows how to write, beginning with his own name and including personal and basic words. It works well to take your class into the gym or a space where there is no print around for reference. The child has ten minutes for the task, and the score is the number of words spelled correctly. Verbal prompts are allowed. For example, the teacher can ask, "Do you know how to write _____?" (See Clay, 1993a, pp. 58–59, for suggested prompts.) This is an easy test to adapt to whole-class use and a quick way to find out who the readers and writers are. We find the writing score correlates highly with reading ability. Take your papers and rank them from high to low. The high scorers will be the proficient readers and the lowest scorers the struggling readers.

Another of Clay's diagnostic tests that is easy to use whole class is the "Dictation Test." The teacher reads a sentence, and the children are asked to write it. The child is given credit for every sound written correctly. For example, if the child wrote "hav" for "have" or "todae" for "today," he gets credit for correctly writing all the sounds in the word, even though the spelling is not correct. The score gives some information on the child's ability to hear sounds in words, indicating graphophonic ability, and to make sound-letter connections. (See Clay, 1993a, pp. 65–70, for specific directions.)

Running Records and Miscue Analysis

Running records are a form of miscue analysis. The teacher observes, records, and analyzes any unexpected words the child says in the process of reading aloud a connected text. Running records are used for instructional purposes to evaluate the child's reading behaviors and set directions for teaching, to check the difficulty of a text for a child, and to monitor progress.

While initially taking a running record seems quite complicated, with lots of practice and attention to detail it becomes second nature. It is very difficult to teach yourself to take a running record, but it is possible. (See Clay, 1993a, pp. 20–42.) The easiest and best way to learn is to have a trained Reading Recovery teacher demonstrate for you and practice with you.

As part of my job, I have taught classroom teachers how to take running records, and they have found it enormously useful for reading diagnosis and reporting to parents. Other Reading Recovery teachers in our district have done the same. I recommend combining running records with retellings and using running records with your good readers about three times a year and with your struggling readers about every six weeks.

At some point in your transition to more meaningful evaluation strategies, you will want to include some form of miscue analysis. Again, this is not an easy transition in whole language teaching, especially for those teachers who have had no specialized training and practice in this area, but it is an important component. In order to know what reading strategies students are and are not using—so you can plan effectively for instruction and evaluate intelligently—being able to do an analysis of reading behaviors is extremely useful. Give yourself time to handle this further transition. Connie Weaver (1993) has done a comprehensive job of explaining miscue analysis, building on and referring to the work of Kenneth Goodman, Yetta Goodman, Dorothy Watson, and Carolyn Burke. Once you understand the concepts and procedures of miscue analysis, you may want to work out your own variations of the procedure.

Informal Evaluations of Reading and Writing

When my principal requests information about a child in our building, I no longer obtain the information through formal assessment or norm-referenced testing. I can find out everything I need to know through informal assessment. I always take several running records using book texts. Based on what the teacher has told me about the child, I have a variety of books on hand. Usually I pick one I think might work and say to the child, "Take a look at this book. Does it look just about right for you? Does it seem too easy, too hard?" After the child is comfortable with the book, both in terms of readability and interest, I ask the student to read orally a 100–300 word passage. (I count the words later.) With older children, choosing a passage closer to 300 words is a good idea, because as the reader begins to get a sense of the story, he may read the last section considerably better than the beginning section. This will have a positive effect on the child's comprehension and overall miscue rate. Following the reading, I ask the child to do a retelling of the story as described in "Retellings," earlier in this section.

For writing evaluation, I may ask to see a favorite piece of the student's writing, the child's journal, or a sample of "anything you might like to write about." For young children, I might use the "Dictation Test" and the "Writing Vocabulary Test." The entire informal evaluation usually takes about twenty minutes.

Finally, I share my observations and findings with the teacher and principal and write up an informal summary. (See Figure 13–15 for the informal reading evaluation of a new grade 2 student who entered school in late spring.)

Recently I have begun to add an informal interview (where I talk with the child and record responses) to the informal evaluation as I have become more aware of the importance of including the child's attitudes, behaviors, and understandings of himself as a learner.

Teacher-Made Tests

While most of our comprehension checks in reading center around student responses in logs, discussions, and other related book activities, teachers sometimes

Figure 13-15   Informal Reading Evaluation

INFORMAL READING EVALUATION
(Using running records, retellings, and writing samples)

Name: Myra B.
Grade: 2
Date: 5-19-89
Birthday: 5-21-81
Age: 8-0   Examiner: Regie Routman

READING

Based on three passages in the context of a story, Myra's oral reading and comprehension level are well above grade level. She reads fluently and generally has good word attack skills and understanding of what she's read.

Strengths

1. When in trouble, Myra keeps going and maintains the flow of the story.
2. She reads with good phrasing and cadence.
3. She comprehends main ideas and can do a simple retelling that includes major points of the story in sequence.
4. She sees herself as a good reader.

Weaknesses

1. Her self-correction rate is low, indicating she sometimes reads the words without thinking about overall meaning.
2. She has difficulty with words of three syllables or more.
3. She does not always use the context to help herself when she comes to an unknown word.
4. At times, she ignores punctuation.

WRITING

Based on a writing sample, Myra's writing is below grade level for handwriting, punctuation, content, and maturity—closer to a first grade level for this time of year than a second grade level. Myra reported that almost all the writing she did at her previous school was copying from the board.

RECOMMENDATIONS

1. Recognize Myra's excellent reading ability, and use that strength to connect to the writing areas.
2. Demonstrate to Myra how she can use the meaningful context of a story to figure out unknown words.
3. Continue to give Myra help in cursive handwriting.
4. Conference with her parents regarding the writing process and writing activities that can be encouraged over the summer.

give a written test after a book has been completed in group. Questions are open-ended and are designed to encourage a variety of thoughtful responses. (See Figure 13–16 for a test developed by fourth grade teacher Nancy Schubert and a student's responses.)

When teachers give tests, students need to know what is expected without, at the same time, being given a lot of rigid guidelines. Nancy Schubert gives her students as much time as they need to take tests and also encourages them to use the book. She comments,

> In most of life, you can go back to the source for reference, so why not here? When students can use the book, they think it's not a test. However, you have to know the book to use it well. Also, if I give a test, I no longer say, "Time is up." I might say, "We have gym now, but you'll have time later." I don't want kids to feel pressured. I want them to do well.

In place of a formal test, Nancy sometimes has students write and illustrate the six to eight main events of a book in sequence. Students write sentences or short paragraphs in a booklet format, and accompanying illustrations may be optional. Students enjoy this variation on a test, and the teacher learns a great deal about what the student has understood about the book. As long as students can justify their responses, different interpretations are accepted.

For older students, you may want to include student-developed questions. My favorite final exam in graduate school was in a philosophy of education class where the professor presented several important, global questions but also gave the option for the student to write and answer his own important question. I still recall the fun I had creating and answering my own question.

Passage Reading of a Book

One nonthreatening way to evaluate oral reading is to have students pick a favorite part of a chapter or a book that they have read recently and read it to you. You could also choose to photocopy a section from a book that the students have read as a group and observe a student reading the passage to you in a one-to-one setting.

Journal Writing

Journals may be used to evaluate spelling, phonics, handwriting, and writing abilities, in addition to content and ideas. Some teachers keep a checklist in the front or back of the journal and note the date the child used a particular skill—for example, capitalizing "I" or using question marks or possessives correctly. Other teachers encourage students to look through their journals and note these findings. First grade teacher Peg Rimedio involves her students and parents in using journals to evaluate writing (see Appendix J11).

Critical Issues in Meaningful Evaluation

Portfolio Assessment

Portfolio assessment is one of the current directions in evaluation. The International Reading Association 1990 conference included many opportunities for teachers to hear about the topic. Articles in professional journals are talking about portfolio assessment as the state of the art in evaluation. And in several states

Figure 13–16 Teacher-made Test for James and the Giant Peach *by Roald Dahl*

Name: Natalie   "James & the Giant Peach"

1. Explain how James changed during the story. How did his character develop during the book? In the beginning of the book James was sad. He had two very mean aunts, that hated him. He cleaned, cooked, washed and did art the aunts told him to do. (Not asked him.) At the end when he lived in the peach pit, he had all the playmates in the world. Many came to see James's famous home. The children asked him to tell his story again and again. So he wrote the story in the form of a book by R. Dahl.

2. Where in the book did you feel happy about something that happened? Give 2 examples. ① I felt happy when Aunt Spiker and Aunt Sponge got crushed by the peach. Centipede cut the stem) and it rolled off what was called "a ghostly hill." The two aunts scrambled to save themselves, tripped over each other and "CRUNCH!"
② I was glad when the peach landed on top of the Empire Terminal Tower instead of smashing into a zillion tiny pieces. I was glad nobody was hurt badly.

3. Who was your favorite character in the book? Give at least 3 reasons for your choice.
I think Centipede was my favorite character because
1. He was smart
2. He helped the peach
3. He's a rascal
4. He makes me laugh
5. He is mischevous
6. He says funny stuff

4. Name one hero in this story. Explain why you think this character is a hero.
I think James was a hero because He saved the peach from the sharks. He used the earthworm for bait. He attracted gulls. Then he tethered them to silk, made by the silkworm.

(5) What do you think the crocodile tongues really were? Explain: I think the crocodile tongues were really some of Aunt Spikers dead skirt, that had fallen off of her hand. Then the old man dipped them in green paint, and then put them in a → brown paper bag.

(6) In the next adventure what will happen to James? Explain: His mother and father will not be eaten by a rhino. He will be happy forever. Aunt Spounge and aunt spiker will be eaten by the rhino. But the two are so gross; the rhino spits them up. They are taken to the cemetery, and put into their graves. The two tombstones say DRIP. (which means Dont Rest in Peace

(7) Pretend you are talking with Roald Dahl. What are some (3 or 4) questions you would like to ask him?
1. How long have you been writing books?
2. How many have you written so far?
3. Is writing fun?
4. Where do you get your ideas?
5. Do you watch TV?
6. Are you rich
7. What is your favorite food? Is it chocolate or peaches? Thankyou Mr. Dahl Its been nice meeting you!

(8) Will you read this story to your children? Why or why not?
Yes I will. It may encourage them to read or write books of their own. And also Roald is a very good author

One day the giant peach will roll down the hill, in to the cemetery and squash the two graves. They will sink into to earth and never be seen again!

portfolio assessment is mandated or is in the process of being required. With all of this, one would think portfolio assessment is everywhere. Not so. Most school districts are only just beginning to look at and think about portfolio assessment.

Portfolio assessment, as I understand it, is based on the selection of a representative, ongoing, and changing collection of work samples. Usually the pieces are stored in a large folder or portfolio, much in the same way an artist or writer saves sketches, drafts, and completed pieces. The concept behind portfolios is a powerful one and can be consistent with whole language teaching as long as it is a natural process that serves the students and guides the teacher. Ideally, students look at their work over time and make reflective decisions about what might go into their classroom portfolios. Thus, students are at the center of the assessment process. Through continued student examination, discussion, and reflection, the portfolio can become a vehicle for continued growth in the learning process.

The problem is in carrying out the concept. There is a real danger, especially when the procedure is mandated, that portfolios will become collection silos—storage bins filled with data serving no useful purpose. Just because work is in folders or on tapes, or check marks and grades are in a teacher's record book, does not mean evaluation is taking place.

At present, the notion of portfolio assessment seems to overemphasize collections of things. I think this is probably a normal part of the initial transition process, much the same way as teachers are initially overconcerned about activities when first teaching with literature. However, and this is the important factor, the only way we will move to evaluation in the highest sense—valuing and analyzing the process, the product, and attitudes about teaching-learning—is to make evaluation consistent with our philosophy. What is significant is not the collection itself but what the collection represents, or how it demonstrates the learning process that has taken place and, especially, the insights the learner has gained.

Because I worry about the misuse of the term "portfolio assessment," I prefer "portfolio approach to evaluation." By that I mean using multiple indicators and data sources to inform and guide instruction and to put the learner in charge of the evaluation process. The portfolio as a particular physical holding place need not even exist. What would exist is knowledgeable employment of various observations, measurements, and records that are assimilated to create a profile of students, their progress, and their learning needs. Students would be initially guided in looking carefully at their work over time. Self-evaluation of their work would focus on process and change, on what is significant and not just their best work. A portfolio approach to evaluation assumes knowledgeable teachers who understand and integrate language and learning processes in their teaching and who are ready to give up some control and entrust ownership of the learning-evaluation process to students. See Appendix Q for some possibilities for portfolios.

Many of us are already using a portfolio approach in our teaching. We rely on reading records, reading logs, journals, writing samples, discussion groups, collaborative projects, and other authentic reading-writing-listening-speaking activities as responses to literature and content area texts and material. We need to take the approach beyond the response level to the evaluation level. With a portfolio approach to evaluation, students examine their responses and thoughtfully select and appraise representative and significant work samples. This is a sophisticated concept that is not easy to implement. A portfolio approach goes beyond keeping a collection of work samples; it includes a way of thinking about evaluation. This highest level is necessary if students are to become independent learners and critical thinkers.

Probably having students examine and collect selected writing samples over time is a good place to begin with a portfolio approach. In the beginning, or until teachers and students are ready for students to do most of the selecting and evaluating, a compromise might be to balance the selection process, with the teacher sometimes choosing, the teacher and student sometimes deciding together, and the student sometimes selecting. In any case, students and teachers need to know and be able to articulate why they are choosing a particular piece for the portfolio.

For example, in getting started, the teacher could guide the student in verbalizing what is significant about a selected piece. Some questions to help students think about and evaluate their work might include: "Do you notice anything about this piece of writing that is significant for you?" "What are your strengths?" "What do you think you have improved on?" "How might you have made this piece better?" Even a kindergarten student may be guided to look at journal entries over time and note her specific growth as a writer. Eventually, students should be able to identify on their own their progress, strengths, needs, and future goals.

Beginning to adopt a portfolio approach to evaluation is no easy matter. In our district, we struggled this past school year in our weekly language arts support groups trying to decide if and how to implement writing portfolios. The year before, based on an idea from Upper Arlington, Ohio, schools, we had talked about the possibility of saving three "significant" pieces of writing from each child each year. The pieces could be kept in a permanent folder that would follow the child from kindergarten through twelfth grade and be part of the permanent record.

In three of our five k–4 buildings, we spent several months looking at children's writing samples from a school-wide writing prompt (kindergarten used journal samples) in an attempt to establish criteria by which to judge the quality of student writing at each grade level. While the holistic scoring and analysis were valuable for looking at children's writing, we continued to wrestle with how to utilize portfolios, and we came to no consensus or decisions concerning implementation.

After an entire year of ongoing discussion, looking at children's writing samples, and talking about possible implementation procedures, we had not resolved the following issues related to setting up writing portfolios:

- How would the pieces be selected?
- Who would select them?
- How many pieces would be selected?
- How would the portfolio be used in the total evaluation process?

Part of the problem is that many of our teachers and administrators are not yet highly trained or experienced in the writing process. Even establishing criteria for good writing became difficult. At some grade levels teachers wanted to give mechanics equal or greater weight than content. Unless the approach is based on an understanding of how children learn language processes, portfolio assessment is likely to be a "catch-all" folder for work samples. Until teachers are at a point where they are reflective about their own teaching-learning and classrooms are collaborative communities, work samples are likely to be selected by teachers without ownership by students. Teachers need to be asking questions about their own teaching and looking at alternative possibilities in problem solving before they can expect students to do the same.

Another constraint to portfolio assessment is the problem of teacher management—finding time for periodic review of the contents of the portfolio. Optimally, students would take time to look through their portfolios and make judgments about their own learning. Students and teachers would conference with each other and with parents and note progress, changes, and new directions for teaching and learning. For teachers to encourage student self-evaluation and for students to assume responsibility for their portfolios is a big step. Teachers have to be ready and willing to give up some control of the learning process and to guide students toward independence.

Despite these constraints, we probably need to stop discussing and jump in and "have-a-go." Rob Tierney, a professor at The Ohio State University in Columbus, reports encouraging news about teacher change on the basis of a group of Ohio teachers he has worked with over the past several years. He notes that just about all the teachers who became involved in portfolio assessment found enough benefits for students and themselves to choose continuing involvement in the project. Furthermore, by observing students, teachers became more effective decision makers and problem solvers and were able to put in place aspects of evaluation that never existed before in their classrooms. By carefully looking at their students, teachers began thinking about what meaningful evaluation is. The portfolios became a way of grounding assessment in the classroom—facilitating ongoing thinking and talking about evaluation, promoting ownership of evaluation by students, and contributing to ongoing learning.

Whatever a school or district finally decides about a portfolio approach, student self-selection and optional elements must be included along with the required components. All aspects of students' thinking processes, not just written work, need to play a part. For example, if teachers and administrators who decide to go with portfolio assessment decide that three writing samples should be part of each permanent portfolio, students should also have an opportunity to select for their portfolios work samples that are significant to them—whether these are illustrations, sample literature response log pages, or reading records.

Rob Tierney is one of the few U.S. researchers who has collected data on the impact of portfolio assessment on teachers, parents, and students. He has looked at how students view themselves as writers and readers and the extent to which portfolios facilitate the achievement of ongoing learning goals. Rob sees portfolios as a "vehicle that gives students opportunities to get involved in self-assessment." He stresses that student ownership and student self-assessment must be the first priority, but also admits that "the hardest part is the issue of student self-assessment" (conversation, August 1990).

The verdict is not yet in on portfolio assessment. It may be that it's a great idea that many of us are not quite ready for yet. There is no formula for implementation or one best method. Teachers as skilled observers who are highly knowledgeable about language processes have to be ready to place students, even young students, at the center of the evaluation process. Portfolios can then be used as intended—as vehicles for students' self-evaluation, reflection, and learning.

The process could easily fail if it serves only the needs of teachers and administrators. We need to move slowly in setting up thoughtful objectives and guidelines, or we and our students will end up amassing collections of work for somebody else's purposes. If the evaluation process is truly to serve learners and their needs, then the learners must be central to the process.

Report Cards and Grading

Concern about report cards and grading scares off potential whole language teachers. Many teachers already feel tremendous pressure to keep grades and to report to parents four times a year. Having to deal with a new way of reporting can be overwhelming. In my own district, we use a checklist and narrative format for reporting in kindergarten through grade 3 and letter grades for grades 4 through 12. We continue to struggle with the grading process and the design of holistic report cards. One teacher told me, "I understand meaningful evaluation, but I don't understand how I can possibly give grades."

We need to keep in mind that grading is not evaluation. A student's abilities can never be described by a single letter. At best, grading is a narrow, arbitrary measuring system that fosters competition, discourages cooperation, and does little to promote understanding. Like standardized test scores, grades are scores that do not carry any real meaning for instructional purposes. Yet grades continue to drive instruction and learning in our schools. "Grades are the sole reason that most school activities are undertaken, requiring or enticing students to engage in tasks they would never otherwise go near" (Smith, 1988, p. 69).

My preference is to dispense with grades entirely, or at least until junior high school. I constantly hear that we can't do away with grades because the parents want them. The only parents I know who like grades are the parents of the "A" students. I believe the rest would be pleased to consider an alternative, especially if teachers and students took the time to keep records of performance-based evaluation and shared these with parents.

Nonetheless, grading is a fact of life for most teachers. We can work to change the system, but in the meantime, most of us have to deal with grades. While recognizing that the giving of grades is inconsistent with whole language philosophy, teachers can give grades in a fair and holistic manner. When grades are used, they should be used for looking at a child in relation to himself and for comparing and analyzing the child's growth over time.

Consistent with whole language philosophy would be involving the child in the grading process. I recommend using a rubric, a format of criteria that the student and parent see at the start of the grading period. An "A" in a subject must mean more than just that the teacher thought the work was excellent. What specific criteria were used to determine the grade? With a rubric set up ahead of time, every student and parent know the expectations for the course and, technically, every student has the potential to get an "A."

In addition to the teacher filling in the rubric, it is a good idea to have students fill it in at the end of the project or grading period or at interim periods. Where interim reports are required, rubrics can be completed as self-evaluation forms by students and co-signed by the student, teacher, and parent. The teacher and student could then conference—individually or with parents—and note strengths and weaknesses, discuss differences in perceptions, and set realistic goals for the next semester. With the exception of very low-achieving students who may have difficulty perceiving where they are, most students evaluate themselves quite fairly. If anything, they are tougher on themselves than the teacher is.

Following is an example of a rubric for reading based on independent, self-selected reading (WEB) and in-class reading (log, discussion, and related activities):

Rubric for Reading

- Reads and understands nightly WEB book (independent reading)
- Completes WEB folder (record of daily and monthly reading)
- Completes assigned reading on time
- Completes literature response log on time and to the best of his or her ability
- Contributes thoughtful comments to literature group discussion
- Refers to log in discussion—uses text to support statements
- Listens attentively and responds to peer comments in discussion
- Completes literature-related activities and assignments to the best of his or her ability
- Takes good care of books

Grades might be allocated as follows:

A—consistently for all areas	(9 out of 10)
B—consistently for most areas	(8 out of 10)
C—consistently for some areas	(6–7 out of 10)
D—inconsistently for most areas	(5–6 out of 10)
F—inconsistently for all areas	(5 or less out of 10)

Note that on the rubric, "consistently" means "most of the time," or you could define the term more specifically to meet your needs. Teachers and students would support their judgments on the rubric through anecdotal records, work samples, and other evidence from the "Data Gathering Profile." All the evidence could be utilized to complete specific report cards.

See Figure 13–17 for a reading rubric, Figure 13–18 for a sample writing rubric, and Figure 13–19 for a spelling rubric based on an integrated spelling program as described in Chapter 10. While ten categories were selected to make the grading easier, any number of categories could work. See Figure 13–20 for the first-time use of the reading rubric by fourth-grader Doris (discussed at the beginning of this chapter) as a self-evaluation at the end of the first grading period.

A rubric need not be formal. Fourth grade teacher Joan Servis combines the following components, with each worth a certain percentage, to arrive at student grades on a major topic of study in social studies or science. Students and parents are informed at the start of the project about the expectations and scoring system.

- Group work (may account for as much as 50 percent of grade)
  cooperation, collaboration, note taking, research, use of references, participation in group discussion
- Presentation
  explanation of research project to class, optional format, organization, effort

Figure 13-17   Reading Rubric

Name _____   Date _____

READING RUBRIC

Category	Consistent	Inconsistent	Comments
Reads and understands nightly WEB books (independent reading)			
Completes WEB folder (record of daily and monthly reading)			
Completes assigned reading on time			
Completes literature response log on time and to the best of his/her ability			
Contributes thoughtful comments to literature group discussion			
Refers to log in discussion-- uses text to support statements			
Listens attentively and responds to peer comments in discussion			
Completes literature related activities and assignments on time			
Completes literature related activities and assignments to the best of his/her ability			
Takes good care of books			

FINAL GRADE _____

GRADING SYSTEM

A--consistent for all areas (9 out of 10)
B--consistent for most areas (8 out of 10)
C--consistent for many areas (7 out of 10)
D--consistent for some areas (6 out of 10)
F--inconsistent for many areas (5 or fewer out of 10)

- Essay test on understanding of major concepts of topic
    open-ended questions
    complete sentences, best spelling, punctuation, legibility expected

The essay test questions have included:

- Name five facts you learned about _____.
- Choose a presentation you observed and tell what you learned.
- What else would you like to know about this topic?
- What did this unit cause you to think about?

Samples of other informal rubrics (not necessarily used for grades), which are first attempts by teachers, are given in Figures 13–21 and 13–22. Note in Figure 13–22 that third grade teacher Karen Horton has added a column for student self-evaluation two years later.

The examples shown are meant to serve only as possibilities. Notice that they do include both process and product in various contexts and go way beyond workbook pages and weekly or unit tests. The rubrics will undoubtedly need to be revised

Figure 13-18   Writing Rubric

```
Name _____        Date _____

                         WRITING RUBRIC

Category                          Consistent   Inconsistent   Comments

Able to write a coherent draft

Willingly takes suggestions
from peers and teacher

Able to give constructive feed-
back to a peer's draft

Attempts to incorporate
colorful language

Takes responsibility for
revising

Proofreads for _____

Adheres to writing deadlines

Keeps writing folder organized
and up to date

Learning to take meaningful
notes

In content areas, incorporates
and seeks out multiple
references


FINAL GRADE     _____

GRADING SYSTEM

A--consistent for all areas (9 out of 10)
B--consistent for most areas (8 out of 10)
C--consistent for many areas (7 out of 10)
D--consistent for some areas (6 out of 10)
F--inconsistent for many areas (5 or fewer out of 10)
```

after use. For example, they are probably too achievement oriented and need also to include improvement and effort.

For your first attempt at creating a rubric, you may want to do some brainstorming with a colleague. Though your first efforts may require lots of revision, you will get better through trial and error and feedback from colleagues and students. Give it a try. Teachers who begin to use rubrics seem to experience less conflict about having to give grades.

Fourth grade teacher Linda Cooper had this to say after using the reading, writing, and spelling rubrics for the first time: "I was absolutely shocked that the rubrics ended coming up with probably the same grades I would have given. I really didn't expect the results to be appropriate. It was only my trust in you and Dr. Stokes [our principal]—and your support—that enabled me to take a risk."

After employing your rubric for a semester, you may want to ask for student feedback and make revisions. The point is that students and parents have a right to know how grades will be determined at the start of a course. They also should know what is not being graded, because not everything requires a grade. Students need lots of opportunities for ungraded practice. They also have a right and responsibility to be part of the total evaluation process. Even if you have to use grades, you can still promote a climate of reflection and self-evaluation. For

Figure 13-19   Spelling Rubric

Name _____   Date _____

SPELLING RUBRIC

Category	Consistent	Inconsistent	Comments
Proofreads for identification			
Proofreads for corrections			
Attempts standard spelling on Have-A-Go sheets			
Consults multiple resources for standard spelling			
Uses file boxes and spells words correctly			
Uses file boxes and alphabetizes			
Takes informal tests -- dictation			
Takes informal tests -- proofreading paragraphs			
Takes formal tests -- high frequency words			
Takes formal tests -- content area words			

FINAL GRADE _____

GRADING SYSTEM

A--consistent for all areas (9 out of 10)
B--consistent for most areas (8 out of 10)
C--consistent for many areas (7 out of 10)
D--consistent for some areas (6 out of 10)
F--inconsistent for many areas (5 or fewer out of 10)

secondary teachers, Nancie Atwell provides guidelines for evaluation and grading (see *In the Middle*, Heinemann, 1987, especially pp. 113–121).

In reporting to parents, it works well if you can also meet personally with parents, or provide an accompanying narrative, since grades by themselves tell nothing specific about the student. In our elementary grades, we have required teacher-parent conferences in the fall and optional conferences in the spring. While traditionally the conference has been between the teacher and parents, I believe the student—even a young student—should attend and participate in at least part of the conference. The student's work samples, drafts, processes, and goals could be shared with the parents, and new directions could be set for teaching and learning with the student actively involved in the plan.

With traditional assessment we have often left the student out of the process; with holistic evaluation the student is central to the process. Even when grades are required, this can be done. Dana Noble, a high school English teacher, now includes the writing conference he has with a student along with the child's final papers in determining the writing grade. The student is also expected to turn in all drafts and revisions, not just the completed final copy.

Finally, and perhaps most important, work out an evaluation system you feel is fair and with which you are comfortable. Try to balance your scoring system with

Figure 13-20   Reading Rubric Used by a Fourth-grader

Name Doris   Date 10-24-90

READING RUBRIC

Category	Consistent	Inconsistent	Comments
Reads and understands nightly WEB books (independent reading)	√		
Completes WEB folder (record of daily and monthly reading)	√		
Completes assigned reading on time	√		most of the time
Completes literature response log on time and to the best of his/her ability	√		
Contributes thoughtful comments to literature group discussion	√		tries hard
Refers to log in discussion-- uses text to support statements	√		
Listens attentively and responds to peer comments in discussion		√	most of the time
Completes literature related activities and assignments on time		√	need to improve
Completes literature related activities and assignments to the best of his/her ability	√		
Takes good care of books	√		

FINAL GRADE   B—

GRADING SYSTEM

A--consistent for all areas (9 out of 10)
B--consistent for most areas (8 out of 10)
C--consistent for many areas (7 out of 10)
D--consistent for some areas (6 out of 10)
F--inconsistent for many areas (5 or fewer out of 10)

observations, interviews, and performance samples. Also, try to make your grades more process-performance-based than product-based.

Improving Report Cards

Report cards in our district have undergone major revisions in the elementary grades, especially in kindergarten through grade 3, where we use a checklist and a narrative. We have a separate report card for each of the k–3 grades and one design that uses letter grades for grades 4–6. Once we moved to more meaning-based strategies in our teaching, the descriptors on the old forms no longer fit the way we were teaching. Committees made up of teachers and administrators worked together to improve our methods of reporting to parents. Then teachers at each grade level had an opportunity to give feedback.

In a three-year period, we have been through two major revisions, and there's no doubt there will be more in the future. Improvements have involved changing, adding, and deleting descriptors and categories, especially as they apply to reading

Figures 13-21 and 13-22   Informal Rubrics

NAME _____   DATE _____

__/10 - NEATNESS

__/20 - GRAMMAR (spelling, punctuation, correct
                        usage)

__/30 - ART WORK

__/40 - CONTENT (story, information)

__/100 - total grade

COMMENTS:

Evaluation of a 3rd grade Book

1. Vocabulary appropriate for 3rd graders   ☐

2. All papers turned in   ☐

3. Written on every other line   ☐

4. Illustrations were planned   ☐

5. Spelling corrected on dummy copy   ☐

6. Sentences corrected on dummy copy   ☐

Grade on project - _____

and writing. In our first revision, we added observational categories such as shared reading, reading strategies, and writing process, but we kept the old marking system: "O" (outstanding), "S" (satisfactory), "I" (improving), and "N" (needs improvement). That system did not work well for two reasons. First, the marks did not fit philosophically with our beliefs about language learning; and, second, they fostered competition. Many teachers felt the marks were not developmentally appropriate, and they did not like the way the system fostered comparisons on the part of parents. Some parents whose children had received an "O" during the first marking period wanted to know why the mark wasn't "O+" the next report period. Or parents who saw an "S" (satisfactory) the first marking period wanted an explanation of why the child had not received an "O."

The descriptor terms we are now using include "consistently," "occasionally," "seldom," and "not evaluated at this time." Many teachers and administrators feel this is a significant improvement because the system is more compatible with our philosophy and teaching.

Our second revision encompassed fewer but broader categories, including atti-

Figure 13-22   Informal Rubrics

Name _Saul C._   Date _Sept. 24, 1988_

Project _Compound Word Booklet_

　　　　+ Excellent　　　　　✓ Satisfactory　　　　　－ Needed Work

		Comments
Syllabication of Compound Words	+	
Illustrations	+	*You have clever illustrations most were large enough to see easily.*
Capitalization	+	
Punctuation	+	*Good attempts at spelling.*
Spelling	✓+	
Neatness	✓+	*neatly done.*

This is an excellent first third-grade project!

Name _Nathan Yancey_   Date _9/18/90_

Project _Freckle Juice_

　　　+ Excellent   child   Mrs. Horton ✓ Satisfactory   － Needs Work

	child	Mrs. Horton	Comments
Cover	+	+	*Great cover.*
Illustrations	－	－	*Illustrations could use more detail*
Creativity	✓	✓	
Sentence Sense	✓	✓	
Overall spelling	✓	✓－	
Capitalization	✓	✓	*Sometimes you put a capital letter in the middle of a sentence for no reason.*
Punctuation	+	－	*Many periods are missing at the end of sentences.*
Neatness	✓	✓	

You evaluated yourself very honestly, Nathan. This was a good project for the beginning of 3rd grade. Work for more details.   B

tudes toward reading and writing, and our language-related categories are now consistent across grades 1–3. We found that our first revised k–3 report card was taking too long to fill out, and parents became bogged down by having to look at so many sections. Figure 13–23 shows the whole language section on the report card for grade 2. The grades 4–6 committee decided to combine reading and writing processes with spelling under the category whole language.

One step that teachers can take, whatever form is in use, is to avoid negative statements, note what the child is doing well, and discuss the child's progress in relation to where he once was and where he is now. Other information, for example, that the child is reading a year below grade level, can be given *after* the teacher's positive statements about what the child can do.

Teachers can also work to change the words that go along with the descriptor lists so they do not foster competition and comparison among students. For exam-

Figure 13-23 Whole Language Section on Grade 2 Report Card

WHOLE LANGUAGE

EFFORT			SPEAKING & LISTENING		
READING STRATEGIES/COMPREHENSION			Can express ideas orally with fluency		
Uses picture clues			Listens and comments appropriately		
Uses context clues			**HANDWRITING**		
Uses structural clues			Forms manuscript letters and numerals appropriately		
Uses phonetic clues			Forms cursive letters appropriately		
Self-corrects			Spaces letters and words appropriately		
Learns, understands & utilizes new vocabulary			Writes neatly		
Recalls main idea, details and sequence			**SPELLING**		
Follows plots & sees relationships between characters			Moves from invented spelling to conventional spelling		
Takes risks in predicting and in discussions			Learns spelling words		
Formulates questions from material read			Applies correct spelling		
Is able to find proof to answer questions			**REFERENCE SKILLS**		
Recognizes different story forms			Uses reference sources for reading and writing		
Reads orally with fluency			**READING/WRITING ATTITUDES**		
WRITING PROCESS			Demonstrates an interest in reading		
Generates topics for personal writing			Chooses to read silently		
Writes with thorough development (beginning, middle, end) to observe unity			Demonstrates an interest in writing		
Makes use of descriptive language			Chooses to write		
Is developing correct capitalization, punctuation & sentence structure					
Is beginning to revise					
Has begun to edit for mechanics					

ple, to indicate that the child is performing at a very competent level, words such as the following may be used: "proficient," "consistently," "usually," "most of the time," "secure," and "effectively demonstrated." To indicate a middle level, these words may fit: "sometimes," "demonstrated some of the time," "developing," "occasionally," and "generally." To indicate that a skill or strategy is not yet understood or mastered, terms such as the following may be used: "not noticed yet," "not yet," "working on," and "infrequently." As much as possible, try to keep the wording positive.

Finally, parents must be informed about any changes in reporting practices. If our most recent changes had not been clearly explained, a parent might easily have interpreted an "O" for "outstanding," whereas "O" now represents "occasionally." Parents also need to understand why the reporting system has been changed so they feel they are part of the evaluation process.

Reflections

As teachers, we need to stop complaining about the evaluation process and start contributing to it. Too often we have complacently given over our power for decision making and change to others. Knowledgeable teachers who use common sense, experience, and a collaborative approach can make the evaluation process more meaningful.

While we are working to improve report cards, we should keep in mind that eventually a total narrative, nongraded report format, or even no report card at all, may be possible. Whole language teachers find that a single report card does not give an adequate or accurate profile of a student. Including a portfolio approach to evaluation provides a more complete student portrait as well as an opportunity for reflection, both for teachers and students.

Reporting to parents can be an opportunity for improved, open-ended communication between parents and teachers. One school I visited in Australia did not have report cards. Parents came to the school four times a year to meet with the teacher and student and discuss the student's progress. All manner of student work samples were shared and discussed. In looking to improve reporting to parents, we need to be asking, "What do we want to achieve with parents in informing them? How can we best achieve this?"

Self-Evaluation for Teachers and Students

The foremost goal of evaluation is self-evaluation, that is, the analysis of our own attitudes and processes so that we can use the information to promote continued growth and learning. The purpose of self-evaluation is the purpose of education— to enable an individual to function independently, intelligently, and productively. This is not just a worthy goal for students. If we are to be expecting self-evaluation by our students, we teachers must also be demonstrating it and practicing it ourselves. Self-evaluation implies trust of ourselves and of our students, and that is often the hardest part of the teaching-learning process.

Self-evaluation by teachers is a difficult, but necessary part of the evaluation process. By taking a look at what you choose to evaluate, you get a picture of what you value. For example, when I filled out "What Do I Want to Know?" (Figure 13–2), initially I had included only oral reading, spelling, and reading comprehension on the grid. I added reading-writing attitudes and the student's view of himself as a reader-writer after talking with Rob Tierney and Andrea Butler. I realized that my orientation was more toward a skills model than I had recognized or wanted to admit. The same is true of my informal reading evaluation (Figure 13–15). I have not connected reading and writing, nor have I taken the time to interview the student to determine how he views himself as a reader. I am now aware that my evaluation process needs to reflect more accurately students' attitudes, behaviors, and understandings. Several years later (1993), listing what I value in good readers and writers forced me to think again about my beliefs and examine my teaching. (See Appendix M1 and M2.)

Good teaching fosters self-evaluation by students. Capable readers self-monitor and self-correct while reading. They self-select much of what they read and often keep records of their reading. Even a first-grader can begin to keep track of books read. A competent writer is able to choose his own topics, effectively proofread, and know why he chose a particular piece of writing for publication. A portfolio approach—student centered and properly implemented—has potential for high-level self-evaluation. Engaging in self-regulation and self-examination of multiple data sources gives the learner the message, "I am better at this today. Here is my evidence."

This section examines various procedures that can be effectively used for self-evaluation by teachers and students. Certainly the list provided here is not exhaustive, but these are procedures that have helped to increase teachers' and students' awareness of attitudes, strengths, weaknesses, areas needing improvement, and directions for future teaching and learning. In this section, too, teachers who have been in transition toward whole language for three to five years share their thoughts on teaching and learning. Finally, some former students in a first grade literacy program (Routman, 1988) share their present attitudes toward reading, writing, and literacy.

Self-Evaluation Procedures

Self evaluations can take many forms, such as class responses to teachers' evaluation questions, a self-evaluation checklist for teachers, individual evaluative responses for literature-group discussions, reflection logs, weekly evaluations, report cards, self-evaluations by students, and report cards on teachers by students. See Appendix N for samples of self-evaluation forms and ways to involve students in self-evaluation.

Class Responses to Teachers' Evaluation Questions

Individual student and whole-class responses to questions can be used by teachers to evaluate the kind of instruction that is going on in our classrooms. By carefully analyzing students' feedback, teachers can find out whether what they think they are teaching really is what they are teaching. Teachers who are able to value students' opinions about what has gone on in the classroom are truly reflective practitioners.

Some questions we can ask to inform our teaching might include:

- How is reading taught in this class?
- How is writing taught in this class?
- What do you do when you come to a word you can't read?
- What do you do when you want to spell a word you're not sure of?
- How do you decide what to take notes on?
- How do you study for a test?
- What do good writers do?

Ellen Rubin, a second grade teacher who implemented writing workshop (Calkins, 1986) for the first time, wanted to know what her students had learned about writing. I offered to ask her class what good writers do. The purpose of the question was to help guide her self-evaluation of the year's writing program. I called on students in random order and then wrote down their responses. Their first responses (out of many) follow:

What We Have Learned About What Good Writers Do

1. Don't put too many thoughts into the same sentence.
2. Skip lines when you're writing so you have room to make changes.
3. Use punctuation at the end of sentences.
4. Start a new paragraph when you have a new thought.
5. Use capital letters for names and at the start of each sentence.

Ellen and I spoke honestly about what the students stressed first—predominantly mechanics. While how and when they get ideas for stories (such as "asking classmates")—as well as how they write interesting stories (such as "conference with a classmate or the teacher")—eventually surfaced, their first emphasis was on editing. Ellen took a hard look at her teaching. While she believed she had been stressing writing for meaning and content first, the children's responses made her think about the messages she had actually been sending.

She set conscious goals for the second year of writing workshop. She would emphasize content before form, and she would consciously listen to the language she was using. Ellen's growth as a writing teacher is reflected in the students' responses the following year when they were asked what good writers do. There is far greater evidence of writers immersed in writing and concerned about the quality of their writing.

What We Have Learned about What Good Writers Do

1. They think up a story and then they write it.
2. After they write a story, they read over it to see if it makes sense and it's the way they want it.
3. They check their spelling.
4. They use expression—"good words" like Roald Dahl uses; instead of "said"—"muttered."
5. They write good sentences by using interesting words.
6. They write with detail. They tell what happened.
7. They make their writing clear so that people can read it—legible handwriting.
8. They try to improve their story as much as they can—put in different words if they don't like some of the words.
9. They put in words that you might have to ask what they mean—like "grieved"—and they use words that might help it get published. Instead of "she was very sad," use "she grieved."
10. They put capital letters, exclamation marks, and other marks where they need them to make sense.
11. The author sometimes needs to find an illustrator or a photographer, for most information books.
12. Good writers let somebody else read their story. If one part doesn't make sense the reader can suggest how to fix it.
13. On your first time writing a story, you don't worry about spelling. You just write your thoughts down so you don't forget your thoughts.

In another whole-class evaluation, Joyce Pope's first-graders did a shared writing experience following a visit by a doll maker. With their teacher's guidance, the students wrote a story telling about the doll maker and how she made dolls. After the detailed story was completed on large chart paper, Joyce asked the students what they had learned about the writing they had just done. She used the shared writing experience to extend and confirm the learning that had taken place. It is important for students to be able to verbalize what they have learned so they are aware learning has taken place. I believe if we did this more often in classrooms, parents would get fewer "nothing" responses to the question, "What did you learn today?"

What Did We Learn?

- A story needs an interesting beginning and a good ending to show it's over.
- We had to remember the order.
- We couldn't start to write until we started to think.
- When you rough draft, you can cross out.
- If you read aloud, you catch your mistakes.
- The words had to match the pictures.
- We had to print neatly for the reader.
- Apostrophes tell someone owns it, like "Elizabeth's shoes."
- Use a full stop (.) if you tell, a question mark (?) if you ask, and an exciting mark (!) to show you feel strongly.
- We can say good things about ourselves or other kids.
- We can spell by sounding out, writing in chunks, looking in a book, asking a friend, using a dictionary, having-a-go at it, or looking back at a page already done.
- We can use what we know to explain, like "It looks as big as my two-year-old cousin."
- We can investigate to find facts for our story, like using a yardstick to measure the doll.
- We can print in special ways to give a message, like "long-g-g" and "VERY BIG!!!"
- We learned to work longer than ever before.

Second grade teacher Mary Pryor wanted to know what her students thought about the core literature books they had read and discussed so she could effectively plan her reading program for the following year. After Mary discussed and demonstrated good questioning strategies, the students worked in pairs to come up with their own important questions. See Figures 13–24 and 13–25. Then they responded to each other's question formats (see Figures 13–26 and 13–27). In another attempt to look carefully at her teaching, third grade teacher Linda Cooper asked her students for feedback on the reading program (see Figure 13–28).

Self-Evaluation Checklist for Teachers

In looking at our daily teaching, teachers may find having a list of important and desirable teaching behaviors is helpful. You may want to adapt the list I put together (Appendix N7) for your own purposes.

Individual Evaluative Responses to Literature Group Discussions

Joan Servis and I devised the form shown in Figures 13–29 and 13–30 (Appendix N3) to use occasionally with students after a literature discussion group. We have tried checklists and more involved formats and find that the simplicity and open-ended quality of this form is both easy for students to use and very informative. The same format works well for evaluation of small-group work in the content areas.

5-17-9

Reading

Write 5 evaluation questions with a partner.

1. Do you think the words are like poetry?

2. What was your favorite activety in the book?

3. Did you like the chartecters?

A 4. What was your favorite charter?

o Why?

5. What - wa's- your favorite chapter?

6. Would you like to read the book again!

Figure 13-25

najah
5-12-89

Reading

Write five evaluation questions with a partner

1. What was your favorite chapter? Why did you choose that person?

2. Was the lanuege aporpreat in the nXne book you read?

3. Were the words hard for second graders?

4. Were the nine books exiting? Why were they exiting?

5. Do you think kids will like these books? othepades

6. Would you like the book to be made into a video

Evaluation   5-24-87

The Courage of Sarah Noble

1. Yes. I think the words are like poetry because the book has beautiful words.

2. I liked when we wrote what happened to Sarah when she grew up.

3. I liked the charecters because they are kind and loving.

4. My favorite chareder was Sarah because she was nice, loving and caring

4. Her job was to make sure that her father and herself were fed. And take care of the horse.

5. My favorite chapter was FRIENDS becaus Sarah made friends with the indians and wasn't afraid of them anymore.

6. I wan't to read the book again because it was a true storry and Sarah was the kind of person who would do anything for her family.

7. Yes. I think they should make the book into a movie becase it would attract a good audience.

Figure 13-27

Charlotte's Web

5-25-89

1. Yes I thigh the words are like poetry because the authour is such a good writer

2. I liked it when we did our special activity for the end of the book.

3. Yes I liked charecters because they where all special in thier own way.

4. My favorite chaecter was Charlotte because she was graceful and beautful.

4. Charlottes job was to save Willbur from dieing around Christmas.

5. My favorite chapt. was chapt. 22 because Willbur had Charlotte's children to keep him company.

6. Yes, I'd like to read the book over again because I liked the reasone he wrote ther story.

7. Charlotte's Web was already made into a movie but even though I've already seen the movie I'd would like to see it again.

8. I think E.B.White's purpose of writing this book was so it could entretain children.

9.

Figure 13-28   Students' Feedback to the Teacher on the Reading Program, Grade 3

Reflection Logs

Some teachers are finding that reflection logs, a place for students to think about and comment on their learning, are important tools for fostering self-evaluation. Having to put thoughts into writing seems to help clarify what has, or has not, been learned. Not only do students think about their learning; teachers have an opportunity to understand what concepts have been understood and what needs to be retaught. As with all journal writing, no corrections are made in these logs. Reflection logs can be used the last fifteen minutes of the day or week and/or in the content areas. After a while the teacher will not need to ask specific questions, but at the beginning, some guiding questions could be:

- What did I learn today? (new insight or confirmation)
- What am I still confused about?
- What would I like to know more about?

See Figure 13–31 for a page from a fourth-grade student's reflection log on what he has learned that day and how he has used his time.

Some teachers also keep personal reflection logs as a way to think about and self-evaluate their teaching.

Weekly Evaluation

Even very young children are capable of looking at their work and progress and putting their thoughts into writing. Weekly evaluations can be a vehicle for students to reflect on their attitudes, strengths, and weaknesses and can be used to communicate with parents and inform our teaching. With regular use, students become conscious of their strengths and what they need to improve. You will first want to demonstrate how the form might be filled out. The overhead projector works well here.

Whatever form or method you use, keep it simple and allow for open-ended comments and flexibility. (See Appendix N6 for a sample form.) Some space may also be left on the form for teacher and parent comments. After a while, you may want to do a shared writing and design your own format with the students. Adapted for kindergarten, the weekly evaluation form may be used at the end of the week as a whole-class activity and then sent home as a newsletter.

Report Cards and Student Self-Evaluations

I think it makes sense to have students write a narrative of how they see their progress in a particular subject to go along with the teacher's comments. Certainly that provides a more balanced picture. Students generally enjoy the opportunity to be part of the reporting-to-parents process. Even first-graders can evaluate themselves with some insight (see Figures 13–32 through 13–35).

Some teachers attach the students' evaluations to their own when reporting to parents. Third grade teacher Julie Beers asked her students to evaluate themselves in reading. First she demonstrated on the overhead projector by evaluating her own reading (Figure 13–36). Then students volunteered to write on the overhead projector with her guidance (Figure 13–37). Finally, they were ready to write on their own (Figures 13–38 and 13–39). Sylvia Tallentire, a third grade teacher, has her students design their own report cards when evaluating themselves. (See Figures 13–40 through 13–43.)

Figure 13–29 and 13–30   Self-evaluations in Literature Discussion Group

Self-Evaluation

Literature Discussion Group

Name Briana   Date 4/17

Book/story Fairy Tale

1. What did I do well today (and/or improve on) during group discussion?

I think that we do well on cooperating together and contributing to all discussions. We improved on listening to each other's ideas and asking questions on them so that we understand them and aren't just writing them down on our sloppy copy.

2. What do I still need to improve on during group discussion?

We need to work on staying on one subject so we don't get confused.

Figure 13–30

Self-Evaluation

Literature Discussion Group

Name Elizabeth   Date 4-17-90

Book/story Fairytale

1. What did I do well today (and/or improve on) during group discussion?

We talked over if we should change any titles and the topics. Our group got a little hectic but we maneged it. I maybe got a little bossy. I tried to control myself and respect others when they were talking. I think I improved on giving sugestions on what to do. I think that I'm begining to feel comfatable in a group.

2. What do I still need to improve on during group discussion?

Maybe not being so bossy when I'm not captain of the group.

351

Figure 13–31   A Page from a Fourth Grade Student's Reflection Log

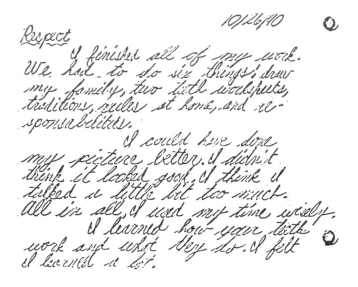

Figure 13–32   First-grader's Response to "How I Grew as a Learner This Year"
Format by Peg Rimedio.

Figures 13–33, 13–34, and 13–35   First-graders' Self-evaluations

5-29-90
My writing has got
alot better then it use to
be. I wrixe in conventional
spelling. I know how to spell
attention author money and
lots of other words.

Figure 13–34

6-8-90
When I came
to Boulevard I
stred to read. I
jiat read pichers.
New I can read
book. Lose
of book. I read
books with no
pichers.

Figure 13–35

6-8- 90

I The fert day
came to school
I cod not read
to good but now
that we have
reading prtners I can
read good. by Lauren

Figure 13–36   A Teacher Evaluates Her Own Reading

Reading

I read very fast. I usuall
read about 1-2 books
per week. ✓ I need to
read books other than professional
books. I always read during
RAP but on occasion, I
have not been interested in my
book so I'm not too excited
about reading it.
   During reading group, I
actually participate in the
discussions. I listen to
others ideas although there
are times I get distracted
because. I worry too much
about what the other children
not in reading group are doing.

Figure 13–37   Students' Reading Self-evaluations on the Overhead Projector with Teacher Guidance

<u>Reading</u>

I read chapter books.
I read a veity of books.
I try to read as much as can each day.
I have improved reading longe books in shorter times.

At rap I mostly read but some times I don't feel like reading my books. I look at a pichure book. (I think rap is a good idae to rest after lunch to have peace and quiet)

During reading groups I read my chapters. In my Reading Log I write in complete sentences. I try not to forget not to write without punctuation. When I pridict I try hard to come up with the right answer. I need to work on my paragrahs. During Reading group I try to stay in the descuion. Also. I give my prediction.

Figure 13–38 and 13–39   Third Grade Students' Self-evaluations of Reading Behaviors

Self Evaluation

Feb 1, 1990

Darrell

reading: I read books at my own level. I read chapter books and I read short books. I enjoy reading. I think I am improving. I am improving in rap because I am doing more reading and less talking. I am Starting to read more books than I did in the beginning of the year.

355

Figure 13–39

Reading Assessment
Xavier
June 7, 1994

I like to read. But not that
much. I do not read every minute.
I read book at my level, which
is grad 3. The reason I do not
read books at higher levels is because
I get frustrated on some words.
One book at my level now is
Alens for lunch. Because it does
not have that many hard words.
But once or twise a moth
if I finish the book I was
reading I will read a book
at a bigger level. over a books.
I use different strategies for hard
books. One of the strategies I use
for picture books is looking at the
picture. If there is not a picture
I look at the word next
to the word. But if that does
not work I read on and go back
to that word and it's most likely
that you will figure the word out.
I discuss good thing in reading
group like why did Dan get hit.
My favorite author is John
Reynolds Gardiner because
he writes interesting books like
Top Secret and stone Fox.

Figures 13–40 through 13–43   **Student-Designed Report Cards**

Figure 13–41

Figure 13–42

3:rd grade

Mrs. Tallentire

Journal
Math
Spelling
Language
Reading
Science
Spictal studies
Silent Reading
Gym
Division
Music
Art
tardy
portsmanship
riendly
addition
ubtration
Book it
Multiplacation
addentance
Time Line
Minature
~~totlography~~
Creative Writing
Book Reports
Tree Repot

Teachers Note

Hallie J is a very good student. Tho I think she could work on her science. She is very friendly and smart. Afte her math group is done wit Multiplacation we will learn divison so Hallie s dosint have anything to worry about. This is a Report card to be proud of. I'm sure you will have many more.

Thank you

Mrs. Tallentire

Good/Bad chart

| Good | — | ☺ ✓ |
| Bad | — | ☹ |

Figure 13–43

Jerome

p. m A
language X
SciEncE ✓
math ✓
Spelling ✓
Studies X
Book Report ✓
Gym ✓
Flag ✓
mizic X
Act ✓
Reading ✓
Spelling spid ✓
Journal ✓
Creative Writ ✓
proJects ✓

Some times
Jerome is bat
but most of
the time he
is good his reading
is good he gose
to the bathroom
a lot.

Report Cards on Teachers by Students

Teachers find that when they take the risk and ask students to evaluate their teaching, the results can be informative and insightful. One teacher told me, "The children's comments made me rethink some of my behaviors." A first grade teacher was surprised by the number of "C"'s she received in "fairness." A third grade teacher did not realize that she was not focused on the students in reading group until she read her "N"—"needs improvement" comments. Until teachers saw those comments, they had no idea students perceived them that way. (See Figures 13–44 through 13–49 for samples of report cards on the teacher for grades 1, 2, and 3.)

Figures 13–44, 13–45, and 13–46   Report Cards on the Teacher in Grade I
(Based on an idea and format developed by R. Anthony, T. Johnson, N. Mickelson and A. Preece.)

Report Card

Molly

grate

	Grade	
Friendiness	A+	you are varry frendle to me.
Helping	A+	you do a grate gob on Helping me.
Fairness	C	you need a Lot of inpravmint
Reading Stories	A+	I love The way you read.

Figure 13–45

Report Card   David

	Grade	
Friendiness	A+	Grate keep up the gad wrok.
Helping	A	Grate wrok
Fairness	B+	gatd trie next trie to get a A
Reading Stories	A+	you read beuute te keep up the good wrok.

Figure 13–46

Report Card Emily

	Grade	
Friendiness	A+	good Joñob.
Helping	A+	You halp us puplish uer books.
Fairness	C+	not so good
Reading Stories	A.--	You Riede good to us.

Figure 13–47   A Report Card on the Teacher in Grade 2

Grade 2	Grade	My Teacher's Report Card. Comments
Friendliness	B+	You aren't like other teachers you care about us. And I care about you to.
Fairness	A-	I think it is fair if some body bes bad and you put them in the hall I under stand that. It is becuse there messing up your class.
Teaching	B-	I think if you say any questions and somebody don't under stand. And then you exsplani it and they slel dont get. I think you shouldent yell at them. You should give them a trie.
Explaining	A+	I think some times you can explane things. But give them a trie. ☺
Encourage-ment	A	I think I have encouragemen I keep on working some-times when you say STOP.
Helping	C+	Because sometimes when somebod needs help and rase there hand. You don't answer them for a long time.

362

Figures 13–48 and 13–49   Report Cards on the Teacher in Grade 3

Dane

EXPLANATION OF MARKS
O-Outstanding
S-Satisfactory
I-Improving
N-Needs Improvement

		Comments
1. Demonstrates an interest in books	O	You Demonsrate outstanding interest in books.
2. Teaches the writing process	S	You teach writin and Process very good.
3. Listens in group situations	N	You do not Listen in reading groups well. You need to listen
4. Fairness	N	You are not fair but to the boig you. need to Improve.
5. Willing to help	O	you are willing to help on anythin
6. Friendliness	I	You are improvein. in Friendliness to the boys

Figure 13–49

REPORT CARD
ON THE TEACHER

Alison M.

EXPLANATION OF MARKS
O-Outstanding
S-Satisfactory
I-Improving
N-Needs Improvement

		Comments
1. Demonstrates an interest in books	O	You alwas tells as good book to read and why to read books.
2. Teaches the writing process	O	Alwas explains about writing if someone dosen't understand
3. Listens in group situations	N	Needs to not worry about the other children around.
4. Fairness	S	Some times gets the boys in trouble then the girls.
5. Willing to help	O	Alwas willing to help if you can understand.
6. Friendliness	O	Alwas in the morning you greet like you were our mother.

Taking a Look at Teacher and Student Attitudes

Teachers

Teachers Who Have Been in the Process of Becoming Whole Language Teachers for Three to Five Years

In this section, elementary school teachers who have been immersed in professional reading, literature in the classroom, the writing process, and more meaningful teaching talk about their attitudes, their growth, their frustrations, and their goals. These are experienced, knowledgeable teachers who have been in the process of becoming whole language teachers for at least three to five years. All are active participants in our weekly language arts support groups.

Karen Sher taught first grade in an inner-city school for five years, using dull texts and a heavily phonetic approach to reading. Realizing "intuitively" that the curriculum was not relevant to students' lives, she incorporated art and writing activities into each day's program to make school more interesting. After teaching preschool for three years, she moved into kindergarten, where she has taught for the last four years.

> I'm less tied to programs and teachers' guides now, and this is a new feeling for me. All of a sudden, things are popping into my head—coming from me—and I don't need the security of having to read it somewhere first. I'm starting to trust myself more, and that's a powerful feeling. Teaching has become more fun and creative for me. I was so impatient and frustrated with myself for so long, I never thought I'd get to this place.
>
> I'm also more forgiving of my mistakes. In watching myself grow as a teacher, I have also learned what helps children grow. I used my principal's supportive relationship with me as a model for my behavior with children. Her praise and positive comments left me feeling good about myself, and I thought, "If she can do this to me, I can do this to kids." That kind of positive feedback was instrumental in allowing myself to make mistakes. Because I was given freedom to grow and develop at my own pace, I want to give that to the children in my classroom. When you give someone freedom, you send them the message, "I have faith in you."

Pam Anderson has taught for fifteen years in grades 2, 3, and 6, with the last seven years in sixth grade. While she began as a traditional teacher, she always strived for students to have a say in what was going on in the classroom and to make school interesting.

> I have appreciated that I've had the freedom to slowly evolve. When I heard what was going on in the k–4 buildings, I wanted to learn more about it. I think people thought I was doing more than I was. I see now that I really didn't have a sense of what whole language was.
>
> Now, I feel good that I have a better grasp about what whole language may be about. This past summer, I read Frank Smith's *Joining the Literacy Club*, and I also attended a week-long whole language workshop. That really brought things together for me, for thinking about what I want to be as a teacher. I'm going to try to give my students more choice this year.
>
> I'm fearful that I probably want to do too much. I still feel that I have to do everything to make the day go smoothly. It's hard to let go of some control.

Joan Di Dio has taught for twenty years in grades, 2, 4, 5, and 6, with the last seven years in fourth grade. She began as a traditional teacher but always tried to make her teaching meaningful in spite of reliance on basal texts.

> I feel best about my deeper understanding of whole language. Whenever I get off track and doubt what I'm doing, professional reading helps get me refocused. At the same time, I feel an inadequacy and frustration at not being able to immediately implement everything that I'm reading about. I want to do it all at once, and I realize I can't.
>
> I'm still struggling with a number of issues. I didn't have reading groups last year, and it's bothered me. I had whole class reading and individualized reading. I just couldn't fit in the groups with my fragmented schedule. Management of groups is a concern too—being able to think up meaningful activities that will take kids long enough so I can devote myself totally to a group.
>
> Evaluation is a big issue for me. Grappling with grades is a horrendous burden to a whole language teacher. I feel guilty knowing that what I've done with letter grades is not indicative of my students as readers and writers. I see now if I can work out a rubric, I can tackle it. I'm trying to get the courage to trust myself and look at evaluation differently. As in every school, there are colleagues who have a very different approach in their teaching philosophy. Sometimes, I have a feeling of isolation which makes it difficult for me to implement what I really believe in.

Linda Cooper has been teaching for thirteen years and has spent the last five years in third grade. She began as "a good basal teacher who followed the manual." About five years ago she began to make changes in her teaching.

> When kids started asking me what dictionary definition I wanted for the vocabulary words because the vocabulary was done before the story, and I also saw the amount of time I spent explaining worksheets that were done in one-third the time it took for me to explain them, I knew I was ready for change.
>
> At about the same time, I observed our school's first grade literature program, and I became convinced that there were more exciting ways to teach language arts than what I had been doing. Even though I was scared to death the first year, I moved away from the basal. Having you take a reading group in my room—at the same time I did—was very reassuring. I could hear some of the questions you asked, and that helped me. It made my transition easier and more secure. Also, when a lesson we both thought was wonderful died, I realized I didn't have to know it all. I saw that when we could talk out what went wrong, we could work out the problems. That was most valuable.
>
> Then I started professional reading and getting the philosophy behind my thinking. I slowly gained the confidence to set up my room and interpret whole language my way. I was going along fine till I was just moved to fourth grade. I spent the entire summer in a panic worrying about having to put letter grades into a whole language program. I began feeling better after proofreading your chapter on evaluation and understanding that evaluation and grading are not the same. I saw I was further along in understanding whole language philosophy than I thought. I feel more willing to give evaluation a try now.

Students

Former Students in Our First Grade Literacy Program

At the suggestion of my former principal, Delores Groves, in June 1989 I interviewed fifth and sixth grade students who had been in our first grade in a reading-writing classroom where they had been immersed daily in authentic literature and self-selected writing (Routman, 1988). We were interested to find out what, if any, effect they felt their first grade experience had had on them and how they viewed their education to this point. While initially I asked about twenty students to complete a written interview form, I found their comments—limited to the space and questions provided—gave little in-depth information. I therefore selected seven students of varying abilities, three fifth-graders and four sixth-graders, to interview personally. Four representative interviews follow.

Martin had been in our district Headstart program and had qualified for Chapter 1 in the fall of first grade. His daily journal writing had been a favorite activity and a springboard for his learning to read (see Routman, 1988, pp. 96–103). As a fifth-grader, Martin exuded confidence and a positive attitude about himself. It was clear from his comments that writing was still very central to his life.

ROUTMAN: What are your best memories of school so far?

MARTIN: Grades 1 and 2 because that's when I did the most writing. We don't do so much writing now. I published a whole bunch of books in first and second grade. Now, hardly anything I write gets published.
First and second grade were also important to me because we had a good reading program. I don't remember how I learned to read, but I know I read a lot of books. The books influenced me to write more because I saw all that good writing of authors.

ROUTMAN: I remember you used to prefer writing to reading and most other activities. Is that still true?

MARTIN: I still like writing best because it lets me put my thoughts on paper. Sometimes I write when I'm bored, and then I'm not bored anymore. I write stories and draw pictures. I write mysteries and adventures and everyday life stuff. I write lots of stories at home. I don't bring them in to share because the teacher doesn't read them.
The way I was taught, it was exciting and made me want to write. Ideas came easily to me because of all the stories we read. I always got good ideas for characters. Also I wanted to go to the Young Authors' Conference. When you took me in first grade, I still remember that. I was so proud to share my books. I felt like an author.

ROUTMAN: What's writing in school like for you now?

MARTIN: The teacher chooses most of the topics. Some of them are all right, but I don't like a lot of them. It takes longer to write when she chooses the topic. Like we had to write a myth. I had no ideas but the teacher said we had to write a myth, and get graded on it. It was very hard for me because I didn't know a lot about myths. Other people in my class suggested ideas to me, and that helped.
I don't like to get graded. It makes me nervous. You shouldn't be graded when you're trying to use your imagination. Using your imagination is more fun than something the teacher has thought of. This whole year, I could only choose my own topic once. That story is my favorite because I got to use my own imagination. I think it's the best thing I've written so far. Would you like to see it?

Martin very proudly showed me a story where the cover was a cut-out cardboard from a box of bran flakes. The story was humorous, expressive, and adventurous. The main character was called Natural Flake. Martin had been in school a whole year and felt he had completed only one meaningful piece of writing.

Quita was one of our most remarkable writers in first grade. In second grade, when she was not in a reading-writing classroom, the principal and I noticed little growth and less interest in writing on her part. As a fifth-grader, she was a strong student and was in the gifted math program.

ROUTMAN: What are your best memories of school so far?

QUITA: Probably math has been most significant to me, especially learning division and decimals.

ROUTMAN: What do you remember about your early school writing experiences?

QUITA: I don't remember how I learned to write. I loved the daily journal writing in first grade. But after that, I didn't get to write as much.

ROUTMAN: What about reading? How do you feel about reading, and do you choose to spend time reading?

QUITA: When I get home from school, I read about fifteen minutes or more by choice. I usually pick a novel. I think I became a reader because there were lots of good choices at Moreland. There were no boring books that the teacher made you read. Now, I read at least two or three chapters a day on my own. I go with the emotions of the book. If it's a sad part, I get sad. If it's a happy part, I feel happy.
I like reading, but I'd prefer more choice. With my teacher this year, we have to read each book with the whole class, and we have to read two assigned chapters each night. I'm in a high reading group. We change classes; there's also a middle and a low group. We also have book reports due every two weeks on our free reading. We have to do oral and written book reports. I don't think kids should have to write book reports. It takes away from the fun of reading.

Oscar presented himself as a fairly confident sixth-grader. He clearly saw himself as a "reader." In first grade, he had struggled with learning to read, and he continued to struggle through the grades. For several years he had received Chapter 1 reading support. In third grade, it was suggested he be evaluated for possible learning disabilities. Oscar's parents had refused, saying he just needed to apply himself more.

ROUTMAN: How is school going for you?

OSCAR: Science and social studies are hard for me. I'm a good reader, but I don't like some of the books we're reading in class. I don't like when we have to do summaries and book reports. I like to write stories, especially when I can decide what to write about.
Before I didn't like school at all. Now I do. We play a basketball game when we study for tests. And when we have comprehension assignments, you can work with a partner.

>First and second grade were really hard for me. As I got older, I kept trying and school got easier.

ROUTMAN: How do you feel about reading? What kinds of books do you like to read, and when do you read?

OSCAR: I like to read books that are funny and have illustrations. I just read *The Little Fishes* (by E. C. Hauggard, Houghton Mifflin, 1967). (*He proceeded to tell me the whole story, excitedly.*) At home I read before I go to bed, until I fall asleep.

ROUTMAN: What do you remember most about your early school years?

OSCAR: I remember the *Mr. Men* books (by Roger Hargreaves, Price/Stern/Sloan, 1982) in first grade and liking them. I liked journal writing and publishing books.

ROUTMAN: What has been the most significant thing in your education so far?

OSCAR: My improvement.

ROUTMAN: What do you do if you can't read something?

OSCAR: When I come to a word I don't know, I try to figure it out. I skip it and read the next sentence to see if the word will come to my mind. If not, I'll ask my mother, and she'll tell me. Skipping words and coming back to them works best for me.

Nicky was a conscientious, achieving sixth-grader; she had been like that since first grade. Raised by her mother and grandmother, school and learning remained an important focus in her life. Nicky told me she wants to be a doctor, lawyer, or basketball player when she grows up.

ROUTMAN: What are your best memories of school so far?

NICKY: This year has been most significant to me. With Mr. H. we go over everything we don't understand. We switch papers and grade each other's. Then Mr. H. goes over all the work.

ROUTMAN: Tell me how you feel about reading and writing.

NICKY: I like to read most of the time. I don't like that we have to do so much writing on every book: summaries, focuses, what we'd change about the book. Then we have to hand those in every two weeks. If I were the teacher, I'd have students read the book without interruption and require less writing.

ROUTMAN: When do you read?

NICKY: Most of my reading is done at school. I have no time at home. On weekends, I have to watch my cousin. Sometimes I pick up a book when I'm mad at my mother, and I have nothing else to do. I like fantasy, mystery, and some nonfiction.

ROUTMAN: Do you still like to write, and when do you write?

NICKY: I have written a lot of stories. I spend about an hour a day writing stories at home. I like writing better than reading. I remember doing a lot of writing at Moreland. At Moreland I learned how to write and read books and reading helped writing. If you read and then write it down, you understand it more. I like to write songs and stories about people—how kids relate to school and their parents. Some of the stories I wrote were based on *Sixth Grade Can Really Kill You* [by Barthe DeClements, Viking, 1985]. I choose parts I like from books I've read and put them in my own stories. I learned that in first grade at Moreland.

You know, we read lots of books in school, but instead of essays and book reports, we could write our own stories and books. I think that makes more sense.

Observations

From interviewing these students, it became clear to me that being immersed in a reading-writing classroom in first grade was very significant for their view of literacy even four and five years later. In spite of the fact that these students all wished they had more choice in and ownership of their reading and writing, their attitudes about reading and writing remained fairly positive. These students were very aware of the influence of reading on writing, the power and enjoyment of journal writing and publishing, the importance of self-selection in reading and writing, and the need for time set aside for reading.

These positive attitudes and self-awareness seem to indicate that even one year in a whole language classroom can make a difference in a child's reading-writing attitudes and behaviors. That one year—no matter when it comes—is still better than never being in a whole language classroom. This should give some comfort to the teacher who may be the only whole language teacher in a school.

At the same time, it is also quite clear that just because a district makes a written commitment to more meaning-centered approaches and moves from the basal to literature, unless ongoing staff development takes place across all the grades, teachers will teach as they have always taught. What came through from the interviews was that reading was largely whole class, there was some ability grouping for reading, there were lots of required written book reports and summaries, and most writing topics were assigned by the teacher. While choice and ownership were primary to the students, they were not yet highly valued by some of the teachers. That would only come when teachers acquired a strong theoretical understanding of language learning and whole language principles.

Reflections on Evaluation

Balancing evaluation means relying not only on multiple sources to inform instruction but on sources that rely heavily on observation and process. Meaningful evaluation means an extremely knowledgeable teacher looking at how students apply knowledge in different contexts. On the highest level, meticulous documentation would be done largely by the learner. The teacher-learner or student-learner would be observing and talking about his own learning processes—including strategies being used, changes being noticed, progress being made, strengths and weaknesses observed, past and present levels of functioning noted, and new goals needing to be established.

Evaluation will no doubt continue to be an area educators grapple with. Self-evaluation is still the hardest part for me. While I strive to improve my evaluation procedures, it is a struggle. Although I am continually examining my teaching philosophy, behaviors, and methods, I have not yet taken the risk of asking for feedback from my colleagues on how I do my job. I plan to make that one of my new goals.

If evaluation is to move to a place where it is valid and valued by teachers, students, parents, administrators, and policy makers, then teachers need to stop waiting for someone else to make the necessary changes. We can no longer rely on test constructors, state departments of education, and administrators to set evaluation policy. If we want evaluation to be consistent with our theory of how children learn, teachers must get together and actively work for better assessment and evaluation procedures. One teacher working alone is not likely to have much effect, but groups of teachers can write letters, influence administrators and board of education members, share recent research with parents and policy makers, change testing procedures, and work to make evaluation more balanced, informative, and useful. It is an effort worth making. Until meaningful evaluation becomes an integrated part of all teaching and learning, tests and decontextualized measures will continue to drive, misinform, and misguide instruction.

Resources

For professional books dealing with evaluation, see *Resources for Teachers*, especially:

Barrs and others. 1990. *The Primary Language Record: Handbook for Teachers*

Cohen. 1988. *TESTS: Marked for Life*

Goodman, Goodman, and Hood. 1989. *The Whole Language Evaluation Book*

Kamii. 1990. *Achievement Testing in the Early Grades: The Games Grownups Play*

Tierney, Carter, and Desai. 1991. *Portfolios in the Reading-Writing Classroom*

The following journal articles, chapters, and booklets have been particularly useful in personal exploration and in our weekly language arts support groups for deepening understanding of evaluation in a meaning-centered classroom.

Anthony, Robert J., Terry Johnson, Norma I. Mickelson, and Alison Preece. 1991. *Evaluating Literacy: A Perspective for Change.* Portsmouth, NH: Heinemann. See annotation, p. 74b.

Au, Kathryn H., Judith A. Scheu, Alice J. Kawakami, and Patricia A. Herman. April 1990. "Assessment and Accountability in a Whole Literacy Curriculum," *The Reading Teacher*, pp. 574–578.

> *This informative article addresses teachers' concerns about assessment and accountability with a "whole literacy" approach. Based on their work in the Kamehameha Elementary Education Program (KEEP) in Hawaii, the authors recommend a portfolio approach incorporating a curriculum framework based on six aspects of literacy: ownership, reading comprehension, writing process, word identification, language and vocabulary knowledge, and voluntary reading. Five major assessment tasks and procedures are suggested for providing information on the six aspects of literacy: questionnaire on attitudes for reading and writing, response to literature task, student's writing sample, running record, and voluntary reading log. Some specific examples of assessment tasks are provided. This is an excellent article for understanding and implementing holistic assessment strategies.*

Austin, Terri. 1994. *Changing the View: Student-Led Parent Conferences.* Portsmouth, NH: Heinemann. See annotation, p. 74b.

Bailey, Janis, Phyllis Brazee, and others. April 1988. "Problem Solving Our Way to Alternative Evaluation Procedures," *Language Arts*, pp. 364–373.

> *A group of teachers describe their attempts to move toward evaluation that is consistent with their meaning-centered approaches to reading and writing. This is a terrific article, both for understanding holistic evaluation and for the literacy evaluation forms and checklists that are shared.*

Barrs, Myra, Sue Ellis, Hilary Tester, and Anne Thomas, all of the Centre for Language in Primary Education, London. 1988. *The Primary Language Record: Handbook for Teachers.* Portsmouth, NH: Heinemann. See annotation, p. 75b.

Batzle, Janine. 1992. *Portfolio Assessment and Evaluation: Developing and Using Portfolios in the K-6 Classroom.* Cypress, CA: Creative Teaching Press. See annotation, p. 75b.

Bouffler, Chrystine (ed.). 1993. *Literacy Evaluation: Issues and Practicalities.* Portsmouth, NH: Heinemann. See annotation, p. 75b.

Bredekamp, Sue, and Lorrie Shepard. March 1989. "How Best to Protect Children from Inappropriate School Expectations, Practices, and Policies," *Young Children,* pp. 14–24.

   This important position statement, from the National Association for the Education of Young Children, on the uses and misuses of standardized testing with young children complements and follows the NAEYC position statement on developmentally appropriate practice (Bredekamp, 1987). Based on research findings, the authors address inappropriate assessment-curriculum–related policies in kindergarten and the primary grades: readiness testing, raising the entrance age, transitional classes, increased academic demand in kindergarten, and retention. They note that they are not opposed to all standardized testing—for example, reliable screening measures that are used for instructional planning in meeting children's special needs are valid. However, standardized tests used to exclude, admit, or place children in special classes are viewed as harmful. "If no beneficial outcome for children can be demonstrated, then using a standardized test is not justified" (p. 15). The article concludes with suggested guidelines for decision making in testing and placement. Use these specific guidelines and resources to promote appropriate practice in your school district. Every teacher, administrator, parent, and policy maker concerned with early childhood education should read this powerful article.

Clay, Marie. 1993. *An Observation Survey of Early Literacy Achievement.* Portsmouth, NH: Heinemann. See annotation, p. 75b.

Clemmons, Joan, Lois Laase, DonnaLynn Cooper, Nancy Areglado, and Mary Dill. 1993. *Portfolios in the Classroom: A Teacher's Sourcebook.* New York: Scholastic Professional Books. See annotation, p. 76b.

Cohen, S. Alan. 1988. *TESTS: Marked for Life?* Richmond Hill, Ontario: Scholastic-TAB. See annotation, p. 76b.

Cooper, Winfield and B.J. Brown. February 1992. "Using Portfolios to Empower Student Writers." *English Journal,* pp. 40–45. See annotation, p. 76b.

Davies, Anne and others. 1992. *Together is Better: Collaborative Assessment, Evaluation and Reporting.* Winnipeg, Manitoba: Peguis Publishers. See annotation, p. 76b.

Eggleton, Jill. 1990. *Whole Language Evaluation: Reading, Writing and Spelling.* Bothell, WA: The Wright Group.

   This 80-page resource by a New Zealand educator is full of practical ideas for evaluating and monitoring children's progress in the "emergent," "early," and "fluency" stages of reading, writing, and spelling. Lots of sample checklists, forms, suggested approaches, and ideas for use in the early grades.

Farr, Roger and Bruce Tone. 1994. *Portfolio and Performance Assessment: Helping Students Evaluate Their Progress as Readers and Writers.* Fort Worth, TX: Harcourt Brace. See annotation, p. 76b.

Fisher, Bobbi. November/December 1989. "Assessing Emergent and Initial Readers," *Teaching K–8,* pp. 56–58.

   A practicing kindergarten teacher describes the systematic way she observes, records, and assesses each of her students' early literacy behaviors through a tape recorded reading and writing interview, various reading and writing observations and conferences, and procedures to assess letter, sound, and word-sound identification. Kindergarten and first grade teachers will find this a practical, invaluable article.

Francis, David (executive director). 1994. *English—A Curriculum Profile for Australian Schools.* Carlton, Victoria: Curriculum Corporation, and Portsmouth, NH: Heinemann. See annotation, p. 77b.

Gill, Kent (ed.). 1993. *Process and Portfolios in Writing Instruction.* Urbana, IL: National Council of Teachers of English. See annotation, p. 77b.

Glazer, Susan Mandel and Carol Smullen Brown. 1993. *Portfolios and Beyond: Collaborative Assessment in Reading and Writing.* Norwood, MA: Christopher-Gordon Publishers. See annotation, p. 77b.

Goodman, Kenneth, Lois Bridges Bird and Yetta Goodman (eds.). 1992. *The Whole Language Catalog: Supplement on Authentic Assessment*. Blacklick, OH: SRA Division of Macmillan/McGraw-Hill. See annotation, p. 77b.

Goodman, Kenneth, Yetta Goodman, and Wendy Hood (eds.). 1988. *The Whole Language Evaluation Book*. Portsmouth, NH: Heinemann. See annotation, p. 78b.

Graves, Donald H. and Bonnie S. Sunstein (eds.). 1992. *Portfolio Portraits*. Portsmouth, NH: Heinemann. See annotation, p. 78b.

Harman, Susan. 1989–1990. "The Tests: Trivial or Toxic?" *Teachers Networking: The Whole Language Newsletter*. Vol. 9, no. 1, pp. 1 and 5–9.

> *The author, who is project director of the American Reading Council, refutes claims that standardized tests are objective or useful for diagnosis, accountability, and placement. She points out the monopoly of the three major elementary school test publishers who are also the same three (out of four) major elementary basal reading text publishers. Harman notes the damaging effects of tests on many levels of education and calls for evaluation that respects teachers as professionals and that thoughtfully observes children's performance over time.*

Harp, Bill (ed.). 1994. *Assessment and Evaluation for Student-Centered Learning. Second Edition*. Norwood, MA: Christopher-Gordon Publishers. See annotation, p. 78b.

Harp, Bill. November 1988. "When the Principal Asks: 'When You Do Whole Language Instruction, How Will You Keep Track of Reading and Writing Skills?'" *The Reading Teacher*, pp. 160–161.

> *This brief response gives the rationale for more meaning-based assessment, with some specific examples of holistic measures.*

Herman, Joan L., Pamela R. Aschbacher, and Lynn Winters. 1992. *A Practical Guide to Alternative Assessment*. Alexandria, VA: Association for Supervision and Curriculum Development. See annotation, p. 78b.

Hill, Bonnie Campbell and Cynthia Ruptic. 1994. *Practical Aspects of Authentic Assessment: Putting the Pieces Together*. Norwood, MA: Christopher-Gordon Publishers. See annotation, p. 79b.

Hornsby, David, and Deborah Sukarna, with Jo-Ann Parry. 1988. "Record Keeping and Evaluation." In *Read On: A Conference Approach to Reading*. Portsmouth, NH: Heinemann, Chap. 12, pp. 129–143.

> *Lots of practical and visual examples are given for evaluation in the classroom along with learning principles supporting holistic evaluation of individual children. Very helpful to the teacher who wants to "see" what holistic record keeping might look like.*

Jett-Simpson, Mary and Lauren Leslie (eds.). 1994. *Ecological Assessment: Under Construction*. Schofield, WI: Wisconsin State Reading Association (94809 Sternberg Ave., 54476). See annotation, p. 79b.

Johnston, Peter H. 1992. *Constructing Evaluation of Literate Activity*. New York: Longman. See annotation, p. 79b.

Johnston, Peter. April 1987. "Teachers as Evaluation Experts," *The Reading Teacher*, pp. 744–748.

> *Johnston affirms that the current preoccupation with testing does not further instruction. Instead, he recommends that knowledgeable classroom teachers—interacting with and observing individual students—should evaluate students and make appropriate instructional decisions. He describes what a teacher who is an expert in literacy evaluation would know and be able to do. This article is a personal favorite; read it and discuss it with colleagues for information and inspiration.*

Kamii, Constance (ed.). 1990. *Achievement Testing in the Early Grades: The Games Grown-Ups Play*. Washington, DC: National Association for the Education of Young Children. See annotation, p. 80b.

King, Dorothy F. 1989–1990. "My Word! Real Kids or Unreal Tasks: The Obvious Choice," *Teacher's Networking: The Whole Language Newsletter*, Vol. 9, no. 1, pp. 14–15.

> *After getting back low test scores from a thoughtfully literate second grade class, an administrator takes a careful look at the tests and the students and decides to ignore the test results. Share this article with your administrator.*

Koskinen, Patricia S., Linda B. Gambrell, Barbara A. Kapinus, and Betty S. Heathington. May 1988. "Retelling: A Strategy for Enhancing Students' Reading Comprehension," *The Reading Teacher*, pp. 892–897.

This compact article cites the research that supports the beneficial outcomes of retelling and gives suggested models for how to use retelling in the classroom. Useful for all classrooms.

Linek, Wayne M. February 1991. "Grading and Evaluation Techniques for Whole Language Teachers." *Language Arts*, pp. 125–131. See annotation, p. 80b.

Little, Nancy and John Allan. 1988. *Student-Led Teacher Parent Conferences.* Toronto, Ontario: Lugus Productions Limited. See annotation, p. 80b.

Ministry of Education, Victoria, Australia. 1990. *Literacy Profiles Handbook: Assessing and Reporting Literacy Development.* (A U.S. version, *The American Literacy Profiles* by Patrick Griffin, Patricia G. Smith, and Lois Burrill, will be available from Heinemann in spring 1995.) See annotation, p. 80b.

Murphy, Sandra and Mary Ann Smith. *Writing Portfolios: A Bridge from Teaching to Assessment.* 1991. Markham, Ontario: Pippin Publishing, and Portsmouth, NH: Heinemann. See annotation, p. 80b.

Neill, D. Monty, and Noe J. Medina. May 1989. "Standardized Testing: Harmful to Educational Health," *Phi Delta Kappan*, pp. 688–697.

Share this carefully researched article on the negative effects of multiple-choice standardized testing with other educators and policy makers in your district. Unfortunately, the authors' research reveals that "the number of states that mandate testing has increased greatly in recent years" (p. 689). Some adverse effects of testing include placing disproportionate numbers of minorities in remedial, special education, and lower-track programs; focusing on basic skills and isolated facts instead of on integration of information and critical thinking. "[T]esting must become an occasional adjunct, used for obtaining basic but limited information about education—and for nothing else" (p.695).

Perrone, Vito (ed.). 1991. *Expanding Student Assessment.* Alexandria, VA: Association for Supervision and Curriculum Development. See annotation, p. 81b.

Reardon, S. Jeanne. Winter 1990. "Putting Reading Tests in Their Place," *The New Advocate*, pp. 29–37.

A first grade classroom teacher acknowledges that while the results of standardized tests are not particularly useful to students or the teacher, the results are used to make decisions about children and reading programs. Therefore, students should be taught "reading-test-reading" as a separate reading genre to prepare them for test taking. The author describes how she manages to weave the reading-test genre into her reading program without compromising the high-level thinking and joy of reading that goes on in her reading-writing classroom.

Rhodes, Lynn K. (ed.). 1993. *Literacy Assessment: A Handbook of Instruments.* Portsmouth, NH: Heinemann. See annotation, p. 81b.

Rhodes, Lynn K. and Nancy Shanklin. 1993. *Windows into Literacy: Assessing Learners, K-8.* Portsmouth, NH: Heinemann. See annotation, p. 81b.

Rogers, Vincent. May 1989. "Assessing the Curriculum Experienced by Children," *Phi Delta Kappan*, pp. 714–717.

This is a superb and highly useful article for k–12 teachers by the director of the Alternative Assessment Project at the University of Connecticut. Rogers gives many creative, workable strategies and activities for assessing the "curriculum of the mind." To probe and assess what students have actually experienced and learned in the content areas, Rogers describes a range of activities and interview probes that can be applied successfully to any classroom in which the teacher is looking to incorporate alternatives to traditional testing. Don't miss this valuable resource!

Seidel, Steve. December 13, 1989. "Even Before Portfolios: The Activities and Atmosphere of a Portfolio Classroom," *Portfolio: The Newsletter of Arts Propel*, pp. 6–9.

A portrait of a ninth grade portfolio classroom gives valuable insights into the conditions and strategies that put students at the center of their own assessment as writers and learners. Applicable and useful for all grade levels.

Sharp, Quality Quinn (compiler). 1989. *Evaluation: Whole Language Checklists for Evaluating Your Children. For Grades K–6.* New York: Scholastic.

This 38-page booklet provides many useful checklists in various areas: reading behaviors, reader response, writing and spelling, miscue analysis, students self-evaluation, and literary appreciation.

Stenmark, Jean Kerr (ed.). 1991. *Mathematics Assessment: Myths, Model, Good Questions, and Practical Suggestions*. Reston, VA: The National Council of Teachers of Mathematics. See annotation, p. 82b.

Teale, William H. November 1988. "Developmentally Appropriate Assessment of Reading and Writing in the Early Childhood Classroom," *The Elementary School Journal*, pp. 173–183.

> An expert researcher in emergent literacy cites the theoretical rationale and calls for assessment programs and procedures for four- and five-year-olds that are based mostly on performance samples and observational methods. The major concepts and skills that are significant in children's emerging literacy are identified and ways to assess students' knowledge of those concepts and skills are demonstrated. This is a useful article for prekindergarten and kindergarten teachers who are looking to tie teaching and assessment together in a developmentally appropriate and meaningful manner.

Traill, Leanna. 1993. *Highlight My Strengths: Assessment and Evaluation of Literacy Learning*. Crystal Lake, IL: Rigby. See annotation, p. 82b.

Turbill, Jan and Brian Cambourne (eds.). 1994. *Responsive Evaluation*. Portsmouth, NH: Heinemann. See annotation, p. 82b.

Valencia, Sheila W., Elfrieda H. Hiebert, and Peter P. Afflerbach (eds.). 1994. *Authentic Reading Assessment: Practices and Possibilities*. Newark, DE: International Reading Association. See annotation, p. 82b.

Weaver, Constance. 1994. "Portfolios, Reading, and Miscue Analysis." In *Reading Process and Practice: From Socio-Psycholinguistics to Whole Language*, Second Edition. Portsmouth, NH: Heinemann, Chap. 6, pp. 216–285.

> This outstanding chapter will guide the teacher in assessment procedures. Particularly valuable are the detailed procedures and guidelines for miscue analysis.

Wiggins, Grant. May 1992. "Creating Tests Worth Taking." *Educational Leadership*, pp. 26–33. See annotation, p. 83b.

Wolfe, Dennie Palmer. April 1989. "Portfolio Assessment: Sampling Student Work," *Educational Leadership*, pp. 35–39.

> The author, a researcher involved with portfolio assessment, advocates making school assessment more in keeping with real life, which is full of long-term projects that need ongoing reflection and monitoring. Modeled on the working processes of musicians and artists, the suggested goal is for students to be guided in taking the responsibility of thoughtfully judging their own work over time. Educators interested in the use of portfolios as part of the assessment process will want to read this article.

Wood, George (coordinator). Fall 1990. *Democracy in Education: Alternatives to Standardized Testing*.

> Read and discuss this issue for insights from teachers and students on standardized testing. (See "Themed Journals," p. 55b, for a full description.)

Woodward, Helen. *Negotiated Evaluation: Involving Children and Parents in the Process*. Portsmouth, NH: Heinemann. See annotation, p. 83b.

14

The Learning Disabled Student:

A Part of the At-Risk Population

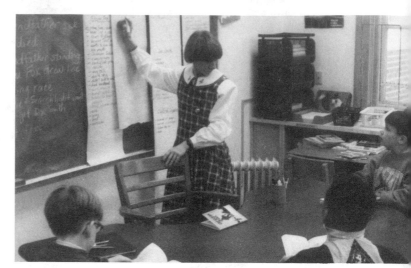

L.D. teacher Margie Glaros noting students' insights during a discussion of Stone Fox *(Gardiner, 1980)*

"I believe there are very few true learning disabled students. We have made them learning disabled by focusing on their deficits, instead of their strengths." There was a loud round of applause. It was obvious I had touched a nerve. No other comment I made as the opening speaker at the whole language conference had aroused so much emotion and support.

I am a certified teacher for children who have been identified as learning disabled (L.D.). For eight years I worked in my local school district as an L.D. tutor where I saw students on a one-to-one pull-out basis for thirty minutes a day. Based on my graduate-level training, I taught reading with a heavy emphasis on phonics. I taught most skills in isolation, and I taught mainly to the students' deficits. I did frequent task analysis, keeping charts and records documenting skills growth, and I used behavior modification techniques to motivate and reward students. I worked hard, and my students made real gains. Yet in all that time, I have very few recollections of dismissing a student from the L.D. program. Almost all students continued to need and receive supportive services throughout their school careers.

It is, therefore, not surprising to me that the number of students identified as learning disabled has continued to increase since 1975 when the Education of All Handicapped Children Act became federal law. The public law, P.L. 94-142, requires that school districts identify and provide appropriate education for all handicapped children. Since the law was enacted, the number of students identified as learning disabled has remained at 6 to 10 percent of the total U.S. school population.

It is interesting to note that the L.D. population is often partly defined by a "definition of exclusion." That is, these are students who are *not* achieving in school in spite of the fact that they are *not* mentally retarded, *not* deaf or blind, *not* emotionally disturbed, and have *not* had inordinate obstacles to learning such as poor teaching and frequent absences.

I do not believe that becoming learning disabled is a predetermined condition. Even with the few students who have been identified as having biological or neurological dysfunctions, the way students are perceived, taught, and interacted with has dramatic effects on achievement. Teachers who view a child as having learning abilities, as opposed to disabilities, will usuallly find a way to be successful in teaching the child.

I strongly believe the number of children identified as L.D. could be greatly reduced if educators focused on students' strengths instead of on their deficits. While the Individual Education Plan, required for each identified student, is intended to remediate the deficits and teach to the strengths, more often than not the main emphasis on this written plan focuses only on goals and objectives to remediate the deficits.

This chapter takes a close look at some students with learning disabilities and discusses related issues: teaching strategies, evaluation, the pull-out program, changing attitudes of the L.D. teacher, and communicating with parents. Since students with learning problems are a part of every classroom, the intended audience is the classroom teacher as well as the L.D., or Resource Room, teacher and parents. In addition, since the L.D. student is part of the broad at-risk population, the issues discussed are relevant and applicable to the special education population, Chapter 1 students, second language learners, limited-language–proficient learners, and other remedial learners, including illiterate adults. My hope is that while recognizing the problems in dealing with at-risk learners, teachers, administrators, and parents will feel encouraged by the possibilities.

A Look at Three Students

Expectations for Success: Paul

Several years ago, on a mid-January day, I received a call from a learning disabilities teacher in our district. She was very concerned about one of her students and asked if I would work with Paul.

> Paul was a fourth-grader who had entered our school district in second grade and had then repeated that grade. Despite caring teachers and varied teaching strategies and materials, he was a virtual nonreader and nonwriter after nearly four years in our district. In addition, Paul had begun "acting up" in the classroom. These days, he was receiving few positive comments from teachers.
>
> Theo Husband had been Paul's L.D. teacher since second grade, and she and Paul enjoyed a warm and caring relationship. Her classroom was the place where Paul felt most consistently valued and successful. Paul often sought her out at lunch time and after school, when he talked to her for hours. She, in turn, was a good listener and constantly worked at building his self-esteem after a tough day in school. In fourth grade, during one of their talks, Paul spoke about how the kids were teasing him, and then he blurted out, "I really want to learn how to read." It was at

that point that Theo decided to call me. She hoped that together we might make a difference in Paul's learning.

Theo was completely dedicated to seeking the best for Paul. She had tried many programs and methods and consulted colleagues for advice. She had spent years being an advocate for Paul—attending school conferences and keeping in close contact with his mom. Now, mid-year in fourth grade, Theo was experiencing anxieties because Paul would be leaving at the end of the school year to enter another building where all fifth- and sixth-graders were housed. At the same time, Paul's mother was expressing some anger about her son's failure to learn to read and write in the public school and was threatening to send him to a private school.

As the only information I had about Paul at our first meeting was that he was having severe difficulties, I had no preconceived notions about what he could or could not do. I met him with the expectation that he was whole and able and that he could learn. I spoke with him in language and tone uncharacteristic of me. I told him that I was a well-known reading expert and that I had never failed to teach a child to read—*never*. I told him that I would be teaching him in a way that was totally different from what he had experienced so far and that he would be successful.

Paul had agreed to meet with me only after much encouragement by Theo. We spent the first half hour just talking and getting to know each other. I knew that after many years of frustration with reading and writing, he doubted his abilities. Paul's expectations about becoming a successful reader and writer would need to change before any new learning could take place.

In the course of our conversation, I asked Paul about reading in school, and he told me about the basal texts and worksheets he'd had. When I asked him to show me what he was working on now in reading, he brought me his Phonics C workbook. I asked Paul if his own language and stories had ever been used to try to teach him to read. Because he said no, I decided to begin with the most predictable text of all—his own language.

That first day together Paul and I wrote our first book. I folded several sheets of blank, white ditto paper together and asked Paul what he would like his first story to be about. I suggested he write about something he was interested in and knew a lot about. With very little hesitation, he told me he wanted his book to be called *The New Space Shuttle*. I served as his scribe as he dictated the story, told me how much print he wanted on each page, and where the writing and the illustrations would be placed. I began with a title and author page, followed by an information page that included where and when the book was being published. His completed story was forty-two words spread over four pages of text and illustrations. It read as follows. (See Figure 14–1 for reproduction and layout.)

- p. 1: I want to improve space travel so we can get farther away from the earth.
- p. 2: Then we can meet other people.
- p. 3: Technology will improve the way we live.
- p. 4: This is a drawing of the way I think the space shuttle should be.

Figure 14-1   Paul's First Book

As Paul dictated one page at a time to me, I had him watch me write as I slowly verbalized and stretched out the sounds of each word. Then I asked him to read the page back to me. Because it was his own language on a topic that was important to him, he read the page without difficulty. We continued, one page at a time. I slowly verbalized each word as I wrote it. Paul carefully observed the process and read each completed page.

Next, I suggested to Paul that it might be a good idea to have an "About the Author" page for this first book. We looked at several book jackets and discussed the kinds of information that might be included. He dictated: "Paul is eleven years old. He is a nice guy. He can be friendly and funny. He likes to draw. He knows a lot about science and history. He wants to be an

Air Force pilot when he grows up. When he retires he will design ships for outer space."

I was surprised that he would risk having that much print on a page (it took up eleven lines when it was handwritten), and despite the fact that there were no picture cues, he was able to read it. I was even more surprised by his last line: "When he retires he will design ships for outer space." That statement told me that Paul was an imaginative and inquiring student.

Working with Paul that first day, I was struck by his strong oral language, his delightful sense of humor, and his knowledge of things scientific. I had expected him to be of normal intelligence; I had not expected him to be above average. Because of my own prejudices about literacy, I assumed that if he was a nonreader and nonwriter after so many years in school, he probably wasn't overly bright. How wrong I was!

After we completed the text and Paul had read each page, we went back and read his book together. He followed my voice so he would know how a story should sound in its pacing, phrasing, and overall fluency. I assured Paul that he would always be able to read his own stories, and eventually these reading skills would transfer to commercial books and other reading materials.

After reading his completed text, Paul began to add illustrations. Paul was an excellent artist, and he loved to draw. Incorporating his artistic ability to complement his story served as a boost to his confidence by acknowledging his special talent.

Before Paul started to draw, we talked about how important it was for the illustrations to match the text, both to help him when reading and to support the story line. We were very specific in talking about how certain pictures would help him remember words in the text. He carefully worked on the illustrations after our visit and had them completed when I saw him the following week.

I encountered a changed student in our second session. Paul, who had never been able to read even his own writing, was bursting with pride at his first reading success. He proudly read me *The New Space Shuttle*, including the author page, which he had practiced and reread in school and at home over and over again. His L.D. teacher, Theo, was absolutely joyful. It was the first time she had ever seen Paul believe that he could read.

Much later Theo told me of the significance of my first session with Paul. "He really felt he accomplished something that day." Paul had carried his book around with him all day, never letting it out of his sight. Even during his math lesson, the book sat beside him on the table, and he kept flipping through it.

I continued to work with Paul, about forty-five minutes every Thursday until the end of the school year in June. If he hesitated when reading a word, we discussed how he could use the context of the whole sentence and his picture to help him work it out. He could also, finally, utilize the phonics he had been drilled on for so many years. To read "Technology" in his first book, *The New Space Shuttle*, all he needed was to see the "T." To

Figure 14-2   Paul's Second Book

He has a brown shell. He
is fast. He is lazy, but I
keep him in good shape with
an amusement park in my
room.

read "should" on page 4, he needed to be helped to see that it began like "shuttle." The familiar context and structure of his story, his picture, and his memory for text would work together to do the rest.

Each week Paul gained a little more confidence and risked putting more print on the pages of the successive books he wrote. The second book we wrote together was *My Pet Turtle.* It was, by his choice, 237 words spread out over eleven pages. (See Figure 14-2 for a sample page.) The book also included, as did all his new books from that point on, a dedication page. This one read "Dedicated to George" (his turtle). His next book, written during our third session the following week, was *How I Would Teach My Friend to Draw.* The book was dedicated to his friend Yusef, and it took Yusef, step by step, through sequenced stages in drawing a horse. It was fifteen pages and 184 words.

In February, over the span of four once a week meetings, Paul composed *My Friend P. J.,* a charming story about friendship, shared adventures, and life's happenings beginning in nursery school. The book was eighteen pages of text and 1,175 words! While Paul's beginning pages had less than 50 words on a page and were carefully illustrated, the last three pages had well over 100 words on a page with no illustrations. He practiced until he could proudly read each page.

Shortly thereafter, a parent volunteer word-processed *My Pet Turtle* and *My Friend P. J.*, made ten copies of each, and bound them into books. We introduced Paul as the author in several second and third grade classrooms, where these stories were used as reading materials with small groups. Paul was buoyant. What a boost to his self-esteem! He practiced reading these typed versions and began to dictate a science fiction story, *War Adventures*, at our next meeting.

I now sensed that Paul's growing confidence and risk taking would enable him to try reading an unknown book. At our meeting during the third week of February, I brought some trade books with me—three picture books of varying difficulty and several easy chapter books. We looked through them together as I told him something about the story line of each book. When I asked him to choose which book he'd like to read, I had no idea what he would pick. Paul enthusiastically decided on the delightful picture book *Louis the Fish* by Arthur Yorinks, with pictures by Richard Egielski (Farrar, Straus and Giroux, 1980). Paul loved the richly colored graphic illustrations as well as the fanciful text about a butcher who yearns to be a fish. After I read the entire book to him, he was eager to try it. I assured him that with practice he would be able to read it. We began with reading just the first few pages over and over again. Paul never seemed to tire of reading *Louis the Fish*. Four months later, he still seemed to love that book.

At our first session in March, Paul announced that his reading was getting better, but that the school librarian didn't know it yet. He asked me if I would go with him during library time to choose a science fiction book. I told him I would speak to the librarian so she could help him choose more appropriately. At the same time, his mother reported that Paul was beginning to choose to read in his spare time at home, and Theo reported similar behavior in school. He was beginning to see himself as a reader for the first time in his life.

Additionally, Paul's work habits began to change. Whereas previously he would use avoidance behaviors and never attempt any work on his own (except for math computation), Paul now began to complete assignments and to be responsible about bringing back homework. His mom reported coming home from work and being surprised and pleased to find Paul already working on his spelling pages. His usual behavior had been to wait for her help before starting any assignments.

Paul continued to read and reread all his books—at home, with his L.D. teacher, during sustained silent reading in his regular classroom, and with me. At first, during classroom sustained silent reading time, he would only illustrate, but as his confidence in his ability to read slowly began to grow, he gave up drawing for reading.

In early March, I brought Paul *More Stories Julian Tells* by Ann Cammeron (Knopf, 1986). I knew Paul would appreciate the subtle humor in the stories of this black family and identify with the main character, Julian. It was one of our third grade core books, and it would be the first chapter book Paul would read. Sometimes he would reread a page three and four times until he could read it smoothly. By the beginning of April his improved fluency was noticeable. He could read the first two chapters in *More Stories Julian Tells* without help, with reasonable speed, and with about 90 percent accuracy.

At the end of April, Paul signed out his first chapter book from the school library. It was *Russell Sprouts* by Johanna Hurwitz (Morrow, 1987). It was the first book he picked up and started reading on his own without guidance. There were few pictures, yet he tackled it boldly. He was very proud of himself. He had chosen an appropriate book for himself, and he stayed with it until he finished it about four weeks later.

While Paul was feeling some confidence as a reader, it was also necessary that he begin to see himself as a writer. By mid-February, I began writing weekly letters to Paul. I wanted a way to increase our contact, but I also wanted him to begin to risk writing for himself, which, up to now, he had been reluctant to do. I told him not to worry about his spelling, but just to do the best he could and that I would be able to read it. When he received my first letter through the interschool mail, he asked the L.D. teacher for help reading it. But when he received another letter from me the following week, he refused help, read it privately, and didn't want to share its contents with anyone. He began writing to me regularly (see Figure 14–3).

In early April we began writing Paul's sixth book, *My Vacation*, and for the first time, Paul was willing to do the writing himself. I sat right next to him and encouraged him to put down the sounds he heard and to try to remember the way words looked in books. When he made a mistake, I would ask him if the word looked right. Usually he could tell if the word was misspelled. If he was unable to spell the word correctly on subsequent attempts, I wrote the word for him. Whenever possible, I would encourage him to relate the known to the unknown, to use a pattern he already knew in one word and apply it to a new word.

At the same time, Paul continued to reread all his old, familiar books. When he got stuck, he now relied on meaning strategies combined with phonics to self correct. For example, from his *War Adventures* he read, "We *could* our vehicle Euto 3." He immediately self-corrected "could" for "called." Several lines later he read, "*Both* was coming from his nose." He quickly self-corrected and reread, "*Blood* was coming from his nose." His ability to monitor his own reading was a major breakthrough in his being able to begin to read independently.

In late May there was a conference about Paul to discuss the results of his recent re-evaluation. The school psychologist, speech therapist, L.D. teacher, classroom teacher, Paul's mother, and myself were in attendance. Paul's I.Q. was reported as average. The psychologist indicated that Paul had experienced normal developmental milestones, had average intelligence, evidenced distractible behavior, and suffered from asthma. He was taking ritalin to control hyperactive behavior and medication for asthma.

A language assessment revealed average to above-average vocabulary skills, which served to mask a language disability, making it difficult for Paul to retrieve single words. Tests of auditory processing and written

Figure 14-3   Increasing Contact with Paul through Letter Writing

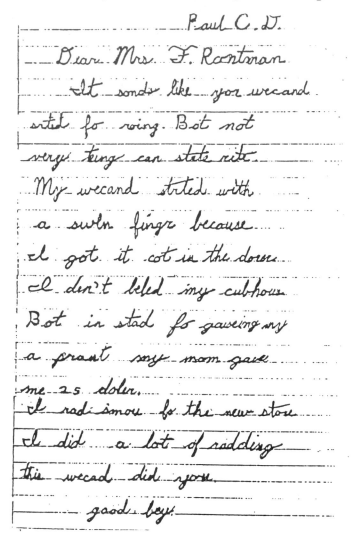

Dear Mrs. F. Routman,

   It sounds like your weekend started off wrong. But not everything can start right. My weekend started with a swollen finger because I got it caught in the door. I didn't build my clubhouse. But instead of giving me a present, my mom gave me 25 dollars.

   I read some of the new stories. I did a lot of reading this weekend. Did you?

   Good by.

language both revealed low average scores relative to his ability. A diagnostic reading test yielded significantly below average scores—two standard deviations below his expected performance level. At the end of the conference, Paul's mother spoke of how proud she was of Paul's progress, explaining, "He will read to anyone now."

I have not worked with Paul since he completed fourth grade and moved to our grades 5 and 6 building. However, we have kept in regular contact through letter writing. As Paul has grown older he has used a word processor with a spelling checker, and he has sent his letters out in edited form. I am always pleased when he refers to books he is enjoying.

Paul and his mother both report that he reads and writes over vacations and in his free time. He still prefers books with interesting pictures and enjoys reading games magazines as well as the movies and comics sections of the newspaper. Vicki Griminger, his present L.D. teacher, notes that Paul willingly picks up books to read in class. As long as Paul chooses to read and write, I feel confident that his literacy skills will continue to develop.

Teaching Skills in Context: Chris

"He doesn't know anything. He doesn't know how to read and write. He's very low." Those were among the first comments made by Chris's mother to his new teacher when Chris transferred to our school district near the end of second semester in second grade.

Chris, who had already been in four other schools, received little support from home. His mother was usually at work, and his older brothers picked physical fights with him. In his new classroom, he was quiet and unmotivated. Still, it was clear he was a capable child. During discussions, his oral contributions, though infrequent, were on target and meaningful.

In the fall of third grade, his L.D. teacher, Margie Glaros, asked me if I could work with Chris on the day I was in her building. Chris was receiving services in the L.D. resource room for up to two and a half hours daily. Margie reported that it seemed as though Chris had been taught reading only phonetically. He had no idea what else he could do when he couldn't figure out a word.

When I first met Chris he seemed ready to learn. He told me, "This is the first school I've been in where anyone really cares." As with Paul, I began with his own language and interests. I acted as scribe for his first book, *My Two Cats*, and for his next two books, *About My Grandpa* and *About My Friend Brian*. For his last book, *About the Gerbils*, he did most of the writing himself. He illustrated each of his books and practiced reading them many times.

At the suggestion of his L.D. teacher, Chris taped himself reading his stories. Margie told me the taping originally came about as a result of Chris's disappointment over a missed session with me. Because he wanted to share his improvement in reading, Chris taped his latest book and sent it to me in the school mail. When I saw him the following week, I complimented him on his efforts. We also talked about how choppy his reading sounded, and I demonstrated what "fluent" reading sounds like. He practiced, retaped himself, and was able to notice his improvement.

I had worked with Chris for only a few months when he suddenly moved to another school district. Working cooperatively with Margie, even in our short time together, I saw a marked change in Chris's attitude and ability. Chris was coming to see himself as a potential reader and writer, and he was beginning to take risks. Relying on context he created, he was beginning to learn and apply literacy skills. His improvement was most noticeable working one-to-one or in a group with younger students. He was still somewhat resistant in groups of grade-level peers.

Margie and I believed that Chris would learn to read and write high-frequency words if they came from the context of his stories. Years of skills in isolation had not contributed favorably to his literacy development. If he began with the whole, he could deal with the parts. Therefore, all work in word analysis came directly from the familiar language of his own text.

Chris's brief story is included because strategies that were working with Chris are applicable for other L.D. and special education students. (See "Selected Reading-Writing Strategies," pp. 391–393, for specific strategies utilized with Chris.) Hopefully, Chris will continue to build on his successes. We know it will not be easy for him. The same school year he transferred, we were contacted by two additional schools. Margie wrote to them and shared goals and methods that had worked for Chris. Margie, I, and the students in Margie's lab also wrote to Chris, but we never received a reply from him.

Focusing on the Strengths: Onajé

When I first met Onajé, he didn't smile. He kind of dragged himself down the hall, shoulders down, with a pout on his face. Onajé was a fourth-grader, and he had been receiving pull-out services for learning disabilities since second grade.

Onajé was presently working one-to-one with a tutor thirty minutes daily. It was clear that he did not see himself as a capable learner. Except for his oral contributions to classroom literature discussions, he did not appear to enjoy school, and he certainly didn't see himself as a reader or a writer.

In early fall, Onajé's L.D. tutor, Ellen Potter, asked me if I would model lessons for her on the day I was in her building. Ellen expressed concern that she was focusing more on what Onajé couldn't do and felt she might be contributing to his continuing lack of confidence. She was also aware of her skills-based orientation and felt ready to include some holistic strategies.

For our first lesson, we took a piece of writing Onajé had completed in the classroom (see Figure 14–4). I began our lesson by telling Onajé how much I liked his piece of writing and how well he had stuck to the topic. Knowing that spelling was a significant problem area for Onajé, I pointed out that most of his words were spelled correctly. I went through his paper, one line at a time, and pointed out each word that was correctly spelled. Out of the seventy words in his story, almost 80 percent were spelled accurately. I shared that information with Onajé and his tutor, and they both looked at me in disbelief. They were used to looking at his papers and seeing only the errors.

Next, I asked Onajé to read orally from *My Robot Buddy* by Alfred Slote (Lippincott, 1975), the science fiction book (in our grade 3 core collection) that he was reading with Ellen. His reading was choppy and hesitant, but based on his oral retelling, he seemed to get the overall meaning. I attended to everything he did well when he read. For instance, when he

Figure 14-4   Writing by Onajé

Here is something I'll never
forget

Some, I'll never
forget, was when my mother
was cleaning out the cabinets.
She was standing
on a chair. and the
chair sliped and my
mother fell. My father
had to take my mother
to the Hospital. She had
to get stithes. The
reason why I'll never forget
is becaues I was shocked and the only
thing I could do was call
my dad

substituted a word that made sense for a word he couldn't read, I praised him and told him, "That's what good readers do." Then I asked him, "What did you just do that good readers do?" Onajé was almost unable to talk about a reading strength. I had to restate what he had just done well and prod him to repeat what I'd said. When I came back the second week, Onajé again read orally from *My Robot Buddy*, and I focused once more on the positive things he did while reading. When he had difficulty, I showed him how he might help himself.

I asked him what kinds of books he might be interested in and he told me "science fiction" and "adventure." We talked about how important it was to read every day in order to become a really good reader.

The following week I brought three chapter books for him: *The Ghost of the Dutchman* by Cruz Martel (Scholastic, 1979), *The Twits* by Roald Dahl (Knopf, 1980), and *The Magic Finger* by Roald Dahl (Harper &

& Row, 1966). I told him something of the story line of each, and I asked him to choose one for nightly, independent reading. He chose *The Ghost of the Dutchman*.

I asked Onajé to begin reading orally. I wanted to demonstrate what he could do when he got into difficulty. When he couldn't read "rested" on page 1, I said, "Go on. Finish the sentence." Then, on his own, he went back and read the whole sentence from the beginning. I had him verbalize what he had just done. He said, "I skipped the word I couldn't read and read to the end of the sentence."

On page 2, I told him to read silently and "jot down any word that gives you trouble but only if it interferes with the meaning of the story." He read and wrote down "sailor." I asked, "What did you do when you came to that word?" He said, "I read it as 'soldier.' " Again, I stressed that what he had done, substituting a word that would make sense, was an excellent strategy. We did not work on "sounding out" the word "sailor." This would not have been the most efficient use of our time because Onajé's meaningful substitution did not affect his overall comprehension.

We were about to close the book when Onajé asked if he could continue reading. Ellen indicated that during the previous week he had also asked her, "Can I read today?" These were the very first times Onajé had ever requested to read. He was beginning to believe he could be a reader. However, it would still be some time before he chose to read voluntarily.

At about this time, I suggested to Ellen that we invite Onajé's mother in to observe me working with her son. Previously she had communicated to Ellen that she felt "bitter" about "whole language." It was also evident from talking with Onajé that his mom was giving him a lot of help at home. She didn't believe he had the necessary skills to figure things out for himself.

During our session she observed some teaching for strategies. For example, when Onajé circled "anoter" as recognition of a misspelling on a writing paper, I asked him if he knew "brother." He wrote it correctly, and then connected it to writing "another." When reading, he was not interrupted when he made an error. He was given time to self-correct, was guided to incorporate meaning-based strategies, and was asked to verbalize higher-level strategies he was using. He also received lots of praise for his efforts.

Following our session, I asked Onajé's mother how she felt about the way we were teaching spelling and reading. She said with a smile, "Now I understand what you're trying to do, and I like it." She admitted she had found it difficult to notice what Onajé does well: "When I see his papers, I see only the errors. I comment on them, and I want to take over." Gradually, over the coming months, Onajé's mother was able to focus more on the positive and to believe that Onajé was developing the necessary skills to read and write successfully. Her change in attitude contributed to Onajé's growing self-esteem.

After a while, I suggested to Onajé's classroom teacher that he probably didn't need to use the time with his L.D. tutor to work on reading, that perhaps the focus should be on writing while the tutor monitored his reading. What had become clear in working with Onajé weekly was that he utilized enough meaning-based and grapho-phonic strategies to make overall sense of what he was reading. When this message was given to his classroom teacher, she was initially disbelieving. She had heard him read only orally in front of the class, which all of her students were required to do. Based on his public oral reading, he was a poor reader. I told her it was like asking a stutterer to make a speech. I believed he should have to read orally only for diagnostic purposes in a one-to-one setting or if he chose to read orally. I explained that Onajé might never be a fluent oral reader, but all of his required and voluntary reading could be done silently. Silent reading was not only a situation that afforded him the opportunity to work through difficulties at his own pace, it was also the desired goal for all independent readers.

Onajé had become quite proficient in incorporating higher-level reading strategies, and Ellen and I noted his self-correction rate was much improved. For example, in observing him while he read silently, he continued to jot down words interfering with his reading, such as "incredible" and "practice," but more often than not, he would wind up erasing those words. As he continued reading, he seemed to work out the difficult words or make meaningful substitutions. We would also see him move his line marker back to the beginning of a sentence or phrase and then reread to get the meaning. In addition, we observed him skipping a word after softly pronouncing the beginning letters. Then, moving his line marker, he would read on to the end of the sentence and then head back to the beginning of the sentence again. We could tell by his pleased expression that he had figured out the troublesome spot. As Onajé began to see that he could rely less upon his teachers and his mom and more upon himself, his confidence began to grow.

Nonetheless, getting Onajé to invest in reading independently took much encouragement by Ellen, his mother, and me. He eventually finished *The Ghost of the Dutchman* on his own. Although it was only thirty-eight pages, it took him about three weeks. One of the things we had to do was discuss realistic expectations about nightly reading. Onajé complained that because of nightly homework, he had little time to read. He thought if he read one or two pages a day, that was adequate. We said that reading for pleasure was the most important homework he could do and that he should read for twenty to thirty minutes each evening. Eventually, he became convinced. One morning, about a month later, Onajé proudly announced he had completed and very much enjoyed *The Twits* by Roald Dahl. It was the first book he had chosen to read and complete independently. His face broke into a broad smile as he told about the book.

Shortly thereafter, I talked with Onajé about his reading. Looking back on our talk, I see that what struck me most was the pride and success he felt, clearly visible by the ever-present smile on his face. He seemed peaceful, not at all the agitated, moody student from just several months ago. Part of our conversation follows:

ROUTMAN: How are you feeling about reading?

ONAJE: Good. It's not fun when you can't read. You can't stick your hand up like the other kids. It's scary when you can't read. Now I can read like the other kids, and I don't mind if the teacher calls on me. It's fun to read like everyone else.

ROUTMAN: What's different for you now?

ONAJE: I can read better now, and I like to read. I read faster, too. I like to read hard words on signs and directions. I read at home now sometimes when I don't have too much homework. And my mom leaves me alone now to do my work.

ROUTMAN: You seem a lot happier.

ONAJE: Yeah, because I don't need as much help in my reading as I did at the beginning of the year.

ROUTMAN: What do you do now when you come to a hard word?

ONAJE: I either go past it and come back to it, or I see what would fit there, or I try to sound it out.

Onajé's classroom teacher, always supportive of his efforts, commented that he had begun volunteering to read aloud in class. She noted that though he wasn't fluent, he was no longer a hesitant reader who lacked confidence. Ellen Potter, his L.D. tutor, noted that Onajé was "reading like crazy!" She noted that it used to take Onajé fifteen minutes to "go through" two pages. Now he was much quicker, more fluent, and was integrating cueing systems. Perhaps, best of all, he was excited about starting new books because he believed he could read them. On an author page in a book he wrote, he had written, "I like to read in my spare time."

By the end of fourth grade, Onajé's new Individual Education Plan for the following year reflected his reading strengths. A norm-referenced educational achievement test indicated Onajé had gone from the 3rd to 7th stanine in reading comprehension in one year. He would now be receiving all reading instruction in the regular classroom. Ellen remains convinced that if she had not begun to change her emphasis from focusing on the deficits to building on Onajé's reading strengths, he would still be a learning disabled reader.

Selected Reading–Writing Strategies for L.D. and Other At-Risk Students

This section encompasses selected strategies I and other teachers have used successfully with L.D. and remedial students to teach reading and writing. However, these strategies are not just for the L.D. or special education teacher. The classroom teacher also has the responsibility to teach the L.D. student—usually the major responsibility. As such, the classroom teacher must be knowledgeable and flexible enough to set up a learning environment in which every student becomes literate.

I believe all of us learn language most easily when the language is whole, and when the experiences, contexts, and texts are meaningful and relevant to the learners' lives. Therefore, the strategies for teaching L.D. students and other at-risk learners should be similar to the meaning-based, holistic strategies recommended for teaching all students.

Fragmented instruction is particularly difficult for at-risk learners. While efficient language learners figure out what makes sense regardless of the instruction and ignore what doesn't fit, the at-risk population becomes further handicapped by splintered instruction. These are the students who do not learn language efficiently. They are often unable to filter out what doesn't make sense.

For example, at-risk students may be able to complete phonics or language workbook exercises but still be unable to apply those skills in a meaningful context. When instruction has focused on disconnected parts and isolated skills, students often find the bits and pieces insufficient to enable them to make sense of language and texts. These students need better instruction, more of it, and lots of opportunities to practice and apply meaning-based strategies.

Paul's mother told me,

> If the teacher or I take the time to give Paul an overall sense of what the story is about, or to discuss what the main concepts or questions to be answered are in a social studies or science text, he can pretty much figure things out for himself—even if the reading level is hard for him. But if he is just given an assignment without any background information, he is at a loss to make sense of it.

While the strategies discussed in this section may be used successfully with all students, they are especially helpful for the at-risk children. When applicable, I have used specific examples from working with Paul, Chris, and Onajé, as well as from a group of L.D. students, to demonstrate how a strategy has been used. Although the strategies that follow are presented one at a time, in the actual teaching-learning situation, they are often integrated and used interactively.

Creating Predictable Text from the Child's Language

This is a sure-fire technique that has never failed me. The child's own language becomes his beginning reading material. The approach has worked successfully for first-graders as well as for high school students, and I believe it can also work well for illiterate adults. By encouraging the student to talk and write about what is important to him, and by writing for and with the student, by hand or on the word processor, the student engages in the material. The "skills" are taught as they come up, in the context of reading and writing together. (See "Expectations for Success: Paul," at the beginning of this chapter, for specifics.)

Although the specific examples cited come from working with one student, predictable text can easily come from a group of students. A common experience, a series of books by an author, or a favorite book can all be used as a springboard for a shared writing. The story can then be reproduced so each child has a personal copy for reading and illustrating.

The following techniques have been successfully utilized with a child's natural language, predictable text:

Cutting apart a sentence from the child's story   A sentence from the child's story is written with a marker on a vertical strip. The words, and in some cases the word parts, are cut apart. The student attempts to put the sentence in proper sequence. If necessary, the student goes back to the text to check or correct herself.

With Chris, L.D. teacher Margie Glaros or I would choose a sentence that had one or more basic sight words that we knew Chris would encounter often in other contexts. We would write the sentence from his illustrated story on a sentence strip that had been cut lengthwise from the photocopy paper. Next, we would cut the sentence apart, word by word. (Later some words might also be cut apart to emphasize a teaching point, such as a consonant digraph or blend, for example, *wh en*, *th ird*, *gr ade*.) Although Chris saw words in isolation, they always went back into the context. Chris was expected to put the sentence back together in sequence and read it aloud as he did so. He would then check himself against the written text. If he had made a mistake, he was expected to self-correct using his book's written model.

Chris kept all sentences from each book (cut apart and held with a paperclip in a large envelope labeled with the book title) so he might practice often on his own.

Referring to other texts the child can read   When a student gets stuck reading or writing a word that has been known in another context, he is guided to go back to a familiar source, read the particular word in context, and then apply it to the new situation. Students get very proficient at locating the unknown word, reading it in the familiar context, and applying it to the new context.

When beginning to write *About the Gerbils*, I asked Chris, "Where have you seen 'About' before?" He was able to find his previously written book, *About My Friend Brian*, and read and write "About" for himself in the new title.

Making a "Words I Can Write" booklet   When it appeared that Chris was reading a high-frequency word without any help, I would ask him to try writing it. If he wrote it correctly, he was able to add it to his "Words I Can Write" booklet. He could eventually read all these words in isolation. If he got stuck, he referred to one of his books for help. He was very proud of his growing list of words and seemed eager to add new words to his booklet (see Figure 14–5).

Teaching some short vowels, or other phonics generalizations, through the child's name or other well-known words   Many children like Chris have a difficult time applying short vowels, particularly "e" and "i," to reading and writing words. When Chris was unsure of what letter to put in the middle of words such as "with" and "get," which came from his stories, he referred back to his name, "Chris Jenesin." With guidance, he could make the correct connection. Eventually, he would do this on his own. (For specifics on teaching phonics, see "Phonics in Perspective," pp. 149–155.)

Sharing the scribing process   For some L.D. students, writing has been so difficult that the teacher needs to sit right next to the child to provide emotional and physical support. An environment in which the child feels valued and safe enough to take a risk must already exist. Even students who have been reluctant to write can usually be persuaded to give it a try if the teacher takes over when the child falters. If a word processor is available, the child is even more willing to get started.

Once Chris knew he could read and write some words, he was willing to risk writing for himself with some support. In his third book, *About the Gerbils*, he was encouraged to write as much of each word as he was able and to use all of the above strategies. For his sentence "Sometimes I get to pick them up," he was able to write all of the letters that are underlined.

Sometimes I get to pick them up.

Figure 14-5   Chris's "Words I Can Write" List

Words I Can Write

Then Them
when
Cars smart far yard
Very
get
with
play. Say day
lab
go

___

we me he be
my by
Dad sad mad bad

___

boYs toYs
Sometimes
fill will pill Rill ill
                    sill
up   hill
                bill
                mill
                Jill
                Lill
            still
            Grill

On a subsequent page, "Sometimes I get to go down to the boy's bathroom to fill up the bottle," he referred back to the above page and was able to write "Sometimes," "get," and "up" in their entirety.

He decided "sometimes" was a word he wanted to have in his "Words I Can Write" booklet. In spite of its length, he mastered the word after looking at it many times, writing it, and referring back to his stories when he got stuck.

Creating Predictable Text from Patterned Language

Little books that repeat a pattern such as "I can . . ." or "This is . . ." can be used as a springboard for writing and reading original stories. Using simple patterned text with matching pictures, Mary Leo's developmentally handicapped students in grades 2–4 did the first reading and writing they had ever done using an "I Can . . ." text as a model. Prior to that time, all skills and sight words had been taught in isolation. (See *Recommended Literature*, "Books Which Invite Readers into Print" for suggested publishers and titles.)

Using Predictable, Well-Written Literature

Special education teachers who formerly used basal texts report a big difference in interest level and motivation, not only by the students but by the teachers themselves, when quality literature is used to teach reading. Both teachers and students were bored with dull materials. At the secondary level, this also means supplementing the literature of the 1970s with more relevant and interesting texts.

Onajé became a reader only when the emphasis of his instruction shifted from structured texts and skills sheets to predictable texts and books at his interest level. Then the pleasure of reading could be combined with skills instruction arising from his on-site needs.

Allowing the student to self-select reading books is especially important. A high school teacher reported her first success with a student who had a keen interest in all aspects of building. She brought in everything she could find on the subject, and all the student's reading and writing emanated from those books.

Creating Predictable Text from Literature

Working in a small group, students can create their own text to use as reading material. Because the language is their own, students are highly motivated to read it. After students have heard or read several poems, stories, or books by an author, they can be encouraged to create their own text in that author's style. The teacher acts as guide and scribe. Because students are already familiar with the characters, settings, and plots in a series, they feel confident developing a sequel or related chapter or story. A group of second-graders enjoyed writing their own *Nate the Great* text, based on the series by Marjorie Sharmat (Putnam, 1977), while a group of sixth-graders created an epilogue to *The Great Gilly Hopkins* by Katherine Paterson. The text can be written on overhead transparencies or large chart paper for group reading or photocopied so each student has a copy to read. Students' original texts may take the form of a conversation between two characters, a scene in a play, a chapter, or a complete story.

Using wordless picture books   Wordless picture books work wonderfully well with elementary and secondary students as a springboard for developing oral language and for creating original stories to read. (See "Wordless Books" in *Recommended Literature* for appealing selections.) Students begin by orally retelling the story through the pictures. The original text can then be written by the teacher or another student. Older students can create text for younger readers. Students can also work in pairs to create original wordless books, with one student creating the pictures and the other writing the text.

Besides wordless books, familiar picture books can also be used, and the existing text can be covered up. The new text becomes a retelling or new version in students' own language. Even in schools where the basal text is the mainstay of the reading program, students can cover up the text of a dull story, rewrite it, and practice reading the new, improved version.

Reading Aloud to the Student and by the Student

Reading aloud *to* the child—for vocabulary development, literature appreciation, exposure to literary-level language and authors' styles, and comprehension—continues to be of utmost importance for attitude, motivation, and just sheer enjoyment.

Reading aloud by the teacher is important even at the secondary level where lack of vocabulary and word meanings interfere with comprehension. Reading aloud helps build needed vocabulary and lets the student hear what fluent reading sounds like. In addition, it is recommended in a test-taking situation where the student is unable to read the test.

Reading aloud *by* the child, in a one-on-one or small-group setting where the child feels safe enough to take a risk, provides the teacher with information on the strategies the child is using or not using. The teacher can then guide the child to employ various strategies that good readers use. At times, the child's reading aloud can be documented with a running record or tape recording.

Relating the known to the unknown Whenever possible, it is advisable to use what the child already knows and apply that knowledge to a new situation. When Chris could not read "them," we went back to "then" in one of his stories. When he could not write "by," we used "my," which he already knew. After he was able to read and write "play," we wrote and read "say," "day," "may," and other words that fit the pattern.

Shared Reading

Shared reading, as described on pages 33–38, is an excellent technique for getting the student engaged in reading. I find using a transparency on the overhead projector invaluable for maintaining attention, focusing eyes on the print, and immersing the student in reading without singling her out. Students get to hear and feel the appropriate phrasing and fluency for poems, songs, raps, or excerpts from a book. The reading is always invitational; students are expected to follow the text with their eyes and join in orally if they choose to do so. While the emphasis is always on enjoyment in a social setting, one or two teaching points—such as calling attention to conventions of print—may be made on subsequent rereadings.

Repeated Reading

Reading a selection over and over again increases fluency and improves word-attack skills, building confidence and enabling the student to focus on comprehension. Working alone, with a partner, or with the aid of a tape recorder, the student chooses a paragraph or excerpt and practices it until he can read it fluently. Students can tape record themselves, evaluate where they need to improve, and then rerecord themselves.

Paired Reading

Paired reading occurs when one reader supports another in the reading of the text. The student has a personal copy of the text and follows along visually as he:

    Hears the text on tape

    Listens to a peer read the text

    Has the support of a peer when needed in reading the text for himself

    Follows the voice of the teacher or reader

Once the student is familiar with the text he can try it again on his own. More important, he can be included in group discussion of the text. Paired reading assumes that a reader will be able to understand the text even if he is unable to read it all independently.

Having books available on tape   Many L.D. students who have difficulty reading do quite well understanding text and contributing to oral discussion if they can hear the text and follow along with a tape. Students can then "read" literature that is at their listening comprehension level, even though the text is above their instructional and independent levels. Literature and content area tapes are made by the teacher or parent volunteer or are available free from the local public library through the federally funded "Talking Book" program.

   Paul's mother reported that her son experienced success when his L.D. teacher sent home tapes from chapters in his science and social studies texts. When the key vocabulary and focus of the chapter were discussed prior to reading-listening, Paul was able to answer orally questions about the chapter without difficulty.

Sustained Silent Reading of Self-Selected Text

Sustained silent reading, where the student engages in uninterrupted reading of a book of his choice, is one of the most important strategies for increasing fluency, vocabulary, and overall reading ability. Students need to do lots of reading of easy books for pleasure to become fluent, confident readers. Before students willingly and successfully engage in this activity, they must be able to help themselves— beyond "sounding out"—when encountering an unknown word. They must be integrating all cueing systems—using semantics and syntax along with graphophonics.

Promoting independent silent reading and self-monitoring   Using a line marker, verbalizing the strategies used when in difficulty, jotting down important vocabulary that interfered with understanding the text, and connecting the known to the unknown all helped Onajé read more independently.

   In reading *My Robot Buddy* by Alfred Slote, Onajé had difficulty with the sentence "I couldn't really believe they'd hear me, but suddenly the air cruiser started its descent onto the road" (p. 58). He could not read and did not know the exact meanings of "cruiser" and "descent." Thinking while reading, he was able to substitute "vehicle" for "cruiser" and "landing" for "descent." Because he had jotted down both those words, we worked on them grapho-phonically and for meaning. For "cruiser" I wrote the word "bruise," which was in his vocabulary, and related it to "cruise." We talked about what kind of vehicle an air cruiser could be. For "descent" he could read "de," but could not apply "sc." I wrote down "sc-ience," "scene," and "scent," which he could read, and had him apply what he already knew to "descent." We used "ascend" and "descend" together, and I graphically demonstrated the opposite meanings by moving my body and my arms.

Providing books at Onajé's interest and reading level helped him begin to read on his own. Setting realistic expectations with him and his mother contributed to his success.

Promoting reading comprehension   Some L.D. and classroom teachers note that many at-risk learners have difficulty grasping the major points of a story once they move into longer books where most of the reading is done independently. These children need to understand why we read. They also need to be carefully monitored and held accountable for what they have read. I have found that assigning only a few pages of silent reading at a time works well. In severe cases, silently reading and monitoring one paragraph at a time may be necessary until the student begins to self-monitor and think about what he is reading.

I was recently asked to work with Robert, a third-grader, who could read the words in a grade-level book but could not say what he had read beyond giving some unrelated details. When I asked him, "Why do we read?" he replied, "to know the words." Because he viewed reading only as reading the words, he did not stop when something didn't make sense, and he never went back to reread or refocus.

I asked Robert to read a passage orally (pp. 15–16) from *Mr. Popper's Penguins* by Richard and Florence Atwater (Little, Brown, 1938), a book he had never seen before. Before he began reading, I gave him some general background information about what he was about to read, and then I took a running record of his reading. Although he read with 92 percent accuracy, indicating the book was at his instructional level, when I asked him to tell me what he had just read (what Mr. Popper wanted to do and why), he gave me misinformation. I sent him back to the text to reread. When he again gave me inaccurate information, I sent him back to the specific paragraph and asked, "Where does it say that? Find the line that says that, and read it to me." He finally replied, "It doesn't say that anywhere." I asked him, "What does it say? Now put that into your own words." With prodding, and my insisting he reread, think about his reading, and stop every time something didn't make sense or sound right, Robert could eventually come up with an intelligent response.

By continuing to ask Robert very specific questions that focused on main ideas, by verbally modeling thinking processes aloud, and by guiding him to reread a small chunk of text silently and do a retelling, Robert gradually improved in overall comprehension. Although he had been expected to be reading a chapter book as part of his independent, nightly reading, he had never received guided instruction in understanding what he was reading silently. He was now asked to slow down and read only several pages a night. He knew his teacher would be asking him to do a retelling, and that if he could not do it, he would be asked to reread. He was also asked to verify his oral responses. He would be asked, "How do you know that? Where in the text does it say that?" By being held accountable on a daily basis, by talking through specific passages with his teacher, and by being shown where he needed to reread, Robert gradually improved his comprehension abilities.

Emphasizing Silent Reading as Part of Instructional Time

Typically, most of the reading instruction time for remedial students is spent in oral reading and practice exercises. Even when L.D. and remedial learners use real literature, the tendency is to have students read aloud. Since most of the reading students will do in school is silent reading—and since silent reading is how reading is used in the world outside school—students need to be guided in the transition from oral to silent reading. As teachers, we tend to feel slightly uncomfortable allowing silent reading during "teaching" time, but it is necessary if students are to become successful, independent readers. When students find that they can begin to monitor their own reading and work out trouble spots on their own, their reading confidence, along with the amount of time they spend reading silently, increases.

I was asked to work with a group of third grade L.D. students reading *The Mouse and the Motorcycle* by Beverly Cleary (Morrow, 1965). Up to this time, their reading in the L.D. class had been done mostly round-robin style, with each child taking a turn reading orally. At the same time that I asked them to read several pages silently, I asked them to "write down any words you can't read or don't know the meaning of." Then we took the words they had trouble with and worked them through together. Mostly, they worked them through after I asked them, "What could you try that might help you?" As they worked through their difficult words, I kept asking, "What can you do?" and then, "What did you do to work that out? What could that word mean? Reread that paragraph, and see if you can figure it out." Margie Glaros, the L.D. teacher, and I had already spent a lot of time putting the responsibility for learning on them and emphasizing meaningful language strategies.

Donald had written down the word "automatically" from the sentence "He did not even have to think what to do—he automatically grabbed for the motorcycle and held on with all his strength" (pp. 82–83). When he went back to work it out, he skipped it and got the meaning through the context by predicting what the word could mean. He substituted "quickly." Because what he put in made sense, it was not significant that he could not read the exact word.

Below is the chart that came out of several short sessions and stayed posted in the L.D. classroom for referral. It is shown exactly as the students wrote it.

What to Do When You Can't Read a Word

1. Look at that word again—ending, middle, beginning.
2. Read on, and then come back to the hard word and try again.
3. Stretch out the letters; take the word apart.
4. Think about what would make sense.
5. Think about what would sound right.

6. Substitute a word that makes sense.
7. See if it looks like a word you've seen before.
8. Put word parts together (re lief).
9. Skip the word and go on.

It is very valuable to take the time to get students to verbalize what works for them. The list you and your students come up with will be worded differently but will be even more valid because it will come from your students. If the strategies they come up with are limited, the teacher needs to guide them and demonstrate meaningful alternatives.

When, after several silent reading sessions of short passages, it became clear these students were reading for meaning and using the above strategies, I asked them to read an entire chapter in *The Mouse and the Motorcycle* silently (pp. 79–85). Before they started reading, I explained that we would begin to use a reading log. (See "Literature Response Logs," pp. 103–122, for a complete explanation of the reading log.) The students were asked to answer the following question: "What's the most important thing that happened in this chapter?" They were told they needed to write only one sentence. To help focus their attention, I sat with them and read the chapter silently at the same time. Damon wrote, "Ralph got caught in a vacuum cleaner but he chewed himself out." It was clear from each of their individual responses that they had gleaned the main ideas of the chapter.

After the students had moved almost totally into silent reading during their instructional reading time in the L.D. class, I asked them, "How do you feel about reading silently versus reading out loud?" These were their responses:

"You can go faster."

"I like reading in my mind."

"You don't have to express yourself, or change the tone of your voice."

"I like it 'cause if I don't know a word, I can ask someone who is also reading silently."

"If I don't know a word, I can figure it out myself without anyone helping me."

Self-Selected Writing

For many L.D. children, their own writing—in language that is predictable and familiar to them—leads to their first successful reading. Teaching needs become apparent from a close look at the child's self-selected, frequent writing. Journal writing, as described in Chapter 9, is a powerful vehicle for evaluating the child's phonics, spelling, use of syntax, and ideas. Writing as a response to reading also indicates the thought processing and connections the child is making.

Using Post-its or a copy of an original piece of writing   Students are sensitive to "marks" made by the teacher on their writing. Leaving the original writing intact sends a message of respect and value to the student. I find students more receptive to working out problem areas when the "marks" are made on a copy. Instead of a reproduced copy of the original, some teachers write on Post-its and place them strategically on the original writing to draw attention to particular strengths and concerns.

Using self-selected writing to teach spelling   Onajé's L.D. tutor, Ellen Potter, used his personal writing to teach phonics and spelling. For example, in the piece in Figure 14–4, she took "thair" and "stithes" as an opportunity to teach "ch." They kept a chart of "ch" words as they came across them, and several weeks later we noted the correct usage of "ch" in Onajé's journal writing.

Many L.D. students are able to find their own misspelled words from journal entries or other writing and use the Have-a-Go sheet (see Appendix I) effectively. Ellen often used a Have-a-Go sheet to help Onajé work out his misspellings. First he would find and circle those words that "looked" wrong. Then he would work them out with help from his tutor, a spelling dictionary, and other resources available.

Typing or word-processing the student's writing   Students are more willing to make revisions and corrections when the text is clean and easily readable and spaces are left between lines. In addition, a typed copy sends a message to the student that the writing is appreciated.

Valuing Oral Responses

When Paul had to respond to a test by writing, he stated, "I know the information but it doesn't come out right."

Some L.D. students can really shine when they are encouraged to contribute their thoughts orally. Students need to know that verbal responses are just as valid and valued as written responses. A student who is unable to read and write sufficiently well to complete a test should be given the test orally. When the spelling and handwriting are poor, the student should be allowed to dictate to the teacher or volunteer. In addition, some students find when they can tape their original story or responses and go back to the tape at their leisure, they can write adequate responses.

Using a tape recorder in the content areas   Older students who cannot copy well from the board or take notes quickly or in an organized fashion benefit from taping the discussion in the content areas. On their own, or with assistance, they can work at their own pace to write down necessary information.

Using a tape recorder for a final copy   Some teachers allow students to put their final copy of a story on tape, so that writing and editing are not required.

Writing Aloud

Writing aloud is an excellent, nonthreatening way for students to observe frequently the conventions of writing. Seeing words formed, spaced, spelled, and used in context with correct capitalization and punctuation eventually imprints on the students. The teacher can incorporate and highlight conventions and words that students need or are struggling to learn.

Shared Writing

Shared writing is appropriate and desirable even at the high school level. The teacher, in collaboration with the students, guides the students in the composition of a common interest and demonstrates the process of writing. While the chalk-board may be used, Magic Marker on large chart paper or a transparency on the overhead projector is even more attention getting.

Sustained Silent Writing for Teachers and Students

Typically, because writing is an area of difficulty for L.D. students, much encouragement is needed. Margie Glaros and I have found students will make a much greater effort and maintain attention longer when teacher and students write simultaneously in a shared setting.

Valuing time for talk and sharing before writing   Margie and I asked a group of five third grade L.D. students to write about their relationship with a sibling or other family member. Our purpose was to get these students, who normally wrote very little and who stopped writing after just a few minutes, to write for a sustained period. We began by sitting around a table with the students. Margie and I each spoke in detail about our relationship with one of our siblings. We then encouraged the students to verbalize their thoughts about a sister, brother, or family member—what they liked about them, what drove them crazy, special interests shared. If they got stuck talking, we asked questions to help stimulate thinking. We allowed about fifteen to twenty minutes just for talking. The students later told us that talking over what they might write about made the writing "easy." Not only did their talking to the group help clarify what they already knew and could write about but listening to their peers triggered memories and generated fresh ideas for their own writing. Later, they were also eager to share orally their completed stories with each other.

Writing while students are writing   When Margie and I wrote with the students, we found that they were less distracted and more willing to invest in their writing. They saw each of us look up as we stopped to think and put out heads down and be seriously quiet as we engaged in the writing. When a student looked up as though she was finished, even though everyone else was still writing, we reminded the student—based on her oral sharing—that she probably had more she could write. Eventually, the student went back to adding to her piece. The students later acknowledged feeling pleased with and surprised by the quantity of their writing. We teachers were surprised that each student was able to stay with the writing for about twenty minutes

Demonstrating   Once the students were convinced they could write a substantial amount on a topic they knew about, we moved into refining the writing. We asked them to choose one small part of their sibling story and try to develop it in some depth. First Margie and I talked about what parts of our stories we would pick. I told them I was going to expand on one line in my story: "When my sister Adrienne and I were little, we used to fight all the time except when we built cities together in our bedroom." Then I went on to explain in detail how we moved our furniture, spread blankets and bedspreads across desks and beds, fortified our "city" with comic books, games, and snacks, and played happily secluded "under wraps" until our parents insisted we clean up. Margie told about an incident in a restaurant as an example of how her brothers always teased her. Then each of the students, with guidance when necessary, talked about a part that could be expanded into its own story. We then wrote quietly together for about thirty minutes. Again, seeing teachers writing was a powerful inducement for students to write.

Conferencing with Peers

We have found students are more willing to make revisions if feedback is given in a group setting. Working with a group of L.D. students in the middle grades, Margie and I noted that when we demonstrated positive comments and questions to each other about our writing, students were eager to participate and were very willing and able to provide appropriate feedback to each other.

In one situation, we gave the students a choice. Did they want to put the piece away, revise it, or edit it? We were surprised that even though they didn't want to do revisions, they opted to edit their pieces so they could be published. Because the choice was theirs, they were willing to make the required effort.

Since we wanted most of the responsibility to rest with the students, we first spent time making a chart of what to look for while editing. We wrote the chart using their responses in their own language. To our surprise, the students knew what needed to be done in the editing process. After going over their chart, they began by circling all misspelled words, and with guidance and encouragement, they went on to self-edit their pieces with a greater effort and involvement than usual.

Perspectives on Teaching for Strategies

Learning disability teachers who move toward more holistic models do not give up skills teaching. They come to believe that comprehension and meaning must be part of all teaching-learning situations. As such, they incorporate the skills teaching they have always done in meaningful contexts so that students use the skills strategically. Students no longer *practice* skills through exercises and drill. With guidance, they learn how and when to apply skills strategically as they *use* them in authentic contexts.

For example, a traditional, multisensory approach that includes seeing, sounding, tracing, and writing might well be employed, but not with the belief that isolated, decoding skills in a prescribed hierarchy is necessary *before* the child can read or write a story. The structured letter and word study would be related to, and part of, the authentic reading and writing experience. A child needing work in a particular phonics skill would work on the deficit areas in the context of reading real stories and/or writing for real purposes.

Finally, if learning disability students are to become learning ability students, they must receive large doses of meaningful instruction that facilitates their understanding of language. Teaching for strategies, where students learn how and when to apply skills in a thoughtful manner, must become the major instructional approach. Their language arts experiences—in and out of the classroom—must be purposefully integrated and include reading all types of literature as well as writing on a variety of relevant topics. The definitions and expectations of literacy we hold for regular students must also apply to at-risk students.

Evaluation and the L.D. Student

I feel strongly that evaluation techniques for L.D. and other special education students should be the same as they are for all students. (See Chap. 13, "Evaluation.") In this section, I highlight some concerns about present methods of evaluation as well as discuss several holistic evaluation techniques that are particularly useful for L.D. students.

The Multifactored Assessment

For more than fifteen years, I attended before-school weekly meetings as a member of the special services team in my elementary building. Our primary function was to assess the needs of students recommended for special services and to determine whether or not the students qualified for such services. More often than not the student was being assessed for a possible learning disability in one or more areas. And more often than not the student's deficits, based primarily on standardized test scores, were the focus of discussion.

To be eligible for special support services from the L.D. teacher or tutor, a student must demonstrate significant discrepancies between cognitive ability and academic achievement. Prior to beginning a multifactored assessment, a recommendation—usually by the classroom teacher—is formally written stating the reasons for referral as well as the instructional methods and services that have been employed. Then, with signed permission from the child's parent, the school psychologist, classroom teacher, L.D. teacher, speech pathologist, and other members of the special services staff take a careful look at the whole child.

I am pleased to note that special services teams in our district are currently making concerted efforts to look at the child more holistically. They are noting strengths as well as weaknesses and are attempting to obtain a profile of the child that goes beyond standardized test scores. In addition to various standardized tests and assessment instruments (including an individually administered cognitive assessment), informal measures of evaluation and teacher observations are becoming more highly valued as equally important parts of the assessment. Eventually, as more holistic assessment becomes the norm, fewer students should end up diagnosed as learning disabled.

Even so, because of unfavorable classroom practices and the types of standardized tests presently being used, a child with adequate learning abilities may wind up being referred to the special services team. For the child who does not do well with part-to-whole learning and exercises and subtests in isolation, a "learning disability" may show up unnecessarily. In some instances, where the classroom teacher is teaching reading primarily through phonics, a child that could probably learn to read with a holistic, multisensory approach might be labeled L.D. prematurely. In one case, a first grade teacher stated that a particular student would *never* make the transfer to content-reading materials in the middle grades. This prediction was based on the student's difficulty with phonics in isolation and recall of isolated sight words. The student in question is presently functioning well above average in the fourth grade and has been phased out of L.D. after several years of immersion in reading real literature and dealing with phonics and meaning-based strategies in the context of reading.

Further distortions of a student's abilities are common when the diagnostic instruments used to assess the student only measure skills in isolation. Paul, who is discussed at the beginning of this chapter, did extremely poorly on the *Woodcock Reading Mastery Tests—Revised* (American Guidance Service, Inc., 1987). His severely depressed total reading score was a combination of his performance on five separate subtests: letter identification, word indentification, word attack, word comprehension, and passage comprehension. Taking isolated tests and combining them to get a reading ability score is common practice but is of questionable value because the assessed tasks do not constitute meaningful reading. The results cannot be used diagnostically, and they give no realistic picture of what the child *can* do.

Furthermore, when parents are given the information that their child is weak in a subtest such as word-attack skills and they are not given the total picture, the parents often intepret that to mean that the child needs work on word-attack skills in isolation. The parent comes to view reading in segments rather than as a process of constructing meanings.

Taking a Close Look at a Diagnostic Reading Test

Looking closely at the *Woodcock Reading Mastery Tests—Revised*, one sees that this test—and many similar diagnostic reading tests—is of limited use for evaluation purposes. The tasks students are expected to perform do not occur in meaning-based classrooms. The word identification test involves naming words presented in list format. Yet the only time students are expected to read words in list format is on such a reading test.

The word-attack test requires the student to read nonsense, phonetically regular syllables (such as "ift" and "vunhip"). It is significant that the Examiner's Manual states:

> Nonsense words have been chosen as the main stimuli for this test because the task faced by a subject encountering a nonsense word closely simulates the real-life task of a person encountering an unknown—though real—word. A correct response to a real word would not provide evidence that a subject has applied word attack skills to that word, only that he or she has identified it (p. 6).

This is nonsense! The creators of the test are telling us that being able to sound out a word is the most valid way to approach unknown words. Indeed, a full page word-attack error inventory has the examiner target every error by sound and syllable.

Low scores on these two subtests indicate students' difficulty with nonsense syllables and words in isolation. Conversely, high scores indicate a child's facility with nonsense syllables and words in isolation. Such overemphasis on one cueing system—grapho-phonics—reflects a traditional view of reading that does not include important research on how good readers process print. High scores on these tests have nothing to do with real reading and the integrated strategies that good readers use in processing print in meaningful context.

The subtests that purport to measure comprehension are also in question. The word comprehension test consists of three subtests—antonyms, synonyms, and analogies. The Examiner's Manual indicates that these subtests provide "another measure of the subject's comprehension of reading vocabulary" (p. 7). Such tests may well measure a student's ability to read a word in isolation and respond with a synonym or antonym, or to complete a word-pair analogy, but I fail to see how such tests correspond to comprehending meaningful texts. Regarding the analogies task, the manual suggests that the word comprehension task closely resembles "real-life reading." But a format such as

mechanic–vehicle   dentist–

is not real-life reading.

The final subtest on the *Woodcock Reading Mastery Tests—Revised* is the passage comprehension test. It consists of multiple items of one or two sentences with one word missing. The student is expected to fill in a blank space in this context-in-isolation exercise. Certainly such an exercise cannot be considered genuine reading. In the meaning-based classroom, we would never expect a child to read one unrelated two-sentence passage followed by as many as eighty similar sentence passages and call it reading. Yet the manual states: "a correct response demonstrates that the subject has comprehended the entire passage" (p. 8).

I do not have a problem with using such a diagnostic reading test *as long as* real reading is also being assessed. Test reading, with its bits and pieces of unrelated words out of meaningful context, is only test reading. The student encounters such exercises *only* in taking the test. Real reading is what the student does every day, so most of the reading assessment must come from authentic, continuous, meaningful text. Within that text, we need to be looking at how the student samples, predicts, confirms, and self-corrects while in the process of reading.

This kind of assessment is especially important to use with L.D. students, who characteristically do not do well with phonics and isolated skills. Keeping in mind that phonics is a low-level strategy and that poor readers go to phonics while good readers rely on meaning, assessment must become more meaning based. As educators, we must begin to press for more balanced and meaningful assessment; the sum of the testing parts do not make a whole. At the same time, we must also educate parents about what meaningful reading involves and put decoding skills into proper perspective.

The thoughtful and thorough examiner needs to note the strategies—not just the skills in isolation—the reader is using or not using. What else, if anything, does the student use besides phonics when he gets into difficulty? One way to note the strategies the reader uses is to take a running record of the child's oral reading. (See *An Observation Survey of Early Literacy Achievement* by Marie Clay [Heinemann, 1993a] for directions on taking a running record.) Taking a running record from meaningful text, where the child has the opportunity to use picture cues with the written context and syntax—as well as grapho-phonic cues—can yield very different results than a standardized test. By noting the strategies the reader is using or not using, the teacher can establish meaningful and realistic teaching goals.

Using the Running Record Diagnostically: Dennis

Dennis was a third-grader who was in a pull-out L.D. classroom for daily reading instruction. Because he was experiencing great difficulty reading in the classroom, his teacher asked me to take a running record of his oral reading.

> I showed Dennis several books and asked him which one he thought "looked about right" to him. He chose *Stone Fox* by John Gardiner, a core book in our third grade literature collection. I asked him to stop reading

after it had become apparent the book was far too difficult for him. He could only read a few small words in the first several sentences.

"Let's try *Nate the Great* by Marjorie Sharmat" (Putnam, 1977), I told him. "This book is about a boy detective who solves cases. Start reading here, and see if you can find out what Nate the Great is up to now." Before Dennis started to read, I asked him how this book "looked," and he said it looked easy. As Dennis read, he relied totally on "sounding out" words. He read the entire passage at a consistent pace and did not stop when he made an error.

This book, which he said was "easy," turned out to be at his frustration level, indicating not only his poor reading skills but his inaccurate perception about his reading abilities. In examining his running record of 192 words, I saw that Dennis had made fifty errors, or miscues, giving him an accuracy level of about 75 percent. His self-correction rate was severely low, with one self-correction for every twenty-five errors.

When I asked him to tell me what the passage was about, I was amazed Dennis could tell me anything coherent about what he'd read. I complimented him on his good comprehension despite his excessive word-attack difficulties and said that it indicated he was smart. I talked honestly to him about how difficult the passage really was for him and about his over-reliance on phonics. I suggested that he slow down, reread for meaning, and think about what makes sense when reading—all strategies that good readers use. The tears he was trying to hold back indicated he was upset by what I had told him. I then showed Dennis how, if he thought about what he was reading at all times, he would be able to figure out most of the words. As an example, he had started (his errors are in italics):

> I am a detective
> I *know*/work *all*/alone.
> Let me tell you about my last case:
> I had just *ate*/eaten breakfast.
> It was a good breakfast. *Pan*/*pick*/*pack*/pancakes, *jus*/juice, *p. . .*/pancakes, *make me*/milk,

His error "ate" for "eaten" did not affect the meaning so I chose to ignore it at this time. I asked Dennis, "What had Nate just done?" He replied, "ate breakfast." I continued, "So what was in that good breakfast? Try this line again." With that guidance, he read the entire line correctly. I praised him and said, "That's what good readers do. They think about what they're reading, and when something doesn't make sense they slow down, go back to the beginning, and try again. You did that. Good for you."

Because I wanted Dennis to begin to see himself as a reader who could read for meaning, I told him I would be back the following week so he could try the same passage again. On the re-evaluation of the same passage the next week, his accuracy level was 93 percent and he had one self-correction for every three errors. We were both pleased with his greatly improved performance.

Because it is important for a child to verbalize what he is doing well so he is conscious of his actions and will repeat them, I asked him, "When you have trouble reading a word now, what else will you do besides sound it out?" He was able to tell me three good strategies:

> If it doesn't make sense, go back and look at it again.
>
> Look at the picture.
>
> Skip over it, and then come back to it, and see what makes sense.

I told Dennis, "There's one more thing you can do. Put in a word that will make sense when you can't figure it out."

When I shared his running records with his L.D. teacher, she said that she had been trying to teach Dennis meaning strategies but that his mother insisted on his "sounding out" every word at home. Nonetheless, several weeks later, Dennis' classroom teacher reported that he had shown increased confidence and interest during free reading time. Dennis was voluntarily reading many of the books in the *Nate the Great* series.

Perspectives

Assessment practices nation-wide continue to focus far too much on students' deficits. In addition, traditional attitudes and practices that overvalue standardized testing results still prevail. While the research and philosophy of how children learn to read and write has evolved and changed, the old assessment paradigm is still firmly in place. Part of the problem is that meaningful standardized tests are not yet readily available. Also, teacher education at both the undergraduate and graduate levels often does not include training in more holistic, informal evaluation measures. Learning how to take anecdotal records, running records, or do miscue analysis is not commonly taught in many universities. Learning how to administer a norm-referenced test is taught as standard procedure. Teachers, psychologists, parents, and administrators must become active in the movement to make assessment procedures and Individual Education Plans (IEP's) consistent with current research and views of the language processes.

In evaluating L.D. students—and all students—we need to get a fair and accurate picture of how the student functions over time. We need to employ and develop assessment and Individual Education Plans that rely not just on standardized tests given on one day but on the student's continuing learning processes. Running records, anecdotal records, oral tapes, journals, writing samples, reading records, retellings, student self-evaluations, and teacher and parent observations need to carry greater weight.

Whatever evaluation techniques we use, they must utilize the whole—the whole functioning student, the whole context, and whole literacy acts. If we continue to focus on the parts in teaching and evaluation, we will continue to identify and maintain a large population of learning disabled students.

The Pull-Out Program

Most students identified as learning disabled in the United States receive daily instruction in reading and language arts from a specially certified teacher. In almost all cases the L.D. teacher works outside the regular classroom in a resource room pull-out setting. Pull-out instruction is also the norm for Chapter 1 and other remedial programs across the country. While in some situations the pull-out program is advisable, too often it is used as a place for children who do not quite fit into the classroom setting and who require attention and instruction the classroom teacher feels unable to provide. More important, the majority of the children that are pulled-out remain in the special education program most of their school careers.

For the truly learning disabled children, estimated to represent not more than 2–3 percent of the population (two to three times less than the actual identified population), a separate setting for part of the day may be advisable. Thus, specific, specialized instruction may be provided for children who are not only unable to function in the classroom but who may feel "different" because they cannot do classroom work. Many L.D. teachers believe that some students must have a highly structured, multisensory approach in a setting with few distractions. Basically, if a student is way behind classmates or feeling too frustrated to confront regular classroom work, a "replacement" program that is offered in another setting may be necessary. Also, in fairness to the classroom teacher (who is already expected to be an expert in reading, math, computers, cooperative learning, current events, social studies, science, health, behavior, and so on), expecting proficiency in yet another highly specialized field may be unrealistic and even unfair.

A pull-out setting may also allow many moments of glory for a child who has few opportunities to shine in the regular classroom. Additionally, some L.D. teachers provide a safe, nurturing environment that may not, unfortunately, be available in the regular classroom. The resource room may be the only place in which the student feels completely comfortable and understood.

Paul's mother told me she preferred having Paul pulled out for reading instruction, but not because she believed he would be served better academically. She stated that Paul is very sensitive about his reading, and she worried about his being teased and feeling embarrassed among his peers. In the resource room, he did not feel uncomfortable about reading an easy book, and he did not have to read aloud in front of his peers.

I do not object to the pull out when it is a highly specialized, interim situation. In my four years as a Reading Recovery teacher working with first-graders, I was completely comfortable with the pull out. These children needed the quiet, intensive, one-to-one setting with very specific teaching techniques. However, once the children were "recovered" after twelve to twenty weeks of instruction, they went back into—and remained in—the regular classroom. The pull out was a stopgap measure, employed just long enough to give the student the skills and confidence necessary to function in the regular classroom. It was not a school lifetime placement, as often becomes the case for L.D. and Chapter 1 students.

The pull-out model is also desirable if the child is receiving skills-based instruction in the classroom but in the resource room setting is meeting success with a more holistic, meaningful model of instruction. In some cases, the L.D. teacher, or supportive services teacher, can share what's working and influence the classroom teacher to make some meaningful changes. In some school districts, the Chapter 1 teachers or reading specialists have initiated the movement toward more meaning-based, whole language teaching. (For a successful model, see Walmsley and Walp, 1990, in "Resources" at the end of this chapter.)

The pull-out program seems to be most successful when the classroom and supportive services teachers work cooperatively and are in agreement in terms of philosophy and methodology. The programs complement each other, with the child receiving similar messages and techniques from both teachers. For example, a child is pulled out during writing workshop time and works on writing while classmates are writing. Unfortunately for the student, this is not the usual case. Too often the pull-out and classroom programs are totally different, so that the child is sent confusing and conflicting messages. These different programs coexist in spite of the fact that regular education initiatives in special education and recent Chapter 1 guidelines point to greater coordination.

For some students, being pulled out of the regular classroom is a greater drawback than it is a support. Mark, who had been identified as learning disabled in third grade and who had been leaving the classroom to work with a tutor daily, rebelled against such treatment after one year. "I never liked it because I missed what was going on in class," he said. "I felt I was always behind. I felt pressure. When you go to the tutor, it makes you feel singled out—like you're not part of the whole class. And it's sort of embarrassing."

Onajé (discussed early in this chapter) also felt embarrassed about leaving the classroom but was never able to express his feelings until his mother observed him one morning in the pull-out setting. She observed that Onajé kept his head lowered and never smiled throughout the lesson. She was surprised when the tutor said this was how he presented himself each day. When she spoke to Onajé that evening about the need to have a good learning attitude, he said he felt ashamed about being pulled out.

Neither Onajé's classroom teacher, nor his L.D. tutor, nor I was aware of his very sensitive feelings until his mother shared them. We then took several steps to partially alleviate his feelings of embarrassment. Onajé's classroom teacher moved his desk from the back of the room to the front, so that when he left and re-entered the room he was less conspicuous. And when possible—for example, when the class was working on writing—his L.D. teacher tried to come into the classroom and give assistance in that setting. As a result of those changes, Onajé began coming to his tutoring sessions more frequently on his own and on time. Previously, his tutor had been having to call for him daily.

Onajé and Mark felt embarrassed about being pulled out in spite of the fact that they were leaving meaning-based classrooms. Their teachers did not expect them to make up work when they returned. For students who are expected to complete the worksheets they missed while they were "down the hall," feelings move beyond embarrassment to resentment.

Then, too, even spending time with a specially trained teacher does not ensure that students will receive more or better instruction. A recent study documents that L.D. students who are being served in a special education program receive more seatwork than active teaching. The L.D. teacher, it said, spends most of the time monitoring progress, checking responses, and recording performances (Richard Allington and Anne McGill-Franzen, "School Response to Reading Failure: Chapter 1 and Special Education Students in Grades Two, Four, and Eight," *The Elementary School Journal*, May 1989, pp. 529–542). If this study is representative of what occurs in L.D. classes, the fact that the L.D. population continues to increase should come as no surprise.

Additionally, much instructional time is lost while the student is in transit—when the student goes "down the hall." The student spends at least fifteen—more realistically thirty—minutes a day in such tasks as packing up, leaving the classroom, walking down the hall, getting settled in the Resource Room, getting ready to read, focusing, exiting the Resource Room, traveling back and re-entering the classroom, refocusing, and figuring out what's going on. That means that instruction in the pull-out program actually has to be accelerated and more efficient to make up for loss of instructional time. In reality, this is rarely the case, contributing to keeping students in special education programs (Richard Allington, "The Redesign of Remedial and Special Education Interventions," presentation at the national Reading Recovery Conference, Columbus, Ohio, February 1990).

The content of instruction for L.D. students is also in question. As I have worked and talked with many teachers around the country, I have found that in teaching L.D. students to read, phonics continues to be the major strategy being taught. Since phonics is a major weakness for most of these students, overemphasis on decoding and skills in isolation practically ensures a student's continued disability. On the surface, it would seem logical that if phonics is the problem for these students, then phonics instruction should be the solution. What happens in many L.D. programs, however, is that phonics instruction occurs as an isolated activity—unconnected to authentic reading and writing. Students neither see the purpose for what they are doing nor meet much success. Many minority students and second language learners (ESL students) have difficulty hearing and identifying vowel sounds. Struggling with daily phonics exercises only heightens their already existing feelings of inadequacy. Eventually, most of them learn to pronounce the words, but they take little pleasure or pride in reading. They rarely choose to read, so that their reading continues to be slow and ineffectual. To become a reader, one has to read continuous, meaningful material. Until the teaching of grapho-phonics strategies is integrated with meaning-based strategies—and until reading is viewed as getting meaning from print and not just reading words—many of these students will fail to reach their potential reading levels.

The lack of reading progress for some L.D. students also has to do with the fact that classroom teachers may use the pull-out program as a way of relinquishing responsibility for reading instruction. If the L.D. teacher is the teacher of record in reading, very likely the student will be pulled out during classroom reading time. If the student is unable to read the words of the classroom reading books, the teacher may assume the student cannot be included in a reading group. However, this deprives the student not only of taking part in a high-level discussion he may be capable of joining but also of participating as a member of a group.

Peter was a fifth grade student with a third grade reading level; his L.D. teacher was the teacher of record for reading. Even though his Individual Education Plan recommended that he be included in a classroom reading group, his inclusion was not mandatory because the classroom teacher was not responsible for instructing or evaluating him in reading. Despite the fact that he had an excellent oral vocabulary and strong listening skills, Peter was never included in a classroom literature group. Had he been paired with another reader or given the opportunity to hear the book on tape, Peter would have benefited greatly from being part of a group discussion of such books as *The Great Gilly Hopkins* by Katherine Paterson and *The Sign of the Beaver* by Elizabeth Speare. Peter missed out on the opportunity not only to read these great books but also to share his personal reactions to the reading, to learn from his peers, and to connect good literature to his life. Then, too, his classmates and teacher missed the unique insights Peter would have brought to the group.

Despite growing concerns about the possible ineffectiveness of pull-out programs, there is little current data to support the practice of the L.D. teacher—or any supplemental services teacher—going into the regular classroom. In addition, in most states, the division of special education does not give local school districts funding at high enough levels to make this a feasible option. The funding is far greater when there is a pull-out program, a situation that in itself helps to perpetuate the traditional model. Unfortunately, L.D. service can depend more on funding organizations than on educational theories and children's needs. Still, in spite of the lack of data and funding, school districts need to be exploring alternatives.

School districts need to consider seriously the implementation of holistic, collaborative models where the L.D. or Chapter 1 teacher works in the regular classrooms in cooperation with the regular teacher. The L.D. teacher would, more likely, be seen as a valid instructor and teacher, not just as an adjunct person, as has often been the case in the pull-out model. In one school district, where administrators and teachers are committed to a language-based integrated day, the L.D. teacher goes into the classroom and team teaches with the classroom teacher. At the secondary level, where much of what goes on in the pull-out setting involves help with assignments, the L.D. tutor or supplemental teacher in the classroom could help students better understand classroom teacher expectations as well as background information and organizational skills needed to complete assignments.

We need to examine those L.D. models of school districts that have been successful in moving from skills-based to meaning-based instruction and from a pull-out to an in-class setting. Finally, we need to be open minded about all possibilities and use what works best for kids. We must place remedial and L.D. students in situations that enhance and increase their learning opportunities. In some cases, for the supportive services teacher to pull out students may be desirable. However, I believe that in far more cases, working within the classroom—providing additional, high-quality instruction coordinated and shared with the classroom teacher—may be the more desirable route.

The L.D. Teacher: Changing Attitudes

> I think the biggest thing is to be willing to try whole language, even if it's just with a few kids. I never got the reading results with the basal and skill sheets. The kids read far better now that I use good literature. And once you see how much more the kids enjoy learning, you become convinced.

Teachers in Transition

Vicki Griminger, a well-respected L.D. teacher in grades 5 and 6 in our school district, who also was Paul's L.D. teacher for two years, made the comments above. As Vicki tells it, she started out as a very traditional L.D. teacher eighteen years ago—lots of worksheets, skills in isolation, heavy phonics emphasis. But she always read aloud to her kids.

She credits her transition to more holistic teaching to being at Moreland School and seeing the first grade program (see Routman, 1988) and to reading and discussing professional books and articles with colleagues. Initially a total skeptic, Vicki became a believer after several years. She says:

> I watched what was happening in the first grade. I saw it working, and eventually I got caught up in the excitement of it all. The kids and teachers were having so much fun, and everyone was learning. Gradually, my thinking began to change. I started slowly, with journal writing. Initially I had the most success with first-graders. It was harder to do with my older kids due to the lengthier books they were reading.

For Ellen Potter, an L.D. tutor, the transition to whole language with L.D. students has been difficult but personally rewarding. An L.D. tutor for three years and a classroom teacher before that, Ellen was entrenched in the skills model. She began to change her thinking when she observed Onajé in a teaching situation in which he was viewed as able to read. She started attending weekly language arts support groups where we were discussing the philosophy behind whole language, and she began to take a critical look at her teaching. One day she told me proudly that she had removed all the dittos from the kids' folders. She had filed them; she wasn't ready yet to throw them out.

Ellen comments,

> I used to do every page, every ditto, and every workbook page in the basal reader when I was teaching second grade. I used to feel kids would learn more if we did every page. Also, I felt it was a way for parents to see what we were working on in class so that they could give help at home if it was needed. When I moved into L.D., whatever I could get my hands on that was tangible, I put in the kids' folders. Even now, when I've moved away from all that, I sometimes find myself sliding back into the skills model when someone gives me materials that look new and exciting. However, I'm able to catch myself, and now I'm able to select the activities that will be most appropriate for the lesson I want to teach.

When Ellen moved into L.D., she continued to rely on dittos and story starters, but she was also beginning to look carefully at students' needs. At the same time, she used literature in her reading program right from the start because she believed she needed to support what was going on in the classroom and because our district had made a commitment to teaching reading with literature.

As Ellen began slowly to examine her teaching, read articles, and talk with colleagues, she made changes in both her philosophy and her teaching. A major shift was in how she taught reading. While she had added trade books to her program, she used to write down every word Onajé missed and would constantly interrupt him when he was reading. A list of missed words was regularly sent home for Onajé to master. Even though she knew Onajé was upset by the interruptions and the home drill with his mom, Ellen believed this drill in isolation was necessary. In addition, she wasn't ready to give up any control. She felt she had to be with Onajé every step of the way.

As she observed Onajé in a reading situation in which he was guided to use strategies to figure out words and meanings for himself, as well as encouraged to read silently, Ellen began to question her methods:

> I used to think if a child could read out loud fluently, that meant he was a good reader. Comprehension came later. But, if it didn't sound very fluent, I assumed he was a poor reader. I never realized Onajé could make mistakes and still understand what he reads. Now, even though he's making fewer and fewer mistakes, I find it difficult to give him wait time, allow him to read silently, and trust he will find his errors. I still stop Onajé and tell him the word. I know I need to improve on how to help him, but I am much better at complimenting him now for what he does well, and that has made a big difference.

Ellen has become reflective in her teaching. She continues to seek answers, try out new ideas, meet with colleagues, and trust herself and her students more. Increasingly, she is using more meaning-based materials and strategies and is making every effort to keep language whole.

Margie Glaros has been an L.D. teacher for seven years. She had been an L.D. tutor for five years and a classroom teacher for three years. As a starting L.D. teacher, she was initially skills-based, with lots of structured phonics work and structured reading texts.

For the majority of the kids a skills approach to reading "seemed to work," but for the really severe kids, "no program worked." As for writing, most of Margie's students were not eager to attempt it in any form. Spelling was taught by drilling the weekly classroom lists. While students might show improvement on the weekly tests, there was no transfer. They were memorizing skills but could not apply them.

A particularly hard-to-reach fourth grade student made Margie think about looking for alternatives. She began to use taped books and repetitive readings. Looking back, she notes, "While there was some improvement, there was no real instruction going on. The student was following the text with his eyes while listening to the teacher or a tape. But that wasn't enough. No strategies were being taught." Margie admits to feeling defeated, incompetent, and terribly frustrated.

At about the same time, our district was in the process of making a commitment to more meaning-centered teaching approaches through literature and whole language. A reorganization closed some elementary buildings and moved many teachers to different buildings. Contact with new teachers encouraged Margie to think about trying new approaches. She began attending the weekly language arts support group and began to view herself as an extension of the classroom.

> I tried to start doing things more like the classroom teachers were doing. Having the same philosophy made it easier to communicate with classroom teachers. I feel it helped me be viewed as a colleague, not "just" a special services person. Teachers began to see me as someone who was interested in doing the same things. And it did seem as though the kids could succeed with similar materials and methods. The whole thing just made sense.

Margie began adding literature to her reading program, and by the following year she was teaching all reading through literature. By observing a colleague pattern lessons from the literature and teach the skills in context, she began to try similar lessons herself. "Before that, I'd never had any instruction in teaching strategies."

At the same time, Margie added journal writing to her program and began pulling all the children's spelling words from their writing. (See Chap. 10 on spelling for specifics.) Writing, spelling, and reading became interrelated activities for Margie and the children.

Walking into Margie's L.D. resource room today, one sees students engaged in reading literature and doing all kinds of writing. The room is filled with wonderful books, cozy corners in which to read them, writing materials, tape recorders, a computer, charts made by and with the children, and displays of children's work. Most important, the children are happy and filled with pride at what they are accomplishing.

Margie's move toward more meaningful teaching has been gradual. Interacting with colleagues at weekly support meetings, working cooperatively with classroom teachers in the building, and doing lots of professional reading and thinking about her teaching have all contributed to her professional growth. Margie is still struggling with the teaching of phonics. Some of her students use a structured phonics workbook, but she is also consistently teaching phonics in the context of real reading.

Theo Husband has been a special education teacher in our school district for twelve years. She believes that each child is entitled to the gift of learning and that we as educators must help students find and develop their strengths. She sees whole language as another way of becoming involved with her students.

> Whole language has forced me to examine my beliefs about learning and teaching. It confirms my beliefs that an eclectic approach to education meets the needs of our students. Learning is multimodal! I'm learning with my kids and looking at them to see what their needs are so I can help them reach their full developmental potential. I'm able to be creative in my teaching, and I find myself enjoying using varied resources.

Best of all, Theo finds that her students are also more excited and motivated about what they are learning. She feels that whole language has helped develop a sense of self-esteem in her students and has allowed them to take risks with their learning.

Parents: The Need for Effective Communication

Parents of L.D. children often feel separated from the educational process. One mother told me she signed all the papers so her child could be serviced but never really understood what she signed. She felt too "embarrassed" to ask the necessary questions.

As educators, we need to take the time to make parents feel comfortable and well informed. Too many parents never really comprehend what L.D. means. One parent told me, "After six years in the L.D. program, I'm still not sure what all the terms mean and what L.D. really is."

Bonnie Daniels, Paul's (see beginning of chapter), mother, is a social worker, well accustomed to group meetings and agency procedures. As such, she has never felt insecure or inadequate at meetings with the psychoeducational team at Paul's school. She has freely voiced her opinions and asked hard questions about her son's Individual Education Plan, but she knows she is not typical. She is concerned that inexperienced parents may just listen quietly and assume the professional team has all the answers.

Bonnie suggests a fifteen-minute preconference for parents with the L.D. teacher or psychologist just before the "big" meeting. She comments, "As a social worker, I would never bring a client into a room without first saying, 'This is what to expect. This is what you're going to hear.' It's too threatening for most people to walk into a room full of professional strangers."

Bonnie Daniels also suggests that teachers focus on specific educational progress when talking with parents. For years she had heard what a "wonderful" child Paul was and what a great personality he had. "The attitude seemed to be that because of his great vocabulary and articulation skills, he would suddenly wake up one morning and be reading. It was never explained to me how this was going to happen."

Other parents feel a sense of exasperation with teachers who fail to recognize the child's disability. One parent said, "Because they can't see the handicap, some don't acknowledge it. At times, they see it as the child's fault." This mother saw her child as making strides, for example, when he got three words right on a spelling test when previously he had never spelled even one word correctly. The parent's praise was not echoed by the teacher. "My son is not getting enough positive feedback for what he's doing well," she said.

Parents really appreciate it when they find their child's efforts are acknowledged by the classroom teacher. One parent told me that out of six teachers her child had had, only one had been sensitive to her child and made him feel good about himself. Among other things, on written tests that teacher had graded the child only on the content of his answers, not on his spelling or handwriting. The teacher had also taken the time to give the child extra help after school.

It is not only teachers who need to send positive messages to students; parents too need to be sensitive about giving criticism. Paul Daniels and his mother related a situation that illustrates this point. Paul had brought home a writing paper, and because his mom immediately commented on his poor spelling (after Paul had been humiliated by a substitute teacher in front of the class for the same thing), he never heard her say the content was excellent. He was mad for days, and his mother had no idea how upset her son was until he finally told her.

Robin Grimes, Onajé's (pp. 386–390) mother, admits to having put a lot of pressure on her son.

> If the teacher sent work home, I felt he *had* to get it. When I looked at his papers, I only saw the errors. Onajé was afraid to make a mistake with all the pressure I was putting on him. Working together, we both ended up in tears. I was feeling very stressed out. Watching you focusing on the positive really turned things around for me. I realized he needed support and that I had to compliment him for doing his best. I'm still involved, but now I try to focus on what Onajé's doing right. That has made all the difference.

Finally, Paul Daniels gives this advice to parents: "Be more positive. Put yourselves in your child's shoes. Encourage them. Congratulate them on what they do well. Listen to your kids 'cause sometimes they have a lot to say." It's good advice for teachers too.

Reflections

Looking closely at Paul, Chris, and Onajé—*all considered by their L.D. teachers to be as severely disabled as any students they had* ever *worked with*—one sees that literacy is possible when the expectations for success are constantly present, when the focus of instruction stems from the student's strengths, when the skills are taught strategically in the context of the learning situation, and when the student is provided additional time and quality education by knowledgeable practitioners.

It is not enough to care about the students, have a trusting relationship, and hope that years of skills instruction will finally take hold. Teachers, parents, administrators, and students must first believe that L.D. students can and will learn. All must work together to find what the student can do and build on those strengths, no matter how small they initially seem to be.

Each student, regardless of age, must be taken at his readiness and interest level, whatever that happens to be. The learning program must then be designed for the child; the child cannot be fitted into a commercial program. And as much as possible, instruction needs to be holistic and strategically based, with educational needs determined cooperatively by the learner, teacher, and parent—in the context of an authentic, reading-writing situation.

In addition, even though difficult to achieve, efforts between regular and remedial programs must be better coordinated in curriculum design and implementation. Administrators need to exert their leadership and take strong initiatives in their local school districts so cooperative and congruent programming between regular and special education programs becomes the norm instead of the exception.

For all of us, the impossible task seems possible only when we begin to believe we *can* do it and appropriate guidance and support are available.

Resources

For more information on holistic approaches to working with at-risk and learning disabled students see the following books and articles.

Allen, JoBeth, Barbara Michalove, and Betty Shockley. 1993. *Engaging Children: Community and Chaos in the Lives of Young Literacy Learners.* Portsmouth, NH: Heinemann. See annotation, p. 2b.

Bartoli, Jill, and Morton Botel. 1988. *Reading/Learning Disability: An Ecological Approach.* New York: Teachers College Press.

The authors propose understanding learners' behaviors through broad social contexts that include the classroom, school, and community. Specific suggestions to support this "ecological model" include an integrated language approach to reading and writing across the curriculum. A substantial portion of this scholarly text (272 pp.) is devoted to strategies for teaching that include specific case studies and lesson plans. Important reading for educators and policy makers ready to question and change traditional understandings of learning disabilities.

Carbo, Marie. November 1987. "Deprogramming Reading Failure: Giving Unequal Learners an Equal Chance," *Phi Delta Kappan,* pp. 197–201.

The author discusses the importance of matching reading instruction with students' learning styles and notes that poor readers have been most successful with teaching that has accommodated their global, tactile, and kinesthetic strengths. Teachers will find the specific recommendations and activities, based on research findings, applicable for increasing students' chances for reading success.

Church, Susan, and Judith M. Newman. 1985. "A Case History of an Instructionally Induced Reading Problem." In *Whole Language: Theory in Use,* Judith M. Newman (ed.). Portsmouth, NH: Heinemann, pp. 169–179.

This is a case history of a ninth grade student reading on a second grade level after years of intensive, supplementary instruction in word analysis (phonics) and word identification (skills). The student learns what he is taught, reflecting his teachers' beliefs about the reading process, but he never views reading as a meaning-getting process. Only when the focus of his instructional program shifts to developing strategies in the context of classroom reading materials does this student begin to understand texts. Must reading for teachers ready to look at reading for L.D. students as a constructive process.

Fielding, Linda and Cathy Roller. May 1992. "Making Difficult Books Accessible and Easy Books Acceptable." *The Reading Teacher*, pp. 678–685. See annotation, p. 44b.

Five, Cora Lee. 1991. *Special Voices*. Portsmouth, NH: Heinemann. See annotation, p. 15b.

Gersten, Russell, and Joseph Dimino. February 1989. "Teaching Literature to At-Risk Students," *Educational Leadership*, pp. 53–57.

The authors describe an instructional approach that uses "scaffolding" and "story grammar" to teach literacy analysis to low-achieving secondary students. This is a useful article for incorporating story grammar elements (stating the problem and main characters; noting character clues, reactions, themes, resolution) to improve students' comprehension of literature. The teacher "thinks aloud" and demonstrates his language processes and decision making to the students. Eventually, with guidance, students are able to use this approach on their own.

Hasselriis, Peter. January 1982. "IEPs and a Whole-Language Model of Language Arts," *Topics in Learning and Learning Disabilities*, pp. 17–21.

The author examines the requirements of IEPs (written Individual Education Plans required by Public Law 94-142 for all handicapped students) and suggests that there is nothing in the law that mandates an emphasis on skills-oriented goals and objectives. He states, "Objectives should be written so as to lead to instructional strategies that keep students in constant touch with language (either oral or written) that is unfragmented—language that is interesting, practical, worthwhile, and functional" (p. 19). The practitioner who wants to write IEPs that are reflective of the whole language philosophy and current view of reading will find sample IEPs included.

Heath, Shirley Brice and Leslie Mangiola. 1991. *Children of Promise: Literate Activity in Linguistically and Culturally Diverse Classrooms*. Washington, DC: National Education Association. See annotation, p. 20b.

Hiebert, Elfrieda H. and Barbara M. Taylor (eds.). 1994. *Getting Reading Right from the Start. Effective Early Literacy Interventions*. Boston, MA: Allyn and Bacon. See annotation, p. 21b.

Krogness, Mary Mercer. 1995. *Just Teach Me, Mrs. K! Talking, Reading, and Writing with Resistant Adolescent Learners*. Portsmouth, NH: Heinemann. See annotation, p. 23b

Lee, Nancy G. and Judith C. Neal. Dec. 1992/Jan. 1993. "Reading Rescue: Intervention for a Student 'At Promise.'" *Journal of Reading*, pp. 276–283. See annotation, p. 46b.

Maria, Katherine. January 1989. "Developing Disadvantaged Children's Background Knowledge Interactively," *The Reading Teacher*, pp. 296–300.

Various strategies are discussed for helping disadvantaged students understand a text. The teacher selects several main concepts from a text, estimates what kind of background knowledge students will need for comprehension, and then demonstrates one or more prereading strategies to develop background knowledge.

Means, Barbara and Michael S. Knapp. December 1991. "Cognitive Approaches to Teaching Advanced Skills to Educationally Disadvantaged Students." *Phi Delta Kappan*, pp. 282–289. See annotation, p. 47b.

Mills, Heidi, and Jean Anne Clyde (eds.). 1990. *Portraits of Whole Language Classrooms: Learning for All Ages*. Portsmouth, NH: Heinemann.

Five chapters in this text describe whole language in use with remedial students: a resource room setting in an elementary school, an ESL elementary school classroom, a middle school remedial program, an English class of "reluctant learners" at a high school, and a university "Ed Lab" servicing students with learning difficulties. I found the interviewing of peers assignment described by middle school teacher Betty Ann Slesinger and the individually designed final English exams described by reading consultant Donelle Blubaugh working with students in Marianne Dalton's tenth grade English class illustrative of some alternative reading-writing possibilities that work. "[R]eluctant students . . . are not reluctant learners when the school agenda is kid-centered, when they are given time to read and write about things that matter and for authentic audiences, when they are provided with realistic language models, and when their voices are as important as our own" (Donelle Blubaugh, p. 274).

Pogrow, Stanley. January 1990. "Challenging At-Risk Students: Findings from the HOTS Program," *Phi Delta Kappan*, pp. 389–397.

This powerful article with supportive data advocates that the way to develop and apply thinking skills in at-risk students who "do not understand what it means to understand" *is through changing the way teachers ask and respond to questions. Instead of typical, brief, recall responses, students should be engaged in high-level intensive conversation where thinking processes are initially modeled by the teacher. "[T]he constant probing by the teacher gradually increases the students' confidence in their own ability to express ideas, and the quantity and sophistication of their speech increases" (p. 393). Some specific interventions for increasing the learning capability of at-risk students are suggested.*

Rhodes, Lynn K. and Curt Dudley-Marling. 1988. *Readers and Writers with a Difference: A Holistic Approach to Teaching Learning Disabled and Remedial Students.* Portsmouth, NH: Heinemann.

 See the complete annotation in Resources for Teachers, *p. 31b. See especially instructional strategies for developing reading and writing fluency, pp. 102–121.*

Sears, Sue, Cathy Carpenter and Nancy Burstein. May 1994. "Meaningful Reading Instruction for Learners with Special Needs." *The Reading Teacher,* pp. 632–670. See annotation, p. 48b.

Stires, Susan (ed.). *With Promise: Redefining Reading and Writing Needs for Special Students.* Portsmouth, NH: Heinemann. See annotation, p. 36b.

Taylor, Denny. 1993. *From the Child's Point of View.* Portsmouth, NH: Heinemann. See annotation, p. 37b.

Taylor, Denny. 1991. *Learning Denied.* Portsmouth, NH: Heinemann. See annotation, p. 37b.

Thistlewaite, Linda L. May 1990. "Critical Reading for At-Risk Students," *Journal of Reading,* pp. 586–593.

 The author defines critical reading and offers seven activities for teaching and promoting it. Specific strategy lessons are presented for use of tabloid articles, advertisements, editorials, movie reviews, comparison of a book and movie, and descriptions of two historical events. Very useful for promoting critical reading and thinking for intermediate through college age students.

Trachtenburg, Phyllis, and Ann Ferruggia. January 1989. "Big Books from Little Voices: Reaching High Risk Beginning Readers," *The Reading Teacher,* pp. 284–289.

 This article describes how skills instruction can be incorporated through shared book experiences of favorite books. An enlarged text version of Cordoroy *by Don Freeman is used to develop sight vocabulary, phonics, fluency, and self-confidence with a class of at-risk first-graders.*

Wheeler, Nancy S. 1990. "Showing the Way: Using Journal Writing to Develop Learning and Teaching Strategies." In *Coming to Know: Writing to Learn in the Intermediate Grades,* Nancie Atwell (ed.). Portsmouth, NH: Heinemann.

 An L.D. teacher in a resource room setting describes how she developed a program of journal writing for both herself and a fourth grade student as the major strategy for improving very depressed reading and writing abilities.

Zucker, Carol. May 1993. "Using Whole Language with Students Who Have Language and Learning Disabilities." *The Reading Teacher,* pp. 660–670. See annotation, p. 52b.

15

Classroom Management and Organization

Enjoying the cozy book corner in the classroom

"I'm in a downward spiral. Each day, I feel myself losing more control of the classroom. What's more, I find I keep lowering my expectations for the kids because it's taking longer to get everything done."

A dedicated first-year teacher talked with me after five months into the school year. She had started school full of enthusiasm and with high hopes of having a whole language classroom. Fresh out of the university, she was ready and eager to try out what she had learned about whole language and teaching. She attended our weekly whole language support group, worked long hours trying to create meaningful learning contexts, and dedicated herself to the students and her job.

Now, however, the rules and point systems she had established no longer seemed to work. As soon as her back was turned, someone was out of control. Praising the appropriately behaved students and hoping the rude ones would get the message to fall in line was having no effect. By the end of the day she was exasperated, and lately she had given some thought to changing professions.

While this new teacher understood and could apply many whole language strategies to reading and writing, her management system was based on the traditional belief that children need tight controls set by the teacher. Yet, just as many of us are working to help children take more responsibility for their reading and writing, we also need to help children take more ownership of their behaviors.

Some experts tell us it is no harder to have order in a whole language classroom than it is in a teacher-dominated one. I disagree. I believe it is much harder in the whole language classroom because the children are expected to take responsibility for their own behaviors—even when the teacher is not looking. Having that inner self-control, which is necessary for the free movement and effectively operating learning centers that whole language classrooms often have, does not just happen. It takes many months of modeling, self-evaluation, setting expectations, and trial and error.

Most of us, including myself, have had behaviorist training. As long as we are in control—giving rewards and points, putting names on the board, and granting and taking away privileges—things seem to run smoothly. Many of us have spent years trying to bribe children into being interested by appealing to their stomachs, their sense of competition, and their desire for tangible rewards. But when we are absent, student self-control often disappears. It's as if an entirely different group of children is in the room when a substitute appears. The children are well behaved only when the classroom teacher is present and asserting authority. This teacher-dominated classroom looks orderly, and it is—as long as the teacher functions as overseer.

By contrast, the whole language classroom may well be using rewards but the rewards do not usually foster competition, and they are less likely to be tangible ones. Rewards might include reading to the kindergarten, having extra time on the computer, being a gym helper, writing collaboratively with a partner, or working in the hall.

As opposed to coercion and bribery, the whole language teacher uses persuasion and problem solving. Built into effective classroom management are the principles of whole language, including collaboration, demonstrations, self-evaluation, and teacher as facilitator. Motivation to behave appropriately comes from within the students. Students know what to do, where to find resources, where everything belongs, and what behaviors are acceptable in the classroom. Rather than being a method, management is a way of thinking and an approach that is consistent with whole language beliefs about learning.

For example, instead of "tattling" and relying on the teacher to solve a problem, students will often first problem solve through writing. Writing encourages students to think through a problem independently and to assume some responsibility for the solution. Before the teacher intervenes, the student may fill out a form that lists such questions as the following:

- What is the problem?
- What did I do?
- How can I help solve this problem?

Developing a system of management that is contrary to the traditional teacher-in-control approach is a difficult and slow process for most of us. It takes an understanding of whole language philosophy, the desire to have a collaborative classroom, time, experience, trial and error, risk taking, and trust in students. The transition process can be frustrating, and, in the beginning, it often seems easier to just continue to give orders and set the rules ourselves. However, if the goal of education is independence, then children need to learn to behave and interact without teacher supervision. Initially, constant modeling and role playing are required, and, for a while, it does take longer to get everything done. This is time well spent because once children assume responsibility for expectations and procedures, the teacher is freed to observe and work with children.

To the untrained eye, a whole language classroom often looks less structured than a traditional classroom because there is much talking and movement as well as children involved in different enterprises. However, just the opposite is true. For things to flow well, the teacher is highly organized, students have had a part in setting up the environment, and students understand, respect, and share responsibility for classroom management.

Some visitors to our whole language classrooms have asked, "What is the discipline policy?" They are amazed when we say we don't have one, that we share responsibility with students. Visitors also note, "It seems so natural," referring to the way students converse and work together. What the visitors do not see is that the naturalness, which looks so easy, has taken months of cooperative work and problem solving to set up.

Establishing the Climate of the Whole Language Classroom

The amount of choice students have, the importance of opportunities to collaborate with each other and with the teacher, the number and relevance of teacher demonstrations, as well as other important issues, have already been discussed in "Becoming a Whole Language Teacher" (pp. 12–25). All of these factors, and others related to them, contribute to a supportive, nurturing learning environment in the classroom. Putting theory into practice, however, takes time, experience, and patience.

Setting Up the Collaborative Classroom

Walking into Joan Servis' fourth grade room, one quickly notices that this is a collaborative classroom. Children work cooperatively, problem solving and supporting each other in the learning process. Joan is a facilitator and a learner, guiding and stretching her students to find and support their own meanings. There is a feeling of community and caring between the students and teacher, and one senses that this is a happy and literate environment.

Joan says it takes about five weeks for her to begin to feel that her classroom has become a collaborative community: "I know I have it when I tell the class it is time for physical education or recess and they moan because they would rather continue with math or writing or with whatever academics we're involved in. When that happens, I know I have the cohesiveness going. But at the beginning of the year, without it, I feel very frustrated."

High school English teacher Holly Burgess felt she had the cohesiveness of a comfortable, safe community two months into the school year. She notes,

> After a class of reluctant readers had read and discussed *The Learning Tree* by Gordon Parks, I asked them to write their own questions for a final test on the book. The questions they wrote were all so good I typed up the entire set and asked students to choose four to answer. When time was up, students wanted more time to write. That had never happened before. Students felt nonthreatened because the questions were their own, they had access to the questions and the book, the book related to their lives, and they really wanted to stay involved with the book.

First grade teacher Karen Shiba says that establishing a collaborative classroom requires "consistency and routine." Karen moves slowly and takes the first few months of school to introduce procedures and expectations. She says, "I don't introduce a new center until everything is running smoothly, and the children are working well independently." She and other primary teachers note that the excitement and sense of community in their classrooms often emanates from the daily shared reading experiences. The literature, poems, songs, and chants provide opportunities for innovations on text and other motivational activities that generate success and collaboration.

Joan Servis begins working for collaboration the first week of school by getting children used to working with each other. Her class is a racially integrated one, with children at extreme ends of the scale in terms of economic background, behavior, and academic ability. In working to establish a collaborative community, she notes, "You never get 100 percent, but if you have 95 percent, that's wonderful."

While Joan likes collaborative groups of three and four, she begins by having children work in pairs after she has demonstrated what they are to do, whether the activity is peer conferencing, note taking, or responding in a literature log. After several weeks, the students begin working as a cooperative group. (See Hill and Hill, 1990, for procedures for setting up groups and for establishing a collaborative classroom.)

Joan says that she constantly employs the following strategies to establish a collaborative classroom. She notes, "If the task is worthy of collaboration, that is, if it is interesting and relevant and the materials are engaging and not too difficult, then collaboration works."

- *Expecting self-evaluation of behaviors*   When students finish working together, for example, in math or social studies, they are asked to reflect upon their behaviors. (See Figures 12–5 and 12–6 in Chap. 12, "Integration," and Figures 13–30 and 13–31 in Chap. 13, "Evaluation.") With teacher guidance, orally and in writing students are constantly examining how they might improve the functioning of the group, and gradually they take more responsibility for their behaviors.

I have found that promoting continuous self-evaluation eventually leads students to assume more responsibility for their behaviors. For example, when I am teaching a demonstration lesson and a student misbehaves or the noise level of the class gets too high, I say something like, "I'm having difficulty hearing students in reading group. What can you [rest of class] do that would help the situation?" In the past, I would have said something like, "It's too noisy in here. Jason, you need to be in your seat. Kara, quiet down and get to work." I find that having students problem solve puts the responsibility on them and takes the teacher out of the role of placing blame and taking over. It also makes students more aware of what behaviors are appropriate.

- *Stressing cooperation*   Through oral discussion and shared writing, Joan Servis and her students discuss specific behaviors that foster respect and cooperation, for example, making eye contact, listening to one another, and taking turns.

Additionally, students are encouraged to help each other. For example, Joan does not check daily reading logs (explained in "WEB Reading," Chap. 3) until the group (usually four students) has completed recording in their logs and all raise their hands (an idea she picked up from fifth grade teacher Jim Servis). The stronger students have assisted and encouraged the others, so that when Joan comes over to check, the entire group has completed the logs satisfactorily.

• *Praising positive behaviors* Orally and in writing, Joan comments on what students are doing well. Commenting on positive behaviors encourages students to repeat the behaviors.

• *Making sure students completely understand the task* Through repeated demonstrations and specific instructions about what the group is to accomplish, Joan makes sure each group member knows what to do and that each group has a spokesperson.

• *Modeling and role playing appropriate and inappropriate behaviors* To establish a collaborative classroom, demonstrations are often not enough. With teacher guidance, students need to move from teacher demonstrations to role playing appropriate behaviors and interactions. For example, the class looks on as a group of students role play how to use the reading center. Following their role playing, the teacher guides a class discussion about appropriate and inappropriate behaviors.

Many teachers have found it works best to demonstrate and role play one activity at a time and to take many weeks to establish classroom routines. While initially this can be very time-consuming, following this plan pays dividends later on. For teachers who feel routines have not been well established, it works well to think of the current week as week one, and just start again.

The Physical Climate and Room Arrangement

Along with learning expectations and the emotional climate, the physical layout and setup of the classroom support the teacher's philosophy of learning and teaching. The way we organize our classrooms affects children's views of themselves as readers and writers and has an impact on their attitudes toward school and learning.

A whole language, collaborative classroom has a distinctive look and feel that is noticeable when you walk into the room. There are displays of children's work and books everywhere. There is space for exploration, learning centers, and a classroom library, and the room is full of attractive, purposeful print.

While each whole language classroom is unique, they often have a number of physical factors in common. These physical changes are not easy to implement because they go hand in hand with our development of learning theory. As with the development of theory, we need to give ourselves time to become comfortable with a new physical setup. Most teachers make these changes slowly and gradually over a period of many years. The following are suggestions and alternatives for consideration.

Room Arrangement

In a whole language classroom, the room is set up so students can read, write, and collaborate comfortably by themselves or in a small group. There are open spaces where the class can gather or small groups can meet. There are centers of designated areas where students have opportunities for talk, exploration, writing, reading, and sharing. In a small room, or in a secondary classroom, the hallway is sometimes used for conferences and paired collaboration. See Figure 15–1 for the setup of Joan Servis' fourth grade classroom and Figure 15–2 for the arrangement of Karen Sher's kindergarten classroom.

Figure 15-1   Joan Servis' Fourth Grade Classroom

Figure 15-2   Karen Sher's Kindergarten Classroom

Sink

Door

Paint storage table

Easel

Manipulatives

Math center materials

Block corner

Art center

Counter displays children's work

Storage shelves

Art materials

Science center

Teacher's desk

Chalkboard

Listening center

Rice or water table

Math tubs

Children's table

Conference table

Low storage cabinets (cooking, science, math materials)

Children's table

Computer

Writing center

Children's table

TV

Children's table

Extra writing supplies (chalkboards, chalk, clipboards)

Book baskets (by theme and/or author)

Poetry chart stand

Teacher's chair

Long bench divider and counter space for storage (journals, art projects, etc.)

Tall metal storage cabinet

Housekeeping corner

Dress-up clothes baskets

Books on display shelves

Big Book easel stand

Space for children to sit during shared reading, story times, etc.

Storage cabinet countertop - parent's lending library

Reading cushion

Toy stove

Sink

Table & chairs

Doll's high chair

Door

Record player

Turtle tank

Doll's crib

Windows

Calendar board

Chalkboard

Bulletin board

File cabinet

Desks

Desks are usually clustered so students have opportunities to collaborate with a partner and with a small group. Clumps of four desks work well; more than five can be difficult for small-group work. Some teachers have begun to replace all desks with large tables, an arrangement that allows for greater flexibility and more work space for projects but that requires separate storage areas for students' books and materials. Stackable bins or personal baskets have worked well here.

Eliminating the teacher's desk is an option for getting more space since some teachers find that in a whole language classroom they rarely sit at their desks. Adding another file cabinet, with extra file folders and organizers, may be necessary, but teachers who do get rid of their desks find they prefer having an extra table that provides additional space for collaborative work and conferencing. Teachers who keep their desks use them more as a place for a student and teacher to confer undisturbed rather than as the focal point for the teacher in the classroom.

Whole-Group Area

Whole language classrooms, especially at the elementary level, include an area where the whole group can gather. Some teachers define such an area with a carpet; others use furniture to block off space. Some teachers move desks out of the way just before whole-group time and have students sit on carpet squares. An easel for Big Books, a stand to hold enlarged-print poetry charts, a rocking chair, and an author's chair are often part of this space. Sometimes the cozy reading corner is part of this area or adjacent to it.

Secondary classrooms often have mobile, lighter-weight furniture. Some teachers prefer chair arrangements in semicircles, u-shapes, or clusters of armchair desks. Such clustering promotes a feeling of community.

Bulletin Boards

A teacher's beliefs about learning and teaching are evident in the format and content of the classroom bulletin boards. When the classroom is a collaborative one, children's work is everywhere, and the bulletin boards—which are done by and for the students—reflect meaningful and relevant reading-writing processes. By contrast, in traditional classrooms, bulletin boards are most often "done" by the teacher. I still remember the last-minute, time-consuming scramble to have all bulletin boards complete for the first day of school and the constant pressure throughout the year to change the bulletin boards so they would be current and attractive.

By giving students some ownership of the bulletin boards, they take more pride and responsibility for how the room looks and functions. By using children's work instead of commercially prepared materials, the teacher is sending a message that the classroom is student centered. This transition is not an easy one for most of us, and it does not occur until we are ready to share control and responsibility for learning with our students.

However, putting students in charge of the bulletin boards saves the teacher lots of time. In one Australian classroom I visited, the teacher reported starting school with empty bulletin boards each year and saying to students, "This is going to be our room together for an entire year. How do you want to use our bulletin boards? What do you want our room to look like?"

Sixth grade teacher Pam Anderson tried this approach for three out of her five bulletin boards this past fall and found that students did a better job than she had anticipated. She recalled, "I really had reservations about turning over the bulletin boards to the students because I thought it would be difficult to establish cooperative work habits so early in the school year. But most of them took the project seriously and did well." Beginning with a class discussion led by Pam, students decided to have a holiday bulletin board, a calendar bulletin board, and a behavior/rules bulletin board. Then students worked together in groups—based on the bulletin board they wanted to work on—discussing and sketching out their plans, which were subject to Pam's approval.

Some teachers effectively use bulletin boards to feature students' writing. Based on an idea in *Creating Classrooms for Authors* (Harste, Short, and Burke, 1988), Joan Servis uses her largest bulletin board to spotlight the writing of each class member. Each student—and the teacher—has a space on a 9 by 12 inch sheet of colored paper on which a piece of monthly writing is selected by the writer to be posted. Each month a new piece is tacked on top, and a collection of dated writing samples results. Other teachers keep students' writing samples in a transparent, plastic folder and staple it to the wall.

A permanent bulletin board that promotes self-esteem and interpersonal relationships is "Person of the Week" or "Author of the Week." Each week a different student is highlighted with family photographs, writing samples, interviews, and anything significant about the student. With teacher guidance, the student can be in charge of planning and creating the bulletin board. The student is also often the special classroom helper for that week.

Another idea that works well and gives a personal touch to the classroom is to replace the usual commercial borders on bulletin boards with student-designed borders. For example, students can design a class logo at the beginning of the school year and reproduce it on plain borders or paper strips.

At the secondary level, where classrooms are usually shared with other teachers, hallway display cabinets can be used to exhibit student writing. At our high school, a recent hallway display showed students' writing alongside the teachers'. Another display demonstrated high school readers. In the same window case, readers—both teachers and students—displayed favorite books recently read, along with a description of why these books were significant to them.

Message Board

In addition to legitimizing note passing, the message board can serve as a permanent bulletin board that promotes within-class communication, fluency in writing, and self-esteem. At designated times, students write and receive signed messages to and from each other and the teacher. Some teachers use the message board to have students communicate and work out classroom problems. For example, a student who is upset about something or someone may write a message through the message board to the teacher, or a student may be asked to write a message explaining what he has done to try to solve a particular behavior or discipline problem. If a student in Joan Servis' class wants to have her seat changed, the reasons are stated, and the request is put in writing through the message board. Some teachers use the message board as a way to recognize students' positive behaviors. Joan says that about one quarter of her class receives a positive written message from her each morning and that students eagerly await those messages.

The message board was developed by Carolyn Burke of Indiana University, and specific procedures and ideas for its use are given in *Creating Classrooms for Authors* (Harste, Short, and Burke, 1988, pp. 309–312). Some teachers use mailboxes, especially in the younger grades, to serve the same purposes as the message board.

Display Areas

Children need lots of space to display their own work. To get additional display space for children's work, many teachers have found that fishing line or nylon string, attached to the wall or woodwork with small eyehooks and strung across the room or in levels across the window wall works well. The line is light, transparent, flexible, and easy to put up. Clothespins work well for attaching work samples to the lines. Window shades may also be utilized for posting charts.

Cozy Reading Corner

A whole language classroom usually has an attractive area, not only for display of many books, but a "cozy corner" where students can read in a relaxed, comfortable manner. Just as we adults do not do all our reading sitting upright at a desk, children also need to have space in which to curl up comfortably with a book. Along with attractive book shelves, book racks, and/or book spinners, the corner may include beanbag chairs, cushions, a rocking chair, a throw rug, reading posters, and even a sofa or bench for reading. Many parents are willing to donate some of these items. Books and materials are always easily accessible to students.

The amount of time and effort spent establishing an attractive library center pays off. Researchers Lesley Mandel Morrow and Carol Simon Weinstein found that students, even those who were poor readers, chose to read more during free-choice time and have more interaction with books when there was a well-designed, inviting reading corner (Morrow and Weinstein, "Encouraging Voluntary Reading: The Impact of a Literature Program on Children's Use of Library Centers," *Reading Research Quarterly*, Summer 1986, pp. 330–346).

In addition to all types of fiction and nonfiction books—both commercial and student written—the reading corner may include magazines, plays, poetry, newspapers, reference books, and dictionaries. While many teachers prefer to limit reading workshop, or sustained silent reading time in class, to books, these other resources are available when students have "free" time or when they are working on special projects. For younger children, there will need to be many titles with predictable structures, favorite storybooks, and counting and concept books. In the reading corner there may also be puppets and felt boards to dramatize stories. Books should be attractively displayed, many of them with covers cleary visible.

One hundred to 150 books in various genres is a good number to aim for in the classroom library. Involving students by checking with them for particular titles, authors, and subjects that they would like to see included in the library gives them ownership of reading. Even when funds for books are very limited, teachers can establish classroom libraries by signing out books from the school and public libraries. Often librarians are willing to rotate sets of about fifty titles to help establish classroom libraries. Asking parents to donate books from home that children are no longer reading has worked well in helping many teachers build libraries. Other teachers have checked out local garage sales and library sales for books. Some teachers also accumulate many books for the classroom through bonuses from book clubs such as Trumpet (Scholastic).

Writing Center

The writing center has a table and chairs, pencils, pens, markers, crayons, chalk, all types of paper, booklets, envelopes, book making materials, a computer or typewriter, and chalkboards. Students know how to use the materials, and the center is open to them. (Some teachers have been able to get parents to donate an old typewriter to the center.) Where space is tight, a small table or ledge that houses writing supplies works well.

Listening Center

An area is set aside for small groups of students (using headphones) to listen to cassette recordings of favorite books while they follow along in individual copies. The listening center may also be used for students to hear a text over and over again before they are about to read, and also to reread a text to gain fluency. The teacher, or another proficient reader, may also record a small portion of text that has already been discussed in reading group, so that students can listen and follow along visually. Additionally, the tape recorder may be used to record student reading of text and original stories. Students enjoy creating a final copy without worrying about editing.

Other Learning Areas/Centers

Depending on what is going on in the elementary classroom, there may also be areas for math manipulatives, science projects, and other curriculum/theme study. While these centers will not be discussed in this book, they are briefly noted so as not to be overlooked.

Messages, Directions, Jobs, and Rules

In a whole language classroom, many of the notices, announcements, and schedules are written by the students. With teacher guidance, even very young children can write appropriate explanatory labels and messages on displays, equipment, cabinets, and other classroom items. Jobs are often designated on a volunteer basis. Students sign up for the jobs they want to do, and because the choice is theirs, they are motivated to do the job well. Other teachers prefer to identify classroom jobs with the students and then rotate the jobs. Many teachers find it works well to co-establish classroom rules through a shared writing experience. There are usually few classroom rules, and they are always stated positively. For example, one rule might say, "Be courteous" (instead of "Don't be rude").

Classroom Organization

Lesson Plans and Schedules

Whole language teachers often find that traditional lesson plan formats are too confining. In addition to the required curriculum, because much of what goes on in the whole language setting springs from the children's needs and interests—which are always subject to change—a flexible framework seems to work best. For the teacher, this requires a solid theory base, confidence in oneself and the children, and a flexible, supportive principal who understands whole language.

Many whole language teachers design their own formats for lesson plans. Sometimes these plans are done in pencil and may be "messy" because of ongoing changes and additions teachers make. Instead of traditional lesson plan books, some teachers use three-ring notebooks, large spirals or oversized blank books in which they can create their own formats and spaces. Often the major components or areas of study are blocked out for the day or week, with the specifics to be filled in one day at a time (see Figure 15–3). For example, there may be blocks for shared reading, guided reading, independent reading, sustained silent reading, and writing workshop. Often there are separate folders for each area of study. For example, under reading-writing workshop or language arts, the plan might indicate a biography unit. The objectives and specifics are listed in the particular folder. The folder also may contain reproduced samples of well-done projects by students from past years to use as demonstrations.

Kindergarten teacher Karen Sher has designed an innovative, flexible lesson plan format that works well for her and may be easily adapted across the grade levels. Karen writes a broad, comprehensive plan for the week and then writes daily on large Post-its (which she overlaps in the corner of her large spiral notebook) what she specifically hopes to do that day. The weekly plan and Post-its give her freedom. If a project is not finished one day, it easily carries over to the next day (see Figure 15–4).

Flexible planning represents a major change for Karen. She says,

> If I used to breathe, I wrote it down. As I became more secure, I relaxed and wrote down less. But I was still spending a lot of time trying to fit everything into those little boxes in the plan book. I felt so frustrated by my plans, but, at the time, I didn't know why. Now my lesson plans match my teaching. My plans provide me a framework so I can easily weave everything together. I always have at least several units or themes going on at one time, perhaps an author study, a unit on feelings, and a science unit that has arisen naturally from the children's interests.

First grade teacher Jim Henry also uses a flexible format. While Jim has a broad, overall weekly plan, the bulk of his planning is done daily on a 3 by 5 inch pad of paper. He notes, "Our class projects and successful motivational activities stem from our daily shared reading experiences. The planning of these experiences often hinges upon the previous day's efforts, so that planning for the next session happens at the end of each day."

Teachers I have worked with have taken at least three to five years to develop a schedule and lesson plan format they feel comfortable with. All of these teachers expect their daily plans to change. Joan Servis calls her daily schedule a "forecast."

Figure 15-3   Susan Mear's Grade 1 Schedule/Plan

MONDAY

9:05   Entry Bell - Meet children at Front Door

9:10   Begin reading poems and jokes

9:15-9:20   Announcements and Pledge on PA

9:20-9:45   Reading to and with Children and Calendar (Calendar information in
               substitute folder)
               Story: Optional Big Book:

               Poem:

               Objective: To immerse children in literature, to see reading
                            demonstrated, to point out conventions of language,
                            punctuation, sentence structure, phonics in context, etc.
               Evaluation: Are they involved? Do they read poems later by their choice
                            and use the strategies? Do they transfer knowledge to
                            their own writing using language conventions, punctuation,
                            phonics and sentence structure correctly?

9:45-11:10   Reading in Small Groups - Guided Reading (20-25 min. per group). The
               reading material for the groups is contained in the folders in the
               basket behind my table marked Reading. Please be flexible with the
               order of the groups because of the pull-outs. Some groups may be
               reading independently. (During this time later in the year the children
               can put their things to share on my chair -- stories they wrote,
               Journal page, etc. -- About six children will have time at the end of
               reading period.)
               Objective: To match children and books, to demonstrate reading
                            strategies, language conventions, phonics and grammar
                            in context and develop reading competence.
               Evaluation: Children will read independently, transfer strategies to
                            new material, understand what they have read and appreciate
                            the author's craft.
               Seatwork:

11:10-11:15   Restrooms (Recess Optional)

11:15-11:50   Math Their Way and Box It, Bag It - Children are doing hands-on activities
               contained in Tubs at the Math bookcase - The children are familiar
               with this and can set it up and proceed on their own.
               Objective:

               Evaluation:

11:50-12:15   Story Writing for Publication (Folders contained in tub under cubbies.)

12:15   Lunch (Mrs. Mims will come to the room and pick them up.)

1:05   Entry Bell

1:05 1:20   Quiet Time/Reading (SSR)
               Objectives: To allow for choice, to establish regular reading
                             habits, to enjoy reading, etc.
               Evaluation: None
               Read with:

1:20-1:30   Story:

1:30-2:10   Social Science -- Text:
               Objective:

               Evaluation:

2:10-2:30   Box It, Bag It - hands on addition and subtraction contained in the
               school boxes on the math shelf - Number Operations
               Objective: To use computational skills
               Evaluation:

2:30-2:45   Handwriting either on desk with chalk, on transparencies, on paper
               or with shaving cream on desk.

2:45-3:15   Physical Education

3:25   Dismissal

Theme of the week:

Figure 15-4   Proposed Weekly Schedule for Karen Sher's Kindergarten Class

week of October 1, 1990

Proposed Weekly Schedule for Kindergarten
Karen Sher, Teacher

LANGUAGE ARTS ACTIVITIES	MATHEMATICS
Poetry → Turtle Poem } on chart Autumn Poem } stand	Graphing 1. graph Rosemary Wells books 2. Apple Tasting Party → graph favorite kind
Shared Reading → ① Read class made book: Our Trip to Sage Fruit Farm ② Introduce - The Monster's Party (Big Book) ③ Sing song & read Big Book: Miss Mary Mack	Free Exploration Add tubs: mirrors, tiles, toothpicks
Phonics, Penmanship Focus → Tt - relate to our turtle Penmanship → Practice writing our first names; the letter Tt Reinforcement → Ff → make class book Our Favorite Food Book; Cooking- fruit salad	Stuffed Animal Theme Activities Counting/Estimation: count stuffed animals (use graphing mat) with numeral cards. Children estimate first. Story Problems: develop with stuffed animals
Phonics (Tt) reinforcements 1. Draw pictures beginning with Tt 2. note Tt items brought in by children & Tt words in reading & conversation 3. Toothpick art 4. Cut magazine pictures beginning with Tt 5. Invite children to play 'teacher'	Comparing: weight & height of children's animals with mine. Use balance scale. Vocab: heavier lighter taller shorter the same Concept Instruction: Pattern ① Introduce people sorting: the pattern a/c categories used for sorting ② Snap/Clap patterns → translate to words, shapes, letters, etc
Literature ①Closure on Rosemary Wells - graph our favorite ② New author - Pat Hutchins ③ Get from library → Fall Books, Turtle books ④Book Look → daily opportunity for children to enjoy books alone or with friends	③ Pattern fruit salad on skewers New Tubs ① Begin to introduce pattern tubs: stamp & ink pad patterns
Writing ① Journals → model diff. ways of writing ② encourage writing during activity time ③ photograph children engaged in writing	- unifix patterns

She notes, "Like the weather, it is subject to change." See Figures 15–4 through 15–6 for three elementary teachers' schedules/plans.

Plans for the Substitute

Since it may be difficult to have a substitute who does not understand or accept whole language principles, whole language teachers try not to be absent a lot. Of course, the reality of life is that we are sometimes absent. Some teachers keep a set of alternative, more traditional plans in a substitute folder. Others try to find a substitute who understands whole language and works well with the class. Then, they request that same substitute consistently.

Some teachers find that having separate folders of procedures for the substitute works well—for example, folders of explanation for WEB reading, sustained silent

Figure 15–4   Continued

Social Studies/Science	Art/Music
S.S. : Developing an understanding of ourselves and others (OUSO) Obj: To become aware that we do things to achieve goals; to examine our own purposes & to determine results Stories - ① Frowny Brown - people who are dejected are not fun to be with ② The Box - dealing with rejection. Science - ① Apple Experiments - lemon juice; covered vs not covered ② FALL - (literature) - Walk in Southerly Park: collect signs of fall Begin leaf & seed collections, SORT A/c different attributes	1. Flip Face - relate to OUSO themes - children will express times when they felt happy or sad and flip face to appropriate expression 2. Toothpick Art 3. Fancy Foil Magnets { Ff 4. Make flowers to decorate room 5. Begin giant leaf mobiles - FALL 6. Nature Collage - after our walk 7. Music ① introduce children to Raffi and his music ② rest to Firebird Suite (Stravinsky)

10-1-90 Monday - Tentative Plan
Special Classes - Art - 9:20 - 10:15
                             PE - 11:15 - 11:45

A.M.
- Greet children, take attendance, gym shoes, snacks
- ART
- Calendar
- Group Time
      - Poetry → Turtle Poem, Fall Poem
      - read Apple Farm Book together
      - Sing & read Miss Mary Mack
- SNACK, BATHROOM, BOOKLOOK
- Physical Education
- Math - Free Exploration Tubs
      - small groups will work with me comparing stuffed animals (height & weight)
- STORYTIME - non-fiction - Box Turtle book
      - discuss difference between fiction & non-fiction
  LUNCH
- Shared writing → LUNCHTIME STORIES
- Literature/Math - review book by Rosemary Wells. Which was your favorite? Why? Graph
REST → music - Firebird Suite
SCIENCE → Walk in Southerly Park - observe and collect signs of fall
Independent Activities - children choose room centers. Include at art center - making flowers to decorate room.

Figure 15–5   Ellen Rubin's Flexible Schedule

Flexible Schedule for Heterogeneous Class   Grade 2   Ellen Rubin

9:05–9:30 A.M. *Taking Care of Business*
  •write note to classmate and put in classmate's mailbox
  •write daily "News of the Day"
   large piece of newsprint is posted daily, and students can write their news throughout
      the day. For example, "My tooth came out last night." (1 or 2 sentences on anything
      important to student.)
  •read
  •class meteorologist does weather report ⎫ Jobs change
  •class mathematician takes self-designed class survey ⎭ every 2 weeks

9:30–10:00 *Reading Aloud* (and occasional Shared Reading)
   teacher reads excellent literature to class—content oriented (social studies/science);
      theme oriented (author, seasonal, mystery, nonfiction); predicting, reasoning, dis-
      cussing—focus on author's "voice" (style, individuality)

10:00–10:30 *Independent Reading*
  •using self-selected books, students read alone (SSR) or "buddy read"—books, peers'
      published pieces, magazines
  •student records selection in daily reading log
  •teacher holds individual reading conferences

10:30–11:30 *Reading-Writing Workshop*
  (opening)   •mini-lesson (modeling, usually whole class, 5-10 minutes)
            ⎡ •class continues with work in progress
            ⎢ free choice 90% of time (1/2 of time within teacher specified parameters
            ⎢   [genre writing, content area writing, focused writing—setting, devel-
            ⎢   opment, using interesting words, proofreading, etc])
  (ongoing) ⎨ •peer conferencing
            ⎢ •small group and/or individual conferencing with teacher (anecdotal
            ⎢   records taken)
            ⎢ •word processing
            ⎣ •special projects (plays, puppetry, book projects, content area projects)
  (closing)   •sharing circle (students can share any writing)
[Note: Spelling is integrated with writing {see Chap.10}. Once a week, parent volunteers
assist.]

11:30–12:00 *Guided Reading*
   whole class and/or small group reading using core books

12:00–12:10 teaching mechanics of cursive handwriting or working on final copy of piece

1:05–1:30 *Whole Class Project Sharing*
   students share favorite poems, talk about favorite books, share published books,
      share content area projects

1:30–2:15 *Mathematics*
   Math textbook program supplemented with open-ended problem solving and monthly
      graphing from weather reports (meteorologist) and math surveys

2:30–2:50 *Science/Social Studies/Health*
   Content areas are integrated into literature program and writing as much as possible.
      This is "spillover" time for what has not been integrated.

2:30–3:10 *Day Books (Journals)*
   "Capture the day—you'll never get it back again." Students write about their day, and of-
      ten refer to this journal for writing ideas; occasionally, journal is used as a literature
      response log.

3:10–3:15 *"News of the Day" and Wrap-Up*
   Students read what they have written throughout the day

Figure 15-6   Joan Servis' Grade 4 Class Schedule

Schedule for Heterogeneous Class—Grade 4

Joan Servis

MONDAY	TUESDAY	WEDNESDAY	THURSDAY	FRIDAY
9:15–9:45 W.E.B. — Independent reading and bookcheck. See Chapter 3 for procedures.				
9:45–10:00 Class announcements. Children and teacher plan activities for the day.				
10:00–11:00	10:00–11:00	10:00–11:25	10:00–11:00	10:00–11:25
Opportunities/Independent Worktime/Process Writing From list on the board which was generated from teacher and students, the students select an opportunity. Teacher circulates, holds writing conferences, and provides needed materials and guidance. Some examples of opportunities are: projects relating to current literature books (see Reading below), teacher and peer writing conferences, journal writing, pen pal letters, writing drafts or final copies of current book/story/article/letter, and editing revised stories. (Spelling is taught as part of writing, see Chap. 10.)				
11:00–12:00 Social Science	11:00–11:45 Social Science	11:25–12:10 Physical Education	11:00–11:45 Social Science	11:25–12:10 Physical Education
Social Studies and Science are combined. Students work in interest groups, reading, researching, and presenting orally to the class the results of their findings. Some units of study have included: Prairie Life and Land, the Amazon Basin, Ohio, and Life in the Deserts of the U.S.				
12:00–12:15 Sharing	11:45–12:15 Music	11:45–12:15 Physical Education	11:45–12:15 Music	11:45–12:15 Physical Education
Sharing—Whole class gathers for oral sharing of successes accomplished in the morning.				
12:15–1:05 Lunch/Recess				
1:05–1:15 Poetry Class poet (volunteer job) reads aloud previously selected poetry to the class				
1:15–2:15 Reading Students read (independently, in pairs, or occasionally teacher reads aloud) the current class selection from core literature. Children read with 1 or 2 open-ended questions in mind (questions are on board). Procedures are followed for Literature Response Logs and Literature Discussion Groups (see Chap. 6).				
2:25–3:15 Art	2:15–2:45 Mathematics	2:15–2:45 Mathematics	2:15–2:45 Mathematics	2:15–2:45 Mathematics
Mathematics Students primarily work on problem solving of word problems in groups of four. Computation is assigned as homework. Concepts are taught in class.				
Art	2:45–3:15 Teacher Reading Aloud	2:45–3:15 Teacher Reading Aloud	2:45–3:15 Teacher Reading Aloud	2:45–3:15 Teacher Reading Aloud
Reading aloud by teacher—picture books, novels, various genres. Class makes predictions, reacts to selection read with comments and discussion.				
3:15–3:25 Self-evaluation Oral or written, of contributions to the class either as a team member or as an individual. (See Figures 13-30 and 13-31 in Chap. 13, "Evaluation," for sample written self-evaluations.)				
3:25 Dismissal				

reading, spelling, literature response logs, and literature discussion. If a collaborative classroom has been established in which children work well together and take responsibility for their behaviors, tasks, and routines, a substitute may be able to carry on the regular program.

High school English teacher Holly Burgess notes, "The first time I had to be absent this year—three days all together—I created substitute plans and then scrapped them! How could I encourage and trust students to follow the reading/writing plan I had taken such pains to establish if I were still in such rigid control of who could do what, when?!" The note from the substitute indicated that most of the students had stayed committed to the usual tasks for most of the period.

Getting around Time Constraints

Especially at the secondary level, where rigid time frames (forty-five- to fifty-minute periods) affect the "flow" of the curriculum, some teachers and schools have begun experimenting with more flexible time blocks in order to establish some continuity. For example, ninth grade teacher Dana Noble schedules writing workshop daily for several weeks and then moves to responding to literature for several more weeks (see Figure 15–7). Additionally, some teachers and administrators are working to create larger time frames by scheduling classes twice or three times a week but for longer time periods, as is the practice at some colleges and universities. Middle school English teacher Mary Krogness says, "Think of class time as being on a continuum versus its being so many little parcels used rigidly."

Most whole language teachers at the elementary level prefer to keep their classes

Figure 15–7   Dana Noble's Grade 9 Writing Workshop and Response-based Literature Study Schedules

Schedules for Writing Workshop and for Response-Based Literature Study
Grade 9   English

Dana Noble

Each schedule of a 50-minute period is in effect for approximately a two-week span, intermittently throughout the year. (Or schedules could alternate M,T,W [writing] and T,F [literature study]) Time spans are approximations only. In actuality, schedule reflects a daily routine which flows together as one time block.

I   **Schedule for Writing Workshop** (based on model by Nancie Atwell, 1987, *In the Middle*)

MONDAY	TUESDAY	WEDNESDAY	THURSDAY	FRIDAY
8:05	Students have picked up their writing folders before the bell rings.			
8:05–8:15	Mini-lesson: Rehearsing, writing leads, giving response, paragraphing, editing, common punctuation errors, etc.			
8:15–8:20	Silent write: Read your piece in progress, consider the next step in the process of writing, and begin writing, revising, editing and thinking.			
8:20–8:25	Schedule the day: Each student announces his/her progress in the current piece: Draft 2, ready for response, editing for final draft, starting a new piece, etc.			
8:25–8:50	Writing time: Writers write, get and give response in conference area, edit, finish pieces of writing.			
8:50–8:55	Group share: A student reads work in progress or talks about problems and asks for ideas in whole group session.			
8:55	Students place drafts in their folders on their way to next class.			

Individual reading and response

At home, students read books they have chosen from book talks, book sharing, or other sources. Students write responses in journal: comments on plot, personal connections, observations about author style and story structure, and ideas for writing in writing workshop.

II   **Schedule for Response -Based Literature Study**   (See Chap. 6.)

MONDAY	TUESDAY	WEDNESDAY	THURSDAY	FRIDAY
8:05	Students reread journal responses to prompts about current literature they are studying.			
8:10	Students form groups to read their responses, compare and discuss ideas. Groups are formed by various factors: common book choices, common prompt choices, or common interests. Other small group activities may include the following: 1. Students exchange journals, read another student's response to the same or different prompt. (or an undirected response to the literature) and write a reaction to their response: confirming facts, providing an opposing viewpoint, or contrasting their reading. 2. One small group discusses their responses while the rest of the class carefully listens and observes without interrupting. At a signal from the teacher, other students are invited to offer new or contrasting observations about the literature.			
8:30	Students rejoin the whole group for discussion, dramatic interpretation of the literature, brief writing assignments using the literature as a model, individual reading, etc.			
8:50	In the last five minutes, students write down a prompt written on the board for the night's reading or discuss and choose one question from a list of open-ended questions.			

Note: Be flexible! Setting up a definitive time schedule has been done only for the purpose of giving some time-management guidance to teachers.

Figure 15-8   Encouraging Self-Evaluation

Name of project _____

☐ **My pictures go with my story.**
☐ **I have used my best handwriting.**
☐ **I have used capitals and periods.**
☐ **I practiced reading this once.**

_____
signature

self-contained (and to avoid switching classes). This plan affords maximum flexibility, with time to establish a collaborative classroom community and to build in opportunities for integration across the curriculum. Teachers also try to work with their principals to obtain blocks of uninterrupted time.

Setting Aside Time for Sharing

Many teachers in reading-writing classrooms find there is never enough time for children to share. Students, creating their own projects and stories, want to share everything. We have found it works well to set aside time daily and/or weekly (at the end of the morning, afternoon, or week) for students to share their work. Even at the secondary level, sharing is important.

Holly Burgess, a high school English teacher, plans time after a writing prompt, especially with all-class reads, for students to either read their journal responses or tell about what they wrote. She notes, "Surprisingly, I have about 95 percent of students sharing, even with reluctant readers/writers. All gain from each others' insights."

Jim Henry found that in his first grade classroom he had to move away from allowing students to share everything. Being allowed to share everything seemed to encourage students to rush through their work. Then, too, students became frustrated because there was never enough time for everyone to share. Instead, Jim put in place a whole-class weekly share where students had an opportunity to share one piece every week or every other week. The specialized sharing invited children to do and choose their finest work and also encouraged self-evaluation. Jim also developed a simple form that encouraged his first-graders to do their best work on all required and optional projects (see Figure 15–8).

Providing Reading-Writing Opportunities That Allow for Choice

Planning for Unstructured or Independent-Choice Time

A critical component of whole language is allowing and promoting student choice and decision making. We need to provide and value time for students to select options. Peg Rimedio, a first grade teacher, notes, "The most important thing in first grade is to plan the unstructured time. If you give children constant activities to do, they are not going to have time to explore. Everything doesn't need to be checked and marked by the teacher. The main thing that kids need—that we don't give them—is time and choice." Peg has built many student-selected activities into her daily program. However, before giving students options for their unstructured time, she sets up materials and procedures and carefully explains how they may be used.

Most teachers find it takes at least the first six weeks of school to set up routines and procedures with students. In setting up learning centers and explaining optional and expected activities, teachers find that when activities are introduced slowly, one at a time, week by week, and when the use of centers and activities is carefully and repeatedly demonstrated, role played, and monitored, students learn to use them appropriately.

First grade teacher Karen Shiba has a daily block of time when students have unstructured, independent choice time. During most of that time, Karen is meeting with reading groups or conferencing with students. Students not in group are involved in optional reading, writing, or listening activities. Available options are gradually introduced and explained. For the first two weeks, students are expected to spend the entire independent work time reading Big Books and little books, independently or with a friend anywhere in the room as long as they use "inside voices" and do not disturb the teacher. The third week Karen introduces and demonstrates the use of the mailboxes. The following week she introduces the listening center with its tape recorders and headphones. The fifth week, Karen demonstrates the use of the computer, with two students working collaboratively. At the same time, students also have the option to continue journal writing or illustrate their published books. The only requirement is the illustration of the week's poems (from shared reading) that become part of each student's poetry notebook. Self-evaluation is a big part of the successful management of unstructured time. If a student is off task, Karen will ask, "Are you reading, writing, or listening?" The student has to say what she is doing and could be doing. (For more specifics on Karen's first grade reading and language block that allows for flexibility and choice, see Routman, 1988, pp. 36, 37, 200, and 319.)

Even with careful planning, we will often need to demonstrate more than once. One high school teacher found that after many weeks she finally had reading workshop functioning well. Then she introduced writing workshop, only to find that some students forgot about completing their reading journal. While she had expected students to continue doing their reading journals (along with writing workshop), she had not made that expectation explicit.

Involving Students in Planning

In planning, in addition to meeting the requirements of the curriculum, students in whole language classrooms have options. Kindergarten teacher Karen Sher asks her students, "What do you want to learn about today?" and includes her own input and direction. An author study of Steven Kellogg emerged initially from the children's hearing the story *Can I Keep Him?* and wanting more books by the same author. The study of Kellogg included obtaining information and photographs of the author, finding lots of books by the author for reading aloud and independent reading, making a whole-class graph of favorite books by Kellogg, and discussing the language the author uses and how he does his illustrations.

Karen also uses Friday mornings and many afternoons as opportunities for students to choose "meaningful educational" activities. Children decide what art, reading, writing, math, manipulative, or curriculum-related acvitity they want to do, and Karen is available to provide materials, set up the environment, conference with students, and give help as needed.

Giving students more options connected to what they are interested in is a recent change for Karen. She notes that the half day of flexible time or "independent choice" allows her to observe children and then set directions in her teaching. She states, "I have found that children will take me where they need to go."

Karen also provides unstructured time through daily sharing. At the beginning of the year, children are assigned their day of the week for sharing, and approximately four to five children have an opportunity to share daily. Sharing time sometimes leads to a curriculum focus. One afternoon a student brought in two beetles in a paper bag. A lively class discussion led Karen to bring in books about beetles. One student chose to make an elaborate beetle out of art supplies found in the room.

Examples of Reading-Writing Opportunities

Joan Servis' fourth grade students have daily reading-writing opportunities, and Joan is available during that time to conference with students. See Figure 15–6 for Joan's weekly schedule.

The following were the opportunities listed on the chalkboard one morning early in the school year just before Halloween and again near the end of the school year when a folk/fairy tale unit was in progress (see Appendix A). Asterisks (*) designate required activities.

Opportunities—October 25

1. *Halloween book (original Halloween story for first-graders)
2. Reader's Theater (poem or picture book)
3. Cleveland Electric Illuminating Company Contest (poster on how electricity affects our lives)
4. Letter to Robert Munsch (follow-up reading-hearing many of his books)
5. Memorize Halloween chant to do with first-graders
6. Message for message board
7. Letters to American servicemen and servicewomen in Saudi Arabia (during the Middle East crisis in Kuwait)
8. Newspaper activity (to go along with local daily newspaper)
9. Rods (cuisennaire rod puzzles)

Opportunities—May 15

1. *Young Authors book—finish
2. Fairy tale—choose new one to read
   Storymapping
   Picture of characters and setting
   Sloppy copy of original fairy tale
3. "Once Upon a Time" project
   Optional activities to go along with fairy tales (see Appendix A)
4. Read—independently or with a partner
   Books for Young Authors that have been completed by other students
   Optional activities to go along with fairy tales
5. Messages for message board
6. News articles for "Onaway Outreach"
7. Journals

See Figures 15–9 through 15–11 for additional examples by other teachers.

Figure 15-9 *One Day's Invitations to Meaningful Independent Activities in Grade 1*
From Jim Henry's first grade classroom.

Today's Invitations   5·31-90

Continue journal
Listening center
Reading center
Letters to:
    Jake the Snake (garden snake)
    Nipper
    Cuddles } guinea pigs (classroom pets)

Projects   (literature adaptations)
    The Tenth Good Thing About _____
    Frog and Toad Are Friends
        chapter 6
    The Longest Journey in Shaker Heights
    Jake the Snake Manual
    Blueberries for _____

Figure 15-10   Independent Work in a Grade 3 Classroom

From Linda Cooper's third grade classroom.

**The following appears on the chalkboard
and the items shown below are on a table under the chalkboard**

LANGUAGE WORKSHOP

Independent Worktime Activities *(required)*	Book Projects *(optional)*
1. Reading Assignment	Make a diorama
2. Homonyms	Write a letter to/from
3. Thesaurus	a character
4. Personification Story	Make a mobile
5. Riddle Book	Make a puppet show
	Write a reaction to the book
	Make a poster advertising
	· the book
	Write a commercial
	Make a book jacket
	Make up your own extension
	project (clear it first)

1. **Reading Assignment** – the assignment made in reading group which may be a reading and/or a written activity.

2. **Homonyms** – (skill project) – every day for about two weeks four new homonyms were solicited from the students. Each pair of homonyms was recorded on the pears in alphabetical order. The students then used each homonym correctly in a sentence. (Dictionaries were used as references). Another class period was given to cutting out all the pears, punching a hole in each, and arranging them in alphabetical order on a ring. (This project is evaluated by the homonym being used and spelled correctly, and the proper use of capitals, punctuation and alphabetical order).

3. **Thesaurus** – Each day a new word is added to the thesaurus. This word is usually an "overused" word from their writing. They may use dictionaries, reading group books, library books, or any other written material as a resource to complete this activity. The thesaurus is then used by the student as a reference.

4. **Personification Story** – After studying an author and his/her books, such as William Steig's picture books leading up to the core reading book, Abel's Island, each student then writes his/her own personification story.

5. **Riddle Book** – On each page of the book, three clues and an illustration about a main character are given so that we can guess the character and novel.

Figure 15-11   Suggestions for Independent Activities
From Julie Beers's third grade classroom.

Name: _____

* Homonym Book	* Indian Research Report	* Draw a picture for each chapter of Stone Fox. Write 3 or more sentences for each picture.
Write a letter to the author of a book and explain your reaction to the book.	Draw a comic strip of your book.	Readers Theatre for any book. Perform for class.
Make a poster advertising your book.	Write out your title decoratively and for each letter write a phrase about the book.	Make a time line of the events in the life of the main character.

* <u>Must</u> <u>Do</u>

Managing Multiple Reading Groups

Teachers who are accustomed to teaching literature with a whole-class approach panic at the thought of juggling multiple reading groups. Especially worrisome is the independent work, the seatwork component. How to design reading time so students are productively involved in meaningful activities when the teacher is meeting with a reading group has been a challenge for all of us.

We are constantly reminded how difficult the transition is from workbooks and packaged activities to more meaningful independent work when we have visitors. Third grade teacher Linda Cooper and I have noticed that many visitors to her classroom spend most of their time examining the independent work the children are doing, even when they could be observing her facilitating an interesting reading group discussion. We are reminded that until teachers feel they can manage the independent work component, multiple reading groups do not seem possible for many teachers.

Organizing for Reading Groups

We find that we can meet with three reading groups in about one hour. When getting started with groups and using three different books, some teachers find that rotating the three books among the heterogeneous groups works well to give everyone a chance to read each book. Most of us try to meet with groups daily. Others work out a system they are comfortable with, for example, meeting with reading groups three days a week and conferencing with students individually two days a week. As long as students have lots of daily opportunities for reading and writing, with teacher guidance and independently, there is no one right or best way to set up groups. Because reading groups are used mostly for discussion once the child is reading fluently, all the important points about the reading surface in a fifteen-minute period. (See Chap. 6, "Responding to Literature: Later Transitions," for specific procedures and management of the reading group.)

In addition to heterogeneous grouping, it is also important to meet with the student or a small group of students who are experiencing difficulty reading the common text. While heterogeneous grouping works well for discussion and collaboration, it is still our job to teach students at their instructional level. We need to take time daily to guide students in figuring out unknown vocabulary, attacking new words, integrating all cueing systems, and practicing reading for fluency.

Multiple Reading Groups in Grade 1

As previously mentioned, until children are reading easily, I like to meet with homogeneous groups for at least the first several months of school. I find that we go through about one book a week per group and that most of the independent activities spring from the books and from the children's own ideas. When the classroom is child centered, the students are deeply involved in developing activities and creating projects right along with you.

I have found it works well to do as much as you can during group time so you are not spending a lot of time on outside planning. In addition to on-the-spot teaching, independent work can be created in group. For example, the final copy of an innovation on a text can be done during group time. This also has the advantage of students seeing the teacher modeling and writing in front of them. As an example, early in the school year, after a group of struggling first-graders had read *I Climb* (DLM, 1976), using blank ditto paper we did a shared writing modeled on the simple text. The students decided to write an *I Jump* book following the same pattern and number of pages but using the names of students in the group. (" 'I can jump,' said Katie" was a typical page.) Reproducing the completed booklet so students could illustrate it and use it as another reading text took only five minutes. (See "Teaching for Strategies," pp. 138–144, for examples of strategy lessons in primary grade reading groups.)

Reading Group Rules, Grade 1

- Don't tell another person a word. Give the person time to try to figure it out.
- Follow along even if it's not your turn to read.

Finding a Comfortable Noise Level

Moving from a silent classroom to a classroom full of conversation is an adjustment for most of us. When I am with a reading group, I cannot concentrate if there is loud talking. I am comfortable only with students whispering, and I make that an expectation of students. With young children who have difficulty keeping their voices to a whisper, role playing seems to help.

Independent Work Time

As the whole language classroom evolves, students know what is expected of them and how and where to seek help when they need it. Usually there are some required activities, but there are choices as well. Many of us have found that a good plan is to expect the reading assignment to be done first. Above grade 1, this assignment frequently involves silent reading and response in the literature response log. There may also be a required project connected with the read-aloud book or curriculum. For example, activities may be related to a field trip or care of classroom pets, or communicating-writing to parents or people relevant to a topic of study. Included also are optional activities, such as are described in "Literature Extension Activities" (pp. 87–102), or skills booklets connected to literature (pp. 135–138). See Figures 15–9 through 15–11 for three teachers' expectations during independent work time while reading groups were taking place and pages 439–440 for samples of "opportunities."

Some choices and opportunities have included, but are not limited to, sustained silent reading, writing a draft, journal writing, listening to a tape of a story, using the overhead projector (placed on the floor with the week's poems on transparencies), responding to literature (through the reading log or literature extension activities), editing, peer conferencing, working at the computer, following a filmstrip, and making a tape.

While demonstrations will be necessary for some of what will be done during independent work time, most of reading time will be spent reading and writing. With traditional seatwork, it typically takes at least fifteen to thirty minutes daily just to explain what students are to do. We need to be questioning that kind of time being spent on activities of questionable value.

A difficult transition for many of us has been to think of the time children spend reading and listening to books during their independent work time as valuable. Used to seeing products and completed pages, teachers need time to value activities where the results are not so concretely visible. Even more difficult for many of us is the concept of allowing children choice in the work they do. Providing choice allows children to pursue a highly engaging activity without interruption.

First grade teacher Jim Henry notes that when his students were given more choice during independent work time—including choosing the format and the project—more students became engaged with their work, more time was spent on the task, and the quality of work improved. Jim moved from mandatory projects, where he set up the format and was requiring a certain number of completed pages a day, to offering students "invitations" to choose from a variety of options. Jim comments, "Looking back, I see that I was giving kids a lot of 'busy work.' I spent a lot of time trying to convince them that the dittos and fragmented writing were important when they weren't."

Jim notes that students did not automatically monitor their time well. A weekly form we developed proved to be an effective management tool (see Figure 15–12). Students kept all their contracts and work in a folder Jim looked at daily and collected weekly. He took anecdotal notes on students' projects and conferenced with students as needed. (See also Figure 15–13 for a daily management plan developed by second grade teacher Elaine Weiner to put students in charge of their work.)

Another effective management tool for promoting appropriate behavior during independent work time is first to do a shared writing of behavioral expectations. I find it works well to treat the shared writing as a draft and make modifications with students as problems arise. The following was a first draft from a grade 2 class.

Rules for Independent Work

1. Work quietly.
2. If you have a question, use a whisper voice and ask someone at your table.
3. Work at your seat on
     reading
     journal
     any other assignment given.
4. When you finish your work
     read free choice book
     listen to a tape
     go to art center
     use the computer
     practice cursive handwriting
     work on Have-a-Go sheet
     illustrate published book
     get a game to play quietly (up to four people).

Organizing for Visitors

We have many visitors that come to find out more about whole language and a literature approach to reading. We are very careful to tell all visitors that we are in transition, that we are still at the beginning stages of moving toward whole language, and that we are all learners too. After several years of trial and error, we have worked out a system for visitors that works well for both the visitors and us teachers. I share our procedures so that you may adapt what is useful to your own school.

Visiting teachers and administrators are first invited to attend our weekly whole language support group with the hope that they may see it as a possibility for

Figure 15–12   Weekly Plan: Two First Grade Students

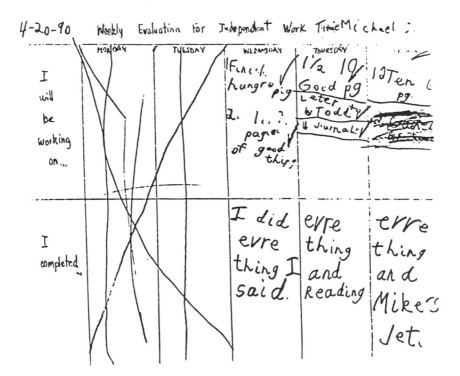

Figure 15-13   A Second-grader's Daily Management Plan

MY WORK PLANS   (daily)

NAME _____ alexander _____

DATE June 7 _____

THIS IS WHAT I NEED TO DO:

1. Scence EXPeriment _____
2. √Fairy tale. _____
3. √Reading _____
4. Reading log _____
5. Wether EXPEriments _____
6. √Wether PuZZle _____

Check off all items that you have finished.

Take home any work that is not finished for homework.

Please have your parents initial this paper after your homework is finished.

support and staff development in their own building. Then visitors have the opportunity to visit classrooms and explore the WEB, where our literature collection is housed. Finally, the principal, myself, and whatever teachers are available meet with the group of visitors to answer their questions, clear up any confusions, and to learn from each other.

While at the beginning certain teachers were selected to have visitors, in the last few years any teacher who chooses to have her classroom open may do so. In keeping with whole language philosophy, which respects all learners, no matter where they happen to be in the process, this more democratic format presents a realistic picture of the change process and is fair to and respectful of all teachers.

Also in keeping with whole language philosophy, our visitors are not assigned to particular rooms but may choose the classrooms they want to visit. They receive a welcome letter describing the makeup of the building and school district, some general information about whole language in our district, a map of the building, a schedule, and a brief description of what will be going on in the classrooms that are open for visitation.

Additionally, some visitors also receive a detailed description of what is going on in a particular classroom. Some teachers have taken visitations as an opportunity for an authentic writing experience. The teacher and students do a shared writing of what visitors can expect to observe in the classroom. Some of these pieces are detailed and include an explanation of procedures in reading, writing, and other areas. These handouts—along with encouraging visitors to talk with students about their questions—allow the teacher to continue teaching without interruption. The descriptions of language learning also allow the visitor to better understand what is happening in the classroom. These shared writings may also serve as self-evaluations for teachers. Teachers note how their students are perceiving reading, writing, and other language-curriculum processes in the classroom.

Utilizing Library Services

Librarians are valuable resources available in every community. They are aware of the latest and best books published and have a wealth of information on these books. They are experts at finding the books and resources teachers need.

Even if your school does not have a library or librarian, you can use your public libraries to enrich your curriculum and support your teaching. Susan Scheps, supervisor of the children's department at one of our local public libraries, says, "I have never met a children's librarian from a public library who wouldn't be thrilled to be approached by a teacher for any kind of help at all—read-alouds, special projects, research, anything."

In addition to our public libraries, we are fortunate in our district to have libraries and librarians in every school building as well as a district library media office that supports and facilitates the operation of all our libraries. Most book and media orders and requests for laminating and spiral binding of Big Books and blank books go through the district library office under the leadership of Ellen Stepanian.

While the services discussed in this section relate to our district, my hope is that you will see possibilities and options for your own school and district.

• *Check your public library resources.*   Most public libraries will arrange for you to sign out multiple copies of books for your literature program if given sufficient notice. With limited school or district budgets, the local public library system may be used to supplement the school and library resources. In an effort to support literature-based reading, some public libraries now have available twenty or so paperback copies of many titles, and often the books can be signed out for three or four weeks. If such a service is not yet available in your area, you may want to work with your local schools and public libraries to make it a reality.

• *Communicate with your librarian.*   Let your librarian know what kinds of books and resources you need. For example, if you are looking for predictable books or various versions of a familiar tale, your librarian can alert you to books already existing in the collection as well as new and recently acquired books.

Share bibliographies from workshops and professional books with librarians. Many of the books you are interested in may already be in the library collection, and your librarian can locate them for you.

Also, share articles and information from workshops about whole language. Include librarians in staff development efforts. Librarians will be better able to assist you if they understand the principles of whole language and how those principles apply to teaching and learning in the classroom.

• *Establish a classroom library.*   Support your independent reading program by using your school and/or public library to bring books into the classroom. Often books may be borrowed for an extended period of time, and you will probably be able to sign out thirty to fifty books at once.

- *Begin a professional library.*   If you do not already have a professional library for teachers in your school, be the impetus for starting one. You might want to begin by subscribing to newsletters and journals. (See *Resources for Teachers* for recommendations.) If a professional library already exists, recommend to the librarian outstanding new titles for purchase.

- *Find out about available media.*   Check with your librarian for video, filmstrips, cassettes, public television programs, and other resources to enrich literature and content area study. Find out about programming and scheduling for "Reading Rainbow," "Long Ago and Far Away," and other exceptional public broadcasting opportunities.

- *Become familiar with authors.*   Librarians can gather many books by one author, information about authors, and addresses to write to authors, and they may be willing to help arrange an author visit or a Young Authors' conference in your school or local area. Public librarians also inform teachers of author visits to local schools and bookstores.

- *Incorporate nonfiction books into your reading program.*   Consult your librarian to learn about and to incorporate nonfiction into your reading program. With a literature approach to reading, most of the emphasis has been on fiction, but children also need to appreciate nonfiction as an important genre. Fortunately, more and more high-interest, beautifully illustrated and easy to read nonfiction books have been published. Librarians are more likely than teachers to be familiar with the latest and best in nonfiction—including books in enlarged print, books with outstanding illustrations, and books on timely topics. Your public library budget will usually allow for a more extensive nonfiction collection than your school library.

- *Let librarians know what your classroom needs are several weeks in advance.*

Multiple copies of books   If your school district has libraries in each building, often your librarian can get you multiple copies of a desired title by borrowing from other buildings. Your local public library may be able to do the same and may even be able to extend the usual loan period.

Resources for a unit of study   Librarians are terrific resources for planning and implementing thematic units. Not only will they help gather resources, but often they are willing to come into classrooms and work with teachers if the teacher requests it. Some school librarians will also prepare written bibliographies for content areas or thematic units. For example, a librarian can compile a list of math-related literature, books on handicapped people, environmental issues, or whatever topic is being studied.

When the local public library is notified ahead of time that a teacher will need lots of books for an upcoming project, the librarian can temporarily extend the loan period on books related to the topic and can designate certain titles as reference books for a set amount of time. In that way, more students have access to the books, and librarians can provide better service to students.

• *Talk to your public librarian about the arrangement of easy readers.*   Our local public libraries have recently changed the way beginning reading books are organized. All grade-level designations have been removed from books. Books—up to chapter books—are now categorized to reflect readability levels based on multiple factors, rather than just readability formulas. Books for children are divided into three sections—"Get Ready" (easier), "Get Set" (medium), and "Go" (harder) —roughly based on the readability and book-leveling system given in *Transitions* (Routman, 1988). Picture books and chapter books are organized into separate sections.

Local librarians were finding that strict adherence to grade levels to categorize books was inconsistent with what the schools were trying to promote with literature use and was giving parents the wrong message. Parents were coming to the library asking for "hard" books, believing their children would become better readers with books at a higher level. The librarians find that the new organization system supports what librarians have always done when helping connect children and books. With a young reader, they are likely to ask, "What have you read lately?" and then suggest, "Take a look at this book. Read this sentence." Librarians find that this more natural approach to books has promoted wider reading among students and a more relaxed approach to book selection with parents.

• *Support a summer reading program.*   Our school librarians publish an annual annotated reading list that goes home with students at the end of the school year. Such a list gives guidance to children, parents, and teachers and narrows the selection when there are so many books to choose from. Most public libraries sponsor motivational summer reading activities. Invite your local public librarians into your classroom to talk about summer reading and the programs they offer. We find that when students read widely over the summer, they make gains in fluency, vocabulary, and comprehension. Communicate with parents to make them aware of summer reading opportunities.

Organizing a Book Collection

Getting Money for Books

Jean Sylak, our director of elementary education, notes that the cost of moving from a basal-workbook reading program to a total literature program initially cost approximately the same amount as adopting a new basal series. In addition, the thousands of dollars that used to be spent annually for workbooks have gone toward replacing books and updating the schools' collections. However, our district budget for art supplies doubled after we made a commitment to move toward whole language.

Some teachers in other districts have been able to use the money that used to go for consumable workbooks and worksheets to purchase paperback literature. Other teachers have written grant proposals for books and/or enlisted the help of their Parent-Teacher Association to raise funds.

My recommendation is that whatever your budget, put most of the available funds into books, not programs. Except for the very early levels, where children need lots of easy reading material that is not always available as literature, books are your best investment. We have also chosen to invest in paperbacks that have not been specially coated for durability—and cost more—so that we can buy as many books as possible.

Selecting Titles for Purchase

Before ordering books for a literature collection, it is important to be familiar with the best of children's literature. The "Recommended Literature" by grade levels (k–12) and categories (blue pages) will be helpful in guiding you in organizing and ordering your own classroom, building, or district collection. Also, use your own personal favorites, and check with your librarian and other teachers for suggestions.

A collection of quality literature has become a priority in our district. We started with a core collection of books in each elementary building, which included approximately seven titles per grade level with enough copies to be used whole class or in small groups. (Each kindergarten class also received *The Story Box* [Stage 1, The Wright Group], which included twenty-four Big Books and accompanying little books.) In general, if there were four classes at a grade level, then enough copies of a title were purchased for two full classrooms. In addition, a supplemental collection, based on teacher and librarian recommendations—and titles suggested in *Transitions* (Routman, 1988)—were purchased for each k–4 building. Ten copies of more than 300 titles were purchased. The quantity was less for Big Books. The grade level assigned to the books is based on teacher input and is determined within each building. While the core books are used only at the designated grade level, or at a higher grade level, the supplemental books are used by the entire building.

We continue to meet by grade levels several times yearly to discuss the use of the books and to update our collections. Based on the recommendations of teachers and librarians, our district library media office orders books to be evaluated for possible purchase. For example, grade 1 teachers felt they needed a nonfiction book in the core collection. Thus, *Chickens Aren't the Only Ones* by Ruth Heller was purchased in Big Book and little book form after first grade teachers had had an opportunity to discuss possible titles. In grade 4, teachers decided they no longer wanted to use one core book that had been originally selected. In its place, teachers chose to use Cynthia Rylant's book of short stories, *Every Living Thing*, and copies were ordered through the library media office.

In addition to the common core collection in each building, every building orders titles, through each principal's budget, to meet student and teacher needs. For example, in the building where I am based, teachers sought more multicultural titles, especially African-American literature. Several teachers took the responsibility for recommending quality titles, and approximately twenty new books, in multiples of ten, were ordered. We have also been able to secure new titles through the generosity of the Parent-Teacher Association.

Housing the Collection

Each of our elementary buildings has a central location for housing the literature collection and a committee that is responsible for managing the collection. Often it is parent volunteers who oversee the organization of the book room. In the building where I am based, we house all our books in a former book storage room, and we call the room the WEB. Conduit pipe, secured by eye bolts, has been installed to hang our Big Books on skirt hangers. "Notes on the Use of the WEB" are given to all teachers the first week of school. (See Appendix F for specifics on our WEB procedures and organization.)

I believe that a central storage area, open equally to all teachers, is necessary for the successful functioning of a literature program. In the building where I am based, our literature collection—which includes core books, commercial books, teacher-made Big Books, and supplemental literature in various genres—is open to all classroom teachers, the L.D. teacher, the L.D. tutor, the Chapter 1 teacher, tutors, parent volunteers, and the teachers of the behavior-disordered class and the developmentally handicapped class. Books are signed out as needed. Teachers looking for a particular book need only look at the sign-out book (see Figure 15–14 for a sample page) to see who has the title and how long it has been signed out. All books are returned to the WEB at the end of the school year.

That all teachers should have equal access to all books cannot be emphasized enough. In that way, all teachers have an equal opportunity to sign out as many books as other teachers, and new teachers to the building—or teachers who have just moved into a literature approach—are not at a disadvantage. In one building a lot of resentment built up when a teacher refused to house "her" books (which had been purchased with district funds) in the central book area. One teacher even

Figure 15-14   A Page from the "Literature Collection" Sign-out Book

MERCER SCHOOL LITERATURE PROGRAM PAPERBACK BOOK COLLECTION

Note: Title* indicates reading group book.
Big Book* indicates teacher-made book.

GRD	TITLE	#	TYPE	Initial	# Books	Date Out	Date In	Initial	# Books	Date Out	Date In	Initial	# Books	Date Out	Date In	Initial	# Books	Date Out	Date In
1	I Was Walking Down the Road	1	BB																
1	I Was Walking Down the Road*	19	Fic																
1	I Wish I Was Sick Too	13	Fic																
1	I'll Be the Horse If You'll Play With Me	3	Fic																
1	I'll Fix Anthony*	10	Fic																
4	Ida Early Comes Over the Mountain	9	Fic																
	If A Poem Bothers You	9	Poetry																
1	If I Had*	7	Fic																
2/3	If I Were in Charge of the World	10	Poetry																
	If Kids Could Ask the President One Question	2	NFic																
2	If the Dinosaurs Came Back	1	BB*																
2	If the Dinosaurs Came Back	13	Fic																
1	If You Give A Mouse...	9	Fic																
1	If You Meet A Dragon	10	Fic																
2	If You Sailed on the Mayflower	3	NFic																
3	Iggie's House	2	Fic																
1	In a Dark Dark Wood	1	BB																
1	In a Dark Dark Wood*	7	Fic																

transferred to another building the following year, largely because of the negative feelings of inequity that resulted. Even though the teacher with all the books said that anyone could borrow those books from her room, it is a lot easier to take books from a central location where no special permission is needed.

Caring for and Repairing Books, and Book Sign-out

Without special handling and attention, our core books have on average lasted three years. Where teachers have taken time to talk with students about book care and handling and have made caring for and repairing books a priority, titles have lasted much longer. In the school where I am based, most of our collection is still in use after seven years of heavy use. That extra durability is due to the responsibility teachers put on students to take care of books and to the dedication of parent volunteers who spend many hours repairing our books.

Most book repairs involve the use of transparent book tape of various widths to reinforce bindings, covers, and inside covers. To facilitate the repair process, we have several tape system applicators (ordered from an office supply company) for volunteers and students to use. Additionally, our Parent-Teacher Association recently purchased us a plastic binding system that allows spiral binding of books where the pages are still usable but the binding cannot be repaired. The binding system is also used extensively in the publishing process in grade 2 and up and for school-wide publishing needs.

Under the leadership of Judy Heiskell, our parent volunteer WEB room coordi-

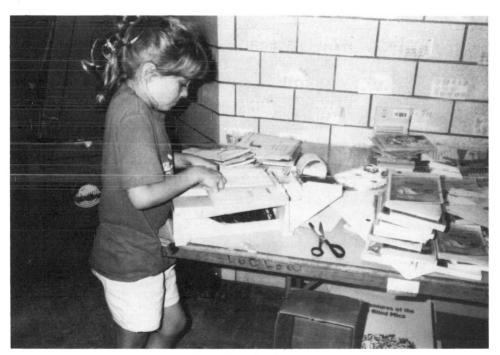

End of year book repair

Parent volunteer Judy Heiskell organizing the WEB

nator in the building where I am based, all books in our collection are inventoried, repaired, and reshelved at the end of the school year. Other volunteer parents and some older students work with Judy for several weeks in this time-consuming but worthwhile effort. For easy storage and handling, books are grouped by title with rubber bands. Books that can no longer be repaired and need to be replaced are returned to the library media office with a request for new copies.

Our school secretary, Bev Scoby, has entered our entire collection on computer, and she updates it each summer and prints out a new sign-out book for the upcoming school year. We are also extremely fortunate that Donna Jackson has assumed the responsibility for putting the new sign-out book together and to have it ready for the first week of school. Donna Jackson is our new WEB room coordinator.

Ordering Paperback Books

Wholesalers

If you are fortunate enough to have two or three hundred dollars or more, you probably want to order from a book wholesaler in order to receive a sizable discount. Also, even though you may be ordering books from many different publishers, it is a great time saver to be able to place your entire order with one source. Most wholesalers will special order titles when they are not in stock. Additionally, many wholesalers are now stocking Big Books. Plan to order about 25 percent more book titles than the money allotted to allow for titles currently out of print and out of stock. You can often expect delivery on your order within a few weeks.

There are hundreds of reputable wholesalers across the country, and many have regional locations as well. Before choosing a wholesaler, check with your school librarian and find out who the school uses to purchase its books. Check to see if there is already a catalog available for you to look at. You may want to place your order directly through your school or district library to save opening up a new account. Also, if your order is included with a library order, you may be able to get a greater discount. Three reputable wholesalers with relevant information are listed below. Wholesalers usually have toll free 800 numbers for obtaining information and offer free catalogs on request. Inquiries should be directed to the school marketing department.

See also "Book Clubs," p. 105b, as a source for discounted books.

BAKER & TAYLOR BOOKS
652 East Main Street
Bridgewater, NJ 08807–0920
(908) 218-0400

- Stocks over 50,000 titles in paperback—includes mass market and trade books
- Will create customized lists according to subject needs; call or write customer service
- Minimum order—ten assorted books
- Discount—negotiable, based on volume, with the following minimum level discounts:
  30% trade and hard cover
  10% single copies
- Ships within 48 hours of receipt of order

THE BOOKMEN INC.
525 North Third Street
Minneapolis, MN 55401
Phone (800) 328-8411
Fax (800) BOOKMEN or (800) 266-5636

- Well-organized catalog *Paperbacks for Young People* annotates the 3,000 most popular children's K-9 paperbacks, ready for 24-hour shipment.
- Over 25,000 paperback titles in stock, including titles for senior high and adults
- Free *Monthly Paperback News* annotates 800 new releases ready for 24-hour shipment, including each month's new juvenile and young adult releases.
- Minimum order of 25 assorted books; will special order titles not in stock with a five-copy minimum (allow about three weeks).
- Will provide customized bibliographies at the request of the school; please call or write customer service.
- Discount—customer choice of 40–43% plus freight, or 36% with free delivery.

H. P. KOPPELMANN INC.
Paperback Book Service
P.O. Box 145
Hartford, CT 06141
(800) 243-7724

- K–8 catalog includes Trade Paperbacks from many publishers; grades 7–12 catalog also available, stocks about 20,000 titles; school and library oriented
- Quality literature titles, some arranged in collections by recommended grade level, authors, and various categories
- Well-done teacher book guides (by notable educators) for over 100 titles; teacher guides may be requested free with an order of 20 copies or more of a title or purchased for $1.00 each
- Videos available for many titles
- Discount: Net, 1–2 copies of the same title
  20%, 3–9 copies of the same title
  25%, 10–29 copies of the same title
  30%, 30 or more of the same title
- Shipping within 72 hours of receipt of order

Transitional Resources for Literature

For teachers and school districts that need a guided framework in the change process, the following publishers produce commercial programs that contain high-quality, balanced anthologies that use unabridged, authentic literature (that now includes quality multicultural literature) and also have helpful, accompanying teacher resource books. While these collections are useful for organization in getting started in whole language, teachers are advised to supplement these programs with quality trade books, particularly at the upper grade levels where literature excerpts are common. Additionally, teachers and administrators are asked to look carefully at how the anthologies are organized and connected to be sure there is depth. Consider the anthology as a way of sampling books and literature in different genres.

DELMAR PUBLISHERS INC.
Two Computer Drive West
Box 15–015
Albany, NY 12212–5015
(800) 347–7707
> *Publishes* Early Bird *for k-1 (geared more to k) and a variety of teacher resources.*

GINN PUBLISHING CANADA INC.
P.O. Box 261
Tonawanda, NY 14151–0261
(800) 361–6128
> *Publishes* Journeys *(k-6). Accompanying teacher resource books are excellent.*

HARCOURT BRACE & COMPANY
School Division
6277 Sea Harbor Drive
Orlando, FL 32887
(800) 787–8707 (East and Midwest)
(800) 426–6577 (West, Southwest, and Southeast)
> *Publishes* Treasury of Literature *(k-8).*

HOUGHTON MIFFLIN COMPANY
222 Berkeley Street
Boston, MA 02116–3764
(Write for your regional sales office and the 800 number that serves your state.)
> *Publishes* Houghton Mifflin Literature *(k-8).*

MACMILLAN/McGRAW-HILL
220 East Danieldale Road
DeSoto, TX 75115
(800) 442–9685
> *Publishes* A New View *(k-8).*

SCHOLASTIC INC.
P.O. Box 7502
Jefferson City, MO 65102
(800) 325–6149
> *Publishes* Bookshelf *(k-2).*

SCOTT FORESMAN AND COMPANY
1900 Lake Ave.
Glenview, IL 60025
(800) 554–4411
> *Publishes* Celebrate Reading *(k-8) and accompanying resources.*

Reliable Sources for Literature
for the Reading-Writing Classroom

The following selections have been found to support a literature approach to reading. Other materials from each publisher will need to be carefully examined to determine whether they are consistent with a whole language philosophy. Some of these companies only publish their own "literature collections," and you have to be choosy in making selections.

CHILDREN'S PRESS
5440 N. Cumberland
Chicago, IL 60656
(800) 621–1115

Children's Press publishes its own beginning reading books (see Rookie Readers, p. 118b), "Adventures in Storytelling," science and social studies collections (see Rookie Read–About Science, p. 95b), books about our states, and biographies. Many titles are available in Spanish.

DLM/SRA
250 Old Wilson Bridge Road
Suite 310
Worthington, OH 43085
(800) 843-8855

DLM publishes literature by Bill Martin, Jr., including a wonderful selection of poetry, Big Books, and a recent edition of the original Sounds of Language series with teachers' editions for grades k–6. Big Books for grades k–2. Audio cassettes are available for k–4. Predictable science books in 9 by 12 inch format for grades k–2 are beautifully photographed and written. Poetry by Leland B. Jacobs is available on 12 by 18 inch posters and in small books. Two sets of six–eight-page predictable books for emergent readers, This Is the Way I Go *and* Can You Do This? *are excellent for practicing early reading strategies.*

HARCOURT BRACE & COMPANY
6277 Sea Harbor Drive
Orlando, FL 32887
(800) 237-2665

Especially notable are the beautifully illustrated Bill Martin Big Books, which include such classics as Brown Bear, Brown Bear, What Do You See? *and* The Longest Journey in the World. *Each Big Book is sold only with eight small books, an audiocassette, and a teacher's guide. "Lap Books" (12½ by 16³⁄₁₆ inches)—high-quality wordless books and picture books by notable authors—are available for k–1 with accompanying small books and cassettes. HBJ also packages trade book libraries for grades k–6.*

HOUGHTON MIFFLIN COMPANY
222 Berkeley Street
Boston, MA 02116-3764
(Write for your regional sales office and the 800 number that serves your state.)

Houghton Mifflin Literature is a collection of multiple copies of six to ten quality paperback books for grade levels k–8, with Big Books included for k and 1. The program is a good transition for teachers moving away from the basal who still want some structure and guidance with authentic literature.

Author Videotapes of ten authors (Russell Freedman, Eve Bunting, Marvin Terban, Lois Lowry, Bill Peet, Scott O'Dell, James Marshall, Elizabeth George Speare, David Macaulay, and Bernard Waber) give students a glimpse of how authors go about creating their books. Houghton Mifflin also publishes multiple titles available in paperback—consult a Houghton Mifflin Children's Trade Book catalog or call a regional sales office 800 number.

MODERN CURRICULUM PRESS
13900 Prospect Avenue
Cleveland, OH 44136
(800) 321-3106

Modern Curriculum Press is an elementary, supplemental publisher that offers choices to teachers and students. They have extensive lines of multicultural, whole language, and language arts products. Over three hundred fiction and nonfiction Big Books are included in their catalog.

NELLIE EDGE SEMINARS AND RESOURCES INC.
P.O. Box 12399
Salem, OR 97309-0399
(800) 523-4594

Nellie Edge is the creator and distributor of predictable Big Books of folksongs, rhymes, poetry, and chants for kindergarten and grade 1. Each spiral-bound Big Book—at an average cost of $13—is constructed of black and white tagboard for teachers to color. Every Big Book order also includes a black line master, allowing teachers to make accompanying personal copies for each student to "read." The company also has high-frequency word stamps for use with young children getting started with writing. Sponsors workshops for grades k–2.

RICHARD C. OWEN PUBLISHERS INC.
P.O. Box 585
Katonah, NY 10536
(914) 232-3903

Richard C. Owen is the distributor for Ready to Read books, a core program of real books— the national reading program in New Zealand—intended for five-, six-, and seven-year-olds. For the upper elementary grades, a quality collection of Canadian poetry and literature—as well as School Journals, a periodical with a variety of genres from New Zealand—is available. A delightful selection of Big Books and an excellent selection of professional books for teachers are also available. The company also sponsors high-quality whole language workshops.

RIGBY EDUCATION
P.O. Box 797
Crystal Lake, IL 60014
(800) 822-8661

This is a reliable source for quality Big Books and accompanying small books. "Contemporary Stories and Traditional Tales" are popular titles for shared book experience. Particularly appealing are "The Informazing Books" by Steve Molene, beautifully photographed informational texts for the elementary grades in Big Book format and accompanied by an extensive teacher resource guide. Eight-page books, for guided and independent reading at the earliest levels, are very useful for gaining fluency and confidence at the emergent reader stage. Rigby also sponsors quality whole language workshops. See the "blue pages" p. 117b, for Rigby collections to use at the emergent "learning to read" stage.

SCHOLASTIC INC.
P.O. Box 7502
Jefferson City, MO 65102
(800) 325-6149

Scholastic is one of the world's largest companies dedicated to the education of young people from preschoolers to secondary school students. It is best known for its magazines, books, software and video. The company is the largest publisher and distributor of children's books in the English-speaking world. Scholastic books are distributed through four major channels: book clubs, book fairs, retail stores and catalogs to schools. Titles include predictable books, chapter books, multicultural books (including Scholastic's Big Multicultural Tales), "Reading Rainbow," and more than 120 Big Books. Among the best known of Scholastic's books are its best-selling paperback series, The Baby-sitters Club; the new hit Goosebumps series of thrillers for pre-teens; The Magic School Bus, a science adventure series; and its many Clifford the Big Red Dog books for younger children.

Teachers and students can access Scholastic authors and books online through Scholastic Network, the first full-service online network connecting schools to a nationwide learning community. Scholastic also publishes a wide range of instructional materials including textbooks, workbooks, classroom paperback reading programs, professional books for teachers, and audio cassettes used as part of the classroom curricula in schools nationwide.

SHORT STORY INTERNATIONAL
6 Sheffield Road
Great Neck, NY 11021
(516) 466-6091

Short Story International is a nonprofit organization that publishes high-quality, multicultural short stories by living authors from countries all over the world. These well-written, contemporary stories—*often accompanied by illustrations—appeal to both reluctant and avid readers and are a nice change of pace from full-length chapter books.*

There are three separate ongoing series. Annual subscriptions, single issues, or back issues are available. With an order of twenty or more subscriptions, a teacher's guide (which may also be ordered separately) is included.

Seedling Series—*geared to grades 4–7 (may be used in grade 3 as a read-aloud or for independent reading); includes seven to eight individually illustrated stories per issue; published four times a year.*

Student Series—*aimed at junior high to high school, grades 8–12; includes ten to twelve stories per issue; published four times a year.*

Short Story International—*for high school advanced placement, college, and adult readers; includes twelve to fifteen stories per issue; published six times a year.*

SUNDANCE
P.O. Box 1326
Newtown Road
Littleton, MA 01460
(800) 343-8204

Sundance publishes and distributes quality trade books, most of which are "multicultural" and also available as Big Books. Some titles are also available in Spanish. Offers individual titles and classroom library collections.

TROLL ASSOCIATES
100 Corporate Drive
Mahwah, NJ 07430
(800) 526-5289

Troll publishes its own reading collections for k-8 including "First Start Easy Readers" (see p. 117b), concept science and social studies books, mysteries, folk tales, and biographies.

21ST CENTURY EDUCATION INC.
1128 Morton Blvd.
Kingston, NY 12401
(800) 866-5559

This source provides k–8 integrated, literature-based units of excellent titles in various genres, grouped by theme and grade level. The typical thematic teaching unit is priced between $100 and $200 and includes books, audios (if applicable), and instructional resources. On average, a unit contains thirty books (six to twelve individual titles) in hardcover and paperback. Units are customized and are meant to be used flexibly across grade levels and special groups. This is a very valuable source for teachers who want to use high-quality literature but are unsure of titles to choose and need support to develop an integrated instructional program centered around literature.

THE WRIGHT GROUP
19201 120th Ave. N.E.
Bothell, WA 98011
(800) 523-2371

The Wright Group publishes more than 2,000 supplemental books in various genre for the emergent, early fluent and fluent reader. Many books are available in Big Book, sets of six student size books, and/or audio cassettes, and class packs. Perhaps The Wright Group is best known as the publisher of The Story Box and The Sunshine Series that they brought to the United States from New Zealand more than ten years ago. Each series features delightful short stories for beginning readers.

Other integrated learning materials include the non-fiction TWIG, and the Story-Basket featuring the beloved and well known character Mrs. Wishy-Washy. An extensive line of traditional, historical, contemporary, and science songs are presented in The Song Box. Professional teacher resource books are now available, and quality integrated learning workshops are offered nationally for teachers of k-6.

For information on ordering books through Book Clubs, see page 105b.

THE WRIGHT GROUP
19201 120th Ave. N.E.
Bothell, WA 98011
(800) 523-2371

The Wright Group is the publisher of The Story Box, *a collection of Big Books and accompanying little books from New Zealand. Especially delightful are the predictable titles for kindergarten and grade 1, Level 1, Emergent Level. Many eight-page little books, which are good for beginning reading practice and developing fluency, are included in the* Sunshine Series *and nonfiction TWIG books. The Song Box includes traditional children's songs (such as "The Eensy Weensy Spider" and "She'll Be Comin' 'Round the Mountain")—available as Big Books with accompanying small books. Various resource books for teachers are available. The Wright Group offers integrated language workshops, k–6.*

16

Establishing Support Networks

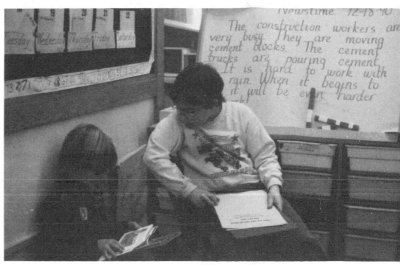

*Using older students: a fourth-grader
helping a first-grader with his reading*

I believe teachers must take the lead in staff development and in establishing support networks in their districts. Traditionally, staff development has been undervalued in this country, with many school districts having no long range plans for professional development. In order to move forward in our teaching, however, we must become knowledgeable practitioners. We need to understand sound staff development practices so we can put our theory and potential resources into effective practice.

This chapter explores effective staff development as well as support resources for teaching. While the examples given come from my school district and experiences, my hope is that you will be stimulated to think about investigating possible resources for staff development and support in your own school and district. No doubt, your available resources will be somewhat different. Nonetheless, you can use this chapter as a way to think about your own workable possibilities for establishing support networks.

Staff Development

We are a society conditioned to the quick fix, the one-shot workshop led by the expert from out-of-town. In education, change has traditionally meant new materials with, perhaps, some in-service on the use of those materials. Then, the following year, the focus usually shifts to a new subject. Rarely has change in school districts focused on an ongoing commitment that emphasizes educational philosophy and how we teach. Rather, the emphasis is usually on methodology and what we teach. Since whole language implementation necessitates a strong evolving theory base, the one-shot approach is particularly ineffective. For change to be effective, comprehensive, and lasting, staff development must occur cohesively over an extended period of time.

461

Staff development has traditionally been done *to* teachers and *on* teachers instead of *with* teachers and *by* teachers. My own personal philosophy views teachers as knowledgeable professionals who should be actively involved with planning and implementation. Teachers have a clear sense of what they need for growth and development; these needs must be seriously considered. Besides aiming at increased professional knowledge, staff development programs should include opportunities for teacher leadership, collegial interaction, decision making, and problem solving. Most important, effective staff development should lead teacher-learners toward continued inquiry and independence.

The terms "in-service" and "staff development" need clarification because they are sometimes used interchangeably. However, they do not refer to the same thing. While in-service may encompass more than one session and be a part of staff development, its goal is to provide specific information to staff with little or no follow-up. Usually the information is transmitted to the audience with minimal opportunities for interaction. On the other hand, staff development is an ongoing program that focuses on specific needs—for example, the district's, the students', or the teachers'. Staff development provides not only information but the time to process and integrate knowledge and practice. The goal of staff development is to improve conditions, whether it be the climate of the school or skills of the teacher.

My Beliefs and Goals about Staff Development

Because I believe it's important to be able to articulate one's philosophy, I state my personal beliefs and goals as an example of how you might explore your own. As you read this, I hope you will reflect on your own beliefs and develop your own theoretical framework.

Beliefs	*Goals*
• Staff development must be ongoing.	• Establish support groups that meet regularly. Put in place a three- to five-year staff development plan.
• Teachers must have choices.	• Allow voluntary attendance at support groups. Provide options in required staff development.
• Program change must be research and knowledge based.	• Read and discuss professional literature, attend conferences, and provide other opportunities for acquisition of theory.
• Teachers should be encouraged to attend professional conferences and participate in professional organizations.	• Allocate adequate discretionary funds, and make professional growth a priority. Have clear expectations for resourcing these opportunities.
• Teachers should be involved in district decision making.	• Include teachers in curriculum design, district evaluation procedures, and hiring new teachers.

Beliefs	*Goals*
• A teacher-to-teacher component is desirable and necessary.	• Recognize and utilize talented classroom and resource teachers for potential teacher leaders, staff developers, and coaches.
• Teachers need support in the change process.	• Give release time for in-service, and provide support staff to facilitate the change process.
• First-year teachers need additional support.	• Provide a mentor teacher/internship for at least one year.
• Teachers need opportunities to observe and interact with other teachers.	• Provide release time for peer observation and collaboration. Provide training for peer coaching.
• Teachers need time for collegial reflection during the school day.	• Use specialists, paraprofessionals, and parents to create blocks of time for discussion and planning.
• Effective change takes lots of time.	• Establish reasonable time lines for both staff development and teacher change.
• Different people need different support and time expectations.	• Make provisions for individual differences.
• All of these beliefs and goals also apply to administrators.	• Provide staff development opportunities for administrators. Expect administrators to participate actively.

Components of Effective Staff Development

Bruce Joyce and Beverly Showers, well-known researchers on effective teacher change, have outlined principles and components of effective staff development that have been widely accepted. They have found that for new concepts and strategies to transfer to classroom teaching, the components discussed below need to build on each other and be used in combination (Joyce and Showers, 1980). The following discussion applies their components to whole language teaching.

1. Presentation of Theory

Understanding the research and theory of literacy learning provides the rationale for a whole language instructional approach to teaching and learning. In-service by "experts" can fit here. Interactive discussion of professional reading and theory takes place regularly at our weekly language arts support groups. Development of theory is ongoing.

2. Demonstration or Modeling

Demonstrations show the learner how to do the skill or strategy and also increase understanding of the theory. Usually multiple demonstrations are necessary.

Teachers demonstrate for each other at our weekly language arts support groups as well as view effective professional videotapes. A major part of my job is demonstrating strategy lessons for teachers.

As a language arts resource teacher, I go into classrooms and demonstrate how shared reading, shared writing, journal writing, literature discussion, or any other component of whole language might be taught. I first meet with the teacher to discuss her needs and where she is in the change process. After the teacher has observed the demonstration lesson or specific intervention strategies, we discuss what has gone on and what the teacher is comfortable with and has questions about.

3. Practice under Simulated Conditions

The teacher tries out the new strategy when circumstances do not require managment of the whole class. Peer coaching is very effective here. In my role, I encourage and attempt to give the teacher confidence while she is trying out a new strategy. Then she takes time to practice on her own. Repeated practice will be necessary.

4. Structured Feedback

Structured feedback through careful observation gives the teacher an opportunity to reflect on teaching behavior. Structured feedback should be presented in a way that encourages teachers to draw their own conclusions. Feedback can come from peers, administrators, or self. I often observe a teacher trying out a new approach, and, afterwards, I meet with the teacher to give constructive feedback. I try to avoid the one-shot deal. For effective change, practice-feedback on the new instructional practice needs to happen at least several consecutive times. Before this can happen, there has to be a high level of trust between teachers.

5. Coaching for Application

For maximum transfer of new learning, coaching is the critical component. I define coaching as a collegial process where support, assistance, and companionship are given along with demonstrations and constructive feedback. Without coaching, strategies that have been tried out may never reach the application-to-teaching stage. This is what is inherently wrong with a one-shot approach to staff development; there are no personal support systems built in for employment of new knowledge.

Coaching is the largest and most satisfying part of my job. As a nonjudgmental coach, I try to be an encourager, cheerleader, and supportive and empathetic assistant. While I may try to guide the teacher in analyzing and interpreting teaching behaviors, I am not an evaluator or supervisor in any way. I am a peer working and collaborating with peers.

Coaching does not work if it is tainted by "evaluation," actual or implied. The "threat" of evaluation can hinder or destroy the mutual trust needed for effective change.

Teacher Support Groups

One of the most effective staff development vehicles that employs some of the principles just listed is the teacher support group. All over the country teachers are getting together and forming groups to support and encourage each other as they move toward meaning-centered, whole language teaching. In these meetings, teachers talk frankly about issues and concerns in their teaching and try to integrate theory and practice. Many of us have found that meeting with our peers has lessened our anxiety, fostered collegiality and collaboration, and promoted and confirmed professional growth. Perhaps, above all, we find out we are not alone; others have struggled along with us.

There are now many state and local understanding whole language networks, and even a Confederation of Whole Language Support Groups, called the Whole Language Umbrella, which provides a network for groups across the United States and Canada. Many of these groups are called TAWL (Teachers Applying Whole Language). I prefer the designation used by some California teachers I met; their TAWL stands for Teachers Attempting Whole Language. I also like the TAWL that stands for Teachers Approaching Whole Language, or Talking About Whole Language, or Ohio's Teachers Advocating Whole Literacy. We have simply called our school and district groups Language Arts Support Groups or Whole Language Support Groups. Whatever name is used, it should be inclusive and welcoming to all interested teachers.

Getting Support Groups Going

Weekly Building Support Groups

When I first began my job as a teacher supporting other teachers in transition to whole language, I saw a need for teachers to have time to be together to share issues and concerns and to support each other. In addition, there was no way I could provide full support to all interested teachers in the school district. By meeting collegially, we could all learn from each other and grow professionally. Our meetings are a form of peer coaching. Through ongoing dialoguing and sharing with each other in the change process toward more effective teaching, we have become supportive communities.

Our weekly language arts support groups have been in place in each of our k–4 buildings since the fall of 1987. Since school does not begin until 9:15 A.M., we meet from 8:30 to 9:00 A.M. in the library or in a classroom. I serve as facilitator at four of the buildings; fourth grade teacher Joan Servis serves as facilitator in her building. For me this has meant five meetings a week. For teachers who choose to attend, this means one morning a week. Attendance ranges from about 50 to 90 percent of the staff, depending on interests, needs, and time demands. Some teachers attend faithfully every week; others have never come. This open door policy is an important aspect. It protects teachers' rights to attend voluntarily; it treats teachers as adults. The focus and agenda are set by the group, based on teachers' expressed needs. A copy of the agenda and applicable articles are distributed with the principal's weekly bulletin. The time and location of the meeting is announced over the public address system by the school secretary just before it is ready to begin.

We began haphazardly. The first year our district made a commitment to more meaningful approaches to reading and writing through literature, our agenda was fragmented and scattered, reflecting our own confusion and disorganization. Most of our concerns were related to practical and organizational matters—materials, activities, and management. One week we talked about one issue; the following week the agenda would be totally different. Looking back, that seems quite normal for the change process. We needed time to find our own way. That first year principals did not generally attend the meetings. They were sensitive to the fact that teachers needed time to express concerns and insecurities.

Getting started did not always go smoothly. At the first meeting in one building, a teacher dominated the half hour with complaints about teaching and students and almost sabotaged the entire effort. Not wanting to dominate or interfere, I let the teacher continue speaking. Teachers left very depressed, and several expressed unwillingness to return the following week. I wrestled with what to do. While I didn't want to quell free speech, the purpose of the group was teacher support, and this clearly wasn't happening. The next week, when the teacher returned and again tried to preside with negative comments, I intervened and said, "I'm sorry, I appreciate your concerns. However, what you're talking about are building concerns. The purpose of this group is teacher support." While I was sorry the teacher never came to another meeting, my intervention allowed the rest of us to move ahead in positive directions.

By the second year, we knew our needs better and, quite naturally, each building chose to focus in depth on an issue of concern. By the second or third years, principals were making an attempt to attend meetings, and most teachers welcomed their presence, input, and support. For the second and third years, a building focus might go on for several months. Usually I gathered journal articles, professional books, and resources and made copies of articles for interested teachers. Often we would begin by discussing a journal article that had been "assigned" the week before. An interest in and examination of whole language theory began to evolve in the second and third years.

Recently, we have focused on such issues as explaining whole language to parents, integrating spelling, portfolio assessment and evaluation, writing process, schoolwide holistic writing and scoring criteria, vocabulary and questioning, using a core literature book, taking a close look at standardized testing, strategies for at-risk students, and phonics. We have also used this time to share ideas and materials from conferences and to discuss activities and concepts that are effective and ineffective as well as to give feedback about new professional books and significant upcoming conferences.

One of our most successful focuses took place this last school year. All teachers and administrators in the k–4 buildings had an opportunity to view and discuss four whole language videotapes by Andrea Butler. This was the third year teachers were moving toward whole language, and there seemed to be a readiness to understand the theory better and relate it to classroom practice. Attendance was high, not only by classroom teachers and administrators but by special teachers, who agreed that Brian Cambourne's conditions of learning also apply in math, art, music, and physical education.

The art teacher said that she was becoming more conscious of children's needs to have some choice. The music teacher confirmed that if she wanted her students to do a research report on a composer, it was her responsibility to demonstrate report writing in music. The physical education teacher began to add writing to his program. For example, he asked students to write about their experience with the wind chimes, and when he talked about a forward roll with first-graders, he wrote "forward roll" on the chalkboard. Amazed first-graders told their classroom teacher, "Gosh, he can write too!"

One of the surprising outcomes of our weekly meetings has been seeing ourselves as experts. In one building, we focused on evaluation for three months. The interview forms, anecdotal records, and evaluation procedures we talked about, created, tried out, and eventually came up with were as good as any I have found in books on evaluation. Of course, we did our homework first. We observed our students carefully, and we read and discussed relevant journal articles before adapting many of the idea we came upon.

Another unexpected outcome has been finding out that when teachers act responsibly, we have some power. The push to do away with standardized testing in first grade began in one of our support groups and picked up momentum throughout the district. We continue to be activists on the standardized testing issue. One of our groups wrote a letter to the head of the corporation that publishes the standardized tests we use. We asked some hard questions about why the reading tests were not more compatible with recent research findings about reading as an interactive, constructive process. In addition to a detailed response, several representatives from the company came to one of our meetings, did a slick presentation, and answered our questions. When we learned that the company's newest tests could be normed for reading comprehension only—without the fragmented word study skills and phonics-in-isolation—we were vocal and successful in making that change a reality in our district. Based on research that calls for no standardized testing before grade 3 (Kamii, 1990), some of us hope to be influential in doing away with testing in grade 2.

Perhaps most important, we have become teacher researchers—reflective inquirers who have enough theoretical knowledge to look at our own teaching, ask and explore our own questions, and begin to trust and value what we are observing and finding. Our practice has continued to change as our theory has grown, so that now theory and practice seem less separate. Becoming a teacher researcher—with resulting effective and long-lasting change—may very well be the highest form of staff development we can hope for.

It is not difficult to get a support group started in your building. Even if there is only one other teacher to begin with, set up a regular time to meet. Keep your doors open and invite others to join you. Try to meet weekly, but even meeting monthly—or every few months—is better than not meeting at all. The hardest part is getting started for the first time.

An example of a weekly language arts support group   Two months before school ended, teachers in one k-4 building requested a meeting devoted to "sharing." A second grade teacher started that meeting by talking about, and passing around, the letters her students wrote from the point of view of Sarah as part of their literature study of *The Courage of Sarah Noble* by Alice Dalgliesh. She commented that all the important points of the story came out in the letters.

A third grade teacher then shared a new poetry book she had just read, *Sunrises and Songs* (McClure, Harrison, and Reed), and told how she was going to have her students keep poetry journals the next year. She also spoke about the influence of the book *For the Good of the Earth and the Sun* (Heard) on her teaching of poetry this year and how encouraged she had been by the poetry writing of children who had had no previous experience. She passed around poetry anthologies by her students.

A second grade teacher concurred and talked about what had happened since she had begun to immerse her students in poetry. Another second grade teacher told how she begins each day with a child (or teacher) reading aloud a favorite poem and how sometimes the whole class memorizes a preferred poem.

A third grade teacher expressed a need to talk about our new report cards. She felt further revisions were still needed. Discussion followed, and several teachers also spoke of the need for our district to come to some decision regarding portfolio assessment.

A fourth grade teacher shared resources and ideas from a hands-on science and environment conference she had attended the previous week.

Finally, we discussed future directions for our group. Several teachers requested a bibliography of recommended professional books for summer reading. (I shared with them the list and the books several weeks later.) One teacher spoke about the influence of Frank Smith's *Essays into Literacy* on her teaching and recommended we continue to read articles and discuss theory as it applies to our teaching. In closing, we decided to leave time near the end of school to discuss setting up the whole language classroom in the fall.

Looking at the diverse agenda of the meeting, it would be easy to dismiss it as unfocused. While most of our meetings tend to stay fairly focused on a topic we are exploring in depth, occasionally devoting whole meetings to the sharing of ideas and concerns fills an important need. Teachers request and enjoy the opportunity to share valuable teaching ideas based on reading and experience. Often books and ideas we share wind up being used and applied by other teachers. Allowing time to express concerns helps us understand each other's needs, redirect meetings so they stay meaningful to the group, and set new focuses. All of this is important for meeting the needs of the support group.

Sampling of support group agendas   Following are some notices of recent meetings that appeared in weekly bulletins in our k-4 buildings and which may be helpful for your own groups. It is important to keep the tone invitational and nonthreatening. On one bulletin, I had written, "Please come prepared to discuss . . . ," and some teachers took that to mean they were expected to do methodical readings of the attached journal article. After I have received feedback from some teachers, I was careful to say in the future, "We will be discussing . . . ." Even if teachers did not have the time to read the article, or had read only part of it, it was important that everyone felt welcome to attend.

- In continuing our focus on the writing process, we will be discussing the attached article, "Encouraging Meaning Making in Young Writers" by Juliebo and Edwards. Starting with kindergarten, we will also begin sharing expectations and processes by grade level.

- Come celebrate the writing process with your colleagues! We will begin going through the process as adults. Bury your fears, take a risk, and join the process movement. Everyone welcome!

- In our continuing focus and critical discussion and questioning, we will begin discussing *Danny the Champion of the World* by Roald Dahl. Please come prepared with questions and strategies for Chapters 1, 2, and 3 as well as with ideas for how you might introduce the book. We will begin promptly at 8:30 A.M. You may obtain a personal copy of this book from the office. That way you can write in it and keep the book.

- The Whole Language Support Group has been discussing the need for writing folders to be passed on to the next grade at the end of the school year. These folders would contain samples of the students' writing (probably three or four samples). To help us select samples, we have been discussing common criteria for evaluating writing. On January 31, the group will meet at 8:30 A.M. to develop broad criteria for evaluation. We will be developing criteria specific to each grade level, after examining students' writing samples on a topic that has been agreed upon across grades 1–4.

- Based on the concerns which emerged about testing and the group discussions on October 25, we will begin to work on organizing our ideas about having standardized testing consistent with whole language teaching. Please read the attached article, "Evaluation in the Holistic Reading/Language Arts Curriculum" by Richard Ammon.

- We will be viewing the first of four Andrea Butler videotapes on elements of whole language. This 35-minute videotape discusses Brian Cambourne's conditions of learning. Following the viewing, there will be small-group discussions. This is an excellent tape that is applicable to all teachers across the curriculum. You are always welcome to attend.

  In order to view the tape and have follow-up discussion, we need to begin promptly at 8:15 A.M. Those that attend may leave school fifteen minutes early. Your attendance is encouraged.

- We will begin demonstrating how to take a running record of a child's oral reading. This will be our focus for the next four weeks. If you are interested in this topic, it would probably be most beneficial to plan to attend all four sessions.

A District or Local Support Group

In addition to our weekly building support groups, we also have a district support group. Since the early 1980s, a group of teachers from across the district have been meeting about every six weeks. While our meetings began over lunch hour in one elementary building, we now meet in homes in the evening, and attendance averages twenty to twenty-five teachers. Recently, what has been particularly encouraging and exciting is the high school involvement. We now have at least several high school teachers and a professor from a local university in attendance regularly.

For our first district home meetings, invitations went out only to those teachers we felt were interested and committed. After a while, that approach seemed exclusive, and we now invite all professional staff in the district. Joan Servis has continued to act as secretary and to ensure that the meeting notices are sent out.

She sends a flyer to a representative in each school building, who duplicates and distributes the invitation to the staff. People who are planning to come let the host/hostess know. We also count on about five or six people showing up without having responded.

We also open our meetings to any teacher in any outside district who needs support and does not have a local group. At most meetings, we have teachers from three to five other school districts, occasionally from several hours away. Everyone is made to feel welcome. We have gained much from the experiences of our fledgling members, who keep us humble by reminding us how difficult and scary the starting process is. After a while we encourage visiting teachers to start their own local groups. At times, we have calls requesting on-the-spot help in starting a new support group. We invite the teachers requesting help to one of our meetings to see how the group functions, and usually they feel confident enough to go back and start their own group.

Our meetings have a relaxed, conversational format. We have no set agenda, and we charge no dues. We begin at 7:30 P.M. and end at 9:00 P.M., with a new meeting date set and someone volunteering a home for the next meeting. We alternate evenings of the week to allow people with commitments on a particular evening to be able to attend most of the time. While our meetings are very informal with no preset agendas or speakers, you may well prefer a more structured approach with topics planned for each meeting and occasional speakers. Use what works well for your group.

We usually begin by sharing a new professional book or two and passing it around. I, or another member, act as facilitator, which means only that we make sure everyone who wants to gets a chance to speak. Teachers share frustrations, concerns, activities, journal articles, techniques, questions, and anything that seems relevant to them. The small group size has allowed for lots of talk and exchange of ideas. The hour and a half format has encouraged high-level discussion.

Particularly exciting has been the sharing among cross-grade level teachers k–12. One English teacher commented, "I hear an idea from a second grade teacher, and I think, I could do that at the high school." A learning disabilities teacher shared how she had successfully tried working in the regular classroom after listening to a discussion on the harmful effects of pull-out programs.

During one meeting, high school English teacher Bill Newby shared his frustration with not being able to get many senior high school students to invest time in the revision process. He stated, "I'm working at trying to create an attitude, a tone for revision, but it's very difficult." Susan Mears, a first grade teacher, suggested Bill try a technique she uses. First, Susan has a parent come into her classroom and, in front of the children, the parent asks Susan questions and makes suggestions for a piece Susan has written. Then Susan models her revision process on the overhead projector. Students see two trusting adults talking knowledgeably and honestly about a piece of writing. Six weeks later, at our next meeting, Bill shared how, based on Susan's idea of adults modeling the writing process, he had invited high school teacher Dana Noble into his classroom to respond to his own writing. Students saw the struggle of two adults giving and receiving feedback. After the demonstration, Bill noted that more students were willing to share and respond to their own writing without feeling they were being criticized.

As a direct result of attending our district support group, a small group of our fifth and sixth grade teachers began a support group in their elementary school. Additionally, as a follow-up to a workshop he presented on whole language to the secondary English faculty, Bill Newby took the initiative to purchase Tom Romano's *Clearing the Way* for members of the high school English department who began devoting some of their meetings to discussing the book. Furthermore, influenced by the success of our weekly language arts support groups, math support groups have begun to meet every other week in several of our elementary schools.

Teachers' attitudes   Nan Bonfils, an American teaching in Malaysia, was visiting with me and other teachers in one of our schools recently. As visitors often do, she attended our langauge arts support group and commented on how struck she was by the level of commitment and reflective inquiry of our teachers. When she asked teachers why they come to these meetings, they spoke eloquently about the opportunities for inspiration, refocusing, rethinking, reflecting, and sharing successes and failures.

Darla Carlson, a first grade teacher, says she found the weekly support group meetings in her building "solid" and very helpful. She commented,

> At first, as a new teacher, I was too self-conscious to ask questions and speak up at our meetings. When I heard other people talk about their concerns and what wasn't going well, it helped to know I wasn't the only one. Probably what was most helpful were the other colleagues on my grade level who were so willing to be supportive.

Kindergarten teacher Karen Sher comments,

> Without question, the weekly support groups have been one of the most important stimulants for my growth. Sharing ideas and concerns with peers on my grade level and other grade levels has been invaluable. The literature— books and articles—that came my way, via the support group, helped to satisfy an intellectual hunger and provided me a framework to connect practical classroom teaching to theory. I appreciated having the readings spread out over time so I did not feel overwhelmed. Understanding the *why* in my teaching has helped me define where I wanted to go next.

Often at our meetings, teachers' confusions about an issue are cleared up. For example, one teacher said she was relieved to hear she could allow kids to read more than one chapter at a time or just let them read and discuss. She had been feeling guilty for not having more seatwork. On another occasion, a fourth grade teacher admitted she no longer felt guilty reading aloud to her class, but she was still struggling with whether it was all right to read aloud sometimes in place of having reading groups. Third grade teacher Lee Sattelmeyer comments, "One of the reasons the support groups worked is because once the idea of support was broached, teachers were able to acknowledge their own needs and confusions without feeling guilty."

Teachers also share positive happenings. Fourth grade teacher Janet Houk acknowledged her appreciation for the fine job primary grade teachers were doing in reading and writing. She noted, "I have no nonreaders. I've never before had a group of kids who all love to read. They like to write, too."

Finally, we still have our frustrations. Some teachers feel that having dialogues about theory and philosophy through reading and discussing journal articles and professional books needs to be a far greater priority. One teacher told me, "Far too few of our group see the value in understanding the theory behind whole language. I think we're still too activity focused." Some mornings teachers arrive late, and it seems as though we have barely gotten started when our time is up. Other teachers say they have felt threatened occasionally when a peer has disagreed with them. Some weeks teachers have been so busy that few have read the "assigned" journal article. Our meetings are not perfect. We are in process and probably always will be. We will continue to have dialogues and to meet and share our beliefs, frustrations, concerns, and goals.

Reflections   Undoubtedly, in spite of our occasional frustrations, the weekly support group has been one of our best staff development efforts. It is relevant, teacher centered, and voluntary, and development occurs slowly and deliberately over long periods of time. The support group attempts to address our needs as teacher learners and to promote leadership in our teaching as well as in district decision making. It has given us a chance to talk with each other, share ideas, and get to know each other better. The support group has diminished the isolation of teaching and fostered respect for colleagues. Cross grade-level sharing has given us an appreciation and understanding of the learning and language processes from grade to grade. While we recognize we have lots of room for growth, our support groups have been an important impetus for change for many teachers.

Administrators as Staff Developers

While support groups make a significant impact on teachers' professional growth, teacher growth and change are even more powerful when strongly supported by the building administrator. The most effective administrators are staff developers. They have frequent, nonthreatening communication with their staff, work with their teachers on a collaborative plan of action, and raise teachers' self-esteem by recognizing and valuing their individual strengths and teaching styles. They also are actively involved in the change and learning process. They read professionally, attend workshops, make an effort to demonstrate effective teaching strategies, and take a leadership role in the change process. Additionally, the most effective administrators have moved away from the traditional boss-employee relationship to a collaborative partnership based on shared decision making.

Elementary principal Rebecca Kimberly is an effective staff developer. Literally, she provides opportunities for her staff to develop to their full potential. When she reads professional journals, she thinks of her teachers' interests and abilities. If she reads an article that she thinks will particularly interest one of her staff, she makes a copy for that teacher. She lets her staff know of upcoming conferences, encourages their attendance, and attends conferences with her teachers. She also attends conferences to promote her own development as an effective administrator. She is frequently—as are the other administrators in our district—an active participant in our weekly language arts support groups. Additionally, she encourages and provides opportunities for peer observation. She has facilitated teachers' interest in learning from one another by hiring a substitute teacher for a half day so a teacher can spend the morning observing in classrooms in the building or in another building.

In place of the traditional faculty meetings that deal solely with details of running the school, Rebecca's bimonthly faculty meetings include opportunities for professional growth. Teachers report on conferences they have been to and share successful teaching strategies. An advisory committee, composed of grade-level representatives and others, meets with her monthly to resolve building issues. A written weekly communication provides detailed information of events, policies, and procedures.

Rebecca also involves teachers in the hiring process. When three kindergarten aides were to be hired, all three kindergarten teachers participated in the interview process and gave feedback. Each of the three teachers received the aide that was his or her first choice. When there are openings for new teachers, Rebecca uses a committee process that includes and respects her teachers' recommendations.

Finally, every few years she asks her staff to do an extensive, anonymous evaluation of her performance and to make recommendations. Based on that feedback, she sets goals for her own professional development. This past year, based on that feedback, Rebecca made a greater effort to spend more time in classrooms and provide feedback to teachers about progress toward their goals.

Jean Church is another example of an administrator who has taken a leadership role in the staff development process. As a curriculum coordinator in Indiana, she has been instrumental in getting her district to make a five-year staff development plan for the implementation of whole language. Starting with a district-wide language arts committee, workable long-range goals were established, and specific goals were outlined for the first three years. The goal for the first year was to build a knowledge base of whole language theory among teachers, administrators, parents, and students. To back up that commitment, the district bought a professional library for every school with at least a dozen current titles, some in multiple copies. Every faculty member was expected to read one self-selected professional book each semester and to try to implement some of the book's ideas. One faculty meeting a month was devoted to discussing and reacting to those professional readings. The second year's goal was continued reading and study at building levels as well as implementation of a process writing approach through trained peer colleagues. Goals for the third year included continued reading and study, refinement of the process writing approach, and implementation of a literature-based conference approach to reading. To accommodate the specific needs of teachers and principals, all participants completed a survey at the start and close of each school year to help identify needed revisions in the staff development plans.

Valuable Resources for Support

The reality is that whole language, or any effective approach to teaching and learning, cannot be fully implemented without administrative support. Unfortunately, that support is not always available. This section looks at the importance of administrative support and how to foster it and examines other available and valuable resources for teachers and schools, including peer tutoring, older students, Reading Recovery, parents, and grants. The chapter concludes with some thoughts on teacher education and future directions for whole language.

Getting Administrative Support

I believe that significant curricular and social change in a school environment cannot be put in place without administrative understanding and support. I think one of the reasons support from administrators has traditionally been slow in developing is that most administrators lack university training and experience in early childhood education. In general, while the literacy movement in schools has evolved in the primary grades, most principals have had experience and training at higher grade levels. Even when administrators seem to understand whole language philosophy, moving beyond mere knowledge of whole language to providing effective support is sometimes difficult to achieve. However, unless administrators become actively involved, whole language cannot survive.

We teachers can do several things to try to facilitate support from administrators.

• *Attending workshops and conferences*   Make every effort to get your administrator to join you at conferences. Often what happens is that teachers attend workshops, come back to school excited about new possibilities, and then try to convince their administrators of the changes they want to make. The change process is a lot easier if you can get your administrator involved at the ground level. If your administrator says there are too many things to be done at school, and she cannot take the time, offer to assist with a task or two so "time" can be created. If administrators are unable to attend, try to bring back tapes of presentations and share handouts and books. Take time to share aspects of the conference with your administrator; the importance of open communication cannot be overstated.

In my experience, it's the rare administrator who goes to conferences with her teachers. Ann Scholl, a principal of an urban elementary school with 800 students, attends conferences with her teachers several times each year. When I asked her how she was able to leave such a large building, she said, "I just make it a priority. Staff development is one of my major goals, and I find supporting my teachers in this way pays big dividends in the long run. It helps us work and plan as a team and become more effective educators."

Another exception is assistant superintendent of schools Bob Justice. When Bob invited me to facilitate a three-day workshop on the implementation of whole language, not only was he very involved in the planning, he also attended all the sessions. Based on my experience, this is quite exceptional. Typically, central office administrators are present for the introductions, and then they are in and out briefly at various points during the day. Bob's uninterrupted attendance gave a powerful message to teachers: He valued the workshops; he too was a learner; he was interested in teachers' questions and reactions; and he would be there to support the change process.

Some conferences have made attendance by the principal or an administrator a prerequisite for teacher attendance. This is not a bad idea. Some reluctant administrators have come to understand some of the theoretical basis for whole language through mandatory attendance.

• *Keeping administrators informed*   Make it a point to invite your administrator into your classroom regularly to see the reading-writing-speaking-listening process in action. Make your principal aware of any curricular changes you are thinking of making. Make copies of noteworthy journal articles, with your underlinings and highlighting, and let your administrator know a discussion of the articles would be welcomed.

I am constantly putting important articles in my principal Bernice Stokes's mailbox and sharing with her new ideas, current research, and information about upcoming conferences. Such sharing is a way for us to have a continued dialogue about news of the profession and possible educational directions. Bernice is interested and knowledgeable and seems to appreciate this opportunity for us to grow in understanding and applying whole language principles.

When I returned from the annual Reading Recovery conference in Columbus, Ohio, in January 1990, I shared in detail (through my notes and a tape I purchased) the research Richard Allington had presented on the negative effects of most pull-out programs on at-risk children. Based on that research and on our common interest in better serving the at-risk population, I proposed that I work with small groups of children as a supportive teacher *in* primary grade classrooms for the next school year. This proposal became a reality. I don't believe it would have happened without our close communication.

I am also careful to keep my principal well informed about daily happenings. If I am having a visitor, if a parent has contacted me, or if I am having a problem with a student, I place a brief note in my principal's mailbox. In that way, she is kept up to date, and she has no chance of being embarrassed by lack of knowledge of a situation.

It is not only principals whose support we need. Invite your superintendent and board of education members to in-services and support groups. As they come to understand the theory underlying whole language, they tend to commit more moral and material support.

Support for Administrators:
What to Look for in Classrooms

To support their teachers, administrators often want to know what to look for when observing in whole language classrooms. One principal told me, "The teachers are leading, and I am following." Many teachers are more knowledgeable about whole language theory and practice than their administrators. However, in a sincere effort and desire to be better able to support their teachers, administrators have asked, "What are some evidences I might look for in a brief classroom observation to assess the application of whole language principles?" What follows are some questions that may be helpful to keep in mind during a classroom observation. In just ten or fifteen minutes, an administrator would be able to "read" the whole language climate of the room. Teachers may want to share these questions with their administrators and may also want to think about them for their own self-evaluation.

• *Who's doing the talking?*   Is the teacher's voice the main voice, or are students doing most of the talking? Does every child have an opportunity to be heard? Are teachers directing with authority or guiding and leading from behind?

• *Do the students know the routines and procedures?*   Do the students go to the teacher every time they have a question, or do they know the routines, assume responsibilities, use peers as helpers, and assume some self-management? Do things seem disorganized, or is there a well-planned flow from one activity to another?

• *Are the bulletin boards by and for the children?*   Is children's work displayed everywhere? Are the bulletin boards done by the children, with samples of writing, illustrations, and projects, or are they commercial, perfect, and cute?

• *Does the seating arrangement and teacher control allow for collaboration?*   Are students isolated in rows, or are they grouped so they can conference and assist each other?

• *Is the teacher with the children?*   Is the teacher always standing front and center or sitting at his desk, or is he mostly among the children, demonstrating and guiding as needed?

• *Is there an orderly hum of activity?*   Is the classroom silent, or are students quietly talking with each other and actively engaged in various enterprises?

• *Is reading time focused on comprehension and understanding?*   Are children spending most of reading time oral reading, working on "skills," and responding to literal level questions, or do they have frequent opportunities for responding to open-ended questions and participating in high-level discussion?

• *Is the independent work the children are doing meaningful?*   Are worksheets and workbooks being used with fill-in-the-blank formats, or are there other purposeful activities that encourage open-ended responses that require thinking and application of experience and knowledge?

• *Do the children have choices?*   Is everyone doing the same activity, or are there opportunities for children to make decisions about their work for the day? Are there self-selected reading and writing activities?

• *Are there opportunities for students to work together?*   Are all activities being completed individually, or are pairs and groups of children reading, writing, and problem solving together? Is there time for sharing?

• *Is there a classroom library and cozy reading corner?*   Are there all types of literature attractively displayed and easily accessible? Are there reference books, dictionaries, and thesauruses available? Is there a pleasant reading area where children can read in a comfortable position and with a friend?

• *Are there learning centers, especially a writing center?*   Is there an area where children can find different kinds of paper and writing supplies? Are there many opportunities for writing? Are there opportunities for exploration on topics of study?

• *Does the teacher use anecdotal records and observational data in evaluation?* Does the teacher use only checks and grades in a grade book? Is there also evidence of informal, observational data?

• *Do the students seem happy and actively involved?*   Are the children passively completing assignments, or are they excited about the opportunities for learning in their classroom?

Peer Tutoring

When small groups of children learn how to work together cooperatively, teachers sometimes reap great benefits. However, putting students in groups does not automatically result in productive learning or successful group interaction. With peer tutoring, a child who has grasped an idea helps a child who has not mastered the concept. Peer tutoring, which is carefully organized by the teacher, may have the most potential as a paired reading technique. With paired reading, the student to be tutored selects any book or reading material to read out loud, and a trained tutor provides needed support and positive feedback in a relaxed setting. In addition to children's positive attitudes toward paired reading, the evaluation research confirms strong gains in reading for both the tutor and the student who is tutored (Topping, 1989; for organization and procedures, see Topping in *Resources for Teachers*).

Paired reading can occur within a class or between classes on the same grade level or across grade levels. We use paired reading on a regular basis in our literature program. Many teachers, believing that all students should have the opportunity to discuss the literature being read whole class or in small groups— even if it is above their reading level—pair students as needed. The more able student reads the text aloud while the less able follows along visually, or the students read out loud together, or the less able student listens to the book on tape and follows along in the book. Paired reading is also used simply for enjoyment, anytime two students choose to pair up to read a book.

Using Older Students within the Support Network

When first grade teacher Peg Rimedio had exhausted all possible resources for getting reading support for the large number of at-risk children in her room, she enlisted the help of Nancy Schubert's fourth grade class. Peg felt that if each of her students had an interested partner willing and able to listen to him or her read, students would become more engaged and competent in their reading. Peg reflected, "I was desperate. I wasn't reaching all the kids, and this partnership provided the vehicle."

Peg and Nancy began by carefully pairing their students. Then Peg showed the fourth-graders how to introduce the book the student had selected, how to guide the student in reading, and how to record the book in the child's reading folder once it had been read successfully. Fourth-graders also wrote books for first graders to read. Toward the end of the school year, the tutoring sessions were expanded to help first-graders locate books and complete their individual animal research reports. The partner sessions took place twice a week for thirty minutes and were so successful—for both the younger and older students—that the teachers decided to repeat the program.

The surprise dividend was the positive impact the sessions had on the fourth-graders. While it was expected that the first-graders would thrive on the special attention, the fourth-graders enjoyed an equal sense of importance and purpose. Before the shared sessions, Nancy Schubert reviewed the strategies students might use to help the first-graders. Not only did the fourth-graders learn to ask good questions ("Look at the picture. What could it be?"), Nancy noticed a carryover to their own work. In addition, several fourth-graders who had difficulty with interpersonal relationships seemed to become more confident and outgoing. Students also expressed a new appreciation of their teacher. They spoke of how hard it was to be a teacher; many came back exhausted after the thirty-minute one-to-one session.

Another successful first grade–fourth grade partnership was created when first grade teacher Kay Dunlap teamed up with fourth grade teacher Maria Padovani. Kay, a highly experienced teacher who had writing workshop well established in her classroom, engaged the fourth-graders in supporting the editing component of the writing process. Again, the teachers carefully paired the students and established guidelines for the fourth-graders. Teacher modeling was a critical aspect of the initial phase of this partnership. Kay discussed editing with the fourth-graders and gave them a sheet of items to look for, including punctuation, capitalization, and coherence. Besides editing, partners occasionally collaborated on writing stories together. Editing-sharing conferences took place every other Friday for forty minutes.

Once again, benefits for both first- and fourth-graders included empowerment. The fact that teachers let first-graders "go at it together" without imposing ideas seemed to give them much confidence. Fourth-graders were surprised at how well first-graders could write, and that seemed to motivate and assist the fourth-graders in refocusing on their own writing. Maria Padovani noted that her students became more attentive to mechanics and took more responsibility for their own writing. She comments, "I was surprised at how well they could edit. They took it more seriously than with their own writing. The kids also felt very important; the first-graders looked up to them. My kids would get upset if there was a Friday when we couldn't meet."

Another surprise was an excellent management solution that came from a fourth-grader. A mid-year survey of students indicated much concern about the noise level with the two classes working in one room. A student's suggestion of using both classrooms proved remarkably effective. Students that needed to be with their classroom teacher (mostly for behavioral reasons) stayed in their own classroom. Other student pairs were divided between the two rooms. While the new arrangement meant the two teachers had to find a separate time to communicate with each other, they believed the new arrangement was worth that extra effort. The noise level was substantially lowered, and teachers felt they could give more and better assistance to students.

At the end of the school year, first- and fourth-graders filled out a written evaluation form that Kay Dunlap had developed. The evaluations indicated that every student but one liked working with his or her partner. Asked what they had learned about doing writing workshop with partners, first-grader Claire Long responded: "I learned how to make stories better by using things you know about and your imagination and when to put in periods and questions marks" (see Figure 16–1). A number of the fourth-graders' comments pointed to affective outcomes:

"I have learned that my partner has good ideas and different ideas that I could write about."

"I have learned to be patient with my first-grader because this is very hard for them."

"I have learned how to cooperate with my partner."

"I have learned to work better with children younger than me."

Figure 16-1   A First-grader's Evaluation of Writing Workshop with a Fourth Grade Partner

I Lrde How to
Make Sroes, BeTr
by yosing fhins
you Know abowT
and ro Imajnashan
And
When To PoT
pereis, and quasid
mrx.

Reading Recovery: Support for At-Risk First-graders

Reading Recovery is an exemplary model of a short term early intervention designed to reduce and prevent reading failure. Starting where the child is and building on existing strengths, the child is skillfully guided to make accelerated progress in reading whole predictable texts and writing self-generated sentences.

To qualify for the program, the lowest 15 to 20 percent of a beginning first grade population (in the United States) is identified through teacher observation, the results of an individually administered Observation Survey (Clay, 1993), and, in some cases, standardized test results. Then Reading Recovery teachers, who have received highly specialized training from a teacher leader who has participated in a year-long academic training program, provide daily one-to-one instruction for fifteen to twenty weeks. The thirty-minute lessons, meticulously tailored to the child's responses, consist of reading and rereading "little books" and applying reading and writing strategies in the context of authentic reading and writing. In every lesson, the Reading Recovery teacher also takes and analyzes a running record of the child's oral reading of the book introduced the day before. The teacher notes the strategies the child is using and neglecting to use and carefully plans instruction based on the child's needs. The instructional sessions are noteworthy for their rigorous pace, time on task, and independence-fostering behaviors. The goal of the program is to accelerate the student to the average level of his classroom peers, make him an independent reader with a continuing self-improving system, and make further intervention unnecessary.

The program was developed in New Zealand in the 1960s by child psychologist and researcher Marie Clay. In 1979, after twelve years of longitudinal data indicated that once children were "recovered" about 85 percent rarely needed reading support again, the program become nationally funded. Reading Recovery sites

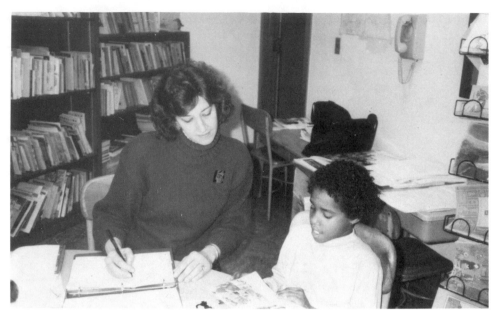

Regie Routman teaching a Reading Recovery lesson

spread to Australia in the mid-1980s and to the United States in 1985 when it came to Ohio through the The Ohio State University. As of 1990, the results of five years of research on Reading Recovery students in Ohio have supported the original findings, and these findings have remained consistent across diverse populations. The program continues to expand; as of the summer of 1990, sixteen states and several Canadian provinces had at least one training site. Being designated a training site means that a teacher-leader, who lived and worked at The Ohio State University in Columbus for one year, was educated to train and supervise new Reading Recovery teachers in his/her home state.

For four years I worked as a Reading Recovery teacher every afternoon in the school where I was based. These teaching experiences were among the most satisfying and the most demanding I have ever had. I saw firsthand the power and potential of Reading Recovery for changing how a student is perceived and for positively affecting an entire school career.

Daniel was one of the last students I worked with. I started seeing him in early February after he had been in the first grade for five months. At that time he was a nonreader, the lowest-functioning child in his class, and a severe behavior problem. Daniel was very immature, was easily distracted in a group, and had poor gross and fine motor control. His limited ability to form letters appropriately and hear sounds in words made it difficult for him to write in his journal. His Observation Summary indicated he could identify almost all the upper and lower case letters of the alphabet; he could read three words ("and," "the," and "yes"); he could write five words ("Daniel," "mom," "no," "yes," and "my"); he knew print contained the message in a book, and he had one-to-one matching of spoken words to printed words on a page; he could hear and write a limited number of beginning and ending consonants in words; and he could use picture cues and memory to "read" a simple text if he heard part of the story pattern first.

Like all Reading Recovery lessons, every lesson began and ended with books that were carefully selected to meet Daniel's instructional needs and interests. We began with Daniel rereading several books he had previously read with 90–100 percent accuracy. I then took a daily running record of the new book introduced the previous day by observing, recording, and analyzing his oral reading—his accuracies, errors, and self-corrections (see Clay, 1993a, for taking a running record). Each lesson also ended with reading a book, a new text carefully introduced through talking about the pictures and language in the story before Daniel attempted reading. In each lesson, reading instruction included making just a few teaching points by focusing on observed strengths and weaknesses. Unique to the Reading Recovery lesson, and all good teaching, are noticing and commenting on what the child has done well. By commenting favorably on Daniel's reading behavior, he was being encouraged to repeat it, and his confidence grew. Typical comments I used, and that Reading Recovery teachers often use, were:

"I like the way you worked that out."

"I saw you looking at the picture to check yourself. That's what a good reader does."

"You went back to the beginning of the sentence and tried again. Good for you."

Also typical of Reading Recovery is the implied message, constantly given to the child, that he needs to take responsibility for most of the problem solving. While the teacher utilizes opportune moments to make relevant teaching points, she is careful to leave sufficient wait time and intervene only when necessary. In a Reading Recovery lesson, the child rarely looks to the teacher; independence is fostered from the very beginning. Some regular prompts I used to get Daniel going on his own were:

"What can you do to help yourself?"

"Can you find the tricky part? Go back and look for it."

"Go back to the beginning of the sentence and try that again."

"Look at how that word starts. Get your mouth ready to say it. Now try it."

"What else can you do?"

With specific guidance, Daniel learned to effectively use meaning and structure cues in reading text. It took longer for him to integrate grapho-phonic cues and orchestrate all three cueing systems interdependently. Once that happened, he was on his way toward independence.

Following the familiar rereadings and the taking of the running record, with my support Daniel dictated and wrote a short message each day. I would then write his message on a sentence strip, cut it apart, and ask Daniel to put it back together. It was in this part of the lesson that Daniel focused heavily on visual cues (graphophonic) and on bringing high-frequency words to fluency.

In our beginning writing lessons, Daniel and I had to spend much time on letter work. See Figure 16-2 for his practice and story page in his second lesson. (The connected boxes are formed to help him hear sounds in words.) Even though he

Figure 16-2   Daniel's Practice and Story Page in His Second Reading Recovery Lesson

could already write "mom" and "my" independently, Daniel was confused about upper and lower case letters and direction in letter formation. Note his writing page at the beginning of May (Figure 16–3). Although his writing vocabulary was not yet keeping pace with his reading, he independently spelled and correctly formed the letters for all the words except "when" and "get."

Daniel was discontinued from Reading Recovery after fourteen weeks and fifty-seven lessons. He was reading *Clifford* books by Norman Bridwell fluently in class, was writing independently in his journal daily, and was just beginning to read *Frog and Toad* books by Arnold Lobel with me. His success had been a joint effort among Daniel, his mother, his classroom teacher Karen Shiba, Cindy Brodsky (a tutor who took her own time to listen to him read regularly), and myself.

When I first met Daniel, he kept his head lowered and seemed very sad. Now he was a happy, confident student. Initially a nonparticipant in reading group, he now prodded his teacher daily, "Is our group next?" He was still a behavior problem but never in reading group.

When Daniel was about to be discontinued, I interviewed him.

Figure 16-3   Daniel's Practice and Story Page in May

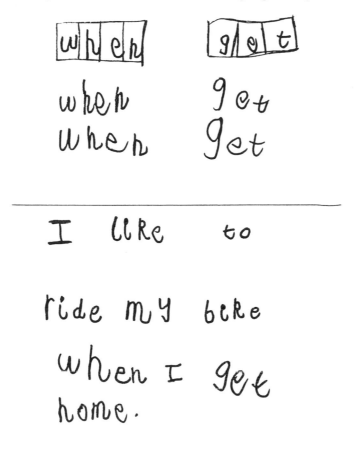

ROUTMAN: What was it like for you when you couldn't read?

DANIEL: Not too good. I couldn't read, and all the other kids could read. I was thinking, I'm not smart. I felt really bad, *real* bad. The teacher would say, "You can read a book," but I couldn't read!

ROUTMAN: Were you worried?

DANIEL: I was thinking I would never be able to read. I was really scared.

ROUTMAN: When did things change for you?

DANIEL: When I came into Reading Recovery, I started to read better, write better. I began to feel proud of myself because I was doing good.

ROUTMAN: Do you feel like you're smart now?

DANIEL: I feel much better because I can read now. I'm a good reader. I think I'm a smart person.

Daniel's mother, initially very upset about her son's nonreading, was enthusiastic about his progress and confidence. Some excerpts from a long letter I received from her follow.

June 12, 1990

Dear Mrs. Routman,

I just wanted to take some time before the school year is out, and the possibility that we may never see each other again, to extend my thanks to you. . . .

Daniel's reading and writing has improved *110%*. He can now pick up books that he has around the house and read them without much help, if any. As you were helping him, you were helping me as well. I love Daniel very much and as I told you before he is my best friend.

I am a single parent and at times it is hard to sit down and work with him as much as I should. Before Daniel started working with you, I was very worried about his reading and writing, and when he came home and told me he was going to be working with a special teacher, and I began to see the results, you cleared away one less worry.

I wish you much luck in your career, and I hope that you continue to help other children as you have helped my son. May God bless and keep you always! Thank you!

Darlene Goodwin

Reading Recovery is not a panacea; it does not work for every child. No program does. It is, however, the best early intervention program I have ever seen, and school districts would do well to investigate its implementation. Reading Recovery is an expensive program that requires at least a three-year commitment, but it is cost effective in the long run. The program also requires strong support, education, understanding, and flexibility on the part of administrators. Administrators must be willing to release teachers part of the school day to work one-to-one with students, and they must be able to look at more than standardized test scores to judge reading success.

Some states now say they have Reading Recovery and that they can train teachers, but this is not so. The Reading Recovery training program is a year-long commitment and includes the theoretical underpinnings upon which this program is built. This critical training can be guaranteed only through the National Diffusion Network for Reading Recovery. Program developer Marie Clay has authorized The Ohio State University in Columbus as the only official U.S. site to educate trainers of teacher leaders.

Finally, besides reducing early reading failure, one of the greatest benefits of Reading Recovery is improved reading instruction. Reading Recovery teachers often have an impact on the way reading is taught in the classroom and in the school. When Reading Recovery teachers are able to work cooperatively with classroom teachers, classroom teachers with a skills-based approach to reading begin to approach the teaching of reading more strategically and more analytically.

This discussion of Reading Recovery is only a brief conceptual framework. For more complete information on the program, see the following resources:

Clay, Marie 1993a. *An Observation Survey of Early Literacy Achievement.* Portsmouth, NH: Heinemann. See annotation, p. 75b.

Clay, Marie. 1993b. *Reading Recovery: A Guidebook for Teachers in Training.* Portsmouth, NH: Heinemann. See annotation, p. 9b.

DeFord, Diane E., Carol A. Lyons and Gay Su Pinnell (eds.). 1991. *Bridges to Literacy: Learning from Reading Recovery.* Portsmouth, NH: Heinemann. See annotation, p. 13b.

Lyons, Carol. Director of the National Diffusion Network for Reading Recovery, The Ohio State University, 200 Ramseyer Hall, 29 West Woodruff Avenue, Columbus, OH 43210-1177. (Write for information.)

Lyons, Carol A., Gay Su Pinnell, and Diane E. DeFord. 1993. *Partners in Learning: Teachers and Children in Reading Recovery.* New York: Teachers College Press. See annotation, p. 25b.

Ohio Department of Education and The Ohio State University. *Reading Recovery Conference.* Columbus, Ohio; held annually in early February.

   This high-level conference for teachers, administrators, parents, and policy makers offers sessions on the research, funding, and implementation of Reading Recovery as well as on related issues and strategies for early literacy. Barbara Watson, Director of Reading Recovery in New Zealand, and/or Marie Clay, Developer of Reading Recovery, have often attended and given presentations. (For conference information, write to Reading Recovery, Division of Inservice, State Department of Education, 65 Front Street, Columbus, OH 43266-0308.)

Pinnell, Gay Su, Mary D. Fried, and Rose Mary Estice. January 1990. "Reading Recovery: Learning How to Make a Difference," *The Reading Teacher,* pp. 282–295.

   The authors, all trained in Reading Recovery—a teacher trainer and professor, a state coordinator, and a teacher—describe the program, the components and teaching procedures in a Reading Recovery lesson, the teacher-training model, the program's research base, and the pilot study in Ohio. A case study documents one student's success with the program.

Promoting Parent Education and Involvement

Strong parent involvement is not a question of "Should we?" but rather a question of "How should we?" The importance of ongoing, well-planned involvement of parents is backed by research on effective schools. Effective parent involvement programs—all of which have elements in common—positively affect school achievement across diverse populations. (Henderson, and Williams and Chavkin, 1988).

We need to welcome parents into our schools and classrooms and keep them well informed about their children's education. We need to create opportunities for parents to see themselves as a vital, continuing part of their children's education. We need to keep the lines of communication open and to build trust. Not only will parents be better able to support the learning process at home but the message will get out to the community and to the principal that the students are learning and happy and that the teachers care. Parents are our best public relations agents. They can do more to sell whole languaage, or any educational program, than anyone else in the school district. They have far greater power to effect change than the teacher does. Parents are a resource we must use wisely.

Some things we can do to promote education, understanding of whole language, and cooperation among parents include the following:

• *Recognize what parents have done well.*   When we are explaining whole language to parents, a good plan is to start by congratulating parents for what they have done well. We can begin by explaining how parents have successfully taught their children to speak. The research and theory behind whole language are based on the language learning that has taken place in the home. Parents relate easily to the notions of demonstration, approximation, practice, and learning over time when these issues are explained in relation to their child's learning how to talk. Then the transition to applying the same principles to invented spelling and learning to read is a natural one for parents.

• *Provide opportunities for parent education.*   Use open houses, conferences, parent newsletters, and Parent-Teacher Association meetings to increase parents' understanding of the language processes. Besides the regular curriculum statement given to parents at our annual fall open house, third grade teacher Lee Sattelmeyer hands out a language arts philosophy statement (see Figure 16–4 for a recent statement). Also, as much as you feel comfortable with the idea, have your classroom open to parents. Bring them into the literacy process by inviting them to help with journal writing, editing, special projects, and field trips.

Our school sponsors an annual "Family Literacy" night, a workshop on effective strategies for helping parents help their children become successful learners. After a

Figure 16-4   Language Arts Philosophy Statement Given to Parents

LOMOND SCHOOL
SHAKER HEIGHTS, OHIO

THIRD GRADE

I. LANGUAGE ARTS (Whole Language Approach)

Premise

* Language is a composite of three systems: semantics
  (meaning), syntax (grammar), and graphophonemics
  (letter-sound correspondence). Learning to read
  becomes more difficult when systems are taught in
  isolation. Language is best learned through its use.

* Learning to read requires sharing, interaction, and
  collaboration involving parent/child, teacher/child,
  and child/child relationships.

* Placing importance on reading for meaning and reading
  for enjoyment will develop life long readers.

* When applicable, choice and self-selection in reading
  and writing activities are important factors in
  building confidence in language experiences.

* Reading involves an interaction between the reader
  and the text. Meaning is constructed by the reader
  based on prior experience.

* Literature can be used as a springboard for writing
  experiences.

* Learning to write is facilitated when writing
  exercises are purposeful and communicate ideas
  rather than practicing isolated skills.

* Where possible, other curriculum areas, e.g., science
  and social studies, are integrated with the language
  arts program.

* As much as possible, skills are taught in the context
  of the literature as the need arises.

brief presentation by several teachers, parents and teachers meet in small groups by grade level to ask questions and discuss concerns about working with their children at home. Some of our kindergarten and first grade teachers sponsor their own classroom literacy workshops as a way to educate parents and make them a welcome part of the literacy process.

The first year that our district made a commitment to whole language, each building devoted a Parent-Teacher Association meeting to explaining whole language and allowing time for questions and answers.

• *Provide parents suggestions for what they can do at home.*   Send home a communication that gives parents a framework for worthwhile home activities. (See "Parents as Allies in Children's Education," Appendix J5, for a model.) Probably most important is getting the message out that parents should continue to read to their children, serve as reading role models themselves, and provide quiet time and space for leisure reading.

• *Start a library for parents.*   Easy access to books about language learning is one way to clarify and expand parents' understanding of language develoment and the language processes. See if your public or school library will fund, organize, and reserve a corner for parents. Use relevant book titles in this book and in Routman (1988) for recommended educational resources for parents. Also check with your local libraries and book stores for recommended titles. Scholastic Inc., and the American Reading Council in New York City, and the International Reading Association in Newark, Delaware, all publish pamphlets, brochures, and books for parents.

• *Utilize parent volunteers.*   Parents may be used in the publishing process to listen to children read, as supports for journal writing, to put together projects for teachers, or for a host of other tasks. Be sure parents are clear on what you want them to do and that they understand the program philosophy. If parents from your classroom are not available, contact grandparents, other relatives, or senior citizens.

• *Let parents know when their child does something well.*   Some teachers make it a point to telephone or drop a short note to parents during the first week of school and, on occasion, throughout the year to note something positive about the child. If parents are contacted when their child does something well, not only are good relations established between the parent and teacher but the parents are likely to be more receptive if you call with a problem.

• *Explain standardized testing and evaluation procedures.*   Jerry Harste of Indiana University recommends having parents take part in the standardized tests their children take. For example, one of the subtests could be given at fall open house. Once parents actually go through the testing process themselves, they are less likely to place so much significance on the test results. Be sure your grading and evaluation procedures are clear to parents, and make parents part of the process. (See Chap. 13, "Evaluation.")

• *Explain how reading is being taught.*   Teachers need to explain how reading is being taught—to the children as well as to the parents—especially when there has been a major change in philosophy. Robin's mother was feeling a lot of anxiety when her first-grader wasn't using "sounding out" as a major strategy. She also expected to see lots of phonics worksheets coming home. It had never been explained to this mother that meaning-based strategies were being emphasized in the classroom, that phonics was being taught in the context of reading and through journal writing, and that phonics sheets were not being used. See Appendix J2, "Ways to Help Your Child with Reading at Home," which gives parents meaning-based strategies to use with their children in the reading process.

It's also a good idea to communicate to parents the kinds of high-level questions that teachers are trying to ask in order to foster the same kind of question asking at home.

• *Explain the writing process.*   Talk to the children about the writing process so they can talk about it to their parents. Some parents think the teacher has shirked responsibility when papers come home with mistakes. Many of our teachers have a stamp, marked "unedited," and we stamp papers that have not gone to final copy. When a final product does go home, you may want to also attach the drafts. See Appendix J1 for a letter to primary parents explaining invented spelling.

• *Communicate regularly in writing.*   A newsletter written by you and/or the students lets parents be part of the learning process. Use the newsletter to communicate class happenings, strategies being taught, and successes to celebrate.

English teacher Dana Noble guides his reluctant ninth grade readers and writers in writing a newsletter to parents describing what's going on in the classroom. Students choose their own format and events, and engagement and interest are high in this authentic writing project. Third grade teacher Julie Beers's students also write a monthly newsletter to parents (see Appendix J9). Julie also writes a newsletter to parents at the start of the school year to explain her philosophy, curriculum, and goals (see Appendix J8 for the reading-writing portions).

• *Encourage good book selection.*   Many parents need guidance in choosing books for children or in helping their children choose. Let parents know about *Teens' Favorite Books: Young Adults' Choices 1987–1992* by Anne Kenney and others, *Hey! Listen to This: Stories to Read Aloud* by Jim Trelease, and *The New York Times Parents' Guide to the Best Books for Children* by Eden Ross Lipson, all published recently (see *Resources for Teachers* and *Parent Books and Resources*). If you use a book club so children can buy trade books inexpensively, recommend some good titles (see Appendix J10). Also, let parents know about favorite authors and popular series for your particular age group so they can look for them with their children at the local library.

• *Avoid any negative reinforcement or reactions to students whose parents are not involved for some reason.*

Support through Grant Money

Many teachers have been resourceful in getting funds for trade books, materials, equipment, additional personnel, curriculum design, and staff development by applying for special grants. Unfortunately, most teachers are unaware that money exists—in some cases big money.

In my own school district, some teachers, with strong administrative support, have been highly successful in the leadership role they have taken in writing proposals and getting approval for grants, in amounts ranging from several hundred dollars to one hundred thousand dollars. Some recent grants include:

- A private foundation grant for a summer literacy outreach program for entering first-graders deemed at risk by their kindergarten teachers
- An effective schools grant to assess building needs—guiding philosophy, teaching-learning climate, expectations, leadership, delivery of instruction
- A matching funds grant with a commitment of equal hours from community leaders in private business and industry to develop a math program more congruent with the current math *Standards* (see p. 89b) and real-life needs
- A state grant to fund a language enrichment program for at-risk kindergartners in every school
- A foundation grant to bring in resource personnel to support middle school teachers in working with at-risk students

Check with your administrators, superintendent, and other teachers who have been successful in obtaining grant money. Contact community groups and service organizations, as well as private corporations, to determine whether grants are available. Also check out local, county, federal, and state resources, including your state department of education. See if your city has a library for obtaining information on grants, and check to see what public and private foundations in your town offer educational grants.

Some districts, including my own, have begun their own foundations to further educational development. In addition, our Parent-Teacher Association and our Teachers' Association also offer small annual grants for teacher projects that will enhance teaching and learning.

Some Thoughts on Teacher Education

One would expect recruitment of teachers with a whole language background to become easier as more and more colleges and universities are providing the underlying theory. However, unless universities also move from the traditional transmission model of lecturing truths to an interactive model of sharing understandings, espousing the theory won't be enough. Teacher educators must begin to employ the whole language model in their undergraduate and graduate classes. We teachers need to exert our influence with our local colleges and universities to make sure this begins to happen.

Specifically, for university professors, this means conducting their undergraduate and graduate classes as whole language classes. Just as classroom teachers cannot expect students in their classes to go through processes they have not sufficiently demonstrated, university professors cannot expect their students to become whole language teachers without being whole language teachers themselves. I see that changing the traditional model would mean:

- Employing Holdaway's "Developmental Model of Language Learning" (pp. 9–10)—not just lecturing and giving assignments
- Allowing teachers choices (based on their interests) in required professional reading—for example, choosing any two out of five approved texts

- Journal keeping by students and teachers to record reactions to reading
- Using class time for sharing and collegial interaction
- Encouraging teachers to demonstrate their new knowledge in a variety of forms
- Evaluating university students from a multifaceted perspective

When Jerry Harste of Indiana University visited our district in May 1990, I was impressed with the commitment he told us he has made to changing his own teaching. He gives teachers a choice of professional texts to read, has them keep a journal of their reactions, and devotes class time to discussion of issues raised. He puts his students through the literature discussion process by having them read adult literature and then break into small groups for discussion. In that way, teachers come to understand the process they want to facilitate with their students. In addition to his own evaluation of students, Harste places high value on both peer evaluation and self-evaluation. For example, students are required to turn in a paper describing the classmate they learned the most from. Because this requirement is made clear at the start of each course, students take listening to and learning from each other quite seriously.

In addition to the fact that few educators at the university level employ a whole language teaching model, there is also a scarcity of whole language classrooms in which to place student teachers. To aid the placement process, some universities are pairing up and working closely with teachers and local school systems that have made commitments to whole language. Universities and colleges should then take the opportunity to ask supervising teachers what they think is needed for better preparatory education for classroom teaching. Professors and teachers need to respect and utilize one another's knowledge in looking to create better teacher education models.

Finally, some states are now requiring a four-year liberal arts degree and a fifth year for teacher certification. This makes sense. If teachers are to be models of knowledge and critical thinking, they must have a broad education in the liberal arts as well as basic education courses.

Future Directions

While our school district has made some commitments to furthering whole language on an ongoing basis, we are still working on putting a long-range plan into effect. On the plus side, our teachers are involved in curriculum design, writing new report cards, and ongoing committee work related to the language processes. Reading Recovery is in place in every k–4 building, and classroom teachers are expressing interest in learning how to employ Reading Recovery strategies and assessment procedures. Our weekly language arts support groups are vital and active. Many of our teachers have made presentations at local, state, and national conferences. A small number of our teachers have initiated new programs through obtaining grants and receiving special funding and approval.

We have much room for growth. While our teachers are encouraged to attend conferences, it has been rare for administrators to attend with us. For the most part, workshops with "experts" still tend to be the one-shot deal. Most of our staff development has been in the form of the voluntary efforts of teachers meeting and collaborating. Release time during the school day for staff development has been rare. Teachers are still generally not included in the hiring process, and teacher-administrator relationships often need to be more collaborative. Nevertheless, we are slowly but surely moving forward, and there is no turning back.

On the national scene, existing TAWL groups are active and networking, and new groups are springing up in every state. A national networking exists through the Whole Language Umbrella, which began sponsoring annual conferences in the summer of 1990. Coaching and mentoring programs are being tried out in many districts. Some districts have begun to make hiring of new teachers conditional on their having a whole language background. Districts are also offering early retirement incentives to encourage weeding out more traditional teachers.

There is much work still to be done. Teacher education needs an overhaul, and we need to be doing more as a society to attract the best and the brightest to the teaching profession. In most school districts, reading instruction is still driven by basal readers, skills sheets, and standardized testing. Administrators need to become more involved in understanding and supporting whole language theory and practice if it is to become an approach to teaching and learning that is here to stay. Teachers need to take the initiative to be afforded their rightful and responsible place as decision makers and leaders in the staff development process.

Resources: Staff Development Opportunities

E.L.I.C. (EARLY LITERACY INSERVICE COURSE)
Robyn Platt, Director
685 Industrial Drive
Cary, IL 60013
(800) 822-8661

> *Based on the staff development program that has trained the majority of teachers in Australia since 1983, this literacy course for groups of up to twelve teachers in grades k–3 offers school districts a proven model for effective teacher change. The course includes taking a close look at language learning, reading and writing processes and strategies, evaluation, and more. Teachers meet weekly for twelve weeks with a trained facilitator for one two-hour interactive session, usually after school. Teachers discuss that week's assigned professional readings and specific classroom-based tasks. In addition, the facilitator is available on request to work in classrooms with teachers.*
>
> *In place in many states, E.L.I.C. has had an impact on teachers' literacy beliefs, attitudes, and practices. E.L.I.C. training also benefits districts using Reading Recovery by helping develop supportive classroom environments for children to return to. By participating and completing E.L.I.C., teachers learn about children's reading-writing processes and how to become kid watchers.*

LLIFE (LITERACY AND LEARNING INSERVICE: FOUR-EIGHT)
Robyn Platt, Director
Jackie Danley, ELIC/LLIFE Manager
685 Industrial Drive
Cary, IL 60013
(800) 822–8661

> *LLIFE follows the same philosophy and format as E.L.I.C., considers reading and writing to learn as the main focus, and supports teachers working with grades 4–8. Strategic teaching/learning is demonstrated in classroom support sessions.*

FRAMEWORKS
Staff Development Office
Wayne-Finger Lakes BOCES
3501 County Road 20
Stanley, NY 14561

> *Frameworks is a whole language staff development program that has been designed by Australian educators Andrea Butler, Brian Cambourne, and Jan Turbill to support literacy learning in grades*

k–8. Frameworks uses the same interactive, teacher-facilitator model as E.L.I.C.; teachers closely examine many aspects of learning, language, reading, and writing in making connections between their beliefs and their practices.

STAFF DEVELOPMENT SERIES ON WHOLE LANGUAGE
Andrea Butler, Presenter
Rigby Education
454 South Virginia Street
Crystal Lake, IL 60014

These four videos—conditions of natural learning, application of those conditions to the classroom, components of a whole language classroom, and shared book experience—have application in k–12 for understanding the theory and practice behind whole language. A facilitator's guide, several handouts, and recommended professional reading are included. For districts desirous of understanding whole language principles, these videos provide an excellent staff development package.

See also "Reliable Sources for Literature for the Reading-Writing Classroom" in Chapter 15 for publishers that offer whole language workshops.

17

Any Questions?

A reader

The following questions are representative of teachers' concerns that have come up repeatedly at workshops and through letters I have received.

What are your feelings and experiences regarding retention?

Unfortunately, years ago I was unaware of the unequivocal research against holding back low-performing students. When I was coteaching language arts in the first grade, I was responsible for the retention of Sheila. Sheila arrived at school late on most mornings, had trouble learning to read and write, and always seemed disorganized. I remember calling several conferences with her mother and trying for hours to persuade her that Sheila needed to be retained. I have no doubt that my convincing arguments finally persuaded Sheila's tearful mother to agree to retention.

While Sheila appeared to do well the first months repeating first grade, she slowly fell further and further behind until by third grade she was not only one of the lowest-achieving children in her class but also one of the unhappiest. That retention decision continues to haunt me. I have never recommended retention since that time.

Under the guise of raising educational standards, we hold back 5 to 7 percent of public school children each year and contribute to even more negative academic achievement, a higher drop-out rate, and damaged self-esteem. While there are rare cases of students who benefit from retention, they are the exception. Current research on retention concludes that there is no benefit in just about every case from kindergarten through high school (see Shepard and Smith, 1990). As responsible educators, we must take this research seriously.

It seems that handwriting of students has gotten poorer with whole language and its acceptance of invented spelling. Do you agree? How do you feel about the need for teaching formal handwriting?

493

I do think we are seeing less beautiful penmanship these days, but I don't think that's all bad. Some of that perfect penmanship came at the expense of lots of board copying and vacuous writing. We need to remember that, like spelling, the only reason handwriting is necessary is for writing. Writing must come first.

I have relaxed on my teaching and acceptance of handwriting. If it's legible, and neat, I accept it. I have the poorest handwriting of anyone I know, but if I need something to be carefully handwritten, I can do it. Otherwise, I make sure it's typed. Legible writing will always be important, as the current use of handwritten fax communications demonstrates.

If a child can form the letters so they're readable, I leave the handwriting alone. However, I believe it's important to demonstrate the formation of all the letters. This can be done in group minilessons and individually as needed—to encourage legible and attractive letter formation and help with specific problems. For very young children, demonstrations are appropriate as long as mastery is not the goal. I would keep practice handwriting exercises to a minimum and make sure children have lots of opportunities to use handwriting through purposeful writing experiences.

What are your beliefs about homework? Are we assigning too much or not enough? How much should parents have to be involved?

I believe that homework should be based on concepts the student already understands. It should be a practice time, to confirm and extend learning, and, as much as possible, homework should be self-checking. Above all, it should be worth doing, and students and parents should see the purpose of it. Unfortunately, that is not what usually happens.

When I was reading *Growing Up Literate* by Denny Taylor and Catherine Dorsey-Gaines, I remember being very struck by the authors' descriptions of children doing their homework. What struck me was how seriously these children and parents took this work. Homework was done right after school, and parents took the time to check it and give feedback. What disturbed me was how meaningless the exercises were—mostly workbook pages, dittos, and penmanship papers. The parents received no explanation about the work; it just came home and was expected to be completed. It was clear that homework was considered important, so it was done despite its questionable value.

Because many parents and students do take homework seriously, we must be sure that what we are sending home is worth doing. Instead of narrow and boring tasks, we should be providing opportunities for problem solving that are relevant to the children's lives. We must also be cautious about the amount of time we expect children to spend on homework. There is no reason to assign fifty math problems when a student can demonstrate his understanding with ten.

Most of the research on homework (Cooper, 1989) suggests that no more than fifteen to forty-five minutes of homework a week should be assigned students in grades 1–3. I was relieved to have that confirmed. Many of our primary teachers do not assign homework except for the expected, nightly independent WEB reading (p. 43). However, many parents question why more homework is not assigned.

Regarding homework in the elementary grades, Cooper (1989) states,

...homework for young children should help them develop good study habits, foster positive attitudes toward school, and communicate to students the idea that learning takes place at home as well as at school. As such, homework assignments in elementary grades should be short, should employ materials commonly found in the home environment and should lead to success experiences (p. 90).

At the high school level, where one to two hours of homework a night is recommended, it is still necessary that assignments take the form of practice and review to extend and confirm what the student already understands. Harris further recommends that, at all levels, parental involvement and grading be kept to a minimum.

Unfortunately, few school districts and teachers subscribe to the policies the research promotes. Martha Anderson, a parent with a son at a public middle school, has this to say:

> My ideas about homework crystallized the year my son Derrick changed schools because of reorganization in our district. Previously my son had little homework, and he was quite positive and self-sufficient about doing it. Then, in his fourth grade year, he had a significant amount of homework—the usual worksheets but also a lot of what I call showcase projects: reports, posters, games, maps, dioramas, the sort of work always in evidence at open house. It was not Derrick's happiest year in school, and more than once his teachers found his work deficient, although in the preceding years he had been a happy and successful student.
>
> What I finally put together spring of that year was that *parents* were doing the projects as much as the children. I came to that conclusion after Derrick and a friend's child had been partners on a project, had to my knowledge worked diligently on it, and had been criticized by the teacher for carelessness and poor presentation. By comparison with projects done with and by parents, work done solely by children looked sloppy and immature. Derrick received a very false and possibly damaging message about his work during fourth grade; his own efforts weren't good enough; he wasn't competent to do his assignments himself and do them successfully.
>
> This had not been the case in earlier grades. Perhaps because Derrick's previous school was the poorest in the district in terms of family income (which means not only families less able to buy supplies, but also parents who may be less available because of shift work or being single parents, who may have less access to transportation, who may have less knowledge of how to use libraries or where to buy supplies, and who may have fewer resources within the home), and because teachers in that school were very sensitive to their students' situations, the assignments he had there didn't presuppose a lot of parent involvement.
>
> As far as homework goes, I am in a bind I have yet to resolve. Many of Derrick's classmates' parents become very involved with their children's school work. While interest is appropriate and, I think, valuable to the child, I don't think it should extend to taking an active role in the child's homework. To do so confuses the matter of whose work it is; I don't think it benefits the child who is "helped." It also plays havoc with the evaluation of children's work, rewarding and penalizing children on the basis of their parents' resources rather than on the children's own efforts. But the bind: given that other parents are helping

their children with homework, do I disadvantage my son by taking myself out of it because I have sound reasons for thinking that he is better off doing it himself?

Only teachers and administrators can cut the knot. I have the impression that homework, especially in k–6, is something that the various adults—teachers, administrators, and parents—pass around among themselves to impress each other. The child's interests and how the homework enhances the child's learning appear to be the last considerations. No one can prevent a parent from helping his/her child with homework. However, screening each assignment against the question, Can a child in this class successfully complete this assignment *by him/herself?* would go a long way toward correcting the well-intentioned but mistaken perception that more homework, complicated homework, and inappropriately advanced assignments are the hallmarks of a rich school experience.

We need to take this parent's comments seriously, examine our own homework practices, and make sure they support what the research recommends.

My greatest roadblock has been the concern of parents who feel their children are somehow not receiving their full complement of education when the "trivial pursuit" daily drill pages do not come home. How do you overcome this when workbook pages are replaced with more significant independent activities?

Parents, used to basing education on visible products, have to be reeducated and reoriented to a process approach to learning. The first year our district made a commitment to move toward whole language, each elementary school had a Parent-Teacher Association meeting devoted to explaining whole language, the research it was based upon, the use of literature and accompanying meaningful activities, and the change in the way phonics would be taught. Parents also had opportunities to ask questions and raise concerns.

Even for parents who do not attend Parent-Teacher Association meetings, on-going communication is possible through weekly newsletters, open house, conferences, and phone calls. We find that when teachers and administrators have taken the time to explain a whole language philosophy of teaching, parents are very quick to embrace this style of teaching. Parents are delighted that their children are reading real literature at school and at home, completing worthwhile projects, and are excited about school. I have never had a parent ask for worksheets once they have understood what whole language is all about.

If I am already doing shared reading, journal writing, and reading literature and poetry daily to my class, what would be a good next step or two?

If you are already doing shared reading, shared writing is a natural next step. You may also want to think about doing some guided writing and allowing more choices for students in both reading and writing activities. You may be ready to add an individualized and independent reading component, as described on pages 41–50. You may also want to think about moving into heterogeneous discussion groups if your literature has been taught mostly whole class. Also, you may want to look at your evaluation procedures and think about adding some observational, process-based aspects.

Continue to do professional reading to stay vibrant as a professional and to question how your theory ties into meaningful practice. Perhaps most important, just focus on one or two new aspects each year. Remember, you don't have to do everything at once. Everyone I know is still in transition—even after many years.

Is there such a thing as a whole language program or whole language text?

There is no such thing as a whole language program or text. Since whole language is a philosophy and approach to teaching and learning, each teacher—with the collaboration of students—creates a program based on curriculum requirements and children's needs and interests. The best commercial text or program can be used only as one resource.

Scheduling still plagues me. How do I fit it all in? I'm afraid, too, that giving children large blocks of time to write may lead to chaos in my classroom.

Scheduling is a problem for most teachers. Even when teachers manage to get uninterrupted blocks of time in their day, they are often disrupted by students leaving and entering from special programs. Many teachers find the only way to fit it all in is to have reading and writing go across the curriculum. For example, if your children are doing research reports in science, the reading and writing they are doing in science could take place during language arts time, with students receiving guidance and practice in reading and writing informational texts.

Allowing time to write means setting up an environment that is structured but not rigid and controlling. Teachers that establish writing workshop or extended writing periods take many weeks and months to demonstrate procedures, set expectations, and give students time and practice to take responsibility for their topics, drafts, revisions, and completed pieces.

I still have trouble with the idea of everyone doing somewhat unstructured activities while I'm conducting a reading group. How can the teacher come up with enough daily activities to keep them all busy? It seems as though it would take so much time.

You are right. It would take too much of the teacher's time to try to "think up" daily activities. However, we are not looking to keep students "busy." We are looking to keep them productively involved with text and responding to it in a way that enriches them and brings deeper connections to the literature. Moving to more unstructured activities is a gradual process. Give yourself time. Teachers find that once they have internalized a whole language philosophy of teaching and learning, ideas come naturally, and options for students make sense. Also, once you begin to share responsibility for learning with the students, they come up with many ideas.

I'm having a hard time moving away from homogeneous grouping. You mentioned it took you ten years. What are some intermediate steps I could take?

Even if you are not comfortable with moving away from ability grouping most of the time, you could still provide some opportunities for heterogeneous grouping. For example, take one month out of your usual reading program, choose a book that will appeal to your students, and divide the class into mixed ability groups. Pair your less able readers with better ones for the reading of the text so everyone can then participate in discussion. Try adding shared book experience, as described on pp. 33–38, to your program. Also, begin to take a careful look at the research on grouping practices (see pp. 71 and 77–78) and then try to examine your own beliefs in light of the research. Change is slow and difficult for most of us, but eventually you will be able to make your theory and practice congruent.

It seems as though I have a noisier classroom as I begin to work with whole language activities. Although in most cases I find it to be productive noise, I worry what others will think as they come into my room. Is this a normal feeling?

Perfectly normal. It seems to take most of us several years to adjust to a noisier classroom. I remember worrying for years about the noise level. I used to query visitors, "Does the noise level bother you?" Most commented on how engaged the children were in their activities, and I would feel relieved. One first grade teacher was particularly bothered because the first grade class next to hers was always quiet. I asked her, "Which classroom would you rather have your own child in?"

Language does not flourish in a silent space. Students need and enjoy opportunities to discuss, share, listen to one another, and communicate. However, go with a noise level with which you are comfortable. For example, when I am guiding a literature discussion, I expect students not in group to work quietly because I find too much noise distracting. I am comfortable with students working together as long as the noise level stays very low. However, if I am not working with a particular group and students are collaborating on various projects where I am available for guidance, I can accept a higher noise level.

I'm trying to eliminate some of the basal drill and skill worksheets but worry that I'll eliminate something that is really important and will cause problems down the line for the students. Are there any guidelines on what to eliminate?

Gradually, as you develop and can articulate your own philosophy of teaching and learning—through observing children, professional reading and reflecting, staff development, sharing with colleagues—you will also develop confidence and trust in yourself to decide what to keep and what to eliminate. I find it always helps when I ask myself, "What is the purpose of this activity? Why am I giving it to students? What do I hope to accomplish? Could this be done in a more meaningful way?" If the skills sheet is not meaningful, don't use it. Keep in mind that mastering a set of skills has nothing to do with being a thoughtfully literate person.

Go slowly. Many teachers hang on to phonics worksheets for years until they become convinced that phonics can be taught more meaningfully and naturally in context. Especially during the first years teachers are moving from the basal to literature, they want the assurance that the "skills" are "covered." This is a normal part of the transition process.

What many of us did initially to ease our worry about "covering" all the skills was to list all the skills required by the curriculum course of study. Then, as we taught those skills through the literature, we checked them off. After a while we relaxed as we saw we could teach all the skills through our daily authentic reading and writing activities.

Once you trust yourself and become a knowledgeable, observant, and reflective teacher, you won't need the skills sheets as an insurance policy that learning is really occurring.

I'm enjoying working with "books" in my classroom but still have that feeling of doubt when the skeptics in the teachers' lounge say that the whole thing is just a fad that will be gone in a year or two. Do you think whole language is here to stay?

Whole language, or whatever one chooses to call meaningful teaching and learning that respects principles of language learning, is not a fad because it is based on solid research over the last several decades on how children learn language. I find the only people that see whole language as a fad are those that are tied to "programs" and mistakenly view whole language as another program instead of as a way of thinking about learning and teaching. However, I believe that unless administrators and policy makers get behind whole language, unless teachers become highly knowledgeable, and unless parents are well educated about whole language, it could well disappear and be considered another passing fad.

I have a couple of gifted students who read several years above the other kids. However, when I did some pretesting, I found that they did not have a few of the skills. Does it matter if they can read fluently with good comprehension but may not know a few of the skills?

If reading is viewed as a constructive, interactive process in which the reader gets meaning from text, being able to "do" isolated skills exercises is meaningless. Take a close look at what the student *can't* do on a test and see whether the student *can* apply the same skill in a meaningful context. If a student is using and applying a skill in a meaningful context, I don't worry about the results of isolated subtests.

I remember a gifted kindergarten student who was a fluent, comprehending reader. As a fluent reader, she had to be integrating the three cueing systems—semantics, syntax, and grapho-phonics. However, when presented with daily phonics worksheets, she rebelled. She could not and would not do them. It became a battle of wills between the teacher—who insisted the child needed phonics to read—and the child, who grew increasingly unhappy in the classroom. I believe it was the teacher's lack of knowledge of the reading process that caused the problem. The teacher was not phased by the fact that the child was already an excellent reader. To be a proficient reader, the child was effectively using and applying skills on a strategic level. However, to that teacher reading meant being able to do the skills on isolated tasks.

When is it okay to teach grammar and parts of speech?

I believe that the same principles apply to teaching grammar as apply to phonics teaching and formal handwriting. It makes more sense *after* you are already reading and writing. Once you have the fluency and conceptual understanding, you can benefit from analysis. It is not necessary to be able to define and label parts of speech in the elementary grades in order to use them appropriately. Students seem to be ready for this by junior high. In the elementary grades, students *internalize* the structure of language through immersion and guidance in authentic daily reading and writing experiences. It takes most of us years to believe this, but once teachers can articulate and apply beliefs about language learning, they find this latter statement to be true.

18

Final Reflections

*District whole language support group:
an evening meeting in a teacher's home*

Becoming a whole language teacher is no easy journey. There is no blue-print, recipe, or formula for success. There are few shortcuts and no ready solutions, and each teacher's route is slightly different. There is no best class to take or classroom to visit to get all the answers. There is not even a commonly understood definition, for whole language is a philosophy, a way of thinking. Becoming a whole language teacher is more about learning than it is about teaching. It is more about asking questions than it is about finding answers. Most of all, it is about making a profound philosophical shift in beliefs about learning and teaching. It is a highly personal, intellectual, and thoughtful endeavor.

Recently I was struck by the sense of frenzy in a group of visiting teachers. Spurred on by their district's new commitment to whole language, these dedicated and hard-working teachers were expected to attend workshops, implement new techniques and literature, take running records and anecdotal records, and revise the report cards—all in one year! There was no time set aside for professional reading and teacher collaboration. Neither was there time for thoughtful reflection about their teaching. Concern with accountability and rapid change was the district's first priority.

In talking with these earnest teachers, I understood that they had little idea why they were doing what they were doing. Instead of operating from a firm theory base, they were simply implementing a new set of procedures and activities. In the district's conscientious efforts to have them become whole language teachers immediately, these teachers had lost the joy of teaching and learning. They were going through the motions of change but without personal commitment and understanding. Allowing and valuing time for change in the process cannot be overstated. Unless teachers are encouraged to take time for reading, risking, and reflecting, no meaningful change will occur.

501

It takes most of us a long time to feel confident about the changes we have made and are making in our teaching and to begin to trust ourselves. In the process of becoming whole language teachers, most of us find that we are continually struggling and questioning what we are doing. Just when we think we have some answers, new questions arise.

It has taken me about ten years to feel confident with my own philosophy and teaching. I am kinder to myself now when one of my lessons doesn't succeed. I use the failure as an opportunity for reflection, and I often solicit feedback from students as well as other teachers. Based on such ongoing evaluation and reflection, I know there is a lot of learning going on, and I know that this learning is relevant and connected to the students' lives. I am no longer upset when I provide choices and some students abuse them. I no longer believe that time has been poorly spent when there is a lot of conversation between students, and some students seem to be off task. I have realized there is no perfect democracy or perfect classroom.

In the continually evolving process of becoming whole language teachers, my colleagues and I continue to read professionally, think about our teaching, observe our students, attend conferences, and collaborate with each other. We are feeling more courageous in our risk taking, more confident in the decisions we make, and more tolerant of our mistakes. It is a joyful struggle that keeps us energized and excited about our teaching and learning. I wish you continued success and risk taking in your own joyful struggle. I hope that you move slowly and thoughtfully enough to savor and appreciate the lifelong learning process.

The Blue Pages

The Blue Pages

Resources for Teachers

from

INVITATIONS

Regie Routman
Shaker Heights, OH City Schools
language arts resource teacher

with

Susan Hepler
Alexandria, VA
children's literature specialist

Vera Milz
Bloomfield Hills, MI Public Schools
elementary school teacher

and

Dana Noble
Shaker Heights, OH City Schools
English teacher

HEINEMANN
Portsmouth, NH

Introduction

I am a fanatic about being well informed professionally. Partly it's because teachers are often not held in the same high regard as other professionals. Partly it's because I'm largely self-educated in the teaching of reading and writing and continue to be so. Mostly it's because I believe we teachers must be knowledgeable in order to get our message across and be taken seriously by other teachers, administrators, parents, policymakers, and other educational stakeholders. And, of greatest importance, we teachers must take responsibility for being well informed so that we provide the kinds of excellent learning experiences and environments that allow all our students to thrive.

When I wrote *Invitations: Changing as Teachers and Learners K–12* (Heinemann, 1991), I shared my and other teachers' experiences in moving toward whole language and more authentic teaching, learning, and evaluating. I dealt in depth with such issues as responding to literature, teaching for strategies, writing and spelling, integration, evaluation, learning disabled students, classroom management and organization, and establishing support networks. The response to the book from educators across the United States and Canada has been overwhelming. I am often told that the "blue pages" at the end of the book are a particularly helpful resource for supporting our teaching and professional growth.

The hope for these updated, expanded, and revised "blue pages" is that you have easy access to some of the best and most relevant current professional books, resources, and children's literature. To that end, *The Blue Pages: Resources for Teachers from Invitations* is offered as a stand-alone volume for educators who already own *Invitations*. In this 1994 edition of *Invitations*, the original white pages are mostly unchanged except for the updated resources in the body of the text and at the end of chapters.

The Blue Pages is organized with integrated teaching in mind. For your easy referral, separate, annotated listings are included for evaluation, spelling, mathematics, social studies, science, author/illustrator, and parents. Many resources are provided for choosing and using quality literature in the classroom. The extensive recommended literature and supplemental literature lists for K–12 support a balanced literature/reading program. The expanded appendices include practical material for classroom use. Professional books, journals, newsletters, and articles are useful for independent reflection and for collaborative talk in your building or district. Use the table of contents to locate what you are interested in.

Because our field is changing so quickly, it is difficult to know and keep up with all the latest and most useful resources that are now available. I hope you enjoy reading through these pages, locating the resources that are just right for you, and incorporating them into your teaching and learning.

The Blue Pages

Resources for Teachers

The following annotated resources—professional books, journal articles, themed journals, journals, newsletters, and literacy extension resources—have been carefully selected to support teachers in continued professional growth in teaching and learning. A (•) before a title indicates a resource that has been found to be particularly useful, thought provoking, and outstanding in quality.

Almost all of the new professional books and resources that are included in this edition have publication dates of 1991 and beyond, and more than 60 percent of these are new to this edition. The professional books and resources from the "blue pages" of *Invitations: Changing as Teachers and Learners K–12* (1991) that are excellent, current, and worth teachers' time have been kept. Many older, less useful resources have been deleted, especially when there is an updated book by an author. For other recommended resources, up to and including 1988, see *Resources for Teachers* (Routman, 1988).

Professional Books

Annotations with Vera Milz

The following is an annotated bibliography of books other teachers, Vera Milz, and I have found helpful in furthering our knowledge of language learning, literacy, and teaching. Vera Milz, a highly talented elementary teacher and reviewer of professional books, has annotated many of the titles, and her initials *(V.M.)* appear after the annotations she has written. All titles, unless otherwise noted, are available in paperback.

Note, also, because there is enormous interest in spelling and evaluation and so many of us struggle with these issues, professional books and resources related to spelling and evaluation are listed separately for your easy reference in "Literacy Extension Resources" on pages 83b–86b.

Being Professional

Teachers ask me how I find the time to read professionally. I make it a priority, as the reading is absolutely necessary to my continued growth and development as a teacher-learner. Without exception, every teacher I know and admire who has made great professional strides in moving ahead in thinking and practice reads professionally and talks about those books with other colleagues. I, and they, deliberately set aside time to read professionally, and we consider it a necessity. For Vera Milz, professional reading breaks the isolation of teaching. By hearing the voices of others through their texts, Vera's beliefs are often confirmed. She says, "It gives me the strength to do things that are right for children." Reading widely also makes it possible for us to question assumptions, acknowledge weaknesses, try new approaches, and move toward new goals. Just as we ask our students to take increasing responsibility for their learning, we must also take responsibility for our own. So how do we find the time?

For myself, when I am working in classrooms, I try to do as much as I can when I am right there with the students. For example, during reading time, if I am meeting with a small group who needs an activity to work on independently, I try to put it together on the spot (for example, scribing an original story using the children's language) with just minimal time required later on for reproducing and assembling. In elementary writing workshop classrooms, I read and respond to the children's writing during individual or group conferences with the student(s). I do not take the papers home. In my planning in school, after school, and at home, I make an effort not to do much "busy work" but rather to get materials and plans ready that engage students and teachers to work as independently as possible. I think you will find that as your classroom becomes more student centered, and as you are negotiating curriculum and classroom decisions with your students, you will be able to make time to read and grow professionally—in spite of ever-increasing demands across the curriculum.

My recommendation is that you read through the titles and annotations, see what interests you, and choose one or more titles to get started on. You may want to choose a topic or book you're interested in or curious about, one you feel is a weak area for you, or one that is an area you're moving toward. With the busy work and family schedules that we have, it often motivates us to make time for reading if one or more colleagues is reading the same book. I always get more out of a book when I can discuss it with a colleague. One of the most wonderful things that our district did towards the close of a recent school year was to buy a copy of a professional book (from a committee-recommended list of about a dozen titles) for every K–12 teacher and administrator who chose one. Teachers had the summer to read the book. Then, a part of a professional day was set aside for teachers to get together around a table and talk about the book they had read. Those that took advantage of the opportunity found it a terrific experience for collegial exchange and professional growth.

Finally, perhaps most important are the political issues. Beyond the personal benefits to me and my students of reading professionally are the political considerations. If we teachers are to have a voice that is heard, respected and taken seriously by other educators, parents, administrators, and policy makers, we *must* be knowledgeable about current research, theory, and practice in language learning. We must be able to think for ourselves, be intelligent decision makers, and take a stand on important issues. Only when we teachers become more articulate through reading, writing, and speaking on a wide range of educational issues will we be trusted to make decisions for children and freed from the external pressures that continue to drive curriculum and evaluation.

Allen, JoBeth, and Jana M. Mason (eds.). 1989. *Risk Makers, Risk Takers, Risk Breakers: Reducing the Risks for Young Literacy Learners.* Portsmouth, NH: Heinemann.

This is a thought-provoking book with chapters by classroom teachers and university researchers who discuss how schools and parents can provide the most effective support for children labeled at-risk. Stereotypes about social class and educational expectations are examined in light of new evidence of early literacy acquisition by these children. The book is divided into four sections, moving from detailed accounts of successful individual children to descriptions of teachers and their positive learning environments to strategies for parental support, and, finally, to suggestions for literacy policies and practices designed to reduce risks for all children. The book is important reading for anyone developing programs that will increase the potential of every young child to be successful in becoming literate. (V.M.)

Allen, JoBeth, Barbara Michalove, and Betty Shockley. 1993. *Engaging Children: Community and Chaos in the Lives of Young Literacy Learners.* Portsmouth, NH: Heinemann.

This book is the story of what two classroom-based and one university-based researcher learned about six children chosen because they were the ones that they were concerned for the most in a school with many at-risk children. The teachers wanted to study the effects of whole language instruction on children who were experiencing extreme hardship in the educational setting. Each of the children's stories is compelling and unique with many successes, but no magical "learned happily ever after" ending for any of them. In the words of the authors, "Maybe one teacher can't make all the difference. But teachers can make a difference, a lasting difference, for the children we worry about the most." The book is important reading for anyone dealing with children who are at risk of failing to become literate. (V.M.)

Armour, Maureen W. 1994. *Poetry, the Magic Language: Children Learn to Read and*

Write It. Englewood, CO: Teachers Ideas Press.

Designed to take the mystery out of enjoying and writing poetry, this book is a joy to read. Using anecdotes, many examples of poetry by children, and a conversational tone, the author invites you to use poetry in a variety of fresh and interesting ways. Various poetic forms are explored, and directions for integrating poetry into the content areas are included. Poetry is also integrated into themes, such as food, pets, oceans, trees, and families, with suggestions for poems to use with the children, and examples of student poems inspired by them are given. The entire book is a delightful resource. (V.M.)

- Atwell, Nancie (ed.). 1990. *Coming to Know: Writing to Learn in the Intermediate Grades*. Portsmouth, NH: Heinemann.

Practicing teachers in grades 3–6 in Maine enthusiastically describe fresh approaches to writing in the content areas. Social studies, science, math, and art are integrated with reading and writing through the use of learning logs based on personal experiences and observations. Teachers looking for alternatives to traditional book reports and research reports will find well-documented alterative methods. The seventy pages of appendices, which include "Genres for Report Writing," "Prompts for Learning Log Entries," "Bury Yourself in Books: Children's Literature for Content-Area Study," and "Resources for Writing and Reading to Learn," are wonderfully helpful.

Atwell, Nancie. 1991. *Side by Side: Essays on Teaching to Learn*. Portsmouth, NH: Heinemann.

If you have ever had the privilege of reading an article by Nancie Atwell, or hearing her speak, this book will be a welcome reminder of her insights. It speaks of her loving involvement with her adolescent students, as well as her young daughter. She explores the conditions that allow children to become readers and writers, and proposes new revisions of the workshop model described in her book In the Middle. Other topics include the teaching

of poetry, including special education students in the reading and writing workshop, the implications of reader response theory in literature-based classrooms, and the importance of reflection through teacher research. As always, a visit with Nancie Atwell is a stimulating experience. (V.M.)

Atwell, Nancie (ed.). 1989–1990. *Workshop 1, 2, 3, by and for Teachers*. Portsmouth, NH: Heinemann. (See Newkirk, Thomas for *Workshop 4, 5* and Barbieri, Maureen, for *Workshop 6*.)

1, *Writing and Literature*.
2, *Beyond the Basal*.
3, *The Politics of Process*.

This annual series of books each features about ten articles by knowledgeable, practicing teachers representing grades K–8, a discussion between an expert teacher and a professional leader, an article by a children's author, and an interview with another children's author to be shared with your students. Each issue is themed in order to give a focus that might be explored by educators and students. For example, in the first volume, Donald and Carol Carrick share their insights into writing and illustrating children's books. Cora Five shares her fifth grader's poetry, while Tom Newkirk interviews a fifth-grade teacher, Jack Wilde. Each article gives insight into the use of wonderful literature in the classroom writing program. In the second volume, Jack Prelutsky is interviewed, as well as first-grade teacher Carol Avery. Cynthia Rylant describes how easily writing comes to her, and what this might mean for the teaching of writing in school. In the third annual, Mem Fox gives her perspectives on the exercises that children must perform, instead of real writing and reading in the classroom. Patrick Shannon shows how so-called reading reformers are making their voices heard, and how educators need to use their own literacy skill to make their views known. Toby Curry and Debra Goodman are interviewed about their efforts to obtain community support for a whole language magnet school. The above are but a sampling of the thought-provoking articles by the many authors in this collection.

Each volume deserves your careful attention. (V.M.)

Avery, Carol. 1993. *. . . And with a Light Touch: Learning About Reading, Writing, and Teaching with First Graders.* Portsmouth, NH: Heinemann.

Primary-grade teachers will love this book! The author takes you inside her first-grade classroom, and shows the day-to-day interactions of teaching and learning between herself and her students at schools in Lancaster County, Pennsylvania. In the book, she shares how she organizes the classroom environment, helps children to begin writing, lists possible minilesson topics for writing, gives suggestions for reading aloud to children, structures a reading workshop, and documents student growth. Children's literature, how it is used and enjoyed, is cited throughout the book. As each of the topics is explored, case studies are used to demonstrate how the children are learning in this rich environment. (V.M.)

Barbieri, Maureen, and Linda Rief (eds.). 1994. *Workshop 6: The Writer as Teacher.* Portsmouth, NH: Heinemann. (See Atwell, Nancie, for *Workshop 1, 2, 3,* and Newkirk, Thomas, for *Workshop 4, 5.*)

The importance of personal and professional writing is considered in this sixth volume of the series. As the editors say, "Writing helps us understand why we do what we do. Writing brings us closer to our students. And writing connects us to one another." Mary Mercer Krogness begins the book with her eloquent poem, "Voice." Mike Steinberg illustrates how writing nourishes his teaching and his life. Teacher-author Susan Benedict and author Betty Green are interviewed and share their insights on how writing contributes to the richness of their lives. The editors hope that the book will inspire teachers to take their writing beyond the classroom—I believe it meets their goal! (V.M.)

Barth, Roland S. 1990. *Improving Schools from Within: Teachers, Parents, and Principals Can Make the Difference.* San Francisco: Jossey-Bass Publishers.

For all those who have become fasci-

nated with school change and staff development, as I have, this is an inspiring book. Barth sees collegiality as central to a healthy school where everyone is a teacher and a learner. He defines collegiality as teachers and principals talking to each other about practice, observing each other in their work, sharing their knowledge with each other, and teaching each other what they know. "The quality of adult relationships within a school has more to do with the quality and character of the school and with the accomplishments of students than any other factor" (p. 163). Barth's faith in teachers seems to make it possible for us to break the isolation of teaching and develop more collegiality.

• Baskwill, Jane. 1989. *Parents and Teachers: Partners in Learning.* Richmond Hill, Ontario: Scholastic Canada.

The author, who is a whole language teacher, parent, and principal, honestly shares how she went about improving parent-teacher communication. Using the "family model" built on trust, understanding, and open communication, Baskwill describes the projects and procedures she initiated in her move toward a reciprocal communication model. Specifics are given in the text and the appendix for how she used a survey, booklets for parents, notes to parents, dialogue journals, newsletters, book bags, parent bags, "lunch box launchers," special kits, and more. An extremely valuable resource for any teacher wishing to significantly improve parent-teacher communication. Be sure your school library and administrator have a copy of this book.

Bayer, Ann Shea. 1990. *Collaborative-Apprenticeship Learning: Learning and Thinking Across the Curriculum, K–12.* Mountain View, CA: Mayfield. Co-distributed by Richard C. Owen, Katonah, NY.

This terrific text (156 pp.) discusses, demonstrates, and applies a collaborative teacher-learner model that is relevant for teachers at the kindergarten through university level. Teachers ready to shift more responsibility for learning to students and to use language and writing as a tool for learning—especially in the content areas—will find much support here. Specifics for management, eliciting prior knowledge (especially through focused free writing), focused reading, writing to learn, and peer interaction are invaluable for revising approaches to planning and implementing curriculum.

Bissex, Glenda L., and Richard H. Bullock (eds.). 1987. *Seeing for Ourselves: Case-Study Research by Teachers of Writing.* Portsmouth, NH: Heinemann.

Bissex defines a teacher-researcher as "an observer, a questioner, a learner, and a more complete teacher" (pp. 4–5), while Bullock discusses the power of teacher research to change the way teachers regard their students, themselves, and their profession (p. 27). Case-study research is described as a powerful tool to discover what is happening to the children we teach, as well as a way of looking at both ourselves and our profession. Classroom teachers from first grade to university level then present their findings from their studies of poetry usage, writing process, writing conferences, journal usage, and so on. An especially interesting chapter brings the various authors together for a roundtable discussion on their research. (V.M.)

Bloome, David (ed.). 1989. *Classrooms and Literacy.* Norwood, NJ: Ablex.

Twenty researchers examine literacy activity and learning in natural settings— classrooms in elementary schools. The researchers explore the relationships between classrooms and literacy through four related issues: the classroom community, intellectual consequences, access to literacy, and distribution of power. Educators and teacher-researchers interested in how the functions and functioning of classrooms affect students' literacy will be interested in these long-term, descriptive studies.

Two quotes:

"Children from low-income and working class communities tend to have a literacy curriculum different from that of their middle and upper class counterparts" (Bloome, p. 19); "In order to move into a higher group, students must not simply work harder and learn more; they must also learn qualitatively different reading skills, participation styles, and teacher orientations" (Borko and Eisenhart, p. 124).

- Boomer, Garth, Nancy Lester, Cynthia Onore, and Jon Cook (eds.). 1992. *Negotiating the Curriculum: Educating for the 21st Century.* London: The Falmer Press.

  Teachers and learners are advised to ask four questions about a topic of study and together negotiate the answers.

  1. What do we know already?

  2. What do we want, and need, to find out?

  3. How will we go about finding out?

  4. How will we know, and show, that we've found out when we've finished? (p. 21)

  This book is must reading for all educators struggling to move to a more student-centered, meaningful curriculum. It is also the most helpful book I have read for creating an integrated, inquiry-based curriculum that both engages students' interests and meets district requirements. Very provocative reading for coming to grips with sharing power in the classroom (as compared to limited decision making by students), real choice for students (as opposed to required choosing from options), intention (as compared to external motivation), collaborative talk and learning (as compared to planned cooperative learning) and integrated learning contexts. Terrific for discussion and rethinking your teaching.

Bredekamp, Sue (ed.). 1987. *Developmentally Appropriate Practice in Early Childhood Programs Serving Children from Birth Through Age 8.* Expanded ed. Washington, DC: National Association for the Education of Young Children.

This position statement (91 pp.) has become a highly acknowledged document for looking at appropriate and inappropriate practices for infants, toddlers, preschoolers, and primary-grade students. It is an outstanding reference for all teachers, administrators, parents, and policymakers who want to ensure the development of favorable early childhood practices in language and literacy learning. Be sure your school library has a copy of this publication.

Bredekamp, Sue, and Teresa Rosegrant (eds.). 1992. *Reaching Potentials: Appropriate Curriculum and Assessment for Young Children. Volume 1.* Washington, DC: National Association for the Education of Young Children.

Guidelines are presented to determine what is included in early childhood curriculum and assessment decisions. One chapter addresses the relationship of child development and curriculum while giving many examples of age-appropriate and individually appropriate curriculum decisions. Another section is concerned with antibiased, multicultural curriculum in general. Finally, educators describe their own growth as teachers as they implemented more appropriate classroom practices in their primary classrooms. This book takes learning beyond just "hands-on" activities, and its suggestions are bound to stimulate discussion among educators looking to improve programs for young children. (V.M.)

• Brooks, Jacqueline, and Martin Brooks. 1993. *In Search of Understanding: The Case for Constructivist Classrooms.* Alexandria, VA: Association for Supervision and Curriculum Development.

The authors elaborate on the guiding principles of constructivism:

"(1) posing problems of emerging relevance to learners

(2) structuring learning around 'big ideas' or primary concepts

(3) seeking and valuing students' points of view

(4) adapting curriculum to address students' suppositions

(5) assessing student learning in the context of teaching" (viii).

If you agree with these principles and the accompanying constructivist view that children formulate their own understandings of the world, then we teachers must provide meaningful learning environments that foster inquiry and speculation. The authors of this outstanding text (144 pp.) elaborate on each of the guiding principles and provide excellent informa-

tion and examples for becoming constructivist teachers. Don't miss reading this fascinating book!

A few quotes to think about:

"In order to understand, students must search for meaning. In order to search for meaning, students must have the opportunity to form and ask questions" (p. 54).

"Posing narrow questions for which one seeks a singular answer denies teachers the opportunity to peer into students' minds" (p. 86).

• Brown, Rexford. 1991. *Schools of Thought: How the Politics of Literacy Shape Thinking in the Classroom.* San Francisco: Jossey-Bass Publishers.

For educators and policymakers interested in creating schools that promote a "literacy of thoughtfulness," this is one of the best books I have ever read. Brown visited a representative sampling of North American schools and classrooms "where thinking and problem-solving activities were supposed to be a major part of the curriculum." In seeking to determine how and if educational policy impacted a "literacy of thoughtfulness," Brown and his team interviewed, observed, and talked extensively with elementary through secondary teachers and administrators. The results, while disturbing, were not surprising. With the exception of an Ontario school district and small pockets of whole language classrooms, there were few classrooms where a literacy of thoughtfulness was observed, that is, a literacy "that goes beyond basic skills and includes enhanced abilities to think critically and creatively; to reason carefully; to inquire systematically into any important matter; to analyze, synthesize, and evaluate information and arguments; and to communicate effectively to a variety of audiences in a variety of forms" (xiii). Despite the fact that educators believe that you have to aim at students' higher mental processes and profess to do so, most instruction relied on the textbook and aimed at the lower mental processes. The book ends with a copy of "Resource Guidelines for Program Review from the Ontario Ministry of Education." Use these excellent guidelines, which are listed on a continuum, to self-evaluate where you and your school are in having a child-centered, subject-integrated, problem-solving, instruction/evaluation program that leads to learner independence.

Some quotes to think about (from pp. 232–233):

"If you want young people to think, you ask them hard questions and let them wrestle with the answers. If you want them to analyze something or interpret it or evaluate it, you ask them to do so and show them how to do it with increasing skill. . . . If you want them to think the way scientists or historians or mathematicians do, you show them how scientists and historians and mathematicians think, and you provide opportunities for them to practice and compare those ways of thinking."

"Schools and districts that are farthest along in developing more thoughtfulness among students have also created more thoughtful environments and conditions for the adults in the system."

Browne, Ann. 1993. *Helping Children to Write.* London: Paul Chapman Publishing.

For teachers who struggle with how to implement and sustain a developmental approach to writing, this practical guide (158 pp.) incorporates the best of current research and practice and presents it in a readable, well-organized manner. "There are three important elements of designing a writing curriculum for children: firstly, that they are given tasks that involve real reasons to communicate meaning through writing; secondly, that they are initially given time to work on a piece of writing and time to return to it later either alone or with the teacher's help; and, thirdly, that they have opportunities to write in different styles and with different degrees of concentration depending on the task" (p. 21). Browne analyzes children's writing samples with in-depth comments on content, handwriting, and spelling, and she suggests future teaching directions for the child's continued progress. She answers common questions about writing in practice, addresses the teaching of writing to bilingual pupils, discusses explaining developmental writing to parents, and much more. If you are planning a writing curriculum for young children (preschool through primary), you will want to track down this book.

Caine, Renate Nummela, and Geoffrey Caine. 1991. *Making Connections: Teaching and the Human Brain.* Alexandria, VA: Association for Supervision and Curriculum Development.

How the brain functions, and how the brain (and learning) are affected by health, stress, and teaching approaches is the subject of this fascinating book. Over and over, the authors demonstrate how rote practice on isolated skills is inappropriate for acquiring knowledge. Instead, they show how a deeper understanding of the complexity of the brain supports holistic education. For example, content to be taught when spelled out in state curriculum frameworks can be fragmented and meaningless to individual students. Instead, subject matter to be studied should be organized around themes developed in the classroom setting to allow students to relate new and unfamiliar information to their background of experience. The book complements the work of Frank Smith, and also provides theoretical support for integrated, meaning-centered education. (V.M.)

Calkins, Lucy McCormick. 1994. *The Art of Teaching Writing.* New Edition. Portsmouth, NH: Heinemann.

In this new edition of her original breakthrough book, Calkins writes about helping students find and develop the significance in their lives through writing. "In this new edition I describe writing episodes that do not begin with a topic and a draft but instead with noticing, a question. When writing begins with something that has not yet found its significance, it is more apt to become a process of growing meaning" (p. 8). In rethinking her ideas, Calkins shares with us how to create a writing workshop in the elementary classroom that delights in what children can do and encourages them to find meaning in the moments and stories of their lives.

Among some of the topics she discusses in depth are rehearsal for writing, development of conventions in writing, conferencing, revising, publication ("the beginning, not the culmination of the writing process"), writing poetry, writing memoir, reading/writing connections through author and genre study, and writing nonfiction. She also addresses issues in assessment, theme studies, curriculum, and home-school connections. Each chapter ends with an excellent recommended bibliography of children's literature and professional literature.

• Calkins, Lucy McCormick, with Shelley Harwayne. 1991. *Living Between the Lines.* Portsmouth, NH: Heinemann.

This is an unusual, personal, and thoughtful book on the teaching of writing. There is no index to look up minilessons, conferencing, or specific procedures to follow. Instead, the reader is completely immersed in the recent work, thoughts, images, and writings of the teachers and students of the Teachers College Writing Project in New York City and is asked to rethink the teaching of writing.

In this sensitively and beautifully written text, the reader gets a feel for what the promise of writing can hold when writing workshop moves from writing folders and published pieces to notebooks and projects. We are asked to reexamine the writing workshop in broader, more flexible ways so we provide—among other elements— "silent spaces," "commitment," "genre study," "longer, slower conferences," ourselves as joyfully literate role models, real-life connections and purposes for writing, and lots of opportunities to help children develop their most promising "seed ideas." "In a sense, everything in this book addresses how we can help youngsters write with an intensity and life force" (p. 271). The changes Calkins has made in her own thinking and teaching since she wrote The Art of Teaching Writing *(Heinemann, 1986) are humbling and inspiring for us all.*

• Cambourne, Brian. 1988. *The Whole Story: Natural Learning and the Acquisition of* Literacy in the Classroom. Richmond Hill, Ontario: Scholastic-TAB.

In whole language circles, Brian Cambourne is to Australia what Don Holdaway is to New Zealand and Ken Goodman is to the United States. For teachers ready to take the time to understand the theory behind whole language, this text (201 pp.) offers detailed insight into the language learning process. The in-depth discussion of Cambourne's eight conditions of learning is thought provoking and applicable to the classroom. While mostly a theoretical text, the reader is taken into a grade 5 Australian classroom and given a picture of theory into practice. There is a useful section on evaluating literacy development. There is no index.

Cazden, Courtney. 1992. *Whole Language Plus: Essays on Literacy in the United States and New Zealand.* New York: Teachers College Press.

This collection of essays on language learning is challenging, thought-provoking reading. Cazden takes the view that as children become literate, "they need deliberate help in attending to parts as well as wholes" (ix). She believes that children do not learn to read in school just as easily as they learn to speak at home (a tenet of whole language) because schools cannot duplicate the conditions of oral language immersion that exist in the home. Along with Marie Clay, she suggests the "instructional detour"—a momentary diversion, when needed, on the main road of meaningful language use (pp. 14–15). The last section of this text deals with education in New Zealand, and I found the essay "Richmond Road: A Multilingual/Multicultural Primary School in Auckland" especially fascinating. It is the remarkable story of an unusually successful, inner-city, multicultural school and how the vision of its educational leader, Jim Laughton, powerfully influenced the entire school community—even after his death. It is worth getting a hold of this book just to read this uplifting essay, originally published in Language and Education: An International Journal *in 1989. We see what is possible when "kids always come first," and teachers respect and value families' cultures and each other while also taking responsibility for their own learning.*

Chase, Penelle, and Jane Doan. 1994. *Full Circle: A New Look at Multiage Education.* Portsmouth, NH: Heinemann.

Increasingly, schools are restructuring with multiage groupings in order to have more developmentally appropriate programs and to reap the benefits of children of various ages learning from each other. Two teachers who have collaborated in teaching a primary-grades, multiage classroom since 1988 describe how they structure their day, support children as learners, use ongoing assessment strategies, use thematic units to integrate the curriculum, incorporate a workshop approach to learning, and involve parents in their program. What comes through in this 197-page text is the caring, secure community the children and teachers develop together and the responsibility the children assume for their behavior and learning. Additional perspectives are offered on multiage groupings in chapters written by a parent, a principal, and other teachers. The book ends with an extensive review by Diane McClellan of the literature on multiage grouping and useful appendices for classroom use. Valuable for educators interested in multiage classrooms, holistic teaching, and co-teaching.

Christenbury, Leila. 1994. *Making the Journey: Being and Becoming a Teacher of English Language Arts.* Portsmouth, NH: Boynton/Cook.

As an experienced, reflective teacher of English, Leila Christenbury has written this thorough, theoretical and practical text (247 pp.) to help prepare middle and high school teachers for the realities and demands of the profession. Christenbury discusses various teaching models and recommends "exploration and discussion" instead of "teaching by telling." She explores and discusses a myriad of ongoing issues such as fear of not knowing enough, classroom management, literature young people should read, characteristics of a reader-response classroom, guidelines for dealing

with average, gifted, and alienated students, teaching Shakespeare, teaching language and grammar, questioning techniques, and much more. Christenbury raises philosophical questions, gives suggestions, and encourages the reader to reflect on the ideas presented in the text by engaging in personal journal writing and further exploration with cited resources. Lots of practical ideas for teaching literature, including an annotated bibliography of recommended young adult novels and selected, multicultural literature.

Clay, Marie. 1991. *Becoming Literate: The Construction of Inner Control.* Portsmouth, NH: Heinemann.

To become a reader and writer is a complex process! This book looks at the acquisition of literacy from the preschool years to the early years of school when a child reaches the stage that allows them to read independently from new texts. Clay argues that successful readers develop an inner control, and a self-extending system, that allows them to work with print even though they have been taught by very different programs. Children who do not develop strategies to organize and control their reading processes will fail to become literate. She pleads that teachers recognize that "some children need extra resources and many more supportive interactions with teachers." One example would be the Reading Recovery program developed in New Zealand. The book is very detailed in tracing how children learn to write and read, and it will be very useful to primary teachers attempting to understand the process in an effort to support the children in their classroom. (V.M.)

Clay, Marie. 1993. *Reading Recovery: A Guidebook for Teachers in Training.* Portsmouth, NH: Heinemann.

This is the guidebook that is used by all Reading Recovery teachers in training and in practice and that replaces Early Detection of Reading Difficulties (Clay, 1985.) The intensive program that this text outlines in great detail is for the small percentage of first graders in any classroom that are hardest to teach. Marie

Clay cautions that 80 to 90 percent of all children will learn to read without the meticulous and rigorous procedures of Reading Recovery. While I had read this difficult and comprehensive text before becoming a Reading Recovery teacher, it was most useful to me after I had received the teacher training. See also the companion volume, An Observation Survey of Early Literacy Achievement *(Clay, 1993), which presents ways of observing young children's literacy development, (annotation p. 75b). (If you are unfamiliar with Reading Recovery, see pages 479–485 in* Invitations *for information.)*

Cochrane, Orin (ed.). 1992. *Questions and Answers About Whole Language.* Katonah, NY: Richard C. Owen.

Twenty-one questions about whole language are answered by educators from England, Canada, Australia, and the United States. The book is substantial in content, yet informal enough for a relaxing read. It covers such topics as defining whole language, the role of literature study, evaluation in a whole language classroom, and where whole language is going in the future. The answers will be helpful to parents, teachers, administrators, and anyone inquiring about whole language methodology. (V.M.)

Cochrane, Orin, and Ethel Buchanan (eds.). 1993. *Teachers' Stories: Starting the Year with Whole Language.* Winnipeg, Manitoba: Whole Language Consultants.

This quick, enjoyable read includes stories by sixteen teachers from kindergarten through university. They each explain how they begin the school year in their classrooms. Their routines, structure, struggles, parent communications, and honest sharing give teachers support and ideas for a successful beginning.

Collerson, John (ed.). 1988. *Writing for Life.* Portsmouth, NH: Heinemann.

I found this Primary English Teaching Association publication a very welcome addition to books on the teaching of writing. This practical, readable, 120-page book goes beyond the process-conference approach and gives specific suggestions for teaching writing across the curriculum. There are lots of ideas for teaching children to write in different genres: reports, scripts, descriptions, and factual accounts, as well as narratives. The point is well made that we need to demonstrate expository as well as narrative forms of writing to have a balanced writing program. Applicable for secondary school too.

• Cordeiro, Pat. 1992. *Whole Learning: Whole Language and Content in the Upper Elementary Grades.* Katonah, NY: Richard C. Owen.

This book shows what worked for the author in her self-contained classroom as she began to utilize whole language techniques through her use of process writing methods. As a learner, she describes how she changed, why she was proceeding the way she did, and how her upper elementary students learned. A flexible schedule allowed her students to focus on thematic work centered around the content areas of social studies, science, and math. Suggestions for literature books to support the various topics abound in every chapter. A very important section is her thoughts on reflection and assessment. It includes ways of documenting student growth through portfolios and self-evaluations, as well as her own narrative accounts of the student's progress. This is an important book for teachers who are seeing whole language students enter the upper levels of elementary school. (V.M.)

Crafton, Linda K. 1994. *Challenges of Holistic Teaching: Answering the Tough Questions.* Norwood, MA: Christopher-Gordon.

This is a practical book that can be used in many ways. It could be read from cover to cover, but probably will be used to find information as a concern becomes pressing and needs a response. A wide variety of topics are covered from ability grouping to writing workshop. A unique feature of the book is the Related Questions section, which allows readers to network their way through the book. Suggestions for further reading and any children's books cited are listed at the end of each question. I especially enjoyed the sections on Skills and Strategies, Parents, and Literature Discussions. (V.M.)

Crafton, Linda K. 1991. *Whole Language: Getting Started . . . Moving Forward.* Katonah, NY: Richard C. Owen.

This is a comprehensive handbook dealing with the realities of starting and continuing a whole language classroom. It is grounded in theory, yet is full of practical ideas. Beginning with the differences between traditional, product-oriented, teacher-controlled education and holistic, student-centered, process-driven, language-based teaching, the author notes that the two philosophies are total opposites. She then lists six guiding principles and how they are applied in the whole language classroom. Crafton worked with six classroom teachers from various grade levels, including a high school teacher, and their stories are told throughout the book. One especially valuable chapter contains twenty-five strategies that can easily be integrated into the classroom setting. Another tells how each teacher begins the school year with her students. This is a supportive as well as challenging book for evolving whole language teachers. (V.M.)

Crawford, Leslie W. 1993. *Language and Literacy Learning in Multicultural Classrooms.* Boston: Allyn and Bacon. (hardbound)

The student population in the United States is rapidly changing as children who were considered representative of minority groups are now becoming the majority. This book is a comprehensive resource for teachers who are concerned that students from varied ethnic, cultural, and language backgrounds become literate in a pluralistic society. Strategies for learning that benefit all children are identified, as well as suggestions for assessment and evaluation. A "Teacher's Resource Kit" contains a fine selection of children's books for multicultural teaching themes and topics. (V.M.)

Cullinan, Bernice (ed.). 1992. *Invitation to Read: More Children's Literature in the Reading Program.* Newark, DE: International Reading Association.

Information to build or strengthen your use of children's literature in the reading program is presented in this thoughtful book. From Tomie dePaola's opening words to Bill Martin, Jr.'s afterword, it is loaded with vital information for teachers. The first section deals with genre studies, including books for emergent readers, poetry appreciation, realistic fiction, and informational books. In the next section, suggestions for enriching the arts and humanities, conducting author studies, extending multicultural understandings, and introducing award-winning books are given. The last portion considers reader response, at-risk readers, censorship, resources to find children's books, and suggestions for organizing a literature/reading program. Throughout the book, practical and innovative teaching ideas are featured. All in all, this is a very helpful book for busy classroom teachers. (V.M.)

Cullinan, Bernice, and Lee Galda. 1994. *Literature and the Child.* 3rd ed. Fort Worth, TX: Harcourt Brace. (hardbound)

This is an updated and more concise edition of one of my favorite reference books. I often refer to it when I am developing a thematic unit, studying an author or illustrator's work, or considering a genre study. As with Charlotte Huck's Children's Literature in the Elementary School, *a landmark anthology of children's books, books are described, criteria are given as to what to look for in a children's book, and many suggestions are given for their use in the classroom. Yet this book has several unique features, which make it especially useful in the classroom, such as a chapter on the readers of children's books— the children themselves, and how they respond to reading, read to learn, and read to enjoy. Another strong chapter is one that focuses on multicultural books as a distinct genre. Brief profiles of authors/illustrators are placed throughout the book, as well as a list of their birthdays in one of the appendices. Though the book is expensive for an individual teacher to purchase, it is well worth requesting as an addition to the school library. (V.M.)*

• Dahl, Karin L. (ed.). 1992. *Teacher as Writer: Entering the Professional Conversation.*

Urbana, IL: National Council of Teachers of English.

The voices of teachers are needed for sharing their insights and knowledge about educational issues, but many do not know where to start. This book begins with the personal accounts of teachers who are writing for the profession, and encourages others to take the plunge. Advice for tackling all aspects of the writing process, how to find support within writers' groups, as well as how to develop articles and get them published, is offered by teacher educators from all levels of education. This book is a treasure chest of practical support and encouragement for anyone planning to write for publication. (V.M.)

Davidson, Jane L. (ed.). 1988. *Counterpoint and Beyond: A Response to "Becoming a Nation of Readers."* Urbana, IL: National Council of Teachers of English.

This publication was written to explore concerns that the NCTE Commission on Reading found in the highly publicized BNR (Becoming a Nation of Readers), which was released in 1985. They believed that while BNR presented some sound theoretical positions and offered practical suggestions, it had several serious faults that needed to be addressed in a new publication. Commission members felt BNR was biased, did not present a full picture, and was inconsistent in the theory of reading presented and in the suggestions made for beginning reading instruction. BNR blithely dismissed whole language theory and research with the statement, "In the hands of very skillful teachers, the results can be excellent. But the average result is indifferent when compared to approaches typical in American classrooms, at least as gauged by performance on first and second grade standardized reading achievement tests" (p. 45, BNR). Several chapters describe how minority concerns were largely ignored in BNR. The place of literature in the reading program was barely mentioned beyond suggesting that parents should read to their children. Another problem was the relationship between phonics and comprehension. In one statement, BNR stressed that children construct meaning

from their first experiences with reading, while the report stressed that children be taught basic letter-sound relationships first, or they would be unable to comprehend. Both the original report and Counterpoint should be read together and the dialogue continued! (V.M.)

DeFabio, Roseanne Y. 1994. *Outcomes in Process: Setting Standards for Language Use.* Portsmouth, NH: Boynton/Cook.

Acknowledging that national standards and outcomes are present realities and that "someone" will be setting the standards, the author, who is a language arts consultant at the State Education Department in New York, contributes to the national conversation by explicitly defining and recommending standards for the language arts. She also reports the results of a pilot study of a group of teachers who used specific standards, outcomes, and criteria in their high school classrooms to assess students' language learning. This is a thoughtful, useful text for educators and stakeholders interested in standards and outcome-based assessment as well as in improving instructional practices.

I appreciated the clarification of common terms as these terms have taken on different meanings depending on one's educational context and past experiences. Outcomes are defined as the "knowledge, skills, and understandings that individuals can and do habitually demonstrate as a result of instruction and experience." Outcomes without standards are insufficient. "While the outcome describes what an individual knows, can do, or is like, the standard indicates how well or to what degree the individual knows, can do, or is like the behavior indicated in the outcome." Furthermore, DeFabio asserts, in order to make the standard clear, some specific criteria or performance indicators of observable behaviors are necessary. I found chapter 4, "Standards, Benchmarks, and the Continuum," particularly definitive and relevant to my own school district's debate on curriculum/assessment standards and outcomes. The Appendix, "Revised Draft of Outcomes with Eight Levels of Performance," will be helpful to groups writ-

ing their own outcomes. This text is applicable across the grades even though most examples come from secondary level.

DeFord, Diane E., Carol A. Lyons, and Gay Su Pinnell (eds.). 1991. *Bridges to Literacy: Learning from Reading Recovery.* Portsmouth, NH: Heinemann.

For teachers, parents, administrators, and school districts who want to know how Reading Recovery training and teaching operate and are implemented, reading this text will give much information and insight. Marie Clay's unique early-intervention program for the lowest-achieving readers in a first-grade class is detailed. The New Zealand and Ohio research bases are summarized. In the chapter, "Reading Recovery Surprises," Marie Clay notes the long-term, surprising outcomes/successes for "slow-learning" children and thus makes a convincing case for implementing Reading Recovery. In Part 2 of the book, Diane DeFord, Kathy Short, Barbara Peterson, and Kathleen Holland describe rich literary experiences and contexts in school and in the home that promote strategic reading and success for "at-risk" children. Many of the principles, examples, and strategies they cite and use are applicable to all students learning to read and write. In fact, since many teachers (myself included, until I became a Reading Recovery teacher) have never had good instruction in understanding and teaching the beginning reading process, this 240-page text can serve as an invaluable resource. Early primary teachers will find that the explanations of leveling of books for Reading Recovery and the bibliography of leveled books provided by Barbara Peterson in chapter 6 are very useful. In Part 3, Gay Su Pinnell, Daniel Woolsey, Carol Lyons, and Charlotte Huck address Reading Recovery teachers as learners and describe the powerful impact of Reading Recovery training and teaching on teacher thinking, attitudes, and classroom practice. The final section, "Constructing Literacy Lessons" (pp. 222–231), provides an essential framework of six components that some experienced Reading Recovery teachers in Ohio adapted to their classrooms:

reading aloud, shared reading, rereading stories, writing—including shared writing, dictation, independent writing, ongoing assessment, and honoring children's reading and writing.

Dyson, Anne Haas, and Celia Genishi (eds.). 1994. *The Need for Story: Cultural Diversity in Classroom and Community.* Urbana, IL: National Council of Teachers of English.

In this book, the basic need for story to organize and bring meaning to our life experiences is vividly illustrated. Nineteen contributors look at many aspects of storying—from its nature to its power in the classroom. I was especially interested in how Vivian Gussin Paley used an ongoing story she wrote to influence the way three African-American kindergartners viewed their racial identity. Courtney Cazden looked at the critical role of teachers in responding to the stories children tell at sharing time. Other essays looked at the performance of African-American student writers, the influence of gender in what children write, and teachers as authors of children's literature. The questions raised within these pages will increase the potential that the power of story has in your classroom. A very thought-provoking volume! (V.M.)

Edelsky, Carole, Bess Altwerger, and Barbara Flores. 1991. *Whole Language: What's the Difference?* Portsmouth, NH: Heinemann.

This book has been written with the intention of helping educators become more knowledgeable about the theoretical bases of whole language. For the teacher who already has some understanding of whole language, the detailed theoretical framework that is presented—as well as the scenes from whole language classrooms—makes whole language theory very explicit.

Elbow, Peter. 1990. *What Is English?* New York: Modern Language Association of America.

This book is a very personal and challenging picture of the English profession from early elementary to college. Reflecting on the 1987 English Coalition Conference, Elbow identifies the major issues con-

fronting our profession: what does "English" mean?, theory and practice in the teaching of reading and writing, should there be a "canon" of books that all students should read?, and assessment. Interspersed between Elbow's reflections are pieces by participants who attended the conference. This is a thought-provoking book for teachers of any grade or age level. (V.M.)

• Ernst, Karen. 1994. *Picturing Learning: Artists and Writers in the Classroom.* Portsmouth, NH: Heinemann.

The author was an eighth-grade language arts and social studies teacher for many years when a budget crisis eliminated her job; but since she was certified as an art teacher she was assigned to teach art to K–4 elementary school students. Having used the principles of the reading/writing workshop for many years, she decided to apply them in her art program. She says, "Just as writing led my students into the process of discovery, learning, and making meaning, I wanted creating pictures to do the same." This book is the exciting journey she and her students undertook together. It is also the story of an unusual collaboration between Ernst and the classroom teachers she worked with. She often visited their classrooms and wrote notes to the children that reflected on her visits. Their teachers in turn often stayed as the children began their art classes. In the classroom, as children began to write they were already often planning how they would express their written thoughts in art projects they could do when they could go to the art room. Choice of projects, writing, or pictures to create meaning became a central issue, just as choice of topics is important in a reading/writing workshop. Ernst illustrates the book with her own line drawings and notes, which adds another level of understanding to her work. This is an important book in considering the integration of art into the curriculum, and should be read both by classroom and art specialist teachers alike. (V.M.)

Fearn, Gloria Wilber. 1993. *Building the Good School: Participating Parents at Charquin.* Hayward, CA: Ohlone Press.

This book is a tribute to the empowerment of students, parents, and teachers in creating a holistic environment that is growing and changing to meet the needs of the learners within its walls. The Charquin Program is an alternative school within the Markham Public School that dates back about twenty years. It began with the active participation of parents in developing a philosophical base utilizing the open-classroom model, and has evolved into one also using whole language practices. Both theoretical and practical, this book shows how a school community can work together to support educational programs that will allow children to meet the demands of the future. It will be enjoyed by educators who might be interested in creating a school within a school, and shared with parents who support their vision. (V.M.)

Feathers, Karen. 1993. *Infotext: Reading and Learning.* Markham, Ontario: Pippin Publishing, and Portsmouth, NH: Heinemann.

By infotexts, the author means the oral and written texts that we read (such as books, journals, newspapers, speeches) to gather information on specific topics. In Feathers's words, this book is about "strategies that will help students read infotexts of all descriptions with greater understanding and better retention of information." I especially appreciated this book for its student-centered approach and all the current, excellent, and usable information on content reading.

Fisher, Bobbi. 1991. *Joyful Learning: A Whole Language Kindergarten.* Portsmouth, NH: Heinemann.

This book describes what an observant, knowledgeable kindergarten teacher does in her classroom in a typical day and why she does it. It is a remarkably clear and pragmatic explanation of a classroom based on Don Holdaway's Natural Learning Model. Each chapter highlights a specific aspect of the classroom. The chapters on assessment, dramatic play, and questions teachers ask are especially strong. Although the book is focused on the kindergarten level, teachers from pre-kindergarten through grade 2 will find many ideas, routines, themes, and record-keeping suggestions that will directly apply to their whole language classrooms.

Five, Cora Lee. 1991. *Special Voices*. Portsmouth, NH: Heinemann.

The stories of eight children with special needs are told as they lived in a regular classroom instead of an isolated setting. Their teacher describes how she helped the children develop into readers and writers while learning from them. She began by building an accepting, supportive environment that allowed children to have time to create, ownership of their ideas, and response from herself and fellow students. As this design worked for general education students, she began to question if it would nurture special children and enable them to do their best. Each year for six years, she had one or two students who were labeled ESL, were disruptive, or labeled "learning disabled." All proved they could work and learn in a language-rich environment with their peers. Their stories will provide many answers to problems facing learners in our own classrooms. Their successes can become those of our special learners. The possibilities are endless. (V.M.)

Fletcher, Ralph. 1991. *Walking Trees: Teaching Teachers in the New York City Schools*. Portsmouth, NH: Heinemann.

This is a sensitively written, honest account of the author's struggles and successes during one school year when he worked as a staff developer for the Teachers College Writing Project. In a book that reads like a novel, Fletcher poignantly describes his daily experiences in teaching the writing process to administrators, teachers, and children in the New York City schools. Compelling reading.

• Fletcher, Ralph. 1993. *What a Writer Needs*. Portsmouth, NH: Heinemann.

This is one of my favorite books on the teaching of writing. It is short, personal, well written, original, and terrifically useful. Fletcher, a talented writer and teacher, shares anecdotes and details of the craft of writing, and, in so doing, helps us become better writers and better teachers of

writing. Some of the writing topics he discusses and develops in individual chapters include: character, setting, specificity, voice, tension, beginnings, endings, unforgettable language, playfulness with time, and significant subjects. The Appendix gives many examples of books, poems, and stories that develop each of those topics well. Elementary and middle school teachers will appreciate the wealth of strategies and supporting examples of Fletcher's and students' writing. A wonderful resource for getting students and ourselves to write well.

Some favorite quotes:

"The writing becomes beautiful when it becomes specific" (p. 47).

"Voice in writing has to do with a unique personality-on-paper" (p. 77).

"We need to teach students how to write small, not just in terms of detail . . . but also in terms of moments, time" (p. 132).

• Forester, Anne D., and Margaret Reinhard. 1989. *The Learner's Way*. Winnipeg, Manitoba: Peguis.

This outstanding text (315 pp.), based on the belief that children learn from models and by being immersed in doing, combines a strong theory base with very specific practice. For the primary teacher, especially in K–2, who wants to visualize the whole language classroom and make it a reality, there is no book that is more helpful. Teachers will find the details and scheduling of actual classroom teaching presented in a clear, relaxed, applicable manner.

Activities and strategies such as story time, book time, reading groups, unison reading, individualized reading, writing workshop, author's circle, and news time are fully explained. News time is viewed as "our most comprehensive way of modeling all of the writing skills" (p. 90). During news time, children share their news of the day orally as the teacher writes and demonstrates the reading-writing connection through spelling, phonics, handwriting, punctuation, capitalization, and re-reading.

Forester, Anne D., and Margaret Reinhard. 1991. *On the Move: Teaching the Learn-*

ers' Way in Grades 4–7. Winnipeg, Manitoba: Peguis.

Theory and practice are blended into a comprehensive handbook that supports teachers who are attempting to bring holistic teaching methods into the intermediate grades. It continues the work the authors began in their text designed for primary-grade teachers. They encourage teachers to learn by doing and observing their students, and give many suggestions to start with. Topics include: Establishing a Climate for Learning, Classroom Management, Aspects of Reading and Writing Workshops, Moving Across the Curriculum to Teach Social Studies, Science, the Arts, Combination and Nongraded Classrooms, and Assessment. All of their suggestions are grounded on their research in the classrooms of three outstanding classroom teachers, which makes the book even more useful to busy teachers wanting to make substantive changes in their classrooms. (V.M.)

Foster, Harold M. 1994. *Crossing Over: Whole Language for Secondary English Teachers.* Fort Worth, TX: Harcourt Brace.

English teachers in middle and high school settings who are beginning to receive whole language–oriented students will appreciate this resource. The opening chapters define and describe the growing whole language movement in the secondary schools. The next part of the book is used to illustrate aspects of whole language teaching in the classroom setting. Topics such as conducting a reading workshop, leading a reader-response book discussion, and assessing writing are included. Last, becoming a whole language teacher, planning for the classroom, and remaining a whole language teacher are considered. This book would be very helpful as a guide for a discussion group of teachers interested in learning more about, or beginning to implement, whole language methodology. (V.M.)

- Fox, Mem. 1993. *Radical Reflections: Passionate Opinions on Teaching, Learning, and Living.* San Diego: Harcourt Brace.

Written in a humorous, engaging style, this collection of a well-known author's articles and presentations makes thought-provoking, inspiring reading for what it means to be a teacher of reading and writing. Two favorite quotes:

"If you don't open up and share who you are with your students, they will not learn to trust you as a teacher and as a fellow human being; this will limit their engagement in class" (p. 163).

"The best 'teacher' you will ever have is careful reflection on your own experience as a teacher of whole language in your own classroom" (p. 165).

Freeman, Yvonne S., and David E. Freeman. 1992. *Whole Language for Second Language Learners.* Portsmouth, NH: Heinemann.

The authors do not believe that whole language instruction is a panacea that will cure all problems facing bilingual students, but they are convinced that the application of seven principles found in whole language will give each of their ESL students a better chance for school success. They are the following: lessons should proceed from whole to part, lessons should begin with what the student knows, lessons should be meaningful to the students, lessons should encourage students to share their ideas, lessons should develop both oral and written language together, learning should take place in the first language before English is acquired, and teachers should believe that their students will learn. These principles are each developed in a supporting chapter with an explanation of underlying theory, as well as possible practices. This is essential reading for any teacher with ESL students in his or her classroom. (V.M.)

Galda, Lee, Bernice E. Cullinan, and Dorothy S. Strickland. 1993. *Language, Literacy and the Child.* Fort Worth, TX: Harcourt Brace. (hardbound)

Beginning teachers, as well as those wanting to learn the latest information on language learning and literacy development, will enjoy this resource. It brings theory and practice together in a careful and thoughtful manner. The opening chap-

ters look at oral language, listening, reading, and writing from the beginnings to proficiency. Later chapters apply these concepts through descriptions of teachers and students in their classrooms, along with suggestions for planning and implementation. Scattered throughout the text are helpful teaching ideas, which are conveniently listed on the front endpapers of the book. (V.M.)

Glover, Mary Kenner. 1993. *Two Years: A Teacher's Memoir.* Portsmouth, NH: Heinemann.

This little book gives a glimpse of life in a private, alternative school in a first, and then second, grade taught by the author. The value of having one teacher for two consecutive years is beautifully illustrated as Glover describes her classroom experiences in such a setting. Many anecdotes and examples of children's work bring the classroom to life, and will provide inspiration to build a child-centered curriculum. This is a rich environment filled with a love for learning and a stimulating academic atmosphere. (V.M.)

Goswami, Dixie, and Peter R. Stillman (eds.). 1987. *Reclaiming the Classroom: Teacher Research as an Agency for Change.* Portsmouth, NH: Boynton/Cook.

This exciting collection of essays addresses the "how's" as well as the "why's" of classroom research. The importance of teacher-researchers can be summed up in James Britton's statement, "What the teacher does not achieve in the classroom cannot be achieved by anybody else." Though the book is not a step-by-step procedure manual, a teacher can gain valuable information on how to carry out classroom research. Essays such as "A Quiet Form of Research," "Research as Odyssey," "Class-Based Writing Research: Teachers Learning from Students," and "Planning Classroom Research" were quite useful to me. The final section of the book documents the practices and insights of seven teacher-researchers learning in their classrooms. (V.M.)

• Graves, Donald H. *A Fresh Look at Writing.* 1994. Portsmouth, NH: Heinemann.

What I love about Don Graves's newest book is his stance, "I'll show you how to do this so you can do it too." We hear and see Graves's thinking, verbalizing, and writing before he asks us to undertake what he calls "ACTIONS." "An ACTION is something you do that will help you become an active teacher of writing." We are also privy to the changes in thinking and practice Graves has undergone since Writing: Teachers and Children at Work was published by Heinemann in 1983. Bothered by some of the orthodoxy that resulted from that landmark book, he gives us the conditions for creating good writing and relooks at conferencing, sharing, revising, and writing fiction in detail. One of the early quotes I was glad to see was, "We've learned that teachers need to teach more, right from the outset." By this Graves refers to teaching children how to read their own writing, how to share their writing, how to listen and respond to others' writing, and how to teach spelling and other conventions writers use.

One of the most important ACTIONS for optimal learning that Graves models for us is how to get to know our students well and learn from them. Throughout the text, he models that by letting us get to know him well—not just as a writer but as a person who is always learning and changing. Graves's book is a gift to us and our students.

Some quotes to ponder:

"If students are not engaged in writing at least four days out of five, and for a period of thirty-five to forty minutes, beginning in Grade One, they will have little opportunity to learn to think through the medium of writing."

"You, the teacher, are the most important condition for creating learning in the classroom. Your students will observe how you treat writing in your own life, how you learn, and what is important to you through the questions you ask of the world around you."

"The purpose of the writing conference is to help children teach you about what they know that you may more effectively help them with their writing."

"Our data show that when a writer makes a good choice of subject the voice booms through. When the voice is strong, writing improves as well as all the skills that go to improve writing. Indeed, voice is the engine that sustains writers through the hard work of composing, the drafts and redrafts."

Graves, Donald H. 1989–1992. *The Reading/Writing Teacher's Companion.* Portsmouth, NH: Heinemann.

> *Investigate Nonfiction*
> *Experiment with Fiction*
> *Discover Your Own Literacy*
> *Build a Literate Classroom*
> *Explore Poetry*

> This series of books brings together Graves's thoughts and insights since his groundbreaking book Writing: Teachers and Children at Work *(1983). Whereas his earlier book focused more on the process of writing, these books explore the richness of reading and writing together in a literate classroom. Examples of teachers and children sharing both fiction and nonfiction books they enjoy and writing in various forms are given. Teachers are encouraged to examine their own reading and writing, what they do as listeners and speakers, to rethink their own learning and their use of time in the classroom, and to read aloud as well as help children write poetry. Throughout the series, actions/reflections are suggested to encourage teachers to reach out to new possibilities in their language arts teaching. (V.M.)*

Graves, Michael, and Bonnie Graves. 1994. *Scaffolding Reading Experiences: Designs for Student Success.* Norwood, MA: Christopher-Gordon.

> A scaffolded reading experience is an instructional procedure that assists students to learn by allowing them to meet a goal or carry out a task that could be beyond their unassisted efforts. Just as a mother sharing a book with a young child might page through to familiarize the child with the general content before reading, a teacher provides essentials that will make the reading experience worthwhile and more meaningful. This book contains prereading, reading, and postreading activities, as well as comprehensive ones that incorporate all three types, for a particular group of students reading certain texts. Various chapters discuss the reasoning behind such experiences, how to incorporate them into the classroom, and how they fit into a total reading program. Two helpful appendices suggest ways to choose appropriate text material, as well as where to locate information on books. Author, title, appropriate grade level, and subject are indexed for children's books, as well as author and subject for professional books. This book has a wealth of strategies that can be accessed to meet the needs of various students from first to eighth grade. (V.M.)

Hall, Nigel. 1987. *The Emergence of Literacy.* Portsmouth, NH: Heinemann.

> For the educator who wants to examine the worldwide research behind emergent literacy but who doesn't have time to read all the primary sources, this 101-page volume provides a solid foundation. This remains an important book for increasing your knowledge about language learning and for implementing meaningful literacy instructional practices.

• Hansen, Jane. 1987. *When Writers Read.* Portsmouth, NH: Heinemann.

> This comprehensive text brings writing and reading instruction together based on insights found in writing process classrooms. It begins with Hansen's own questioning as she learned new methods of reading instruction while observing in Ellen Blackburn Karelitz's first-grade classroom. However, much of the book is based on her research at Mast Way, a public school in New Hampshire. Guidelines are given for structuring the classroom, evaluation, the teacher's role, the place of phonics, and basal readers based on real happenings in the classrooms where Hansen was working. Chapters are devoted to the ways that librarians, administrators, Chapter 1 teachers, and even college professors can support the classroom teacher. Teachers who are looking for alternatives to basal programs will find this book an invaluable resource. (V.M.)

• Harp, Bill (ed.). 1993. *Bringing Children to Literacy: Classrooms at Work.* Norwood, MA: Christopher-Gordon.

The reader is taken into exemplary grades 1–6 literacy classrooms to see whole language principles and practices in action: theme cycles, literature study, shared reading, portfolios, journaling, to name a few. In great depth, classroom teachers describe their organization, planning, management, teaching and evaluation strategies, and reading-writing programs. Second-grade teachers Deborah Manning and Jean Fennacy broaden our understanding and use of shared reading in a primary classroom. First-grade teacher Mary Giard explains her role and the students' in her excellent guided-reading program. Mary Kitagawa demonstrates how she sets up her excellent writing program and responds to her fifth- and sixth-grade writers. Donna Byrum and Virginia Lazenby Pierce describe how they organize for theme cycles as a way to involve their fifth graders in investigation of meaningful, self-chosen topics. Kittye Copeland shares how she organizes her multiage (ages 5–12) classroom for reading and writing. Each chapter provides a wealth of information and workable ideas for teachers. Don't miss reading this valuable resource!

Harris, Violet J. (ed.). 1992. *Teaching Multicultural Literature in Grades K–8.* Norwood, MA: Christopher-Gordon. (hardbound)

This is a collection of essays by writers reflecting both their expertise and their cultures. An especially helpful chapter by Rudine Sims Bishop presents guidelines for teachers who are trying to select authentic multicultural literature. In other chapters, African-American, Asian Pacific, Native American, Puerto Rican, Mexican-American, and Caribbean children's literature is discussed with great insight. Each author presents the development of children's literature within his or her culture while helping the reader to become aware of stereotypes and negative images that might inadvertently be promoted. Annotated lists of highly recommended books are given at the end of each chapter. The final chapter has an excellent listing of small presses, related organizations, journals, and bookstores for finding multicultural books. The entire volume is a fabulous resource for the selection of, discussion of, and debate on appropriate multicultural literature for children. (V.M.)

• Harste, Jerome C., and Kathy G. Short, with Carolyn Burke and contributing teacher-researchers. 1988. *Creating Classrooms for Authors: The Reading-Writing Connection.* Portsmouth, NH: Heinemann.

This is an in-depth text (416 pp.) for the experienced reading-writing teacher who already applies the theoretical knowledge of language learning in the classroom along with effective management techniques. The authors view "The Authoring Cycle" as a model for all learning in a curriculum that focuses on life experiences. The reader is given much direction to get and keep the cycle going. Teachers will find the second section of the book, where many specific classroom activities are described, especially valuable. "Author's Chair," "Classroom Newspaper," "Family Stories," "Learning Logs," "Literature Circles," "Reader's Theatre," "Save the Last Word for Me," "Sketch to Stretch," and "Written Conversation" are among some of the curricular activities delineated.

• Harwayne, Shelley. 1992. *Lasting Impressions: Weaving Literature into the Writing Workshop.* Portsmouth, NH: Heinemann.

This book is bound to become a well-used and well-worn classic in an elementary teacher's professional library. It is filled with practical ideas based on the author's experiences with Antoinette Cinno's fifth graders in P.S. 148 in Queens, New York. However, as a co-director of the Teachers College Writing Project, Shelley Harwayne also explores the relationship between reading and writing at many grade levels, thus giving the book a universal appeal. She explores the writing workshop structures over a school year, and includes thoughts on minilessons, conferences, author visits, book talks, and assessment. Literature is brought into every aspect of the classroom setting. As she completed the book, Harwayne moved into *a new position as the director of an alternative public school that will have literature as the heart of the curriculum. She outlines her hopes and dreams for the new school, and ends this valuable resource with the words, "To be continued." I look forward to her future comments. (V.M.)*

Heald-Taylor, Gail. 1989. *The Administrator's Guide to Whole Language.* Katonah, NY: Richard C. Owen.

This is a handy text (189 pp.) to give to the administrator who wants to know more about whole language and how to facilitate its implementation. Especially useful is the extensive section on the research supporting whole language teaching, the comparison between whole language and skills-based approaches, the activities and strategies principals should expect to see in whole language classrooms, the suggestions for informing and educating parents about whole language, and the section on assessment. Excellent for teachers as well.

• Heard, Georgia. 1989. *For the Good of the Earth and Sun: Teaching Poetry.* Portsmouth, NH: Heinemann.

A practicing poet and teacher with a love of language and respect for students takes us "inside" the process of poetry writing by describing her own thinking-writing-reading processes. In so doing, she makes reading and writing poetry seem natural, desirable, and possible for us all. The book is practical, inspiring, and lovely to read. For the classroom teacher, there are suggestions and strategies for reading poetry, getting started writing poetry, creating visual images with words, choosing original words, revising, conferencing, and creating line-breaks and white spaces as well as examples of various minilessons. Although Heard sees a place for rhymed poetry, as well as haiku and cinquain, which she calls "the hamburger and hot dog of American poetry classrooms" (p. 96), she goes beyond formula writing to encouraging exploration with various forms and ideas in a poetry-rich environment. Lots of examples of what actually transpires in her poetry workshops with children are included along with many poems by chil-

dren. There are also useful bibliographies of poetry books for children and reference books for teaching poetry. Reading this extraordinary and powerful book will change the way you approach the teaching of poetry.

Hearne, Betsy, and Roger Sutton (eds.). 1993. *Evaluating Children's Books: A Critical Look: Aesthetic, Social, and Political Aspects of Analyzing and Using Children's Books.* Urbana-Champaign, IL: University of Illinois Graduate School of Library and Information Science.

Taken from a conference devoted to evaluating books for children and young adults, the speakers/writers of this text take us inside the book review process. Reading this text sensitized me to the criteria and issues surrounding the selection of nonfiction books, picture books, and especially books about minority groups. With literature being the mainstay of the reading program in many schools and classrooms, teachers—as well as librarians—are making decisions about literature to purchase. This is an important text for developing a "culturally conscious literature" collection. The chapter "Evaluating Children's Books for Whole-Language Learning" by Violet Harris is particularly helpful to teachers.

A favorite quote: "Books can make a difference in dispelling prejudice and building community: not with role models and recipes, not with noble messages about the human family, but with enthralling stories that make us imagine the lives of others. A good story lets you know people as individuals in all their particularity and conflict; and once you see someone as a person—flawed, complex, striving—you've reached beyond stereotype" (p. 134).

• Heath, Shirley Brice, and Leslie Mangiola. 1991. *Children of Promise: Literate Activity in Linguistically and Culturally Diverse Classrooms.* Washington, D.C.: National Education Association.

This sixty-four-page publication urges us to address the literacy education needs of culturally and linguistically diverse students by seeing them as "children of prom-

ise" rather than "at risk." Citing several literacy programs that have dramatically influenced the literacy skills and attitudes of low-achieving, language-minority students by involving them in cross-grade tutoring, lots of opportunities for talk, and other specific approaches to language-based learning that are powerful for all students, this is a must-read book for all educators. Detailed suggestions for developing literate behaviors—for example, successful small-group conversations in the classroom—are included. Practical for all K–12 teachers.

- Hickman, Janet, and Bernice E. Cullinan (eds.). 1989. *Children's Literature in the Classroom: Weaving Charlotte's Web.* Norwood, MA: Christopher-Gordon.

   Designed as a tribute to Charlotte Huck's teaching and her philosophy about literature for children, this book reflects the influence this remarkable teacher has had on her students. Following the opening tribute describing Huck's career and her vision of literature as the heart of the school curriculum, the book is divided into three sections: understanding the uses of literature in the classroom; celebrating books and authors in the picture book, fantasy, historical fiction, and poetry genres; and developing literature-based programs. The various chapters are contributed by her former students and several children's authors. The Epilogue, "No Wider Than the Heart Is Wide," is a piece by Huck herself. The entire volume is a rich and unique legacy for all of us to savor and treasure. (V.M.)

- Hickman, Janet, Bernice Cullinan, and Susan Hepler (eds.). 1994. *Children's Literature in the Classroom: Extending Charlotte's Web.* Norwood, MA: Christopher-Gordon.

   This book is a companion book to Children's Literature in the Classroom and continues with the fine scholarship and tone of the first volume. It covers completely new topics, such as poetry in the classroom, responses to literature, learning from the illustrations in picture books, literature across the curriculum, using literature in Reading Recovery programs, as well as adapting Reading Recovery principles for adults. The prologue is by Charlotte Huck, who cites many uses and abuses of children's literature. These fine authors leave the reader with much food for thought. (V.M.)

Hiebert, Elfrieda H., and Barbara M. Taylor (eds.). 1994. *Getting Reading Right from the Start: Effective Early Literacy Interventions.* Boston: Allyn and Bacon.

   The purpose of this book is to show that early literacy intervention programs with the focus on authentic reading and writing tasks can prevent many first-grade children from failure to learn to read. Seven different successful programs, designed to accelerate the literacy learning of children who enter school behind their peers in emergent reading skills, are discussed in the various chapters of the book. The programs take various forms, such as tutoring efforts, small-group efforts, and classroom/school restructuring, but all stress the need for activities like reading stories aloud, using big books, extending text through drama or art, and writing experiences in print-rich environments. (V.M.)

- Hill, Susan, and Joelie Hancock. 1994. *Reading and Writing Communities: Co-operative Literacy Learning in the Classroom.* Portsmouth, NH: Heinemann.

   While we know that classroom climate is especially important for developing readers and writers, most of us struggle with how to attain a classroom where students assume responsibility for their own behavior and for the successful functioning of the class. Australian educators Hill and Hancock clearly show us—through words, charts, and photographs—how to organize our classrooms and build a cohesive community. Specific strategies for getting students to successfully read and write in different genres are demonstrated. An easy-to-read, theoretically sound "how-to" book for the elementary grades.

Hill, Susan, and Tim Hill. 1990. *The Collaborative Classroom.* Portsmouth, NH: Heinemann.

   Based on the cooperative learning work of David and Roger Johnson, the authors present lots of detailed examples of activities for successful cooperative group work. Very useful for the teacher who wants children to work together but who needs specific classroom management information to set up the collaborative classroom.

Holland, Kathleen E., Rachael A. Hungerford, and Shirley B. Ernst (eds.). 1993. *Journeying: Children Responding to Literature*. Portsmouth, NH: Heinemann.

Major and current research based on Louise Rosenblatt's transactional theory of reader response is reported in this book about children's responses to literature. Studies are cited from early and upper elementary, middle school/junior high, and across grade levels. Practicing teachers will be able to find many ideas on how to use literature more effectively in their classroom. The whole book is a stimulating blend of theory and practice that will be useful to those reading it, and is especially helpful in noting how the children's responses develop as they grow older. (V.M.)

• Hubbard, Ruth Shagoury, and Brenda Miller Power. 1993. *The Art of Classroom Inquiry: A Handbook for Teacher-Researchers*. Portsmouth, NH: Heinemann.

This is a wonderfully supportive book for any teacher contemplating teacher research. I loved the quote: "Research is a high-hat word that scares a lot of people. It needn't. It's rather simple. Essentially research is nothing but a state of mind . . . a friendly, welcoming attitude toward change . . . going out to look for change instead of waiting for it to come" (xv–xvi, quoting Charles Kettering). Some of the important topics the book deals with include finding and framing the research question, designing the research study, collecting and analyzing the data, writing up the research, getting rid of writer's block, and finding funds for your research. An appendix lists the names and addresses of over forty teacher-researchers and invites you to write to them. We need more teachers writing for teachers. This book invites you to become a teacher-researcher and share your story.

• Huck, Charlotte, Janet Hickman, and Susan Hepler. 1993. *Children's Literature in the Elementary School*. 5th ed. Fort Worth, TX: Harcourt Brace.

This updated edition of an acclaimed text (866 pp.) should be readily accessible to all teachers and librarians as it is one of the most comprehensive and outstanding reference books on children's literature. Part 1 discusses the value of literature and gives guidelines for evaluation of literature. Chapter 2, "Understanding Children's Response to Literature," is valuable for understanding, observing, encouraging, and examining what goes on between a book and its reader. In Part 2, all types of literature are discussed in depth: books to begin on including wordless books, ABC books, and concept books; picture books; traditional literature including folktales, fables, myths, legends, and the Bible; modern fantasy; poetry; contemporary realistic fiction; historical fiction; biographies and informational books. Some of these are complete enough to stand as individual anthologies. Part 3 focuses on developing a literature program in the school. The specific suggestions and examples for guiding in-depth studies of books with webbing and questioning techniques are especially helpful. Numerous charts list books that share similar patterns and may be taught together. "Teaching Features" focus attention on actual classroom programs. At the end of each of the thirteen chapters are "Suggested Learning Experiences" that give ideas that can be adapted to the classroom, "Related Readings" with a brief description of each reference cited, and "References" with recommended book titles specific to each topic.

Karelitz, Ellen Blackburn. 1993. *The Author's Chair and Beyond: Language and Literacy in a Primary Classroom*. Portsmouth, NH: Heinemann.

This author takes us into her first-grade classroom over the period of one school year. She describes what she does, her students' responses, and her own questions and decision making. It is easy to picture a "typical" day, as examples of children's writing, transcripts of confer-

ences, and samples of record keeping illustrate the various points that the author makes. I especially enjoyed the chapter on note writing between the students and their teacher, as well as the information about the integration of reading and writing across the curriculum. The significance of the "author's chair," where children gather to talk about their books and those of professional children's authors, is discussed in the last chapter. Throughout the book, transcripts of the children's conversations reveal things that are important to them, and show how they bring the written word into their own perspectives. This is a valuable book for primary-grade teachers with many practical ideas based on a solid theoretical framework. (V.M.)

Kasten, Wendy C., and Barbara K. Clarke. 1993. *The Multi-Age Classroom: A Family of Learners.* Katonah, NY: Richard C. Owen.

The multiage classroom model has been used for many years in England and New Zealand, and, of course, in the one-room schoolhouses scattered across the U.S. Yet, only recently are researchers taking a second look at the benefits that such groupings of children might have. These authors have been doing research in this field for several years, and in this book have summarized the history and benefits of multiage classrooms. In all instances, they advocate multiage groupings as very positive environments for learning language. They describe several outstanding classroom communities with intermediate, K 1, K 3, or grade 5–6 students, and give advice for implementing them. The last chapter contains questions frequently asked by teachers and parents. (V.M.)

Katz, Lilian G., Demetra Evangelou, and Jeanette Allison Hartman. 1990. *The Case for Mixed-Age Grouping in Early Education.* Washington, DC: National Association for the Education of Young Children.

Multiage grouping is explored and advocated for young children. Both academic and social benefits are seen for the youngest as well as the oldest members of the classroom, and the benefits are explained in detail. Teaching strategies, such

as peer tutoring and cooperative learning, are suggested. Several programs are described, and areas of future research are suggested. (V.M.)

Kirby, Dan, and Carol Kuykendall. 1991. *Mind Matters: Teaching for Thinking.* Portsmouth, NH: Boynton/Cook.

This book is not a "how-to" manual. Instead, it is a book that challenges you as a teacher to "embark on adventures of the mind that may or may not have anything to do with your students." Its central premise is "it takes thinking teachers to develop thinking students." There are many "assisted explorations" designed to take you into the territory of thinking, as well as models to spark ideas that might be implemented in your classroom. Designed almost as a conversation between friends, this book is stimulating but informal. It's the kind of book that would be enjoyable on a summer break when you have time to dream and stretch, or it could be the focus of a discussion group between colleagues. Whatever way you choose to use it, both you and your students will benefit by considering the challenges it presents. (V.M.)

Kobrin, Beverly. 1988. *Eyeopeners! How to Choose and Use Children's Books about Real People, Places, and Things.* New York: Penguin.

Kobrin views fiction and nonfiction as "literary coequals" and states that children need TLC—the total literature connection. Asserting that children have natural curiosity and are fascinated by facts, she discusses over 500 engrossing nonfiction books and groups them by categories such as biographies, dinosaurs, grandparents, and holidays, to name a few. Each book annotation includes a brief summary, recommended age ranges, and teaching tips. This valuable resource book for teachers, parents, and librarians also includes criteria for evaluating nonfiction as well as an extensive "Quick-Link Index" to aid the teacher looking for specific topics or themes.

• Krogness, Mary Mercer. 1995. *Just Teach Me, Mrs. K! Talking, Reading and Writing with Resistant Adolescent Learners.* Portsmouth, NH: Heinemann.

"Resistant learners deserve a good intellectual and creative workout even if they claim not to want it." So believes Mary Krogness, an extraordinary teacher of low and underachieving seventh and eighth graders who are anxious, angry, and fearful about school learning. Taking us inside her classroom, she shares her story of how she attempts to hook these students on talking, reading, and writing through nurturing their imaginations, respecting them as individuals, and getting them to take responsibility for their behavior and their learning. Believing that a language arts class must deal with everything that touches the lives of students, Krogness helps her students feel free to talk and use language to learn through interviews, improvisational drama, theater games, word play, language exercises, reading aloud, conversations, listening, field trips, questioning, literature discussions, reading and writing poetry, plays, personal histories, fairy tales, and more.

While much has been written about the teaching challenges of nonmainstream students with language learning problems, little has been written about successfully engaging these students. In this elegantly written account, Krogness writes about "the class that made me question my worth as a teacher and as a person" and how with great effort and compassion she reaches many of these recalcitrant, yet mostly able, adolescents. The voices and increasing self-esteem of the students shine through in their conversations and in their writing.

Lane, Barry. 1993. *After THE END: Teaching and Learning Creative Revision.* Portsmouth, NH: Heinemann.

In answer to the question, "I can get them to write, but how do I get them to revise?" Lane addresses many concerns of teachers of writing. He carefully takes us through lots of activities, approaches, and questions we can use in the classroom to encourage and help students to write well. Some of the topics for writing and revision he discusses and demonstrates include writ-

ing leads, writing with descriptive detail, creating characters and building scenes using dialogue, "exploding a moment," conferencing, editing, freewriting, and writing with voice. Very helpful to teachers of grades three through college and beyond.

Langer, Judith A. (ed.). 1992. *Literature Instruction: A Focus on Student Response.* Urbana, IL: National Council of Teachers of English.

This book brings together a series of essays advocating student-response literature instruction from elementary years to college. In a piece especially helpful to elementary teachers, Jayne DeLawter presents the idea that teachers must become exploration leaders in order to lead students into and beyond the author's text. She deplores the use of patterned and sequenced instruction guides for literature, and instead focuses on a classroom where children discuss and reflect as they work through their understandings of a particular piece of literature. Other essays provide a picture of what a response-based classroom might look like, as well as call for changes in literature instruction and new ways of evaluation of day-to-day learning. This book will be especially useful to upper elementary through high school teachers. (V.M.)

Lott, Joyce. 1994. *A Teacher's Stories: Reflections on High School Writers.* Portsmouth, NH: Boynton/Cook.

Joyce Lott, a senior high English teacher, began keeping a daily journal as a way to reflect on her teaching and on students who were not progressing with traditional methods. While on a sabbatical, she examined and analyzed her journal entries and the stories they told about individual students and herself. In this engaging, retrospective telling of stories, she comes to realize that "knowing who my students were as people not only affected my interaction with them, it also affected their writing and whether it progressed or not." Lott is able to acknowledge cross-cultural dilemmas and the importance of knowing, valuing, and accepting a student's culture in order to understand and appreciate his or her writing style. She questions her approaches to peer editing, grading, and responding to students' writing. She also acknowledges her many successes and realizes, "My task had been not so much to teach *them* as to encourage *learning*" (p. 94). In Part V, she shares why and how she uses portfolios and how it has shifted the focus away from grades and towards improving the writing. Secondary teachers will find the information on portfolios excellent for getting students to have more ownership and involvement in their writing. This 202-page book is interesting reading for all reflective teachers.

Lyons, Carol A., Gay Su Pinnell, and Diane E. DeFord. 1993. *Partners in Learning: Teachers and Children in Reading Recovery.* New York: Teachers College Press.

For the many educators interested in Reading Recovery (the early-intervention program developed in New Zealand by Marie Clay to prevent reading failure), this significant text discusses the research base, implementation, principles, teacher training, lesson elements, teaching strategies, and change process. Excellent for clear insights into Reading Recovery, teacher and institutional change, the reading process, and literacy education.

• Manning, Maryann, Gary Manning, and Roberta Long. 1994. *Theme Immersion: Inquiry-Based Curriculum in Elementary and Middle Schools.* Portsmouth, NH: Heinemann.

The authors define theme immersion (TI) as an "in-depth study of a topic, issue, or question" that is of importance and interest to many members of the learning community. The topic, materials, activities, direction, and outcomes are determined by a negotiated partnership between students and teachers through a process that fosters student exploration, choice, risk taking, social interaction, knowledge construction, and autonomy. Manning, Manning, and Long differentiate between a theme immersion and theme unit, viewing the latter as mostly a teacher-designated, skills-oriented topic study where all areas of the

curriculum are often forced into a unit. In their TI focus, the authors realistically consider district and state requirements, what areas of the curriculum can be taught through a TI, and how to plan, manage, implement, and evaluate a TI. Chapter 4 is devoted to demonstrating and developing research skills such as raising questions, note taking, and interviewing. Chapter 5 presents many multimedia suggestions from ancient arts to modern technology for demonstrating and sharing knowledge. A list of over a hundred ways students can express their knowledge through writing is also included. Chapter 7 details two theme immersions—environment in a fourth-grade class and oceanography in an eighth-grade classroom. Interviews with theme-immersion teachers follow in the next chapter. The final chapter consists totally of TI photographs. The book ends with an extensive listing of resources to support the TI process, including annotations of recommended professional texts and journal articles, titles and authors of literature for selected theme immersions, and names and addresses of magazines and selected organizations for student research and information. What I especially appreciated and admired about this 206-page resource is its emphasis on meaningful principles, guidelines, and strategies. The authors continually demonstrate how we can effectively apply the theme-immersion, inquiry process to our own classrooms. A first-rate resource!

• Marzano, Robert J. 1992. *A Different Kind of Classroom: Teaching with Dimensions of Learning.* Alexandria, VA: Association for Supervision and Curriculum Development.

This is a captivating, enlightening book for expanding your thinking and your current instructional paradigm about how children learn. "Dimensions of Learning" is Marzano's highly respected, research-based, K–12 model of classroom instruction. "The Dimensions framework is structured on the premise that the process of learning involves the interaction of five types, or dimensions, of thinking: (1) positive attitudes and perceptions about learning, (2) thinking involved in acquiring and integrating knowledge, (3) thinking involved in extending and refining knowledge, (4) thinking involved in using knowledge meaningfully, and (5) productive habits of mind" (vii). Marzano defines and discusses each of these dimensions and makes them come to life through classroom stories that explore teachers' and students' thinking and decision making. The final chapter, "Putting It All Together," presents specific, helpful guidelines to help teachers use the "Dimensions" to organize instruction. An excellent resource for curriculum development in all areas and for learning-centered schooling.

McClure, Amy A., with Peggy Harrison and Sheryl Reed. 1990. *Sunrises and Songs*. Portsmouth, NH: Heinemann.

The reader is taken through a school year in a fifth- and sixth-grade whole language classroom where students are immersed in poetry daily. The teachers, avid readers and writers of poetry, inspire their students to read and respond to poetry; to write, critique, revise, and publish poetry; and to write daily in their poetry journals. For teachers ready to connect poetry meaningfully to children's lives, this text is a valuable resource.

Meek, Margaret. 1992. *On Being Literate*. Portsmouth, NH: Heinemann.

This book is a companion book to Learning to Read (1982) and is designed to help parents understand reading and writing and their importance in today's society. It is also valuable for teachers of any grade level to read. Traditional views of literacy are being challenged by universal schooling, the advent of television, and computer technology. Meek helps the reader to understand that literacy has never been static, and that the definition changes as society makes new demands to meet current conditions. It is up to us to help children deal with these new challenges. (V.M.)

• Mills, Heidi, and Jean Anne Clyde (eds.). 1990. *Portraits of Whole Language Classrooms: Learning for All Ages*. Portsmouth, NH: Heinemann.

Whole language teachers in varied settings—home day care, preschool, elementary, middle school, high school, university education lab—describe their experiences with students in their classrooms. The book assumes the reader already has a good understanding of whole language theory and classroom management. The final chapter, by John McInerney and Jerome Harste, nicely clarifies some beliefs about whole language. For description of chapters dealing with holistic teaching in remedial settings, see "Resources" at the end of chapter 14.

• Ministry of Education (Wellington, NZ). 1993. *Dancing with the Pen: The Learner as a Writer*. Katonah, NY: Richard C. Owen.

This is a handbook designed to help teachers understand how children learn to write as well as provide ways to help them facilitate the learning process. Many samples of children's writing illustrate the various stages of development. The ways that children write—from personal experiences to poetry—are considered in one chapter. Classroom environments, scheduling tips, and resources are suggested, as well as ways to monitor individual writing development. The format of this book will be familiar to readers of the outstanding book on reading published by the Ministry, Reading in Junior Classes. All in all, this is a very complete guide that would be very useful to a beginning elementary teacher. (V.M.)

Mooney, Margaret E. 1990. *Reading to, with, and by Children*. Katonah, NY: Richard C. Owen.

Teachers, especially K–2, who want a full description and understanding of approaches to reading (reading aloud, shared reading, language experience, guided reading, and independent reading) and how these approaches can be used in the classroom will treasure this guide (92 pp.). Sample lessons for emergent, early, and fluent readers model strategies and questions teachers can use to get children to enjoy literature as well as predicting, sampling, confirming, and self-correcting on text.

Morrow, Lesley Mandel. 1993. *Literacy Development in the Early Years*. 2nd ed. Boston: Allyn and Bacon.

For educators interested in current research and theory in early literacy development and how to apply that knowledge to the preschool through grade 1 classroom, this academic text (411 pp.) discusses the development of early literacy in depth and includes strategies for promoting oral language development and reading and writing development. Chapter 5, "Developing Positive Attitudes Toward Reading Through the Use of Children's Literature," deals with promoting voluntary reading and organizing well-planned library corners/literacy centers. Also, particularly useful to classroom teachers are chapter 7, "Developing Reading Through Learning About Print," and chapter 9, "Organizing and Managing the Learning Environment for Literacy Development at School." Pages 183–188 are very specific for how to guide a child's story retelling.

Murray, Donald M. 1989. *Expecting the Unexpected: Teaching Myself—and Others—to Read and Write*. Portsmouth, NH: Boynton/Cook.

This is a diverse collection of twenty-four pieces full of introspection and sharing. Divided into four sections—Listening to the Page, Learning by Sharing, Exploring Form, Sitting to Write—it reveals Murray's thinking about his own process of writing and teaching writing to others. Along with essays and speeches, he even includes handouts used with his students— one of which was a piece written to describe revision by revealing it, "Revision as Visible Craft." He shares how he wrote and later revised a very personal piece, which he submitted to the Boston Globe for his "Over Sixty" column. In another piece, he answers questions from high school students. In paging through the book, I'm sure that you will feel the joy of learning through the writing of this distinguished teacher/writer. (V.M.)

• Murray, Donald M. 1990. *Shoptalk: Learning to Write with Writers*. Portsmouth, NH: Boynton/Cook.

As a teenager, Murray was fascinated by writers talking about their writing, and he began a collection of quotations that eventually filled twenty-four thick notebooks. This book is a selection of his favorites organized into sixteen categories, such as "Why Write," "The Beginning Line," "Waiting for Writing," and "The Writing Habit." However, it is not just a book of quotations, for each section begins with a personal essay on Murray's own experiences with the topic. Both we and our students can join the company of writers as we browse through this book. Murray described it well: "I am comforted by what they say to me as we leave the writing desk together. My collection of quotes allows me to learn from fellow writers, to laugh and mourn with them, to know that others have experienced what I have often thought was eccentric or inappropriate." I'm glad that he took the time to share his quotes and insights with us! (V.M.)

• Nagy, William E. 1988. *Teaching Vocabulary to Improve Reading Comprehension*. Urbana, IL: National Council of Teachers of English and Newark, DE: International Reading Association.

This concise book (42 pp.) is the best I have read for combining research and practice in the teaching of vocabulary on a conceptual level. While the author states that "the single most important thing a teacher can do to promote vocabulary growth is to increase students' volume of reading" (p. 38), he also makes it clear that there is an important place for intensive instruction. Three necessary properties of vocabulary instruction are defined: integration ("tying in new words with familiar concepts and experiences"), repetition (having many encounters with a word), and meaningful use. Many useful activities for classroom application are included.

Neuman, Susan B., and Kathleen A. Roskos. 1993. *Language and Literacy Learning in the Early Years: An Integrated Approach*. Fort Worth, TX: Harcourt Brace.

Neuman and Roskos examine oral and written language processes in young chil-

dren's development and suggest appropriate practices for creating effective learning environments. This text takes a balanced approach in its comprehensive analysis of how children acquire language and literacy. Topics addressed include setting up the physical environment for learning, child-centered activity planning, integrated learning activities, and assessment, to name a few. Packed with usable information and activities for pre-K and K educators, parents, and childcare providers.

• Newkirk, Thomas. 1989. *More Than Stories: The Range of Children's Writing.* Portsmouth, NH: Heinemann.

Every once in a while I find a book that makes me think, "Ah, that says what I am thinking, but I haven't been able to put it into words yet." This book is one of that kind for me. Newkirk clearly explains the semiotic position on language development in the opening section, and then he carefully describes the diversity of writing done by young children as they develop the ability to write expository prose. An especially meaningful chapter is an interview of Kathy Matthews, a second-grade teacher, who focuses on the many uses for writing found in her classroom. The book blends theory and practice in a way that stretched me as a teacher and gave me a lot to think about. (V.M.)

Newkirk, Thomas (ed.). 1992–1994. *Workshop 4, 5 by and for Teachers.* Portsmouth, NH: Heinemann. (*See Atwell, Nancie for* Workshop 1, 2, 3 *and Barbieri, Maureen, for* Workshop 6.)

4, The Teacher as Researcher
5, The Writing Process Revisited
The need for and purpose of teacher research in the language arts is explored in the fourth volume. It challenges teachers to consider what they should include and omit in their writings, and encourages teachers to reflect on what they do. The teacher interview is with Regie Routman, and this issue's author interviews are Jean Craighead George and Barbara Cooney. Cross-age tutoring, writing across the curriculum, and assessment are just a few of the topics addressed by the teacher-

researchers. As with the other workshop volumes, teacher writers are encouraged to submit their professional writing for publication. In the fifth volume, Donald Graves is interviewed, as well as two African-American educators, Dawn Harris-Martine and Isoke Nia. Portfolios, fiction writing, integration of writing and the arts, and the importance of storytelling are considered in light of the writing process movement. (V.M.)

• Newkirk, Thomas, with Patricia McLure. 1992. *Listening In: Children Talk About Books (and Other Things).* Portsmouth, NH: Heinemann.

In this little book, Newkirk visits McLure's first/second-grade classroom where he focuses on her 9:30 A.M. book discussions of thirty to forty-five minutes each. In these daily sessions, the children's understandings of their reading developed as they connected literature with their own everyday lives. The rich "talk" of this classroom challenges the teacher-dominated comprehension questioning with one right answer that occurs in many classrooms. You have to read this book, and its fascinating transcripts, to begin to realize the depth of understanding that these children reach. (V.M.)

• Newman, Judith. 1991. *Interwoven Conversations: Learning and Teaching Through Critical Reflection.* Portsmouth, NH: Heinemann.

This is a remarkable text for rethinking how we teach reading and writing in our classrooms! Judith Newman takes us inside her university classroom during a two-week institute and shows us her thinking, process, and practice in teaching and setting up conditions for learning. The reader becomes an "insider" in seeing how Newman helps establish a community of learners, how she organizes and manages her classroom, how she responds to teachers by conferencing with them about their own writing as well as how she handles revising and editing, literature discussions, reading/writing relationships, and evaluation. We not only hear the honesty of Newman's voice; we also hear the voices of the K–12 teachers as they interact and reflect with Newman, each other, and themselves through conversations and written reflections. More than any other book I have read recently, this book caused me to reflect on my practice and read and think "with pencil in hand." (I wrote all over the margins.) This is a provocative text for extending your thinking and learning about whole language and language processes and for becoming aware of your own questions and contradictions in your teaching.

- Norton, Donna E. 1991. *Through the Eyes of a Child: An Introduction to Children's Literature.* 3rd ed. New York: Macmillan. (hardbound)

    This comprehensive text (779 pages) about all aspects of children's literature is a first-rate resource that you will want to have access to. The organization of the book is unique. The content includes such topics as history of children's literature; selecting and evaluating children's literature; artists and their illustrations; picture books; traditional literature including folktales, fables, myths, and legends; modern fantasy, poetry, contemporary realistic fiction; historical fiction; multicultural literature; and nonfiction biographies and informational books. Following each chapter on the characteristics, history, and discussion of books for each genre is a chapter on involving children in that genre. These chapters present many activities and strategies for webbing, extending, and appreciating the literature and give teachers lots of terrific, practical ideas for use in the classroom.

    *Also unique to this text are the controversial issues raised in each chapter, the personal portraits and statements by well-known authors and illustrators about themselves and their books, and the illustrated flashbacks that highlight significant people, books, and events in the history of children's literature. Each chapter also ends with a summary, suggested activities, references, and an annotated bibliography of children's literature with approximate reading level by grade and interest level by age. Useful appendices to the text in-*clude book-selection aids, publishers and their addresses, and a bibliography of book awards.

Ohanian, Susan. 1994. *Who's in Charge? A Teacher Speaks Her Mind.* Portsmouth, NH: Boynton/Cook.

In this book is an inspiring collection of materials written by a practicing teacher that include letters written to editors, articles published in magazines, and poetry. You may not always agree with Ohanian, but her concerns for children and the profession are very real and her voice shatters a mood of complacency. In past years, I have read some of the articles, and spoken with the author, and I have come to see her as a "conscience" for teachers. It is quite an experience to see her work brought together, and to look at what she has written over the last twenty years. As she has touched the lives of her students, she has touched mine as she writes about topics as diverse as Japanese educational methodology, bringing real reading into the reading program, the basalization of literature, problems with a literary canon, and much more. This is a book for educators of all kinds who want to improve schools and our profession. It will validate concerns you have, stretch your thinking, and cause both some laughter and some tears.

Pappas, Christine C., Barbara Z. Kiefer, and Linda S. Levstik. 1990. *An Integrated Language Perspective in the Elementary School: Theory into Action.* White Plains, NY: Longman.

Educators wanting to plan and implement thematic units will find much support in this scholarly, comprehensive text (384 pp.). The authors present the theoretical and practical aspects of an integrated language perspective that includes integration of the language arts as well as integration across the curriculum. Marginal notations throughout the text cite references, note useful resources, and highlight and explain concepts. Chapter 4, "Prototypes for Integrated Language Classrooms," includes eight prototypes (thematic units). Each prototype includes a WEB, a weekly schedule, a typical day in an actual classroom, a summary, and a bibliography of children's literature and resources. The one thing I found missing in the prototypes were the major concepts and understandings. Teachers will find the thematic units excellent models but will need to be sure to put the "big understandings" into their own integrated language units. I found the chapters "More Ideas to Integrate Curricular Areas," "More on How-to: Ideas for Implementation in Integrated Language Classrooms," and "An Integrated Language Perspective Effecting Change" to be particularly useful for the classroom teacher.

Patterson, Leslie, Carol Minnick Santa, Kathy G. Short, and Karen Smith (eds.). 1993. *Teachers Are Researchers: Reflection and Action.* Newark, DE: International Reading Association.

If you believe that "teachers are professionals who should take an active role in educational change" (p. 173), this supportive text for elementary through college teachers makes teacher inquiry possible in the realm of day-to-day teaching. Teachers describe their inquiry processes, beginning with finding and framing their questions and continuing with their various methods of observation and data collection to their reflections and changes in practice as a result of their teacher research.

Peregoy, Suzanne F., and Owen F. Boyle. 1993. *Reading, Writing, & Learning in ESL: A Resource Book for K–8 Teachers.* White Plains, NY: Longman.

In this concise text, you will find a practical resource to help teachers provide literacy instruction for second-language learners. Several chapters are devoted to background information on how second-language acquisition occurs. Process writing, literature-based reading instruction, and reading across the curriculum are discussed with an emphasis on adapting instruction to the child with limited English. In so doing, the classroom environment can be a richer place for all students. (V.M.)

Perrone, Vito. 1991. *A Letter to Teachers: Reflections on Schooling and the Art of Teaching.* San Francisco: Jossey-Bass Publishers.

Perrone, director of programs in teacher education at the Harvard Graduate School of Education, eloquently urges us to carefully reflect on our teaching and to construct for ourselves "a more powerful voice." He challenges us to discuss and rethink such critical issues as deciding what to teach, engaging students, valuing differences, making school more accessible to parents, evaluating and grading, and empowering teachers. The chapter "Refining the Craft of Teaching" offers specific questions and helpful suggestions to us for continuing our own professional growth. "Only when teachers themselves assume the dominant position in regard to issues of teaching and learning in their classrooms, and begin to speak more broadly and authoritatively on matters of education, will we see significant improvement" (xiii). Each time I reread parts of this inspiring book (160 pp.), I rethink some of my assumptions about teaching and learning.

Peterson, Ralph. 1992. *Life in a Crowded Place: Making a Learning Community.* Portsmouth, NH: Heinemann.

Peterson quickly makes the point that "life in classrooms is an intense social experience." Many teachers cope by restricting everything they can think of, yet he notes there are some teachers who trust students, expect them to take the initiative, and value what they think. These teachers' expectations are nurtured and used to support learning in the best way possible. In this book, the author identifies ways that teachers can work with students to make a learning community that supports language acquisition. Vignettes of teachers and students working together are used throughout the book to illustrate the various points. I especially enjoyed the chapter on "Authority: Empowering Students." If students are to become lifelong learners, they must assume the authority to think for themselves, and to be responsible for their actions. (V.M.)

- Peterson, Ralph, and Maryann Eeds. 1990. *Grand Conversations: Literature Groups in Action.* Richmond Hill, Ontario: Scholastic-TAB.

For teachers who are already comfortable with a literature approach to reading, this eighty-page text dealing with literature study of "books that have layers of story action and meaning" (p. 26) gives inspiration, organization, specific techniques, and lots of examples for constructing meaning through dialogue and interpretation. Developing children's awareness of, and response to, literary elements—story structure, plot, characters, place, tensions, point of view, mood, time, symbols and metaphors, theme—is fully discussed and demonstrated with examples from excellent literature. Examples of teacher-developed forms for organization and evaluation are also cited. A terrific, high-level resource.

Pierce, Kathryn Mitchell, and Carol J. Gilles (eds.). 1993. *Cycles of Meaning: Exploring the Potential of Talk in Learning Communities.* Portsmouth, NH: Heinemann.

Twenty teachers and teacher educators share their perspectives on "talk" in the classroom setting. This is a thoughtful text considering various aspects of talk in the learning community, talk as a strategy to explore writing or content-area reading, the role of the teacher in literature discussion groups, and evaluation of talk in the literature discussion group. Lots of classroom examples are found in the individual essays, making this a very helpful book for teachers who have established collaborative literature studies in their classrooms. (V.M.)

• Probst, Robert. 1988. *Response and Analysis: Teaching Literature in Junior and Senior High School.* Portsmouth, NH: Boynton/Cook.

This book brings literature into students' lives. Probst believes literature should be a vital, personal experience and not presented as the object of tests and exercises. Drawing heavily on Louise Rosenblatt's work of almost fifty years ago, this text tries to show that literature should be personally significant, that readers be respected as they respond in different ways, and that readers acknowledge the role of literature in their world. The book is or-

ganized into three parts: a rationale of response-based teaching, literature choices, and the overall program. Many suggestions for the classroom are given, and there is an excellent listing of literary works that will stimulate students to think. Two sensitive themes, sexuality and violence, are discussed in detail, while representative books are listed under various themes. Other useful chapters include suggestions for response-based evaluation, as well as one in which film and television are considered as visual literature. Lots of practical and theoretical information for a teacher wanting a response-based literature program. (V.M.)

Raines, Shirley C., and Robert J. Canady. 1990. *The Whole Language Kindergarten.* New York: Teachers College Press.

Early childhood teachers will appreciate this handbook for creating a learning environment to support literacy development. Play, group time, library corners, thematic teaching, science areas, and art guidelines are just some of the many topics considered in a whole language framework. Many anecdotes of actual happenings from various kindergartens support the suggestions and strategies suggested by the authors. (V.M.)

Rathbone, Charles, Anne Bingham, Peggy Dorta, Molly McClaskey, and Justine O'Keefe. 1993. *Multiage Portraits: Teaching and Learning in Mixed-Age Classrooms.* Peterborough, NH: Crystal Springs Books.

The opening section of this book contains University of Vermont researcher Charles Rathbone's observations in Anne Bingham's multiage classroom. In the second part of the book, the four coauthors' voices are heard as they each write a chapter about their multiage classrooms. The last portion of the book contains Rathbone's reflections and questions about multiage classrooms. The book will be useful to teachers who are considering this type of organization, as well as teachers who are looking for support for what they do. The book will stretch and inspire you. (V.M.)

Rhodes, Lynn K., and Curt Dudley-Marling. 1988. *Readers and Writers with a Differ-*

ence: A Holistic Approach to Teaching Learning Disabled and Remedial Students. Portsmouth, NH: Heinemann.

For the teacher ready to look at teaching learning disabled and remedial students holistically, this well-documented, comprehensive text (329 pp.) provides a wealth of information on all aspects of language learning. The authors discuss many instructional approaches for assessing, teaching, and extending meaningful reading and writing. The chapter "Developing Fluency in Reading and Writing" provides specific, detailed instructional strategies such as assisted reading, repeated reading, Readers Theatre, choral reading, sustained silent reading, freewriting, journal writing, and written conversation. Most of the strategies and activities recommended are appropriate for all learners. An extensive list of predictable trade books for young children is included.

* Rief, Linda. 1992. *Seeking Diversity: Language Arts with Adolescents.* Portsmouth, NH: Heinemann.

This highly respected, acclaimed text by an exemplary, eighth-grade language arts teacher has already influenced many teachers' practices across the grades. With a passionate, caring voice, Linda Rief takes us into her classroom and the literate lives of the adolescents she teaches to share how she organizes the literacy environment, immerses her students in reading and writing in all genres, encourages students to express themselves through writing and the visual arts, and gets students to take responsibility for their learning. A few of the many areas she gives teaching strategies for are conducting an interview, getting to know your students better, having students take more responsibility for reading, and reading and writing about grandparents and the elderly. The sections on evaluation, which include grading, portfolios, and "close-up snapshots" from student portfolios (in Appendix A), are outstanding and provide a wealth of information for getting students to be the primary evaluators of their writing. References at the end of each chapter, and extensive appendices at the end of the text, include all

kinds of useful information and practical support for literature, reading, writing, book-making, communicating with parents, and evaluation. Wonderful student writing samples abound throughout the text.

Everything Rief does connects to a well-grounded theory of language learning, reading and writing as reciprocal processes, wonderful literature, and the real lives of her students. By sharing what she has learned from other experts and from her students, what strategies and activities she uses, and what is working and not working in her classroom, she invites us to look at our own classrooms and build rich learning environments. Rief writes, "At the end of every year I ask students, 'If you had to pick the one thing I did that helped you the most as learners, what would it be?' They inevitably say, 'You write with us, and you read with us'" (p. 10). Rief helps us and challenges us to do better with our own students. Don't miss reading this powerful book!

Robb, Laura. 1994. *Whole Language, Whole Learners: Creating a Literature-Centered Classroom.* New York: William Morrow. (hardbound)

Based on thirty years of classroom teaching, this book is a treasure trove of practical ideas for bringing literature into the classroom. Some of the topics considered are getting support, getting started, reading and writing experiences, inquiry and content-area journaling, authentic assessment, and planning theme cycles. A unique feature of this book is the fifteen essays by children's authors and illustrators—Steven Kellogg, Jerry Pinkney, Lois Lowry, Karla Kuskin, and others—that are placed throughout the book. The appendix contains a series of forms to stimulate the development of your own parent letters, newspapers, and evaluation forms. (V.M.)

* Romano, Tom. 1987. *Clearing the Way: Working with Teenage Writers.* Portsmouth, NH: Heinemann.

"Our responsibility as writing teachers is to help students learn personal processes for creating writing that enable them to create their best writing" (p. 52). Draw-ing on his own experiences as a high school English teacher, Tom Romano eloquently describes how in a safe writing workshop, he enables students to use language to dis-cover thought and to find their individual voices and styles. Romano demonstrates his craft with samples of his own and stu-dents' writing—drafts, revisions, and finished pieces in which meaning comes before correctness and form—examples of purposeful writing prompts, and mean-ingful ways of evaluating and grading with the goal that "above anything else, we want them to write again" (p. 128).

I began this book because I had been invited to speak with interested secondary teachers in our district. I had intended to skim the book, to get a feel for it. The power of Romano's voice grabbed me and never let up until I had ingested every word. I was surprised to find many refer-ences to Don Graves and Lucy Calkins and to see high school practice in an effec-tive writing workshop very similar to what we are striving for at the elementary level. I savored fresh insights, new visions, clear writing by a teacher-learner, and validation that the writing process is in-herently the same from kindergarten through grade twelve. This is a remark-able book that should be read by every serious teacher of writing.

Routman, Regie. 1988. *Transitions: From Lit-erature to Literacy*. Portsmouth, NH: Hei-nemann.

A personal, honest account of a public school teacher's transition from basal texts and worksheets toward a literature pro-gram in reading and a process approach in writing. Some of the topics that are fully discussed include the use of predictable books, how to teach reading and writing with children's books, the place of phonics in the reading-writing program, journal writing, parental involvement, and evalu-ation. While the book's emphasis is on the primary grades, the theory, ideas, and ex-tensive annotated resources are applicable across the grades. Educators beginning to move toward whole language have found this book both practical and inspiring.

Rudman, Masha Kabakow (ed.). 1993. *Children's Literature: Resource for the Classroom*. 2nd ed. Norwood, MA: Christopher-Gordon.

This book is an updated paperback ver-sion of the first edition. Many of the origi-nal chapters have been reprinted in this edition along with three new ones. Experts in the field share their insights about cen-sorship, multicultural literature, technol-ogy, poetry in the classroom, and global education. Two chapters feature interviews with noted children's authors Virginia Hamilton, Eve Bunting, Ashley Bryan, and others. This is a reference book that should be in every library. It is helpful for teachers to consider current issues in the field, as well as for sharing information with your students. (V.M.)

- Semler, Ricardo. 1993. *Maverick: The Suc-cess Story Behind the World's Most Un-usual Workplace*. New York: Warner Books.

Although this is not a book about edu-cation, I found it such fascinating, stimu-lating reading, with so much that could apply to teaching, that I have included it. The author is the head of Semco, one of the most successful companies in Brazil, a company that manufactures and distrib-utes industrial parts for heavy machinery. In fact, the company is so successful and well thought of that one-quarter of all graduating college students in Brazil ap-ply to work there. Semler describes his unorthodox, common-sense philosophy and methods for running a company where employees set their own hours and sala-ries, design their own working environ-ments, examine all financial statements, and decide with their coworkers how to run their particular section of the com-pany. In Semco, the power does not reside at the top; decisions are made by consen-sus, and flexibility, respect, and freedom are part of the fabric of the company. Some basic premises of the company that schools would do well to think about and adopt are the following: change is normal and necessary; the need for many rules and the need for innovation are incompat-ible; all memos are restricted to a single page with the most important information at the top; put quality of life first, and

*quality of product and productivity of work-
ers follow. The book includes the company's evaluation questionnaire, given to
employees twice each year to evaluate their
supervisors. I recommend all supervisors
in education give this excellent questionnaire to teachers and use the responses as
a self-evaluation tool.*

A few quotes to think about:

*"We simply do not believe our employ-
ees have an interest in coming in late,
leaving early, and doing as little as possible for as much money as their union can
wheedle out of us. After all, these same
people raise children, join the PTA, elect
mayors, governors, senators, and presidents. They are adults. . . . We treat them
like adults. We trust them. . . . We get out
of their way and let them do their jobs"*
(p. 59).

*"Democracy has yet to penetrate the
workplace" (p. 170).*

*"Most businesses today are still organ-
ized much the same way they were in
1633, with stultifying top-down management, close and dutiful supervision, and
little room for creativity. . . . Technology
is transformed overnight; mentality takes
generations to alter" (pp. 283–284).*

Shannon, Patrick. 1989. *Broken Promises:
Reading Instruction in Twentieth-Cen-
tury America.* Granby, MA: Bergin &
Garvey.

*A must for every classroom teacher and
administrator to read! The message is that
commercially packaged basal reading materials control reading instruction and are
doing a "good job of teaching students to
decode words and to reproduce the meaning of texts." However, this goal is prevent-
ing children from becoming fully literate—"able to understand the connections
among their lives and those of others, and
to act on their new knowledge to construct
a better, a more just, world" (viii). Shannon describes the technologizing and marketing of reading in a detailed history of
the basal reader and shows how these systems have actually de-skilled teachers by
their detailed instructions on how to manage the worksheets, reading selections,
and students. He cites research, some of it*

*his own, as to why so many teachers rely
on basal materials and follow their directions, yet want to be professionals able to
make critical judgments to meet student
needs. Finally, he devotes the last chapter
of the book to the "possibilities of constructive change," such as collective seminars in which teachers analyze their de-
pendence on basals or conduct research in
their own classrooms. Although he believes
that it will not be easy, Shannon thinks
that it is possible for teachers and students
to resist the management of their literacy
and lives and to "gain their rightful place
in reading programs." (V.M.)*

• Shannon, Patrick. 1990. *The Struggle to Continue: Progressive Reading Instruction in
the United States.* Portsmouth, NH: Heinemann.

*This book was written to describe the
underlying practices and promises of the
child-centered and critical literacy programs—mentioned as positive alternatives to the controlling technological management of literacy decried in* Broken
Promises. *Shannon also gives a historical
perspective to the whole language movement by noting it as a recent development
of a hundred-year-old movement to provide literacy programs based on the child
within a social context. This is a challenging book but worthwhile reading for any
teacher who has lived with the domination
of reading instruction by the basal reader
industry and is attempting to struggle
with alternatives. As he helps teachers
make connections with the rich progressive past, Shannon encourages teachers to
continue to work for better and more com-
passionate literacy programs for their students and future generations. (V.M.)*

• Shannon, Patrick, and Kenneth Goodman
(eds.). 1994. *Basal Readers: A Second Look.*
Katonah, NY: Richard C. Owen.

*This book is a follow-up to the ground-
breaking* Report Card on Basal Readers
*(1988). After its publication, basal reader
companies attempted to change their materials, often claiming that they had met
the recommendations at the end of the
Report Card. However, when a group of*

educators was assembled to analyze the latest basal editions, various problems still were inherent in the materials. Each author examines one aspect of basal reader production, such as workbook exercises, multiculturalism, poetry inclusion, and others. Four classroom teachers also respond with their concerns. A particularly provocative chapter is written by Mem Fox in which she pleads for the use of real writing, real books, and real relationships in our classrooms. This book should be read by anyone involved in determining what books children will be given in the classroom. (V.M.)

• Short, Kathy Gnagey, and Kathryn Mitchell Pierce (eds.). 1990. *Talking About Books: Creating Literate Communities*. Portsmouth, NH: Heinemann.

Fourteen teachers and teacher educators share their experiences with literature study. This is a very thoughtful text for the teacher who already has a collaborative atmosphere in a whole language classroom. Literature circles, which include small-group discussions in which students read and react to the same book or small-group discussions on text sets in which students read different but thematically related texts, are discussed fully. Lots of specific examples are given, not only for individual books but also for integrated literature study across the curriculum. The introductory chapter by Charlotte Huck sets the tone for the power of literature.

Sloan, Glenna Davis. 1991. *The Child as Critic: Teaching Literature in Elementary and Middle Schools*. 3rd ed. New York: Teachers College Press.

This book supports the belief that the use of literature is the best way to support genuine literacy development. It combines theory and practice to show how to implement reading/writing programs that support the study of literary works or literary criticism. The first section of the book argues that literature must be central in the reading program. Research evidence for the positive effects of literature programs in reading is clearly presented in chapter 2. The next portion gives teachers a theo-

retical framework on which to base the teaching of literature. It examines the work of Northrop Frye to show that even young children can understand the universal patterns present in literature. The final part gives specific examples of techniques and strategies that may be appropriately undertaken in elementary and middle schools. An excellent bibliography will help teachers locate appropriate books for their classroom. (V.M.)

• Smith, Frank. 1990. *To Think*. New York: Teachers College Press.

The process of thinking is examined from all angles in this comprehensive book. As with his previous books, Smith celebrates the power of humans to learn! He expresses concern about complaints that students are unable to think, and, therefore, must be carefully taught, and believes that attempts to teach "thinking skills" can actually hamper the development of thinking. Two especially interesting chapters, "Thinking Creatively" and "Thinking Critically," demystify these aspects of thinking and show how they are not so difficult and distinctive after all. Finally, he looks at educational implications for both teachers and students. He suggests, "Students—and teachers—must learn to doubt. . . . Certainty stunts thought, in ourselves and others. . . . Thought flourishes as questions are asked, not as answers are found" (p. 129). Smith also stresses the importance of functional, relevant reading and writing when he states, "Reading and writing are two activities that promote thought provided that what is read is worth thinking about and that writing is used for extending the imagination of the writer" (p. 128). Last, he warns that "thinking cannot be broken down into parts, specified in objectives, and taught in isolated exercises and drills. All of this interferes with thought" (p. 128). This is a relevant, challenging book with implications affecting the entire school curriculum. (V.M.)

Smith, Frank. 1994. *Understanding Reading: A Psycholinguistic Analysis of Reading and Learning to Read*. 5th ed. Hillsdale,

NJ: Lawrence Erlbaum Associates, Publishers.

In this new edition of his classic text on how reading is learned (not how it is taught), Smith provides a theoretical analysis of all aspects of reading—linguistic, psychological, social, and physiological—based on current research and Smith's own brand of brilliant thinking. "Reading is seen as a creative and constructive activity having four distinctive and fundamental characteristics—it is purposeful, selective, anticipatory, and based on comprehension, all matters where the reader must clearly exercise control" (p. 3). Smith also deals with recent developments, issues, and alternative points of view in reading—especially the ideological clash between whole language and direct instruction. As well, he gives ways to support learners' reading until they are able to take over the process. Noting that reading defies "simplistic analysis," he believes it is up to sensitive teachers, who he views as "the essential element in literacy instruction," to have a solid understanding of learning to read and an understanding of their students. Then teachers can make the necessary decisions about reading in the classroom.

Spear, Karen, and others. 1994. *Peer Response Groups in Action: Writing Together in Secondary Schools.* Portsmouth, NH: Boynton/Cook.

English teachers describe their struggles, efforts, and strategies to establish successful peer-response groups in the writing process classroom. The power of collaboration, the constraints of time and scheduling, the need for modeling, the ways to teach students how to communicate in writing-response groups, and the benefits of peer review are just some of the issues they tackle. The first-person accounts from mostly middle and secondary school teachers provide engaging reading and workable ideas for the writing-response process. Applicable for the intermediate grades through postsecondary.

Stires, Susan (ed.). 1991. *With Promise: Redefining Reading and Writing Needs for Special Students.* Portsmouth, NH: Heinemann.

This is a book about teaching reading and writing to any elementary students considered to be "at risk" of failure. All of us have encountered children who learn in unique ways, and how to help them to learn in the best possible way is always a major question. This book asks those hard questions, and it shares the insights of educators who are attempting to meet the needs of these children. Issues of testing, labeling, effective environments, and programs are considered. In an especially moving piece, Donald Graves pleads that children with learning problems not be disenfranchised from literacy, that they can and should be encouraged to write. (V.M.)

• Strickland, Dorothy S., and Lesley Mandel Morrow (eds.). 1989. *Emerging Literacy: Young Children Learn to Read and Write.* Newark, DE: International Reading Association.

This book is highly recommended for preschool–grade 2 teachers for developing a meaningful literacy program. Kindergarten teachers, especially, will find this book particularly helpful for tying theory and practice together and for incorporating appropriate classroom practices. In addition to gaining a current and broad understanding of issues and principles of early literacy, teachers are presented with a wealth of practical ideas and activities. The importance and application of oral-language experiences, story book reading, and all kinds of writing for promoting children's language and literacy growth are clearly delineated.

Strickland, Kathleen, and James Strickland. 1993. *Uncovering the Curriculum: Whole Language in Secondary and Postsecondary Classrooms.* Portsmouth, NH: Heinemann.

For high school and college teachers who want to understand and implement whole language principles and practice to make their teaching more relevant to students' lives, this is a fine text. Practicing secondary and postsecondary teachers share stories and strategies that lend support and specifics to the reading/writing workshop, application of reader-response theory, classroom management, questioning in literature discussion, conferencing in writing, writing to learn, grading, and evaluation. The final chapter, "Whole Language—A Political Issue" is important reading for dealing with resistance to whole language and the change process. Also applicable to the elementary and middle grades.

Sumner, Deborah (ed.). 1993. *Multiage Classrooms: The Ungrading of America's Schools: The Multiage Resource Book.* Peterborough, NH: Society for Developmental Education.

> This resource book contains a collection of articles reprinted from educational journals and research reports on multiage grouping and supportive practices. An extensive bibliography and descriptions of multiage models provide a wealth of material for teachers or administrators wanting to explore this program for their school. Finally, an assortment of forms and charts currently in use by schools with multiage classrooms are reprinted for adaptation to your educational settings. This compilation provides a good starting point in organizing your own program. (V.M.)

• Taylor, Denny. 1993. *From the Child's Point of View.* Portsmouth, NH: Heinemann.

> In this provocative collection of her papers, Taylor uses rich ethnographic portraits of learners to show that simplistic testing methodology does not tap the complex ways that children become literate. All of the children with whom she has worked have thick special education folders focusing on the errors that these children have made—not on how they use language in nontesting situations. She shows how we must observe children and learn from their strengths—not from what is missing—before beginning to define practice and assessment of curriculum. The final section addresses an "Advocacy Model of Instructional Assessment," in which support teams focus on what students can

do, along with problem solving from the student's point of view. I found myself considering my students with new eyes after reading this book. I encourage you to make this book required reading. (V.M.)

Taylor, Denny. 1991. *Learning Denied.* Portsmouth, NH: Heinemann.

> This little book is the story of a family's bitter clash with the public school, and special education bureaucracy, that their son attended. It shows the wrongness of assessments that reduce learning to scores on tests administered and interpreted by "experts" who rarely work with the child and only focus on what the child is unable to do. As doubts about Patrick's abilities increased in the school setting, the testing became a self-fulfilling prophecy—he met the low expectations and stopped performing in school. Yet at home, and in sessions with Taylor, he read and wrote increasingly difficult material. He was finally abandoned to a home-schooling program, and the school district washed its hands of this child. Taylor questions whether the school district will ever acknowledge his literacy, and make room for him. This book raises more questions than it answers. I wonder how many other "Patricks" are in our schools. (V.M.)

• Taylor, Denny, and Catherine Dorsey-Gaines. 1988. *Growing Up Literate: Learning from Inner-City Families.* Portsmouth, NH: Heinemann.

> This poignant, moving ethnographic study of urban black families living well below the poverty line focuses on families who have first-grade children successfully learning to read and write. Through their carefully documented observations, the authors dispel the common myths and stereotypes of poor, black families. We see overwhelming confirmation that the families effectively use reading and writing daily for their survival, to communicate with others, to fulfill educational requirements, and for pleasure. The authors state, "it is evident that the families with whom we are working are more than the fillers in of forms—they are active members in a print community in which literacy is used for a

wide variety of social, technical, and aesthetic purposes, for a wide variety of audiences, and in a wide variety of situations" (p. 200). *Educators, researchers, and policymakers are urged to take a close look at these families—and other functioning families—to begin to close the wide gaps between home and school literacy.*

- Thomas, Joan Krater, Jane Zeni, and Nancy Devlin Cason. 1994. *Mirror Images: Action Research in Multicultural Writing Classrooms.* Portsmouth, NH: Heinemann.

"What can we as teachers do to improve the writing of African-American students in our classrooms?" This was the action research question that a group of white, female, middle school (grades 7–10) teachers working in integrated classrooms sought to answer. Looking closely at their own role in lower black achievement, this personal, inspiring account tells the story of how they question their assumptions, come to value and build on the strengths of black males, and transform their attitudes and daily classroom teaching so all students benefit. "We realized that if we were committed to teaching all students, we must change how we view our 'mirror reflections'—the kids who most differ from us in race, class, and gender." "Individualizing and personalizing" is what they call their approach of stressing relationships, valuing of culture, and developing self-awareness. It is affirming a child first for who he is, not what he does. And it is being willing to make adjustments for students' needs and interests in the reading/writing process classroom. This is a powerful book for taking a critical look at our own instructional contexts and for finding ways to maximize the potential of alienated, struggling students. This moving account is also testimony to the fact that major change is possible if we are willing to look critically at our own behaviors and get to know and value our students and their cultures. Lots of excellent teaching strategies and sample lessons are woven into this extensive text and the appendices. Don't miss reading this remarkable story of teacher/student change and

growth! Also encouraging for starting your own action research. Applicable and practical for all grades.

Tierney, Robert J., Mark A. Carter, and Laura E. Desai. 1991. *Portfolio Assessment in the Reading-Writing Classroom.* Norwood, MA: Christopher-Gordon.

Based on research and practice, K–12, of the use of reading and writing portfolios in several school districts, this scholarly and practical text provides teachers with a flexible framework for implementing and using portfolios in the classroom. The text fully discusses and gives specific examples for topics such as the following: getting started with portfolios, selecting pieces for the portfolio, involving parents in the portfolio assessment process, understanding the teacher's role in the portfolio process, fostering students' self-evaluation of selected items in the portfolio, sustaining portfolios over time, and using portfolios to evaluate students. Lots of specific examples and ideas.

- Tobin, Lad. 1993. *Writing Relationships: What REALLY Happens in the Composition Class.* Portsmouth, NH: Boynton/Cook.

"Why haven't we been more honest about how hard it is to teach writing?" (p. 144). I guess that's why I appreciated this book so much. In a first-person, confessional tone that is refreshing, engaging, and unconventional, Tobin takes us inside his process-oriented, college composition classes and private thoughts to share honestly the frustrating and rewarding daily interactions and decision-making processes with his students. In telling us "stories about actual situations from my classes that evoked powerful responses from me and my students" (p. 16), he invites us to identify our own unconscious behaviors, biases, problems, and successes. Tobin moves beyond the simplistic assumptions of process classrooms and examines provocative issues about grading, collaboration, competition, power, and peer review with new lenses, suggesting, for example, that "our grades reflect our own attitudes and tastes as much as they reflect something about

the essay in front of us" (p. 68) and that "competition and cooperation are not mutually exclusive or even necessarily conflictual" (p. 90).

Tobin's premise, that supportive interpersonal relationships in the classroom are necessary for improving student writing, is an important one for all classrooms: "writing students succeed when teachers establish productive relationships with—and between—their students" (p. 6). He challenges us as writing teachers to examine the central role we and other students play in students' composing processes when we give students guidelines, suggest changes, and read their essays. All of us who struggle with establishing and sustaining successful process writing classrooms will find much support and ideas for reading student essays, responding to student writing, leading a discussion of an essay, running a writing workshop, grading, setting up peer and coauthoring groups, conferencing, and publishing. Most importantly, though, by acknowledging and understanding what is really going on in our writing classrooms, we can take the first, necessary step to improve and change how we help students learn to write. Written for secondary and postsecondary teachers; also recommended for elementary and middle school.

Tompkins, Gail E. 1994. *Teaching Writing: Balancing Process and Product.* 2nd ed. New York: Macmillan.

Many practical strategies for teaching writing are found in this comprehensive text on the writing process. However, it is not just a recipe book! The author worked closely with classroom teachers and has included many vignettes to show how the ideas are implemented in classrooms. Many student samples are used to show possible outcomes of the various lessons and projects suggested in the book. (V.M.)

Vacca, Jo Anne L., Richard T. Vacca, and Mary K. Gove. 1991. *Reading and Learning to Read.* 2nd ed. New York: HarperCollins. (hardbound)

For educators who want to understand and implement a current view of reading, this scholarly and practical text connects beliefs with practice in an informative, readable fashion. The hallmarks of a literate environment for early readers are described along with workable recommendations for creating such an environment in the classroom. Approaches, guidelines, and strategies to teach and promote beginning reading, connect writing and reading, reading comprehension, vocabulary knowledge, oral and silent reading, literature use across the curriculum, and authentic assessment are described. Activities in Appendix A and B are very helpful for determining and assessing your own theoretical beliefs about reading and reading instruction. Vacca, Vacca, and Gove have taken the best of reading research and practice and organized it into a 616-page text with lots of useful strategies for guiding the reading process.

Vacca, Richard T., and Timothy V. Rasinski. 1992. *Case Studies in Whole Language.* Orlando, FL: Harcourt Brace.

The authors take us inside the classrooms of preschool through grade five teachers who are moving towards whole language and describe their beliefs and practices along with some principles underlying whole language. Each chapter focuses on one teacher and grade, including a multigrade primary classroom, and includes a typical day, organization and management, strategies, and teaching issues. For teachers in various stages of transition to whole language, this is an excellent book for understanding whole language and refining your own beliefs and practices.

Walmsley, Sean. 1994. *Children Exploring Their World: Theme Teaching in Elementary School.* Portsmouth, NH: Heinemann.

The author devotes the first third of this book to a consideration of the theory and practice of teaching through themes. Walmsley looks at different kinds of themes—content area, conceptual, calendar-based, form, and biographical—and then turns the book over to practicing classroom teachers of grades K–6. These teachers share their experiences of developing and teaching specific themes on topics including insects, the human body, a fish hatchery, historical architecture, and Egyptian mummies. Some of the individual stories show how involved children can get in a certain topic if they're given choices about the direction they want their project to take. This book offers professional resources as well as resources for each specific theme.

Watson, Dorothy, Carolyn Burke, and Jerome Harste. 1989. *Whole Language: Inquiring Voices.* Richmond Hill, Ontario: Scholastic-TAB.

This seventy-one-page volume, a companion book to Ken Goodman's What's Whole in Whole Language?, *sees teaching as inquiry as the necessary direction for whole language teachers. Teachers are guided to reflect on their own learning in order to foster a community of inquiring learners. Conditions of inquiry—vulnerability, community, generation of knowledge, democracy, and reflexivity—are discussed and demonstrated. This is a very readable and sophisticated book for the teacher who already has a whole language foundation.*

- Weaver, Constance. 1994. *Reading Process and Practice: From Socio-Psycholinguistics to Whole Language.* 2nd ed. Portsmouth, NH: Heinemann.

For all educators who want the latest tie-in between theory and practice on all aspects of language learning, this comprehensive (731 pp.) and readable text offers a wealth of information in an integrated, useful manner. In addition to detailed discussions of the reading process (including phonics, miscue analysis, research studies supporting whole language practices, Reading Recovery) and extensive, current resources and activities, this new edition also includes two informative chapters on whole language that address whole language principles, common misconceptions, and whole language teaching as a continuing process of development. The chapter "Reading, Literature, and the Dramatic Language Arts" by Ruth Beall Heinig is full of suggestions for combining the dramatic language arts with whole language.

"Whole Language Learning and Teaching for Second Language Learners" by Yvonne Freeman and David Freeman addresses approaches to teaching and supporting second-language students. An amazing resource!

Weaver, Constance. 1994. *Success at Last! Helping Students with Attention Deficit (Hyperactivity) Disorders Achieve Their Potential.* Portsmouth, NH: Heinemann.

Written to help students with Attention Deficit (Hyperactivity) Disorders, this timely book includes articles by and discussions among young adults with AD(H)D as well as articles by parents and teachers. Based on current research and her conversations with students with AD(H)D, Weaver recommends a "system-theory perspective combined with whole language, learning, and teaching." Always valuing and respecting the learner, she and other contributing authors offer many specific suggestions for ways that parents, teachers, and psychologists can work more effectively with AD(H)D students. Fascinating, informative reading that is applicable for all special-needs students.

Weaver, Constance. 1990. *Understanding Whole Language: From Principles to Practice.* Portsmouth, NH: Heinemann.

Weaver provides an extensive research and theoretical background to support a whole language approach to teaching and learning and discusses how whole language principles can be applied to the classroom. For educators who already have a rudimentary understanding of whole language, this thorough, scholarly text (336 pp.) provides as in-depth an understanding of whole language as can be found. Weaver devotes fifty-eight pages to phonics—comprising as complete an overview of the research as exists (including research from whole language classrooms), the implications of the research, and suggestions for teaching. An extensive section on assessment (79 pp.) includes current information regarding standardized testing, reading assessment, and a variety of meaningful assessment procedures.

Weaver, Constance, and Linda Henke. 1992. *Supporting Whole Language: Stories of Teachers and Institutional Change.* Portsmouth, NH: Heinemann.

This provocative text deals with success stories and struggles faced by whole language educators and schools. The first part of the book deals with teacher change, and the second part deals with institutional change. What I found especially worrisome were case studies of places where whole language had once thrived but had now disappeared. "The staff began thinking on the activity level. They continued to do message board, written conversation, book making, graphs, and so on, but the activities were ends in themselves rather than strategies for communication, reflection, and learning" (p. 180). The caution is there for us all. Change in practice without a change in beliefs brings no lasting change. Our practice must be theory-driven. For success, support, and suggestions in the change process, teachers and administrators will want to read and discuss this book.

• Wells, Gordon, and others. 1994. *Changing Schools from Within: Creating Communities of Inquiry.* Toronto: OISE Press and Portsmouth, NH: Heinemann.

For every teacher who seeks to be a teacher-researcher but feels uncomfortable with the title and the process, this book is for you. Wells and a group of teachers in Canada report on their own "action research" in their classrooms. Action research means being deliberately reflective about one's teaching and then using that new knowledge to take specific action to improve one's teaching "so that one's students, in turn, are enabled to become intentional learners" (pp. 30–31). Outstanding for teachers ready to question, observe, analyze, and change their practice and for school-based inquiry and discussion.

Wilde, Jack. 1993. *A Door Opens: Writing in Fifth Grade.* Portsmouth, NH: Heinemann.

I found this to be a very supportive book (138 pp.) for intermediate and mid-dle school teachers, especially those beginning to establish writing process classrooms. Wilde, a fifth-grade teacher, is very explicit on how he teaches poetry, fiction, report writing, persuasive writing, and writing across the curriculum. I appreciated the depth of information on how to write fiction stories—a difficult genre for many students—how to take students from prose to poetry, and how to write a research report. Fast-paced and enjoyable to read, Wilde's teacher stories, assignments, and classroom experiences provide much information and encouragement.

Wood, Karen D., with Anita Moss (eds.). 1992. *Exploring Literature in the Classroom: Contents and Methods.* Norwood, MA: Christopher-Gordon.

Bringing literature and reading education together is the goal of this timely text. It is filled with many suggestions and activities suggested by experts in their respective fields. Lapp, Flood, and Farnan present ways to use trade books and basal readers to complement each other in a well-rounded reading program. Other chapters consider technological support, multicultural literature, use of drama, and ways to turn kids on to reading. Last, children's author Natalie Babbitt traces her own journey as a reader. This is a comprehensive book for elementary teachers who are moving from a basal-equipped classroom to one that includes children's literature. (V.M.)

Zemelman, Steven, and Harvey Daniels. 1988. *A Community of Writers: Teaching Writing in the Junior and Senior High School.* Portsmouth, NH: Heinemann.

The authors, co-directors of the Illinois Writing Project, have written a thoughtful and practical text (288 pp.) for teachers of grades 6–12. Drawing on the research of the integrated language arts movement of the 1970s and 1980s, the authors present a complete theoretical and practical framework for the implementation of a process writing classroom. While they honestly acknowledge the obstacles of implementing process writing at the junior and senior high levels, they also stress its *necessity "because this is the part of school we most desperately need to reform" (p. 11). Teachers from the upper elementary grades onward will find a wealth of usable ideas for developing classroom management techniques, sensitizing students to working in groups, structuring and designing many types of writing activities, and evaluating student writing beyond copyediting. Three approaches to writing are advocated and explained in depth: student-initiated writing (journals, writing workshop), teacher-assigned writing, and writing to learn. A strong rationale and specific suggestions are given for prewriting, drafting, revising, and conferencing. Teachers will find this book very supportive, realistic, and filled with meaningful writing activities.*

Zemelman, Steven, Harvey Daniels, and Arthur Hyde. 1993. *Best Practice: New Standards for Teaching and Learning in America's Schools.* Portsmouth, NH: Heinemann.

This is a tightly organized volume that looks at the best practices in the subject areas of reading, writing, mathematics, science, and social studies. Each of the standards is followed by a description of an exemplary program, and then a summary of how schools should change in this area. Methods for encouraging the implementation of these new approaches, as well as a ten-year program for districtwide staff development, are described. Finally, the Washington Irving School in Chicago is cited as an example of how teachers can be encouraged to work together to enact new curriculum in city school settings. This book should be helpful to administrators and teachers who are looking for an overview of the best educational practices, and places where they are being implemented. (V.M.)

Journal Articles

For other annotated journal articles related specifically to spelling, whole language, journal writing, evaluation, and learning disabilities, see "Resources" at the end of respective chapters in *Invitations.*

Alverman, Donna. October 1991. "The Discussion Web: A Graphic Aid for Learning Across the Curriculum." *The Reading Teacher,* pp. 92–99.

The author defines and describes "the Discussion Web," a procedure that encourages students to work together to make more meaningful and frequent comments in group discussions. An encouraging strategy for getting students to focus critically on the "why" and not just the "what" of an issue.

• Atwell, Nancie. Spring 1989. "The Thoughtful Practitioner." *Teachers Networking: The Whole Language Newsletter,* Vol. 9, no. 3, pp. 1, 10–12.

Atwell encourages us to become teacher-researchers, that is, "thoughtful practitioners" who constantly examine and evaluate our own teaching and learning. Terrific for thoughtful discussion.

Babbitt, Natalie. November–December 1990. "Protecting Children's Literature." *The Horn Book Magazine,* pp. 696–703.

Children's author Natalie Babbitt eloquently reminds us that good fiction is meant to be enjoyed on a human, personal level. She warns against the lessons and discussions designed "to teach" that often accompany the use of literature in the reading program: "Because if we weigh the stories down with the baggage of unrelated lessons, they will sink and disappear" (p. 703).

Braddock, Jomills Henry II, and James M. McPartland. April 1990. "Alternatives to Tracking." *Educational Leadership,* pp. 76–80.

Citing the harmful effects of tracking, the authors offer specific modifications and alternatives. Among them are postponing and limiting tracking, experimenting with different placement criteria, and providing support for teachers in untracked classes.

Brent, Rebecca, and Patricia Anderson. October 1993. "Developing Children's Classroom Listening Strategies." *The Reading Teacher,* pp. 122–126.

Recognizing that effective listening skills do not develop automatically, the authors model how to get students to be good listeners. I have found the suggested activities and strategies especially valuable for improving students' listening abilities during sharing time at the end of writing workshop.

Bruce, Joyce, and Beverly Showers. February 1980. "Improving Inservice Training: The Messages of Research." *Educational Leadership,* pp. 379–385.

Many successful staff-development programs still base their models on the Joyce and Showers paradigm, which evolved from a review of over two hundred research studies. This classic article by two well-respected researchers gives the components of successful staff-development programs—presentation of theory, demonstration of skill, practice, feedback, and coaching. Educators wanting to design effective staff-development programs will find this a very useful article.

Church, Susan. February 1994. "Is Whole Language Really Warm and Fuzzy?" *The Reading Teacher,* pp. 362–370.

Concerns about teachers "doing" whole language without examining their own beliefs prompted Church to explore the complexities of understanding whole language theory and practice. One of the questions she raises is, "Why do so many teachers seem to believe that whole language means they should not play an active role as teacher?" (p. 363). Church convincingly argues that we need ongoing, school-based inquiry that focuses on the "why" of language learning. An excellent article for discussion and reflection.

Cooper, Harris. November 1989. "Synthesis of Research on Homework." *Educational Leadership,* pp. 85–91.

Cooper reviews and summarizes almost 120 research studies on the effects of homework. He concludes that homework has a neglible effect on achievement at the elementary level, a moderate effect at the junior high level, and a positive effect at the high school level as long as the material is not too complex or unfamiliar. Cooper includes a useful recommended homework policy for districts, schools, and teachers. Share these policy guidelines with parents and administrators.

• Copenhaver, Joby. Spring 1993. "Instances of Inquiry." *Primary Voices,* pp. 6–12.

Copenhaver describes how she collaborated with Carolyn Burke and fifth-grade teacher Rise Paynter to help students generate inquiry questions that would sustain their individual research for several weeks. Students then chose a way to share their new knowledge with the class. Self-evaluation was a major part of the inquiry process. I and many of our teachers have used the wonderful self-evaluation idea, "Three Plusses and a Wish," with students and parents as a positive way to hear their voices. Excellent for supporting child-initiated inquiry in the classroom and for promoting self-evaluation.

Cordeiro, Pat. Winter 1992–1993. "Becoming a Learner Who Teaches." *Teachers Networking: The Whole Language Newsletter,* pp. 1, 3–4.

Cordeiro describes how she has moved from integrated curriculum, where the teacher brings separate elements of the curriculum together in a meaningful way, to "generative curriculum," where teacher and students collaboratively shape the curriculum through talk and exploration in the classroom community. "Teachers must be learners first, and teachers second" (p. 4). Great for self-reflection and looking at where you are with curriculum integration.

Cudd, Evelyn T., and Leslie Roberts. February 1989. "Using Writing to Enhance Content Area Learning in the Primary Grades." *The Reading Teacher,* pp. 392–404.

This excellent article is full of specific demonstrations, ideas, and examples for writing in the content areas in grades 1–3. Very useful to teachers who want to move beyond narrative writing.

Daiute, Colette. October 1989. "Research Currents: Play and Learning to Write." *Language Arts,* pp. 656–664.

The importance of collaborative writing and the benefits of playful talk for children's writing development are emphasized. The research indicates that collabo-

rative composing (especially on the computer) is "productive and enriching" and that a "little noise and laughter" contribute to writing.

Donaldson, Gordon A., Jr. October 1993. "Working Smarter Together." *Educational Leadership*, pp. 12–16.

Our K–12 Language Arts Committee found this article very helpful for working together collaboratively through the curriculum-change process. By "working smarter," Donaldson refers to being able to direct our new efforts wisely and monitor what we do so that we benefit children and do not exhaust ourselves in the process. "The cycle of progress requires that a school staff redefine itself as a community responsible for setting and reaching its own goals and capable of managing its own resources" (p. 15). Donaldson helps us achieve this worthy goal.

Dowhower, Sarah L. March 1989. "Repeated Reading: Research into Practice." *The Reading Teacher*, pp. 502–507.

The benefits and procedures of repeated reading ("multiple readings of connected text") are discussed and demonstrated. Specific, practical, and useful for all teachers.

Duffy, Gerald G. February 1992. "Let's Free Teachers to Be Inspired." *Phi Delta Kappan*, pp. 442–447.

The author provides a much-needed, balanced perspective to the debate on which approach to instruction is best. "No matter what is being taught, there seem to be two prevalent approaches to instruction. One is direct; the other, holistic" (p. 442). Rather than carrying one approach to extremes, Duffy recommends that teachers use professional judgment and combine the best of prevailing theory and practice. "Effective teaching is associated with being empowered to combine tenets of various positions in order to arrive at instructional decisions that make sense in a particular instructional situation" (p. 444). Excellent for reflection and discussion.

Farris, Pamela J. Summer 1989. "Story Time and Story Journals: Linking Literature and Writing." *The New Advocate*, pp. 179–185.

The author details specific ways to link literature with writing through story journals, literary journals, and dialogue journals. Useful for the primary-grade teacher.

Fielding, Linda, and Cathy Roller. May 1992. "Making Difficult Books Accessible and Easy Books Acceptable." *The Reading Teacher*, pp. 678–685.

Fielding and Roller recognize the importance of classroom time each day for independent reading and the accompanying reality that some children do not engage with print during this time. The authors offer workable suggestions for getting struggling readers reading the print during independent reading time. Excellent ideas for across the grades.

Five, Cora Lee. Spring 1988. "From Workbook to Workshop: Increasing Children's Involvement in the Reading Process." *The New Advocate*, pp. 103–113.

A fifth-grade teacher describes how she moved to a reading program that complemented her writing program in which students had "time, ownership, and response." Very useful and specific for teachers who want to use literature in a reading workshop approach.

• Fractor, Jann Sorrell, Marjorie Ciruti Woodruff, Miriam G. Martinez, and William H. Teale. March 1993. "Let's Not Miss Opportunities to Promote Voluntary Reading: Classroom Libraries in the Elementary School." *The Reading Teacher*, pp. 476–484.

A quality classroom library positively impacts the amount of voluntary reading students do and increases literacy activities. Yet, the authors found that while most elementary classrooms have library centers, only a very small percentage of these are excellent. Criteria and suggestions for setting up excellent libraries are detailed. Photos and features of some exemplary classroom libraries are included. Read this article, and self-evaluate your own classroom library.

• Fullan, Michael G., and Matthew B. Miles. June 1992. "Getting Reform Right: What Works and What Doesn't." *Phi Delta Kappan*, pp. 745–752.

The authors explain why reforms fail and what must happen in order for reform efforts to succeed. They note that "the implementation dip"—things going wrong before they go right—and anxiety and uncertainty are "intrinsic to all successful change." Use this article in your district, as we did, to help gain support and understanding for the difficult process of change.

Gamoran, Adam. October 1992. "Is Ability Grouping Equitable?" *Educational Leadership*, pp. 11–17.

Negative achievement effects of grouping and tracking are documented with the recommendation that there be less tracking and grouping and an improved use of ability grouping.

Garan, Elaine M. March 1994. "Who's in Control? Is There Enough 'Empowerment' to Go Around?" *Language Arts*, pp. 192–199.

Garan realistically discusses management and control issues in a whole language classroom. Based on her ethnographic study as a participant-observer in a whole language classroom, she urges the sharing of control with students while acknowledging how difficult this is for most of us. Very useful for looking at our own teaching and for effectively structuring the whole language classroom.

• Glasser, William. February 1990. "The Quality School." *Phi Delta Kappan*, pp. 425–435.

A provocative, thought-provoking article on how to manage our teaching so that the majority of students do high-quality schoolwork. Excellent for discussion, K–12.

• Goodlad, John I., and Jeannie Oakes. February 1988. "We Must Offer Equal Access to Knowledge." *Educational Leadership*, pp. 16–22.

"Study after study reveals the dominance of telling, lecturing, questioning the class, and monitoring seatwork. The inquiring, questioning, probing, hypothesizing kind of intellectual endeavor often associated with learning is not usually found in classrooms" (p. 17). Furthermore, poor and minority children, overrepresented in the lowest groups, and with little chance of access to the highest groups, receive the most inferior schooling. Educators are urged to examine tracking practices and consider different ideas: implementing small cooperative learning groups, providing concept-based (rather than fragmented skills) curriculums, and altering the way we perceive individual differences.

Goodman, Kenneth S. Winter 1988. "Look What They've Done to Judy Blume!: The 'Basalization' of Children's Literature." *The New Advocate*, pp. 29–41.

Goodman reiterates that authentic text, the way the author wrote it, is the easiest to read and to learn to read. He decries common tampering with stories by well-known authors to fit basal schemes. Teachers and administrators desirous of using real literature instead of basal texts will find this a supportive article.

• Hammond, Catherine. February 1993. "The Internal Screen: A Powerful Tool for Writing." *Language Arts*, pp. 116–122.

This is the most useful article I have read on getting students to write well. Hammond demonstrates how she gets students to write with specific, powerful images by using their "screens" (the place where we see things in our heads) to capture and visualize exact moments in their lives.

Henke, Linda. Winter 1988. "Beyond Basal Reading: A District's Commitment to Change." *The New Advocate*, pp. 42–51.

For school districts ready to look at alternative reading program options, this article describes how a district that decides against a new basal adoption implements a program that accommodates use of the old basal while adding lots of trade books, daily independent reading, and daily writing workshop time, as well as staff development and parent communication.

• Hepler, Susan. Summer 1988. "A Guide for the Teacher Guides: Doing It Yourself." *The New Advocate*, pp. 186–195.

This gem of an article gives specific guidelines to teachers who want to work together to develop meaningful guides for specific books. Meaningful questions, responses to literature, and appropriate ac-

tivities are discussed and demonstrated. The article is not only useful for making your own guides for books but it is also valuable for looking at commercial guides critically.

Herman, Patricia A., and Janice Dole. September 1988. "Theory and Practice in Vocabulary Learning and Instruction." *The Elementary School Journal*, pp. 43–54.

The authors discuss three approaches to vocabulary instruction—definitional, contextual, and conceptual—while also acknowledging that most words are learned incidentally; "an average reader learns the meaning of 800–1,200 words per year through free reading alone" (p. 44). A combination of the three approaches is recommended, and specifics are provided. The definitional approach, by itself, is seen to be mostly ineffective. With the contextual approach, the importance of teacher demonstration is illustrated through an example of a teacher verbalizing thought processes to figure out the meaning of a word in natural context. A series of activities that demonstrates a conceptual approach to learning a word is clearly delineated. Current research about vocabulary and its effect on reading comprehension is also discussed. An excellent article for gaining perspective on vocabulary acquisition.

Hudelson, Sarah, Julia Fournier, Cecilia Espinosa, and Renee Bachman. March 1994. "Chasing Windmills: Confronting the Obstacles to Literature-Based Programs in Spanish." *Language Arts*, pp. 164–171.

While Spanish-speaking children and bilingual programs are increasing in the United States, the quantity, quality, and cultural authenticity of literature available in Spanish is still very limited. The authors discuss the challenges of getting quality Spanish-language literature into the literature classroom. Excellent criteria, references, and literature cited to aid selection.

• Juliebo, Moira, and Joyce Edwards. January 1989. "Encouraging Meaning Making in Young Writers." *Young Children*, pp. 22–27.

The authors demonstrate what happens when writing tasks are artificially created by the teacher. They concur with already existing studies that support the need for topic choice, real purpose, and a varied audience for obtaining children's best written work. Although the writing samples discussed are from primary children, the characteristics that are found to encourage—or restrict—written composition apply to all the grades. An important article for understanding the need for authentic writing experiences.

Lambert, Linda. May 1988. "Staff Development Redesigned." *Phi Delta Kappan*, pp. 665–668.

Lambert urges expanding the teacher's role in staff development from "passive receiver" to leadership and inquiry. Teachers ready to take an active, decision-making role in restructuring staff development in their school will find lots of support and valuable information in this thought-provoking article. Great for discussion.

Larrick, Nancy. Spring 1991. "Give us Books! But Also . . . Give Us Wings!" *The New Advocate*, pp. 77–83.

Nancy Larrick makes an impassioned plea to keep the joy of reading quality literature alive in the classroom. She notes that many teachers are using real books with students, but many are also using accompanying teachers' guides that ruin the joy and beauty of the books. She cites the problems with many of these guides. Good for discussion and for self-checking your own use of literature in the classroom.

Lee, Nancy G., and Judith C. Neal. December 1992/January 1993. "Reading Rescue: Intervention for a Student 'At Promise.'" *Journal of Reading*, pp. 276–282.

The authors describe how an adaptation of Marie Clay's intensive, 1:1 approach is used successfully with a very poor reader in middle school. The specific components and strategies used are clearly delineated. Guidelines for classroom teachers who work with struggling ("at promise") readers are given. Helpful and applicable across the grades.

Lipson, Marjorie Y., Sheila W. Valencia, Karen K. Wixon, and Charles W. Peters. April

1993. "Integration and Thematic Teaching: Integration to Improve Teaching and Learning." *Language Arts*, pp. 252–263.

Everyone I know struggles with meaningful integration of the curriculum. The authors provide a realistic overview of where we are in the profession and provide a rationale—as well as suggestions—for teaching with integrated, thematic units. Helpful for being able to develop thematic units that deal with important, big ideas that are authentically connected to meaningful content.

- Maeroff, Gene I. "Assessing Alternative Assessment." December 1991. *Phi Delta Kappan*, pp. 272–281.

  "For all its attractiveness, alternative assessment is fraught with complications and difficulties." Maeroff notes, for example, "if students themselves are to take responsibility for their own work, the criteria must be spelled out in ways that are understandable to children." Looking at existing alternative assessments in various states and schools, Maeroff discusses the benefits and the problems. Great for gaining perspective and ideas on alternative assessments.

Manning, Maryann, Gary Manning, and Constance Kamii. November 1988. "Early Phonics Instruction: Its Effect on Literacy Development." *Young Children*, pp. 4–8.

The authors describe what happened to one six-year-old (who entered school reading predictable books) when she received a heavy dose of phonics instruction in kindergarten. "With the exception of digraphs and consonant blends, the instruction caused confusion and reduced her confidence in her own ability to figure things out." The authors are not against phonics instruction, but they do question an imposed, time-consuming phonics program that may not fit the child's stage of development. Rather, they urge an emphasis on meaning with lots of time for reading and writing so children can work out their own system of rules.

Means, Barbara, and Michael S. Knapp. December 1991. "Cognitive Approaches to Teaching Advanced Skills to Educationally Disadvantaged Students." *Phi Delta Kappan*, pp. 282–289.

A summary of the research supporting the teaching of "advanced" skills to "at-risk" learners is presented along with strategies for doing so. Offers helpful suggestions for reshaping the curriculum so all students receive "higher-order" content and thinking.

- Newmann, Fred M., and Gary G. Wehlage. April 1993. "Five Standards of Authentic Instruction." *Educational Leadership*, pp. 8–12.

  Five standards for engaging students in high-quality work that uses students' minds well are presented with specific criteria. The standards are described with a five-point scale for rating lessons and include higher-order thinking, depth of knowledge, connectedness to the world, substantive conversation, and social support for student achievement. Discuss and use this excellent framework in your school, as we did, to self-evaluate current practices and to move toward more "authentic," higher-level instruction and achievement. Applicable to all grade levels and subject areas.

- O'Brien, Kathy L. Winter 1991. "A Look at One Successful Literature Program." *The New Advocate*, pp. 113–123.

  Many teachers now incorporate literature into their reading programs, but, in some cases, not without basalization of the literature. The author describes and recommends specific, successful practices which maintain the integrity of the text and the reader and which promote high level dialogue and analysis. Read and discuss this excellent article, and apply the practices to your own literature program.

- Ohanian, Susan. Fall 1988. "My Word! A Plea for More Disorderliness." *Teachers Networking: The Whole Language Newsletter.*

  Ohanian argues that rather than trusting kids to become readers and celebrating children's literature, many teachers and publishers ruin the literature for kids by trying to extract as many skills as possible. Must reading for teachers tempted to have kids do lots of activities to go along with books!

• Ohlhausen, Marilyn M., and Mary Jepsen. Winter 1992. "Lessons from Goldilocks: 'Somebody's Been Choosing My Books But I Can Make My Own Choices Now!'" *The New Advocate*, pp. 31–46.

Ohlhausen and Jepsen recommend a process for teaching children how to select books that are characterized as "too easy," "just right," and "too hard." Through teacher modeling and guided practice, children learn to independently judge book difficulty for themselves and to choose books to read from all three categories. I, and many of our teachers, use the "Goldilocks Strategy" in the independent reading program. See Appendix D, p. 189b.

Pace, Glenellen. January 1991. "When Teachers Use Literature for Literacy Instruction: Ways That Constrain, Ways That Free." *Language Arts*, pp. 12–25.

Many teachers now use literature to support literacy development. "But frequently what teachers have children do with literature is at odds with a whole language paradigm." Pace identifies key premises from whole language theory, gives supporting examples from elementary classrooms, and asks specific questions about classroom practice as a way for us to evaluate our teaching. Excellent for reflection and discussion and for making our theory and practice congruent with holistic, learner-centered views. Applicable for K–8.

Rasinski, Timothy V. May 1989. "Fluency for Everyone: Incorporating Fluency Instruction in the Classroom." *The Reading Teacher*, pp. 690–693.

This highly practical, research-based article gives the classroom teacher specific strategies for promoting and supporting reading fluency of students. Repetition, modeling, direct feedback, tape recording, choral reading, and use of easy materials are fully discussed. I have found this article to be especially useful for helping "at-risk" students become more proficient readers.

Reardon, S. Jeanne. Winter 1988. "The Development of Critical Readers: A Look into the Classroom." *The New Advocate*, pp. 52–61.

An intermediate-grade classroom teacher describes the necessary elements for development of critical readers. Her specific demonstrations of how she reads to her class every day and how she conducts a small-group literature discussion are extremely helpful to the teacher who wants insight into promoting high-level thinking by connecting authors' purposes to literature. Applicable for all the grades.

Reimer, Becky L., and Leslie Warshow. April 1989. "Questions We Ask of Ourselves and Our Students." *The Reading Teacher*, pp. 596–606.

Teachers who have made meaningful and major changes in their teaching tell their personal stories. Supportive, informative, and inspiring to all teachers in the change process.

Rosenblatt, Louise M. October 1991. "Literature—S.O.S.!" *Language Arts*, pp. 444–448.

Louise Rosenblatt asks us "to be clear theoretically about efferent and aesthetic reading" and to take care not to use literature to teach "skills." Important for understanding Rosenblatt's important ideas on how readers transact with texts and for looking carefully at how we use literature in the classroom.

Scharer, Patricia L., and Deana B. Detwiler. March 1992. "Changing as Teachers: Perils and Possibilities of Literature-Based Language Arts Instruction." *Language Arts*, pp. 186–192.

A sixth-grade teacher describes her transition to literature-based teaching and shares her struggles and successes. Recommendations for supporting teacher change are included. Very helpful to teachers and schools in transition.

Sears, Sue, Cathy Carpenter, and Nancy Burstein. May 1994. "Meaningful Reading Instruction for Learners with Special Needs." *The Reading Teacher*, pp. 632–638.

This fine article details how to balance the need for explicit instruction with whole language principles for special-needs learners. The authors describe a reading program that consists of assisted reading (reading grade-level texts aloud with help), informal assessment (taking running re-

cords and responding to comprehension questions), and contextualized strategy instruction (minilessons based on identified needs). Very helpful to anyone who works with struggling readers.

• Shannon, Patrick. October 1989. "The Struggle for Control of Literacy Lessons." *Language Arts*, pp. 625–634.

The author argues that, in a democratic educational and social setting, the control of literacy lessons should be properly shared by teachers and students. Even when materials are substantially improved over traditional basal texts, publishers still maintain control by predetermining the possible choices. Shannon raises weighty questions about control of literacy lessons and suggests that as long as a commercial program is used, it is the publisher's choices that control the lessons.

Shepard, Lorrie A., and Mary Lee Smith. May 1990. "Synthesis of Research on Grade Retention." *Educational Leadership*, pp. 84–88.

The authors note that "the large body of research on grade retention is almost uniformly negative." Given that 5 to 7 percent of children in public schools in the United States are retained annually at a cost of almost $10 billion a year, this is an article to be taken seriously. Retention leads to increased risk of dropping out of school, poor self esteem, and lower achievement in later grades. The authors recommend "promotion plus remediation" and suggest alternative ways to provide specific and additional instructional help.

Silva, Cecilia, and Esther L. Delgado-Larocco. October 1993. "Facilitating Learning Through Interconnections: A Concept Approach to Core Literature Units." *Language Arts*, pp. 469–474.

For teachers and districts who implement literature and literature-based programs, the authors present a model for developing meaningful literature units with conceptually related books. Helpful for focusing on meaning and enjoyment and avoiding trivialising of the literature.

Slavin, Robert E. September 1988. "Synthesis of Research on Grouping in Elementary and Secondary Schools." *Educational Leadership*, pp. 67–77.

Slavin, perhaps best known for his comprehensive research analysis on ability grouping ("Ability Grouping and Student Achievement in Elementary Schools: A Best Evidence Synthesis." Review of Educational Research, Vol. 57, no. 3 [1987], pp. 213–336), summarizes the research on achievement effects of ability grouping at the elementary and secondary levels. This scholarly article is important reading for all educators. It calls into question many common grouping practices for regular, gifted, and special education students.

• Smith, Frank. February 1992. "Learning to Read: The Never-Ending Debate." *Phi Delta Kappan*, pp. 432–441.

Conflicting views of how children learn to read and how reading should be taught are examined with thoughtful rhetoric and uncommon good sense. Frank Smith elaborates on how children learn to read and on current theories of teaching reading, specifically, the phonics or "skills" approach and the whole language or "naturalistic" approach. "Methods can never ensure that children learn to read. Children must learn from people: from the teachers (formal and informal) who initiate them into the readers' club and from the authors whose writing they read" (p. 440). Read this powerful essay and continue the debate in your own school. You may also want to read the response to Smith, "The Debate Continues" by Kenneth J. Smith, Valerie F. Reyna, and Charles J. Brainerd (Phi Delta Kappan, January 1993, pp. 407–410).

Smith, Frank. January 1989. "Overselling Literacy." *Phi Delta Kappan*, pp. 353–359.

"Individuals become literate not from the formal instruction they receive, but from what they read and write about and who they read and write with" (p. 355). Smith cautions against the promotion of literacy as a cure-all for society's ills and reminds us that literacy is most valuable and productive when it is meaningful and carried out in association with literate people who read and write for pleasure.

Rather than relying on instructional programs and evaluation, school environments need to foster collaborative relationships that free the imagination and empower both teachers and students. A great article for group discussion.

Taylor, Denny. November 1989. "Toward a Unified Theory of Literacy Learning and Instructional Practices." *Phi Delta Kappan*, pp. 184–193.

The author argues that "reductionist" and "hierarchical" research views of children's early literacy development do not take into consideration the complex individual and personal ways children have been observed to learn and use language, and, therefore, these views are too narrow to be taken seriously. Taylor urges educators to establish theoretical frameworks that broaden and enhance children's opportunities for dynamic reading and writing experiences. "Our task is to insure that the voices of children become embodied in the ways in which we teach" (p. 193). An important article for thinking about our own understandings and beliefs about literacy.

Throne, Jeanette. September 1988. "Becoming a Kindergarten of Readers?" *Young Children*, pp. 10–16.

A well-respected kindergarten teacher in our school district argues that good kindergarten teachers have always taught reading—not through formal, decontextualized materials—but through all kinds of authentic language experiences. Throne discusses how she fosters reading through shared book experiences, repeated readings, creative dramatics, related writing and art activities, and group discussions about stories. An excellent article for early childhood educators who want a developmentally appropriate curriculum.

Topping, Keith. March 1989. "Peer Tutoring and Paired Reading: Combining Two Powerful Techniques." *The Reading Teacher*, pp. 488–494.

The author, an educational psychologist who developed a parent-child paired-reading procedure that is widely practiced in the United Kingdom, discusses the bene-fits, organizational procedures, and evaluation research of paired-reading programs in classrooms, in which a more able child assists a less able one in reading. "All the major research reviews on the effectiveness of peer tutoring in reading have shown that the tutors accelerate in reading skill at least as much as, if not more than, the tutees" (p. 489). This very specific article gives complete information to the K–12 teacher who is interested in setting up a paired-reading program.

• Turner, Richard L. December 1989. "The 'Great' Debate–Can Both Carbo and Chall Be Right?" *Phi Delta Kappan*, pp. 276–283.

An educational researcher responds to two extreme positions on the teaching of phonics in beginning reading: "Debunking the Great Phonics Myth" by Marie Carbo (Phi Delta Kappan, November 1988) and "Learning to Read: The Great Debate 20 Years Later—A Response to 'Debunking the Great Phonics Myth'" by Jeanne Chall (Phi Delta Kappan, March 1989). In reviewing the research literature on the place of phonics in beginning reading instruction, Turner reviews the "best evidence" studies—those "that were free from bias, that directly addressed the research question of interest, and that inspired confidence in the results" (p. 276). He concludes, "If systematic phonics influences reading vocabulary and comprehension at all, it does so very, very slightly" (p. 283). Read all three articles for perspectives on phonics in beginning reading.

Urzúa, Carole. Fall 1994. "Faith in Learners Through Literature Studies." *Voices from the Middle*, pp. 19–30.

The rationale and procedures for a literature study—where students meet with their peers to read and discuss an agreed-upon book in "book club" sessions—are described in detail. Excellent for organizing your own literature study.

Walmsley, Sean A., and Ellen L. Adams. April 1993. "Realities of 'Whole Language.'" *Language Arts*, pp. 272–280.

Interviews with a group of teachers confirmed that whole language instruction is very difficult to put into practice, manage, and assess. The authors state, "We had the feeling that most of the teachers were still grappling with a concept that they did not fully understand." This controversial article is important for looking at whole language realistically, for making sure that teachers receive sufficient support for the rigorous demands of whole language teaching, and for addressing the politics of whole language.

Wason-Ellam, Linda. March 1988. "Using Literary Patterns: Who's in Control of the Authorship?" *Language Arts,* pp. 291–301.

The author warns against overuse of literary patterns from predictable texts and suggests that beginning writers need to focus on communicating ideas. While innovating on patterned text can be meaningful (especially in oral-language activities), often it is overworked and restrictive. "At times, this is carried to such an extreme that the task often resembles workbook activities" (p. 292). Teachers who are spending a lot of time having children extend specific patterns should read this article for perspectives and for suggestions of how predictable books can serve as models to promote authentic writing.

Wheelock, Anne. October 1992. "The Case for Untracking." *Educational Leadership,* pp. 6–21.

For schools thinking about "untracking" and giving all students equal access to valued knowledge, this article provides incentive and support. Wheelock identifies characteristics of schools that have successfully eliminated tracking by ability and improved instruction and learning.

Whitmore, Kathryn F., and Caryl G. Crowell. Winter 1994. "What Makes a Question Good Is . . ." *The New Advocate,* pp. 45–57.

The authors describe how literature study in a third-grade community evolved from children's probing questions about a world event. The power of children's questioning as a literature study discussion strategy is demonstrated through the students' conversations and high-level questions.

Wiggington, Eliot. February 1989. "Foxfire Grows Up." *Harvard Educational Review,* pp. 24–49.

The developer of the "Foxfire approach," a democratic, experiential, and hands-on approach and philosophy of education describes Foxfire's core educational practices and how he and others work with teachers to achieve them. The approach believes that all-age students "benefit from examining the culture, traditions, and history of their communities, urban or rural, and then documenting and publishing what they found" (p. 24). The Foxfire approach has much in common with whole language in that education is student centered and connected to the real world. Texts are used as resources as the need arises; group work and collaboration are highly valued; the teacher is a facilitator and guide; self-evaluation is intrinsic to the learning process. A provocative article for educators interested in learning about the Foxfire approach.

Yaffe, Stephen H. March 1989. "Drama as a Teaching Tool." *Educational Leadership,* pp. 29–32.

The benefits of drama as a response to literature for gifted as well as at-risk students K–12 are discussed and demonstrated.

• Zarrillo, James. Fall 1991. "Theory Become Practice: Aesthetic Teaching with Literature." *The New Advocate,* pp. 221–233.

Many elementary teachers are unaware of Rosenblatt's seminal work, The Reader, The Text, The Poem: The Transactional Theory of the Literary Work (Carbondale, IL: Southern Illinois University Press, 1978) and her enormous, worldwide impact. Zarrillo translates Louise Rosenblatt's transactional theory of reading to the elementary grades and demonstrates his interpretation of aesthetic teaching. "Aesthetic teaching relies on literature and supports the personal reading choices and unique responses of students" (p. 231). Be sure to read and discuss this terrific article. Excellent for understanding Rosenblatt's "efferent" and "aesthetic" approaches to reading and for creating a literature *program that is theoretically sound, intensely personal, response centered, and respectful of children's needs and choices.*

Zucker, Carol. May 1993. "Using Whole Language with Students Who Have Language and Learning Disabilities." *The Reading Teacher*, pp. 660–670.

Based on a whole language philosophy, a learning disabilities resource teacher specifically describes her classroom reading-writing activities and the benefits to the children. Helpful and applicable to all learners with special needs.

Themed Journals

These themed journals are wonderful springboards for thinking about practices, processes, and changes in literacy learning and teaching K–12. Many of the articles in these journals have been discussed in our weekly language arts support groups. It is recommended that your school library have a copy of each journal for your reference.

Baumann, James F. (guest ed.). May 1990. *The Reading Teacher: Whole Literacy*. Newark, DE: International Reading Association.

This issue explores possibilities and challenges in implementing whole language. The introductory article, "'Possibilities, Daddy, I Think It Says Possibilities': A Father's Journal of the Emergence of Literacy" by Lester L. Laminack is both scholarly and delightful for taking a look at a preschooler's attempts to interact with print in his world. Preschool, kindergarten, and grade one teachers will find "Dramatic Play: A Context for Meaningful Engagements" by James F. Christie valuable for noting the importance of providing opportunities for literacy-related dramatic play and for specific suggestions on theme centers and teacher involvement. "Language, Literature, and At-Risk Children" by Nancy L. Roser, James V. Hoffman, and Cynthia Farest describes how a literature program was successfully organized and implemented in a large, impoverished county school system. "Whole Language in the Middle School" by Anna M. McWhirter, which describes a reading

workshop approach, will be instructive for middle and high school teachers seeking alternatives to traditional language arts teaching. "Assessment and Accountability in a Whole Literacy Curriculum" by Kathryn H. Au, Judith A. Scheu, Alice J. Kawakami, and Patricia A. Herman will be very useful to teachers, administrators, and school districts looking for accountability in incorporating holistic measures for monitoring and documenting learning. Other fine articles discuss the use of computers, parent involvement, reading-spelling links, and how a grade one teacher incorporated whole language in her classroom.

Brandt, Ronald (executive ed.). April 1989. *Educational Leadership: Redirecting Assessment*. Alexandria, VA: Association for Supervision and Curriculum Development.

If you are interested in improving evaluation and assessment, don't miss this outstanding issue. Lorie Shepard's opening article, "Why We Need Better Assessments" addresses the limitations of standardized testing and points the way to more authentic assessment. "High-Stakes Testing in Kindergarten" by Samuel J. Meisels discusses the harmful effects and misuse of readiness testing for labeling, placing, and retaining children. "There are presently no readiness or achievement tests sufficiently accurate to serve the high-stakes functions they are being asked to perform" (p. 20). "On Misuse of Testing: A Conversation with George Madaus" by Ron Brandt addresses the concerns of the director of the Center for the Study of Testing, Evaluation, and Educational Policy and is a terrific article for group discussion. Among other things, Madaus notes that high test scores do not correlate with high skills levels; measurement-driven instruction makes teaching easier but "deprofessionalizes" it; ranking school districts by test results uses tests in a way that was never intended. In "Testing and Thoughtfulness," Rexford Brown notes that thinking skills cannot be broken down and tested. He calls for more thoughtful tests such as those that students create themselves. Dennie Palmer Wolf's article, "Portfolio As-

sessment: Sampling Student Work," is outstanding for understanding the concepts behind portfolio assessment. In a very significant article, "Teaching to the (Authentic) Test," Grant Wiggins calls for a redesign of assessment procedures at the high school level that reflects authentic literacy behaviors. "Theory and Practice in Statewide Reading Assessment: Closing the Gap" by Sheila Valencia, David Pearson, Charles Peters, and Karen Wixon describes the statewide reading comprehension tests in Illinois and Michigan that are based on current reading theory. "How Do We Evaluate Student Writing? One District's ANSWER" by Melva Lewis and Arnold Lindaman gives specifics on how a district measures students' growth as writers in grades 1–12 using fall and spring writing samples, student and parent evaluative responses of those samples, and holistic assessment of the samples.

- Flores, Barbara (guest ed.). January 1994. *Primary Voices K–6. Challenge for Change: Theme Cycles.* Urbana, IL: National Council of Teachers of English.

  This is a great issue for understanding integration and gaining a meaningful framework for classroom inquiry focused on critical questions, problem solving, and constructing knowledge. In the opening article, Barbara Flores and Bess Altwerger rethink learning and teaching and explain what they mean by "theme cycle." In a theme cycle, "Teachers and students select and negotiate topics of study, and based upon the collective knowledge of the class, they delineate questions and issues of interest, seek out resources, and plan learning experiences." The new knowledge is presented and shared, leading to other questions and further study that continues the learning cycle. In the articles that follow, elementary school bilingual teachers, a principal, a seventh-grade humanities teacher, and a sixth-grade bilingual teacher describe in detail how theme study has evolved and transformed instruction and learning in their classrooms and schools. Don't miss this enlightening issue for rethinking your own curriculum. Lots of usable ideas for the classroom.

Froese, Victor (guest ed.). April 1989. *The Reading Teacher: Empowering Both Teachers and Students.* Newark, DE: International Reading Association.

Each of the articles in this thought-provoking journal is noteworthy for thinking about how literacy is taught and learned in schools and for incorporating recent research into practice. I was particularly impressed by "Building Communities of Readers and Writers" by Trevor Cairney and Susan Langbien, who stress the importance of the social and collaborative nature of learning in all learning environments. "Empowered Students; Empowered Teachers" by William T. Fagan is a very important article for understanding the crucial role teachers play in determining whether or not reading and writing are meaningfully connected to children's lives. "Questions We Ask of Ourselves and Our Students" by Becky L. Reimer and Leslie Warshow describes the struggles and breakthroughs of specific classroom teachers in trying to teach reading and writing with "real life connections." "The Teacher's Role in Students' Success" by Mariam Jean Dreher and Harry Singer calls upon teachers to move from activity managers who follow teacher manuals to professional decision makers who determine goals, materials, and methods.

- Gadsden, Vivian L. (guest ed.). Autumn 1992. *Theory into Practice: Literacy and the African-American Learner.* Columbus, OH: The Ohio State University, College of Education. (1945 N. High St., 43210)

  The collective voices of the authors and researchers in this provocative issue discuss the social and cultural contexts, approaches, and experiences that appear to support and/or hinder literacy learning and access to literacy for African-Americans. I will highlight just a few contributors, but the entire issue is high level, excellent, and worth reading and discussing.

  Violet Harris discusses the historical perspective of literacy and notes that educators working with African-Americans need to know and learn from the lessons of the past and use materials and methods that affirm African-Americans and their culture. In her article, "Acquisition of Literate Discourse: Bowing Before the Master?" Lisa Delpit challenges some conventional views of teaching African-Americans. She believes it is not enough for students to speak and write freely in their own language and voice; they must also be taught to speak and write eloquently with correct grammar, form, and style in the dominant discourse in order to have access to the culture of power. She shares the stories of two successful African-American men who grew up "in an era of overt racism" and who had no aspirations beyond their immediate neighborhoods. These men made major achievements in life because of teachers who had unflappable visions of what they could become and who gave them access to the subtle and mechanical features of middle-class discourse. Their teachers set high standards for them, expected them to meet them, and gave them the necessary, explicit help needed to succeed in mainstream America. Delpit's work is critical reading for all teachers. "In Reading Between the Lines and Beyond the Pages: A Culturally Relevant Approach to Literacy Teaching," Gloria Ladson-Billings describes how two exemplary teachers, who appreciate and celebrate their students "both as individuals and as members of a specific culture" facilitate learning for the African-American students in their classrooms. The descriptions of how these teachers and classrooms operate provide important information for teaching African-American students. So do the articles by Emilie V. Siddle Walker and Michele Jean Sims. The final article, by Patricia A. Edwards, "Involving Parents in Building Reading Instruction for African-American Children," describes a successful book-reading program for low-income, African-American parents that assists and supports them in sharing books with their children. The strategies presented are powerful and workable for other similar communities.

Good, Thomas L. (ed.). November 1989. *The Elementary School Journal: Special Issue on Whole Language.* Chicago: University of Chicago Press.

This is a superb issue for examining the theory, history, and applications of the whole language movement as well as for getting perspectives and implications for teaching and learning. Yetta Goodman begins the issue with a scholarly article that gives a history of the whole language movement. Kenneth Goodman discusses characteristics of whole language and the strong research base for whole language, as well as research possibilities. Other articles define and describe whole language, Reading Recovery, and current and potential views of teacher education. Two commentaries on whole language respond to the articles in this issue and give varying perspectives. The concluding article by Jerry Harste addresses the future of the whole language movement and is important reading for all those concerned with schooling in a democratic society.

Hardt, Ulrich H. (ed.). Fall 1988. *Oregon English. Theme: Whole Language.* Portland: Oregon Council of Teachers of English. (Available for purchase through National Council of Teachers of English, Urbana, IL.)

Favorite articles include "Reflections on Whole Language: Past, Present and Potential" by Dorothy Watson, "Evaluation in the Holistic Reading/Language Arts Curriculum" by Richard Ammon, "Whole Language Teaching: Support from Instructional and Research Models" by Jane B. Braunger. Other articles deal with curricular change, integrating fairy tales into language arts, teaching skills, organizing a student publishing company, integrating letter writing across the curriculum, using children's literature (including picture books) with junior high students, incorporating the arts to reach turned-off high school students, thinking beyond biased textbooks in teaching U.S. history. This entire journal is outstanding for deepening understanding of whole language theory and practice.

Jongsma, Eugene, and Roger Farr (guest eds.). April 1993. *Journal of Reading: Literacy Assessment.* Newark, DE: International Reading Association.

For districts that are ready to question their assessment practices, this provocative issue examines the changes taking place in reading assessment and raises important questions about portfolio assessment systems, creative performance tasks, and national standards. Informed (informal) assessment by teachers, preparation for state-mandated tests, the present practice of portfolios from elementary through postsecondary contexts, and attempts to incorporate more authentic assessments are examined from both problematic and promising perspectives. Because of the national interest in portfolios, I was particularly struck by "Student Portfolios: Opportunities for a Revolution in Assessment" by Robert C. Calfee and Pam Perfumo. In that article and others, the editors and authors caution that without knowledgeable educators and adequate support, the changes taking place in assessment may fizzle and disappear. A terrific issue for discussion and for helping establish workable and meaningful assessment practices.

Shannon, Patrick, and Kenneth S. Goodman (guest eds.). Autumn 1989. *Theory into Practice: Perspectives on Basal Readers.* Columbus, OH: The Ohio State University.

This journal presents varying viewpoints about basal reading materials and raises philosophical questions about literacy learning and teaching. The volume goes way beyond basal texts and raises critical questions about assessment, textbook adoption, reading programs, students' perceptions about reading, reading comprehension, and more. Important reading for all teachers, administrators, and policymakers who are interested in the effects of reading programs on literacy instruction and development and in bringing about constructive change.

Wood, George (coordinator). Fall 1990. *Democracy and Education: Alternatives to Standardized Testing.* Athens, OH: Institute for Democracy in Education at Ohio University.

Don't miss this powerful, thought-provoking issue! This outstanding journal includes articles that discuss how standardized testing demeans and disempowers educators and students by devaluing classroom teachers' judgment and by overrelying on test makers, and it offers alternatives for authentic evaluation. The lead article, "Toward Authentic Assessment," by the editorial board of Democracy and Education, is a clear statement about standardized testing that contains what's wrong with standardized testing (including a statement from Fair Test, the National Center for Fair and Open Testing) as well as options open to teachers to deal with testing. The second essay is a position statement on standardized testing from the National Association for the Education of Young Children. Educators in early childhood programs will find much support here for restricting test use. The remainder of this issue includes inspiring articles by elementary and secondary teachers and students—and a parent—who offer personal and practical insights into the necessity of valuing and involving students in an authentic evaluation process.

Journals

Democracy & Education
4 issues per year/subscription $20
The Institute for Democracy and Education
College of Education
313G McCracken Hall
Athens, OH 45701-2979

A quality journal written by and for teachers that focuses on issues related to democratic practice. For example, recent themed issues have addressed tracking and ability grouping, democratic management, alternatives to standardized testing, classroom and community building, and project-centered learning. The Institute sponsors a conference in Athens, Ohio, every June.

Educational Leadership
8 issues per year/subscription $32
Association for Supervision and Curriculum Development
1250 North Pitt Street
Alexandria, VA 22314-1453

A journal for elementary, middle school, and secondary teachers and administra-

tors interested in being on the cutting edge of current educational theory and practice. For anyone interested in being well informed about good ideas regarding today's educational practices. ASCD offers many excellent professional development opportunities through an annual conference, continuing workshops, and many publications and resources for administrators and teachers.

Elementary School Journal
5 issues per year/subscription $29.50 (individual); $56 (institutions); $22.25 (NAESP); $19.50 (students)
University of Chicago Press
Journals Division
5720 South Woodlawn
PO Box 37005
Chicago, IL 60637

Geared toward a more scholarly audience, this journal contains studies, research reviews, and analyses of ideas for elementary teachers, administrators, teacher educators, and researchers.

• English Journal
8 issues per year/subscription $40 (individual); $50 (institutions) (includes membership in NCTE)
National Council of Teachers of English
1111 W. Kenyon Road
Urbana, IL 61801–1906

By teachers for teachers in middle, junior, or senior high school, English Journal contains quality, thought-provoking articles about theory, practice, and new ideas in learning, reading, and writing in the classroom.

The Horn Book Magazine
6 issues per year/subscription $35 (individual); $42 (institutions)
11 Beacon Street, Suite 1000
Boston, MA 02108

For anyone interested in quality writing about books for children and young adults, The Horn Book Magazine provides the most complete, responsible, and thoughtful coverage. Contains reviews of children's and young adult titles; articles from and about authors and their work; articles on books from parallel cultures, using literature in the classroom, and many more topics of interest.

Journal of Reading
8 issues per year/subscription $38 (individual); $41 (institutions)
International Reading Association
800 Barksdale Road
PO Box 8139
Newark, DE 19714–8139

The audience is adolescent and adult-level teachers. Contains insights into theory, research findings, reviews of professional and adolescent books, and reviews of institutional materials.

• Language Arts
8 issues per year/subscription $40 (individual); $50 (institutions)
National Council of Teachers of English
1111 W. Kenyon Road
Urbana, IL 61801–1096

Theory and practice in language learning are combined with exceptional literary style in monthly themed journals. This official journal of NCTE (for the elementary grades) notes its new publications, forthcoming conferences, and reviews of children's and professional books.

Note that NCTE sponsors an annual conference in late November and a spring conference that focus on current professional issues. State and local affiliates also sponsor meetings of interest to English/language arts teachers at all levels. NCTE also publishes numerous professional publications for teachers.

Learning
8 issues per year/subscription $18
Learning Magazine
Education Center, Inc.
1607 Battleground Avenue
PO Box 9753
Greensboro, NC 27429

PO Box 2580
Boulder, CO 80322 (subscriptions)

This lively journal contains creative suggestions from teachers for teachers, practical applications for the classroom, activities, tips, and a reader exchange. For those interested in teaching K–8. Teachers new to the field should be aware that articles cover a broad spectrum from traditional to whole language approaches.

- **The New Advocate**
4 issues per year/subscription $27
The New Advocate
480 Washington Street
Norwood, MA 02062

Noted authors, illustrators, and educators share their perspectives on children's literature and related issues in this outstanding literary journal. Book and media reviews are included.

Phi Delta Kappan
10 issues per year/subscription $35
Eighth & Union
PO Box 789
Bloomington, IN 47402

Concerned with issues relating to leadership, research, trends, and policy, Phi Delta Kappan (named for the educational fraternity) is a must for those truly interested in what's happening in our schools today. Contains an annual Gallup poll of this country's attitude toward public schools.

- **Primary Voices K–6**
4 issues per year/subscription $15
National Council of Teachers of English
1111 W. Kenyon Road
Urbana, IL 61801 1096

This relatively new journal for teachers (first issue, April 1993) aims to explore current thinking in literacy education and to promote open discussion. Each themed issue is completely written and edited by outstanding educators of a "literacy community" who propose their topic of interest to NCTE. Some topics of past issues include: "Asking Questions/Making Meaning: Inquiry Based Instruction" (Fall 1992), "Making Meaning Through Writing: Writing to Learn" (August 1993), and "Challenge for Change: Theme Cycles" (January 1994). This is a terrific journal—extremely high level and practical with lots of clearly presented teaching strategies. Educators are encouraged to submit a proposal for a themed issue. Submission guidelines and back issues are available.

- **The Reading Teacher**
8 issues per year/subscription U.S. $38
International Reading Association (IRA)
800 Barksdale Road

PO Box 8139
Newark, DE 19714–8139

This practical journal for preschool and elementary teachers focuses on teaching approaches and techniques and also includes reviews of children's books, tests, and other teacher resources. Subscription includes "Reading Today," a bimonthly newspaper on news of the profession.

Note that IRA sponsors an annual conference, a World Congress, as well as state and local conferences; publishes professional publications and brochures for teachers and parents; and identifies and distributes "Children's Choices"—a yearly list of books children vote as their favorites.

Teaching K–8
8 issues per year/subscription $19.77
40 Richards Avenue
Norwalk, CT 06854 (correspondence)

PO Box 54805
Boulder, CO 80323 (subscriptions)

This publication, subtitled "The professional magazine for teachers," carries columns on reading, math, science, technology, professional growth, assessment, school and classroom libraries, parenting—all written by well-known educators. It carries ten reader exchange networks, such as Art Pals, Whole Language Network, Substitute Teachers Network, and Paraprofessionals Exchange. Each issue includes reports on innovative schools and teachers throughout the country, which the editors have personally visited. It also features a monthly personal interview with well-known authors and illustrators of children's books. Editorial content includes emphasis on multiage, whole language, integrated curriculum, and professional growth.

Voices from the Middle
4 issues per year/subscription $15
National Council of Teachers of English
1111 W. Kenyon Road
Urbana, IL 61801–1096

This excellent, new journal (first issue, Fall 1994) written by a team of experienced educators is both reflective and practical and is geared to upper elementary and middle school teachers of language *arts. Each issue focuses on a curricular topic or concept. In the first themed issue, "Students Responding to Literature," the teacher-authors invite you into their classrooms, and readers see the organization, planning, student work samples, and theory-into-practice teaching. Teachers will appreciate the rich descriptions of middle school classrom practices in this journal. Educators are encouraged to write for guidelines and submit a proposal for an issue in literacy education.*

Young Children
6 issues per year/subscription $25
National Association for the Education of Young Children
1509 16th Street, NW
Washington, DC 20036–1426

Early childhood educators will find this journal to be thought provoking, informative, and supportive in the area of professional growth. Major issues and ideas in the field are discussed. Contains such items as a calendar of conferences, book reviews, Washington public policy updates, and a section of reader commentary.

Newsletters/Other Periodicals

Book Links
bimonthly magazine/subscription $20
Booklist Publications
The American Library Association
50 E. Huron St.
Chicago, IL 60611

Aptly described by its subtitle, Connecting Books, Libraries, and Classrooms, *this bimonthly magazine is for teachers, librarians, parents, and anyone else who works with books and children. Each issue explores the connections between literature and the learning experience for children preschool to grade eight, and contains articles, recommended reading lists, and interviews that provide strategies for using books effectively in teaching.*

The Five Owls
5 bimonthly issues per year/subscription $20
The Five Owls, Inc.
Hamline University Crossroads Center
Mailing Code MS–C124

1536 Hewitt Avenue
St. Paul, MN 55104

This publication is intended for teachers, librarians, and parents interested in staying involved and current with the best of children's literature. Includes in-depth book reviews, practical ideas for using books with children, specialized bibliographies, and thoughtful articles, essays, and interviews.

The Kobrin Letter. Concerning Children's Books About Real People, Places and Things.
7 issues per year/subscription $12
The Kobrin Letter
732 Greer Road
Palo Alto, CA 94303

This is the only publication that deals exclusively with the review and recommendation of children's nonfiction. Two or three themes or topics are dealt with in each issue, and information from six to eight books per topic is included. For example, one issue dealt with "Trees" and "About AIDS" and included information from approximately six books for each topic.

Portfolio, The Newsletter of Arts PROPEL
[five back issues published from 1987–1989 (Vol. I, nos. 1–5)/$2 (nos. 1, 2, and 4); $2.25 (no. 3); $2.50 (no. 5)]
Harvard University
Graduate School of Education
Harvard Project Zero
323 Longfellow Hall, Appian Way
Cambridge, MA 02138

This outstanding, occasional newsletter of the Arts PROPEL project (the five-year collaborative effort that involved artists and researchers from Harvard Project Zero and Educational Testing Service, as well as students, teachers, and administrators from the Pittsburgh Public Schools) shares experiences from the project and offers insightful articles on creative approaches to learning and assessment and evaluation in middle and senior high school classrooms. Lots of terrific information on portfolio assessment.

Rethinking Schools
Rethinking Schools Limited
4 issues per year/subscription $12.50

1001 East Keefe Avenue
Milwaukee, WI 53212

Rethinking Schools *is a nonprofit, activist, independent newspaper published by Milwaukee-area teachers. This provocative, thoughtful publication focuses on local and national reform in urban elementary and secondary schools. Articles and issues connect classroom practice with broad policy issues and are written by educators from all over the country. Recent issues dealt with such topics as teaching for social justice, school choice in education, charter schools, the role of teachers' unions, multicultural videos and audiotapes, and funding education. This is an important publication for dealing with equity and social-justice issues in a forthright, constructive manner. Back issues and bibliographies are available.*

- **Teachers Networking: The Whole Language Newsletter**
4 issues per year/subscription $15 (U.S.); $18 (Canada)
For group membership at one address, each subscription over ten ordered is half price.
Richard C. Owen Publishers, Inc.
PO Box 585
Katonah, NY 10536

Features thought-provoking articles by leading whole language educators as well as reviews of professional and children's literature, issues of concern and interest to parents and educators, and a whole language calendar of upcoming conferences. A particularly well-done newsletter.

- **The WEB: Wonderfully Exciting Books**
3 issues per year/subscription $10
The Web, Ohio State University College of Education
200 Ramseyer Hall, 29 West Woodruff
Columbus, OH 43210–1177

Comprehensive book reviews, which include excellent teaching ideas, are presented by teachers and librarians. The center spread in each issue—a teaching web focusing on activities centered on a book, group of books, genre, or theme—is especially helpful for integrating literature across the curriculum. For more examples of well-done "webs," back issues of The WEB *are available for purchase.*

The Whole Idea
4 issues per year/subscription $12 (U.S.); $15 (Canada)
The Wright Group
19201 120th Ave NE
Bothell, WA 98011–9512

Practical articles, activities, and ideas for teachers interested in whole language. Includes ideas from practicing teachers as well as well-known educators. Very useful for the elementary classroom teacher.

Whole Language Special Interest Group of IRA Newsletter
2 issues per year with membership/$5 (U.S.)
WLSIG Newsletter
Margaret Y. Phinney
740 Cherokee Avenue
St. Paul, MN 55107

This thoughtfully literate newsletter has lead articles by well-known whole language educators as well as reprints of newsworthy articles about whole language. Also includes news of the teaching profession as related to whole language, reviews of recent whole language materials, and a calendar of future events.

The Whole Language Umbrella Newsletter
4 issues per year/subscription included with membership in the Whole Language Umbrella, a confederation of Whole Language support groups and individuals ($25 U.S. member; $30 Canadian member per year). Group memberships ($25 U.S. or $30 Canadian plus $1 either per member) include 5 subscriptions, additional subscriptions $3 U.S. or $3.25 Canadian.

The Whole Language Umbrella
Membership Office
PO Box 2029
Bloomington, IN 47402–2029

The newsletter describes the activities and business of the Whole Language Umbrella, primarily helping whole language teachers and support groups to network with each other. Includes articles and news about whole language issues and teaching, information about other newsletters and support groups in the United

States and Canada, support group publications, and upcoming conferences, including the annual Whole Language Umbrella conference.

Literacy Extension Resources

Annotations with Vera Milz

The following resources are ones I, Vera Milz, and other teachers have found especially useful for supporting our teaching and professional growth. Resources in this section can be used to support the integration of the language arts across the curriculum. You will also find much information and many ideas for selecting, using, and responding to quality literature. For your easy reference, this edition of "Literacy Extension Resources" lists separate categories for assessment and evaluation, spelling, math, social studies, science, and author/illustrator. There is also a separate listing for parent resources to promote parent communication and education. Check with your school and public librarians, other teachers, local bookstores, and journals for additional, new, and updated resources for teaching. All resources listed are available in paperback unless otherwise noted.

American Library Association Publishing Services. 50 East Huron Street, Chicago, IL 60611.

> *Publishes professional books for teachers and librarians and* Booklinks *(see annotation, p. 58b). Some recent resources include* Against Borders: Promoting Books for a Multicultural World *by Hazel Rochman (1993),* Handbook for Storytellers *by Caroline Feller Bauer (1993),* The Newbery and Caldecott Award: A Guide to the Medal and Honor Books *(1993, continually updated),* Mock Newbery and Caldecott Election Kit *by Kathleen Staerkel, Linda Callaghan, Nancy Hackett, and Susan Reisner,* Genre Favorites for Young Adults *by Sally Estes (ed.), and* Venture into Cultures: A Resource Book of Multicultural Material and Programs, *edited by Carla Hayden (1992). Because neither Heinemann nor I was able to obtain review copies from ALA, I was unable to read and review these titles.*

Bare Books. 1987. Racine, WI: Treetop Publishing.

> *Publishes reasonably priced blank books (about $1 each) and sturdy line guides for writing in the blank books. Each* Bare Book *contains twenty-eight blank white pages and a hard cover that measures 6 3/8 by 8 1/8 inches. Minimum order ten books. Adds a nice touch for special projects.*

Baskwill, Jane, and Steve Baskwill. 1991. *Language Arts Sourcebook: Grades 5 & 6.* Richmond Hill, Ontario: Scholastic Canada. (hardbound)

> *Four themes and accompanying four week plans for "In the Days of the Knights," "Imagine That," "Take Flight," and "The Sea" make up the major part of this resource. I found the section on routines, which includes minidemonstration routines and activity routines, especially helpful and applicable across the elementary grades. See also* Language Arts Sourcebook: Grades 3–4 *(1988) and* Language Arts Sourcebook: Grades 1–2 *(1986). Three-ring binder format. Expensive.*

• Bauer, Marion Dane. 1992. *What's Your Story? A Young Person's Guide to Writing Fiction.* New York: Clarion.

> *Written for upper elementary and middle school students, this terrific book lets young writers "inside" the fiction writing process. Well-known author Marion Bauer gives a wealth of specific, workable suggestions for getting and developing ideas for stories, for creating realistic characters, and for writing a satisfying story from beginning to end. I plan to lend this book to students who show promise and interest in fiction writing. Bauer's book will also enable me to do a better job teaching fiction writing, a difficult genre for many students.*

Beaty, Janice J. 1994. *Picture Book Storytelling: Literature Activities for Young Children.* Fort Worth, TX: Harcourt Brace.

> *This is a delightful book filled with ways to bring young children and picture books together. Nearly 200 picture books are described, along with ways to extend the enjoyment with songs, projects, and games. Many suggestions are given to enhance*

the presentation of the books through storytelling, and the books are categorized into themes such as dinosaurs, food, space, families, and beauty. A feature I especially enjoyed was the "Authors of Interest" statements scattered throughout the book. Interesting facts about authors and illustrators were given that I could take back to my classroom to share with my students. (V.M.)

• Benedict, Susan, and Lenore Carlisle (eds.). 1992. *Beyond Words: Picture Books for Older Readers and Writers*. Portsmouth, NH: Heinemann.

As an adult reader, I have always loved picture books. It always seemed a shame to hear a librarian label them "baby" books, and encourage children to move on to chapter books. This book is an especially welcome addition to my professional library as it eloquently argues that picture books belong to all ages. Within its pages, teachers of various grade levels show how they use picture books in their reading/writing programs. Several authors and illustrators provide a glimpse into their creative worlds, while two teenage writers detail how they use picture books to enhance their own writing processes. This is an especially helpful resource for teachers of older students, but there are plenty of ideas for every grade level. (V.M.)

Bishop, Rudine Sims (ed.). 1994. *Kaleidoscope: A Multicultural Booklist for Grades K–8*. Urbana, IL: National Council of Teachers of English.

Over 400 books published between 1990 and 1992 explore the lives of people of color, primarily African-Americans, Asian-Americans, Hispanic Americans/Latinos, and Native Americans. Books are grouped and annotated by genre or theme rather than by cultural group and include nonfiction, fiction, picture books, poetry, biography, folktales, myths, and legends. Indexes and multicultural resources are particularly helpful for developing teaching units and locating specific books.

• Blatt, Gloria T. (ed.). 1993. *Once upon a Folktale: Capturing the Folklore Process with Children*. New York: Teachers College Press.

Outstanding contributors—such as Bette Bosma, Patricia Cianciolo, Eric Kimmel, and Margaret Read MacDonald—share how they use folklore to engage and educate children. Folklore, the oldest form of literature, relishes the oral tradition and is the telling of old fairy tales, myths, rhymes, jingles, family stories, urban stories. Believing that, through folklore, we understand literature, and that "folklore fits the intellectual and emotional development of children" (p. 5), the authors give a convincing rationale and a myriad of possibilities for using folklore in the classroom, the home, and the community. Bibliographies of folklore materials are included. Terrific ideas and plans for the classroom.

Bohning, Gerry, Ann Phillips, and Sandra Bryant. 1993. *Literature on the Move: Making and Using Pop-Up and Lift-Flap Books*. Englewood, CO: Teacher Ideas Press.

This resource book offers guidelines for making eight basic pop-up and lift-flap action books, along with numerous variations for you to try with your students. The last part of the book offers many creative ideas that teachers can use to develop thematic units. They are organized by topic and include children's books, as well as springboards for reading/writing projects. Some of the topics are biographies, animals, holidays, sports, and transportation. The directions are so simple and well-written that I have been able to put the book out in my second-grade classroom as an idea book for children to use as they "publish" their stories. (V.M.)

Bosma, Bette. 1992. *Fairy Tales, Fables, Legends, and Myths: Using Folk Literature in Your Classroom*. 2nd ed. New York: Teachers College Press.

For the elementary and intermediate levels, this useful resource can be used to heighten children's awareness of and appreciation for folk literature. Four types of folktales—fairy tales, animal tales, legends, and myths—are explained and elaborated upon. Suggested activities include involving students in reading, writing, storytelling, dramatizing, improvising, and *illustrating folktales. This second edition includes new information on multicultural folktales and an extensive bibliography of recommended folk literature with annotations for 180 books. Lots of ideas and lesson plans for developing units on folk literature are included.*

Brinkerhoff, Stevie Auld. 1993. *Linking: Developing Strategic Readers and Writers in the Primary Classroom.* Grand Rapids, MI: Michigan Reading Association (P.O. Box 7509, 49510).

In an easy-to-read, personal tone, Brinkerhoff and colleagues have put together a useful, eighty-page spiral-bound booklet to help teachers "make the transition from teaching skills to teaching with a strategy focus." Building on the work of Marie Clay and other practitioners, Brinkerhoff discusses and demonstrates early reading strategies in a manner that is helpful and specific to early primary grade teachers.

Bromley, Karen. 1993. *Journaling: Engagements in Reading, Writing, and Thinking.* New York: Scholastic Professional Books.

An elementary teacher has compiled pre-K through high school teachers' experiences using many different types of journals to suggest ways to build a journal-writing program. Some of the journals that are described are the buddy journal, learning log, double-entry journal, home-school journal, writer's journal, and daily group journal. Especially useful to teachers who are new to journal writing and to those looking for fresh ideas. Many examples from student journals are provided.

Bryant, Patricia, and Luceille Werner (compilers). 1992. *Reading and Writing . . . Can Be a Child's Talk Written Down.* Updated ed. Peotone, IL: Early Prevention of School Failure.

Written to assist kindergarten and first-grade teachers to connect reading and writing through language experience and whole language approaches, this sourcebook is full of activities, thematic ideas, and projects for teachers who want to move away from programs and worksheets. Lots of photographs and visuals make the book a functional resource.

Canavan, Diane D., and LaVonne H. Sanborn. 1992. *Using Children's Books in Reading/Language Arts Programs: A How-To-Do-It Manual for School and Public Libraries.* New York: Neal-Schuman Publishers.

The authors have selected quality trade books to use in the K–8 reading program. Sections include many titles and annotations of books for developing beginning reading, vocabulary through word play, text comprehension, language concepts, and literary awareness. This 216-page resource is particularly helpful for teachers moving towards a literature approach. Lots of ideas for using children's books.

Chatton, Barbara. 1993. *Using Poetry Across the Curriculum: A Whole Language Approach.* Phoenix, AZ: Oryx Press.

This amazing reference shows teachers how to integrate poetry across the curriculum. Two thematic units, "Eats" and "Conversation," are given for use in the classroom. Each is filled with suggested poems, books, activities, and projects. Although the purpose of the book is to cross curricular lines, for convenience, most of the chapters have been arranged by content areas, such as science, mathematics, social studies, language arts, health, and music. Each chapter is further divided by subject with many poems listed, along with bibliographic information to help you locate the appropriate poem. The index in the back of the book is invaluable in locating a particular poem, or the work of a certain poet. (V.M.)

The Children's Book Council, Inc. 568 Broadway, New York, NY 10012.

Publishes a newsletter with information about children's books, book publishers, and inexpensive publishers' materials. Sells pamphlets, posters, and bookmarks that support reading and writing; sponsors an annual Children's Book Week and distributes accompanying materials. Distributes annually: "Children's Choices" (a yearly selection of newly published books that children prefer), "Outstanding Science Tradebooks for Children" (first published in spring issue of Science and Children), and "Notable Children's Trade Books in the Field of Social Studies" (first published in spring issue of Social Education).

Cole, Joanna (compiler). 1989. *Anna Banana: 101 Jump-Rope Rhymes,* illustrated by Alan Tiegreen. New York: Morrow Junior Books. (Beech Tree Paperback)

Traditional jump-rope rhymes are great for shared reading and chanting in the classroom and on the playground. Students can also be encouraged to write their own jump-rope rhymes. Sources for finding additional jump-rope rhymes are included.

Cullinan, Bernice E. (ed.). 1993. *Children's Voices: Talk in the Classroom; Fact and Fiction: Literature Across the Curriculum;* and *Pen in Hand: Children Become Writers.* Newark, DE: International Reading Association.

Noting that children's literature is now widely used in classrooms, these three slim volumes with contributions by notable educators give suggestions and examples for meaningfully connecting literature with reading-writing-speaking processes. Some of the many activities that are discussed are literature circles, storytelling, creative drama (in Children's Voices), literature in the science and math program, nonfiction in the social studies program, diversity education (in Fact and Fiction), literature and children's writing, reading assessment through written response, and writing nonfiction (in Pen in Hand). An excellent, practical resource for teachers.

Cutting, Brian. 1990. *Getting Started in Whole Language.* Bothell, WA: The Wright Group.

This is an excellent, all-purpose, highly practical resource (120 pp.) to see, feel, and read about how a whole language classroom looks and functions. Although this resource is based on the commercially produced "Sunshine Books," the verbal and visual examples for shared reading experiences, writing connections, language experiences, paired reading, independent reading, scheduling, and evaluation are very useful to any K–1 teacher interested in whole language.

Cutting, Brian, with Helen Dupree. 1988. *Language Is Fun: Teacher's Book.* Level 2. Bothell, WA: The Wright Group.

This practical collection of ideas for K–2 whole language classrooms extends to drama, art, and literature. Particularly useful are the colorful photographs and samples of children's work from New Zealand classrooms. While many of the literature extension ideas stem from specific books in a reading series, ideas on the resource's theme "I Can . . ." are applicable across the curriculum.

Danielson, Kathy Everts, and Jan LaBonty. 1994. *Integrating Reading and Writing Through Children's Literature.* Boston: Allyn and Bacon.

This 251-page resource focuses on ways to use literature in the integration of reading and writing. In addition to extensive children's literature bibliographies, the authors offer excellent background information on current views of reading and writing as well as many ideas and sample activities for using literature to enhance reading comprehension, responding to literature through writing, involving students with poetry, and dealing with skills and assessment. While some ideas for using the literature are overstructured and directive, teachers can choose the ones that suit their contexts. Especially helpful to teachers who are beginning to use literature as the mainstay of the reading/writing program and for teachers seeking additional ideas.

Davies, Anne, Colleen Politano, and Caren Cameron. 1993. *Making Themes Work: Building Connections.* Winnipeg, Manitoba: Peguis.

For teachers who want to promote learning through meaningful "themes" that capitalize on children's interests, this seventy-six page book is full of practical ideas for beginning, planning, exploring, and evaluating the thematic topic under discussion.

Day, Frances Ann (compiler). 1994. *Multicultural Voices in Contemporary Literature.* Portsmouth, NH: Heinemann.

Information about thirty-nine inspiring multicultural authors and illustrators, their noted works, and optional activities to go along with designated books are included in this comprehensive teacher reference. This is a great resource for planning author or illustrator units and for balancing the literature program with diversity. Also, teachers who struggle with ways to meaningfully extend the literature will find excellent models in the suggested optional activities.

Doiron, Ray. May 1994. "Using Nonfiction in a Read-Aloud Program: Letting the Facts Speak for Themselves." *The Reading Teacher*, pp. 616–624.

Because fiction predominates in the selections teachers make for read-aloud and discussion books in the classroom, this is an important article for balancing our literacy programs. In addition to presenting a convincing case for reading more nonfiction, Doiron provides a starter, annotated bibliography of nonfiction read-alouds.

Eisele, Beverly. 1991. *Managing the Whole Language Classroom: A Complete Teaching Resource Guide for K–6 Teachers*. Cypress, CA: Creative Teaching Press.

If you are a teacher who is just beginning to move to a whole language philosophy, you will enjoy this "how-to" book. It contains basic information on creating a classroom environment, suggestions for professional development, ideas for scheduling the school day, ways to plan instruction, ways to organize classroom materials and supplies, how to evaluate, and ways to inform parents and colleagues. There are lots of guides and forms that can be adapted for classroom use. Very well illustrated and teacher friendly! (V.M.)

Fairfax, Barbara, and Adela Garcia. 1992. *Read! Write! Publish! Making Books in the Classroom Grades 1–5*. Cypress, CA: Creative Teaching Press.

Materials, techniques, and directions are given for making all kinds of books. Teachers looking for creative ways for children to publish will find many clearly written and illustrated ideas that are easy to put into practice.

Fox, Carol, and Margery Sauer. 1989. *Celebrate Literature*. Logan, IA: The Perfection Form Company.

These spiral-bound, comprehensive resource books for each grade level from kindergarten through grade six promote the use of a literature curriculum. Each literature unit is presented by genre—poetry, picture books, traditional literature, fiction, nonfiction, biography—and includes goals and objectives, background information, author study, featured books and resources, lots of student activities, and evaluation activities. Lots of good ideas for the classroom teacher.

Freeman, Evelyn B., and Diane Goetz Person (eds.). 1992. *Using Nonfiction Trade Books in the Elementary Classroom: From Ants to Zeppelins*. Urbana, IL: National Council of Teachers of English.

Informational books are highlighted in this fine collection of articles in which the genre itself is explained, its place in the elementary curriculum is considered, and strategies to use it in the classroom are given. Several award-winning authors, such as Russell Freedman and Patricia Lauber, reflect on their experiences in writing nonfiction. In other chapters, practitioners share how these books are used in their classrooms. The index of titles and authors is helpful in locating a particular book on a topic your class is studying. A listing of Nonfiction Book Awards is useful in finding the highest quality books of this genre. (V.M.)

- Gilles Carol, Mary Bixby, Paul Crowley, et al. (eds.). 1988. *Whole Language Strategies for Secondary Students*. Katonah, NY: Richard C. Owen.

This 208-page resource is very useful to the middle school and secondary teacher wishing to understand and apply whole language teaching strategies in the classroom. The first section of the book lays the theoretical foundation for whole language. The second section consists of specific strategy lessons from whole language classrooms that tie theory and practice together. Each full-page strategy lesson contains the rationale for the lesson, specific procedures, and extensions and variations on the lesson. Strategy lessons encompass literature, the content areas, reading and writing, computers, and other areas.

Goforth, Frances S., and Carolyn V. Spillman. 1994. *Using Folk Literature in the Classroom: Encouraging Children to Read and Write.* Phoenix, AZ: Oryx Press.

This book was written for teachers to encourage children to make connections with literature and respond to it. The first two chapters provide a background for the study of folk literature, and the theoretical base for the literary transaction process. The remaining chapters present summaries of fifty-four stories and verses from twenty countries around the world. The stories are organized by thematic units, such as magical animals, overcoming odds, special gifts, and many more, along with instructional strategies and activities. As I looked over this book, some of the tales were familiar, but many were new to me. This is definitely a book that will stretch your knowledge of folk literature, and expand your use of it in the classroom. (V.M.)

Green, Joseph. 1993. *The Word Wall: Teaching Vocabulary Through Immersion.* Markham, Ontario: Pippin Publishing, and Portsmouth, NH: Heinemann.

A sixth-grade classroom teacher tells how a Word Wall, initially posted for room decoration, became the focus of his curriculum and a terrific way to expand students' vocabulary. Green describes how he uses Word Walls as a daily tool for teaching phonics, grammar, spelling, new vocabulary and as a thesaurus and spell-check. Some teachers will find the approach too structured, but most will be able to meaningfully adapt ideas to their own contexts. Applicable to elementary and secondary classrooms.

Green, Pamela. 1992. *A Matter of Fact: Using Factual Texts in the Classroom.* Winnipeg, Manitoba: Peguis (distributors).

This theory-into-practice book is for the primary-grades teacher who wants students to read and write competently in a range of factual genres such as reports, descriptions, explanations, and procedural texts. Lots of classroom-created charts and children's work samples included. Applicable to the intermediate grades.

Hall, Susan. 1990, 1994. *Using Picture Storybooks to Teach Literary Devices: Recommended Books for Children and Young Adults.* Volumes 1 and 2. Phoenix, AZ: Oryx Press.

The primary purpose for a picture book must always remain in the pleasure of its reading, but, in addition, older students can begin to utilize these books to enhance their own writing skill. These two books are very useful in locating literary elements used by various authors, such as flashback, inference, irony, simile, metaphor, and others. Each reference contains actual quotes from the cited picture book, and is cross-referenced to other devices that the author uses. In volume 2, the author also shows how students can learn to appreciate the color, power, and nuances of picture book art while learning about literary devices. (V.M.)

• Hamilton, Martha, and Mitch Weiss. 1990. *Children Tell Stories: A Teaching Guide.* Katonah, NY: Richard C. Owen.

The authors, professional storytellers, demonstrate how to teach children to tell stories—especially simple folktales—and to make storytelling an essential part of the curriculum. The benefits of storytelling by children, including improvement in self-esteem, expressive language skills, group dynamics, and new learnings, are convincing. Many exercises and strategies for teaching children all aspects of storytelling are clearly delineated. Handouts for students and parents, as well as extensive bibliographies, are included. The book is so well organized and specific, you will feel storytelling is possible and desirable for your classroom. An outstanding resource for all grade levels.

Hart-Hewins, Linda, and Jan Wells. 1992. *Read It in the Classroom: Organizing an Interactive Language Arts Program, Grades 4–9.* Portsmouth, NH: Heinemann.

This little handbook is designed to help teachers incorporate literature into their reading programs. Guidance for theme development, related books, ways of organizing the classroom, and record-keeping forms are given. A series of bibliog-

raphies list books that can be used to focus on a particular topic. The suggestions can be easily adapted to younger or older students. (V.M.)

Heller, Ruth. 1991. *Up, Up and Away: A Book About Adverbs.* New York: Grosset & Dunlap. (Sandcastle)

This gorgeous picture book uses playful, rhymed text to introduce students to adverbs. A wonderful resource for sensitizing students in the intermediate grades and beyond to the interesting use of adverbs. See other equally engaging, language concept/vocabulary books by Ruth Heller: A Cache of Jewels and Other Collective Nouns *and* Many Luscious Lollipops: A Book About Adjectives.

Hill, Susan. 1993. *Jump for Joy: More Raps & Rhymes.* Winnipeg, Manitoba: Peguis.

Hill has selected raps, chants, and rhymes for reading aloud, having fun, and building group cohesion in the classroom. Builds on her earlier Raps & Rhymes *(Peguis, 1990).*

Hill, Susan. 1992. *Readers Theatre: Performing the Text.* Winnipeg, Manitoba: Peguis (distributors).

Hill gives lots of examples on how to bring poems, picture books, and stories to life through Readers Theatre (see Invitations, p. 98). Useful for getting more oral language, drama, and performance of texts into the primary classroom.

Hurst, Carol Otis. 1990. *Once Upon a Time . . .: An Encyclopedia for Successfully Using Literature with Young Children.* Allen, TX: DLM. (hardbound)

This comprehensive, spiral-bound resource (370 pp., 8½ by 11 inches) by a highly knowledgeable children's librarian is written and compiled to assist teachers who don't have time to research authors, illustrators, and themes. The book is well organized into four sections: "Authors and Illustrators," "Individual Picture Books," "Themes," and "Special Pages." Each prominent author and illustrator listing (there are about forty-five) includes a mailing address (when available), biography, books published, awards received, relevant topics to "notice and talk about," and activity ideas for selected books. The "Special Pages" section includes annotated listings of patterned books, wordless books, Big Books, whole language and children's literature resource books, poetry resources, children's records and tapes, children's magazines, books about color, math, social studies, science, the seasons, and more. A wealth of valuable and useful information. Expensive.

Irvine, Joan. 1992. *How to Make Super Pop-Ups.* New York: Morrow Junior Books.

For teachers who are interested in making different types of pop-up books, this resource gives easy-to-follow instructions with clear illustrations. The book includes needed materials, directions for cutting, folding, and measuring and many examples of pop-up projects. See also, How to Make Pop-Ups (1987).

Jenkins, Esher C., and Mary C. Austin. 1987. *Literature for Children About Asians and Asian Americans: Analysis and Annotated Bibliography, with Additional Readings for Adults.* New York: Greenwood Press.

Although this text has not been updated, it is still the most comprehensive resource for books by and about Asians (as of 1994), and therefore, it is included. In addition to recommended literature, the book includes criteria for selecting books for a cross-cultural curriculum.

Jensen, Julie M., and Nancy L. Roser (eds.). 1993. *Adventuring With Books: A Booklist for Pre-K–Grade 6.* 10th ed. Urbana, IL: National Council of Teachers of English.

Nearly 1800 annotations of books published between 1988 and 1992 are included in this latest edition. The book is designed to help anyone introducing books to children to choose those of literary and artistic merit, and it is a sampling of the over 20,000 books actually published during that period. The introduction is especially interesting as the editors note their observations of current trends in the publishing field. The annotations are grouped under headings, such as Celebrations, Sciences and Mathematics, Historical Fiction, Poetry, and more. In addition, the book has a listing of selected literary *awards, publishers' addresses, and descriptions of popular booklists. (V.M.)*

Johnson, Paul. 1992. *A Book of One's Own: Developing Literacy Through Making Books.* Portsmouth, NH: Heinemann.

For a very complete look at every stage of the book-creating process, you will want to check this book. It has everything from simple folded-paper books to hardcover, bound books. There are lots of examples and step-by-step instructions for you to make books with your students. Every classroom publishing center needs one. (V.M.)

Johnson, Paul. 1993. *Literacy Through the Book Arts.* Portsmouth, NH: Heinemann.

With paper, pens, and a pair of scissors, you can learn over fifty ways to make a book. Johnson believes that children can combine writing and visual communication through the book arts, and this book is filled with examples of wonderful student creations. Two basic books are explained in detail, along with many variations: the Concertina from China, and Origami from Japan. No matter what grade you teach, there are plenty of ideas to get your students started on creating unique books to share their writings. (V.M.)

Kaufman, Ronne L. (executive ed.). 1990. *Innovations: Teaching with Literature in the Classroom.* New York: Scholastic.

Lesson plan guides have been developed to go along with quality books such as The Hundred Dresses *by Eleanor Estes,* Nettie's Trip South *by Ann Turner, and* Lon Po Po *by Ed Young. Each guide (there are about fifty available) includes a story overview, information about the genre and the author/illustrator, and many suggested activities for reading and reacting to the book. While there are too many activities suggested, teachers can choose the ones that will work best for them.*

Kenney, Anne, Lori Morgan, Jane Owen, Chris Sherman, and Russell Walsh (team leaders). 1992. *Teens' Favorite Books: Young Adults' Choices 1987–1992.* Newark, DE: International Reading Association.

For anyone looking to choose a high-interest book for a teenager, this useful re-source includes descriptions of over 100 books for young adult readers that are grouped by subject. For recommended books for children aged 4–13, see Kids' Favorite Books: Children's Choices 1989–1991, *also published by the International Reading Association.*

• King, Laurie, and Dennis Stovall. 1992. *Classroom Publishing: A Practical Guide to Enhancing Student Literacy.* Hillsboro, OR: Blue Heron. (Also available from the International Reading Association.)

This magnificent guide to publishing for grades K–12 is one you will not want to miss. It is packed with practical information and limitless possibilities for publishing. The first section of this 224-page guide, "Tales from the Classroom," contains rich examples and successful publishing stories from teachers in diverse K–12 classrooms. The second section, "Publishing: Who, What, When, Where, Why & How," contains a history of modern publishing, a description of how it's done, career options, how to get funding for student projects, and legal and social issues of publishing. The last section of the book, "Resources," provides detailed lists and addresses of contests, publishing programs, markets for young writers, and an extensive bibliography of sources of further information. Even if you are an experienced writing/publishing teacher, you will find inspiration, new ideas, and much to apply in your own classroom from this fascinating, useful resource.

Kruse, Ginny Moore, and Kathleen T. Horning. 1991. *Multicultural Literature for Children and Young Adults.* 3rd ed. University of Wisconsin-Madison: Cooperative Children's Book Center.

Summaries and publishing information of carefully selected literature by and about African-Americans, American Indians, Asian-Americans, and Hispanic Americans make up this notable bibliography. Books are grouped in sixteen broad categories, such as "History, People and Places," "Seasons and Celebrations," "Issues in Today's World," "Biographies," and "Fiction for Teenagers." Appendices include authors and illustrators of color, a listing of the titles categorized by ethnic or cultural groups, annotations of recommended resources, and a public policy statement.

Larrick, Nancy. 1991. *Let's Do a Poem! Introducing Poetry to Children.* New York: Delacorte Press.

This is a handbook with many ideas for bringing poetry and children together. Complete poems are found in each chapter, along with suggestions for movement, music, drama, and pantomime. I especially like the author's suggestions for interactive reading between two or more children. A list of poetry books, by the poets whose works are cited in the book, is found in the back, along with indexes by author, title, subject, and first lines of the poem. This is a valuable resource for teachers who want their students to come to love the sound and feel of poetry. You'll never just "read" a poem again after reading this book. (V.M.)

• Ledoux, Denis. 1993. *Turning Memories into Memoirs: A Handbook for Writing Lifestories.* Lisbon Falls, ME: Soleil Press, and Portsmouth, NH: Heinemann.

Noting the importance of story for entertainment, reassurance, and making meaning, Ledoux encourages us to connect with our own lifestories and write them down. The step-by-step strategies and exercises that are demonstrated make it possible for us and our students to write successful lifestories from our family histories. An intriguing book!

Levine, Michael. 1993. *The Address Book: How to Reach Anyone Who Is Anyone.* 6th ed. New York: Putnam.

This book is continually updated to provide current mailing addresses of thousands of interesting and famous people and organizations. Teachers and students find this a motivating letter-writing resource for the writing classroom. See also Levine's The Environmental Address Book *and* The Kid's Address Book.

Lipson, Eden Ross. 1991. *The New York Times Parent's Guide to Children's Books.* New York: Random House.

This guide of "best books" published in the United States has been written "to help you look for the next book to give to your favorite child." Many book titles, accompanied by brief descriptions, are listed alphabetically by title in each of the following categories: wordless books, picture books, story books, early reading books, middle reading books, and young adult books. Thirty-four indexes allow looking up books in multiple ways. Preschool through middle school (through grade nine) teachers will find this a useful reference to share with parents.

Lynch-Brown, Carol, and Carl M. Tomlinson. 1993. *Essentials of Children's Literature.* Needham Heights, MA: Allyn and Bacon.

This is a wonderful resource text (350 pp.) for learning about and using children's trade books in the classroom and for planning literature units. Lots of background information and recommendations are provided for notable poetry books, picture books, traditional literature, science fiction, realistic fiction, nonfiction, multicultural literature, and authors in various genres. Appendices include an extensive listing of award-winning books, popular children's magazines, and professional resources. A wealth of information for K–8 teachers using a literature approach is provided in this practical, readable text.

McClure, Amy A., and Janice V. Cristo (eds.). 1994. *Inviting Children's Responses to Literature: Guides to 57 Notable Books.* Urbana, IL: National Council of Teachers of English.

Teachers who move to a literature approach and feel they are not doing enough with a book will feel comforted by the solid, yet minimalist, activities included in this resource. Each brief book guide includes suggested grade levels, a plot summary, teaching suggestions, and related books. The "Introduction" and the guides provide rationale and ideas for deepening readers' responses to text through conversation, reading, writing, and listening.

Macon, James M., Diane Bewell, and Mary-Ellen Vogt. 1991. *Responses to Literature Grades K–8.* Newark, DE: International Reading Association.

For teachers who have moved, or are moving, to using a literature approach and trade books as the foundation of the language arts program, this twenty-nine page booklet provides specific support on how to respond meaningfully to literature. The authors discuss theories of response to literature, engagement activities, and management issues. Teachers will appreciate and use the sample writing activities that are included.

Miller-Lachmann, Lynn. 1992. *Our Family, Our Friends, Our World: An Annotated Guide to Significant Multicultural Books for Children and Teenagers.* New Providence, NJ: R.R. Bowker. (hardbound)

This extensive reference text (710 pages) provides a critical bibliography and reference guide for multicultural fiction and nonfiction for children and young adults. Acknowledging that "many of the best multicultural works have shortcomings and blind spots" the authors point out the biases and inaccuracies in these texts so that "with the help of sensitive adults, young people will learn to read critically and to look behind stereotypes to the richness, diversity, and universal elements within each culture" (xi). A wealth of information that is helpful to any educator involved in selecting multicultural books for purchase or use.

Moir, Hughes, Melissa Cain, and Leslie Prosak-Beres (eds.). 1992. *Collected Perspectives: Choosing and Using Books for the Classroom.* 2nd ed. Norwood, MA: Christopher-Gordon.

Over 1000 children's books written between 1984 and 1990 are reviewed in depth in this book. Curriculum suggestions, related books on similar topics, and resources are given for each book. The books are organized according to audience and genre, and an extensive subject index will be very useful for thematic study planning. This is a book written by educators who work daily with children, and their suggestions are very useful to busy teachers. Though the book is expensive for a teacher to purchase singly, it is well worth requesting as an addition to the school library, or asking colleagues to go together to purchase a copy for shared use. (V.M.)

Monson, Dianne (project chair). 1994. *Teachers' Favorite Books for Kids: Teachers' Choices 1989–1993.* Newark, DE: International Reading Association.

This annotated list of more than 150 books of high literary quality for K–8 classrooms is a great guide for selecting and using outstanding books. "These are books that might not be discovered or fully appreciated by children without introduction by a knowledgeable adult." A fine source for families too. (IRA also publishes Children's Choices and Young Adults' Choices.)

Morgan, Norah, and Juliana Saxton. 1991. *Teaching, Questioning and Learning.* London and New York: Routledge.

This unique text offers elementary through postsecondary teachers models, techniques, activities and lots of detailed examples to promote relevant, appropriate, and substantial questioning in the classroom. The authors believe "effective teaching depends primarily upon the teacher's skill in being able to ask questions which generate different kinds of learning." They classify questions into three categories: questions that elicit information, questions that shape understanding, and questions that press for reflection, and then they demonstrate limitless possibilities within these categories. This practical text is particularly useful and specific for getting the language of good questioning into the classroom and for promoting effective classroom discourse.

Moss, Joy F. 1994. *Using Literature in the Middle Grades: A Thematic Approach.* Norwood, MA: Christopher-Gordon.

For use in reading-writing classrooms in grades 4–8, the author has developed integrated literature units (focus units) that are organized around a topic, genre, theme, or narrative element. Each focus unit includes a variety of related texts, reading experiences, dialogue groups, and responses. Complete, detailed plans and suggested activities are included. Some of *the focus units and chapters are: "Friend-ship Stories," "Modern Fairy Tales and Traditional Literature," "Internal Conflict in Realistic Fiction," "Family Stories," and "War and Peace: Historical Fiction and Non-fiction." Each chapter/focus unit ends with a literature bibliography. A terrific resource!*

Moss, Joy F. 1990. *Focus on Literature: A Context for Literacy Learning.* Katonah, NY: Richard C. Owen.

This practical text connects theory and practice and offers in-depth literature units around the following focuses: transforma-tion tales, Baba Yaga tales, devil tales, cat tales, magic object tales, bird tales, wish tales, horse tales, Cinderella tales. Each unit includes plans for daily sessions, meaningful literature extensions, and bib-liographies or tales.

NOVA Books. 1990. New York: Simon & Schuster.

Produced in association with the award-winning public television series "NOVA," these outstanding informational paperback science books on a variety of topics are a visual delight. All books include an index, and all are fascinating reading for inter-mediate grades upward.

• O'Toole, Mary. Illustrated by Ruth Moodie and Nel Pianta. 1993. *Relevant Reading Resources: Strategies for the Teaching of Reading.* Kew, Victoria, Australia: Yarra Publications; distributed in the U.S. by A.U.S.S.I.E. (Australian United States Services in Education, 1636 Third Ave-nue, #292, New York, NY 10128).

This remarkable resource offers a mul-titude of meaningful activities for creating a literary environment, reading to and with children, organizing a language pro-gram, developing positive reading attitudes, developing effective reading and learning strategies, and focusing on how texts work. Each page, which is packed with clearly written text supported by black-and-white illustrations, gives practical in-formation and many suggested teaching activities. Teachers will love all the won-derful ideas in this unique resource! Spiral bound.

• Peck, David. 1989. *Novels of Initiation: A Guidebook for Teaching Literature to Adolescents.* New York: Teachers College Press.

This excellent guidebook for secondary teachers contains analyses of twelve Ameri-can novels commonly read in secondary English classes. Each of these novels is connected by the theme of initiation, that is, the main characters move on a "peril-ous passage" from childhood to adulthood. Each chapter discusses a different novel and includes an analysis of the novel that encompasses story and setting, characters, themes, style, and language; teaching sug-gestions for discussion and writing; and other related literary works that can be used with the particular novel. The useful appendices list other American novels of initiation as well as other thematic unit possibilities with suggested novels to fit each theme.

Raffi. 1989. *The Raffi Everything Grows Song-book.* New York: Crown.

For early-childhood teachers who want to connect reading and singing, this spi-ral-bound book contains the printed music and words of fifteen songs to go along with Raffi's album Everything Grows. *See also* Raffi Songs to Read *for other materials on the singing-reading connection.*

Raines, Shirley C., and Robert J. Canady. 1989–1994. *Story S-T-R-E-T-C-H-E-R-S: Activities to Expand Children's Favorite Books.* Mt. Rainier, MD: Gryphon House.

Story S-T-R-E-T-C-H-E-R-S: Original Volume

More Story S-T-R-E-T-C-H-E-R-S

Story S-T-R-E-T-C-H-E-R-S for the Pri-mary Grades

450 More Story S-T-R-E-T-C-H-E-R-S for the Primary Grades

These four volumes contain exciting lists of children's books that could be used to build a literature program in early-child-hood through primary-grade classrooms. The first two books were especially writ-ten for preschool use, but many primary-grade teachers used them, and requested that the format be extended beyond first grade. The books are organized into themes such as friends, plants, science, seasons, environment, and multicultural concerns. Each cited book is summarized, and several pages of creative ideas to expand its enjoyment are listed from which teachers can pick and choose. These books are a helpful resource for lower-grade teachers who want to integrate learning across the curriculum. (V.M.)

Rasinski, Timothy V., and Cindy S. Gillespie. 1992. *Sensitive Issues: An Annotated Guide to Children's Literature K–6*. Phoenix, AZ: Oryx Press.

This is a fine reference book for teachers to find high-quality literature dealing with serious problems that children often must confront on a daily basis both in and out of school. Often I have found that when children read about someone dealing with a similar problem to their own, it can help them to begin to work through it themselves. Books and possible activities are listed for topics such as substance abuse, death, divorce, cultural differences, relocation, and nontraditional home environments. (V.M.)

Rhodes, Lynn K. (ed.). *LINK PAKS*. 1986 1994. Lakewood, CO: LINK, the Language Company.

A LINK (Language Instruction Natural to Kids) PAK includes meaningful activities to go along with a quality title for pre-K through grade seven as well as a copy of the designated book. Some suggested activities include reading and comparing other versions and other related books, and writing as a response to reading. LINK also publishes guidelines for creating your own book units.

Roettger, Doris. 1986–1992. *BOOK PROS*. Johnson, IA: Heartland Area Education Agency.

Teaching guides for notable picture story books and novels are available for kindergarten through upper elementary grades. Each guide is teacher developed and describes activities to do before reading, during reading, and after reading. These guides are helpful in the transition process to a literature program. Many activities are suggested, so you will need to be selective to keep the focus on enjoying and appreciating the literature.

Roettger, Doris. 1988–1993. *Reading Beyond the Basal Plus*. Logan, IA: Perfection Learning.

Teacher resource guides for novels for upper elementary and middle school levels. Teacher- and student-tried suggestions to involve students in using their own experiences to better understand the concepts and ideas in the story, keeping a journal, exploring the use of language, critical thinking, drama and oral language activities, exploring an author's writing styles, authentic writing activities, and exploring across-the-curriculum activities. Author information and an annotated bibliography are also included.

Sharkey, Paulette Bochnig, and Jim Roginski (eds.). 1992. *Newbery and Caldecott Medal and Honor Books in Other Media*. New York: Neal-Schuman Publishers. (hardbound)

"For librarians, teachers, and parents, this is the place to find the answer to the question, 'What filmstrips, posters, videos, etc., have been made from this Newbery/Caldecott book, or about its author or illustrator?'" (ix). Appendices in this 143-page volume include "Newbery Medal and Honor Books, 1922–1992," "Caldecott Medal and Honor Books 1938–1992," "Bibliography of Resources," "Directory of Media Producers and Distributors," and a "List of Titles by Media Formats."

Slapin, Beverly, and Doris Seale (eds.). 1992. *Through Indian Eyes: The Native Experience in Books for Children*. 3rd ed. Philadelphia, and Gabriole Island, British Columbia: New Society Publishers.

This 312-page resource on Native Americans includes texts written by Native Americans about the Native American experience. This is an excellent book for sensitizing non–Native Americans to Native American issues and points of view and for selecting materials that represent Native Americans accurately. At the heart of the book are "Book Reviews" that point out what is accurate and inaccurate to the Native culture. While my sensitivity to how

Indians are represented in literature has been greatly heightened through this text, note that parts of some book reviews seem overly emotional.

Slaughter, Judith Pollard. 1993. *Beyond Storybooks: Young Children and the Shared Book Experience.* Newark, DE: International Reading Association.

Giving credit to Don Holdaway's original work in shared-book experiences in New Zealand, detailed in his book The Foundations of Literacy *(Sydney: Ashton Scholastic, 1979), Slaughter suggests many ways to make and introduce Big Books and to use shared-book experiences across the curriculum. An excellent resource for teachers new to shared-book experience as well as those looking for additional teaching ideas.*

Smith, Jennifer. February 1988. "Periodicals That Publish Children's Original Work." *Language Arts*, pp. 202–208.

This informative journal article features twenty-two children's magazines that publish children's original writings and art work. Magazines cited are easily accessible and intended for children preschool through grade six. Information for each magazine listed includes the title, address, subscription price, frequency of publication, intended audience, and type of material accepted from children.

Stoll, Donald R. (ed.). 1994. *Magazines for Kids and Teens: A Resource for Parents, Teachers, Librarians, and Kids!* Glassboro, NJ: Educational Press Association of America, and Newark, DE: International Reading Association.

This publication alphabetically includes entries for 249 magazines for preschool through secondary age/grade levels. Each entry includes the goals and philosophy of the magazine, its subject matter, intended audience, whether or not readers' work is published, circulation, and complete publishing/ordering information. An introduction by Bernice Cullinan gives a rationale and suggestions for using magazines in the classroom and at home. Indexes include an age/grade level index, a subject index that lists magazines by topics, and maga-

zines that publish readers' work. Be sure to take advantage of all the sources that welcome and publish student writing. You and your students may first want to write to order sample copies of these appealing magazines. A great resource!

Sweet, Anne P. 1993. *State of the Art: Transforming Ideas for Teaching and Learning to Read.* Washington, DC: United States Department of Education. (Available in packages of 25 from Superintendent of Documents, P.O. Box 371954, Pittsburgh, PA 15250)

This eighteen-page booklet on effective reading instruction is organized into ten interrelated ideas "for transforming the teaching and learning of reading." Ideal to give to teachers, parents, administrators, and policymakers to promote understanding of reading as a strategic and meaning-constructing process.

Thomas, Rebecca. 1993. *Primaryplots 2: A Book Talk Guide for Use with Readers Ages 4–8.* New Providence, NJ: R.R. Bowker. (hardbound)

Thomas focuses in depth on 150 exemplary picture books published between 1988 and 1992. The book is organized into eight broad chapters focusing on such topics as self-image, folktales, illustrations, and everyday experiences. Teachers and librarians will appreciate the plot summaries, information for booktalking, suggested activities for natural extension of the books, and related book titles. See also Primaryplots *(1989). Check with R.R. Bowker for other useful, annotated book guides and bibliographic resources across the curriculum, K–12.*

Trelease, Jim (ed.). 1992. *Hey! Listen to This: Stories to Read Aloud.* New York: Penguin.

A wonderful collection of stories for reading aloud has been gathered in this volume. Each of the selections could probably be easily found in original form, but what makes this book unique is the background information given in each section about the author or the selection itself. The stories are organized by topics, such as School Days, Food for Thought, or Gigantic Creatures. When excerpts are used from chapter books, I found that Trelease has a wonderful sense of what will catch a child's interest. As I read the portions that he chose, I frequently found that my students would track down the full book and begin to read it on their own. It was a great way to introduce children to a wider range of chapter books when I knew I wouldn't have enough time to read the entire book. See also Read All About It! Great Read-Aloud Stories, Poems, and Newspaper Pieces for Preteens and Teens *(Penguin, 1993). (V.M.)*

Trelease, Jim. 1990. *The New Read-Aloud Handbook.* New York: Penguin.

The author of the inspiring and popular The Read-Aloud Handbook *offers this edition for parents and teachers. The first half of the book deals with the need to read aloud to children and how and when to carry through. Trelease offers valuable suggestions to teachers and parents to promote and implement reading aloud and reading for pleasure at home and in the classroom. The second half of the book, the "Treasury of Read Alouds," presents an extensive listing of picture books and novels that includes brief annotations, related books, and other books by the author. A small listing of poetry books and anthologies is also included. As great read-alouds are most often memorable literature, this text is also an excellent resource for choosing books for children to read with teacher guidance or independently.*

Watt, Letty S., and Terri Parker Street. 1994. *Developing Learning Skills Through Children's Literature: An Idea Book for K–5 Classrooms and Libraries.* Volume 2. Phoenix, AZ: Oryx Press.

Don't be mislead by the title of this book, as it is very useful for the planning of a literature study. It is organized by topics, often utilizing the books of an individual author or illustrator. Each unit has suggested books and activities to develop the theme. These activities are varied to meet the needs of individual students, and suggestions are written to be used independently by the upper-grade children. The strength of this book lies in the inter-esting and unusual ways that topics are pulled together. Some of them are Presenting Information with Gail Gibbons, Feelings Shared by Cynthia Rylant, The Surreal World of Chris Van Allsburg, Character Development with Bill Wallace, and It's a Mystery to Me. If you can't get a copy for your classroom, ask your librarian to purchase one for the library. It will be well used. (V.M.)*

Webb, Anne C. 1993. *Your Reading: A Booklist for Junior High and Middle School.* 9th ed. Urbana, IL: National Council of Teachers of English.

Over 600 quality fiction and nonfiction books have been selected for annotation in this latest edition. Junior high/middle school teachers looking to engage their students and update and balance their literature collections will find this a handy resource. See also other quality booklists published by NCTE that are continually updated:* Adventuring with Books *(pre-K through grade six),* Books for You *(senior high), and* High Interest—Easy Reading *(junior/senior high reluctant readers).*

Wells, Jan, and Linda Hart-Hewins. 1994. *Phonics, Too! How to Teach Skills in a Balanced Language Program.* Markham, Ontario: Pembroke Publishers, and Bothell, WA: The Wright Group.

The authors demonstrate lots of activities and strategies for integrating the teaching of phonics and skills into the language-based K–3 classroom. While some teachers may find the approach too structured, teachers in transition especially will appreciate the wealth of specific information.*

Whisler, Nancy, and Judy Williams. 1990. *Literature and Cooperative Learning: Pathway to Literacy.* Sacramento, CA: Literature Co-op.

K–8 teachers who want some structured, yet meaningful, activities to use with literature will find this 176-page resource very valuable. Lots of sample lessons that include strategies for cooperative learning and for moving through literature—before, during, and after reading—are included.*

Wilson, Lorraine, with David Malmgren, Shirl Ramage, and Leanne Schulz. 1993. *An*

Integrated Approach to Learning. Portsmouth, NH: Heinemann.

In this book, the authors show how integrated learning works in the classroom. They outline how they plan authentic activities with real purposes relating to what the children want to learn. Classroom environment and scheduling are also discussed. The appendices contain several integrated learning units developed by the authors with their classes. These units are especially helpful as starting points for building a unit with your own students. (V.M.)

Wilson, Lorraine. *Write Me a Poem: Reading, Writing, and Performing Poetry.* 1994. Portsmouth, NH: Heinemann.

This short, practical resource for the elementary grades gives suggestions and demonstrations for getting children to write various types of poetry: free verse, rhyming poems, noisy poems, poems for two voices, and poems that express emotions.

• Zarnowski, Myra. 1990. *Learning about Biographies: A Reading-and-Writing Approach for Children.* Urbana, IL: National Council of Teachers of English.

In this book written for elementary and middle school teachers, Zarnowski demonstrates how to actively engage students with the nonfiction genre of biographies. Suggestions and examples are given for reading and discussing biographies and encouraging children to research a particular historical figure and then write their own biographical versions. Includes annotated sources for teachers to locate quality biographies, some recommended children's biographies, and samples of biographies written by students.

Assessment and Evaluation Books and Resources

For additional information and resources on assessment and evaluation, see *Invitations,* pp. 295–375.

• Anthony, Robert J., Terry D. Johnson, Norma I. Mickelson, and Alison Preece. 1991. *Evaluating Literacy: A Perspective for Change.* Portsmouth, NH: Heineman.

This remains my favorite book on evaluation. The authors begin with basic principles of language learning and continue with exemplary models of assessment and evaluation. They include a detailed framework for gathering, organizing, interpreting, and reporting information for student learning. They share samples of anecdotal comments, interviews, letters to parents, observational checklists, self-evaluation forms, children's work, reporting forms, language indicators of progress, and more. I am particularly impressed with the indepth inclusion of the child and the parents in the evaluation process. In our school district, many of us initially relied heavily on chapter 10, "Responsive Evaluation: Reporting to Parents," to initiate student-led parent-teacher conferences. For educators moving toward more holistic and student-centered evaluation, this 196-page text is invaluable.

"Assessment procedures should be contextually grounded. Tasks employed during assessment should be as similar as possible to the tasks required during instruction and the demands placed on real people in real language situations. It is unreasonable to expect learners to behave in one way during instruction and another, for which they have not been prepared, during assessment" (p. 70).

Austin, Terri. 1994. *Changing the View: Student-led Parent Conferences.* Portsmouth, NH: Heinemann.

In this engrossing, first-person account, Terri Austin, a sixth-grade teacher in Alaska, describes how she moved from controlling the assessment process to having her students take leadership and ownership. She shares how she first builds community and trust in her process classroom and, then, how she prepares her students to become active participants in assessment. I was struck by how she engaged her class in exploration of what it means to be a "good student" and how those discussions positively influenced students' future efforts. Most of the book concentrates on the student-led portfolio conference with parents and how Austin lays the groundwork for its success. Austin takes us through exactly *how she prepares students for the confer-ences including all the communications with parents, modeling and practice ses-sions with students, student self-formula-tion of their grades and report cards, and individual conferences with Austin. The highlight is the conference evening when families come to class, and students inde-pendently take them through their portfo-lios and explain their strengths, progress, and goals. I was impressed with how Austin ties home knowledge into assessment by continually inviting and including feed-back and information from the parents. If you are sorting out your own evaluation procedures or beginning the process of student-led conferences, this book will give you much information and support. Con-versations, reflections, and forms from the conference process are included. Austin also shares what she is still struggling with and refining. Applicable K–12.*

Barrs, Myra, Sue Ellis, Hilary Tester, and Anne Thomas, all of the Centre for Language in Primary Education, London. 1988. *The Primary Language Record. Handbook for Teachers.* Portsmouth, NH: Heinemann.

This handbook is another tool for edu-cators who are interested in developing holistic evaluative records of a child's pro-gress in language development. It has a detailed explanation of procedures, along with many examples of evaluations of ac-tual children. Copies of the assessment forms are given with permission to photo-copy. A unique feature of the suggested evaluation is the involvement of parents throughout the procedure. Primary teach-ers considering the use of observation-based, anecdotal record-keeping will find this book to be very helpful for organizing their gath-ered information to provide a detailed pic-ture of a child's literacy development. (V.M.)

Batzle, Janine. 1992. *Portfolio Assessment and Evaluation: Developing and Using Portfo-lios in the K–6 Classroom.* Cypress, CA: Creative Teaching Press.

This spiral-bound handbook is an open-ended resource with lots of ideas to get you thinking about possible materials you might ask students to collect in a portfolio.

Many child samples are shown, and one chapter is devoted to a collection of over twenty pages of forms and checklists. Many portfolio concerns are considered in the book: Definition, Kinds, Who Is Involved in the Collection of Materials, Organiza-tion, and Use in Reporting to Parents, and more. This is an easy-to-understand, very practical reference. (V.M.)

- Bouffler, Chrystine (ed.). 1993. *Literacy Evaluation: Issues and Practicalities.* Ports-mouth, NH: Heinemann.

  The author examines issues in account-ability and some of the recent developments in language assessment in the United States, the United Kingdom, and Australia. What authentic evaluation is, how to balance district evaluation demands and whole lan-guage teaching, how to use a portfolio approach to assess students, what the Pri-mary Language Record is and how it has been used in the U.K., how to assess stu-dent writing, how to develop and use lit-eracy profiles, and how to communicate with parents are all delineated with clear language, sample reports, and usable forms. This is a terrific book (116 pp.) for putting classroom-based assessment into practice.

Clay, Marie. 1993. *An Observation Survey of Early Literacy Achievement.* Portsmouth, NH: Heinemann.

Written for educators who work with young children, this ninety-three page guidebook describes the principles and procedures for systematically observing, analyzing, and summarizing the early lit-eracy skills and book behaviors of young children. Explicit directions are given for the following observation tasks: running records (observing and analyzing a child's oral reading behaviors), letter identifica-tion, concepts about print, word tests, writ-ing, and hearing sounds in words (dicta-tion). These are the same tasks that make up "the Observation Survey" for Reading Recovery, used for selecting the children that need supplementary teaching. Espe-cially useful for kindergarten and grade one teachers for making instructional de-cisions. See also the companion volume on p. 9b, Reading Recovery: A Guidebook for Teachers in Training *(Clay, 1993), which details procedures in the Reading Recovery program.*

Clemmons, Joan, Lois Laase, DonnaLynn Cooper, Nancy Areglado, and Mary Dill. 1993. *Portfolios in the Classroom: A Teacher's Sourcebook.* New York: Scholastic Professional Books.

This 120-page sourcebook is very helpful for getting started with portfolio assessment and for getting new ideas to adapt to your own particular school context. Educators in one elementary school share the rationale for using portfolios in the reading-writing classroom, how to get started, possible components of a portfolio, how to engage students in self-evaluation, and lots of management and teaching tips. The extensive, useful appendices offer workable criteria, charts, and checklists for parent communication and student self-evaluation. The organization, photos, and student samples throughout the book make it an easy-to-use resource.

Cohen, S. Alan. 1988. *TESTS: Marked for Life?* Richmond Hill, Ontario: Scholastic-TAB.

This fifty-eight-page book clearly explains norm-referenced and criterion-referenced tests and notes the limitations of the former. Share this book with parents and administrators.

Cooper, Winfield, and B. J. Brown. February 1992. "Using Portfolios to Empower Student Writers." *English Journal,* pp. 40–45.

A junior high and a high school teacher share their research in using portfolios in the writing-process classroom. They discuss the contents of the student-writing portfolio and how categories for inclusion were decided, share results and insights from the portfolio process, and recommend helpful teacher resources on portfolio assessment.

• Davies, Anne, and others. 1992. *Together is Better: Collaborative Assessment, Evaluation and Reporting.* Winnipeg, Manitoba: Peguis.

Written by educators in British Columbia, this terrific resource gives practical suggestions and a wealth of examples for how to meaningfully involve teachers, parents, and students in three-way conferencing and reporting. There are samples of letters to parents, evaluation/reporting forms, goal-setting plans, anecdotal narratives, feedback and reflections from the conference, and more. Blackline masters (18 pp.) of forms used for preparing for the conference and reflecting on the conference are included.

• Farr, Roger, and Bruce Tone. 1994. *Portfolio and Performance Assessment: Helping Students Evaluate Their Progress as Readers and Writers.* Fort Worth, TX: Harcourt Brace.

"Whatever purpose a teacher, school, district, or even state may set for portfolio assessment, it should not in any way override the primary purpose and potential of all language-arts portfolios: to develop the students' inclinations and abilities to evaluate their own language use!" *(p. 39). Farr and Tone see the other role of portfolios as providing a back-up system for informing educational decision makers. With lots of specific examples and strong theoretical underpinnings, the authors detail how portfolios can encourage students to become self-assessors. In this superb 356-page resource, they include materials that can go into a portfolio, samples of record keeping by students and teachers, indicators to look for when examining the portfolio, activities that encourage self-assessment, guidelines to follow in using portfolios for evaluation of student growth and development, suggestions for developing your own performance assessments, and extensive appendices with reproducible forms, information, and resources for putting portfolios into practice. Teachers will appreciate the "nuts and bolts" of portfolio management, including choosing the physical portfolio holder, keeping the portfolios accessible to students, deciding on the variety of materials that go in the portfolio, managing the content of portfolios, succeeding with and finding the time for student/teacher conferences, and communicating with parents.*

The authors recognize that to use port-

folios wisely for ongoing informal assessment in the language arts, we need to have a well-developed understanding of how children develop as language users and a broad understanding of assessment issues. "The bottom line in selecting and using any assessment should be whether it helps students" (p. 167). In addition to cautions about present assessment practices, we are cautioned not to grade portfolios or use portfolios only for best work but to allow students to struggle with the bulk and variety of their materials so they can begin to make sense of their language development. I have not read a more comprehensive, useful text for meaningfully applying the portfolio assessment concept to the classroom. I did wish, however, that parents were included as a more ongoing part of the portfolio process. You may find, as I did, that the sheer amount of information presented in this guidebook is overwhelming. As with any other useful resource, you will want to adapt the information and ideas to suit your own particular contexts.

Francis, David (executive director). 1994. *English—A Curriculum Profile for Australian Schools*. Carlton, Victoria, Australia: Curriculum Corporation, and Portsmouth, NH: Heinemann.

This document provides a detailed framework that is "designed to assist in the improvement of teaching and learning and to provide a common language for reporting student achievement." Specific outcomes are listed for speaking and listening, reading and viewing, and writing in increasingly complex levels. Along with each level, criteria—performance indicators—are provided as evidence to observe for, and some examples of student work used as evidence are included. Teachers and administrators across the grades will find the language used in describing desired outcomes terrifically helpful for curriculum planning and reporting to parents.

Gill, Kent (ed.). 1993. *Process and Portfolios in Writing Instruction*. Urbana, IL: National Council of Teachers of English.

Elementary, secondary, and college-level teachers will find many practical ideas in this book. In the first section, teachers describe their successes with building students' interest in and appreciation of writing. These students faced problems such as reluctance to begin writing, writer's block, and a lack of ideas. I particularly liked the chapter by high school teacher Betty McWilliams who encourages students to share their work with classmates as they develop stories from their own lives. The second part focuses on the use of writing portfolios both for instruction and evaluation. Various authors describe how students take responsibility for selecting the materials to be placed in their portfolios, and how they learn to evaluate their work. These essays are a testimony to the power of reflective teachers who help their students to write better by becoming writers themselves. (V.M.)

Glazer, Susan Mandel, and Carol Smullen Brown. 1993. *Portfolios and Beyond: Collaborative Assessment in Reading and Writing*. Norwood, MA: Christopher-Gordon.

Developing instruments that would help teachers to assess the holistic, literature-based instruction used in their classrooms was the goal of the authors of this interesting text. They provide a theoretical base to explain the step-by-step alternative procedures that have evolved in their work. I particularly liked the chapter that Lynn Searfoss was invited to contribute that places all assessment in relation to the classroom environment. He believes that the classroom must be the context in which language is to be observed and assessed, with products displayed, shared, and saved. He gives many suggestions for determining if the environment truly is a "print-rich" setting. Further chapters look at actual assessment of reading, writing, comprehension processes and products, as well as how reporting should be a collaboration between parents, student, and teacher. A chapter of questions that teachers ask is full of helpful answers. (V.M.)

Goodman, Kenneth, Lois Bridges Bird, and Yetta Goodman (eds.). 1992. *The Whole Language Catalog: Supplement on Authen-*

tic Assessment. Blacklick, OH: SRA Division of Macmillan/McGraw-Hill.

More than 100 whole language educators contributed material to this comprehensive guidebook on authentic assessment. Strategies and suggestions for new ways of evaluation are given that include use of anecdotal records, holistic checklists, portfolios, interviews, and learning logs. Indexes and cross-references allow readers to find information to meet their own particular needs. Classroom demonstrations throughout the book help make the suggested assessment techniques especially useful to teachers. (V.M.)

Goodman, Kenneth, Yetta Goodman, and Wendy Hood (eds.). 1989. *The Whole Language Evaluation Book.* Portsmouth, NH: Heinemann.

This powerful book encourages teachers to value their students and to find ways to help them—instead of showing them they have failed. Whole language practitioners across the United States and Canada contributed the various chapters describing alternatives to traditional evaluation techniques. They believe that evaluation should be a way of documenting the learning growth occurring daily—never as an assessment of decontextualized, abstract skills unrelated to the functional use of language. A variety of evaluation strategies, such as anecdotal records, learning logs, miscue analysis, journal samples, portfolios or folders, writing samples, and teacher notes, are described as they are implemented by the authors in various classroom settings from elementary to senior high school, adult education, and with bilingual and special education students. Many useful suggestions are given for record keeping. The book is an excellent resource for persons who are grounded in whole language practices and who are now interested in making student evaluation an integral part of the learning process. (V.M.)

Graves, Donald H., and Bonnie S. Sunstein (eds.). 1992. *Portfolio Portraits.* Portsmouth, NH: Heinemann.

An informative picture of how portfolios are being developed by educators from first-grade level through graduate education is found in this book. What I really like about this book is that portfolios are not packaged with a bunch of rules or mandates. Instead, the book shows the diversity and potential that keeping portfolios might have. One of the most fascinating chapters was the one where a superintendent developed his own portfolio before asking his staff to consider a portfolio project in their school district. Anyone considering the use of portfolios should read this book! (V.M.)

- Harp, Bill (ed.). 1994. *Assessment and Evaluation for Student Centered Learning.* 2nd ed. Norwood, MA: Christopher-Gordon.

The opening chapters of this book update the first edition by exploring issues about the whole language movement that have arisen in the past three years. Harp begins by looking at the principles underlying whole language instruction and its relationship to assessment and evaluation. Further chapters look at primary, intermediate, special education and multicultural classrooms, and suggest appropriate ways of assessment. This is both a practical and theoretical handbook that should be in every classroom teacher's library. (V.M.)

Herman, Joan L., Pamela R. Aschbacher, and Lynn Winters. 1992. *A Practical Guide to Alternative Assessment.* Alexandria, VA: Association for Supervision and Curriculum Development.

The authors present clear information and a strong rationale for linking quality alternative assessments with good instruction. "Good assessment reliably measures something beyond the specific tasks that students are asked to complete. The results of good assessment identify what students can do in a broad knowledge or skill domain" (p. 9). Alternative assessments examine the processes as well as the products of learning and may include performance testing, portfolio assessment, exhibits, demonstrations, and other authentic assessments. Guidelines and procedures for designing alternative assessments are given, including determining outcomes to be measured, managing the assessment admini-

stration process, deciding the actual question/problem/prompt, developing and evaluating your own criteria and rubrics, and ensuring reliable scoring and validity. I found the brief information on portfolio assessment very helpful for clarifying what must take place if portfolios are to be more than collections and are truly to be used for assessment. For rethinking, redesigning, and balancing assessment strategies in your educational context, this is a very useful guide. (134 pp.)

• Hill, Bonnie Campbell, and Cynthia Ruptic. 1994. *Practical Aspects of Authentic Assessment: Putting the Pieces Together.* Norwood, MA: Christopher-Gordon.

If you want a very specific and practical book full of ways to assess learning in the elementary classroom, you will want to get this book. It contains over 120 reproducible forms for possible teacher use, along with commentary explaining their usage. The forms are organized according to purpose: emergent literacy, writing, reading, content areas, developmental spelling, writing conferences, reading logs, literature circles, problem solving, and many more. Several chapters address the use, collection, and organization of portfolios in a classroom setting. The entire book is a wealth of information for teachers to consider. (V.M.)

• Jett-Simpson, Mary, and Lauren Leslie (eds.). 1994. *Ecological Assessment: Under Construction.* Schofield, WI: Wisconsin State Reading Association (94809 Sternberg Avenue, 54476)

Ecological assessments combine authentic literacy tasks with authentic texts; that is, tasks and materials are natural to what readers, writers, and speakers do in the real world. With this approach, knowledgeable teachers work side by side with students to capture the complexity of language processes primarily by observing, recording, and analyzing reading and writing processes as they occur in the classroom. How and why teachers have moved to ecological assessment is detailed in this impressive, 255-page monograph. In a straightforward, organized manner that combines theory and practice, this guide provides an abundance of information and work samples for observing reading and writing behaviors, strategies, attitudes, and interests. Lots of specific, useful information, sample forms, and work samples involving parent communication, holistic scoring, developing rubrics, and the portfolio process are included. An excellent source for teachers, administrators, and policy makers for understanding and moving to authentic assessment practices in the classroom.

• Johnston, Peter H. 1992. *Constructing Evaluation of Literate Activity.* New York: Longman.

This is a challenging, complex, comprehensive book on literacy and assessment that is worth the effort involved to read it. "I have based this book on the premise that there is one central reason for evaluating children's literate activity, and that is so that we might ensure optimal instruction for all children. *All other reasons are secondary to that goal*" (p. 9). Johnston believes the most important evaluation is self-evaluation—for us and our students—and that teachers obtain their most useful information about students in one to one conferences and through uninterrupted observation in the classroom when students are working independently and teachers can step back. To that end, the author helps us set up contexts for constructive evaluation, look and listen better when we are observing students ("reflection in action"), describe the learner and his development through narrative reports that capitalize on the learner's strengths, match readers with texts, understand the role of choice in learning, analyze children's errors, help our students become good self-evaluators, and much more. Strategies for recording, keeping track, promoting, and analyzing literacy development are explained in great depth. Johnston demonstrates how we can evaluate a student's concepts about print, oral reading, thinking process, written language, and more through the use and analysis of running records (an audiotape for learning how to take a running record of a child's oral *reading accompanies this text), other observational records, the portfolio process, dialogue journals, thinking aloud, to name just a few. Johnston also examines the inadequacy of standardized tests and testing and suggests ways to reduce the amount of testing in schools. For teachers who are ready to rethink literacy assumptions, become more reflective about their teaching, and view evaluation through a constructive perspective, this remarkable book (426 pp.) is important reading. Read this book slowly. It is packed with a wealth of thoughtful information and feasible ideas.*

Some quotes to think about:

"Any evaluation procedure that interferes with or reduces optimal instruction to any child should be regarded as highly suspect, probably invalid, and generally unacceptable" (p. 10).

"The more independent literate activity that is going on in the classroom, the easier and more consistent evaluation will be. *The more students are reading and writing, and talking about the reading and writing, the more examples are available to be observed, and the less critical it is for the teacher to notice every single one" (p. 8).*

"Possibly the biggest obstacle to development in evaluation practices has been the rather restricted view of what constitute appropriate data" (p. 307).

Kamii, Constance (ed.). 1990. *Achievement Testing in Early Grades: The Games Grown-Ups Play.* Washington, DC: National Association for the Education of Young Children.

The contributing authors to this thoughtful text (181 pp.) give research and rationale to demonstrate the harmful effects of achievement testing in kindergarten through second grade. In place of standardized testing with its emphasis on fragmented skills, they recommend evaluation (with teachers in charge) that is rooted in classroom practice and that informs us of students' thinking processes over time. Provocative, important reading for teachers, administrators, parents, and policymakers.

Linek, Wayne M. February 1991. "Grading and Evaluation Techniques for Whole Language Teachers." *Language Arts,* pp. 125–131.

An elementary principal gives specific and realistic suggestions for evaluating and grading in a whole language classroom and focuses on the issues of philosophy/policy and record keeping. "The process you use will be a unique combination of policy requirements, professional knowledge, and personal choice." Linek provides many practical possibilities for reconciling accountability and grading issues with whole language principles.

Little, Nancy, and John Allan. 1988. *Student-Led Teacher Parent Conferences.* Toronto, Ontario: Lugus Productions.

Written to give guidance and motivation to teachers in grades 1–7 to implement student-led parent-teacher conferences, this thirty-seven-page booklet includes preparatory steps, procedures, methods of evaluation, and several sample letters and forms. You will want to adapt the format presented to your own conference contexts. Great for support in getting started.

Ministry of Education, Victoria, Australia. 1990. *Literacy Profiles Handbook: Assessing and Reporting Literacy Development.* (Available in the U.S. from Brewster, NY: TASA [Fields Lane, P.O. Box 382, 10509]. A U.S. version, *The American Literacy Profiles,* by Patrick Griffin, Patricia G. Smith, and Lois Burrill is in the works and will be available from Heinemann in the spring of 1995.)

"A literacy profile is an array of information that describes and evaluates a student's reading and writing." The profile includes attitudes and interests and strategies and accomplishments. When a K–12 language arts committee in my school district met to write a district language arts course of study, we found the profiles to be a helpful reference for language, content, and format.

• Murphy, Sandra, and Mary Ann Smith. *Writing Portfolios: A Bridge from Teaching to Assessment.* 1991. Markham, Ontario: Pippin Publishing, and Portsmouth, NH: Heinemann.

The authors and twenty secondary teach-

ers, all connected with the Bay Area Writing Project in California, collaborated on a research project experimenting with writing portfolios. In this first-rate, ninety-six-page book, they discuss the rationale for using portfolios, the decision making process teachers used in setting up portfolio programs, the pitfalls and successes teachers had, and the practices that worked best. The chapter, "What Can Students Learn from Reflecting?" (pp. 37–45), has pages of excellent questions teachers can ask in conferences and to encourage self-reflection. "The word 'portfolio,' by itself, means little. It's the individual decisions that define the portfolio assessment" (p. 83). While the portfolio context in this book is high school, as an elementary teacher I found the information very useful and applicable.

Perrone, Vito (ed.). 1991. *Expanding Student Assessment*. Alexandria, VA: Association for Supervision and Curriculum Development.

This is a fascinating book that raises questions about assessment and takes the stance that knowledgeable teachers can use observation and performance samples in the classroom context to formally and informally assess student learning. In such authentic assessment, classroom teachers and students are central to the process, and students are empowered as learners. In the first chapter, Kathe Jervis reports on how standardized testing disrupted the everyday rhythm of a grade 3–4 class in New York City and how the classroom teacher made an effort to deemphasize the tests. In chapter 2, Edward Chittenden looks at assessment first as an attitude of "keeping track" and "checking up" and suggests that classroom activities, such as story time and independent reading, are natural settings for reading assessment. In chapter 3, Ron Berger, a sixth-grade teacher, shares his assessment beliefs and practices, which center around conferences, critique, and the use of portfolios. A terrific chapter by Rieneke Zessoules and Howard Gardner deals with the importance of student reflection and shows how two high school teachers encourage

it. These two authors also explore key practices of authentic assessment for teachers and administrators. In chapter 6, twelfth-grade English teacher Patricia Lambert Stock, who integrates teaching, learning, and assessment, describes the impressive improvement of a struggling writing student. In chapter 8, Judah Schwartz raises important questions about the secrecy of mathematics tests and the fact that the media only see the scores (not the questions), and that recognizing a solution on a multiple choice test is not the same as producing a solution. I found this entire 179-page book provocative and thoughtful.

• Rhodes, Lynn K. (ed.). 1993. *Literacy Assessment: A Handbook of Instruments*. Portsmouth, NH: Heinemann.

All of the various assessment instruments discussed in Windows into Literacy, along with directions for administration, are found in this useful handbook. These forms include interviews and attitude surveys, miscue analysis, comprehension checklists, spelling analysis, emergent reading and writing evaluations, and instruments for self evaluation. They may be photocopied by teachers for classroom use, but the editor hopes that they will be reviewed and revised to fit your particular needs. (V.M.)

• Rhodes, Lynn K., and Nancy Shanklin. 1993. *Windows into Literacy: Assessing Learners K–8*. Portsmouth, NH: Heinemann.

This text is a very inclusive look at literacy assessment. It is built on the principle that the most effective assessment takes place most often in the midst of instruction and should inform that instruction. The book values the teacher as the decision maker in determining what materials should be used to support learning after gathering information on the students' strengths and interests. Chapters in this book define assessment and the principles that should guide it. They cover a wide range of assessment methods in order to discover the following: students' perceptions of their own reading and writing strategies, reading ability, writing processes with emphasis on spelling and written products, emergent reading and writing ability. Sugges-

tions are given as to how to use standardized, norm-referenced tests and literacy collections including portfolios, and to deal with educational change as it relates to assessment. Though the book can be overwhelming when viewed as a whole, each chapter stands alone, and teachers can read those sections that address their particular needs. It is an outstanding resource. (V.M.)

- Stenmark, Jean Kerr (ed.). 1991. *Mathematics Assessment: Myths, Model, Good Questions, and Practical Suggestions.* Reston, VA: The National Council of Teachers of Mathematics.

    Geared to teachers, this seventy-one page handbook gives a convincing rationale and lots of practical assistance to implement alternative assessments that focus on student thinking. Some of the useful topics and techniques that are discussed and demonstrated are creating open-ended questions, conducting interviews and conferences, managing the classroom with observational assessment, recording observations, developing criteria for performance tasks, and keeping and evaluating a mathematics portfolio. Sample assessment forms are included. I was struck by the fact that the principles that apply to good assessment in mathematics are the same principles that apply across the curriculum. A first-rate resource for all teachers.

Traill, Leanna. 1993. *Highlight My Strengths: Assessment and Evaluation of Literacy Learning.* Crystal Lake, IL: Rigby.

   This ninety-two-page sourcebook for primary teachers shares assessment procedures and record keeping for observing, recording, and interpreting reading behaviors as well as for taking running records. Some of the information and procedures are adapted from the work of Marie Clay, Richard Gentry, and others. Attractively organized with photos, charts, forms, and student work samples. Easy to use and read.

Turbill, Jan, and Brian Cambourne (eds.). 1994. *Responsive Evaluation.* Portsmouth, NH: Heinemann.

   Seeking a workable model of evaluation that is congruent with language learning theory, a group of Australian classroom teachers, school principals, directors, and university researchers collaborated in a five-year research project. The model of evaluation they adopted, Responsive Evaluation, shares the same fundamentals as a parental model of responsive evaluation in the everyday world. Some of these common fundamentals include opportunities to gather data and observe language learning in naturally occurring settings, a special relationship with and commitment to those who are being evaluated, a sense of responsibility to set up learning contexts that facilitate literacy development, a set of markers or benchmarks that can be used to recognize students' literacy growth and development. With the help of their co-researchers, teachers focused on "episodes" (literacy lessons, such as sustained silent reading or sharing circle) in their daily teaching and examined the following questions:

   1. Why do I have this episode in my daily schedule?

   2. What data-gathering procedures (i.e. assessment procedures) can I employ that won't break into or stop the flow of teaching and learning?

   3. What markers can I use during this episode that will inform me that students are/are not learning within this episode?

   4. What sense or meaning can I make from what I collect? (p. 23)

   Through this daily examination, teachers and principals became more insightful and explicit about their beliefs and practices and more confident, competent, and rigorous in their evaluation procedures. Use this thoughtful, practical resource as a staff-development model and to examine and improve your own teaching/evaluation practices.

Valencia, Sheila W., Elfrieda H. Hiebert, and Peter P. Afflerbach (eds.). 1994. *Authentic Reading Assessment: Practices and Possibilities.* Newark, DE: International Reading Association.

   For everyone who is struggling with the implementation of authentic assessment and portfolios (and who isn't?), this book is for you. Through case studies that are fol-

lowed by thoughtful, analytical commentaries, the reader gains perspective on approaches to authentic assessment that are taking place at the classroom, district, and state levels in parts of the United States and Canada. This detailed, critical account of successes and failures is very helpful to any individual, school, or district tackling nontraditional assessment. Lends support to classroom-based assessment projects.

Wiggins, Grant. May 1992. "Creating Tests Worth Taking." *Educational Leadership*, pp. 26–33.

A national expert on testing and assessment lists questions and criteria to consider when developing authentic performance assessments. He discusses how to design tasks that involve "higher-order" thinking, scoring considerations, constraints of performance assessment, and how to report progress. He argues that quality assessment must be designed locally since good teaching and good assessing cannot be separated.

• Woodward, Helen. 1994. *Negotiated Evaluation: Involving Children and Parents in the Process*. Portsmouth, NH: Heinemann.

This gem of a book (92 pp.) lends practical help to elementary-grades teachers who want evaluation processes to actively involve the child and his or her parents as well as the teacher. I particularly appreciated all the honest information on what works and what doesn't when teachers use informal observation, such as anecdotal records and checklists. This is a must-read book for teachers who want to take responsibility for evaluation in the classroom but who need specific help with the management, organization, and procedures to make it possible. Lots of usable letters and forms included, especially for parents and student self-evaluation.

Spelling Books and Resources

For integrating spelling into the reading-writing classroom and for additional spelling resources, see *Invitations*, pp. 235–262.

Bloodgood, Janet W. November 1991. "A New Approach to Spelling Instruction in Language Arts Programs." *The Elementary School Journal*, pp. 203–211.

Within the integrated language arts classroom, Bloodgood describes how periodic spelling assessments can enable teachers to plan appropriate word study activities for students. Specific word-sorting and word-hunting activities that help students notice particular features and patterns of words are described. Underscores the need for accurate spelling assessment as part of the spelling program. Many good ideas for teaching spelling.

Bolton, Faye, and Diane Snowball. 1993. *Ideas for Spelling*. Portsmouth, NH: Heinemann.

The main emphasis of this book is on creating a balanced spelling program, and teachers will appreciate the multitude of suggested activities that go along with the various stages of children's spelling development. Viewing spelling in the context of writing, Bolton and Snowball first provide a framework for spelling development that connects spelling relationships in the English language (morphemic, phoneme-grapheme, semantics, and syntax) with strategies used by competent spellers. How to assess and evaluate children's spelling development is also included.

Bolton, Faye, and Diane Snowball. 1993. *Teaching Spelling: A Practical Resource*. Portsmouth, NH: Heinemann.

The authors believe that the only authentic reason for students to learn to spell conventionally is to assist others to read their writing. Students must not only write often, but also form hypotheses about words, try out spellings, receive feedback, and refine their hypotheses. Building on Ideas for Spelling (Heinemann, 1993), which documents the nature of learning to spell, in this 154-page resource Bolton and Snowball provide strategies and management for the elementary school classroom spelling program. Strategies that competent spellers use are demonstrated. Many examples of classroom charts, spelling resources, patterns to be taught, games for playing with words, assessment procedures, and student work samples are provided. Teachers *looking for how and what to teach in spelling will appreciate the abundance of word lists (such as homophones, common derivatives, prefixes, suffixes, abbreviations), ideas, and activities in this useful resource.*

Booth, David (ed.). 1991. *Spelling Links: Reflections on Spelling and its Place in the Curriculum.* Markham, Ontario: Pembroke Publishers, and Bothell, WA: The Wright Group.

For the teacher who is unsure of how to teach spelling and which approach to use, the solid, yet varying, perspectives presented in this 157-page text will prove useful and thought provoking. Booth passionately asks us to rethink our spelling programs, to become lifelong spelling mentors who promote word awareness and teach spelling "through writing, through poetry, through puzzles and games, through reading, through discussion and debate about words, through linguistic exploration, through second languages, through reference helps, through modeling by effective and affective teachers" (pp. 9–10). Suggesting that we must first understand how children learn to spell before we can choose words to teach, Part 1 has an essay by Rosemary Courtney dealing with the history of spelling, and Part 2 deals with developmental nature of spelling with chapters by Carol Beers and James Beers, Richard Gentry, and Edmund Henderson and Shane Templeton. Part 3, on choosing a spelling program, presents perspectives by Judith Preen, a whole language advocate, and Robert and Marlene McCracken, who offer a slightly different approach. Part 4, "What Do I Teach Monday?" has chapters by Janice Merrifield and Larry Schwartz, and offers strategies, activities, and games to develop good spellers. Part 5 offers practical help with assessment with chapters by Kristine Anderson and Ruth Scott. Next, a fascinating chapter by Sharon Siamon chronicles her daughter's growth in spelling and is a great piece for thinking about and discussing the development of spelling. Bob Barton's short essay about word consciousness concludes this fine resource.

Cunningham, Patricia M., and James W. Cunningham. October 1992. "Making Words: Enhancing the Invented Spelling-Decoding Connection." *The Reading Teacher,* pp. 106–115.

Believing that writing with invented spelling is important but that some readers and writers will not learn enough about letter-sound relationships from this practice alone, the authors developed the "Making Words" activity for first- and second-grade writing classrooms. In "Making Words," children are given a specific group of letters that they use to make words. The steps for planning and teaching a "Making Words" lesson are delineated. K–2 teachers that I know have used this activity and find it excellent for increasing phonemic awareness and spelling knowledge. I found the management of it so time consuming that I adapted the lesson for easier management.

Gentry, Richard, and Jean W. Gillet. 1993. *Teaching Kids to Spell.* Portsmouth, NH: Heinemann.

This is a great book for teachers who already have a reading-writing classroom where children are reading, writing, risk taking, inventing, and interacting with language and each other throughout the day. For teachers ready to take a workshop approach to spelling, Gentry and Gillet give us the research, theory, rationale, organization, instructional techniques, and activities for developing spellers. We are taken through the stages of invented spelling and shown how to give K–2 students a developmental spelling test, analyze the spellings to determine the child's developmental spelling level, and support the child's growing competence. For older students, we learn that expert spellers internalize phonetic, semantic, historical, and visual knowledge of words, and we are shown many ways to help children acquire all four of these necessary systems. To support that teaching, extensive appendices at the end of the book provide Latin and Greek stems, useful prefixes, familiar sound and letter patterns ("Children learn to spell pattern by pattern, not word by word"

p. 89.), *most frequently used words in children's writing, and words most commonly misspelled. What I especially like about this book is the balanced approach it takes with whole language and explicit teaching. "In addition to reading and writing daily in a language-rich environment, children must be taught phonetic, semantic, etymological, and visual knowledge of words both directly and indirectly in order to internalize them and use them interactively for producing correct spelling" (p. 56).*

Phenix, Jo, and Doreen Scott-Dunne. 1991. *Spelling Instruction That Makes Sense.* Markham, Ontario: Pembroke Publishers, and Bothell, WA: The Wright Group.

For teachers looking for an alternative to weekly spelling lists, the authors of this practical, 103-page book strike a balance between having children write freely and teaching spelling directly. The easy-to-read text includes the logic, history, and development of spelling along with many specific strategies, techniques, and rules worth teaching. Chapter 5, "Evaluation and Record Keeping" is very helpful for the samples of written analyses of children's work that demonstrate "what the student knows" and "what can reasonably be taught." An excellent resource for understanding how to teach, evaluate, and develop spellers in the classroom.

Powell, Debbie, and David Hornsby. 1993. *Learning Phonics and Spelling in a Whole Language Classroom.* New York: Scholastic.

Teachers who are developing a whole language environment for their students often have concerns and questions about the place of phonics and spelling in the classroom. This teacher-friendly book is full of strategies and activities designed to integrate phonics and spelling into the context of literature and other authentic texts. One section I particularly liked was on recording, evaluation, and reporting. It contained many suggestions for evaluation within the context of everyday reading and writing, as well as ways to keep parents informed of changes in instructional meth-

odology. The book also has many forms that could be adapted for your particular classroom use. (V.M.)

Routman, Regie. May/June 1993. "The Uses and Abuses of Invented Spelling." *Instructor*, pp. 35–39.

Routman examines the use of invented spelling in classrooms and notes that it was never meant to be "anything goes." She discusses the need for raising our expectations and expecting students to spell high-frequency words correctly, to utilize reliable rules and patterns, and to apply spelling strategies to their daily writing. Suggestions are given for encouraging students to become good spellers.

Scott, Ruth. 1993. *Spelling: Sharing the Secrets.* Toronto: Gage Educational Publishing.

Scott gives lots of practical assistance on how to set up the language-based classroom to explore the systems of spelling. She clearly explains the spelling stages all children move through and how to analyze and assess these stages and move children forward. I found the strength of the book to be the multitude of activities and spelling strategies (phonological, visual, and morphological [meaning]) that Scott clearly presents. Teachers who are ready to integrate the teaching of spelling into the language arts will find this a very useful resource.

• Tarasoff, Mary. 1992. *A Guide to Children's Spelling Development.* Victoria, British Columbia: Active Learning Institute, and Winnipeg, Manitoba: Peguis.

For teachers who have moved to an integrated approach to spelling but need the structure, rules, and assistance the published spelling program provided, this book is for you. Tarasoff's easy-to-use, well-organized resource (177 pages) gives specific guidance and strategies for supporting children at each stage of spelling development. Extensive tables and appendices provide rules worth knowing, common letter and sound patterns and sequences, most frequently used words, commonly used prefixes and suffixes, and more. A whole chapter is devoted to spell-

ing multisyllabic words. Using annotated samples of children's writing at different stages, Tarasoff notes the knowledge and strategies the child is using to construct words and gives suggestions for helping the child develop further. A favorite resource of many teachers. See also, Mary Tarasoff's Spelling: Strategies You Can Teach (*Peguis, 1990*).

Templeton, Shane. November 1991. "Teaching and Learning the English Spelling System: Reconceptualizing Method and Purpose." *The Elementary School Journal*, pp. 185–201.

Within the language-based, process classroom, Templeton elaborates on the need for systematic, formal spelling instruction that addresses both the structure of words and vocabulary development. Noting that many students do not automatically pick up the structural and semantic patterns of words without teacher guidance, he provides specific strategies and demonstration lessons for the elementary grades. Based on the current concern of teachers and parents regarding the teaching of spelling, this is an important article for educators who recognize the need for some explicit instruction in the context of the reading-writing classroom.

• Wilde, Sandra. 1991. *You Can Red This! Spelling and Punctuation for Whole Language Classrooms, k–6.* Portsmouth, NH: Heinemann.

Teachers who want to understand how children develop spelling and punctuation competencies will enjoy this comprehensive handbook. It will especially appeal to teachers who sense that spelling instruction should be more than using a workbook, or memorizing a weekly list of words. Wilde very clearly shows how development takes place over time, using many examples of student writing. Many practical teaching ideas are given, and a series of sample minilessons are especially valuable. Her insights into the use and support of invented spelling by children will be especially helpful in defining the process to their parents. (V.M.)

Mathematics Books and Resources

• Apelman, Maja, and Julie King. 1993. *Exploring Everyday Math: Ideas for Students, Teachers, and Parents.* Portsmouth, NH: Heinemann.

Many practical ideas that can be used by anyone helping children to understand mathematical concepts are found in this book. It allows teachers and parents to tap and enhance the opportunities for math that surround a child in daily life. An appendix contains reproducible recording sheets and sample letters to parents. Each activity that I have tried with my second graders and their parents has been received with enthusiasm, and I continue to integrate many of the suggestions from this book into my math program. (V.M.)

Baker, Ann, and Johnny Baker. 1991. *Counting on a Small Planet: Activities for Environmental Mathematics.* Portsmouth, NH: Heinemann.

Using a thematic approach, the authors suggest activities to help children develop an awareness of environmental problems, such as trash accumulation, erosion, and water use or abuse. Each topic has a Math Fact File that helps the student to relate local problems to a global level. Upper-grade teachers will find this book useful in developing ecology units. (V.M.)

Baker, Ann, and Johnny Baker. 1991. *Maths in the Mind: A Process Approach to Mental Strategies.* Portsmouth, NH: Heinemann.

Strategies to encourage children to become independent thinkers in math are found in this book. It emphasizes process rather than one right answer, and is filled with examples of children's work. Many of the activities are appropriate for second graders or older students. (V.M.)

Baker, Ann, and Johnny Baker. 1990. *Mathematics in Process.* Portsmouth, NH: Heinemann.

Elementary teachers who are ready to apply the conditions and principles of whole language to the teaching and learning of mathematics will want to read this book.

The authors, Australian educators, advocate applying the writing process and shared-book experience to a process approach to mathematics. Lots of examples of open-ended math activities in which children have opportunities to experiment with ideas, develop their own strategies, and communicate and reflect about their experiences are presented.

Baker, Dave, Cheryl Semple, and Tony Stead. 1990. *How Big Is the Moon? Whole Maths in Action.* Portsmouth, NH: Heinemann.

As they explore real-life problems and issues, young children are encouraged to learn math concepts in this book. It describes how to establish a learning environment in which children take responsibility for their own learning and share in the planning and implementation of the curriculum. Many examples of student projects are shown throughout the book that make the different topics very understandable. A section on evaluation and record keeping has many useful ideas. (V.M.)

Braddon, Kathryn L., Nancy J. Hall, and Dale Taylor. 1993. *Math Through Children's Literature: Making the NCTM Standards Come Alive.* Englewood, CO: Teacher Ideas Press/Libraries Unlimited.

As the title suggests, this book is organized around the NCTM Standards. The first five (problem solving, communication, reasoning, connections, and estimation) are considered processes to be woven into the other eight elementary standards. Each of the content standards (number sense and numeration, measurement, etc.) has its own chapter, which contains appropriate books with suggested activities for K–6 students. A list of related books is included for each standard. This is a wonderful resource with many ideas for busy classroom teachers. (V.M.)

Burk, Donna, Allyn Snider, and Paula Symonds. 1992–1993. *Math Excursions Series.* Portsmouth, NH: Heinemann.

This innovative series of project-based mathematics units for primary teachers will seem prescriptive at first glance, but the activities invite exciting, open-ended exploration in the classroom. The books are organized by grade level (Math Excursions K, Math Excursions 1, and Math Excursions 2). Each book includes five complete units, and each unit creates a delightful story line that sets up situations in which there's a reason to use mathematics. Many of the units are based on children's literature, traditional folktales, or familiar nursery rhymes. The books are generously illustrated and well organized, and provide a wonderful introduction to the kind of open mathematical exploration called for by the NCTM Standards. The authors are all practicing classroom teachers and this is clearly revealed in their thoughtful approach to each of the books in the series.

- Burns, Marilyn. 1992. *About Teaching Mathematics: A K–8 Resource.* Sausalito, CA: Math Solutions Publications. Distributed by Heinemann.

This book argues that math should be taught through problem solving, and clearly demonstrates why traditional math teaching based on pencil-and-paper computation has little relevance for using math in daily life. The author looks at issues in mathematics teaching, how children learn, and how to organize the classroom environment. Many classroom-tested activities are described in each section of the book, and an extensive bibliography of books and resources is in the back. This is an extremely valuable resource for the K–8 classroom teacher. (V.M.)

Burns, Marilyn. 1987–1990. *A Collection of Math Lessons.* Sausalito, CA: Math Solutions Publications. Distributed by Heinemann.

From Grades 1 Through 3, with Bonnie Tank.
From Grades 3 Through 6.
From Grades 6 Through 8, with Cathy McLaughlin.

Each of these wonderful books presents interesting ideas for teaching mathematics through problem solving. Students are encouraged to work cooperatively to find solutions, and to incorporate writing into *each activity. Each chapter contains a lesson presented to real children, shows how the teacher prepared the lesson, and how the children responded. I have tried many of these lessons, and found that my students responded with enjoyment and interest. (V.M.)*

Burns, Marilyn. 1992. *Math and Literature (K–3)*. Sausalito, CA: Math Solutions Publications. Distributed by Heinemann.

This valuable resource gives detailed descriptions of how ten children's books were used in various classrooms. After reading the story, teachers encouraged problem-solving investigations by asking questions and giving children time to think and explore. I especially enjoyed looking at the written responses by children that are included with each lesson. In addition, twenty-one additional books are briefly described with instructional ideas included for each. (V.M.)

Charles, Linda Holden, and Micaelia Randolph Brummett. 1989. *Connections: Linking Manipulatives to Mathematics (Grades 1–6)*. Sunnyvale, CA: Creative Publications.

Each grade-level resource contains twenty manipulative lessons that connect to important mathematical topics. Each lesson is structured to be used with the whole class as well as with a small group. As part of each lesson, students discuss, organize, report, display, and write about their findings. A fine resource for teachers looking to encourage more active learning experiences to help build understanding in mathematics.

Griffiths, Rachel, and Margaret Clyne. 1990. *Books You Can Count On: Linking Mathematics and Literature*. Portsmouth, NH: Heinemann.

This resource for the primary grades takes first-rate children's literature and outlines activities for developing mathematical concepts. Books are presented individually as well as thematically. Two final sections on classroom organization and evaluation are very useful.

• Kamii, Constance. 1985, 1989. *Young Children Reinvent Arithmetic: Implications of Piaget's Theory*. New York: Teachers College Press.

Grade 1, with Georgia DeClark.

2nd Grade: Young Children Continue to Reinvent Arithmetic, with Linda Leslie Joseph.

These two books can be read separately, but together they will trace children's mathematical development across first and second grade. Basing her work on Piaget's theory, Kamii demonstrates that children do not learn math, but instead reinvent it, or construct it from within—with or without direct instruction. Instead of skill and drill, children are encouraged to use arithmetic in daily living situations and in math games. These books explained many of my "gut" feelings about why my students might be having difficulty with certain concepts. For example, learning place value and double-column addition/subtraction is developmentally too difficult for young children. This book gave me alternatives and better ways to work with my students. There is much food for thought, as well as a vast assortment of games and activities, in these two volumes. I would highly recommend them to anyone working with primary-grade children, and I would suggest that teachers of older students watch for volumes at their grade level. (V.M.)

Lilburn, Pat, and Pam Rawson. 1994. *Let's Talk Math: Encouraging Children to Explore Ideas*. Portsmouth, NH: Heinemann.

This book is designed for students in grades 3–6. It contains forty group activities that encourage children to talk and write mathematically about various everyday problems related to number, space, and measurement. Each activity is carefully described and illustrated by examples of student responses and comments by teachers who have tried them. (V.M.)

National Council of Teachers of Mathematics. 1906 Association Drive. Reston, VA 22091-1593. (telephone 703-620-9840)

The National Council of Teachers of Mathematics (NCTM) has been a driving force in the reform of mathematics education with the publication of the Curriculum and Evaluation Standards for School Mathematics *and* Professional Standards for Teaching Mathematics *(see annotations)*. NCTM *publishes several professional journals, including* Teaching Children Mathematics *for teachers of grades pre-K–6,* Mathematics Teaching in the Middle School *for teachers of grades 5–9, and* Mathematics Teacher *for teachers of grades 8–12. NCTM also publishes the* Journal for Research in Mathematics Education *and a wide variety of books and videotapes on all aspects of mathematics education. NCTM sponsors an annual, national conference as well as several regional conferences and many mathematics award programs.*

National Council of Teachers of Mathematics. 1989. *Curriculum and Evaluation Standards for School Mathematics.* Reston, VA: National Council of Teachers of Mathematics.

This comprehensive document (266 pp.) recognizes and addresses the need for major instructional reform in the content and emphasis in mathematics K–12. Fifty-four standards are delineated and divided into four areas: K–4, 5–8, 9–12, and evaluation. Embedded in the Standards is the belief that "First, 'knowing' mathematics is 'doing' mathematics. A person gathers, discovers, or creates knowledge in the course of some activity having a purpose" (p. 7). Also in each standard are the expected student activities associated with doing mathematics. The document bases its curriculum and evaluation of mathematical literacy on five goals for all students: learning to value mathematics, becoming confident in one's own ability, becoming a mathematical problem solver, learning to communicate mathematically, and learning to reason mathematically. All educators interested in improving the quality of school mathematics will want to become familiar with this highly impressive and workable document.

National Council of Teachers of Mathematics. 1991. *Professional Standards for Teaching Mathematics.* Reston, VA: National Council of Teachers of Mathematics.

This document has been created to provide specific direction and support to teachers for creating mathematical environments, actions, and activities that complement the goals set out in the landmark document for reform, Curriculum and Evaluation Standards for School Mathematics *(NCTM, 1989; see annotation). This text provides guidance for the development of professionalism in the teaching of mathematics and includes standards for teaching mathematics and for evaluating the teaching of mathematics, to name a few. Each professional standard for teachers is explained in depth and illustrated by vignettes depicting excellent teaching. For teachers using the NCTM Standards for how and what students should learn and be taught (1989), this companion document for professional development is a must for meeting the challenges and making the changes in mathematics teaching in the classroom.*

Ohanian, Susan. 1992. *Garbage Pizza, Patchwork Quilts, and Math Magic: Stories about Teachers Who Love to Teach and Children Who Love to Learn.* New York: W. H. Freeman. Distributed by Heinemann.

With a grant from the Exxon Corporation Foundation, the author spent a year visiting K–3 classrooms in which exciting math projects were happening. The resulting book reads like a novel, as teachers make the NCTM Standards come alive with innovative, creative teaching techniques, such as making a pie graph of types of environmental waste, which became the "garbage pizza" of the book's title. The book conveys the enthusiasm of teachers, parents, and administrators who are working together to excite children about the potential of mathematical learning. (V.M.)

Rowan, Thomas, and Barbara Bourne. 1994. *Thinking Like Mathematicians: Putting the K–4 NCTM Standards into Practice.* Portsmouth, NH: Heinemann.

This very practical resource will be appreciated by teachers who want to implement the NCTM Standards. Each chapter is filled with strategies that are explained through vignettes and anecdotes. Specific chapters discuss planning and implementing the program, evaluation, and questions that teachers might have. I especially enjoyed the case study of a student who is thinking and growing as a mathematician while using the concepts embedded in the NCTM Standards. (V.M.)

Welchman-Tischler, Rosamond. 1992. *How to Use Children's Literature to Teach Mathematics.* Reston, VA: The National Council of Teachers of Mathematics.

This seventy-nine-page resource, part of the NCTM "how to . . ." series, describes ways to use children's literature to develop mathematical concepts and connections. Specific plans and sample activities are given for many children's books. Elementary teachers, especially primary teachers, find this a helpful resource. See also The Wonderful World of Mathematics: A Critically Annotated List of Children's Books in Mathematics *by Diane Thiessen and Margaret Matthias (NCTM, 1992).*

Whitin, David J., Heidi Mills, and Timothy O'Keefe. 1990. *Living and Learning Mathematics: Stories and Strategies for Supporting Mathematical Literacy.* Portsmouth, NH: Heinemann.

This text brings the reader into a transitional first-grade classroom where children learn about mathematical principles through daily exploration and sharing of their own problem-solving strategies. Mathematics is explored through children's interests, curricular themes, classroom events, children's literature, as well as through graphing. Numbers are used for real purposes as children write original mathematical stories about such everyday concerns as losing and growing teeth and fish living and dying in the classroom. The primary-grade teacher will find this a useful resource for meaningfully connecting mathematics to the lives of children.

Whitin, David J., and Sandra Wilde. 1992. *Read Any Good Math Lately? Children's Books for Mathematical Learning, K–6.* Portsmouth, NH: Heinemann.

In this volume many interesting books are suggested that will support growing mathematical literacy. Each chapter is organized around a topic, such as multiplication, fractions, or estimation. After a general discussion of the suggested books, the reader is taken into a classroom at various levels (K–2, 3–4, 5–6) where children's responses related to specific books are described. Further explorations are suggested, and a comprehensive bibliography ends each chapter. This book is a treasure chest of ideas for bringing literature into the mathematical curriculum. (V.M.)

Social Studies Books and Resources

"If American history is being studied, a novel about colonial life will be valuable, but only as primarily an aesthetic experience, a sharing of what it would have been like to live in those days. If the story has been read with a primarily aesthetic emphasis, one can later, of course, ask students to recall incidental information about, for example, methods of transportation. But it would often be helpful to suggest that the author of the poem or novel had acquired that information through verified historical sources" (Rosenblatt, 1991, p. 447).

For easy reference, both the Social Studies and Science Books and Resources have been listed in alphabetical order by title.

Adventures with Social Studies Through Literature by Sharron L. McElmeel. 1991. Englewood, CO: Teacher Ideas Press.

In integrating language arts with social studies, McElmeel looks at other times and places through such topics as folklore, Laura Ingalls Wilder's books, Gary Paulsen's books, books related to coming to America, and American heroes. For each of these chapter topics and others, she gives background information, concepts to be highlighted, literature and authors to be discussed, and suggested response activities. Many addresses for authors and poets featured in this volume are included to promote student correspondence.

• *Children's Literature & Social Studies: Selecting and Using Notable Books in the*

Classroom, edited by Myra Zarnowski and Arlene F. Gallagher. 1993. Washington, DC: National Council for the Social Studies.

This treasure of a resource for K–8 teachers gives a wealth of practical information for using excellent trade books in the social studies program. Part 1 of the book examines the selection of books; Part 2 addresses ways to purposefully use these books. In-depth information is given for choosing and using nonfiction to read aloud, picture books, biographies, autobiographies, and historical novels. Suggested ways to use these books in discussion and writing about significant social issues are included. Excellent bibliographies, some of which are annotated, abound throughout this terrific book (80 pp.).

Cobblestone Publishing, Inc. 7 School Street, Peterborough, NH 03458.

During the school year, Cobblestone publishes monthly and bimonthly themed magazines for young people, ages 8–16: Cobblestone: The History Magazine for Young People; Calliope: World History for Young People; Faces: The Magazine About People; *and* Odyssey: Science That's Out of This World. *These quality magazines, which contain well-researched, well-written articles supported by photographs and illustrations, can be used to support an integrated curriculum. All back issues can be ordered.*

Constructing Buildings, Bridges, and Minds: Building an Integrated Curriculum Through Social Studies by Katherine A. Young. 1994. Portsmouth, NH: Heinemann.

Any teacher wanting to implement a "learning across the curriculum" project will want to read this book detailing the integration of the curriculum through a year-long classroom social studies project. Two major projects on Washington, DC, and Latin America were undertaken in the upper-elementary classroom taught by the author. The author describes the planning, the children and what they did, and what happened. She does not offer a "how-to" manual, but instead shows the often spontaneous, but carefully planned, activities that took place over the year. This is an

intriguing book with many ideas to consider and think about if we are to help children to take charge of their learning and become lifelong learners. (V.M.)

"Developing Social Studies Concepts Through Picture Books" by Pamela J. Farris and Carol J. Fuhler. February 1994. *The Reading Teacher,* pp. 380–385.

Geared to middle- and upper-elementary students, this article demonstrates how picture books can be used to teach social studies. Criteria for choosing picture books and examples of how these books can be used to extend students' thinking and knowledge are included.

From Sea to Shining Sea: Ohio by Dennis Brindell Fradin. 1993. Chicago, IL: Children's Press.

This is but one title in a clearly written and illustrated series about our states that is written for the upper-elementary grades. In addition to a text of about fifty pages, each book includes a table of contents, a "Did You Know?" section of interesting and unusual facts, an information section of vital facts, a listing of important historical dates and events, a state map, a glossary, and an index. Appealing content and format.

• "Historical Literacy: A Journey of Discovery" by Cynthia Stearns Nelson. April 1994. *The Reading Teacher,* pp. 552–556.

A fifth-grade teacher does a terrific job explaining how she develops historical literacy in her classroom. She begins with three important questions: (1) What are the big understandings or concepts to be developed? (2) What cultural beliefs and values influence our perceptions of this content? (3) What resources are available for studying this content? (p. 553). Nelson's framework and "Sample Unit, the Stories of Mildred Taylor" provide an excellent model for any teacher who wants to meaningfully integrate the teaching of social studies into the curriculum.

History Workshop: Reconstructing the Past with Elementary Students by Karen L. Jorgensen. 1993. Portsmouth, NH: Heinemann.

"I realized that learning about history,

like learning to read and write, was a process in which children create or construct personal and social meaning." So writes teacher Karen Jorgensen who shares her three-year exploration in grades three through five of how she came to apply the writing workshop model to teaching history. This honest, personal narrative (167 pp.) lets us in on classroom conversations between Jorgensen and her students and also gives us many examples of activities employed in the history workshop. Recommended for teachers making the transition to teaching history so it connects with all language learning. Applicable to all the elementary grades.

Literature-Based Social Studies: Children's Books and Activities to Enrich the K–5 Curriculum by Mildred Knight Laughlin and Patricia Payne Kardaleff. 1991. Phoenix, AZ: Oryx Press.

Many themes with suggested books and activities to extend the social studies curriculum are found in this excellent reference text. Topics include Economics of Family Living, Pioneer Communities, Urban Living, World Neighbors, the American Frontier, the Civil War Era, and many more. This is a helpful book that should be in every elementary library. (V.M.)

National Council for the Social Studies. 3501 Newark Street, NW, Washington, DC 20016-3167. (telephone 202-966-7840)

The National Council for the Social Studies publishes Social Studies and the Young Learner *for elementary teachers (see annotation),* Social Education *for middle school and college teachers,* Curriculum Standards for the Social Studies *(Fall 1994), and many other publications related to teaching and learning in social studies. Also holds an annual conference, as well as regional and state conferences, to focus on issues in social studies.*

New True Books. 1990–1993. Chicago, IL: Children's Press.

There are dozens of interesting books with lots of photographs on a wide range of subjects in this social studies and science series. Books deal with such social studies topics as Congress, newspapers, Mexico,

North America, and money. Written for the primary grades.

"Notable Children's Trade Books in the Field of Social Studies." Children's Book Council, 568 Broadway, New York, NY 10012.

Published annually and jointly with the National Council for the Social Studies, this resource is a great way to keep up with the latest and best new books—including folktales and legends. (See Children's Literature and Social Studies [1993] for ways to use these titles in the classroom.) Send a self-addressed, stamped envelope for your copy.

Social Education. Washington, DC: National Council for the Social Studies.

This scholarly journal on the teaching of social studies is published seven times a year. Includes position statements, research, articles, and practical ideas for the teaching of social studies. The annual April/May issue includes "Notable Children's Trade Books in the Field of Social Studies," a specially selected annotated bibliography for children in grades K–8.

Social Studies and the Young Learner. Washington, DC: National Council for the Social Studies.

A quarterly journal for K–6 teachers to support the creative teaching of social studies. Some issues are devoted to a specific theme. Includes related children's literature, reviews of books and resources for the classroom, discussions of contemporary issues, and practical ideas and strategies for the elementary teacher. Very informative journal with lots of applicable information.

Social Studies Through Children's Literature: An Integrated Approach by Anthony D. Fredericks. 1991. Englewood, CO: Teacher Ideas Press.

Fredericks describes many projects and activities for enhancing the teaching of social studies through literature in the elementary classroom. Questions and activities are presented for about thirty titles. While there are too many questions and activities presented for each book, many of the activities can serve as good models for creating your own meaningful exten-

sions. The annotated literature and resources for social studies included in the appendices are excellent.

- *The Story of Ourselves: Teaching History Through Children's Literature* by Michael Tunnell and Richard Ammon. 1993. Portsmouth, NH: Heinemann.

  We are reminded as we read this wonderful resource for making history come alive for students that the word "history" is made up mostly of the word "story" and that historians have always been storytellers of human events and behaviors. The authors of this 204-page text convincingly give the research and rationale for using historical trade literature as the best way to help children develop historical judgment. As compared to textbooks, trade books offer richer vocabulary, greater detail, a more engaging writing style, enhanced coherence and drama as well as broader perspectives.

  This book is terrific for a close-up look at the creative process that writers of historical fiction and nonfiction use, the process of researching and writing historical literature—including a comparison of textbooks and trade books—and useful strategies and units for teaching history with trade books. The extensive, annotated bibliographies include an "Anne Frank Unit" and books specific to "Americans at War," "Human Rights," "Governing America," and "Settling New Lands." This is an invaluable resource for K–8 educators ready to meaningfully integrate the teaching of social studies into the curriculum and for becoming familiar with the best nonfiction and historical fiction writers for young people.

Understanding American History Through Children's Literature: Instructional Units and Activities for Grades K–8 by Maria A. Perez-Stable and Mary Hurlbut Cordier. 1994. Phoenix, AZ: Oryx Press.

  This volume has been organized into two sections: Part 1 for primary grades, and Part 2 for the intermediate and middle school grades. Within each section, units of instruction are planned that explore the history of the United States from

pre-Columbus to the present. In each section, many books are annotated so teachers can easily choose and select appropriate materials for their classrooms. (V.M.)

Science Books and Resources

Following are some selected resources to go along with "big understandings" and independent reading and research in an integrated science program. For understanding integration see pp. 276–294 in *Invitations*, as well as professional books and resources in these "blue pages."

The Astonishing Curriculum: Integrating Science and Humanities Through Language, edited by Stephen Tchudi. 1993. Urbana, IL: National Council of Teachers of English.

  In this collection of essays, teachers from first-grade level through graduate school share classroom practices that bridge the gap between science and the humanities. I especially enjoyed how the students of Karen Gallas use "science talks" and "science journals" to find the answers to difficult questions. Regardless of your teaching level, there are many ideas for educators to consider as they plan science experiences for children. (V.M.)

- *Benchmarks for Science Literacy: Project 2061* by the American Association for the Advancement of Science. 1993. New York: Oxford University Press.

  Carefully written by six school-district teams and extensively reviewed and rewritten, this companion book to Science for All Americans *(American Association for the Advancement of Science, 1990) provides school districts with benchmarks, "statements of what all students should be able to do" in science, mathematics, and technology. Benchmarks are provided for the end of grades two, five, eight, and twelve, and are meant to be used as a tool to guide school districts in designing and developing their own science curriculum and instructional materials for what students should know, understand, and be able to do scientifically. An essential re-*

source and exemplary model for curriculum reform.

Connections: The Living Planet, edited by Jenifer Ludbrook, Sharon Stewart, and Jocelyn Van Huyse-Ludbrook. 1993. Scarborough, Ontario: Ginn Publishing Canada.

This exciting series of twelve books for the intermediate grades is organized around three environmental issues: Life and the Planet, People and the Planet, and Planetary Change. The books explore basic concepts about ecology, requirements of human life, and ways that humans influence the ecosystem. Some titles in-clude Water in Our World, The Remarkable RainForest, *and* The Earth Feeds Us.

Creepy Crawlies and the Scientific Method: Over 100 Hands-On Science Experiments for Children by Sally Stenhouse Kneidel. 1993. Golden, CO: Fulcrum Publishing.

This book for parents and teachers demonstrates how to use insects and crawling creatures to teach children the five steps of the scientific method: question, hypothesis, methods, result, and conclusion. Each chapter is clearly formatted with background information, lots of experiments, and clear procedures. Great for getting kids excited about science and thinking about and testing their own questions. Written for elementary teachers but suitable for secondary also.

Dear World: How Children Around the World Feel About Our Environment, edited by Lannis Temple. 1993. New York: Random House.

A collection of letters, drawings, and photos from around the world beautifully illustrates schoolchildren's concerns about environmental pollution. Students are encouraged to add their own letters and drawings.

Earth Science for Every Kid: 101 Easy Experiments That Really Work by Janice Van-Cleave. 1991. New York: John Wiley.

Students and teachers love this book because the experiments can be done easily at home or at school, and they really work. Experiments and activities are detailed with step-by-step instructions and illustrations. An easily understood scien-

tific explanation is given for the results of each experiment. Check the other books in this workable series.

Exploring Nature by Peter Garland. 1992. Crystal Lake, IL: The Wright Group.

These six twenty-four-page books for the primary grades include vivid color photography and interesting text. Titles include Animals of the Rocky Shore, The Housefly, The Frog, The Ladybug, The Marvelous Mosquito, *and* The Pond.

First Discovery Books by Nancy Krulik. 1992. New York: Scholastic.

These unique, beautifully illustrated little books include brightly colored transparent overlays and laminated pages to entice the reader into making discoveries and seeing connections. Some titles in the series are Airplanes and Flying Machines, The Earth and Sky, The Egg, The Tree, *and* Weather. *Appealing for preschool through early intermediate grades.*

First Library Paperbacks by Kate Petty. 1990. New York: Franklin Watts.

This information-packed picture book series for the primary grades includes six nonfiction books: Crocodiles and Alligators, Dinosaurs, Frogs and Toads, Sharks, Snakes, *and* Spiders.

Green Giants: Rainforests of the Pacific Northwest by Tom Parkin. 1992. Buffalo, NY: Firefly Books.

This is but one book (48 pp.) in a series of Earth Care Books *that are full of accurate text and illustrations that describe the topic, what the problems are, and what we must do environmentally. Other books in the series for the intermediate grades include* For the Birds, Trash Attack!, Garbage and What We Can Do About It, Get Growing! How the Earth Feeds Us, *and* The Heat is On: Facing Our Energy Problem.

Ideas for Environmental Education in the Elementary Classroom by Kath Murdoch. 1994. Portsmouth, NH: Heinemann

This unique guidebook (204 pp.) for the primary grades focuses on activities and strategies to develop key understandings about the environment. Well-organized, workable plans include broad understandings, preparations, procedures, sam-

ples of children's work, and resource materials. Terrific for integrating environmental education across the curriculum and for problem-solving issues related to living on Earth.

Informazing!, edited by Stephen Moline. 1988–1990. Crystal Lake, IL: Rigby.

Eight, sixteen-page, little books and Big Books dealing with topics such as insects, the universe, animals, dinosaurs, and the body captivate children's imaginations with their lively, clear text and bright, realistic photographs. Geared to the primary grades.

Keeping Minibeasts by Barrie Watts. 1989. New York: Franklin Watts.

Simple text and close-up color photographs depict how to care for small creatures (such as caterpillars, frogs, ladybugs, and spiders) in this nature series for the primary grades. Ten titles in the series. Ideal for supporting independent research.

Let's-Read-And-Find-Out Science. 1992–1994. New York: HarperCollins Publishers.

This is a well written and illustrated series of over sixty picture books for the primary grades. Some new titles include Be a Friend to Trees by Patricia Lauber, illustrated by Holly Keller, Where Does the Garbage Go? by Paul Showers, illustrated by Randy Chewing, What Makes a Shadow by Clyde Robert Bulla, illustrated by June Otani, and Baby Whales Drink Milk by Barbara Juster Esbensen, illustrated by Juster Esbensen. Basic science concepts are introduced in an organized manner, and easy to follow hands-on activities are included. Topics include the Human Body, Plants and Animals, the World Around Us, Dinosaurs, Outer Space, Weather and the Seasons, and Our Earth. Great for the classroom library and supporting young children's natural curiosity.

My World. 1989–1992. Austin, TX: Steck-Vaughn.

This high-interest science and social studies, nonfiction collection for grades 1–3 includes 144 titles dealing with animals, sports, nature, and nations of the world. Each sixteen-page book includes sizable

text, full-color photographs, and an index. Some titles are available in Spanish.

National Science Teachers Association. 1840 Wilson Boulevard, Arlington, VA 22201. (telephone 703-243-7100)

The National Science Teachers Association publishes Science and Children for elementary teachers (see annotation), Science Scope for teachers of grades 5–9, The Science Teacher for teachers of grades 7–12, The Journal of College Science Teaching for college teachers, and many useful books and resources to support science teaching. NSTA also publishes Quantum, a student magazine of math and science and "NSTA Reports!," a science education newspaper. Also sponsors an annual, national conference as well as three regional conferences and many science award programs.

Picture Library Paperbacks by Norman Barrett. 1989–1991. New York: Franklin Watts.

This series of about twenty nonfiction books (can be ordered individually) is packed with information, beautiful photographs, and clear, simple text for grades K–4 and is a welcome addition to the classroom library. Some titles include Polar Animals, Elephants, Bears, Airliners, Trail Bikes, and Helicopters.

Primary Ecology Series, edited by Bobbie Kalman. 1993. New York and Toronto: Crabtree Publishing.

Beautifully photographed with elementary school children in natural settings to support the books' subjects, these thirty-two-page picture books are full of information and invite participation in caring for our world. Some titles in the series include How Trees Help Me and The Air I Breathe. Very appealing.

Rookie Read-About Science by Allan Fowler. 1993. Chicago, IL: Children's Press.

A delightful, informative series of thirty-two-page little books on topics that interest young children. Some of the titles in this extensive series include If It Weren't for Farmers, It's a Good Thing There Are Insects, It's Best to Leave a Snake Alone, and It Could Still Be a Dinosaur. Real-life photos, large, clear text, and only several sentences per page make this a welcome addition to the early primary classroom and school library.

Science and Children. Washington, DC: National Science Teachers Association. 1840 Wilson Boulevard, Arlington, VA, 22201

This informative and practical science journal for elementary and middle school teachers and administrators is published eight times a year and is available with membership to NSTA. Provides thoughtful articles, practical and creative teaching suggestions, reviews of books and resources, colorful posters, and inserts as well as the annual "Notable Science Tradebooks for Children" in a spring issue.

Science and Language Links: Classroom Implications, edited by Johanna Scott. 1993. Portsmouth, NH: Heinemann.

Although it was written halfway across the world in Australia, this book could be a companion book to The Astonishing Curriculum: Integrating Science and Humanities Through Language (Tchudi, 1993). This book looks at the relationships between science and talking, writing, and reading. It helps teachers to realize that language supports science learning, and science concepts can be used to develop language. Examples of student projects enhance the insights in this book. (V.M.)

Science for All Americans: Project 2061 by the American Association for the Advancement of Science. 1990. New York: Oxford University Press.

Science for All Americans is the highly respected philosophical treatise on what constitutes adult literacy in science. Literacy in science is defined broadly, to encompass concepts of mathematics and technology as well as the natural and social sciences. Used widely in the U.S. to help guide reform efforts, this scholarly text (272 pp.) deals with the nature of science, basic world knowledge from the scientific perspective, what scientific concepts people should understand, and the "habits of mind" that are necessary for science literacy.

Recommendations for what scientifically literate students should know and be able to do by the time they graduate from high school are stated. See the companion book, Benchmarks for Science Literacy, and watch for the upcoming Blueprints for Reform and Designs for Science Literacy.

Science Through Children's Literature by Carol M. Butzow and John W. Butzow. 1989. Englewood, CO: Teacher Ideas Press.

This useful resource geared to the elementary grades connects fiction books with scientific concepts by describing many activities to go along with specific books. Activities for each science topic are centered around a work of fiction. Related books and references are cited.

Science Workshop: A Whole Language Approach by Wendy Saul, et al. 1993. Portsmouth, NH: Heinemann.

Concepts and ideas developed in the reading/writing workshop are shown to be applicable in the study of science in this book. Wendy Saul provides the introductory theoretical framework in the opening chapter. Four teachers present ways of getting started, developing a questioning atmosphere, and ways of assessing the program. The final chapter gives suggestions for topic development as well as sources for materials and further information. This is a hands-on, practical approach that will be appreciated by classroom teachers eager to bring student-centered learning to the science area. (V.M.)

Sierra Club Books for Children. 1992–1994. 730 Polk Street, San Francisco, CA 94109.

The Sierra Club publishes some first-class books for children. The inspiring books include engaging text and full-color photographs to tackle environmental issues, present accurate information, and share how children and adults can make a difference. A favorite, highly acclaimed book is Come Back, Salmon by Molly Cone, photographs by Sidnee Wheelwright (1992), the compelling story about how a group of fifth-grade students adopted a polluted stream that had once been a spawning ground for salmon and brought it back to life.

Snapshot, edited by Mary Ling. 1994. New York: Covent Garden Books.

Titles in this series for the primary

grades, which devotes one to two pages (a snapshot in enlarged print and pictures) to each subtopic, include Wild Animals, Things on Wheels, Animal Antics, and Funny Faces.

Sunshine Science, Level 2 by Brian Cutting and Jillian Cutting. 1993. Bothell, WA: The Wright Group.

These information books with such titles as Keeping Warm! Keeping Cool!, How Flies Live, The Survival of Fish, and Our Eyes are a good addition to the classroom library. Each twenty-four-page book has sizable text, clear concepts, and color photo/illustrations. First and second graders will enjoy reading these independently or with support.

Author/Illustrator Books and Resources

- *Art for Children.* 1994. New York: Chelsea House Publishers. (hardbound)

Written with conversational text from the viewpoint of inquiring students, this fascinating series of books takes the reader into the life, thoughts, times, and art of some of the most renowned artists: Brueghel, Chagall, Leonardo da Vinci, Degas, Gauguin, Matisse, Picasso, Rousseau, and Van Gogh. Each book is about sixty pages and includes photographs related to the artists' lives along with color reproductions of their paintings. Engaging reading for grades 3–6.

Blair, Gwenda. Illustrated by Thomas B. Allen. 1981. *Laura Ingalls Wilder.* New York: Putnam. See annotation, p. 152b.

Chevalier, Tracy. 1990. *Twentieth-Century Children's Writers,* 4th ed. Chicago: St. James Press. (hardbound)

This useful teacher reference features over 800 contributors in literature. For each author, there is a lengthy, interesting narrative biographical account and a list of publications. Lots of information for in-depth author study.

- Commire, Anne (ed.). 1994: *Something About the Author.* Detroit: Gale Research. (hardbound)

Written for teachers and students, this is the most complete and extensive resource on children's authors and illustrators. Most entries are autobiographical and include the following information: personal, career, writings, and sidelights. Updated every year since 1972, there are over sixty volumes in this reference series, and each volume includes a cumulative index. If your school district does not own this outstanding series, check with your local public library.

Copeland, Jeffrey S. 1993. *Speaking of Poets: Interviews with Poets Who Write for Children and Young Adults.* Urbana, IL: National Council of Teachers of English.

Sixteen poets are interviewed by Copeland about what they hope to accomplish as they write for children. Many of them, such as Arnold Adoff and Myra Cohn Livingston, are recipients of the NCTE Award for Excellence in Poetry for Children. Bibliographies of each poet's works follow each interview. This is a valuable book for background information about the poets, as well as for assistance in locating a selection of their poetry. (V.M.)

Cummings, Pat (ed.). 1992. *Talking With Artists.* New York: Bradbury Press.

Questions asked of artists such as Leo and Diane Dillon, Lois Ehlert, Tom Feelings, Jerry Pinkney, Lane Smith, Chris Van Allsburg, and David Wiesner include where they get their ideas, whether family is included in their work, and how they make pictures. Illustrations include early work by the artists, a childhood and an adult photograph, and art work from a well-known book. Excellent resource material for author background and for discussing how artists get their ideas. Fourteen picture book illustrators are included.

Day, Frances Ann (compiler). 1994. *Multicultural Voices in Contemporary Literature.* Portsmouth, NH: Heinemann. See annotation, p. 63b.

dePaola, Tomie. 1989. *The Art Lesson.* New York: Putnam. (Sandcastle)

The popular author-illustrator tells and draws about growing up wanting to be an artist and his not-very-encouraging early school experiences. Very appealing for K–2 students and everyone who is determined to be uniquely creative.

Fox, Mem. 1992. *Dear Mem Fox, I Have Read All Your Books Even the Pathetic Ones: And Other Incidents in the Life of a Children's Book Author.* San Diego: Harvest/Harcourt Brace.

The best-selling author of Possum Magic *and* Hattie and the Fox *shares her early life experiences, and tells how she came to create her unique books. From lighthearted to serious, this book gives her insights on teaching, authoring, her brush with cancer, and life in general. An inspiring and delightful book to read! (V.M.)*

Gallo, Donald R. (ed.). 1992. *Authors' Insights: Turning Teenagers into Readers and Writers.* Portsmouth, NH: Boynton/Cook.

A group of distinguished young adult writers contributed essays on the subject of teaching literature to teenagers in this book. They cover topics such as the importance of using "readable" books in the classroom, censorship, response to books, teaching writing, and bringing authors into the classroom. Their unique experiences give teachers a lot to think about as they plan for their students. (V.M.)*

Gherman, Beverly. 1992. *E.B. White: Some Writer!* New York: Beech Tree.

Illustrated with photographs, this book gives us a chance to meet the man behind Charlotte's Web, Stuart Little, *and* The Trumpet of the Swan. *White wrote extensively for adults, but these three books he created for children have become classics. I especially enjoyed the chapters describing the creation of these wonderful books. There are many anecdotes that can be shared with your students. (V.M.)*

Holtze, Sally Holmes. 1989. *Sixth Book of Junior Authors and Illustrators.* New York: H. W. Wilson.

This teacher reference, the sixth in the series, offers complete and interesting autobiographical and biographical sketches of about 250 noted children's authors and illustrators. A new volume is published every five to six years.*

Hyman, Trina Schart. 1989. *Self-Portrait:*

Trina Schart Hyman. New York: Harper & Row. See annotation, p. 153b.

Immell, Myra (ed.). 1992. *The Young Adult Reader's Adviser: The Best in Literature and Language Arts, Mathematics and Computer Science. Volume One;* and *The Young Adult Reader's Adviser: The Best in Social Sciences and History, Science and Health. Volume Two.* New Providence, NJ: Bowker.

These volumes have been written to assist students, teachers, and librarians with the wide selection of resources available. Alphabetized by author within the subject category, each entry includes biographical information about the author including books by and about the author.*

Killen, Rosemary (project director). 1988. *The Author's Eye.* Santa Rosa, CA: American School Publishers.

Each complete program—available for authors Roald Dahl and Katherine Paterson—includes an excellent video of the author in his or her writing setting, twenty-five "Author's Notebooks," a poster, and a teacher's resource book. The terrific "Author's Notebooks," which are sold in packages of twenty-five and can be ordered separately, include letters written by the author, first drafts, notes, jottings, and favorite phrases and words. Inspiring for understanding how a writer works and for stimulating students' own writing. Very expensive.*

• Kovaks, Deborah, and James Preller. 1993. *Meet the Authors and Illustrators: 60 Creators of Favorite Children's Books Talk About Their Work. Volume Two.* New York: Scholastic Professional Books.

For each engaging two-page profile of a well-known, favorite author or illustrator, the following is included: some early memories, the creative process each goes through, a picture of the author or illustrator, selected published titles, statements by the author or illustrator, photocopies of the cover of one or two favorite books or illustrations, and a terrific activity suggested by the author or illustrator. See also Volume One, 1991. Both resources are visually appealing and filled with interest-*

ing information for students and teachers. My favorite part about these profiles is that each is written in a way that encourages young writers to write their own stories and/or create their own illustrations.

Lloyd, Pamela. 1990. *How Writers Write*. Portsmouth, NH: Heinemann.

Using a question-and-answer format, the author has put together a book that shows how writers live and work. She interviews authors such as Robert Cormier, Madeleine L'Engle, Jack Prelutsky, Seymour Simon, and Jane Yolen to find out how they write a first draft, where ideas come from, how they conduct research, and why they are writers. There are many ideas that can be shared with your students. (V.M.)

• *Meet the Author Collection*. 1993–1994. Katonah, NY: Richard C. Owen. (hardbound)

Written by the authors themselves for seven-to-ten-year-old readers and illustrated with real-life, color photographs of authors at home and at work, each of these thirty-two-page books is terrific for kids to read on their own. Even as an adult, I found these books fascinating. Readers will notice how and where authors live and write, get many of their ideas, and organize their days. The prominent children's authors in the series include Verna Aardema, James Howe, Jean Fritz, Lee Bennett Hopkins, Jane Yolen, Rafe Martin, Karla Kuskin, Paul Goble, Patricia Polacco, Margaret Mahy, Eve Bunting, Patricia McKissack, and Cynthia Rylant. Great for learning about favorite authors and for motivating reading of their books. Also terrific for motivating children's own writing. Available as individual titles.

Norby, Shirley, and Gregory Ryan. 1989. *Famous Children's Authors. Book Two*. Minneapolis, MN: T. S. Denison.

A grade-two teacher and a children's librarian have written twenty author stories for young readers to enjoy and gain information about popular authors. Each two-page entry ends with a bibliography of the authors' books. Sequel to Book One.

Quackenbush, Robert. 1985. *Once Upon a Time: A Story of the Brothers Grimm*. New York: Simon & Schuster. See annotation, p. 152b.

Rosen, Michael J. (ed.). 1993. *Speak! Children's Book Illustrators Brag About Their Dogs*. San Diego: Harcourt Brace.

Kids and adults love this book. Forty-three famous illustrators brag, in pictures and stories, about their dogs. The personalities of the dogs—and the illustrators—shine through. Editor Michael Rosen invites children to write to him and "send me a little bragging about your favorite dog." A totally entertaining and engaging book.

Rylant, Cynthia. 1993. *But I'll Be Back Again: An Autobiography by the Newbery Award-Winning Author*. New York: Beech Tree.

In this book, Rylant describes the influences on her life: her grandmother, a tiny town named Beaver, the Beatles, and Robert Kennedy. How a little girl from rural West Virginia who grew up without books became an award-winning author becomes clear after you read these words. Her books become even more meaningful as she mentions where some of her ideas and characters come from. (V.M.)

Shapiro, Miles. 1994. *Maya Angelou: Author*. New York: Chelsea House. See annotation, p. 152b.

Tunnell, Michael O., and Richard Ammon. 1993. "The Creative Process." In *The Story of Ourselves: Teaching History Through Children's Literature*, edited by Michael O. Tunnell and Richard Ammon. Portsmouth, NH: Heinemann, pp. 9–47.

Four well-known authors (Joan W. Blos, Milton Meltzer, Pam Conrad, Russell Freedman) and an illustrator (Leonard Everett Fisher) describe their own process of writing and illustrating historical fiction and nonfiction and, in so doing, make elementary through middle school students "insiders" to the process. I found the reading fascinating and saw possibilities for children's writing. For example, in writing nonfiction, Russell Freedman vividly describes his storytelling devices: creating a detailed scene that the reader can visualize, developing a character through explicit word pictures, and using telling an-

ecdotes. For the annotation of the complete text, see p. 93b.

- Turner, Robyn Montana. 1992. *Georgia O'Keeffe (Portraits of Women Artists for Children)*. New York: Little, Brown.

  This is but one in an excellent series of biographies of prominent women artists Rosa Bonheur, Mary Cassatt, Frida Kahlo, Georgia O'Keeffe, and Faith Ringgold. The books are distinctive for the informative, carefully researched text, photographs related to the artist's life, and beautiful color reproductions of the artist's work. Use as a read-aloud for the early grades. Intermediate-grade students can read them on their own. Reaffirming to young women (and young men) who are interested in art and becoming artists. Fills a need for more books on famous women.

Venezia, Mike. 1990–1994. *Getting to Know the World's Greatest Artists*. Chicago, IL: Children's Press.

  A great series for introducing young children to art and artists. Written in enlarged, clear text, the book presents the artist as a real person. Color reproductions of the artist's work plus fanciful illustrations open up the world of art to students in grades K–4. Some of the celebrated artists in the series include: Botticelli, Leonardo da Vinci, Hopper, Goya, Cassatt, Monet, Picasso, Gauguin, Rembrandt, and Van Gogh.

Winter, Jeanette, and John Winter. 1991. *Diego*. New York: Knopf. See annotation, p. 153b.

Parent Books and Resources

Baghban, Marcia. 1989. *You Can Help Your Young Child with Writing*. Newark, DE: International Reading Association.

  This pamphlet is part of a series designed to provide parents with practical ideas to use to support young learners. Beginning with anecdotes of young children writing, it describes how the child's understanding of the writing system differs from that of the adult writer. Answers to possible parent questions, such as "What about correctness?" are given, along with recommended readings for more information. A helpful guide to hand to a questioning parent! (V.M.)

Barron, Marlene. 1990. *I Learn to Read and Write the Way I Learn to Talk*. Katonah, NY: Richard C. Owen.

  Based on whole language theory and practice, this concise booklet (32 pp.) simply and clearly explains early reading and writing behaviors. Excellent to share with preschool through grade one parents.

Baskwill, Jane. 1989. *Parents and Teachers: Partners in Learning*. Richmond Hill, Ontario: Scholastic Canada. See annotation, p. 4b.

- Bialostok, Steven. 1992. *Raising Readers: Helping Your Child to Literacy*. Winnipeg, Manitoba: Peguis.

  This is a terrific book to lend or give to parents who want specific information about how children learn to read, what to look for in their children's reading, and how they can support the process. Bialostok answers the questions parents have about reading aloud, the role of phonics, skills teaching, prediction, literacy development, school, and much more. Viewing reading as a process of making meaning, he gives parents perspectives and specific strategies for helping their young children develop as readers. Every parent I have lent this book to has found it easy to read and understand and incredibly helpful.

Butler, Dorothy, and Marie Clay. 1988, 1987. *Reading Begins at Home, Writing Begins at Home*. 2nd ed. Portsmouth, NH: Heinemann.

  These companion books are very useful in helping parents to understand how young children learn to read and write, and even more important, to help them to support the process before their children enter school. Both are helpful to give to parents of first-grade children, and they are especially appreciated by parents with younger children at home. (V.M.)

Cullinan, Bernice E. 1993. *Let's Read About: Finding Books They'll Want to Read*. New York: Scholastic, Inc.

Here is a companion book to Read to Me: Raising Kids Who Love to Read. *It is filled with ideas for parents to use in creating a reading environment, for reading aloud, for finding time to read, determining appropriate books for children of different ages, and how to find needed books. The final chapters suggest specific books according to subjects of interest to children of certain ages. For example, a seven- or eight-year-old might enjoy a book of poetry, or a book about sports. Under each category, a list of annotated books is suggested. This is a useful book to give or lend to parents. (V.M.)*

Cullinan, Bernice E. 1992. *Read to Me: Raising Kids Who Love to Read.* New York: Scholastic, Inc.

Writing to help parents give a love of reading to their preschool through age twelve children and keep them reading, well-known reading educator Bernice Cullinan gives straight talk, practical ideas, and brief summaries of recommended books. Several teachers I know have ordered these in bulk and given them out to parents at the first curriculum/open house evening.

• Edwards, Sharon A., and Robert W. Maloy. 1992. *Kids Have All the Write Stuff: Inspiring Your Children to Put Pencil to Paper.* New York: Penguin Books.

This is the perfect book to hand to a parent wanting to learn more about children and the writing process. It is filled with practical ideas to support young writers, and it has many samples of what children have produced. A special "Note to Teachers" chapter answers many questions that parents raise about writing in the classroom. There is an extensive bibliography of children's books that support the writing ideas and activities in the body of the text. Although written for parents, this book also deserves a teacher audience. (V.M.)

Henderson, Anne T. October 1988. "Parents Are a School's Best Friend." *Phi Delta Kappan,* pp. 149–153.

Henderson reviews long-term research findings across diverse populations and reports that "parent involvement in almost any form appears to produce measurable gains in student achievement." While training of parents of at-risk children in home teaching proved significant, the average level of achievement for a school rose only when parents were involved in the school. Important findings for raising achievement levels in effective schools through long-term, comprehensive, well-planned parent involvement.

Hill, Mary W. 1989. *Home: Where Reading and Writing Begin.* Portsmouth, NH: Heinemann.

This book is written specifically for parents and extends the idea of parents as partners in literacy development. Many examples of the developmental nature of children's reading and writing are given. Children's literature titles fill the pages, along with many practical suggestions for parents who want to reflect and consider how they can encourage their children as readers and writers. It is a great one to hand to parents in answer to their question, "How can I help my child?" (V.M.)

International Reading Association, Newark, DE. (800 Barksdale Road, P.O. Box 8139, 19714-8139, telephone 800-336-READ)

Publishes many booklets and brochures to assist parents in helping their children develop as readers and writers. Reasonably priced and can be ordered in bulk.

Kenney, Anne, Lori Morgan, Jane Owen, Chris Sherman, and Russell Walsh (team leaders). 1992. *Teens' Favorite Books. Young Adults' Choices 1987–1992.* Newark, DE: International Reading Association. See annotation, p. 67b.

Lipson, Eden Ross. 1991. *The New York Times Parent's Guide to the Best Books for Children.* Revised and updated. New York: Random House. See annotation, p. 68b.

National Council of Teachers of English. Urbana IL (1111 Kenyon Road, 61801, telephone 800-369-NCTE). 1993. "Elementary School Practices."

This popular brochure helps parents, board members, and administrators better understand and recognize the ways in which elementary teachers are incorpo-

*rating current research on language learn-
ing in their classroom practice: single copies are free and can be copied without
permission. Multiple copies are available
for $7.00 per hundred.*

Oxley, Peggy, Jean Sperling, Lynda Mudre,
and Nancy Blume, with Moira McKenzie,
and Martha King. 1991. *Reading and
Writing: Where It All Begins: Helping
Your Children at Home.* Columbus, OH:
The Literacy Connection. (2577 Coventry
Road, 43221)

*This forty-page booklet is terrific to give
to preschool, kindergarten, and grade one
parents. Clearly illustrated and written in
a positive tone, it helps parents support
their children as they learn to read and
write. Lots of specifics are given for what
parents can and should do at home.*

Phenix, Jo, and Doreen Scott-Dunne. 1994.
Spelling for Parents. Markham, Ontario:
Pembroke Publishers, and Bothell, WA:
The Wright Group.

*This eighty-page handbook helps par-
ents understand how spelling is learned
and why we are moving away from weekly
memorization of word lists. What to teach
about spelling and how to help children
become better spellers is clearly presented.
An excellent reference for teachers too.*

Preece, Alison, and Diane Cowden. 1993. *Young
Writers in the Making: Sharing the Process with Parents.* Portsmouth, NH: Heinemann.

*This practical, 130 page book is full of
usable ideas, visuals, letters, newsletters,
and forms for communicating the writing
process of young children to parents.
From the first day of school to classroom
visits to meetings to home-school projects,
Preece and Cowden offer guidelines and
suggestions for getting parents to support
and understand an integrated, literacy-
based curriculum. The primary-grades
teacher will find this a terrific resource for
effectively communicating children's writing processes with parents.*

Stillman, Peter. 1989. *Families Writing.* Cincinnati, OH: Writer's Digest Books. Distributed by Heinemann. (hardbound)

*This is a delightful book about writing
for the very best of reasons—for the family's sake—and pure enjoyment. Beginning with reasons for writing, the book is
filled with suggestions for a lifetime of
family writing activities. It's not a textbook, but a plea to tell your story—to
capture family happenings in words to be
cherished, enjoyed, and passed on to future generations. Stillman's pleasure in
writing shines through the many pieces of
his family history that are scattered
throughout the book. It's a book that I
want to share with parents, and one I
want to return to for ideas and inspira-
tions. (V.M.)*

Stoll, Donald R. (ed.). 1994. *Magazines for
Kids and Teens: A Resource for Parents,
Teachers, Librarians, and Kids!* Glassboro, NJ: Educational Press Association
of America, and Newark, DE: International Reading Association. See annotation, p. 72b.

Trelease, Jim. 1992. *Hey! Listen to This: Stories to Read Aloud.* New York: Penguin
Books. See annotation, p. 72b.

Trelease, Jim. 1990. *The New Read-Aloud
Handbook.* New York: Penguin. See annotations p. 73b.

Williams, David L., and Nancy Feyl Chavkin.
October 1989. "Essential Elements of
Strong Parent Involvement Programs."
Educational Leadership, pp. 18–20.

*Seven essential elements from successful
parent involvement programs in a five-
state area are identified and described:
written policies, administrative support,
training, partnership approach, two-way
communication, networking, and evaluation. A list of parent involvement resources is included. A useful article for
schools intent on improving parent involvement.*

Recommended Literature by Grade Level, K–12, and Supplemental Lists

Annotations for grades K–8 and supplemental lists by Susan Hepler
Annotations for grades 9–12 by Dana Noble

About These Lists

Implicit in a literature/reading program that uses real books are choice, reading for pleasure and information, and sustained daily reading time in school and at home. In addition, we need to provide time for collaborative talk about books that examines text in depth through multiple perspectives and makes connections to our lives and other texts. With high quality literature and teacher guidance, children learn to read and read to learn across the curriculum.

The following K–12, grade-level lists assume a balanced reading program that includes reading aloud, shared reading, guided reading, and independent reading as well as diverse opportunities to respond to text through listening, discussion, further reading, writing, and the visual and dramatic arts. With the exception of the kindergarten list in which books are meant to be read *to* the child, all books are meant to be read *by* and *with* the children in the guided-reading program. Books have been chosen for suitability for guided reading and literary appreciation—that is, these are books that have the power to evoke high-level discussion and personal connections to children's lives. While the grade-level placement of a book is arbitrary, that is, a title could work at several grade levels, what is not arbitrary is the quality of the books.

Balancing the Collection

As much as possible, each grade-level collection is balanced to reflect a wide variety of literature—picture books, poetry, folktales or traditional literature, realistic fiction, historical fiction, science fiction, humor, multicultural literature, and nonfiction. Books have been carefully selected from the best of children's literature, young adult (YA) literature, and, in some cases, adult literature for both their high quality and outstanding illustrations. When a folktale has been included, a "best version" has been chosen—that is, a version that is prizewinning, easily available, and beautifully told.

In this edition, we have made a major effort to locate and include excellent multicultural literature, that is, books by and about people of color that are also books respected within the particular cultures. Recognizing that, in the near future, many more Americans will be African-American, Latino, Native American or Asian-American, we have made an effort to include the best texts and illustrations that authentically represent these ethnic groups. We believe it is important that students see themselves and their culture as connected to school literacy and that all students experience the richness and diversity of other cultures through outstanding literature. As well, we have made a deliberate effort to include more books with females as main characters. Also, picture books are included through the grades as they are not just for young children. Older students enjoy the notable illustrations, beautiful and thoughtful text, and making connections to their lives and other stories.

All titles from the 1991 edition of *Invitations* have been looked at for relevance and current publishing information. Updated comments have been added to some titles; a few titles have been deleted; many new titles have been added.

Organization

Grade-level literature lists are organized alphabetically by title. Each book annotation includes a brief summary, noteworthy characteristics about the literary and artistic quality, and possible suggestions for discussion and response. Key features of each grade-level list precede the list of books, and in the K–8 levels, this information also includes suggestions for author study.

In addition to the grade-level lists, be sure to check the supplemental lists that follow the Grade 6 list and include: "Books Which Invite Writing and Storytelling" (grades 1–6), "Wordless Books" (grades K–6), "Life Stories" (grades 2–6), and, new with this edition, "Bilingual Spanish Books—A Beginning List." Also, note the extensive listing of books and series for emergent readers in the lists between kindergarten and Grade 1: "Books Which Invite Readers into Print" and "Developing Early Reading Strategies." Some titles that previously were listed in "People in Other Lands" and "Books About Our Diverse Population" have been reabsorbed into the grade-level lists as there are now many excellent multicultural titles available, making those separate categories unnecessary.

To help you locate all recommended books easily, this edition has included recommended K–12 literature, as well as the supplemental literature lists, in the main index by title, author, and illustrator. Books on the lists in the following categories are also resorted in a "Multicultural Book List:" "African-American/Black Culture," "Asian-American/Asian Culture," "Latino," and "Native American." (see pp. 167b–169b).

A "+" next to a title means the book is also available as a Big Book. The word "series" after an annotation means that there are sequels or

at least one more book dealing with the same characters in the same setting. The paperback publisher is noted within the parentheses following the original publisher and date. In general, publishers have their own paperback imprint. If the parentheses are empty, the book was not available in paperback when *Invitations* went to press, or it may only be available through a book club. (COP) indicates that a title is currently out of print. Paperback books often go in and out of print and sometimes change publishers, so if a book is not available at a particular time, it may well be available at a later date. So that teachers and schools can afford to purchase multiple copies of books, these lists are almost completely limited to titles that are (or will be) available in paperback.

Also, keep in mind that while each of the following grade-level lists stands on its own, many titles could work well on several levels.

Easy Books

Note that within grade levels 1–12, some texts have been designated easy reading (E). That is, in comparison to the other books at this grade level, these titles should be the easiest for most students to read. This designation is to ensure that your grade-level collections include some easy-to-read titles so that all students not only discuss books (that may have been read to them aloud or through shared reading) but that all students be able to read some books with minimal assistance. One of the disturbing trends with the transition to a literature program is struggling students who never actually receive books that are easy enough for them to read. Note that books marked (E) at a grade level above you may well be appropriate at your grade level.

Building a Literature Program

These literature lists are meant to be used as a reference and starting point for dialogue in a school or district. It is recommended that six to ten copies of each selected title be purchased so books can be used for guided reading and small-group discussion. It works well if groups of teachers, librarians, and administrators sit down together, read and discuss books, and make decisions about what will work best in their own school contexts. There is no one right list or best list.

For use of literature and additional recommended titles, consult your school or public librarian, reading specialists and resource teachers, the recommended texts, journal articles and "Literacy Extension Resources" in these "blue pages" as well as chapters 3, 5, and 6 in *Invitations*. For complete, updated information on ordering trade books and literature collections from wholesalers and publishers, see *Invitations* (1994), pp. 454–459.

Literature-based or a Literature Program?

While some educators do not distinguish between a literature-based program and a literature program, we do. We see a literature program as encompassing complete texts that are each separate, bound books. Many of these books are part of the classroom library collection, housed in an attractive reading area where students are free to choose books they want to read. We see a literature-based program as part of the transition process to an integrated literacy classroom. In a literature-based program, to ease management and choice of multiple texts, a school or district purchases a program that packages authentic literature selections in one text, often with accompanying consumable activities. One of the advantages of a packaged program is that it is often well balanced with nonfiction, fiction, poetry, and multicultural selections. Among the disadvantages are that some of the original illustrations and text may be altered or missing completely, thereby changing some intended meaning. Most important, even if the text is unaltered, part of a book is not the same as reading a complete book. Since as adults we do not regularly read books in anthologies, we need to give our students the same pleasure a whole book encompasses. Especially, let's keep the magic that comes from turning each page of a favorite book in anticipation and wonder.

"Formula Fiction" Books

While we do not include popular culture series books, such as *Baby Sitters Club, Boxcar Children, Encyclopedia Brown, Goosebumps,* and *Sweet Valley High* on our lists, we take the position that these books are an acceptable genre for children. The powerful appeal of "formula fiction" series books and the excitement they generate in young readers make them worth including in children's choices for reading, if for no other reason than children read them willingly and gain confidence in themselves as readers. Because so many children get "hooked" on these series books, where the format of one book follows another and the literary merit may be questionable, they probably need these books for a while as part of a balanced literary diet, much the same way as adults read some popular fiction. It is our job to help readers broaden their reading experiences to include more mature and richer literature.

Book Clubs

Because book clubs have become a major supplier of trade books to elementary classrooms in the U.S. and because they offer a wide range of interesting books across all genres, information about the three major book clubs is included. Within each club, there are different clubs for different grade levels. Prices are discounted with average costs per book of about $1.50 to $3.00. Note that many of the books on the literature lists may first be available exclusively through book clubs but later will be available through trade publishers. Check with your local bookstore or book distributor. For information regarding the nature and use of school book clubs and how they contribute to children's literacy development, see "School Book Clubs and Literacy Development: A Descriptive Study" by Dorothy S. Strickland and Sean A. Walmsley, 1994. (Available from the National Research Center on Literature Teaching and Learning, State University of New York at Albany.)

Scholastic Book Clubs
P.O. Box 7500
Jefferson City, MO 65102–9981
800-724-2424

Scholastic has five clubs, Firefly (pre-K), See Saw (K–grade 1), Lucky (grades 2–3), Arrow (grades 4–6), and Tab (grades 7–9 and up). Monthly brochures offer forty-five to fifty titles and include award-winning books. Also offers books to teachers grouped by theme and special offers for specific curriculum areas.

Troll Book Clubs
2 Lethbridge Plaza
Mahwah, NJ 07430
800-541-1097

Troll has five clubs, Troll Pre-K/K (preschool and K), Troll 1 (grades K–1), Troll 2 (grades 2–3), Troll 3 (grades 4–6), and Troll 4 High Tops (grades 6–9). Each month about forty-five titles are offered as well as different teacher specials, such as award-winning books and theme sets that can be used in the classroom.

Trumpet Book Clubs
P.O. Box 605
Holmes, PA 19043-9865
800-826-0110

Trumpet's three clubs, Early Years (pre-K–K), Primary Years (grades 1–3) and Middle Years (grades 4–6), send monthly brochures that offer forty to forty-five titles, including books by prize-winning authors and special items such as pop-up books, theme-based text sets, books and audiotape sets, and author video visits. An In-Class catalogue for teachers allows them to order books, Big Books, and text sets—groups of quality books gathered around a central concept—at any time during the school year.

Kindergarten

This list features excellent and near-classic titles with strong story lines and themes powerful to five- and six-year-olds. While a few kindergartners may be able to read some of these books, those selected for this list are intended primarily for reading aloud, discussing, and extending in the classroom. (See the next two lists, which support new readers.) First graders and second graders already familiar with these stories will enjoy them once again as they become readers.

Some key ideas among books in this list include solving problems, being in a family, and growing or changing. Traditional literature features cumulative stories, well-known tales, Mother Goose, and patterns such as the tricky fox, threes, and folktale language. Concepts include counting one to ten, the alphabet, and days of the week. Books may also be grouped by topics such as shoes, cats, or other animals, and eating or foods.

Suggestions for kindergarten author studies include Eric Carle, Donald Crews, Lois Ehlert, Paul Galdone, Kevin Henkes, Pat Hutchins, Bill Martin, and Nancy Tafuri, among others.

1. *Annabelle Swift, Kindergartner* by Amy Schwartz. New York: Orchard, 1988. (Orchard)

    This sophisticated look at a precocious child's beginning of school has humor and a gentle treatment of fitting in at school. Annabelle has been tutored by her older sister in what she thinks is important. But it is Annabelle's own skill, being able to count money, that gives her success. Other starting school stories include Mary Serfozo's Benjamin Bigfoot *(New York: McElderry, 1993), and Dorothy Butler's* My Brown Bear Barney *(New York: Greenwillow, 1988), and Kevin Henkes's* Owen *(see p. 108b).*

2. + *Bread and Jam for Frances* by Russell Hoban, illustrated by Lillian Hoban. New York: Harper & Row, 1964. (HarperTrophy)

    Like many young children, Frances the badger has narrow food preferences but changes her mind with the help of parents and an adventurous friend. Excellent discussion starter on the advantages of and difficulties we have in trying new things. (Series)

3. + *The Carrot Seed* by Ruth Kraus, illustrated by Crockett Johnson. New York: Harper & Row, 1945. (Scholastic; HarperTrophy)

    This classic story fulfills a child's need to feel important and successful by showing how a boy plants a seed and raises a huge carrot despite his family's doubts. Works well with The Great Big Enormous Turnip *and* Titch *in a theme of "planting" (see pp. 107b & 109b).*

4. + *Chicka Chicka Boom Boom* by Bill Martin and John Archambault, illustrated by Lois Ehlert. New York: Simon & Schuster, 1989. (   )

Rhythmic narrative and alphabet both upper case and lower case tell a story of disaster when all of the lower-case letters crowd into the coconut tree. The adult capital letters come along to sort out the mess. Chantable text invites children to chime in and move with the rhythm.

5. + *Chicken Soup with Rice* by Maurice Sendak. New York: Harper & Row, 1962. (Scholastic; HarperTrophy)

   A month-by-month rhyming account of one boy's humorous uses for chicken soup that invites children to follow the pattern in making up their own verses.

6. + *Each Peach Pear Plum* by Janet and Allan Ahlberg. New York: Viking, 1979. (Puffin; Scholastic)

   Characters from Mother Goose and well-known folktales appear in an "I Spy" text pattern. As with B. G. Hennessy's The Missing Tarts *(New York: Viking Kestrel, 1989),* children enjoy reviewing the familiar characters while seeing a story unfold.

7. *Feast for 10* by Cathryn Falwell. New York: Clarion, 1993. (   )

   African-American family shops, one to ten, then counts down to supper, ten to one, as they prepare dinner. Consider how families help each other, how meals are prepared; talk about daily ways in which we use numbers, or count down to an event, such as an upcoming holiday.

8. + *Feathers for Lunch* by Lois Ehlert. San Diego: Harcourt Brace, 1990. (   )

   A humorous account of a cat's inability to catch a variety of spring birds is vibrantly illustrated with Ehlert's collage illustrations made from hand-painted paper. Various birds and flowers are rendered to scale, each discreetly labeled with its proper name. Informative in studying birds or in springtime units. Rhyming text supports new readers.

9. + *Freight Train* by Donald Crews. New York: Greenwillow, 1978. (Mulberry)

   This introduction to what a freight train is and what it does also teaches children specific car names and reinforces the naming of colors. With air-brushed illustrations that seem to move across the page,

this is one in a series of Crews's books about transportation.

10. *The Gingerbread Boy* by Paul Galdone. New York: Clarion, 1975. (Clarion)

    This well-told version of a familiar cumulative tale makes a good flannel board story, mural, or story map of the action. It also reintroduces the tricky fox, a standard character of many folktales that children may already know.

11. *The Great Big Enormous Turnip* by Leo Tolstoy, illustrated by Helen Oxenbury. New York: Franklin Watts, 1968. (COP)

    In cumulative pattern, the animals, children, and the old woman line up behind the old man to try to pull the turnip out of the ground. Excellent for a classroom drama or a flannel board story.

12. *It Begins with an A* by Stephanie Calmenson, illustrated by Marisabina Russo. New York: Hyperion, 1994. (Hyperion)

    This alphabetic guessing game gives four verbal and pictorial clues: "You travel in this. / It begins with an A. / It starts on the ground, / and then it flies away." Four pictures enable children to consider naturally the beginning sounds of words and to guess successfully. While some words such as camera, icing, the soft sound of g for giraffe, and q for quarter may be difficult for children, they are eager to play the game of figuring out the mystery. Large gray letters at the end of each page invite children to read and repeat "What is it/she/he?"

13. *Mama, Do You Love Me?* by Barbara Joosse, illustrated by Barbara Lavalee. San Francisco: Chronicle Books, 1993. (   )

    In a reassuring story set in Inuit territory, a little girl tests her mother's love by proposing all sorts of mischief and asking if she would still be loved. Useful in family units, for discussing how we know our parents love us, and for seeing mischief as a universal child behavior. Pictures accurately depict items and motifs of Inuit culture; an afterword provides background for older children. The same setting forms the backdrop for Ann Herbert Scott's On

Mother's Lap, *illustrated by Glo Coalson (New York: Clarion, 1992; Clarion).*

14. "Mother Goose"

    Kindergartners enjoy repeated hearings and chantings of these rhymes. Many collections by well-known illustrators such as Tomie dePaola, Brian Wildsmith, Arnold Lobel, and James Marshall entertain children for hours with these cornerstones of literature. See, too, Each Peach Pear Plum.

15. *The Napping House* by Audrey Wood, illustrated by Don Wood. San Diego: Harcourt Brace Jovanovich, 1984. (Harcourt)

    In cumulative pattern, this humorous story pictures a snoring granny who shares the bed with her grandson and an assortment of animals until a pesky flea climbs aboard. Children enjoy chanting the rhythmical text, noticing the flea draw closer to the sleepers in each picture, and the gradually lightening palette of colors as dawn approaches.

16. *New Shoes for Silvia* by Johanna Hurwitz, illustrated by Jerry Pinkney. New York: Morrow, 1993. (   )

    In a nonspecific Latino country in "the other America," a little girl receives the present of new shoes, but they are too big. She turns them into toys until finally one day they fit. Read the pictures for details of a rural community lovingly depicted in Pinkney's watercolor illustrations. Pair with Red Dancing Shoes *(see below) to discuss feelings about new shoes.*

17. *Owen* by Kevin Henkes. New York: Greenwillow, 1993. (   )

    Owen, a boy mouse, figures out how to take his blanket to kindergarten in spite of a busybody neighbor, Mrs. Tweezer, and her assertion that this just isn't done. (The blanket goes as handkerchiefs). The story appeals to children who are now over kindergarten anxiety as well as to older children who can look back appreciatively at Owen's resourcefulness. Henkes is a popular author whose books such as Julius, the Baby of the World *(New York: Greenwillow, 1990),* Chester's Way *(New York: Greenwillow, 1988; Puffin), and* Chrysanthemum *(New York: Greenwillow, 1991)*

all portray young children's small dilemmas of growing up.

18. *Purple, Green, and Yellow* by Robert Munsch, illustrated by Helene Desputeaux. New York: Annick Press, 1992. (Annick)

    Brigid is crazy about felt-tip markers and convinces her mother to buy 500 each of the ones that are washable, the ones that smell like foods, and finally, the indelible ones. When she can't resist coloring herself, some silly and impossible disasters occur. Children love the preposterous story and the ending joke on daddy.

19. *Read-Aloud Rhymes for the Very Young* edited by Jack Prelutsky, illustrated by Marc Brown. New York: Knopf, 1986. (   )

    Over 200 poems selected from both old and new poets to enjoy all year long. Poems about loose teeth, friendship, the seasons, animals, or holidays, are nicely balanced for humor and thoughtfulness.

20. *Red Dancing Shoes* by Denise Lewis Patrick, illustrated by James E. Ransome. New York: Tambourine, 1993. (   )

    An unnamed African-American girl receives new shoes from her grandmother and displays them by dancing around the small city neighborhood. When she nearly ruins them in the mud, her favorite great aunt helps clean her up. A soothing presentation of a childhood "tragedy" that comes out right because the community cares.

21. + *Rosie's Walk* by Pat Hutchins. New York: Macmillan, 1968. (Scholastic; Macmillan)

    One long sentence with many prepositional phrases tells of Rosie's walk before dinner. But the illustrations beg to be talked about as another tricky fox is foiled in his attempt to catch his dinner. Children can tell alternative stories, provide dialogue for the many animals pictured, or experiment with patterned shapes in their own art work.

22. *The Salamander Room* by Anne Mazer, illustrated by Steve Johnson. New York: Knopf, 1991. (Dragonfly)

    Like many kindergartners, Brian makes a pet of something he has found outside, a salamander. His mother asks various ques-

tions about how he will care for it while the illustrations show Brian in his imagination turning his room into the woods. Fanciful depiction that elicits both wishful and true stories of bug and reptile "pets."

23. *Seven Blind Mice* by Ed Young. New York: Philomel Books, 1992. (   )

    An Indian fable, "The Elephant and the Blind Men," is given a new twist when seven blind mice each set out on a different day of the week to investigate the large Something that has come to their forest pond. Ordinal numbers, colors, and days of the week are concepts appropriate for this age level, and some children will understand the moral: you have to see the whole picture, not just a part. This Caldecott Honor Book is illustrated with Young's clean, brilliant collages.

24. + *Ten Nine Eight* by Molly Bang. New York: Greenwillow, 1983. (Scholastic; Morrow)

    An African-American girl and her father get ready for bed in a countdown counting book. Talk about bedtime rituals and solve the mystery of where the missing shoe from the "seven shoes" page has gone.

25. *The Three Bears* by Paul Galdone. New York: Clarion, 1973. (Clarion)

    A cornerstone of children's literary experiences, this story is told in a straightforward manner and illustrated with plenty of wee-little, middle-sized, and great-big items or print to encourage children to notice them. Compare treatment of the characters, the household, and humorous touches by looking at other versions of the story illustrated by David McPhail, Byron Barton, Lorinda Bryan Cauley, James Marshall, Jan Brett, and Anne Rockwell.

26. *Titch* by Pat Hutchins. New York: Macmillan, 1971. (Aladdin)

    Titch, the littlest in his family, always gets the short end of things until he plants a seed and his plant is the envy of his siblings. Good start for encouraging children to talk about aspects of being small or little or young. See also *The Carrot Seed*. *(Series)*

27. + *The Very Hungry Caterpillar* by Eric Carle. New York: Putnam, 1969. (Scholastic)

A hungry caterpillar eats his way through various foods during one week, spins a chrysalis (here called erroneously a "cocoon"), and emerges as a beautiful butterfly. Children can retell with the actual book as pictures with die-cut holes provide prediction clues.

28. *We're Going on a Bear Hunt* by Michael Rosen, illustrated by Helen Oxenbury. New York: McElderry Books, 1989. (   )

    This chantable, repetitive, predictable text invites children to chime in with hand or body motions as the teacher reads it. Good for shared reading and dramatic play as well. Note the good-natured humor and the clues that suggest this is imaginative play (a snowstorm in July?) rather than a true story.

29. *When Jeremiah Found Mrs. Ming* by Sharon Jennings, illustrated by Mireille Levert. Toronto: Annick Press, 1992. (Annick)

    In the second story in the series, Jeremiah can't think of a thing to do but Mrs. Ming lets him help, often imaginatively, with her many household tasks. Finally, with all the house in order, Mrs. Ming is ready to read a book and Jeremiah is ready to listen. While readers aren't sure whether Mrs. Ming is Jeremiah's mother, a relative, or his babysitter, she is a wonderful character. Quirky illustrations invite children to examine the pictures and talk about the humorous details. *(Series)*

30. *Where the Wild Things Are* by Maurice Sendak. New York: Harper & Row, 1964. (HarperTrophy)

    In this reassuring classic, Max, sent to his room for making mischief, dreams he travels to a land where he controls things. Children can notice how the pictures change, or create a wild rumpus complete with animal masks, but the most powerful aspect of the story is still parental forgiveness and love for children even when they misbehave.

31. *Yo! Yes?* by Chris Raschka. New York: Orchard, 1993. (   )

    Two boy strangers meet. One is bold, the other is shy. One is white, the other is African-American. They chat, become *friends, and go off together. This powerful story of friendship features eloquent pictures and very little text. The one or two hand-lettered words per page invite children to notice print, and while the words are not predictable, many kindergartners are so taken with the book and its message that they memorize the words and "read" it to each other.*

Books Which Invite Readers into Print

The following texts, many of which are only eight pages, are recommended for beginning emergent readers. These texts have consistent and simple structure, familiar and repetitive language patterns, very limited print, which is consistently and clearly placed on each page, and illustrations that are highly supportive of the text. These books are excellent for guiding students in developing one-to-one matching (one-to-one correspondence) of spoken to printed word, correct directionality skills, and utilization of pictures that depict most of the text. Even at this simplest level, each of these stories ends with a twist to delight the reader. Many of these stories also encourage readers to create their own versions.

For greater student success in reading a new book, introduce the new book by "talking through" the pictures and vocabulary *before* students attempt to read the book on their own. For guidelines as well as titles for selecting books for beginning readers, see especially "Selecting Books for Beginning Readers" by Barbara Peterson, pp. 119–147, in *Bridges to Literacy: Learning from Reading Recovery* by Diane Deford, Carol Lyons, and Gay Su Pinnell (Portsmouth: NH: Heinemann, 1991).

1. + *Across the Stream* by Mirra Ginsburg, illustrated by Nancy Tafuri. New York: Greenwillow, 1984. (Mulberry)

   Rhyming text tells of a hen's dream of escaping a fox by crossing a stream on a friendly duck's back. Notice the tiny symbols next to each page number, the many other animals in the illustrations, and discuss whether this is a dream or not. See how many other stories children can recall in which a chicken and a fox appear.

2. *All Fall Down* by Brian Wildsmith. New York: Oxford University Press, 1983. (Oxford)

   "I see" one animal standing upon another until "all fall down." Like 1 Hunter, *this book can be read easily because the pictures make the text predictable. Compare with* "Pardon?" Said the Giraffe *and make your own falling-down story.*

3. *Blue Sea* by Robert Kalan, illustrated by Donald Crews. New York: Greenwillow, 1979. (Mulberry).

   Four fish—biggest, bigger, big, and little—chase each other until finally little fish escapes them all. Although the text is very simple, with repetition, patterned language, and a different color for each fish and the words that refer to it, children will need to hear the book to put the language in their ears before reading this on their own. See also Rain *by the same pair (New York: Greenwillow, 1978; Mulberry).*

4. + *Brown Bear, Brown Bear, What Do You See?* by Bill Martin, Jr., illustrated by Eric Carle. New York: Henry Holt, 1983.
   (   )

   Children enjoy chanting this chain-structured story of an animal of one color who sees another animal of a different color, and so forth. Change the animals to children in the class for a new chant or make another book of differently colored bugs, other animals, or birds. See also this team's Polar Bear, Polar Bear, What Do You Hear? *(New York: Holt, 1991).*

5. + *The Bus Ride* by Anne McLean, illustrated by Justin Wager. Glenview, IL: Scott, Foresman, 1971. (Scott, Foresman)

   "A girl got on the bus. Then the bus went fast." These first two pages are repeated over and over again, but with different characters—a boy, a fox, a hippopotamus, a goat, a rhinoceros, a horse, a rabbit, and finally a bee, which forces everyone off the bus.

6. *The Cat Sat on the Mat* by Brian Wildsmith. New York: Oxford University Press, 1982. (Oxford)

   Pictures clearly show a cat on the mat but each page turn adds another animal until the annoyed cat says "Sssppstt" and everyone leaves.

7. *The Chick and the Duckling* by Mirra Ginsburg, illustrated by Jose and Ariane Aruego. New York: Macmillan, 1973. (Macmillan)

   "Me, too," says a chick as it follows an adventurous duckling's lead until disaster nearly results and the chick finally thinks for itself: "Not me!"

8. *Five Little Ducks* by Raffi, illustrated by Jose Aruego and Ariane Dewey. New York: Crown, 1989. (Crown)

   In this countdown song, five ducks disappear "over the hills and far away," one by one, until they all return to Mama Duck with ducklings and spouses of their own. Repetitive verses and refrains make this a good match for new readers.

9. *The Good Bad Cat* by Nancy Antle, illustrated by John Sanford. Grand Haven, MI: School Zone, 1993. (School Zone)

   A mischievous cat gets in the way of a chess game: "Bad cat!" But when the cat chases a mouse out of the house, it becomes a "good cat!" One sentence or phrase per page, some of which repeat at the end, supports beginning reading strategies.

10. *Have You Seen My Cat?* by Eric Carle. Saxonville, MA: Picture Book Studio, 1987. (Scholastic)

    Carle uses his brilliant collages and the repeated title plus the refrain of "that is not my cat!" to tell the story of a boy who finally finds his lost cat—and more—after a long search.

11. *Have You Seen My Duckling?* by Nancy Tafuri. New York: Greenwillow, 1984. (Viking; Morrow)

    An adventurous duckling leaves his family but is visible in each picture as a mother duck asks various pond animals, "Have you seen my duckling?" Children enjoy the visual game of hide-and-seek. Other books by Tafuri that work at this level include Who's Counting? *(New York: Greenwillow, 1986) and* Spots, Feathers, and Curly Tails *(New York: Greenwillow, 1989).*

12. *I Like Books* by Anthony Browne. New York: Knopf, 1987. (COP)

    A gorilla mentions the kinds of books he likes; among them are scary books, books about pirates, funny books, and alphabet books. *Ask children to talk about "kinds of books." Create a book display on a table in the classroom based on children's categories of books they like.*

13. + *I Went Walking* by Sue Williams, illustrated by Julie Vivas. Orlando, FL: Harcourt Brace Jovanovich, 1989. (   )

    In the same vein as Brown Bear, Brown Bear, What Do You See?, *a child goes walking and sees various animals who all follow her. Vivas's large illustrations can be easily seen even in large read-aloud groups. Be sure to watch for the girl tossing aside her sweater, socks, and shoes as she begins to play.*

14. *Jog Frog Jog* by Barbara Gregorich. Grand Haven, MI: School Zone, 1992. (School Zone)

    Simple story about a frog who jogs and gets chased by a dog is told in large print. Two to six words on a page and a good match between picture and story support readers. Part of a "Start to Read" series.

15. *Mary Wore Her Red Dress and Henry Wore His Green Sneakers* by Merle Peek. New York: Clarion, 1985. (Clarion)

    The verses in the song repeat what critters wore "all day long" when they attended a birthday party. The chantable or singable text is enhanced by humorous illustrations that augment the story line; the story reviews colors cleverly, as well.

16. *Monster Can't Sleep* by Virginia Mueller. New York: Puffin, 1988. (Puffin).

    It's time for bed "but Monster wasn't sleepy" repeats four times. Parents try reading a bedtime story, warm milk, and a goodnight kiss until Monster finally gets sleepy. (Series)

17. *Mouse Views: What the Class Pet Saw* by Bruce McMillan. New York: Holiday, 1993. (Holiday)

    A class's pet mouse explores the school and is seen in a variety of clear, close-up photographs as it sits on unobvious but typical classroom objects (chalk, stack of colored paper, pencil box). Readers are invited to guess what the mouse is on. The next picture confirms the child's guess with a labeled photograph of the close-up now seen in context. A school map over-

view of mouse's route invites children to map their own classroom or school, or to draw a mouse-eye view of something in their own classroom.

18. *My Book* by Ron Maris. New York: Viking Penguin, 1983. (Puffin)

Half-pages inserted change the look of each picture as a child invites the reader to go through "my gate" and finally into "my room." The text, if not the format, invites readers to make their own book of possessions, routes to favorite spots, and so forth.

19. *Oh No, Nicky!* by Harriet Ziefert, illustrated by Richard Brown. New York: Puffin, 1992. (Puffin)

Nicky, an adventurous little cat, is saved from trouble around the house by a bigger cat who leads him to make better choices. A sturdy lift-the-flap book that will survive many readings; large, easy-to-read text.

20. *1 Hunter* by Pat Hutchins, New York: Greenwillow, 1982. (Mulberry)

Clues to the next page's minimal text are found on each preceding page of this counting book. Children enjoy being able to predict by finding the hidden animals.

21. *Today Is Monday* by Eric Carle. New York: Putnam, 1993. (Scholastic Book Club)

Each day of the week is given to a particular food and the animal that eats it. Multiethnic children at the story's end are invited to a banquet: "Come and eat it up!" Carle's glorious collage and paint illustrations invite children to experiment with their own art work. The traditional song is a part of the text but the chorus, "Is everybody happy? Well, I should say," has been omitted. Teachers may want to teach the whole song, but children who experiment with word correspondence should be warned that the text will not match.

22. *What a Tale* by Brian Wildsmith. New York: Oxford University Press, 1986. (Oxford)

Five tails, "spotted," or "bobbed," and so forth, turn out to be animals riding in a kangaroo's pouch. Silly with one small pun on the word "tail." See, too, Tail Toes Eyes Ears Nose *by Marilee Robin Burton*

(New York: Harper & Row, 1989) for more readable fun with animal parts.

23. *Where's Spot?* by Eric Hill. New York: Putnam, 1980. (Puffin)

Finally in paperback, this classic lift-the-flap book provides children with plenty of prepositional phrases within questions: "Is he under the bed?" Whatever the hiding animal is, it answers "No" until readers find Spot. Sure to be read to pieces, so keep glue handy to mend the sturdy flaps as this is an excellent book with great child appeal.

24. *Who's Counting?* by Nancy Tafuri. New York: Greenwillow, 1986. (Mulberry)

A puppy meets a variety of creatures that are counted out in limited, enlarged text: one squirrel, two birds, etc. Look for the puppy or some part of it in each picture plus the identifiable "main character" in the final three pictures of the puppy with his huge family.

25. *Whose Hat?* by Margaret Miller. New York: Greenwillow, 1988. (   )

"Whose hat?", repeated six times in the text, is followed by a picture of a real-life hat (fireman, chef, nurse) with an adult wearing his or her related hat. The adjacent page pictures a child playing in the same role in the hat. Large, clear print with only one or two predictable words on a page. Compare with Ron Roy's Whose Hat Is That? *(Boston: Houghton Mifflin, 1987), which has more text but equally excellent content.*

Because it is difficult to find "literature" at this earliest emergent level and because budding readers need lots of practice on easy books, the following simple, patterned texts, all in paperback, are also recommended:

26. *Piñata: Celebrating Literacy/Celebrando la lectura* by Barbara Flores, Elena Castro, and Eddie Hernandez. Miami: DDL Books, Inc. (DDL)

Well-done eight-page predictable story books featuring North American Latino families and real-life topics such as Mi familia *(My Family),* En la playa *(On the Beach),* La boda *(The Wedding), and* Los tamales. *The forty soft-cover books are* available in Spanish or English and are perfect for bilingual classrooms.

27. *Reading Corners 1, 1992.* San Diego: Dominie Press. (Available in Canada through Toronto: Gage Educational Publishing)

   A set of eleven books of eight pages each with titles such as I Read, I Have a Pet, I Like to Eat, *and* Baby Animals. *Fanciful illustrations support the short, predictable text.*

28. *The Story Box, Level 1.* Bothell, WA: The Wright Group, 1990.

   Some of the simplest books in this series, like In the Mirror *and* The Party, *have only several words on a page and are extremely predictable with good support from the pictures. Twenty-four titles in three sets.*

29. *This Is the Way I Go.* Allen, TX: DLM, 1976.

   A set of six books emphasizes common action words (climb, fly, run, swim, crawl, and play) in consistent, predictable language patterns. For example, in I Jump, *one page reads, "'I can jump,' said the horse." Also a good springboard for writing similar texts based on the same pattern. Works well to begin with shared writing in a small group and duplicate the new text for each student to read and illustrate.*

30. *Tiger Cub Readers* by Robert and Marlene McCracken. Winnipeg, Manitoba: Peguis, 1989.

   A set of eight books of fourteen pages each depicts basic concepts and familiar experiences. For example, in What Is This? *each animal page says, "This is a duck" or "This is a pig" with a colorful, clear illustration directly under the text. Available in little books and in 8½ × 11 size.*

31. *Twig Books* by Rebel Williams. Bothell, WA: The Wright Group, 1990.

   Twig Books, Sets A, B, C, and D, each contain eight nonfiction books of eight pages each. Well done for simplicity, picture match with text, and content material. For example, Champions *(Set A) shows the symbol and a picture of the Olympics on the cover and title page. The text, spread over eight*

pages, reads, "People running. People jumping. People swimming. People diving. People lifting. People throwing. Champions!"*

For students who need support in learning letters of the alphabet by name and sound, *Letter Books* (compiled by Lois Markt and published by Dominie Press, San Diego, 1994) are very useful. Each ten-page booklet focuses on a letter of the alphabet by featuring a color illustration of a thing that begins with the targeted letter on one page and the word that goes with the picture on the adjacent page.

Developing Early Reading Strategies

These are highly predictable books, many with rhyme, rhythm, and repetition that make them especially predictable. Familiar sentence patterns are repeated; illustrations provide excellent support to the text; the print is very clear, sizable, and consistently placed on each page; the language structure and story line are familiar and make sense. In contrast to the highly structured "Books Which Invite Readers into Print," these texts have more words on a page, longer sentences, more descriptive language patterns, and greater narrative development. Most of these titles are also easier to read than titles on the "First Grade" list. Many of these books are songs readily available on tape or record, and chants, which further support readers.

Repeated readings of such books help young readers develop sight vocabulary, fluency, and confidence as well as strengthen early reading strategies such as one-to-one correspondence, left-to-right line sweep, use of picture, meaning, and structure cues, and use of beginning and ending consonants. (See also "Recommended Literature for Beginning Readers: Rhyme, Rhythm, and Repetition," Routman, 1988, pp. 285–290, for additional titles.)

1. *All I Am* by Eileen Roe, illustrated by Helen Cogancherry. New York: Bradbury, 1990. (   )

   In short declarative sentences, such as "I am a friend. / I am a neighbor. / I am an artist. / I am a singer," a child considers all that he is and does. The book invites children to consider what adjectives and roles might describe them. Perfect model for writing about yourself, for considering talents, roles, and qualities such as being a thinker and dreamer that are not so easy to come up with. See also Quick as a Cricket, page 148b, for a similar pattern using similes.

2. + *Bright Eyes, Brown Skin* by Cheryl Willis Hudson and Bernette G. Ford, illustrated by George Ford. Orange, NJ: Just Us Books, 1990. (Sundance)

   Text in verse celebrates the physical beauty of four African-American children as they engage in typical school activities.

3. *Cookie's Week* by Cindy Ward, illustrated by Tomie dePaola. New York: Putnam, 1988. (Putnam)

   On each day of the week, a mischievous cat manages to create a new household upset. Predictable, repetitive, natural language pattern. Excellent for understanding cause and effect and for creating original stories based on the book's format and pattern.

4. + *Crocodile Beat* by Gail Jorgensen, illustrated by Patricia Mullins. Crystal Lake, IL: Rigby, 1988. (Rigby)

   This colorful animal story of a crocodile in search of his dinner naturally lends itself to drama and movement. Children love chanting the rhythmic beat of this story and seeing the surprise ending. The illustrations, comprised of collage made from tissue paper, are superb.

5. *Dear Zoo* by Rod Campbell. New York: Macmillan, 1982. (Aladdin)

   A child who writes to the zoo requesting a pet receives various animals and returns them all as unsuitable until a puppy arrives. Each animal is revealed in a lift-the-flap format that invites children to predict and see what the zoo has sent. Limited print on each page, consistent pattern, and colorful lift-up feature make this a children's favorite.

6. *Everything Grows* by Raffi, illustrated by Bruce McMillan. New York: Crown, 1987. (Crown)

   Another in the "Songs to Read" series that matches music and text with high-quality illustrations. See other books in this series, too.

7. *Five Little Monkeys Jumping on the Bed* by Eileen Christelow. New York: Clarion, 1988. (Clarion)

   The traditional verse is bracketed by getting ready for bed and Mom finally getting all the little monkeys in bed only so she can gleefully jump on her bed. The verse itself is fun to chant using a countdown starting with five fingers raised.

8. *Gone Fishing* by Earlene Long, illustrated by Richard Brown. Boston: Houghton Mifflin, 1984. (Houghton Mifflin)

   A father and son spend a quiet, satisfying day fishing and being together. While there are some complex language structures, most of the text is quite simple with supportive illustrations. "A big fishing rod for my daddy" (p. 8). "A little fishing rod for me" (p. 9).

9. + *Greedy Cat* by Joy Cowley. Wellington, New Zealand: Department of Education, 1983. (Richard C. Owen)

   Children delight in Greedy Cat who continually loots "Mum's" shopping bag and who finally gets what he deserves. "Along came Greedy Cat. He looked in the shopping bag. Gobble, gobble, gobble, and that was the end of that" is spread out over four lines and repeated seven times in the story.

10. *Hush Little Baby* by Aliki. New York: Simon & Schuster, 1968. (Simon & Schuster)

    Popular folk lullaby is easily and enjoyably sung by young readers. This favorite version is illustrated in folk art style with muted colors to support the mood of the text.

11. + *In a Dark, Dark Wood* by June Melser and Joy Cowley. Auckland, New Zealand: Shortland Publications, 1980. (The Wright Group)

    Children love the suspense of finding out what's in the "dark, dark box" in the "dark, dark house." Compare with Ruth Brown's A Dark, Dark House *(New York: Dial, 1981).*

12. + *Is Your Mama a Llama?* by Deborah Guarino, illustrated by Steven Kellogg. New York: Scholastic, 1989. (Scholastic)

    A humorous story in rhyming verse fol-

lows a baby llama on visits and inquiries to various animals in a quest to determine if his mama is a llama.

13. + *It Looked Like Spilt Milk* by Charles G. Shaw. New York: Harper & Row, 1947. (Harper & Row)

    "*Sometimes it looked like Spilt Milk. But it wasn't Spilt Milk. / Sometimes it looked like a Rabbit. But it wasn't a Rabbit.*" Consistent language pattern and simple, accompanying cutouts of the objects one might "see" in cloud shapes make this easy to read and suitable for beginning patterned writing.

14. + *Joshua James Likes Trucks* by Catherine Petrie. Chicago: Children's Press, 1988. (Children's Press)

    Joshua James, a young African-American boy, likes all kinds of trucks—big, little, long, short, red, green, yellow, blue, and trucks that go up and down. Very predictable text with large, clear print and matching picture cues.

15. *Just Like Daddy* by Frank Asch. New York: Simon & Schuster, 1981. (Simon & Schuster)

    A gentle story of a young bear who emulates his daddy—and his mommy. Repetitive phrases and clear illustrations make this an appealing, easily readable book.

16. *Molly* by Ruth Shaw Radlauer, illustrated by Emily Arnold McCully. New York: Simon & Schuster, 1987. (Little Simon).

    A disorganized but happy and independent little girl gets ready for and goes to school. Easy to read because of its limited print, the engaging story gets good support from the illustrations. (Series)

17. + *More Spaghetti I Say* by Rita Gelman. New York: Scholastic, 1987. (Scholastic)

    Although the pictures are barely more than cartoons, children love this playful, rhyming book about the eating antics of two monkeys, Minnie and Freddy. (Series)

18. + *Mrs. Wishy-Washy* by Joy Cowley, illustrated by Elizabeth Fuller. Auckland, New Zealand: Shortland Publications, 1980. (The Wright Group)

    "*Oh, lovely mud,*" say the cow, the pig, and the duck before Mrs. Wishy-Washy cleans them all up. But back they go into the puddle again. Children will sympathize with these mud-lovers. Retell the story with different animals or make a giant mural mud puddle with a variety of dirty or about-to-be dirty animals.

19. *Mud* by Wendy Cheyette Lewison, illustrated by Maryann Cocca-Leffler. New York: Random House, 1990. (Random House)

    Whimsical pictures match the short, rhyming verse describing a boy and girl who are covered with mud everywhere.

20. *My Bike* by Craig Martin. Wellington, New Zealand: Department of Education, 1985. (Richard C. Owen)

    Realistic photographs show a boy riding his bike each day of the week. The story is cumulative with a new episode being added for each day of the week. Good for reinforcing direction words: "over," "under," "around," "through," "up," and "down" and for writing a similar patterned story. (See pp. 142–143 for examples.) Check other titles in this Ready to Read *series.*

21. + *Noisy Nora* by Rosemary Wells. New York: Dial, 1973. (Dial)

    Young readers love the rhythm and rhyme of this popular tale. Children relate to the angry frustration of young Nora who "had to wait" because her mother and father were busy with her younger siblings. Discuss other, more appropriate ways Nora could have gotten attention.

22. + *Oh, A-Hunting We Will Go* by John Langstaff. New York: Macmillan, 1974. (Aladdin)

    This popular rhyming chant with music included on the final page is a favorite classic. In addition to singing the text, children enjoy adding their own original verses.

23. *Old MacDonald Had a Farm* by Glen Rounds. New York: Holiday, 1989. (Holiday)

    This farmer has the usual animals plus a few surprises in the popular song. Bold, black print in four sizes clues readers into the animal's name, the sound it makes, the chorus, and connecting words. See also other versions such as Carol Jones's (New York: Houghton Mifflin, 1989), Holly Berry's (New York: North South, 1994), and Tracey Campbell Pearson's (New York: Dial, 1984), which adds additional verses, too.

24. *"Pardon?" Said the Giraffe* by Colin West. New York: Lippincott, 1986. (Harper-Trophy)

"'What's it like up there?' asked the frog . . . 'Pardon?' said the giraffe." These two language patterns alternate for most of the text as a persistent frog tries repeatedly to talk to a tall giraffe. Children enjoy the humorous ending and finding the frog on the colorful end pages. See, also by West, "Not Me," Said the Monkey (Lippincott, 1987) and Have You Seen the Crocodile? (Lippincott, 1986).

25. *Pizza Party* by Grace Maccarone, illustrated by Emily Arnold McCully. New York: Scholastic, 1994. (Scholastic)

In rhyming text of two to four words per page, children make pizza from scratch with a man who likes to cook with kids. While the text simply states "We push. / We poke. / We roll. / We joke," the illustrations reveal the process from start to finish. Children who have made pizza can dictate or write directions, making this a book that invites writing as well.

26. + *Pumpkin Pumpkin* by Jeanette Titherington. New York: Greenwillow, 1986. (Mulberry)

A boy and his grandfather plant a pumpkin seed and raise, harvest, and carve the pumpkin after carefully saving some seeds for next year's pumpkin in this life cycle book. Identify the animals that watch the pumpkin grow, and plant seeds or carve a pumpkin. (Series)

27. *Roll Over! A Counting Song* by Merle Peek. New York: Clarion, 1981. (Houghton Mifflin)

Toys in bed fall out as a boy sings the song. Finally, when the child is asleep, readers see the animals in a wall frieze. See also the lift-the-flap Roll Over! by Mordecai Gerstein (New York: Crown, 1988).

28. *Stop, Thief!* by Robert Kalen, illustrated by Yossi Abolafia. New York: Greenwillow, 1993. (   )

This circular story portrays the travels of an acorn as each animal snitches it from the previous one until it finally comes back to the original squirrel. Refrain of "stop, thief" invites children to chime in.

29. *Things I Like* by Anthony Browne. New York: Knopf, 1989. (COP)

A chimpanzee tells what he likes to do: painting, riding a bike, playing with toys, dressing up, and much more. Humorous illustrations strongly support the text of one to five words on each page. See also I Like Books by the same author, p. 111b.

30. + *What a Wonderful World* by George David Weiss and Bob Thiele, illustrated by Ashley Bryan. Littleton, MA: Sundance, 1967. (Sundance)

Inspired by the Louis Armstrong rendition, this song of praise to the marvels in the natural world is beautifully illustrated in Bryan's glowing watercolors.

31. *Wheels on the Bus.* Raffi Songs to Read, illustrated by Sylvie Kantorovitz Wickstrom. New York: Crown, 1988. (Crown)

This well-known song invites children to sing the words and follow the people on the bus as they ride to a park. Final page includes the music and additional verses. Other books in the series with pictures by different illustrators bring other well-known songs to life, allowing children to sing their way toward literacy. (Series)

32. + *Who Said Red?* by Mary Serfozo. New York: McElderry Books, 1988. (Aladdin)

Vibrant watercolor illustrations by Keiko Narahashi complement the rhyming and repetitive text. Imaginative use of language for primary color words. (Series)

33. + *Who's in the Shed?* by Brenda Parkes. Crystal Lake, IL: Rigby, 1986. (Rigby)

Increasingly enlarged cutouts give additional clues to "Who's in the shed?" Children love predicting as they go along and rereading many times. The recurring pattern is "So the sheep (and other animals) had a peep through a hole in the shed. What did she see?"

Once again, it is difficult to find "literature" children can actually read at this early level. Emerging readers needs lots of books (literally hundreds) to read and practice on daily to gain book knowledge, sight vocabulary, fluency, and confidence. Therefore, the following published series, all in paperback, are recommended for the classroom collection. Before introducing these books and sharing them with children, it is important to know children's needs and interests and be very familiar with the books. Once the child is secure with beginning reading strategies and has developed some fluency, be sure to expand your collection to include the wealth of wonderful trade books by well-known and award-winning authors and illustrators found in the grade level literature lists, literacy extension resources, your school and public libraries, children's book publishers, book clubs, and bookstores.

You have to be choosy in selecting books from the following series, but many are short, predictable texts with story language, pictures, and topics that make sense and appeal to the young reader. Some of these published series are better than others, and within a series the quality of books may vary. Some of the books in these series are by noted authors and illustrators. Many come with teacher guides of varying quality. Some focus on "skills" teaching. Our recommendation is to ignore the skills and words in isolation and focus on story enjoyment. A number of these titles are also available in Spanish. Some have accompanying Big Books and/or cassettes. Many can be ordered as individual titles, either singly or in six-packs. Others are only available as part of a package. Check with the respective publishers and/or their representatives.

For classrooms that lack sufficient numbers of needed books, try writing your own books with the students. We do this mostly in the small, guided reading group as a shared writing by scribing for and assisting the children in writing a coherent, original story that is often inspired by a book or author we have particularly enjoyed. It works well to then photocopy enough "books" so each student can illustrate and read a personal copy.

34. *Early Learning Paks.* Carmel, CA: Hampton-Brown Books, 1992–1993.

 Seven stories with rhyme and repetition are geared to second-language learners. Books are sixteen pages or twenty-four pages and vary in difficulty. See also from

Hampton-Brown, A Chorus of Cultures: Developing Literacy Through Multicultural Poetry, *an excellent anthology of over 100 poems (1993).*

35. *A First-Start Easy Reader.* Mahwah, NJ: Troll Associates, 1980–1992.

 Some recommended titles in this series of forty-four books with simple sentences and easy vocabulary include Animals at the Zoo, Betsy the Babysitter, Big Red Fire Engine, Harold's Flyaway Kite, Skating on Thin Ice, *and* Stop That Rabbit.

36. *Hello Reader! Series.* New York: Scholastic, 1992–1994.

 Some of the books in this series in levels 1 and 2 are fine for reinforcing beginning reading strategies. Several recommended, predictable books that deal with topics children can relate to are Itchy, Itchy Chicken Pox, Pizza Party *(see p. 116b),* My Messy Room, *and* Hello House! *(see p. 120b).*

37. *Literacy 2000 Satellites.* Stages 1 and 2. Crystal Lake, IL: Rigby, 1993.

 There are twenty-four books in each stage of this popular series of fiction and nonfiction books. Emergent readers enjoy reading these little eight-page books. For many more easy-to-read titles, refer to Stages 1 and 2 of the Literacy 2000 *reading collection. Some titles are more predictable than others. See also the supplemental collection of traditional tales and contemporary stories. Some favorites include* The Gingerbread Man, Who's in the Shed?, Crocodile Beat, Oh No!, Time for a Rhyme, The Enormous Watermelon, *and* Who Sank the Boat? *Teachers find that the* Literacy 2000 Teachers' Resource *has many helpful suggestions for establishing a balanced reading program.*

38. *New Way: Learning with Literature.* Austin, TX: Steck-Vaughn, 1989.

 We initially rejected this series because it is so structured, but struggling readers enjoy their "chapter book" format. Emergent readers experience much success with this series and come to know and enjoy the characters. Illustrations are clear and highly supportive in each sixteen-page text. Level

1, *Red Level, books are the easiest and include nine titles. Beginning readers also have success with Level 2, Blue Level, books.*

39. *Read More Books* by Dianne Frasier and Constance Compton. San Diego: Dominie Press, 1994.

    Sixteen nonfiction titles for emergent readers focus on real life and work situations such as I Am a Photographer, I Am a Dentist, I Live in an Apartment, Shopping, *and* What Do You See at the Pet Store? *Five pages of limited, clear text are supported by five pages of accompanying color photographs of related people and places. A very well-done, appealing series for emergent readers.*

40. *Read-alongs.* Stage 1. Crystal Lake, IL: Rigby, 1988.

    Six, twenty-four-page, predictable titles are available with or without cassettes for listening to and following along with the text.

41. *Reading Unlimited.* Glenview, IL: Scott, Foresman, 1976.

    Books include The Bus Ride, The Lion's Tail, Catch That Frog, Friends, Pat's New Puppy, Cats and Kittens, Victor Makes a TV, Ten Little Bears *and* Happy Faces. *An old series but great for building early reading strategies with meaningful stories.*

42. *Ready to Read Series.* Katonah, NY: Richard C. Owen, 1983.

    Developed by the Department of Education in Wellington, New Zealand, "Ready to Read" titles provide the structure and natural language upon which New Zealand's highly successful reading program is based. Some of the easiest and most notable titles for emergent readers include: T Shirts, Greedy Cat, I Can Read, Old Tuatara, *and* Sam's Mask.

43. *Rookie Readers.* Chicago: Children's Press, 1987–1993.

    Many of the titles in this series of sixty-four books are delightful as they use children's language and experiences along with rhyming verse and predictable text. Ignore the "Word List" at the end of each book. Some of the best in the series include: Bobby's Zoo; A Buzz Is Part of a Bee; Bugs!; Eat Your Peas, Louise; I Love Cats; Katie Couldn't; Katie Did It; Messy Bessey; Messy Bessey's Garden; Sometimes Things Change; Too Many Balloons; Wait, Skates!; Where is Mittens?; Bobby's Zoo; Hot Rod Harry; Hi Clouds; Collecting; Larry and the Cookie; *and* I Love Fishing.

44. *The Story Box Level 1 Read-Togethers.* Bothell, WA: The Wright Group, 1987.

    Twenty-five fiction titles, available as Big Books and little books, are predictable for emergent readers because of their rhyme, rhythm, repetition, and delightful story line. Some classic titles include Hairy Bear, Mrs. Wishy-Washy, The Big Toe, *and* In a Dark, Dark Wood. *A favorite collection for many kindergarten and grade one teachers and children.*

45. *Sunshine Books, Level 1 Fiction.* Bothell, WA: The Wright Group, 1990.

    More than one hundred titles in fourteen sets (A–J) give the emerging reader practice on eight-page stories and sixteen-page stories. Sunshine, Level 1, Teacher Guide *(1992) is excellent for setting up a balanced reading-writing program.*

46. *Sunshine Science, Level 1,* Sets A and B. Bothell, WA: The Wright Group, 1992.

    Topics that young children are curious about, such as skeletons, spiders, and space, are clearly presented with photo illustrations in these sixteen-page books. Eight books in each set.

47. *Tadpole Readers.* Crystal Lake, IL: Rigby, 1984.

    Twenty books written by or about young children captivate young readers with their fanciful illustrations, interesting topics, enlarged print, and easy-to-read text. Some favorites include The Trolley Ride, When Lana Was Absent, Excuses, Excuses, *and* Munching Mark. *Ideal for having children create their own versions.*

48. *Talk-About-Books* by Debbie Bailey, photos by Susan Huszar. San Diego: Dominie Press, 1994.

    Engaging color photographs of children of diverse cultural backgrounds in natural settings support the simple text of these easy-to-read books. Titles include: My Dad, My Mom, Sisters, Brothers, Toys, Shoes, Clothes, *and* Hats.

49. *Windmill Books. Set E.* Bothell, WA: The Wright Group, 1988.

   The six books in this set are ideal for emergent readers. Several of the titles are Lucy's Sore Knee, Goodnight Peter, *and* My Wonderful Chair.

Grade 1

Books on this list include many titles that first graders will be able to read on their own but not, perhaps, in the early months of school. Teachers should consider some titles as read-alouds and shared readings in the fall and as guided or shared readings as children become more proficient. New readers need the content of the previous two lists and may draw on the kindergarten list as well.

Books in this list deal with ideas of what it means to be a friend, occupations and working habits, helping others, and concepts such as egg-layers, fractions, and the nature of rivers and ponds. Traditional literature includes classic folktales in both European and African-American literature, plus the introduction of the trickster pattern.

Suggestions for first-grade author studies include Byron Barton, Tomie dePaola, Denise Fleming, Mem Fox, Arnold Lobel, James and/or Edward Marshall, Bruce McMillan, Maurice Sendak, Audrey and Don Wood, or any of the authors on the kindergarten list introduction.

1. *Alexander and the Terrible, Horrible, No Good, Very Bad Day* by Judith Viorst, illustrated by Ray Cruz. New York: Atheneum, 1972. (Aladdin)

   Alexander has numerous "terrible things" happen to him and considers moving to Australia. Good discussion or story starter about our own terrible, or even very good, days. (Series)

2. *Amos & Boris* by William Steig. New York: Farrar, Straus & Giroux, 1971. (Sunburst)

   Like Aesop's "The Lion and the Mouse," this story shows how a big and a little creature exchange help: a seagoing mouse is saved by a whale but then the beached whale is saved by a mouse. Notice the interesting language of the story, write a diary as if you were the mouse or the whale, make a tiny mouse museum of things important to Amos, and ask children to compare Steig's story with Aesop's fable. (See Teacher's Guide, Appendix B.)

3. *Anansi and the Moss-Covered Rock* by Eric A. Kimmel, illustrated by Janet Stevens. New York: Holiday, 1988. (Scholastic).

   Anansi, a lazy trickster spider from African folk tradition, gains food from all the animals through the use of a magic rock. But little Bush Deer figures out what he is doing and tricks him instead. See also Anansi Goes Fishing *(New York: Holiday, 1992), and Stevens's updated humorous illustrations present animals sitting in lawn chairs sipping sodas and listening to boom boxes. (Series)*

4. *Benjamin* by Anne Matheson. Toronto: Gage Educational Publishing, 1993. (Dancing Sun)

   In pristine photographs, special Benjamin uses his senses to appreciate the world around him. When he tells his friends about his discovery, they ridicule him until he explains how to look, listen, and smell. Good for discussing how we experience the world and, with older children, how authors notice more than simply how things look.

5. + *A Chair for My Mother* by Vera B. Williams. New York: Greenwillow, 1982. (Mulberry)

   A child and her waitress mother save coins to buy a comfortable armchair after their belongings are destroyed in an apartment fire. The community helps them get back on their feet, and the story provides an excellent start for a discussion of how people help each other in neighborhoods, in classrooms, and in the world. Notice Williams's selection of small pictures to highlight aspects of the larger ones. (Series)

6. + *Chickens Aren't the Only Ones* by Ruth Heller. New York: Putnam, 1981. (Putnam)

   Accurate paintings illustrate the rhyming text about all the animals that hatch from eggs: birds, reptiles, fish, insects, and even the extinct dinosaur are mentioned. An excellent discussion starter for ways scientists categorize the world and a fine introduction to a classroom study of animals.

7. + (E) *Dinosaurs, Dinosaurs* by Byron Barton. New York: Crowell, 1989. (Harper-Collins)

   In three to eight words per page, Barton's deceptively simple text tells quite a bit about dinosaurs in words children can read. A triceratops family provides a story subtext that children can make into a separate story. See also the more difficult and informative sequel, Bones, Bones, Dinosaur Bones *(New York: Crowell, 1990).*

8. + (E) *Eating Fractions* by Bruce McMillan. Scholastic, 1991. (   )

   An African-American child and a white child demonstrate fractions visually while graphics support concept of fractions by cutting of pizza, desserts, and so forth. Appetizing foods are cut into halves, thirds, or fourths. Concepts and words are reinforced with mathematical symbols and provide excellent discussion topics and impetus for dividing and depicting other food fractions.

9. *Every Time I Climb a Tree* by David McCord, illustrated by Marc Simont. Boston: Little, Brown, 1967. (Little, Brown)

   The title poem invites readers to do their own dreaming from a high place, and other poems play with words, sounds, feelings, and sights. A fine introduction to a major American poet; Simont's bold illustrations seem just right for the selections.

10. (E) *Flying* by Donald Crews. New York: Greenwillow, 1986. (Mulberry)

    Like other books in Crews's transportation series, this one examines aspects of flying in short phrases: "Take off. / Flying over highways. / Flying over rivers." Look for visual references to his previous titles, the meaning of the dedication, and Crews on the first page carrying a newspaper on which is written the date he completed the book. (He does this with dates, by the way, in most of his books.) Crews is an excellent author/illustrator to study in first grade because of the age-appropriate content and the fact that children can see the many

patterns Crews works with in text and illustration. See two stories from the author's childhood, Bigmama's *(1991) and* Shortcut *(1992, both New York: Greenwillow).*

11. *Frog and Toad Together* by Arnold Lobel. New York: Harper & Row, 1971. (Harper-Trophy)

    The steadfast Frog helps his impatient friend Toad through a series of humorous incidents in this popular series. Children enjoy laughing at Toad's impetuous acts and discussing what they would do in similar situations. Occasionally, Lobel's gentle tales provoke readers to discuss theme, or "big ideas," as well. (Series)

12. *George and Martha* by James Marshall. Boston: Houghton Mifflin, 1972. (Sandpiper)

    The first collection of small stories about two large friends introduces children to this popular hippo pair. (Series)

13. (E) *Hello, House!* by Linda Hayward, illustrated by Lynn Munsinger. New York: Random House, 1988. (Random House)

    Funny Brer Rabbit tale set in large type, with one to two sentences per page, introduces children to this African-American trickster.

14. *Henry and Mudge* by Cynthia Rylant, illustrated by Suçie Stevenson. New York: Macmillan, 1987. (Aladdin)

    In an easy-reader format with full-color illustrations, Rylant and Stevenson tell about Henry, a boy who finally gets a pet dog. Mudge grows to 180 pounds, accompanies Henry to school, and gets lost and is found all in seven short chapters. Like Lobel, Rylant packs a lot into few words, and readers will be moved, will laugh, and will want to talk about the story. There are many books in this excellent series. (Series)

15. *I Need a Lunch Box* by Jeanette Caines, illustrated by Pat Cummings. New York: HarperCollins, 1988. (HarperTrophy)

    While his first-grade sister gets many new things to start school, an unnamed African-American boy only wants a lunch box. He imagines wonderful designs for a different lunch box for each day of the week before he finally receives a present from his father. Children can design their own perfect and outrageous lunch boxes or decide on the ideal contents to fill them after reading this story. Pair with the easy-to-read Harry Gets Ready for School *by Harriet Ziefert, illustrated by Mavis Smith (New York: Puffin, 1991) for a discussion of how we get ready for the start of a school year.* See Jamal's Busy Day *by Wade Hudson, illustrated by George Ford (Orange, NJ: Just Us Books, 1991) for a comparison of an African-American child's school "work day" with that of his parents.*

16. (E) *In a Small, Small Pond* by Denise Fleming. New York: Henry Holt, 1993. ( )

    In this Caldecott Honor Book, the life cycle of a pond is illustrated by bright illustrations made of dyed paper pulp poured through stencils. Minimal text imaginatively placed on the page notes what animals come to life in a pond in the spring and ends with the pond dormant as deep winter sets in. See also *Fleming's other concept books such as* Barnyard Banter *(1994),* Count! *(1992), and* In the Tall, Tall Grass *(1991).*

17. *Ira Sleeps Over* by Bernard Waber. Boston: Houghton Mifflin, 1972. (Sandpiper)

    The universal problem of how to save face even though you want your teddy bear with you on a sleepover is explored in this family story. Ask why Ira decides to take his bear after all. Most children have bedtime rituals and special toys or blankets that they enjoy comparing. In a sequel, Ira Says Goodbye *(Boston: Houghton Mifflin, 1988), Ira's best friend moves away but not so far that the boys can't visit each other. (Series)*

18. *Jamaica's Find* by Juanita Havill, illustrated by Anne Sibley O'Brien. Boston: Houghton Mifflin, 1986. (Sandpiper)

    An African-American girl finds a stuffed dog and contemplates keeping it. But when she takes it to the park office, she makes a new friend. (Series)

19. *Little Bear* by Else Holmelund Minarik, illustrated by Maurice Sendak. New York: Harper & Row, 1957. (HarperTrophy)

    One of the very first early-reader books, as well as one of the finest, presents Little Bear and his friends to children. Elegantly

told but with a controlled vocabulary, the stories have endured for over thirty years. Ask children how Little Bear is like and unlike human children. Jean Van Leeuwen's series beginning with *Tales of Oliver Pig, illustrated by Arnold Lobel (New York: Dial, 1979), provides some of the same reader satisfactions with its humanized pig family growing up. Check other books in the "I-Can-Read" format published by HarperCollins, Macmillan, Dial, Scholastic, Puffin, and others to introduce readers who are ready for more text to beginning "chapter books." (Series)*

20. *The Little Red Hen* by Paul Galdone. New York: Clarion, 1974. (Clarion)

    If you don't do any of the work, then you don't get any of the hen's bread. Notice the words "Not I" are cleverly illustrated. Encourage retelling with pictured seeds, wheat, flour, bread, and the four folktale characters. For another humorous take on working, see Martin Waddell's funny Farmer Duck *(Cambridge, MA: Candlewick, 1991) with beautiful spring-time settings painted by Helen Oxenbury and* A Job for Wittilda *by Caralyn and Mark Buehner (New York: Dial, 1993).*

21. *Little Red Riding Hood* by Trina Schart Hyman. New York: Holiday, 1983. (Holiday)

    This classic folktale features the hungry wolf and the helpful huntsman as well as wonderfully illustrated borders and small vignettes. Watch the cat. See Self-Portrait: Trina Schart Hyman *(Addison-Wesley, 1981, p. 153b) and tell children about the importance of this story to the author. Compare Lisbeth Zwerger's illustrations for the same story.*

22. (E) *My Best Friend* by Pat Hutchins. New York: Greenwillow, 1993. ( )

    Two black friends and one is better at everything than the other one. However, when they sleep over, the second friend can keep her friend from being scared by the blowing curtains. Good story to discuss friendships, differences in competencies, self-esteem, and self-confidence.

23. (E) *My River* by Shari Halpern. New York: Scholastic, 1992. (Scholastic)

    One short sentence per page, such as

"It's my river," shows a turtle on a log. Successive pages of one short sentence and an illustration of a different animal show the diversity of a river ecosystem: "It's everyone's river." Good for discussion of interdependence of species and what one finds in and along a river.

24. + *One of Three* by Angela Johnson, illustrated by David Soman. New York: Orchard, 1991. (Sundance)

    The youngest of three African-American sisters tells how happy she is to be part of this urban family, even if the two older girls leave her behind sometimes.

25. *A Painter* by Douglas Florian. New York: Greenwillow, 1993. (   )

    Part of the "How We Work" series, this book has about one large-print sentence per page illustrated in bold watercolors. Each title features a man or woman at work. Text varies in difficulty from the more detailed but still simple A Chef to the very easy An Auto Mechanic. (Series)

26. *Pierre* by Maurice Sendak. New York: Harper, 1962. (HarperTrophy)

    Originally a part of the four-book Nutshell Library, this is also published separately. Pierre doesn't care about anything until a lion eats him. After the lion coughs him up, Pierre cares! Rhyming text, repetitive phrases, and the saucy Pierre captivate readers, and the five short chapters support the idea that children are reading longer books. A classic.

27. *The Random House Book of Poetry for Children*, edited by Jack Prelutsky. New York: Random House, 1983. (   )

    Over 500 poems are divided into sections on nature, seasons, children, humor, people, and food ("I'm Hungry!"); other poems invite children to enjoy poetry. An excellent selection from which to choose all year long.

28. *Shoes from Grandpa* by Mem Fox, illustrated by Patricia Mullins. New York: Orchard, 1989. (Orchard)

    Jessie, an active girl, is given new clothes by various members of her family. As the cumulative tale builds and she is encumbered by layers of clothes, she asks if someone could just buy her some jeans?

Torn-paper collage illustrations, lines of text with some internal rhythmic verse, the cumulative pattern of the story, plus a modern girl who has a common complaint make this compelling and easy to read.

29. *Three by the Sea* by Edward Marshall, illustrated by James Marshall. New York: Dial, 1981. (Dial Easy-to-Read)

    Three short stories present a girl and two boys who are entertaining each other before they go for a swim. Humor is found in unexpected plot twists and, as usual, in Marshall's droll illustrations. Teachers will appreciate, too, the hilarious contrast between a bland story Lolly reads from her school basal text and the lively story her friend Sam tells instead. (Series)

30. + *Time for a Rhyme* illustrated by Marjorie Gardner, Heather Philpott, and Jane Tanner. Crystal Lake, IL: Rigby, 1982. (Rigby)

    Nursery rhymes, some well known and others not, are presented with lively illustrations for children who may not be familiar with Mother Goose. (See also annotation for "Mother Goose" on the kindergarten list, p. 108b.)

31. *Tom* by Tomie dePaola. New York: Putnam, 1993. (   )

    An autobiographical picture book. Grandfather shows Tommy interesting things about the butcher business and the grocery store he owns. When Tommy takes to school two chicken feet decorated with nail polish, he gets into trouble, but his grandfather just winks and says "We'll just have to think of something else to do." Wonderful relationship and a good introduction to dePaola's many types of books. See his autobiographical The Art Lesson (New York: Putnam, 1989, see p. 97b); an example of his nonfiction such as Charlie Needs a Cloak (New York: Simon & Schuster, 1990); a story that draws on his Italian heritage such as + Strega Nona (New York: Simon & Schuster, 1979; Scholastic); or one of his many traditional stories or picture books. A great author to study at this grade or the next.

32. *Too Many Tamales* by Gary Soto, illustrated by Ed Martinez. New York: Putnam, 1993. (   )

When Maria helps her mother make tamales for the family Christmas Eve celebration, she thinks she has worked her mother's ring into the filling. So she convinces her cousins to help her eat the whole plate of food in order to find the ring. Rich paintings depict this extended Latino family as all begin once again to make the replacement holiday tamales.

33. *Wiley and the Hairy Man* by Molly Bang. New York: Macmillan, 1976. (Aladdin)

In this traditional African-American folktale, the Hairy Man threatens Wiley and his mother until they trick him three times. Trickery, magic, wise mothers, and the number three are common motifs in folktales, and children might think of other stories with these patterns.

34. *City Kids* by Lorraine Wilson. Crystal Lake, IL: Rigby, 1987.

This series of sixty little books about the everyday experiences of children—from the teacher getting mad, to cooking spaghetti, or getting new sneakers or a haircut—are terrific for enjoying reading and encouraging writing. Humorous illustrations and natural language make them kid favorites. Struggling older readers enjoy them, too.

Grade 2

The books on this list reflect a second grader's desire for increasing knowledge of the world, its geography, its people, and its ecology. In addition, a variety of easy-reader formatted books and chapter books encourage readers to take on more text.

Some unifying ideas of books here include living in a family, diversity in relationships, friendship, caring for the earth, valuing cultural diversity, considering nonfiction formats, occupations and work, animal behavior, and periods in American history. Traditional literature includes the comparison of Anansi versions and the introduction of other tricksters; the cross-cultural variants of the "good person rewarded/greedy person punished"; and an echo from the first grade list, a variant of "Red Riding Hood."

New readers at this grade may need to return to the previous three lists to build fluency and confidence. Consider, too, revisiting books on the previous lists that are thematically related to this one as a way of helping children see patterns in idea, genre, or structure.

Suggestions for second-grade author studies include Verna Aardema, Marc Brown, Gail Gibbons, Steven Kellogg, Bill Peet, Brian Pinkney, James Stevenson, Vera B. Williams, plus others on previous lists.

1. (E) *Abuela* by Arthur Dorros, illustrated by Elisa Kleven. New York: Dutton, 1991. (   )

Latino child and her grandmother affectionately spend time together, which the child Rosalba recalls as a flying journey over New York City. Vibrant illustrations, incidental Spanish words translated into English in context support speakers of both languages in this joyous intergenerational adventure.

2. *The Adventures of Spider* by Joyce Cooper Arkhurst, illustrated by Jerry Pinkney. Boston: Little, Brown, 1964. (Scholastic)

Told with the rhythm, sounds, and cadences of African oral tradition, these tales reveal the trickster nature of Anansi, the spider. Look for the interesting features of African folktales. Compare the character of Anansi and the language of the story in Gail Haley's A Story, a Story *(New York: Atheneum, 1970) or Gerald McDermott's* Anansi the Spider *(New York: Holt, Rinehart and Winston, 1972). See also* Anansi and the Moss-Covered Rock, *p. 119b. Invite children to write their own tales. (Series)*

3. *Amazing Grace* by Mary Hoffman, illustrated by Caroline Binch. New York: Dial, 1991. (   )

A black child who loves to read is glowingly depicted in illustration and text. When Grace is told by her classmates that she can't play Peter Pan because she is black and a girl, her grandmother takes her to see a famous black ballerina from Trinidad. Excellence convinces Grace that she can be Peter Pan and her tryout performance convinces everyone that if you put your mind to it, you can do anything you want.

4. *Amelia's Road* by Linda Jacobs Altman, illustrated by Enrique O. Sanchez. New York: Lee & Low, 1993. (Lee & Low)

    As a child of migrant workers, Amelia is tired of moving and wishes for a place of her own. She finally appropriates a giant tree and buries a box of memories as a way of creating her own spot. Also available in Spanish edition.

5. *Animal Fact/Animal Fable* by Seymour Simon, illustrated by Diane deGroat. New York: Crown, 1979. (Crown)

    In a clever guessing-game format, Simon presents simple statements about animals that may be true or false. When the reader turns the page, his prediction is confirmed or not by a paragraph of facts and two factual illustrations, one usually a close-up. In addition to provoking children to reconsider "common knowledge," this book also provides a lively format children may use in their own report writing. See numerous other books by Simon, one of the foremost writers of nonfiction for children.

6. *Borreguita and the Coyote* by Verna Aardema, illustrated by Petra Mathers. New York: Knopf, 1991. (   )

    In this Mexican trickster tale, a sheep outwits a coyote three times in familiar folktale patterns. Coyote is usually the traditional trickster in Southwest Native American tales and the pattern of the tricky one being "outfoxed" can be found in other trickster tales such as those of Brer Rabbit and the Anansi stories on this and previous lists.

7. *Charlotte's Web* by E. B. White, illustrated by Garth Williams. New York: Harper & Row, 1952. (Harper)

    This beloved animal fantasy has become a classic because of its timelessness. A spider's efforts to save a young pig are chronicled in graceful prose. The gentle humor, development of the animal characters, Fern's growth from young child to young girl, the themes of friendship, growing up, and the cycle of life and death make this a powerful book for young readers.

8. (E) *A Country Far Away* by Nigel Gray, illustrated by Philippe Dupasquier. New York: Orchard, 1988. (Orchard)

    A single text is illustrated as it pertains to two different settings. The top half of the page presents a rural African savannah culture; the bottom half, a suburban western culture. Besides demonstrating a good visual format for comparison, this is an excellent discussion book for similarities and differences. Pair with Galimoto *(below) and look at a map of Africa to see what you can discover.*

9. *The Courage of Sarah Noble* by Alice Dalgliesh, illustrated by Leonard Weisgard. New York: Scribner, 1954. (Aladdin)

    Eight-year-old Sarah's courage is proved in many ways when she accompanies her father into the wilderness to cook for him while he builds a cabin for their family. A realistic picture of part of life in "olden days" and a fine discussion of what bravery and courage are. Teachers may want to note the unconscious racist attitudes conveyed when Sarah is annoyed because the Indians don't speak English and her father renames a Native American man John because he can't pronounce his name— reflections of another era's attitudes toward nonwhite populations. It is still, however, an excellent discussion book and a favorite at this grade.

10. *The Day of Ahmed's Secret* by Florence Parry Heide, illustrated by Ted Lewin. New York: Lothrop, Lee and Shepard, 1990. (   )

    Ahmed, an Egyptian boy of about eight, delivers bottled gas to his customers in Cairo. When he finally learns to write his name, it is a big day in the family. Children who look at the mix of ancient and modern aspects of Egyptian life depicted in the illustrations and consider the message of the story gain valuable experience in seeing "like an anthropologist" or reading between the lines. For other books that deal with the theme of valuing literacy, see Patricia Polacco's The Bee Tree *(New York: Putnam, 1993) set in Amish country, the African-American* Papa's Stories *by Dolores Johnson (New York: Macmillan, 1994), and the South Africa–set* Over the Green Hills *by Rachel Isadora (New York: Greenwillow, 1992). Children can draw inspiration from these books to talk about when they learned to read and write.*

11. *Do Not Open* by Brinton Turkle. New York: Dutton, 1981. (Puffin)

   When Miss Moody opens a blue glass bottle she finds at the seashore, an evil genie is let loose. But it proves no match for the tricks of Miss Moody and her cat. Recall the trick and ask children to think of other stories, such as "Puss in Boots" or "The Brave Little Tailor," in which trickery is important.

12. *Dr. De Soto* by William Steig. New York: Farrar, Straus & Ciroux, 1982. (Sunburst)

   A clever mouse dentist tricks a fox patient. Notice the many contrivances that help the dentist in his office, elicit children's knowledge of the fox character from other folktales, and introduce children to other modern tales by this popular author. See also Dr. De Soto Goes to Africa *(New York: Farrar, Straus & Giroux, 1992). (Series)*

13. (E) *Friday Night Is Papa Night* by Ruth A. Sonneborn, illustrated by Emily A. McCully. New York: Viking, 1970. (Puffin)

   Pedro and his Hispanic family wait for Papa, who is working at two jobs, to come home on Friday. When Papa finally arrives, it is after midnight but the family gathers for a joyous celebration because Friday is "the nicest night." Children might talk of their own family celebrations or special times after hearing this story.

14. *Galimoto* by Karen Lynn Williams, illustrated by Catherine Stock. New York: Lothrop, Lee and Shepard, 1990. (Mulberry)

   Kondi lives in Malawi and spends a day constructing a galimoto, a vehicle made from bits of wire. This story of resourcefulness, determination, and enterprise is glowingly depicted in watercolors and reveals much about contemporary village life on the shores of Lake Malawi.

15. *The Great Kapok Tree* by Lynne Cherry. San Diego: Harcourt Brace, 1990.

   (   )

   A Brazilian woodcutter is persuaded not to cut down a kapok tree, the primary source of life for so many animals, when each one comes to him in a dream. Like My River *(see p. 121b), this book encourages children to talk about interdependence of species and the importance of rain forests to our world. See also* Un Paseo por el bosque lluvioso, *page 154b.*

16. *Honey I Love: And Other Poems* by Eloise Greenfield, illustrated by Leo and Diane Dillon. New York: Harper & Row, 1978. (HarperTrophy)

   Greenfield presents a jump-rope rhyme, chants, observations on people and the neighborhood, and thoughts in the voice of a young African-American child. Illustrations in warm browns and sepias are as sensitive as these poems that celebrate a child's world.

17. + *How Much Is a Millon?* by David M. Schwartz, illustrated by Steven Kellogg. New York: Lothrop, Lee and Shepard, 1985. (Mulberry)

   Help for the reader in conceptualizing large numbers. Follow up with estimating, finding funny illustrations, inventing rules for the game suggested in Kellogg's humorous illustrations, and read the sequel by the same team, If You Made a Million *(New York: Lothrop, Lee and Shepard, 1989). (Series)*

18. *How My Parents Learned to Eat* by Ina R. Friedman, illustrated by Allen Say. Boston: Houghton Mifflin, 1984. (Sandpiper)

   A girl recounts how her American father and her Japanese mother each learned to eat with an unfamiliar utensil, which explains why in their house they sometimes eat with knives and forks and sometimes with chopsticks.

19. *I Want a Dog* by Dayal Kaur Khalsa. New York: Crown, 1987. (Dragonfly)

   May badgers her parents for a pet dog but they are firm in their refusal. So May puts a leash on her white rollerskate and treats it like the longed-for pet. Dog lovers will admire the many dogs crowding the pictures, but children will respond to May's persistent "Try, try, try again," which eventually wins her parents over. The "Henry and Mudge" series by Cynthia Rylant (see Grade 1 list) fits well with stories about children who want pets.

20. (E) *Lionel in the Fall* by Stephen Krensky, illustrated by Susanna Natti. New York: Dial, 1987. (Puffin)

 In four short chapters, Lionel goes back to school and deals with new-teacher anxieties, friendships, and Halloween. Like Cynthia Rylant's Henry and Mudge Under the Yellow Moon *(New York: Macmillan, 1987), which is also set in the fall and is presented in easy-reader format, these short chapters enable children to see their daily lives reflected in books. Good for beginning the school year because of the fall setting and the reading level.*

21. *The Little Painter of Sabana Grande* by Patricia Maloney Markun, illustrated by Robert Casilla. New York: Bradbury, 1993. (   )

 Based on an actual incident, this story tells of a Panamanian boy artist who, lacking paper, painted his work on the sides of his house. Neighbors asked him to paint theirs, too, and the resultant beauty moved everyone. Good discussion book, like Galimoto (see p. 125b) for using what you have to make something beautiful.

22. *Lon Po Po: A Red-Riding Hood Story from China* by Ed Young. New York: Philomel, 1989. (   )

 Unlike the story most familiar to children, this one presents three daughters who, in disobeying their mother, let an old wolf into the house. But the eldest outwits the wolf in this Chinese story. Locate China on the map, discuss how this older version and Hyman's (see list for Grade 1) compare, and wonder over the mysterious dedication. Young has also illustrated a Chinese "Cinderella" variant, Yeh Shen (see p. 138b).

23. *Mary Marony and the Snake* illustrated by Blanche Sims. New York: Putnam, 1992. (   )

 Nervous about starting second grade in a new school, Mary is afraid that the children will make fun of her stuttering. An understanding mother, a matter-of-fact teacher, and the speech therapist help Mary gain the respect of her classmates. Six chapters, black and white drawings, and a length of sixty-four pages make this a good choice when readers are ready for chapter books. (Series)

24. *Me & Neesie* by Eloise Greenfield, illustrated by Moneta Barnett. New York: Harper & Row, 1975. (HarperTrophy)

 Janell's imaginary friend, Neesie, causes trouble as Janell deals with anxiety over starting school. But new friends at school solve some of the problem in this African-American girl's small moment of growing up.

25. *Monarch Butterfly* by Gail Gibbons. New York: Holiday, 1989. (Holiday)

 Gibbons introduces the life cycle of the monarch in numerous close-ups, with labels, a migration map, and some monarch lore. Directions for raising a pupa are given. Gibbons is a wonderful author to know for her lively, useful presentation of so many child-popular informational topics.

26. *An Octopus Is Amazing* by Patricia Lauber, illustrated by Holly Keller. New York: Crowell, 1990. (   )

 An excellent informational book in the "Let's-Read-and-Find-Out" series, this uses illustrations, labels, diagrams, and examples to present this fascinating animal. Good for discussion about how nonfiction conveys information. Lauber is an excellent nonfiction author to know. (Series)

27. + *Ox-Cart Man* by Donald Hall, illustrated by Barbara Cooney. New York: Viking, 1979. (Scholastic)

 This lyrical journey from fall to spring in the life of one early nineteenth-century family in New England is a paean to a self-sufficient life. Compare a child's life in this book with that portrayed in The Courage of Sarah Noble, *or with modern children's lives.*

28. *Owl Moon* by Jane Yolen, illustrated by John Schoenherr. New York: Philomel, 1987. (   )

 A girl's owling trek with her father late one winter night is beautifully evoked in stunning watercolors and poetic prose. Children might enjoy writing or telling of their own memorable experiences with the natural or nocturnal world.

29. *Pass It On: African-American Poetry for Children* selected by Wade Hudson, illustrated by Floyd Cooper. New York: Scholastic, 1993. (   )

    A varied selection of well-known contemporary and traditional poets such as Clifton, Hughes, Giovanni, Greenfield, Cullen, and Grimes is accompanied by Floyd Cooper's rich oil paintings. Subjects of poems include family life and play, pain and enduring, history, strength, and hope. Poems were selected for their power to pass on values to children.

30. *The Patchwork Quilt* by Valerie Flournoy, illustrated by Jerry Pinkney. New York: Dial, 1985. (   )

    Tanya, an African-American child, has a new understanding of the importance of family when she and her mother finish a patchwork quilt her ailing grandmother had started. Discuss how families help each other and the special "gifts" people in families share with each other.

31. *Rabbit's Judgment* by Suzanne Crowder Han, illustrated by Yumi Heo. New York: Henry Holt, 1994. (   )

    A bilingual story told in both Korean and English concerns a treacherous tiger who promises not to hurt the man who helps him out of a deep pit. A clever rabbit tricks the tiger and saves the man in this authentic tale whose striking, impressionistic illustrations enlarge a child's artistic eye.

32. (E) *The Smallest Cow in the World* by Katherine Paterson, illustrated by Jane Clark Brown. New York: HarperCollins, 1991. (HarperTrophy)

    When Marvin's family moves to take care of another Vermont farm, he misses an ornery cow that has been sold and becomes a bit ornery himself. When he creates an imaginary and comforting miniature cow and keeps it in a small bottle, he is ridiculed at school until his family and his sister's new friend show their appreciation for his creative solution in adapting to the move. The sixty-four-page easy-reader with eloquent illustrations is a good book for discussing how people help

each other adjust to changes as well as what farm life is like in a rural area.

33. *The Stories Julian Tells* by Ann Cameron, illustrated by Ann Strugnell. New York: Knopf, 1981. (Knopf)

    Six chapters introduce the imaginative Julian, his younger brother Hugh, and their friend Gloria. Strugnell's pictures of this loving African-American family and their often funny encounters are an added plus. First book in a popular series. (Series)

34. *The Talking Eggs* by Robert D. San Souci, illustrated by Jerry Pinkney. New York: Dial, 1989. (   )

    A poor widow favors her lazy daughter over the industrious one, but the good girl is rewarded by a strange old lady while the lazy one gets nothing but snakes, bugs, and scorpions in this Creole variation on a common folktale theme. Let children compare this cross-cultural theme variant in Jose Aruego and Ariane Dewey's Philippine Rockabye Crocodile *(New York: Greenwillow, 1988; Mulberry); Momoko Ishii's Japanese* The Tongue-Cut Sparrow, *translated by Katherine Paterson, illustrated by Suekichi Akaba (New York: Dutton, 1983); Samuel Marshak's Russian* The Month-Brothers, *illustrated by Diane Stanley (New York: Morrow, 1983), and* Mufaro's Beautiful Daughters, *see page 132b.*

35. (E) *Three Wishes* by Lucille Clifton, illustrated by Michael Hays. New York: Doubleday, 1992. (Dell)

    Nobie, in African American dialect, tells of the lucky penny she has found on New Year's Day and the falling out with her best friend as a result. See the Grade 1 list for other books about friendship plus books such as Russell Hoban's A Bargain for Frances *(New York: Harper, 1970; Scholastic; Harper) and Kevin Henke's* Chester's Way *(New York: Greenwillow, 1988).*

36. *A Toad for Tuesday* by Russell E. Erickson. New York: Lothrop, Lee and Shepard, 1974. (Beech Tree)

    The unlikely friendship that develops between a cranky, messy owl and a good-tempered, orderly toad works well as a springboard for other books about friendship. Readers ready for short chapter books will enjoy the first of four adventure stories featuring the toad brothers Morton and Warton. (Series)

37. (E) + *Tommy at the Grocery Store* by Bill Grossman, illustrated by Victoria Chess. New York: HarperCollins, 1989. (HarperTrophy)

A piggy mother loses her son at the grocery store and successive others purchase the boy thinking he is food of various sorts. Silly rhyming fun based on puns on body parts: human ears vs. ears of corn, or bottle necks, or potato eyes, for instance. Easy-reading format assisted by rhyme is great for shared reading.

38. (E) *Wagon Wheels* by Barbara Brenner, illustrated by Don Bolognese. New York: Harper & Row, 1978. (HarperTrophy)

In easy-reader format, the beginning settlement of Nicodemus, Kansas, is seen through the eyes of two African-American boys as they walk toward their new prairie home.

39. (E) + *Where the Forest Meets the Sea* by Jeannie Baker. New York: Greenwillow, 1987. (Scholastic)

Through striking collage illustrations, readers explore with a modern boy a tropical rain forest in Australia. Throughout, the pictures of ghostly images of past life in the forest as well as ghostly images of possible futures for this forest raise questions about how humans value rain forests and wild land in general. A thought-provoking and beautiful book. See also The Great Kapok Tree *(p. 125b), and* Rain Forest *by Helen Cowcher (New York: Farrar Straus & Giroux, 1988; Sunburst) to develop an ecological theme.*

40. *Wump World* by Bill Peet. Boston: Houghton Mifflin, 1970. (Houghton Mifflin)

This delightfully illustrated tale of grass-eating Wumps, peaceful creatures whose world is ruined by pollution and the misuse of natural resources, is both a clever tale and a catalyst for discussion of the pollution of our world. Be sure to check for other Bill Peet titles (over twenty in paperback).

41. "Adam Joshua" Series by Janice Lee Smith, illustrated by Dick Gackenbach. New York: HarperCollins. (HarperTrophy)

This novel series presents in five to seven illustrated chapters a school setting in which second and third graders deal with the fun, dilemmas, and daily occurrences of being in school. Adam's dog gets into school; the science fair is likely to be won by a boy whose father helped him; show-and-tell gets out of hand, and so forth. Once children have read one book, the rest seem easy. Good starts are The Monster in the Third Dresser Drawer *(1981),* It's Not Easy Being George *(1991), or* The Turkey's Side of It: Adam Joshua's Thanksgiving *(1990, all New York: HarperCollins; HarperTrophy). Length varies from 76 to 176 pages.*

Grade 3

Books on this list include chapter books (novels) that present children with diverse fantasy and realism. In addition, nonfiction presented in straightforward fashion, or embedded in a story, is included to show children how information can be conveyed by narrative, charts, graphs, maps, labels, small features enlarged in closeups to show details, and so forth. Children in their own nonfiction writing can be invited to use techniques they discover in guided reading of these books.

Beautifully illustrated picture books for older children introduce important discussion topics such as being of two cultures, the value of taking risks, and the importance of individual principled action. One person may make a difference. Children at this age may need to be reminded that just because a book has illustrations doesn't mean that it is for little kids.

Relationships between generations in a family are a prominent theme of books on this list, as well as on previous lists. In addition, books set in other countries continue to broaden a child's conception of the world. Books from various genres may also be grouped under the very broad topics of animals, humor, or as by or about Latinos (see the "Multicultural Book List," page 168b, and the Bilingual Spanish Books list, page 153b, for books about Latino experiences).

Traditional literature includes selections from the folktales of the United States: Native American, African-American, and tall tales plus a series to introduce folktales by country, an excellent way to help children organize their reading.

Suggestions for third grade author studies include Beverly Cleary, Barbara Cooney, Johanna Hurwitz, Trina Schart Hyman, Dick King-Smith, Giulio and Betty Maestro, Margaret Mahy, Jerry Pinkney, Patricia Polacco, and William Steig plus any authors on the previous grade list introduction.

1. (E) *Abuela's Weave* by Omar S. Castaneda, illustrated by Enrique O. Sanchez. New York: Lee & Low, 1993. (Lee & Low)

    In picture-book format, Esperanza is asked by her Abuela to sell their woven goods in the Guatemalan marketplace because Abuela thinks customers will be scared off by her facial birthmark. But the beautiful weavings speak for themselves and sell quickly in the market to people used to machine-made goods.

2. *Amazing Spiders* by Alexandra Parsons, photographs by Jerry Young. New York: Knopf, 1990. (Knopf)

    With beautiful full-color photographs that reveal multiple details, this informational book series is organized around a dozen topics listed in the contents. Other books in the series invite readers to talk about birds, mammals, and snakes. The parent volumes are "Eyewitness Books," a more densely packed series for older readers. (Series)

3. *Annie and the Old One* by Miska Miles, illustrated by Peter Parnall. New York: Little, Brown, 1971. (Little, Brown)

    Parnall's sensitive illustrations match this story of a Navajo girl, Annie, and her denial and gradual acceptance of her weaving grandmother's eventual death when she completes her work.

4. *Arthur, for the Very First Time* by Patricia MacLachlan, illustrated by Lloyd Bloom. New York: HarperCollins, 1980. (HarperTrophy)

    Sent to visit his relatives on a farm, Arthur retreats passively into being an observer until his friendship with the exuberant Moira, her veterinarian father, and his eccentric relatives pulls him out of his shell. Arthur's transformation from "Mouse" to himself is believable and entertaining. Discuss the meaning of the title. 128 pages, illustrations.

5. *Chicken Sunday* by Patricia Polacco. New York: Philomel, 1992. (   )

    Despite differences in religion, sex, and race, young Patricia is best friend of Winston and Stewart Washington and she considers their grandmother, Miss Eula, her own. The three children earn Miss Eula an Easter hat from a Russian Jewish shopkeeper when they sell Ukrainian decorated eggs in his shop in order to convince him that they have not pelted his shop with eggs. Themes of understanding and friendship across generations and glorious art work make this picture book sing. Polacco is an excellent author/illustrator to study as children can discover how her books draw on her own childhood. Begin with her Meteor! *(New York: Putnam, 1987), the funny* Some Birthday! *(New York: Simon & Schuster, 1991), and* The Keeping Quilt *(New York: Simon & Schuster, 1988) plus her illustrated autobiography,* Firetalking *(New York: Richard C. Owen, 1994).*

6. *Class Clown* by Johanna Hurwitz, illustrated by Sheila Hamanaka. New York: William Morrow, 1987. (Scholastic)

    First novel in a readable, realistic fiction series dealing with the same class of children. In eight large-print illustrated chapters, Lucas changes during the school year from being the class goof-off to a responsible leader of the class minicircus. In each successive novel in the series the class gets older, but the reading levels remain fairly stable so that some readers may wish to tackle the four books. (Series)

7. *The Comeback Dog* by Jane Resh Thomas, illustrated by Troy Howell. Boston:

Houghton Mifflin, 1981. (Bantam Skylark)

Daniel rescues a near-dead dog from a ditch, revives it, and tries to make it love him. Subtly the author gives the reader clues as to Daniel's feelings in this graceful and poignant novel of what loving is all about. (Series)

8. *Crow Boy* by Taro Yashima. New York: Viking, 1955. (Puffin)

Chibi is too shy to participate in school in this Japanese village until a sympathetic teacher helps him to blossom and metamorphose—beautifully symbolized as flower and butterfly by the book's endpapers.

9. *Danny the Champion of the World* by Roald Dahl. New York: Knopf, 1975. (Bantam)

Danny's father's secret poaching in Victor Hazel's wood provides the opportunity for discussion on the morality of poaching. Children enjoy this adventure of a loving, fun-filled relationship between a father and son as told by a master storyteller. See The Author's Eye, p. 98b, for information about how Dahl works as a writer.

10. *The Discovery of the Americas* by Betsy Maestro, illustrated by Giulio Maestro. New York: Lothrop, Lee and Shepard, 1991. (Mulberry)

An in-depth look at how North America became populated starting with the Bering Land Bridge. Evidence is clearly presented in picture book format so that children review possible visits of Phoenicians, Irish monks, Japanese fishermen, Vikings, and so forth. Appendices, tables of dates, large detailed illustrations, and maps are excellent examples of how informational books "work" and provide children with format examples for their own writing. The Maestros write top-rate nonfiction books.

11. + *Earthworms* by Keith Pigdon and Marilyn Woolley, illustrated by Sadie and Suzanne Pascoe. Cleveland: Modern Curriculum Press, 1989. (Modern Curriculum Press)

Clear illustrations in a variety of formats with labels, cross-sections, examples, cutaways, and graphs help readers understand earthworms. By discussing how information is conveyed in nonfiction texts, teachers can help children be better users of reference material. Directions for making a wormery are included.

12. *Favorite Fairy Tales Told in England* retold by Virginia Haviland, illustrated by Maxie Chambliss. New York: Beech Tree, 1994. (1959) (Beech Tree)

Before the era of the single, gloriously illustrated folktale, these collections were and still are the best source for knowing the major folktales from a particular country. The excellent series encompasses sixteen countries. Look to the well-illustrated single-tale editions for authentic, lively pictures, but read these collections for authentic text that reads aloud well.

13. *The Fortune-Teller* by Lloyd Alexander, illustrated by Trina Schart Hyman. Boston: Dutton, 1992. (   )

This humorous trickster story is set in the African country of Cameroon. Rich illustrations provide much local detail, and the clever story shows a smart man quick to take advantage of a profitable situation. Look for accurate depiction of a Cameroon marketplace plus the two little lizards hidden in each double-page spread. For more books set in Africa, see Galimoto (page 125b) and A Country Far Away (page 124b).

14. (E) *The Great White Man-Eating Shark* by Margaret Mahy, illustrated by Jonathan Allan. Boston: Dial, 1990. (   )

A hilarious story of justice delivered is told about a selfish boy who disguises himself as a shark to scare the other swimmers out of his favorite Australian swimming hole. It works until a lady shark falls in love with his disguise. The deadpan telling and the humor of the pictures are fine emphasis to the moral. A good introduction to the humor of this well-known New Zealand author who writes both picture books and novels.

15. *Halmoni and the Picnic* by Sook Nyul Choi, illustrated by Karen M. Dugan. Boston: Houghton Mifflin, 1993. (   )

A Korean grandmother feels embarrassed and out of place in this country until the third graders in her granddaughter's school welcome her and the Korean food she brings to a class picnic. Intergenerational relationship between grandparent and child is part of many books on these lists. See on this list Abuela's Weave, Knots on a Counting Rope, Annie and the Old One, *and* Uncle Jed's Barbershop *for a beginning. Be sure to see previous lists for the topic of grandparents, also.*

16. *I Hate English* by Ellen Levine, illustrated by Steve Bjorkman. New York: Scholastic, 1989. (Scholastic)

    Mei-Mei, a recent immigrant from Hong Kong, refuses to speak English until an astute new teacher helps her by reading to her and taking her places. How does it feel to be in a new place? How do people learn to speak a new language? Other books that help children talk about the difficulties in learning a new language include Muriel Stanek's story of a Latino girl, I Speak English for My Mom, *illustrated by Judith Friedman (Niles, IL: Whitman, 1989) and Bud Howlett's story of a girl from El Salvador,* I'm New Here *(Boston: Houghton Mifflin, 1993.)*

17. *I'll Meet You at the Cucumbers* by Lilian Moore, illustrated by Sharon Woodring. New York: Atheneum, 1988. (Skylark)

    Adam Mouse considers his own country world the ultimate setting until his pen pal Amanda invites him to the city. There, Adam discovers that he is a poet. This simple animal fantasy novel asks children to consider what poetry is and does. Pair with poetry or with a version of the fable "The Country Mouse and the City Mouse." Discuss what poets do. Debate the merits of a city or country life.

18. (E) + *Knots on a Counting Rope* by Bill Martin, Jr., and John Archambault, illustrated by Ted Rand. New York: Holt, 1987. (Holt)

    Stunningly illustrated, this picture book tells of a blind Navajo boy who loves to hear his grandfather recite his birth story and other stories of the boy's life. For each telling, the old man ties one knot on a rope; when the rope is completely knotted, the boy will be able to tell the stories from

his own memory. A perfect catalyst for telling our own birth stories but a fine discussion book, too, for its many layers of meaning.

19. *Koko's Kitten* by Francine Patterson, photographs by Ronald H. Cohn. New York: Scholastic, 1985. (Scholastic)

    In this nonfiction photo-essay, Dr. Patterson tells how she began to teach Koko the gorilla to speak in American Sign Language (ASL). Talk about how gorillas communicate in the wild and what Patterson has taught here. Discuss what the pictures show us, or perhaps give them captions. How might understanding animals be important to humans? (Series)

20. *Mirette on the High Wire* by Emily Arnold McCully. New York: Putnam, 1992. (   )

    In this 1993 Caldecott Award–winning picture book, a Parisian girl in the last century makes friends with a failed high-wire artist. As he teaches her to walk the wire, he regains his strength and courage as well. Good for discussing the ways we gather courage, and how older and younger may help each other. The ending invites reader speculation on what happens next.

21. *Miss Rumphius* by Barbara Cooney. New York: Viking, 1982. (Puffin)

    As a child, Miss Rumphius wishes to see faraway places, live by the sea, and make the world more beautiful. As a grown-up, she accomplishes all three in this picture book set in the previous century. Consider how each of us could make the world more beautiful; talk about dreams we have. Read about others who made some part of the world beautiful, such as Johnny Appleseed, George Washington Carver, or The Man Who Planted Trees *by Michael McCurdy (New York: Chelsea Green, 1986).*

22. *Molly's Pilgrim* by Barbara Cohen, illustrated by Michael J. Deraney. New York: Lothrop, Lee and Shepard, 1983. (Skylark)

    The girls in her turn-of-the-century class make fun of her imperfect English, and Molly thinks she will never belong. When she brings her Pilgrim doll dressed like a Russian immigrant to school for the Thanks-

giving project, her teacher saves the day. Touching story, based on a true incident, and a good discussion book.

23. *More Stories Julian Tells* by Ann Cameron, illustrated by Ann Strugnell. New York: Knopf, 1986. (Knopf)

    Julian, who is about eight or nine, his younger brother Huey, and his friend Gloria think of interesting ways to overcome summer boredom with a little help from the boy's dad. Warm, African-American family with typical family exchanges; the second book about Julian. (Series)

24. + *Mufaro's Beautiful Daughters* by John Steptoe. New York: Lothrop, Lee and Shepard, 1987. (Mulberry)

    The king is choosing a wife, and two beautiful sisters journey to his village. But the mean-spirited sister does not pass the three tests while the kind and gentle Nyasha naturally succeeds. Notice the lush flora and fauna of Zimbabwe. Ask children to compare the good sister/bad sister pattern found in The Talking Eggs, *p. 127b.*

25. *Nathaniel Talking* by Eloise Greenfield, illustrated by Jan Spivey Gilchrest. New York: Writers and Readers Publishing, 1988. (Black Butterfly)

    In a variety of free-verse poetry, some of which borrows from rap and the twelve-bar blues, nine-year-old Nathaniel shares thoughts on growing up, his proud and loving family, tolerance for variety in people and in music, and memories. Each poem is a gem that evokes response and dialogue about what is important. Try choral reading. Greenfield includes directions for writing your own twelve-bar blues.

26. (E) *Nettie's Trip South* by Ann Turner, illustrated by Ronald Himler. New York: Macmillan, 1987. (Scholastic)

    This simple but eloquent, illustrated story is presented as a letter from a white ten-year-old girl to her friend about what she has felt and discovered about slavery in the pre–Civil War South.

27. *Paul Bunyan* by Steven Kellogg. New York: Morrow, 1984. (Mulberry)

    Children need to know about the only folktale tradition indigenous to the United States—the tall tale. Kellogg's series does a fine job of introducing America's tall-tale heroes of Bunyan, Mike Fink, Johnny Appleseed, and Pecos Bill. See, too, another series by Ariane Dewey, in easy-reader format, and recent collections such as Amy L. Cohn's From Sea to Shining Sea *(New York: Scholastic, 1993) and Mary Pope Osborne's* American Tall Tales *(New York: Knopf, 1991.)*

28. *Poem Stew*, edited by William Cole, illustrated by Karen Ann Weinhaus. New York: Lippincott, 1981. (HarperTrophy)

    Over fifty poems celebrate food, funny eaters both real and weird, and our fascination with what we eat. Finger-snapping rhythm, catchy rhymes, and a variety of topics make this an excellent collection for chants, choral reading, before-lunch laughing, and pure enjoyment.

29. *Ralph S. Mouse* by Beverly Cleary, illustrated by Paul O. Zelinsky. New York: Morrow, 1982. (Dell; Avon)

    While earlier Ralph novels introduced the mouse and his boy companions, this fantasy novel is set in a school classroom and, like Mouse Views *(see page 111b), it seems perfectly believable. A prize-winning film was made of this book, combining live action and puppetry (Los Angeles: Churchill Films, 1991). In Elaine Scott's excellent informational* Look Alive *(New York: Morrow, 1992), text and photos explain how this movie was made. (Series)*

30. *Ramona Quimby, Age 8* by Beverly Cleary, illustrated by Alan Tiegreen. New York: Morrow, 1981. (Dell Yearling)

    Ramona deals with changes in her life and grows up a little. Children identify with Ramona's trying to be a third grader, a younger sister, and a decent person all at once. (Series)

31. *Raven: A Trickster Tale from the Pacific Northwest* by Gerald McDermott. San Diego: Harcourt Brace, 1993. (   )

    Simple, rhythmic language and bold, stylish illustrations reflect the oral and artistic traditions of the Pacific Northwest Native Americans in this story of the trickster Raven and how he brought light from the sky world to the people. Seek out other Native American tales that explain natural phenomena, such as those found in the myth collection by Natalia M. Belting, Moon Was Tired of Walking on Air, illustrated by Will Hillenbrand (Boston: Houghton Mifflin, 1992), or other tales of Native American tricksters such as coyote, Mouse Woman, or Paul Goble's "Iktomi" stories.

32. (E) *The Skirt* by Gary Soto, illustrated by Eric Velasquez. New York: Delacorte, 1992. (Dell)

A short novel of eight chapters tells how Miata Ramirez left her tiered folklorico dancing skirt on the school bus and how she retrieved it. Strong Latino family in a situation many third graders can identify with—that of losing something and what to tell your parents. No glossary but most of the incidental Spanish words are translatable. 74 pages.

33. *Stone Fox* by John R. Gardiner, illustrated by Marcia Sewell. New York: Crowell, 1980. (HarperTrophy)

Ten-year-old Willy enters a sled dog race against the legendary Indian Stone Fox in order to pay off the back taxes on his grandfather's Wyoming farm. Readers will never forget this masterfully told and moving story set in the 1800s.

34. *The Tales of Uncle Remus: The Adventures of Brer Rabbit* by Julius Lester, illustrated by Jerry Pinkney. Boston: Dial, 1988.
    (   )

No child should miss these classic stories of the African-American trickster, Brer Rabbit, because they are a part of our cultural history, extremely funny, and so freshly told here that listeners can almost see the storyteller in front of them. The four-book series features collections of familiar and not-so-well-known stories. Be sure you read Lester's introductions so that you know what he is doing and from what historical tradition his retellings spring. Children will enjoy comparing this to the series by Van Dyke Parks, illustrated by Barry Moser, which begins with Jump! The Adventures of Brer Rabbit *(San Diego: Harcourt Brace Jovanovich, 1986.) (Series)*

35. *Uncle Jed's Barbershop* by Margaree King Mitchell, illustrated by James Ransome. New York: Simon & Schuster, 1993.
    (   )

An African-American barber realizes his dream of opening his own barbershop after years of using his savings to help others in crisis. The neighborhood rejoices in his success and the hard work it took to get there. Good picture book catalyst for a discussing tenacity, entrepreneurship, special family members, and how the community supports its members.

36. (E) + *Vejigante Masquerader* by Lulu Delacre. New York: Scholastic, 1993. (Scholastic)

A Puerto Rican boy makes his own costume with adult help so that he can join the older boys in Carnival mischief. When a goat eats part of his costume, it seems like disaster until his mother helps make it right. See also Delacre's song collections Arroz con leche *(1989) and* Las navidades *(1990, both Scholastic) from Latin America.*

37. *What's the Big Idea, Ben Franklin?* by Jean Fritz, illustrated by Margot Tomes. New York: Coward, McCann & Geoghegan, 1976. (Coward)

Jean Fritz has the knack of making facts lively, interesting, and even funny in her series of well-illustrated authentic biographies of famous people. Create a time line of Franklin's life, marvel over his achievements, or compare information in this book with a fiction account, such as Robert Lawson's Ben and Me *told by Ben's mouse companion (Boston: Little, Brown, 1939). (Series)*

38. (E) *Wild Weather: Tornadoes* by Lorraine Jean Hopping, illustrated by Jody Wheeler. New York: Scholastic, 1993. (Scholastic)

This "Hello Reading" book presents information in six short chapters about tornadoes across the United States. Notice tables, diagrams, and the "blow-up" of a map segment to help children see how information is conveyed. Other nonfiction books in this series include books about manatees, ants, and the Titanic.

39. (E) *The Year of the Panda* by Miriam Schlein, illustrated by Kam Mak. New York: Crowell, 1990. (HarperTrophy)

This eighty-page novel addresses the dilemma of mainland Chinese who need arable land but are being raided by the giant pandas who need bamboo as their range is reduced by farming. A boy raises a baby giant panda before turning it over to a rehabilitation and reintroduction center. Pair with Judy Allen's Panda, *illustrated by Tudor Humphries (Cambridge, MA: Candlewick Press, 1993).*

Grade 4

Books in this list include settings other than the United States and books about people of two cultures. As would be expected, these titles often present some of the dilemmas and responsibilities being human entails—our role in preserving endangered species, the comparison of life in third-world countries with aspects of American life, relationships among family members, and our developing values. Be sure to check previous lists for related titles.

Novels include several kinds of fantasy (animal, science fiction, and high fantasy) and realism both thoughtful and humorous. We have also included titles that invite readers to laugh, depend on some maturity to see what's funny, and appeal to a nine-year-old's sense of humor.

Poetry, short stories, picture books for older children, and informational books extend readers' experiences with text. "Cinderella" variants and folktale parodies draw attention to the many ways authors and illustrators help children reflect on and modify their understanding of this genre.

Suggestions for fourth grade author studies include Paul Fleischman, Sid Fleischman, Paul Goble, Eloise Greenfield, Patricia McKissack, Jack Prelutsky, Cynthia Rylant, Jon Sciezska, Chris Van Allsburg, and Jane Yolen, plus any authors on the previous grade list introductions.

1. *Anastasia Krupnik* by Lois Lowry. Boston: Houghton Mifflin, 1979. (Bantam)

Anastasia, a budding poet and a thoughtful fourth grader, is initially annoyed at her parents for having a new baby. But the death of her grandmother, the arrival of baby Sam, and her increasing sense of the importance of family help her change her mind. Anastasia's lists at the end of each chapter suggest by inference her gradual changes of heart in this first Anastasia story. (Series)

2. (E) *Appalachia: Voices of Sleeping Birds* by Cynthia Rylant, illustrated by Barry Moser. San Diego: Harcourt Brace, 1991. (   )

In evocative prose, Rylant presents the mountains and hollers of Appalachia so that readers can feel and sense the place. Pair with Shiloh *(see p. 137b) and let children see how different authors create and evoke a sense of setting beyond appearances.*

3. *Beauty and the Beast* by Michael Hague. New York: Holt, 1989. (Holt)

This classic story of a beast transformed by love invites children to talk about how and why people change both in stories and in real life. Encourage critical thinking by comparing this version with others such as Beauty and the Beast *by Mordicai Gerstein (New York: Dutton, 1989); by Marianna Mayer, illustrated by Mercer Mayer (New York: Macmillan, 1978); or by Jan Brett (Boston: Houghton Mifflin, 1989).*

4. (E) *Best Wishes* by Cynthia Rylant, photographs by Carlo Ontal. Katonah, NY: Richard C. Owen, 1992. (   )

Excellent photographs illuminate the author's discussion of her life as a writer in Ohio and West Virginia. Readers will notice echoes and origins of many of Rylant's ideas, settings, and characters here. See other titles in this "Meet the Author Collection" (p. 99b). See also Rylant's autobiographical But I'll Be Back Again, *Orchard, 1989 (Beech Tree).*

5. *Bunnicula* by Deborah and James Howe. New York: Atheneum, 1971. (Camelot)

What if a pet rabbit really is a vampire? Chester the cat believes he has discovered one and sets out to prove to the human family that he is right. Told by the laconic family dog Harold with doglike observations and concerns for food, this first story in the series is humorous and fast-moving. Chil-

dren enjoy comparing the vampire lore in this book with traditional lore. *(Series)*

6. *Dynamite Dinah* by Claudia Mills. New York: Macmillan, 1990. (Macmillan)

    Ten-year-old Dinah craves attention and thinks of a million creative things to attract others to her. When her baby brother comes along, family relationships become more complex before Dinah can accept responsibility. Good book for discussing relationships with family and friends and the joys and dilemmas of being a person with dramatic flair. (Series)

7. *Every Living Thing* by Cynthia Rylant, illustrated by S. D. Schindler. New York: Bradbury, 1985. (Aladdin)

    Twelve challenging but never sentimental short stories invite readers to consider little moments of growth in children and adults. The first story, "Slower Than the Rest," reminds readers of the wonder of human diversity as it aligns a child with special needs and a turtle against a hurried world. The last, "Shell," uses a common metaphor in a symbolic way that young readers can understand.

8. *The Frog Prince Continued* by Jon Scieszka, illustrated by Steve Johnson. New York: Viking, 1991. (Puffin)

    What happens after the princess marries the frog prince? This silly sequel helps children see how folktales may be turned around and played with. It may be their first experience with the literary device of allusion, as well. Scieszka's collection of The Stinky Cheese Man and Other Fairly Stupid Tales *(New York: Viking, 1992) parodies at least ten well-known folktales. Donna Jo Napoli's novel treatment of* The Prince of the Pond *(New York: Dutton, 1992) is a full-fledged narrative that begins with a frog sitting in the middle of a pile of clothes. (See* Cinder Edna, *page 145b, for more fooling-with-folktale inspiration before asking children to write their own spoofs).*

9. (E) *Go Fish* by Mary Stolz, illustrated by Pat Cummings. New York: HarperCollins, 1991. (HarperTrophy)

    Six illustrated chapters reveal eight-year-old Thomas's learning about his African-American heritage from his grandfather.

Florida Gulf Coast setting, fishing, and storytelling are all part of this quiet story. 73 pages. (Series)

10. (E) *The Gold Coin* by Alma Flor Ada. New York: Macmillan, 1991. (Aladdin)

    A young thief follows an old healer woman around in an effort to steal her gold coin. Set in Central America, this picturebook tale invites children to consider how much money is enough, and the value of work, friendship, and community.

11. (E) *Grandfather's Journey* by Allan Say. Boston: Houghton Mifflin, 1993. (   )

    In the manner of reminiscence, this 1994 Caldecott Award–winner presents Say's grandfather, who came to America from Japan at the turn of the century. This picture book for older readers speaks on many levels. From a mention of the destruction of World War II, to knowing and understanding our grandparents, to the feelings one has on being a part of two cultures, there is much to discuss. See also a sequel written earlier, Tree of Cranes *(Houghton Mifflin, 1991). Themes in this book echo titles found in previous lists, as well.*

12. *The Green Book* by Jill Paton Walsh, illustrated by Lloyd Bloom. New York: Farrar, Straus & Giroux, 1982. (Sunburst)

    Vivid writing tells the story of a family from the future who must leave Earth to colonize a new planet. How do they survive? What is the importance of stories in a new land? This thought-provoking short novel begins and ends with the same sentence, a magical discovery for fourth graders. Paperback edition often omits the illustrations, so be sure to secure at least one hardbound edition for the classroom.

13. *The Hundred Penny Box* by Sharon Bell Mathis, illustrated by Leon and Diane Dillon. New York: Viking Penguin, 1975. (Puffin)

    Michael's great great aunt Dewbet is 100 years old and keeps an old box full of pennies to help her remember each of her birthdays. When Michael's mother wants to throw out the box, Michael tries to save all the stories of her life. This moving story of emotions in an extended African-Ameri-

can family is a catalyst for talking about our own family histories. What would children tell for each year or penny in their lives so far?

14. (E) *Knights of the Kitchen Table* by Jon Scieszka, illustrated by Lane Smith. New York: Viking, 1991. (Viking)

This funny, time-slip fantasy series introduces three boys, "the Time Warp Trio," who visit times past. Uncommitted readers find these stories compelling, hip, and humorous. While there isn't much to discuss, there is plenty to laugh about, and Lane Smith's line drawings and snappy dialogue move the story along quickly. (Series)

15. *The Lion, the Witch and the Wardrobe* by C. S. Lewis. New York: Macmillan, 1950. (Collier)

Four children free Narnia from the spell of the White Witch in this first of a seven-book series. A modern classic. (Series)

16. (E) *The Most Beautiful Place in the World* by Ann Cameron, illustrated by Thomas B. Allen. New York: Knopf, 1988. (Random House)

Seven-year-old Juan struggles with poverty and parental abandonment but is supported by his own intelligence, determination, and the love of his grandmother. Set in Guatemala, this is a universal story of growing into your own skin and up to your own potential.

17. *The Real Thief* by William Steig. New York: Farrar, Straus & Giroux, 1973. (Sunburst)

While stretching the vocabulary of readers, Steig tells the story of Gawain the goose, guard of the Royal Treasury, who is wrongly accused of stealing, until a repentant mouse confesses. Discuss the consequences of accusing without evidence. A good introduction to a popular author and illustrator. Be sure to have Steig's Dominic (New York: Farrar, Straus & Giroux, 1984) and Abel's Island (New York: Farrar, Straus & Giroux, 1985) on hand as well.

18. *The Rough-Face Girl* by Rafe Martin, illustrated by David Shannon. New York: Putnam, 1992. (Scholastic)

A traditional Algonquin story also known as "Little Burnt Face," this "Cinderella" variant supports the Native American belief that only those who walk humbly can truly see. When the Rough-Face Girl is able to do what her two haughty sisters cannot, which is to see the supreme being in all of his glory, she is made beautiful in his eyes and becomes his bride. Some children may recognize the theme, the transforming power of love, as similar to "Beauty and the Beast."

19. (E) *Sachiko Means Happiness* by Kimiko Sakai, illustrated by Tomie Arai. San Francisco: Children's Book Press, 1990. (   )

Sachiko, a child of Asian descent, is angry because her senile grandmother does not know her, but her sympathy overcomes her anger and sadness, at least for a moment. Pair this picture book with The Hundred Penny Box (see above). Loop the Loop by Barbara Dugan, illustrated by James Stevenson (New York: Greenwillow, 1992) also deals with an elderly person's senility and memory loss, but readers get to know the magnificently sassy Mrs. Simpson before she goes into a nursing home. Children born to older parents are increasingly likely to know a senile relative or visit a nursing home, and books such as these help foster open discussion.

20. *Sarah, Plain and Tall* by Patricia MacLachlan. New York: Harper & Row, 1985. (HarperTrophy)

In spare prose, Anna tells how Sarah came from Maine after her father places an ad for a wife in an eastern newspaper. Colors and music form a continuous thread through this touching story of family life on the pioneer prairie. See also a sequel, Skylark (New York: HarperCollins, 1994), in which the drought-ridden family returns to Sarah's beloved Maine. See also Brett Harvey's stories of her grandmother's prairie days in My Prairie Year (New York: Holiday, 1986) and My Prairie Christmas (New York: Holiday, 1990), both illustrated by Deborah Kogan Ray.

21. (E) *Scooter* by Vera B. Williams. New York: Greenwillow, 1993. (Mulberry)

In short, profusely illustrated chapters,

the personalities and relationships of the neighbors in Elana Rose Rosen's apartment building and neighborhood are explored. The exuberant spirit of Elana, the witty drawings, and the theme of making new friends when you've moved give this book child appeal. Good for discussing how the community supports its members, too.

22. *Shiloh* by Phyllis Reynolds Naylor. New York: Atheneum, 1991. (Dell)

     Eleven-year-old Marty shelters a dog from an abusive owner without the knowledge of his parents. The book elicits all sorts of discussion with fourth graders: What is honorable behavior? What are the consequences of lying? Is the "villain" bad? Told in first person in West Virginian regional dialect, this book is an excellent example of how an author creates well-rounded characters and a sense of place.

23. (E) *Skinnybones* by Barbara Park. New York: Knopf, 1982. (Knopf)

     Like Knights of the Kitchen Table *(see p. 136b), this lead title in a series keeps children, especially boys, interested in reading. Wisecracking Alex, the smallest boy on his baseball team, tells his own story about entering a commercial-writing contest and his encounters with the school bully. The first chapter is a side-splitting, laugh-inducing read-aloud. (Series)*

24. (E) *Song of the Trees* by Mildred Taylor, illustrated by Jerry Pinkney. New York: Dial, 1975. (Bantam)

     A short chapter book that depicts an African-American family in the Depression who protect the family's stand of giant old trees from the dishonest white loggers. This introduces the Logans, whose larger story is told in Roll of Thunder, Hear My Cry. *(See Grade 6 list.) (Series)*

25. *Sunken Treasure* by Gail Gibbons. New York: Crowell, 1988. (HarperTrophy)

     In this nonfiction book, Gibbons tells of the sinking in 1622 of the ship Atocha, its discovery and the raising of the treasure, its preserving, cataloguing, and distribution, and other famous treasure-laden shipwrecks. Text is succinct, and information-bearing illustrations invite study and

discussion. See, too, other works of nonfiction by this prolific author on such topics as lighthouses, the building of skyscrapers, the post office, and a host of other subjects.

26. *A Taste of Blackberries* by Doris Buchanan Smith, illustrated by Charles Robinson. New York: Crowell, 1973. (HarperTrophy)

     A young boy describes his friendship with Jamie and his feelings about Jamie's sudden death from a bee sting. Pair this with Mavis Jukes's sensitive and subtle Blackberries in the Dark *(New York: Knopf, 1985; Dell) for another boy who carries on after the death of someone special, in this case, his grandfather.*

27. (E) *Tiger* by Judy Allen, illustrated by Tudor Humphries. Cambridge, MA: Candlewick, 1992. (Candlewick)

     A village in South China hires a man to shoot a potentially dangerous tiger. The man shoots it, but with a camera, not a gun. Elegant and accurate pictures depict the tiger with reverence and sympathy. A "tiger fact sheet" ends this picture-book blend of information contained within a story. Humphries and Allen have also created informative stories about a whale, a panda, and an elephant in this same format. The series provides excellent inspiration to children who have gathered information about an animal and don't want to write a report. (Series)

28. *The Whipping Boy* by Sid Fleischman, illustrated by Peter Sis. New York: Greenwillow, 1986. (Troll)

     The theme is like "The Prince and the Pauper" with a light, humorous touch as Jemmy, whipping boy to Prince Brat, leads his prince through a series of adventures. Fun to read aloud and a good introduction to an author whose quasi-historical settings pique our interest while his humor and apt similies makes us laugh.

29. *Yang the Youngest and His Terrible Ear* by Lensey Namioka. Boston: Little, Brown, 1992. (Little)

     Two boys, one who is Chinese-American, the other white, must balance their passions for baseball and violin playing with their fathers' conflicting expectations for them. Humorously told, this novel al-

lows children to discuss the theme of balancing your own needs and desires with those of your parents as you grow up. It also reveals the cultural contrasts new immigrants to this country encounter.

30. *Yeh Shen: A Cinderella Story from China* by Ai-Ling Louie, illustrated by Ed Young. New York: Philomel, 1982. (Putnam)

    This version predates the European versions and raises the question of where folktales come from and how they travel. Notice the author's prefatory note, the illustrator's use of the fish motif, and of course the comparisons to the German or French "Cinderella." See also Shirley Climo's The Egyptian Cinderella, *illustrated by Ruth Heller (New York: Crowell, 1989) and* The Korean Cinderella, *by the same pair (Crowell, 1993). See also the parodies listed with* Cinder Edna, *page 145b.*

31. The books of Chris Van Allsburg.

    While Van Allsburg's books are unlikely to be available in paperback, he is an author/illustrator all children should know. Check out his books from the library and let children read them in chronological order to see how the artist's themes change, how his endings feature twists, where "Fritz" the dog is hidden, and how the artist's uses of color, frames, and point of view change and develop.

Grade 5

More of the world, its people, and human dilemmas are included in the novels on this list. Books set in China form a basis for possible study of one country. Several books have historical settings: the Revolutionary War, often introduced in this grade, World War II, plus one book that is an outcome of the Vietnam War. In addition, the theme of survival—in history, in realistic fiction, and in fantasy—is introduced here at the age at which many children believe themselves prepared to "go it alone." Realistic fiction includes more complex relationships among families and friends than have been presented in previous lists.

Dragons, both from the East and from the West, and one fantasy novel featuring a dragon,

are introduced to present a continuing character in traditional literature. Parodies of folktales introduced in the previous list work equally well here as a chance for children to play with form and content of folktales with which they are familiar. The *pourquoi* pattern of folktales is included both as an organizer for tales children already know and as a model for writing.

Suggestions for fifth-grade author studies include Mitsumasa Anno, Natalie Babbitt, Betsy Byars, Jean Craighead George, Virginia Hamilton, Lois Lowry, Eve Merriam, Phyllis Reynolds Naylor, Yoshiko Uchida, plus any authors on the previous grade list introductions.

1. *A Blue-Eyed Daisy* by Cynthia Rylant. New York: Bradbury, 1985. (Dell Yearling)

    Like short glimpses into someone else's life, these chapters present a picture of Ellie's eleventh year. Understated prose, the telling phrase, and a way of letting readers see and understand people truly characterize Rylant's writing.

2. *The Borrowers* by Mary Norton, illustrated by Beth and Joe Krush. San Diego: Harcourt Brace Jovanovich, 1953. (Odyssey)

    This classic asks readers to take another point of view, that of people merely inches tall. A believable story with well-drawn characters and aptly described miniature settings. (Series)

3. *Bridge to Terabithia* by Katherine Paterson, illustrated by Donna Diamond. New York: Crowell, 1977. (HarperTrophy)

    A friendship between an impoverished boy and a girl whose parents have come to rural Virginia to reexamine their values grows, then ends abruptly when one dies in a flash flood. A catalyst for discussion of friendship, the story also examines many sorts of bridges: across cultures, across ages, between sexes.

4. *The Cat's Purr* by Ashley Bryan. New York: Atheneum, 1985. (   )

    In the oral language of the storyteller, Bryan explains why the cat and rat are enemies and how the cat got its purr. The explanatory or pourquoi *story pattern is found throughout the world. Use many examples to introduce the genre before asking children to write their own folktales about some natural phenomena. Pos-*

sible choices include Shonto Begay's Navajo *story,* Ma'ii and Cousin Horned Toad *(New York: Scholastic, 1992),* Flora's Brazilian *story of* Feathers Like a Rainbow *(New York: Harper, 1989), and Verna Aardema's tale from Kenya,* Why Mosquitoes Buzz in People's Ears *(New York: Dial, 1975).*

5. *Chi-Hoon: A Korean Girl* by Patricia McMahon, photographs by Michael F. O'Brien. Honesdale, PA: Boyds Mill, 1993.

 Color photographs, a narrative, and excerpts from the life of an eight-year-old Korean girl give children insight into modern-day Korean life. See, too, Peggy Thomson's City Kids in China, *photographs by Paul Conklin (New York: HarperCollins, 1993) for excellent nonfiction about children's Asian contemporaries halfway around the world.*

6. (E) *Class President* by Johanna Hurwitz, illustrated by Sheila Hamanaka. New York: Morrow, 1990. (Morrow)

 The fifth-grade class officer election attracts Cricket, a confident but self-centered girl, and a Latino boy, Julio, who doesn't think he has the talent for the job but proves it to his classmates and, finally, to himself. The fourth in the series, School Spirit *(New York: Morrow, 1994) continues Julio's quiet development as an activist. (Series)*

7. *Dealing with Dragons* by Patricia Wrede. New York: Harcourt Brace, 1990. (Scholastic)

 Princess Cimorene, tired of her passive castle life, apprentices herself to a dragon and helps rid the dragon world of evil wizards. Humorous references to the conventions and content of folktales let children read as insiders who know the references. Introduce it by asking children to round up what they know about princesses and dragons. (Series)

8. *Dear Mr. Henshaw* by Beverly Cleary, illustrated by Paul O. Zelinsky. New York: Morrow, 1983. (Dell Yearling)

 Readers must draw inferences from this story told completely in letters written by sixth grader Leigh Botts to the author of his favorite books. This honest portrayal of a child in a single-parent family also

suggests that readers might discuss the making of a writer and a problem solver. (Series)

9. *The Dragon's Pearl* by Julie Lawson, illustrated by Paul Morin. New York: Clarion, 1993. (   )

 The traditional eastern dragon offers an interesting comparison with the usually better-known western dragon. In an effort to save a valuable dragon's pearl from robbers, a boy swallows it, only to transform himself into a dragon. Collage and highly textured illustrations are burnished with gold, the symbol of Chinese royalty. For other presentations of Chinese dragons, see Darcy Pattison's The River Dragon, *illustrated by Jean and Mou-sien Tseng (New York: Lothrop, 1993) or Deborah Nourse Lattimore's* The Dragon's Robe *(New York: HarperCollins, 1990).*

10. *The Dream Keeper* by Langston Hughes, illustrated by Brian Pinkney. New York: Knopf, 1994. (   )

 "Mother to Son," "Dreams," and "My People" are among the many well-known poems in this collection of this revered African-American poet's work. First published in 1932, this new edition is elegantly illustrated with Pinkney's scratchboard illustrations.

11. (E) *Germy Blew It—Again* by Rebecca Jones. Holt, 1988. (Knopf)

 The second in a popular and funny series about Jeremy Bluett, a budding entrepreneur whose plans to profit from raising and selling gerbils almost work. Jeremy's frequently imagined encounters with newspaper reporters, which appear as italicized text, let readers laugh over the disparity between how Jeremy sees himself and what is really about to happen. A book to keep readers reading. (Series)

12. *In the Year of the Boar and Jackie Robinson* by Bette Bao Lord, illustrated by Marc Simont. New York: Harper & Row, 1984. (HarperTrophy)

 Twelve chapters chronicle the year (1947) that Shirley Temple Wong, newly arrived in Brooklyn from China, becomes an American. Baseball's great Jackie Robinson is an important catalyst in Shirley's Americani zation. Teammates *by Peter Golenbock and illustrated by Paul Bacon (San Diego: Harcourt Brace Jovanovich, 1990) presents the significance of Robinson to the integration of major league baseball in picture-book format.*

13. *Journey to Topaz* by Yoshiko Uchida, illustrated by Donald Carrick. New York: Scribner, 1971. (Creative Arts Book Company)

    Based on the WWII incarceration in American camps of 110,000 Japanese-Americans, this story is told through the eyes of Yuki. See Behind Barbed Wire *by Daniel S. Davis (New York: Dutton, 1982), for more information on the emotional and political aspects of this moving story. See also the picture book,* Baseball Saved Us *by Ken Mochizuki, illustrated by Dom Lee (New York: Lee & Low, 1993) for another view of internment-camp life, this one in Idaho. (Series)*

14. *Jump Ship to Freedom* by Christopher and James Lincoln Collier. New York: Delacorte, 1981. (Dell)

    Continental Congress's problems with redeeming the scrip paid to soldiers to fight in the Revolutionary War form the backdrop for this story of an African-American boy who struggles to gain self-esteem. Historically accurate in period detail, language, and fact, this is one of the few books for elementary children that presents African-American views of the Revolutionary period. Contains the controversial word "nigger," which is explained in an afterword discussing the historical accuracy of the book. Pair with Avi's The Fighting Ground *(New York: Lippincott, 1984). (Series)*

15. *The Land I Lost: Adventures of a Boy in Vietnam* by Huyn Quang Nhuong, illustrated by Vo-Dinh Mai. New York: Harper & Row, 1982. (HarperTrophy)

    The author tells of his boyhood in a Vietnamese hamlet with his college-educated father, his work with a water buffalo named Tank, and the daily life where crocodiles might threaten, monkeys could cause mischief, and the threat of war was imminent.

16. *Me, Mop, and the Moondance Kid* by Wal-

ter Dean Myers. New York: Delacorte, 1988. (Dell)

A lighthearted, fast paced novel concerns an African-American boy's urban experiences on a baseball team with his brother and a girl they met at an orphanage from which the two boys were recently adopted. Introduces a popular author who has written extensively for adolescents. See, also, a sequel called Me, Moondance, and the Nagasaki Knights *(New York: Delacorte, 1992). (Series)*

17. *Morning Girl* by Michael Dorris. New York: Hyperion, 1992. (Hyperion)

A Caribbean Taino Native American girl's life is made believable and engages reader sympathies. The book ends as Columbus and his men are coming to the island for the first time. Young readers, who have some inkling of what will happen to the Tainos next, are irate at Columbus's diary excerpt, which reports that the Tainos are ignorant but friendly and would make good slaves. Pair this with many of the excellent, partial or fictionalized biographies of Columbus; see also The Discovery of the Americas, *page 130b.*

18. *My Side of the Mountain* by Jean Craighead George. New York: Dutton, 1975. (Puffin)

A stirring story about one boy's survival in the Catskills. Authentic details, nature closely observed, and a character who is very much like a fifth grader make this a powerful discussion story and a natural for follow-up with activities. Be sure to have on hand the sequel, On the Far Side of the Mountain *(New York: Dutton, 1989), for interested readers. (Series)*

19. *Number the Stars* by Lois Lowry. Boston: Houghton Mifflin, 1989. (Dell Yearling)

During World War II, one Danish girl's small, brave act saves Jews from the Nazis. Children identify with the main character, and the story serves as an introduction to the historical period as well. Marie McSwigan's popular Snow Treasure *(New York: Dutton, 1942; Scholastic) set in this time period is a story of a brave group of children who smuggled gold out of Nor-*

way under the Nazis' noses. See also Journey to Topaz *(p. 140b).*

20. *On My Honor* by Marion Dane Bauer. Boston: Houghton Mifflin, 1986. (Dell Yearling)

    What is honor? When Joel's best friend Tony goads him into swimming in a dangerous river and Tony drowns, Joel is left to ponder that question. Honor, a sympathetic and honest father, and a responsible boy who makes one mistake he'll have to live with make this a powerful catalyst for discussion.

21. (E) *Onion Tears* by Diana Kidd, illustrated by Lucy Montgomery. New York: Orchard, 1989. (Beech Tree)

    Deceptively simple in appearance, this novel is told in short bits, small vignettes, letters, and poems by a Vietnamese boat person who has made her way to Australia. Good for teaching readers how to read between the lines, how to notice small clues to large ideas, it also presents another view of two cultures coming together.

22. *The People Could Fly* by Virginia Hamilton, illustrated by Leo and Diane Dillon. New York: Knopf, 1985. (Knopf)

    African-American folktales, divided into four sections of animal, fanciful, supernatural, and slave tales of freedom, are richly told and powerfully illustrated. Part of everyone's multicultural American heritage.

23. *The Pinballs* by Betsy Byars. New York: Harper & Row, 1977. (HarperTrophy)

    Three foster children learn to care for each other in this humorous but also moving account of one summer in the Masons' home. Note the way characters remember events, the use of figurative language, and how and why Carlie especially changes her attitude.

24. *Redwall* by Brian Jacques. New York: Philomel, 1986. (Putnam)

    The first book in the series about a crusader mouse and his protection of the Redwall Abbey from Cluny the Scourge, a rat, is a fast-paced, good-guys-versus-bad fantasy. While the book is long, it is not difficult or complex and provides real reader satisfaction. (Series)

25. (E) *Saint George and the Dragon* by Margaret Hodges, illustrated by Trina Schart Hyman. Boston: Little, Brown, 1984. (Little, Brown)

    In addition to telling a story popular in the Middle Ages, this version is painstakingly illustrated to reflect the rich symbolism of medieval art. Look for fairies vying with angels and for the significant flowers. Look, too, for the author delivering the manuscript to the illustrator on the back cover.

26. *Spin a Soft Black Song* by Nikki Giovanni, illustrated by George Martins. New York: Farrar, Straus & Giroux, 1985. (Sunburst)

    Poems about African-American children in families, living and playing in the city, and loving life, are explored. No punctuation or upper-case letters make readers work a little harder for the ample rewards.

27. *The Story of Money* by Betsy Maestro, illustrated by Giulio Maestro. New York: Clarion, 1993. (   )

    The history of our money system, from trade and barter to coins and dollars, is traced. Useful end matter presents money of other countries, unusual money, and other interesting facts. Since making and having money is a preoccupation of this age group, you may want to pair this with books about entrepreneurs, or start a school store or other money-making project.

28. *A Stranger Came Ashore* by Mollie Hunter. New York: Harper & Row, 1975. (HarperTrophy)

    Finn Learson says he is a survivor of a shipwreck, but Robbie and his grandfather don't trust him. Rightly so, because Finn Learson is a Selkie, a man upon the land but a Selkie in the sea, and he is out to steal Robbie's sister in this well-written, mysterious fantasy. Foreshadowing provides many clues. Find out more about Selkies. Keep a class-compiled glossary of Shetland Island terms and clues to help readers stay located in the story.

29. *Tentacles: The Amazing World of Octopus, Squid, and Their Relatives* by James Martin. New York: Crown, 1993. (   )

*Lucid and beautifully illustrated intro-
duction to general characteristics of cepha-
lopods. Separate chapters by animal, diagrams, photographs, a glossary, and an
index do much to teach children about
information format while interesting them
in a biological class of animals. Compare
the density and treatment of information
on the octopus with a book on the Grade
2 list,* An Octopus Is Amazing, *page 126b.*

30. (E) *Toughboy and Sister* by Kirkpatrick
Hill. New York: Macmillan, 1990. (Puffin)
    *A Canadian Athabascan boy and his
    sister survive the summer at the family
    fish camp when their father dies from his
    alcoholism. Short, cliff-hanger chapters
    make this an easier read than* Hatchet, *see
    page 143b.* (Series)

31. *Tuck Everlasting* by Natalie Babbitt. New
York: Farrar, Straus & Giroux, 1975. (Sunburst)
    *Overprotected Winnie Foster makes a
    decision to help the Tucks, and her life is
    changed forever in this fantasy, which
    considers what it might be like to live
    forever. With a preface and an afterword
    that introduce readers to the layers of mean-
    ing and symbolism a well-written story
    may have, this story is a modern classic.*

Grade 6

Survival in many settings is a theme of this list:
Who survives? How? What do they learn?
What do they need beyond satisfying food and
shelter needs? (See books on the previous list,
too.) Books on this level also include diverse
historical periods, settings, genres, themes,
and types of characters. Fables are presented
as a part of traditional literature and as a model
for writing.

Since children mature at differing rates, be
sure to consider titles on the previous list if
readers have missed them. In addition, call
attention to other books by these well-known,
worthwhile authors to encourage children to
keep reading and talking about books.

Suggestions for sixth-grade author studies
include Betsy Byars, James Cross Giblin, Mary
Downing Hahn, Walter Dean Myers, Scott
O'Dell, Katherine Paterson, Gary Paulsen,

Mildred Taylor, Cynthia Voigt, plus any authors
on the previous grade list introductions.

1. *Aesop's Fables* illustrated by Heidi Holder.
New York: Viking, 1981. (Puffin)
    *Nine fables of human foibles follow the
    pattern: animal characters, spare and pre-
    cise telling, and an ending moral. It is often
    easier for children to compose their own
    fables if they first generate a list of morals
    or lessons, since the sole purpose of a fable
    is to teach. See also* Fables, *page 146b.*

2. *All the Small Poems* by Valerie Worth, illustrated by Natalie Babbitt. New York: Farrar, Straus & Giroux, 1987. (Sunburst)
    *Four of the poet's books in one volume.
    Valerie Worth has the knack of condensing
    the essence of things and making the
    amazingly right comparisons between the
    animate and inanimate. A magnet trades
    "secrets with the North Pole"; a jack-o'-
    lantern has a "vegetable skull." This disci-
    plined free verse might encourage students
    to look closely, make connections, elimi-
    nate excess words, and create their own
    small poems.*

3. *Child of the Owl* by Lawrence Yep. New
York: Harper & Row, 1988. (Dell)
    *When the very American Casey is sent
    to live with her Chinese grandmother in
    San Francisco's Chinatown, she begins to
    realize and finally to accept her family
    heritage as well as her own unique
    strengths.*

4. *Cousins* by Virginia Hamilton. New York:
Philomel, 1990. (Scholastic)
    *An African-American Ohio family, di-
    verse in its members, supports Cammy as
    she tries to cope with the death of a cousin
    whom she has hated. This powerful book
    elicits lengthy discussions about family re-
    lationships. One of this excellent writer's
    most readable books. See also* The Gold
    Cadillac *for another story of African-Ameri-
    can extended families.*

5. *Cracker Jackson* by Betsy Byars. New York:
Viking Penguin, 1985. (Puffin)
    *What should eleven-year-old Cracker
    do when he discovers that his favorite for-
    mer babysitter is being abused by her hus-
    band? Byars is an author every fifth and
    sixth grader should know for her under-*

standing of what it is like to be a kid becoming a young adult, her excellent writing, her humor, and her way of dealing with difficult topics sympathetically and fairly.

6. *The Dark is Rising* by Susan Cooper, illustrated by Alan Cober. New York: Atheneum, 1973. (Aladdin)

     On his twelfth birthday, Will discovers he is the last of the old ones and must join the battle outside time against the dark. With many echoes of Welsh myth and legend to ground it, this fantasy draws on many familiar patterns children know from television or movies as well as from other books: the old mentor, the young and unready hero, magical talismans, the struggle between good and evil, and the power of ancient magic. The second in a five-book series. (Series)

7. *Dicey's Song* by Cynthia Voigt. New York: Atheneum, 1983. (Fawcett)

     In Homecoming (*New York: Atheneum, 1981*), a near-orphaned Dicey and her three siblings walked from Connecticut to the Maryland shore to live with their grandmother. This sequel deals with the prickly peace they all must make and with Dicey's growing maturity, independence, and understanding about family. There are many other books in the Tillerman family saga. (Series)

8. *From Hand to Mouth: Or How We Invented Knives, Forks, Spoons, and Chopsticks & the Table Manners to Go with Them* by James Cross Giblin. New York: Crowell, 1987. (Harper)

     This premier author of nonfiction has made a career of taking unusual subjects (milk, chairs, chimney sweeps) or more predictable ones (the Rosetta stone, unicorns) and making them fascinating. Moving through prehistory to present day and across the globe, Giblin shows how utensils evolved out of necessity, style, economics, and social customs. A good way to view world history plus a good example of how asking interesting questions can lead you around the world in search of answers.

9. (E) *The Gold Cadillac* by Mildred Taylor, illustrated by Michael Hays. New York: Dial, 1987. (Bantam)

     This short, powerful novel set in the 1950s reveals the differences between the North and South when segregation was still overt. A family attempts to drive their newly purchased Cadillac from Cleveland to Mississippi only to see the father imprisoned briefly because the local police believe that a black man could not possibly own this car but must have stolen it.

10. *The Great Gilly Hopkins* by Katherine Paterson. New York: Crowell, 1978. (Harper-Trophy)

     Smart-aleck Gilly finally meets her match in Maime Trotter, the last of a series of foster parents Gilly is placed with. Gilly's gradual change of heart and the hilarity of some scenes impel readers to the story's conclusion. Readers may need some help in discussing the ending as Gilly gets exactly what she has wanted . . . but it is not to stay with Trotter. Is this happy or not?

11. *Hatchet* by Gary Paulsen. New York: Bradbury, 1987. (Puffin)

     After a plane crash, thirteen-year-old Brian spends fifty-four days in the wilderness learning to survive with only the aid of a hatchet given him by his mother. He also reconciles his parents' divorce. Group with other survival stories across genres to compare which qualities make a survivor; how a survivor changes; what beyond food, shelter, and safety (e.g., companions, art, music) helps a survivor; and so forth. (Series)

12. *Homesick: My Own Story* by Jean Fritz, illustrated by Margot Tomes. New York: Putnam, 1982. (Dell Yearling)

     A famous author writes of her childhood in China before the Boxer Rebellion and her longed-for trip back to the United States in a humorous and authentic voice. Be sure to discuss why the book is titled "homesick."

13. *Island of the Blue Dolphins* by Scott O'Dell, illustrated by Ted Lewin. Boston: Houghton Mifflin, 1960. (Dell Yearling)

     A California Indian girl, Karana, survives on an island for eighteen years. Based on fact, this popular story raises many questions about whether "rescue" by Spanish priests was necessarily a good thing. (Series)

14. *Journey to Jo'burg: A South African Story* by Beverley Naidoo, illustrated by Eric Velasquez. New York: Lippincott, 1985. (HarperTrophy)

   When the baby suddenly becomes ill, thirteen-year-old Naledi journeys from their village to find her Mma working in far-off Johannesburg. Readers may gain some understanding of the painful struggles South Africans endured in the time of Apartheid. The sequel, Chain of Fire *(New York: Lippincott, 1990), follows Naledi in her fifteenth year. (Series)*

15. *Letters from a Slave Girl: The Story of Harriet Jacobs* by Mary E. Lyons. New York: Macmillan, 1992. (   )

   This fictionalized account of Harriet Jacobs, born a slave in North Carolina in 1813, presents a character who ran away from her three-year-old mistress to hide in her grandmother's attic for seven years. Her observations, written in dialect based on Jacobs's own writing and on other slave narratives, give readers a remarkable picture of this tragic historical period. See *also* Many Thousand Gone, *page 152b.*

16. *Lincoln: A Photobiography* by Russell Freedman. New York: Clarion, 1987. (Clarion)

   Quoting often from Lincoln and using a variety of primary sources, Freedman makes the man come alive. Readers learn "the facts" about this president and come to understand the ideas for which he stood, his background, the tenor of the times, and the legacy he has left. Biography at its finest.

17. (E) *Missing May* by Cynthia Rylant. New York: Orchard, 1992. (Orchard)

   When Summer's beloved May, who has cared for her for the last six years, dies, Summer has to keep May's husband Ob from despair and willing himself to die. This family, eccentric, quirky, and wonderful, makes itself into a new one that includes the memory and the power of May's love in this short but powerful novel by one of our greatest writers of children's fiction. See also Best Wishes, *page 134b.*

18. *Mrs. Frisby and the Rats of NIMH* by Robert C. O'Brien, illustrated by Zena Bernstein. New York: Atheneum, 1971. (Aladdin)

   Where can rats with human intelligence find a place that does not rely on theft and that won't be discovered and destroyed by humans? This complex and fast-moving story deals with the themes of courage and self-determination. Sequels written by O'Brien's daughter, Jane Conly, continue the story. (Series)

19. *Roll of Thunder, Hear My Cry* by Mildred Taylor, illustrated by Jerry Pinkney. New York: Dial, 1976. (Puffin)

   Being an African-American family in rural Mississippi in the 1930s has rewarding moments as well as grim ones for the Logan family. Nine-year-old Cassie observes racial tension, her mother's struggle to maintain her teaching job, and her own father's dramatic rescue of an African-American teenager from a lynch mob. This story invites children to make links between Lincoln's time, the Depression era, and the present in the lives of African-Americans. See also Song of the Trees, *p. 137b. (Series)*

20. (E) *Sadako and the Thousand Paper Cranes* by Eleanor Coerr, illustrated by Ronald Himler. New York: Putnam, 1977. (Dell Yearling)

   Based on the true story of Sadako Sasaki, who died of radiation poisoning when she was twelve. The heroine to the children of Japan is commemorated by a memorial in Hiroshima Peace Park where children leave paper cranes made in her honor. A short but thoroughly moving story. Coerr has also retold a shorter picture-book version, Sadako, *illustrated by Ed Young (New York: Putnam, 1993).*

21. *The Sign of the Beaver* by Elizabeth Speare. Boston: Houghton Mifflin, 1983. (Dell Yearling)

   Left to attend his family's wilderness cabin in Maine, Matt cannot cope without the help of Attean, a woodland Indian. Consider what gifts each boy leaves with the other, who is freer, what qualities help Matt survive, and whether this story portrays Indians fairly. Compare the survival skills and the character of Matt with that of Brian in Hatchet.

22. *Something Upstairs: A Tale of Ghosts* by Avi. New York: Orchard, 1988. (Avon)

Time-slip fantasy in which a boy in Rhode Island discovers that the stain on the floor of his room is really very old blood. He is able to slip back in time and help a young slave boy who is trying to prevent bloodshed of his people. Historically accurate, this story makes the reader wonder what might have happened if one state had abolished slavery years before 1863, as this one nearly did.

23. *Time for Andrew: A Ghost Story* by Mary Downing Hahn. New York: Clarion, 1994. (   )

    The author, best known for her very popular Wait Till Helen Comes *(New York: Clarion, 1986; Avon), tells a riveting ghost story set at the turn of the century when there is no cure for diphtheria. Andrew from the present day trades places with his namesake in the past so that he may recover from this dread disease, only to discover that the cured boy refuses to return to the past. Both boys become stronger in their resolves and change as a result of their experiences. Hahn's satisfying ending is not typical of most time-slip fantasies. Use this story to discuss conventions of this kind of fantasy as well as an introduction to Hahn's work.*

24. *Where the Red Fern Grows* by Wilson Rawls. New York: Doubleday, 1961. (Bantam)

    Billy trains his dogs to be a fine hunting team in the Ozarks in this heartwarming and sentimental tale of the devotion between animals and humans. A long-time favorite with both adults and young readers.

Books Which Invite Writing and Storytelling (Grades 1–6)

The books on this list value storytelling or are natural models for encouraging children to write, either because of strong story models, definitive formats, patterned organization, or some other device. Many of these books appeal to primary children as stories but may be reread and extended on a different level by older children. Check the titles, too, in the Wordless Books list, page 149b, for writing extension possibilities.

1. *Aesop's Fables,* see page 142b.
2. *All I Am,* see page 113b.
3. *All the Small Poems,* see page 142b.
4. Alphabet Books

    Numerous alphabet books suggest ways for children to organize writing. Illuminations *by Jonathan Hunt (New York: Bradbury, 1989) provides medieval information from "alchemist" to "zither," suggesting that children could organize information from a thematic unit study in this manner.* Aster Aardvark's Alphabet Adventures *by Steven Kellogg (New York: Morrow Junior Books, 1987) is told strictly by the letters: "After Aster applied herself and achieved an A. . . ." Chris Van Allsburg's sinister* The Z Was Zapped *(Boston: Houghton Mifflin, 1987) or Mary Azarian's woodcut* A Farmer's Alphabet *(Boston: David Godine, 1981) are other provocative compendiums. Maurice Sendak's* Alligators All Around *(New York: HarperCollins, 1962) suggests two-word phrases a child could attribute to another animal. Assemble a number of alphabet books, look at how they are organized, and invite children to try their hands at the ones that are appropriate to this grade level. See also the kindergarten list, pp. 106b–110b.*

5. *Animal Fact/Animal Fable,* see page 124b.
6. *The Book of Pigericks* by Arnold Lobel. New York: Harper & Row, 1982. (HarperTrophy)

    Zany pigs in all sizes parade through these imaginative limericks. Children can laugh at Lobel's efforts and create their own using this familiar pattern. Be sure to share a few limericks by the masters, Edward Lear and Ogden Nash.

7. *The Cat's Purr,* see page 138b.
8. *Chicken Sunday,* see page 129b.
9. *Cinder Edna* by Ellen Jackson, illustrated by Kevin O'Malley. New York: Lothrop, Lee and Shepard, 1994. (   )

    In a second story, running parallel to the "Cinderella" story, Edna earns her dress, takes the bus that quits running at midnight, wears loafers as better for dancing, and marries the prince's younger brother who runs the palace recycling plant. See also Sidney Rella and the Glass

Sneaker *by Bernice Myers (New York: Macmillan, 1986). Several other updates of traditional folktales with strong feminine heroines include* Princess Smartypants *(New York: Putnam, 1986), Michael Emberley's urban "Red Riding Hood" story,* Ruby *(Boston: Little, Brown, 1990) and Tony Johnston's* The Cowboy and the Black-Eyed Pea *(New York: Putnam, 1992). Collect parodies and show children how authors vary the setting, change the sex, age, or specie of the main character, and play with traditional tales before you turn them loose on their own updates or parodies. See also* The Frog Prince Continued, *page 135b.*

10. *The Day of Ahmed's Secret,* see page 124b.

11. *Dear Annie* by Judith Caseley. New York: Greenwillow, 1991. (Mulberry)

    Grandfather writes to Annie as she grows towards school age until finally she is able to write back to him. Her show-and-tell item is a shoe box of all of Grandpa's letters to her, inspiring the whole class to make a bulletin board of letters from everyone. The book draws attention to diverse written correspondence and invites children to write to someone they care about.

12. *Don't Forget to Write* by Martina Selway. Nashville, TN: Ideals, 1992. (Ideals)

    One long letter written to her mother over a few weeks' time shows how "old Ginger Nut," as her grandfather calls her, changes her mind about visiting her grandparents. Children can write about their own visits, imaginary visits, or simply see an ongoing letter, which is really a form of journal writing.

13. *Everybody Needs a Rock* by Byrd Baylor, illustrated by Peter Parnall. New York: Scribner, 1974. (Aladdin)

    Ten "rules for finding a rock" guide this poetic text. Parnall's black-line illustrations evoke the landscape of special places, as well. Suggest to children that they find a special rock, seashell, flower, or tree and write new rules. Try illustrating in shades of one color and black line as Parnall does. Other titles by this team, such as Your Own Best Secret Place *(1979),* I'm in

Charge of Celebrations *(1986), or* The Way to Start a Day *(1978) (all New York: Scribner) also provide models.*

14. *Fables* by Arnold Lobel. New York: Harper & Row, 1980. (HarperTrophy)

    Following the models of Aesop and La Fontaine, Lobel has created twenty original fables with morals such as "Even the taking of small risks will add excitement to life." It is often easier to start with the moral and work backwards to create the story. Using Aesop, for instance, borrow morals and ask children to create another version that suits this moral. Children who have read such excellent fable collections as Tom Paxton's Aesop's Fables *(New York: Morrow Junior Books, 1988),* Harold Jones's Tales from Aesop *(New York: Watts/Julia MacRae, 1982), or Eve Rice's* Once in a Wood: Ten Tales from Aesop *(New York: Greenwillow, 1979) will have more to bring to this.*

15. *Faint Frogs Feeling Feverish* by Lilian Obligado. New York: Viking Penguin, 1983. (Puffin)

    Alliterative phrases tickle the tongue in this collection of tongue twisters. Susan Purviance's and Marcia O'Shell's Alphabet Annie Announces an All-American Album *(Boston: Houghton Mifflin, 1988) is loaded with alliterative sentences. Nicola Bayley's counting rhyme,* One Old Oxford Ox *(New York: Atheneum, 1977), presents a dozen animals actively engaged.* A Snake Is Totally Tail *by Judi Barrett (New York: Atheneum, 1983) includes clever alliterative and figurative descriptions of animals. Introducing children to literary devices helps sharpen their sensitivity to language use and provides them with ways of enlivening their writing. Expect some overuse first!*

16. *Family Pictures/Cuadros de familia* by Carmen Lomas Garza. As told to Harriet Rohmer. Spanish version by Rosalma Zubizarreta. San Francisco: Children's Book Press, 1990. (Children's Book Press)

    Paintings depict the Chicana artist's childhood in Texas with such details as shopping in the open market, killing a chicken for dinner, and parties. Presented in Eng-

lish and Spanish, the text encourages children to draw, talk, or write about their own "family pictures."

17. *Fortunately* by Remy Charlip. New York: Macmillan, 1964. (Aladdin)

Fortunately, Ned got a party invitation; unfortunately, the party was in Florida and Ned lives in New York. In this strongly patterned story, Ned meets each setback with improbable innovation. Using this model, children can create their own preposterous adventures with dinosaurs, at the circus, under the earth, and so on.

18. *Go Fish*, see page 135b.

19. *Hailstones and Halibut Bones: Adventures in Color* by Mary O'Neill, with new illustrations by John Walner. New York: Doubleday, 1989. (COP)

O'Neill describes not only things that are red or blue or gray; she also evokes the smell or taste or sounds of a color. While children try their hands at their own color poems, return to the book frequently to help writers see how the poet works. An earlier edition illustrated by Leonard Weisgard (Doubleday, 1969), provides more subtle pictures for the same text. See, too, Eve Merriam's "A Yell for Yellow" in Jamboree: Rhymes for All Times (New York: Dell Yearling, 1984).

20. + *A House Is a House for Me* by Mary Ann Hoberman, illustrated by Betty Fraser. New York: Harper & Row, 1978. (Puffin)

What constitutes a house? There are obvious ones in this rollicking, rhyming text, but there are also unique ones; a carton is a house for a cracker, or peaches are houses for peach pits. Children's illustrated examples of other literal or metaphorical houses make a good class book and help introduce figurative language.

21. *I Am Wings*, see page 158b.

22. *I Need a Lunch Box*, see page 120b.

23. *The Important Book* by Margaret Wise Brown. New York: Harper & Row, 1949. (HarperTrophy)

What is important about a flower? This book asks readers to look at essences. Children can generate their own important attributes for a favorite article, something in nature, or a special time.

24. *In a Pickle and Other Funny Idioms* by Marvin Terban, illustrated by Giulio Maestro. New York: Clarion, 1983. (Clarion)

"In a pickle" and thirty other common American idioms are presented and explained. Other titles in the series introduce a variety of literary devices. Ask children to glean idioms from everyday use, such as expressions using body parts ("have a heart") or using "line" ("bee-line," "lining track," "line of vision"). Activities such as this make children much more sensitive to figurative language in their own as well as others' writings. (Series)

25. *The Jolly Postman, or Other People's Letters* by Janet and Allan Ahlberg. Boston: Little, Brown, 1986. (   )

A postman delivers letters to fairy tale and folktale characters. Actual letters in a variety of formats (e.g., advertising circular, invitation, postcard, announcement, lawyer's letterhead, etc.) may be removed from real envelopes. After a study of folktales, brainstorm who might write what sorts of letters. Provide various sizes of envelopes, card stock, different sizes of stationery, and plenty of time for drafts.

26. *Mouse Letters* by Michelle Cartlidge. New York: Dutton, 1993.

This miniature book, about 2" × 2", includes actual small envelopes that hold letters from mice inviting a non-visible child to a garden party. Children can create miniature letters from fairies, from book characters, or from animals, and display them in the classroom. To make your own tiny envelopes, take apart a regular envelope and reduce the size by cutting an equal amount from the original margin. Refold and glue. (Series)

27. *The Mysteries of Harris Burdick* by Chris Van Allsburg. Boston: Houghton Mifflin, 1984. (   )

Fourteen mysterious stories are each suggested with a title, picture, and a single line of text. "Archie Smith, Boy Wonder" shows a sleeping boy observed by five shining lights while the text states, "A tiny voice asked, 'Is he the one?'" Van Allsburg's provocative phrase invites children to provide the beginning and end as they make their own whole stories. On another plane, ask children to think of their own provocative sentences, titles, and illustrations.

28. *Nathaniel Talking*, see page 132b.

29. *One Sun* by Bruce McMillan. New York: Holiday, 1990. (   )

    In what he calls "terse verse," McMillan presents two-word rhyming phrases dealing with the beach: sand hand / lone stone / snail trail, and so forth. Children can generate their own terse verses while older children can sustain the idea within a topic such as a trip to the small mall or the new zoo. See also his Play Day *(New York: Holiday, 1991).*

30. *The Popcorn Book* by Tomie dePaola. New York: Holiday, 1978. (Holiday)

    Information about popcorn is conveyed in a variety of formats suggesting that children might frame their reports in something other than straight narrative: "My report is about. . . ." Labels under pictures, cartoons, conversational balloons, and a recipe are some of the features. See, too, Animal Fact/Animal Fable, *p. 124b, and Joanna Cole's "Magic Schoolbus" series for other challenging informational formats.*

31. *Quick as a Cricket* by Audrey Wood, illustrated by Don Wood. Clarkston, MI: Child's Play, 1982. (Child's Play)

    A child likens aspects of himself to those of animals: "I'm as slow as a snail" or "I'm as loud as a lion." Young children can make their own books of comparisons. Older ones could decide which of these expressions are trite or predictable and write their own fresh similes.

32. *Sister*, see page 156b.

33. *Someday* by Charlotte Zolotow, illustrated by Arnold Lobel. New York: Harper & Row, 1965. (HarperTrophy)

    While many children write their own "someday" stories as wishes for the future, others are able to catch the irony of "Someday . . . my brother will introduce me to his friends and say 'This is my sister,' instead of 'Here's the family creep.'"

34. *Stringbean's Trip to the Shining Sea* by Vera B. Williams and Jennifer Williams. New York: Greenwillow, 1988. (Scholastic)

    This story of Stringbean's trip with his brother in a camper looks like a book of bound postcards. Readers construct Stringbean's trip, his adventures, and his feelings from what the two boys write on the backs of the postcards. Clever stamps, funny pictures on the cards, and the whole novelty of having to infer the story make this a winner with children. Simply retelling the story is a challenge. To recast the format, ask what if some other character who went on a physical or psychological journey wrote back periodically to her family.

35. *Tell Me a Story, Mama* by Angela Johnson, illustrated by David Soman. New York: Orchard, 1989. (Orchard)

    A girl asks her mother to tell stories of when Mama was little, but the girl ends up retelling them all herself. Italic typeface indicates the mother's talk. The way this family has shown its love for its members throughout the generations comes strongly through in the stories the mother has told. Children can write about their own family stories, interview grandparents, or tell favorite family stories.

36. *Tiger*, see page 137b.

37. *The True Story of the 3 Little Pigs by A. Wolf* as told to Jon Scieszka, illustrated by Lane Smith. New York: Viking Kestrel, 1989. (Scholastic)

    For introducing point of view, there is no better book. The wolf tells of how his bad cold and the pigs' rudeness forced him to act. This hilarious story suggests other folktale characters who might tell their true stories if children would be their voices: Jack's giant, Gretel's witch, or Wiley's hairy man. Build on this experience by asking children to consider another character's point of view in a novel.

38. *When I Was Little* by Toyomi Igus, illustrated by Higgins Bond. Orange, NJ: Just Us Books, 1992. (Just Us)

    Noel, a young African-American boy, hangs out at the old fishing hole with Grandpa. The fishing spot is surrounded by condos and houses now, but Grandpa can recreate life as it used to be when he tells Noel stories of "when I was little." The reminiscences about iceboxes, outhouses, phonographs, and first autos are depicted in black-and-white illustrations interspersed among the full-color of the present day. Ask older relatives for their stories of the olden days.

39. *When I Was Little: A Four-Year-Old's Memoir of Her Youth* by Jamie Lee Curtis, illustrated by Laura Cornell. New York: HarperCollins, 1993. ( )

    A backward look told from the advanced viewpoint of a four-year-old with action-packed, detailed contrasting illustrations. Encourage children to tell their own "little" stories. Pair with a forward look, When I'm Big *by Debi Gliori (Cambridge, MA: Candlewick Press, 1992; Candlewick), in which a boy imagines the bizarre and wonderful things he will have, wear, and do when he is older.*

Wordless Books (Grades K–6)

Wordless books must rely on the illustrations to do the work. All of these titles provide excellent discussion possibilities, and some present children with the opportunity to create narratives. They suggest that children become adept at "reading the pictures" and noticing how the illustrator engages us.

1. *The Angel and the Soldier* by Peter Collington. New York: Knopf, 1987. (COP)

    While a young girl sleeps, her toy angel rescues her toy soldier from the clutches of pirates who live in a ship on top of the piano. Richly evoked by the soft, colored-pencil drawings and seen from the perspective of tiny beings, this story suggests how we might see the world through someone else's eyes.

2. *Anno's USA* by Mitsumaso Anno. New York: Philomel Books, 1983. (Philomel)

    Anno's lone traveler makes his way from Hawaii to California and across the country moving freely in time. Each double-page spread may show bits from a region's history, famous people and landmarks, fine arts allusions, and well-known characters from children's literature or from "Sesame

Street," as well as Anno's trademark optical illusions. Older children, with their greater knowledge of the world, spend hours pondering, naming, and laughing over their discoveries. (Series)

3. *Changes, Changes* by Pat Hutchins. New York: Macmillan, 1971. (Aladdin)

    Entirely with block shapes, Hutchins shows a man and woman who build a block house and dismantle it to produce a fire engine, a boat, and various other things.

4. *Deep in the Forest* by Brinton Turkle. New York: Dutton, 1976. (Puffin)

    This is a mirror of "The Three Bears" but it is a little bear cub who crawls into a Colonial log cabin to wreak havoc. Notice the bear crawling into and out of the pictures that neatly frame this clever story. Pair with versions of The Three Bears, p. 109b.

5. *First Snow* by Emily Arnold McCully. New York: Harper & Row, 1985. (HarperTrophy)

    The mouse family goes sledding but the littlest mouse is afraid to go down the hill. When she finally gets up her courage, the family can't get her off the slopes. Other books in the series chronicle the arrival of a new baby, a family picnic, a Christmas celebration, and the beginning of school. All have strong narrative possibilities. (Series)

6. *Follow Me!* by Nancy Tafuri. New York: Greenwillow, 1990. ( )

    A baby sea lion explores his rocky island while curiously following a red crab. But his mother is always watching. Retell the story in a pattern of conversation between the baby and its mother, or make a story in which a language pattern is repeated: "The baby seal did —————. Mother watched from the rocks." See also Tafuri's Jungle Walk *(New York: Greenwillow, 1988).*

7. *Free Fall* by David Wiesner. New York: Clarion, 1988. (Mulberry)

    While studying an atlas, a boy falls asleep and has an adventure in a surreal landscape that curiously reflects aspects of his room furnishings. The dreamlike quality of the story becomes richer the more one studies the pictures. Obtain several copies *of the book and lay the pictures out in a frieze-like sequence to see how one page exactly blends into the next. Children might write their own dream sequences or imagine that several items in their bedrooms come to life in a story.*

8. *Frog Goes to Dinner* by Mercer Mayer. New York: Dial, 1967. (Dial)

   Chaos results when a boy discovers his pet frog has ridden in his pocket to a fancy restaurant. Jealousy is the theme of One Frog Too Many *(New York: Dial, 1975). (Series)*

9. *Is It Red? Is It Yellow? Is It Blue?* by Tana Hoban. New York: Greenwillow, 1978. (Mulberry)

   Hoban's colorful photographs of common city scenes, children doing things, and articles invite talk, not only about colors but about what is going on, about shapes, or about associations. Good for introducing children to this prolific creator of photographed concept books.

10. *Mouse Around* by Pat Schories. New York: Farrar, Straus & Giroux, 1991. (Sunburst)

    A mouse leaves his nest undiscovered in the pocket of a plumber and has a series of imaginative adventures as it goes from pocket to rolled newspaper to shopping bag to paper cup and so on in the everyday world of people. Numerous pictures of various sizes show close-ups and details, making this a good book for small groups of children to work with in a collaborative retelling.

11. + *Niki's Walk* by Jane Tanner. Cleveland: Modern Curriculum Press, 1987. (MCP)

    Niki and his mother go for a walk in this urban setting; celebrate someone's birthday in a park; and see a variety of sights such as a construction site, boats on the river, a tow truck removing a wrecked car, and so forth. Much to talk about with early elementary children. Take a walk and discuss what you see. Write a group story.

12. *Peter Spier's Rain* by Peter Spier. New York: Doubleday, 1982. (Doubleday)

    A brother and sister explore their wet neighborhood and engage in hundreds of activities before returning home for a hot bath and cocoa. Writing possibilities include

telling about the day from the point of view of one of the children or writing about what you would like to do on a rainy day.

13. *The Silver Pony* by Lynd Ward. New York: Houghton Mifflin, 1973. (Houghton Mifflin)

    This long story depicts a lonely farm boy who fantasizes about the trips he takes on his beautiful winged pony. When his family finds him lying ill outside, their present of a real pony helps the boy bring his fantasy and his real world together. Older children can better sustain the narrative possibilities of this story.

14. *The Snowman* by Raymond Briggs. New York: Random House, 1978. (Random)

    A small boy has a wonderful nighttime adventure with his snowman who can fly. In the morning, though, his friend has melted. Observant children may notice that the story takes place in Britain when they see landmarks and other clues.

15. *Sunshine* by Jan Ormerod. New York: Lothrop, Lee and Shepard, 1981. (Mulberry)

    A small girl's morning routine as she prepares for school is speeded up when she shows her parents what time it is. The same warm family feeling is created in the sequel Moonlight *(New York: Lothrop, Lee and Shepard, 1982; Mulberry).*

16. *Tuesday* by David Wiesner. New York: Clarion, 1991. (   )

    As the moon rises, so do frogs on their lily pads. They glide over a sleeping village, through laundry, into an open window to discover late-night TV, and over a surprised dog. The magic stops when the sun begins to rise. A perplexed news crew tries to figure out what has happened. Funny pictures encourage children to make up dialogue for the many frogs and animals who witness the improbable situation. See, too, Wiesner's also nearly wordless June 26, 1999 *(Clarion, 1992).*

Life Stories (Grades 2–6)

With the many fine picture book and novel-sized autobiographies and biographies available, children are no longer confined to the often dry series books of individual lives. This list introduces authors of biographies and involves children in the lives of some people who made the world a different place because of their actions. Many kinds of biographies as well as a partial autobiography are included here.

1. *Alvin Ailey* by Andrea Davis Pinkney, illustrated by Brian Pinkney. New York: Hyperion, 1993. (   )

    From his early beginnings in Texas to his teen years in Los Angeles through his founding of his famous dance theater in New York, the life of this well-known black dancer is chronicled. Pinkney's swirling scratchboard illustrations capture motion and energy of the man during his triumphant years.

2. *Diego,* see page 153b.

3. *The Double Life of Pocahontas* by Jean Fritz. New York: Putnam, 1983. (Puffin)

    This complete biography covers the short twenty-one years of Pocahontas' life lived in the early 1600s. Fritz writes elegantly about the encounters of the Native Americans with Captain John Smith and the early Virginia settlers. See, too, other titles about Stonewall Jackson, James Madison, and Benedict Arnold by our foremost writer of biographies for children.

4. *El Chino* by Allen Say. Boston: Houghton Mifflin, 1990. (   )

    Bong Way "Billy" Wong, a Chinese American raised in Nogales, Arizona, always dreamed of being a great athlete. But it wasn't until he discovered bullfighting that he found his true calling. Say's radiant watercolors illuminate this true story of a man who pursued his unconventional dream.

5. *Flight: The Journey of Charles Lindbergh* by Robert Burleigh, illustrated by Mike Wimmer. New York: Philomel, 1991. (   )

    In poetic text and compelling illustration this book evokes the feelings and emotions of Lindbergh during his famous flight in 1927. Inspiring partial biography also speaks to having a dream and realizing it. See also the more biographical but less beautiful Lindbergh *by Chris Demarest (Crown, 1993).*

6. *The Glorious Flight: Across the Channel with Louis Bleriot* by Alice and Martin Provensen. New York: Viking, 1983. (Puffin)

    With many historical and background details that invite readers to speculate about life in 1909, the authors involve children in this famous flight.

7. *The Great Alexander the Great* by Joe Lasker. New York: Viking, 1983. (Puffin)

    The vividly illustrated life of Alexander, who ruled the land from Greece to India, is highlighted with particular emphasis on his bravado, imagination, and his friendship with his horse, "Bucephalus." See, too, Lasker's The Boy Who Loved Music *(New York: Penguin, 1979) for an imaginative rendering of how Haydn came to compose the "Farewell" Symphony.*

8. *Homesick,* see page 143b.

9. *Indian Chiefs* by Russell Freedman. New York: Holiday, 1982. (Holiday)

    Aspects of the lives of six Indian leaders who led their people in moments of crisis in the middle 1800s. This collection of partial biographies, illustrated with photographs from the period, enables older readers to see the settling of the West from multiple perspectives. See Freedman's many other excellent biographies, including Lincoln: A Photobiography, *p. 144b.*

10. *James Weldon Johnson: "Lift Every Voice and Sing"* by Patricia and Fredrick McKissack. Chicago: Children's Press, 1990. (Children's Press).

    The life of this civil rights leader and author of the famous song of the title is presented in large print with black-and-white photographs from the period. A chronology of events in the person's life ends each book in this useful biography series. (Series)

11. *Johnny Appleseed* by Steven Kellogg. New York: Morrow, 1988. (Morrow)

    The life of John Chapman is based on fact, but many legends surround this famous planter, as well. In this exuberantly illustrated picture book, children might separate the fact from the fiction and compare Kellogg's version with Aliki's The Story of Johnny Appleseed *(Englewood Cliffs, NJ: Prentice Hall, 1963)* or with Reeve Lindbergh's poetic Johnny Appleseed, *illustrated by Kathy Jakobsen (New York: Joy Street/Little, Brown, 1990).*

12. *Keep the Lights Burning, Abbie* by Peter and Connie Roop, illustrated by Peter E. Hanson. Minneapolis, MN: Carolrhoda Books, 1985. (Carolrhoda)

   In easy-reader format, this fictionalized biographical sketch tells of one month in Abbie Burgess's life when a storm left her father on the mainland and Abbie took care of her sick mother and her siblings while keeping a Maine lighthouse working in 1856. A note tells readers more about Abbie's life.

13. *The Land I Lost,* see page 140b.

14. *The Last Princess: The Story of Princess Ka'iulani of Hawai'i* by Fay Stanley, illustrated by Diane Stanley. New York: Macmillan, 1991. (   )

   This sad story of the annexation of the sovereign nation of Hawai'i to the United States is offset by the proud dignity of the young princess, the last of royalty to rule the island, as she tried to convince Grover Cleveland of her people's right to sovereignty. Part of Stanley's biographical series, beautifully illustrated. See also Stanley's Charles Dickens: The Man Who Had Great Expectations *(Morrow, 1993). (Series)*

15. *Laura Ingalls Wilder* by Gwenda Blair, illustrated by Thomas B. Allen. New York: Putnam, 1981. (Putnam)

   In more demanding vocabulary than the type size would suggest, Blair rounds up details that cover but expand upon this well-known author's life as portrayed in her "Little House" books.

16. *Many Thousand Gone* by Virginia Hamilton, illustrated by Leo and Diane Dillon. New York: Knopf, 1993. (   )

   Short biographical vignettes of famous resistors to slavery, African-Americans and others, trace the history of slavery in the United States. Well-known figures such as Harriet Tubman, Frederick Douglass, Sojourner Truth, and Dred Scott as well as those less well-known give readers

background *in the history of slavery and those who protested.*

17. *Maya Angelou: Author* by Miles Shapiro. New York: Chelsea House, 1994. (Chelsea House)

   One of the "Black Americans of Achievement" series, this powerful biography does not spare middle schoolers the details of life for an African-American person in the United States from the 1930s when Angelou was growing up to the present day. Photographs present political, social, and economic aspects of the author's time but do not show her until the 1970s when she became well known for her writing. The publisher also features a series of biographies for younger readers, "Junior World Biographies." (Series)

18. *Once upon a Time: A Story of the Brothers Grimm* by Robert Quackenbush. New York: Simon & Schuster, 1985. (   )

   This lighthearted, simplified biography introduces readers to the two brothers who collected folklore and enabled many now-familiar tales to be rendered into print in the early 1800s. Quackenbush has written and illustrated many simplified biographies of such people as Thomas Edison and Peter Stuyvesant. (Series)

19. *The One Bad Thing About Father* by F. N. Monjo, illustrated by Richard Cuffari. New York: Holt, 1974. (HarperTrophy)

   In easy-reader format, readers see Theodore Roosevelt through the eyes of his son Quentin, who maintained that the only bad thing about his father was that he was president, and so his whole family, including the irrepressible Alice Roosevelt, had to live at the White House. See other simplified biographies by this author about such people as Thomas Jefferson and Benjamin Franklin.

20. *A Picture Book of Simon Bolivar* by David A. Adler, illustrated by Robert Casillo. New York: Holiday, 1992. (Holiday)

   The famous South American liberator's life story is chronicled. David Adler's picture-book biographies fill a real need. They present accurate information, attractively illustrated, in an easy-to-read format of one or two paragraphs per page. Subjects currently feature several U.S. presidents, Harriet Tubman, Frederick Douglass, Helen Keller, Florence Nightingale, and others. "Notes from the author" and a helpful chronology of the subject's life end most volumes. Highly useful for reluctant older readers as well. (Series)

21. *Self-Portrait: Trina Schart Hyman* by Trina Schart Hyman. New York: Harper & Row, 1989. (   )

    In her familiar bold black line and color, Hyman reveals her personal connection with the folktales she has illustrated and discusses her training as an illustrator, her marriage, and her country household. Bound to send children back to her books for another look, and an inspiration to budding artists, as well. (Series)

22. *Shaka, King of the Zulus* by Diane Stanley and Peter Vennema, illustrated by Diane Stanley. New York: Morrow, 1988. (Mulberry)

    The famous leader of one of the largest African armies ever assembled at a period when European explorers were "discovering" the continent is seen in dramatic, detailed illustration and text. This picture-book biography does not ignore Shaka's cruelty but sets it in the context of tribal beliefs of the time. See, too, this team's other titles, such as Good Queen Bess *(New York: Four Winds, 1990) and* Peter the Great *(New York: Four Winds, 1986) by this team.*

23. So Far from the Bamboo Grove, see page 159b.

24. *Traitor: The Case of Benedict Arnold,* see page 159b.

25. *A Weed Is a Flower: The Life of George Washington Carver* by Aliki. New York: Simon & Schuster, 1988.

    In brief, easy-reader format, Aliki captures simply the story of a man born a slave who became a great research scientist. See also her simplified biographies of Benjamin Franklin and Johnny Appleseed.

26. *Where Do You Think You're Going, Christopher Columbus?* by Jean Fritz, illustrated by Margot Tomes. New York: Putnam, 1980. (Putnam)

    In lively but entirely factual detail, Fritz

captures the man's courage and pride, as well as the attitudes of his times. Information-bearing illustrations, end notes, and a helpful index introduce children to the use of these valuable tools. (Series)

Bilingual Spanish Books: A Beginning List

To address the needs of the growing number of Latino students in our schools to read both in their first language and in English, we have included books that are bilingual. That is, the text is in English and Spanish on each page. In order to become literate in their first language and maintain this literacy while acquiring English, children may read texts with both languages. Such texts are also helpful for English-speaking students to learn Spanish.

Be sure to check with mainstream publishers such as HarperCollins, Morrow, Scholastic, and others such as Lee & Low Books who are now providing their own lines of bilingual books. Look, too, for those such as Farrar, Straus & Giroux, who are republishing Spanish translations of their own books, in this case under the "Mirasol" imprint. Children's Book Press publishes many bilingual titles, some of uneven literary or illustrative quality, so be selective.

For strategies and support for the teaching of second-language learners using a whole language approach, see "Whole Language Learning and Teaching for Second Language Learners" by Yvonne Freeman and David Freeman in *Reading Process and Practice: From Socio-Psycholinguistics to Whole Language* by Constance Weaver (Portsmouth, NH: Heinemann, 1994, pp. 558–629).

1. *Carlos and the Squash Plant / Carlos y la planta de calabaza* by Jan Romero Stevens, illustrated by Jeanne Arnold. Flagstaff, AZ: Northland, 1993. (   )

   A humorous, inventive tall tale concerns Carlos who doesn't take a bath when his mother tells him to. A squash plant grows from his ear until finally he scrubs himself. A recipe for a squash dish called Calabacitas *is included.*

2. *Diego* by Jeanette Winter and John Winter. New York: Knopf, 1991. (   )

   Over half of the text of this short biog-

raphy of Diego Rivera depicts his childhood. The rest encapsulates his contributions to art, both in his native Mexico and
in the world. Small, bordered, square illustrations depicting his life open up to
one contrasting double-page illustration
to suggest the scale in which the muralist
worked.

3. *Family Pictures*, see page 146b.

4. *Margaret and Margarita / Margarita y Margaret* by Lynn Reiser. New York: Morrow,
1993. (   )

   *Two parallel stories of little girls who go
to the park with their mothers. English
language is rendered on one page in pink
letters, Spanish on another in blue. As the
two girls play together and begin to use
each other's languages, the intermingled
blue and pink words reflect this blending.
The theme of friendship fits well with
other titles on the kindergarten, first, and
second grade lists.*

5. *The Piñata Maker / El piñatero* by George
Ancona. San Diego: Harcourt Brace, 1994.
(Harcourt Brace)

   *The process by which a Oaxacan crafts-
man makes piñatas and paper puppet
heads is shown in color photographs, pictures, and full paragraphs. While no specific directions are given, children can
easily make their own modified piñatas
following this process.*

6. *Un paseo por el bosque lluvioso / A Walk in
the Rainforest* by Kristin Joy Pratt. Ne-
vada City, CA: Dawn, 1993. (Dawn)

   *In alphabet-book format, aspects and
inhabitants of the South and Central
American rain forests are presented. Elegant paintings and informative short paragraphs provide background and information in child-alluring ways.*

7. *Uncle Nacho's Hat / El sombrero del tío
Nacho*, adapted by Harriet Rohmer, illus-
trated by Mira Reisberg. San Francisco:
Children's Book Press, 1989. (CBP)

   *In this story based on a Nicaraguan
folktale, Uncle Nacho can't seem to get rid
of his old hat when he is given a new one
by his niece. Finally he is able to discard
it when it returns to him in shreds. It is
his niece who encourages him to forget it*

and get on with life. An afterword note
gives further background.

8. *Vejigante Masquerader*, see page 133b.

9. *The Woman Who Outshone the Sun: La
mujer que billaba aun mas que el sol* from
a poem by Alejandro Cruz Martinez, translated by Rosalma Zubizarreta, illustrated
by Fernando Olivera. San Francisco: Children's Book Press, 1991.

   *Based on a legend, this story shows what
happens when people do not honor each
other, and when a river dries up. An ecological tale as well as a story of human values.*

Grade 7

Books at this level continue to deal with friendships, growing up, becoming independent, and
considering consequences of actions. They also
continue to present wider world views. The
short story genre is introduced in two volumes.

As on the previous two grade lists, many of
the authors here have written extensively for
the middle school age group, and once readers
are familiar with an author, they tend to want
to read more of that person's books. Teachers
should introduce many authors and their works
to readers as encouragement and advice. This
is the age at which children, because of school
and extracurricular demands, often stop most
of their recreational reading and do not return
until after adolescence—or perhaps ever.

Suggestions for seventh grade author studies
include Patricia Beatty, Pam Conrad, Paula
Fox, Virginia Hamilton, Gary Soto, Lawrence
Yep, plus many others on the previous three
grade list introductions.

1. (E) *Baseball in April* by Gary Soto. San
Diego: Harcourt Brace Jovanovich, 1990.
(Odyssey)

   *Small day-to-day events in a California
(Mexican-American) Latino community
much like the author's Fresno are presented in this short story collection of eleven
selections. For and about middle schoolers, these stories present themes of friendship, independence, love, success, and family
relationships. See other Soto collections,
too, such as* Local News *(San Diego: Harcourt Brace, 1993) or his novel,* Taking
Sides *(San Diego: Harcourt Brace, 1991).*

2. *Bull Run* by Paul Fleischman, illustrated by David Frampton. New York: HarperCollins, 1993. (Harper)

Fleischman, an innovative writer, introduces aspects of this famous opening Civil War battle as seen in sixteen short first-person vignettes. People include a horse-lover, a black man, a sketch artist, a slave woman, a local landowner, and others whose stories often fold into each other. One event from different perspectives raises the discussion of how our expectations and our experiences color what we see and understand. Also an excellent introduction to the War Between the States. See, too, his historical novels, Saturnalia *(1990 and* Path of the Pale Horse *(1983, both Harper).*

3. (E) *The Burning Questions of Bingo Brown* by Betsy Byars. New York: Viking Penguin, 1988. (Puffin)

Bingo wonders about girlfriends, his use of mousse, his teacher's sanity, and his family. Byars combines humorous dialogue and adolescent concerns deftly and believably. (Series)

4. *Children of the Dust Bowl: The True Story of the School at Weedpatch Camp* by Jerry Stanley, illustrated with photographs. New York: Crown, 1992. (Crown)

Against the backdrop of the Dust Bowl Era, Stanley tells of the Oklahoman migration to an unwelcoming California. Ostracized by Californians as "dumb Okies," the children went without education until one group pulled together in this true story to create their own school. From two derelict buildings it grew into classrooms, a shop, a science lab, and a full curriculum. Children helped build it by selling produce from school gardens and hammering nails. The school still exists today and is a tribute not only to how industry can overcome hardship but to how prejudice can be transformed. Excellent nonfiction and compelling photographs introduce children to a historical period they may know only through the movie "The Wizard of Oz."

5. *A Day No Pigs Would Die* by Robert Newton Peck. New York: Knopf, 1972. (Dell Yearling)

In the Depression, thirteen-year-old Rob comes to understand his Vermont father's quiet dignity, his willingness to admit to errors, and his ability to do what must be done for the family to survive.

6. *Dragon's Gate* by Lawrence Yep. New York: HarperCollins, 1993. (   )

Newbery runner-up. A boy called Otter flees China to work on building the railroads on the Golden Mountain, the Sierra Nevadas of California, only to find that he has been misinformed about life for him here. Disillusioned, he becomes involved in the first strike of Chinese railworkers in a little-written-about period in American history. The title has a literal as well as symbolic meaning for Otter.

7. *A Girl Called Boy* by Belinda Hurmence. New York: Clarion, 1982. (Clarion)

While fingering a family soapstone carving, a sarcastic African-American girl is transported back to the past where her short hair and blue jeans cause her to be mistaken for a runaway slave. This time-slip fantasy is historically accurate but framed within a contemporary viewpoint.

8. *The Giver* by Lois Lowry. Boston: Houghton Mifflin, 1993. (Houghton Mifflin)

1994 Newbery winner and great discussion book about choices. In a future utopian society, children are given their occupational training beginning at age twelve. Jonas's occupation will be to receive the memories of this society—pleasurable but annoying ones concerning snow as well as painful and horrible ones such as war. It is only when he discovers that euthanasia will kill his adopted baby brother that Jonas rebels. An enigmatic ending, powerful themes, the plan and nature of dystopias, and a believable protagonist make this book eminently discussable. See also Z for Zachariah *(p. 157b).*

9. *Grab Hands and Run* by Frances Temple. New York: Orchard, 1993. (   )

Felipe, his mother, and his five-year-old sister flee from a city in El Salvador after his father disappears. His memories of his father (who he learns is dead), his grandparents, and his dog pull back at him as they sustain the fleeing family. The book hints at the massacres and atrocities that propelled so many Central Americans northward, and presents background for why people immigrate.

10. *The House of Dies Drear* by Virginia Hamilton, illustrated by Eros Keith. New York: Macmillan, 1968. (Macmillan)

Weird and terrifying but ultimately explainable happenings threaten an African-American professor and his family, who are staying in a house that was a former Underground Railroad stop. Thomas Small and his family finally solve the mystery in this fast-paced story. (Series)

11. *Jacob Have I Loved* by Katherine Paterson. New York: Crowell, 1980. (HarperCollins)

Louise develops from a jealous and bitter twin sister to an emotionally healthy adult on an island in the Chesapeake Bay in the 1940s. Rich with well-developed characters, allusions, and multiple themes.

12. *Jayhawker* by Patricia Beatty. New York: Morrow, 1991. (   )

Stealing slaves from neighboring Missouri to freedom in Kansas, a Kansas boy, Lije, is part of events stemming from Lincoln's Emancipation Proclamation. Readers also meet other historical figures, such as Jesse James, Jim Hickok, and John Brown. Accurate Civil War background plus a suspenseful introduction to Beatty's many other novels set in the Civil War period and during the settling of the West.

13. *Julie of the Wolves* by Jean Craighead George. New York: Harper & Row, 1972. (HarperTrophy)

Miyax, a thirteen-year-old Eskimo girl, runs away on the tundra and survives with a pack of wolves. Themes of coming of age and ecology, and details of the true behavior of wolves. (Series)

14. *The Middle of Somewhere: A Story of South Africa* by Sheila Gordon. New York: Orchard, 1989. (Bantam)

The struggle of an African family to continue to live in their home village, which white South Africans want for a suburb. A story with strong values of brotherhood and persistence ending with the release of Nelson Mandela. See, too, Journey to Jo'burg *on p. 144b.*

15. (E) *The Monument* by Gary Paulsen. New York: Delacorte, 1991. (   )

One of Paulsen's shorter, nonsurvival stories asks the reader to consider what constitutes a monument to the war dead? Rocky, a mixed-race thirteen-year-old with a bad leg, sees the adult world more clearly and considers what art can do. Good discussion novel and a quick read.

16. *My Brother Sam Is Dead* by James Lincoln Collier and Christopher Collier. New York: Four Winds, 1974. (Scholastic)

Conflicting loyalties and the injuries inflicted on the innocent during the Revolutionary War are seen through the eyes of Sam's younger brother Tim. See also the Colliers' trilogy about African-Americans during this war, which begins with Jump Ship to Freedom, *p. 140b.*

17. *Prairie Songs* by Pam Conrad. New York: Harper & Row, 1985. (HarperTrophy)

Louise's simple pioneer existence is changed forever by the arrival of a doctor and his elegant, though mentally unbalanced, wife. Figurative and descriptive language, as well as an accurate picture of pioneer living, bring this time closer. See, too, Conrad's My Daniel *(New York: Harper & Row, 1989),* told in two settings, present and pioneer days.

18. (E) *The Shooting of Dan McGrew* by Robert W. Service, illustrated by Ted Harrison. Boston: David R. Godine, 1988. (   )

Life at the Malamute Saloon, as told by Dawson City's resident poet, is boldly brought to life by Harrison's vivid paintings. See, too, Harrison's treatment of Service's The Cremation of Sam McGee *(New York: Greenwillow, 1987).*

19. (E) *Sister* by Eloise Greenfield, drawings by Monetta Barrett. New York: Harper, 1974. (HarperTrophy)

Thirteen-year-old African-American Doretha struggles with her identity in the family until she rereads her book of memories that she started when she was nine. Chapter headings reveal the age at which

Doretha wrote the diary entries—a record of hard times, good times, the times that make her strong now. Students might reflect, journal-style, upon their own strong memories that make them who they are now.

20. *Summer of My German Soldier* by Bette Greene. New York: Dial, 1973. (Bantam)
    Told from the viewpoint of a twelve-year-old Jewish girl in a small Arkansas town who befriends a Nazi POW. Amid prejudice and anger, he leaves her to grow up with knowledge that she is a "person of worth." (Series)

21. *True Confessions of Charlotte Doyle* by Avi. New York: Orchard, 1990. (Orchard)
    A girl, through an accident of fate, becomes the only female aboard a ship bound for America from England in 1832. In first-person narrative, Charlotte tells how she became involved in mutiny, a raging storm, and treachery among the sailors before coming ashore a changed person with a new perspective on what it means to be female.

22. *Village by the Sea* by Paula Fox. New York: Orchard, 1988. (Dell Yearling)
    With her father facing surgery, Emma goes to visit her quixotic aunt at the seashore and learns something about love, envy, rage, and finally forgiveness in this powerful psychological novel.

23. *Where the Lilies Bloom* by Vera and Bill Cleaver, illustrated by James Spanfeller. New York: Lippincott, 1969. (HarperCollins)
    A fourteen-year-old Appalachian girl keeps her family together after her parents' death by trying to teach them "wildcrafting" and the art of being close-mouthed in this survival story. (Series)

24. (E) *Within Reach*, edited by Don Gallo. New York: HarperCollins, 1993.
    (   )
    Ten short stories by popular authors, such as Robert Lipsyte, Judie Angell, Constance Greene, and Pam Conrad, join less well-known ones to tell diverse stories for middle-grade readers. Author biographies

included. Good for introducing theme, genre, discussion, and authors quickly.

25. *The Wright Brothers: How They Invented the Airplane* by Russell Freedman, with original photographs by Wilbur and Orville Wright. New York: Holiday, 1991. (Holiday)
    Working from primary source material, Freedman captures interest by making readers feel as if they were eyewitnesses to history. Pair with Lawrence Yep's fictionalized account of a Chinese-American's work with airplanes at the turn of the century, Dragonwings (New York: HarperCollins, 1975).

26. *Z for Zachariah* by Robert C. O'Brien. New York: Atheneum, 1965. (Macmillan)
    Ann Burden, the sole survivor of her valley after a nuclear explosion, contemplates a solitary existence. Her discovery of a sick man brings her initial hope, but her diary in which she tells the story chronicles her disillusionment and her final departure with hope of finding other survivors. See also a very different future imagined in The Lake at the End of the World by Christine MacDonald (New York: Dial, 1988), and The Giver, p. 155b.

Grade 8

Patterns in this list include many titles that help readers consider how a family in any setting can help or impede the growth of its members. Two compelling fantasies deal with individual responsibility and possibilities in a future setting or in an imagined world. As in the previous list, complex themes, characters, and literary presentations put new but not unmanageable demands on young adult readers.

Suggestions for author studies include Avi, Sue Ellen Bridgers, Peter Dickinson, Russell Freedman, Diana Wynne Jones, William Sleator, Cynthia Voigt, plus many others on the previous three grade lists.

1. *All Together Now* by Sue Ellen Bridgers. New York: Knopf, 1979. (Bantam)
    While spending the summer with her grandparents, twelve-year-old Casey makes friends with a retarded man and begins to

consider responsibility, friendship, and the nature of families in this richly characterized, often humorously told, novel.

2. (E) *The Borning Room* by Paul Fleischman. New York: HarperCollins, 1991. (Harper)

A short, powerful novel of the memories of an Ohio farm girl, told solely through scenes centering on the room in the family's house where people die and are born. Besides being a remarkable picture of frontier life from the mid-1800s through into the new century, this story shows how an author incorporates effortlessly the historical research that makes the period come alive. Runaway slaves, seances, electricity, the endless cycles of farm life, chloroform as a wonder drug, and rural entertainment come to life in Fleischman's powerful story of one life cycle. Help readers see the many allusions, metaphors, and similes Fleischman uses so seamlessly. See also the four-generation story Jericho by Janet Hickman (New York: Greenwillow, 1994).

3. *Borrowed Children* by George Ella Lyon. New York: Orchard, 1988. (COP)

Mandy knows her ticket out of her Kentucky hill house is education and is brokenhearted to have to stay home to care for the latest addition to her siblings in the 1920s. But a well-earned trip to Memphis relatives becomes a journey of self-discovery and gives her a new perspective, both on her family and on her dreams.

4. *Crazy Lady* by Jane Conly. New York: HarperCollins, 1993. (   )

Vernon, an academic failure, hangs out in the Baltimore streets desperate to resolve his problems. He is befriended by Maxine and Roland, an alcoholic and her retarded son, both of whom Vernon used to taunt. A retired teacher Maxine finds to tutor Vernon asks as payment that he help the boy and his mother, which tests but eventually reveals Vernon's true strengths. Poignant, contemporary, true, and many readers will identify with the pain of exclusion and the problems and rewards of compassion.

5. *Eva* by Peter Dickinson. New York: Delacorte, 1989. (Dell)

In a future time, a girl's brain is transplanted into a chimpanzee's body, partly to save her life but partly to further research. This passionate and eloquent story raises questions about ecology, responsible science, and the nature of humankind.

6. (E) *The Highwayman* by Alfred Noyes, illustrated by Charles Keeping. New York: Oxford University Press, 1981. (COP)

This tragic narrative poem of love and loyalty is dramatically illustrated. Keeping reverses his striking pictures from black on white to a ghostly white on black after the highwayman's death.

7. (E) *I Am Wings: Poems About Love* by Ralph Fletcher. New York: Bradbury, 1994. (   )

Taken singly, each poem is about some aspect of adolescent love. But, read as a narrative, the collection could chronicle a relationship from first glance to final breaking up from the standpoint of a boy. Good reading and free-verse approach encourages writers to try their own hands at unrhymed poems that convey strong feelings. See also Paul Janeczko's anthology Preposterous: Poems of Youth (New York: Orchard, 1991).

8. *I Will Call It Georgie's Blues* by Suzanne Newton. New York: Viking, 1983. (Dell Yearling)

Controlled by the conservative views of his minister family and expectations of his small southern town, fifteen-year-old Neal secretly studies to be a jazz pianist. A coming-of-age story compellingly told.

9. *The Moves Make the Man* by Bruce Brooks. New York: Harper & Row, 1984. (Harper)

A white boy and African-American boy form a tenuous friendship based on their admiration for each other's sports prowess, one in baseball, the other in basketball. Themes of overcoming prejudice, dealing with mental illness, and growing up, as well as near-poetic descriptions of playing "hoop."

10. *Nothing But the Truth* by Avi. New York: Orchard, 1991. (Avon)

A ninth grader failing English can't participate in sports. His plan to be transferred from both his English teacher and a failing grade is to hum the national anthem when it is played over the loudspeaker. The ensuing events become issues of First Amendment rights and of national attention. Thoughtfully presented ideas in a variety of formats, from letters and memos to newspaper articles, speech transcripts, and diary entries by one of children's literature's most challenging writers.

11. *The Outsiders* by S. E. Hinton. New York: Viking, 1967. (Dell Yearling)

    In this classic gang novel, "Greasers" face death and struggle with peer relationships, poverty, and a search for self. Realistically written and fast paced.

12. *Scorpions* by Walter Dean Myers. New York: Harper & Row, 1988. (Harper Keypoint)

    When Jamal inherits gang leadership and a gun from his imprisoned brother, he can't seem to find a way out. Gritty portrayal of the consequences of impetuous action set in Harlem.

13. *Shabanu: Daughter of the Wind* by Suzanne Fisher Staples. New York: Knopf, 1989. (Random)

    At twelve, the youngest daughter of a modern-day Pakistani camel herder knows her culture demands that she must be married but chafes against her fate. A vivid portrayal of life and death in the desert world and a dramatic coming-of-age story of a brave young girl. (Series)

14. *So Far From the Bamboo Grove* by Yoko Kawashima Watkins. New York: Lothrop, Lee and Shepard, 1986. (Beech Tree)

    This fictionalized autobiography tells of eleven-year-old Yoko's escape from Korea to Japan in 1945, when Korea was ridding itself of anyone with hated Japanese ancestry. A harrowing story of courage with a unique perspective on World War II. See also Year of Impossible Goodbyes *by Sook Nyul Choi (Boston: Houghton Mifflin, 1991), which takes place within the same setting and time period.*

15. *A Solitary Blue* by Cynthia Voigt. New York: Atheneum, 1984. (Scholastic)

    *The gradual development of a loving relationship between Jeff and his divorced father takes place only after Jeff, too, has been psychologically wounded by his irre-*sponsible mother. Dicey Tillerman, from Voigt's other novels, figures in Jeff's healing as well. (Series)*

16. (E) *Toning the Sweep* by Angela Johnson. New York: Orchard, 1993. (   )

    Moving among different perspectives, the author skillfully tells parts of the story of three generations. Fourteen-year-old Emily has come with her mother to move her cancer-ridden grandmother Ola from the desert back to Cleveland. Past events from Ola's Alabama upbringing, Emmie's mother's inability to face the fact of her father's brutal murder as an "uppity nigger," and Emmie's newfound courage blend into an emotional story about facing life squarely.

17. *Traitor: The Case of Benedict Arnold* by Jean Fritz. New York: Viking, 1981. (Puffin)

    Arnold's enthusiastic, impetuous, and reckless personality leads him finally to disappointment and treason. A gripping biography of a complex personality seen against the Revolutionary War period.

18. *A Wizard of Earthsea* by Ursula LeGuin, illustrated by Ruth Robbins. New York: Parnassus Press, 1968. (Bantam)

    Pride and arrogance cause Ged, a young wizard, to call up a shadow that threatens all of Earthsea until Ged can face what he has done. Powerful themes of maintaining balance and harmony, personal responsibility, and self knowledge, as well as an elegant telling, make this classic high fantasy a standard against which others are measured. (Series)

Grades 9 and 10

The concerns, conflicts, pain, and discoveries of adolescents dominate the literature on this list. Characters struggle with pressure from their peers and parents and with the harsh realities of twentieth-century society. Traditional classics and very current fiction are both represented for students to discover great literature and models for their own writing. A special effort has been made to add literature that explores human differences—racial, cultural, physical, and psychological.

1. *Betsey Brown* by Ntozake Shange. New York: St. Martin's Press, 1985. (St. Martin's)

   Thirteen-year-old Betsey is part of a large, boisterous black family living in St. Louis in 1959, the year of forced school integration. Besides the normal problems and wonders of adolescence, sexual awakenings, fitting in with the group, and self-identity crises, Betsey must quickly learn about racial hatred and how to deal with it. The novel raises questions about how cultural heritage affects identity and what social activism costs in human terms.

2. *Bless the Beasts and the Children* by Glendon Swarthout. New York: Doubleday, 1970. (Pocketbooks)

   A group of emotionally handicapped adolescents grow in maturity and self-esteem through their sensitivity to the plight of the buffaloes near their Arizona camp. Readers are challenged by the storytelling through dream sequences and flashbacks in this coming-of-age novel and drawn to its conservationist theme.

3. *The Catcher in the Rye* by J. D. Salinger. Boston: Little, Brown, 1951. (Bantam)

   This classic young adult novel presents the conflicts of innocence and experience and adolescent angst in an irreverent, touching way. Students identify with Holden Caulfield through his run-ins with authority, parents, and insensitive people everywhere. Invites discussion of issues of sexuality, individuality, ethics, and moral values.

4. (E) *The Chocolate War* by Robert Cormier. New York: Pantheon, 1974. (Dell)

   A powerful story of a high school boy who refuses to sell chocolates for his Catholic high school. Jerry stands up against the cold and calculating Brother Leon and the school's secret society. Encourages students to question the uses of power and authority and the responsibilities of the individual to "dare to disturb the universe."

5. (E) *Eight Plus One* by Robert Cormier. New York: Pantheon, 1980. (Dell)

   Cormier's nine short stories are glimpses into the daily lives and concerns of young people: the mystical world of fathers, the shifting of adolescent friendships, discov-eries about love, and the mistakes of youth. Cormier's brief stories are mirrors for students to look into and see themselves.

6. *Fahrenheit 451* by Ray Bradbury. New York: Ballantine, 1953. (Ballantine)

   Told with poetic power, a classic science fiction tale filled with technological wonders and a chilling warning of the dangers of censorship. Montag is a fireman in the cold and ominous future where fires are not extinguished but used to destroy books, the enemy of people in a world where thinking is dangerous. Connects with current issue of language censorship.

7. *Forbidden City* by William Bell. New York: Bantam Starfire, 1990. (Bantam Starfire)

   At age seventeen Alex has the rare opportunity to witness history when his photojournalist father is assigned to cover Beijing during the 1989 student democratic uprising in Tiananmen Square. Along with Alex the reader acquires a quick education in Chinese politics and customs, but when friends and acquaintances become targets of political reprisal and eventually all foreigners' lives are endangered, the reporter's fascination turns to horror and despair. Students will be exposed to the personal loss and destruction that war as presented in history books seldom teaches. See also Emily Neville's The China Year *(New York: HarperCollins, 1991), which takes place in the same time frame.*

8. (E) *The Girl in the Box* by Ouida Sebestyen. Boston: Little, Brown, 1988. (Bantam)

   A sixteen-year-old girl writes notes to the world from a small cellar room where she is being held after a kidnapping. Her only solace is a typewriter; with it she attempts to make sense of the crime, her fear, and, in the process, her life as a teenager. Unusual style and "audience" make for interesting writing model. Issues of mortality and the enduring human spirit may prompt discussion.

9. *A Hero Ain't Nothin' But a Sandwich* by Alice Childress. New York: Coward, McCann & Geoghegan, 1973. (Putnam)

   Benjie is a young African-American boy struggling for identity in the ghetto and rapidly becoming addicted to heroin. Told by a variety of narrators and viewpoints, this short novel offers insights into the roles of friends, teachers, and family in their efforts to help Benjie and the complex forces that propel the boy toward his escape from the bleak world around him.

10. *The Hitchhiker's Guide to the Galaxy* by Douglas Adams. New York: Crown, 1979. (Pocket Books) *(Series)*

A comic science fiction story of the end of the world and one human's consequent outer space adventures. Adams' characters are as likely to say something significant as absurd in this satire of our bureaucratic systems and materialistic values. Readers enjoy the word play and wit of this hip, well-written story, the first of a series by Adams.

11. (E) *Home before Dark* by Sue Ellen Bridgers. New York: Knopf, 1976. (Bantam)

Vivid characterization pulls readers into the world of a family of migrant workers searching for roots. Excellent writing models for teenage writers in this story of a girl's strength and love. It may prompt reactions to issues of sexual desire and family loyalties.

12. (E) *The Island* by Gary Paulson. New York: Franklin Watts, 1988. (Dell)

Very unusual style and structure make this novel of self-discovery an interesting study for young readers. At fifteen, Wil Neuton finds an island one summer that wakens him to nature, meditation, art, and writing as a way to his own growth. Each chapter opens with an entry from Wil's journal, and interspersed with the traditional narration are Wil's own pieces of writing. Students may be led to ask questions about the meanings of their own existence through their reading.

13. (E) *Jack* by A. M. Homes. New York: Macmillan, 1989. (Vintage)

Fifteen-year-old Jack has juggled loyalties to his divorced mother and father for three years after an acrimonious divorce, and is devastated when he learns that his father is gay. Through the help of his friends and the efforts of his parents, Jack begins to accept the circumstances and how they affect him. The need for self-acceptance

and tolerance for differences is particularly important for young people; this novel offers an opportunity to explore this sensitively.

14. *Kaffir Boy* by Mark Mathabane. New York: Macmillan, 1986. (NAL)

Autobiography of an African-American boy growing up with the horrors of poverty and racial persecution in modern South Africa. The experiences of Johannes and his family give students a real glimpse into the struggles that beset blacks in South Africa.

15. (E) *Linger* by M. E. Kerr. New York: HarperCollins, 1993. (   )

When his brother leaves with the other enlisted men to fight in the Gulf War and the town beauty becomes his brother's pen pal, Gary feels nothing but envy for his brother. By the novel's end Gary is wiser about the realities of war, about relationships, and about hypocrisy among the rich and respectable in his small town. Students will find the theme of appearance vs. reality on several levels worth discussion in this story concerning recent history.

16. (E) *Lizard* by Dennis Covington. New York: Delacorte, 1991. (Dell)

Lizard is a remarkable character, a fourteen-year-old boy deformed from birth with eyes that look different directions and a nose flattened to one side. Committed to the state school for the retarded by an uncaring parent, Lizard learns that his future is up to him. When a group of itinerant actors free him to play Caliban in their production of Shakespeare's "The Tempest," Lizard learns about human nature and discovers his own humanity. This finely written novel will prompt discussion about our feelings about people with disabilities and makes an excellent companion to the study of "The Tempest."

17. (E) *The Man from the Other Side* by Uri Orlev. Boston: Houghton Mifflin, 1991. (   )

True story of a fourteen-year-old boy's experience in Warsaw during World War II. Marek discovers for himself how the Nazis are persecuting the Jews as he and his Catholic father sell food and supplies to Jews in hiding. An exciting story of risky intrigues and narrow escapes, this story also provides young readers an insight about the period of the Holocaust from a new perspective.

18. *The Miracle Worker* by William Gibson. New York: Atheneum, 1960. (Bantam)

 Inspiring dramatization of the story of Helen Keller and her remarkable teacher Anne Sullivan. Students are fascinated by the violent struggle between Anne and Helen. Gibson's focus allows students to see the handicaps of each member of the family, and readers gain insight into how we all handicap ourselves. It also invites the study of stagecraft.

19. *Night* by Elie Wiesel. New York: Hill & Wang, 1960. (Bantam)

 A personal account of a teenage boy's terrifying experiences in the Nazi death camps of World War II. Students identify with Elie through the first-person narrative. The stark reality of the events of the Holocaust promotes study of survival behavior and provokes student interest in this important historical event.

20. *Night Kites* by M. E. Kerr. New York: Harper & Row, 1986. (HarperCollins)

 Seventeen-year-old Erick is an average teenager facing the adolescent concerns of dating, friendships, and school, but must come to terms with a much more devastating problem when he learns that his older brother has AIDS. Readers are presented with realistic conflict for discussion of family reaction to homosexuality and disease.

21. *Of Mice and Men* by John Steinbeck. New York: Viking, 1938. (Viking Penguin)

 Classic American novel of the Depression era in our history and a very readable book. Students are drawn into the friendship between the mentally retarded Lennie and his companion George. Offers readers both an important view of America and an opportunity to examine their own needs for attention, love, and friendship.

22. *Reflections on a Gift of Watermelon Pickle,* edited by Stephen Dunning et al. New York: Lothrop, Lee and Shepard 1966. (   )

 A now-classic collection of modern verse by a wide variety of well- and little-known poets arranged in short thematic sections or grouped by subject matter. A wealth of poetic forms and ideas for student writing or talking.

23. (E) *Running Loose* by Chris Crutcher. New York: Morrow, 1983. (Dell)

 The humorous, gently sarcastic tone of the narration pulls readers into this book about adolescent pressures to succeed and be popular. Struggles of conscience of the main character provide excellent entries into discussion and self-questioning for teenage readers.

24. *Somehow Tenderness Survives* selected by Hazel Rochman. New York: Harper & Row, 1988. (HarperCollins)

 These ten stories of the pain and sadness of racial separation in southern Africa are powerful and very moving records of loss felt by both white and black people. Told by such fine writers as Nadine Gordimer and Doris Lessing, each story focuses on relationships strained or torn by the attitudes of apartheid. An excellent personal history, and also an opportunity for students to experience the personal effects of society's unjust laws.

25. (E) *Somewhere in the Darkness* by Walter Dean Myers. New York: Scholastic, 1992. (Scholastic)

 Jimmy Little is a fourteen-year-old boy who lives in New York with Mama Jean, his only known "mother," when suddenly his father who has been in prison shows up at his door. Myers's depiction of a boy discovering what it means to have a father and a man trying to learn to be a father as they travel across the U.S. is sensitive and engaging. The novel offers students a chance to question the responsibilities of children to their parents, and vice versa, and perhaps to reevaluate the power of parental love.

26. *A Summer Life* by Gary Soto. Hanover, NH: University Press of New England, 1990. (Dell)

 These brief stories and essays by and about a Chicano boy growing up in southern California wonderfully present the imagination and energy of youth. Writing with rich imagery and vivid language, Soto conveys the innocence, humor, joy, and pain of children spending their summer days amid rust and garbage on the hot, weed-covered asphalt of Los Angeles. These pieces are excellent models for student personal writing.

27. (E) *Visions*, edited by Donald R. Gallo. New York: Dell, 1987. (Dell)

Nineteen short stories by authors familiar to and loved by young adults explore issues of acceptance by peers, asserting independence, desire and longing—a full range of adolescent and human concerns. Variety in tone runs from tragic to comic, in subject from fantasy to gritty reality. Valuable source to engage teens in literature and the genre of the short story.

28. A *Yellow Raft on Blue Water* by Michael Dorris. New York: Holt, 1987. (Warner)

This stylistically interesting story, told through three narrators, a daughter, mother, and grandmother, presents the struggles of an American Indian family to accept the bleak remains of their heritage on the reservation. Rayona is fifteen, the daughter of a black man and Indian woman and trying to understand a mother who seems not to care for her, but when the same events are revealed through other points of view, the novel takes on tragic power. The book may prompt exploration of diverse points of view and acceptance of differences.

Grades 11 and 12

War and survival, mental illness, social injustice, and personal versus societal responsibility are some of the many themes explored in the literature from this list. Students nearing adulthood may satisfy their needs to answer questions about the world through their reading of serious, thought-provoking literature. Again, new books have been selected to reflect racial and cultural diversity for students to explore.

1. *After the First Death* by Robert Cormier. New York: Pantheon, 1979. (Dell)

Political thriller about terrorists who hijack a busload of children. Readers view the situation through the eyes of Miro, a young, well-trained killer; Katie, the teenage bus driver; and Ben, the son of a patriotic general. These young views bring into a public drama the issue of what matters more, human life and emotion or political systems and loyalties.

2. *Black Ice* by Lorene Cary. New York: Knopf, 1991. (Vintage)

True account of the life of a teenage African-American girl from a poor family dealing with the challenges and pressures of attending an Ivy League prep school in New Hampshire. The author, who eventually became a teacher herself, confronts social and racial stereotypes with respect to education. An inspiring story of success in overcoming barriers, this account will help young people understand the social pressures black teenagers face today.

3. *Black Voices*, edited by Abraham Chapman. New York: New American Library, 1968. (NAL)

A lengthy anthology of poetry, short stories, fiction, and nonfiction by African-American writers, with biographical sketches. Provides serious readers with a survey of African-American literature. Also offers humor, engaging narratives, and thought-provoking short pieces for important discussion of racial conditions in this country.

4. *Children of a Lesser God* by Mark Medoff. Salt Lake City: Gibbs M. Smith, 1987. (Gibbs M. Smith)

An award-winning play about a teacher who falls in love with one of his students, a young deaf woman, and tries to bridge the gap between the hearing and deaf worlds. In the process, he learns about the strength and dignity of deaf people. This very readable and engaging drama will enable students to gain an understanding of deaf attitudes and culture.

5. (E) *Fallen Angels* by Walter Dean Myers. New York: Scholastic, 1988. (Scholastic)

Told by a young African-American man from the streets of New York, this story of a tour of duty in Vietnam evokes the boredom and terror of soldiers thrown into a war they do not understand or know how to fight. Racial conflict mixes with the conflicts of conscience and courage that characterize war novels. Provides valuable context for understanding contemporary American history.

6. *The House on Mango Street* by Sandra Cisneros. New York: Vintage, 1989. (Vintage)

A personal account of a girl and her Mexican family growing up in Chicago. Told with poetic language and sensitive detail, this series of brief vignettes documents the pain and joy of adolescent longings amidst the poverty and prejudice experienced by the Latino community. The creativity and power of these stories will serve as writing models for young writers and offer experiences for discussion about the point of view of a minority group.

7. *I Know Why the Caged Bird Sings* by Maya Angelou. New York: Random House, 1969. (Bantam)

An African-American woman tells her moving story of childhood and adolescence. Angelou's writing is fresh, engaging, and poetic. She offers insights about African-American values and culture as well as the pain and joy of being young. Invites personal response from students.

8. (E) *I Had Seen Castles* by Cynthia Rylant. New York: Harcourt Brace, 1993. (   )

As an old man, John Dante recalls his life at seventeen as he experienced America's reaction to Pearl Harbor and the emotional build-up to his enlisting to fight in World War II. This sad, poignant story brings out the cruelty and terrible injustice of war as it affects two young people in love. Very simple and moving, the novel may prompt students to think of war in real and personal terms.

9. (E) *If Rock and Roll Were a Machine* by Terry Davis. New York: Delacorte, 1992. (Bantam)

Bert Bowden is a seventeen-year-old boy who has suffered a year of humiliation from a grade-school teacher who was trying to cure his impulsive behavior, but who has destroyed his spirit and self-confidence. Through the love and parenting of a high school teacher and a middle-aged biker, he begins to value himself. The novel's interesting style may inspire some

student experimentation with narration; the concept of gaining self-respect through integrity will appeal to teenage readers.

10. *In Country* by Bobbie Ann Mason. New York: Harper & Row, 1985. (HarperCollins)

Coming to terms with the scars from the Vietnam War in small-town Kentucky during the 1980s, this book shows the pain and confusion of vets and their families. Well-drawn characters and an interesting narrative style. Provides students with insights about conflicting attitudes toward this war and may prompt comparisons to current global events.

11. (E) *Join In*, edited by Donald R. Gallo. New York: Delacorte, 1993. (   )

Seventeen short stories of characters from a variety of ethnic backgrounds, this collection examines the lives of American Indians, Puerto Ricans, Vietnamese, and others as they deal with life in America. Told by well-known and respected young adult writers and others, these stories offer insights to student readers about a variety of cultures and ways of looking at the world as well as prompt self-examination of attitudes Americans have about people of other cultural backgrounds.

12. *A Lesson Before Dying* by Ernest J. Gaines. New York: Knopf, 1993. (   )

Set in Louisiana in the 1940s, this novel about a young black man seeking dignity amid racial intolerance demonstrates the power of helping our fellow man. A young black teacher visits a condemned teenager in prison to teach him how to die and gains his own reward, an understanding of his own sense of humanity. An excellent historical document and, more importantly, a fine work of fiction that offers students an opportunity to explore the question of what it means to be human.

13. *Lord of the Flies* by William Golding. New York: Putnam, 1954. (Perigee)

Classic British novel of the ancient struggle between civilization and chaos. Rich details of setting offer students opportunities for seeing craftsmanship while physical and moral conflicts provide for discussion topics.

14. (E) *Memory* by Margaret Mahy. New York: Macmillan, 1987. (Dell)

    Students may empathize with the plight of the elderly in this story of a teenager's reluctant involvement with an Alzheimer's disease victim. From the New Zealand setting readers also get a glimpse into political unrest there. Especially well-drawn characterization will engage students and spur inquiry into their social responsibility to the elderly.

15. (E) *Midnight Hour Encores* by Bruce Brooks. New York: Harper & Row, 1986. (HarperCollins)

    Offers readers a glimpse into the life of a young musical prodigy through authentic details. Ideals of the hippie movement of the 1960s contrast with present-day realities of divorce and materialist values and raise worthwhile questions for young readers.

16. *The Nick Adams Stories* by Ernest Hemingway. New York: Scribner, 1972. (Scribner)

    Hemingway's stories of the young Nick in Michigan bring up issues important to young people: friendship, loyalty, love and sex, and peer pressure. Very readable. Hemingway's powerful narratives are filled with the ambiguity and mystery of adolescence. An excellent source for discussion and writing ideas.

17. *One Flew over the Cuckoo's Nest* by Ken Kesey. New York: Viking, 1962. (NAL)

    Kesey's antihero, R. P. McMurphy, is both a scoundrel and a saint as he helps a group of beaten men overcome the system that has destroyed their manhood. The uses and misuses of power and the belief in oneself are important questions for students to consider in this classic contemporary novel.

18. *Ordinary People* by Judith Guest. New York: Viking, 1976. (Viking Penguin)

    Story of a teenager's struggle to accept his brother's death and find his own identity. Conrad learns to face the demons of guilt and rejection that torture him and face up to his family, which is falling apart. Catalyst for study of family dynamics and pressures on young people today.

19. *A Raisin in the Sun* by Lorraine Hansberry. New York: Random House, 1959. (NAL)

    The voices of an African-American family struggling against poverty and with one another's needs pull readers into this drama. Family loyalty, the need for a strong black identity, and the frustration of the American dream just beyond the grasp of the Younger family are relevant for discussion.

20. (E) *Remembering the Good Times* by Richard Peck. New York: Delacorte, 1985. (Dell)

    First-person narrative of a young man recalling his bittersweet memories of junior high and high school, the powerful bonds of friendship forged with two friends, and the horror of dealing with the suicide of one. Very engaging prose style will pull readers into the story. May inspire study of psychological pressures of family life and society.

21. *A Separate Peace* by John Knowles. New York: Macmillan, 1959. (Bantam)

    The global conflict of World War II is the backdrop of this story of prep school students discovering their own sources of conflict. Shifting friendships and loyalties, peer pressure, and confusion about identity complicate the last days of youth before the war. High school students faced with pressures of the real world connect with these lives powerfully.

22. *Slaughterhouse-Five* by Kurt Vonnegut, Jr. New York: Delacorte, 1969. (Dell)

    The story of Billy Pilgrim's life, affected as it is by the devastation he witnessed in the bombing of Dresden, Germany, in World War II. The horrors of war and issues of government hypocrisy, individuality, and family intrigue students, and Vonnegut's humorous, offbeat style is engaging to young sensibilities.

23. *Soul Catcher* by Frank Herbert. New York: Putnam, 1972. (Berkley)

    An American Indian takes revenge against the white man for the oppression of his people by kidnapping the son of a state official. Authentic details of Indian culture and philosophy invite comparison to popular American thought and values.

Narrative techniques of multiple first person, letters, and news reports may offer students models for their own experimentation.

24. (E) *Staying Fat for Sarah Byrnes* by Chris Crutcher. New York: Greenwillow, 1993. (   )

    A novel about young people dealing courageously with the difficulties of child abuse and alienation. "Moby," a high school senior who has struggled with obesity since early childhood, fights to save his friend Sarah, whose scars from a terrible childhood burn have made her a social outcast. Young readers will find the novel engaging, and the themes of loyalty in friendship and dealing with the evil of child abuse worthy of discussion.

25. *The Tao of Pooh* by Benjamin Hoff. New York: Dutton, 1982. (Viking)

    This funny and thought-provoking explanation of ancient Chinese philosophy through the stories of Pooh, Piglet, Eeyore, Rabbit, and Christopher Robin are lessons about how to live our lives from a refreshingly offbeat point of view. Students will gain a rudimentary understanding of Daoism, enjoy the wit and humor of Hoff, and find in these parables rather esoteric concepts to be explored.

26. *Wide Sargasso Sea* by Jean Rhys. New York: Norton, 1966. (Norton)

    A prequel to Brontë's Jane Eyre, *this novel tells the story of a young native Caribbean girl's life as a mixed child of British and Jamaican heritage from childhood through marriage and immigration to England. A finely written account of the attitudes and prejudices of traditional views toward "natives" told in stream-of-consciousness style, the novel will provoke discussion about various types of prejudice in a male-dominated world.*

Multicultural Book List

For full publishing information and annotations for the following titles, please refer to the page numbers given below.

African-American/Black Culture

Something Upstairs. See page 144b.

Song of the Trees. See page 137b.

Somewhere in the Darkness. See page 162b.

Spin a Soft Black Song. See page 141b.

Stories Julian Tells, The. See page 127b.

Tales of Uncle Remus, The. See page 133b.

Talking Eggs, The. See page 127b.

Tell Me a Story, Mama. See page 148b.

Ten Nine Eight. See page 109b.

Three Wishes. See page 127b.

Toning the Sweep. See page 159b.

Uncle Jed's Barbershop. See page 133b.

Wagon Wheels. See page 128b.

Weed is a Flower, A. See page 153b.

What a Wonderful World. See page 116b.

When I Was Little. See page 148b.

Wide Sargasso Sea. See page 166b.

Wiley and the Hairy Man. See page 123b.

Yo! Yes? See page 109b.

Asian-American/Asian Culture

Chi-Hoon. See page 139b.

Child of the Owl. See page 142b.

Dragon's Gate. See page 155b.

Dragon's Pearl, The. See page 139b.

El Chino. See page 151b.

Forbidden City. See page 160b.

Grandfather's Journey. See page 135b.

Halmoni and the Picnic. See page 130b.

How My Parents Learned to Eat. See page 125b.

I Hate English. See page 131b.

In the Year of the Boar and Jackie Robinson. See page 139b.

Join In. See page 164b.

Journey to Topaz. See page 140b.

Lon Po Po. See page 126b.

Onion Tears. See page 141b.

Rabbit's Judgment. See page 127b.

Sachiko Means Happiness. See page 136b.

Sadako and the Thousand Paper Cranes. See page 144b.

Seven Blind Mice. See page 109b.

So Far from the Bamboo Grove. See page 159b.

Tiger. See page 137b.

Yang the Youngest and His Terrible Ear. See page 137b.

Year of the Panda, The. See page 134b.

Yeh Shen. See page 138b.

Latino

Abuela. See page 123b.

Abuela's Weave. See page 129b.

Amelia's Road. See page 124b.

Baseball in April. See page 154b.

Borreguita and the Coyote. See page 124b.

Carlos and the Squash Plant. See page 153b.

Chair for My Mother, A. See page 119b.

Class President. See page 139b.

Diego. See page 153b.

El Chino. See page 151b.

Family Pictures. See page 146b.

Friday Night is Papa Night. See page 125b.

Gold Coin, The. See page 135b.

Grab Hands and Run. See page 155b.

Great Kapok Tree, The. See page 125b.

House on Mango Street, The. See page 164b.

I Speak English for My Mom. See page 131b.

I'm New Here. See page 131b.

Join In. See page 164b.

Little Painter of Sabana Grande, The. See page 126b.

Margaret and Margarita. See page 154b.

Most Beautiful Place in the World, The. See page 136b.

New Shoes for Sylvia. See page 108b.

Picture Book of Simon Bolivar, A. See page 152b.

Piñata. See page 112b.

Piñata Maker, The. See page 154b.

Skirt, The. See page 133b.

Summer Life, A. See page 162b.

Too Many Tamales. See page 122b.

Uncle Nacho's Hat. See page 154b.

Vejigante Masquerader. See page 133b.

Walk in the Rainforest, A. See page 154b.

Woman Who Outshone the Sun, The. See page
154b.

Native American

Annie and the Old One. See page 129b.
Courage of Sarah Noble, The. See page 124b.
Discovery of the Americas, The. See page 130b.
Double Life of Pocahontas, The. See page 151b.
Indian Chiefs. See page 151b.
Island of the Blue Dolphins. See page 143b.
Join In. See page 164b.
Julie of the Wolves. See page 156b.
Knots on a Counting Rope. See page 131b.
Last Princess, The. See page 152b.
Mama, Do You Love Me? See page 107b.
Morning Girl. See page 140b.
Raven. See page 132b.
Rough-Face Girl, The. See page 136b.
Sign of the Beaver, The. See page 144b.
Soul Catcher. See page 165b.
Stone Fox. See page 133b.
Toughboy and Sister. See page 142b.
Yellow Raft on Blue Water, A. See page 163b.

Appendix A:
A Folk/Fairy
Tale Unit for
Grades 3–6

Folk/fairy tales are stories that have been handed down through the years in oral or written form.

Older students may enjoy and appreciate a unit focusing on comparative analysis of variants of popular folk and fairy tales. Tales such as *Cinderella, Rumpelstiltskin, Sleeping Beauty, Beauty and the Beast, Hansel and Gretel, and Little Red Riding Hood* have popular versions from different countries. Check with your librarian for titles.

Younger students also enjoy listening to and comparing different versions of favorite fairy tales such as *The Three Bears, Little Red Riding Hood,* and *Stone Soup.*

Rationale for Doing a Unit on Folk and Fairy Tales

1. Folk/fairy tales are a literary genre that is part of children's cultural heritage.
2. Folk/fairy tales deal with important themes: good triumphs over evil, perseverance and hard work pay off; lucid thinking solves problems; unselfishness is rewarded; justice will be done.
3. While some fairy tales are very violent, they provide an acceptable way for children to deal with violence.
4. Children feel connected with parents and grandparents by reading the same tales that past generations have read.
5. Folk/fairy tales have a wonderful, rich vocabulary.
6. Folk/fairy tales are appealing to all children.
7. Folk/fairy tales stimulate children's imagination.
8. Children of varying abilities are exposed to different levels of meaning.
9. Folktales are important for understanding various customs and cultures.
10. A large selection of fairy tales is readily available from the school and/or public libraries, making it easy for the teacher to gather a classroom collection. (You do not need special funds to do a folk/fairy tale unit.)
11. If your school mandates the basal text, you can still supplement it—or set it aside for a month—with an authentic literature unit.

Larger Understandings/Major Concepts

1. Folk/fairy tales can be interpreted many different ways depending on point of view, country of origin, and culture.
2. A clearly defined differentiation between good and evil—as presented in folk/fairy tales—can heighten awareness of consequences of behavior and help students make connections to problems in our society that are not so clearly defined.

170b

3. Some things in life, like folk/fairy tales, have remained consistent through the ages for parents and grandparents and can be a vehicle for connectedness between generations.

Planning

Plan on four to six weeks for an in-depth study. Divide the class heterogeneously into three groups for literature discussion, and be sure each student has a literature response log for recording reactions to the folktales. (See "Literature Response Logs" and "Literature Discussion Groups" in chapter 6 for procedures.) While some books will be read aloud by the teacher, most will be read silently by the students. Students keep a record of all folk/fairy tales read in their literature response log or in a separate folder (see Figure A-1).

Gather a collection of folk/fairy tales for the classroom, allowing at least four books per student. A class of twenty-five students should have about one hundred books. Some of these should be duplicate copies to allow for paired reading and small-group discussion. Try also to get as many different-quality versions of the tales as you can to allow for comparative analysis. See the bibliography at the end of this appendix for a sampling of folktales from our libraries that have worked well. You may also want to consult the following resources for specific titles, ideas, and other recommended resources. The unit presented here acknowledges the following valuable resources for some of the ideas and activities.

Figure A-1   Record of Folk/Fairy Tales Read by A Student

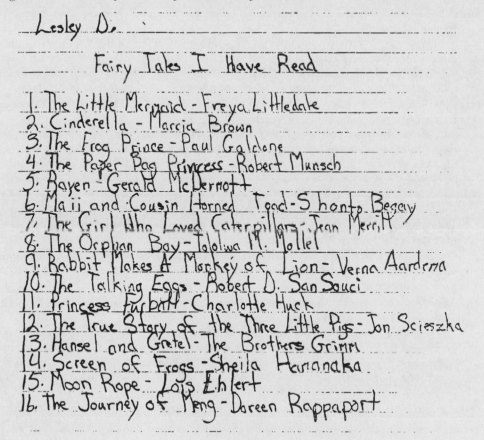

Lesley D.

Fairy Tales I Have Read

1. The Little Mermaid - Freya Littledale
2. Cinderella - Marcia Brown
3. The Frog Prince - Paul Galdone
4. The Paper Bag Princess - Robert Munsch
5. Rayen - Gerald McDermott
6. Maii and Cousin Horned Toad - Shonto Begay
7. The Girl Who Loved Caterpillars - Jean Merrill
8. The Orphan Boy - Tololwa M. Mollel
9. Rabbit Makes A Monkey of Lion - Verna Aardema
10. The Talking Eggs - Robert D. San Souci
11. Princess Furball - Charlotte Huck
12. The True Story of the Three Little Pigs - Jon Scieszka
13. Hansel and Gretel - The Brothers Grimm
14. Screen of Frogs - Sheila Hamanaka
15. Moon Rope - Lois Ehlert
16. The Journey of Meng - Doreen Rappaport

Resources

Blatt, Gloria T. (ed.). 1993. *Once Upon a Folk Tale: Capturing the Folklore Process, with Children.* New York: Teachers College Press. See annotation, p. 61b.

Bosma, Bette. 1992. *Fairy Tales, Fables, Legends, and Myths: Using Folk Literature in Your Classroom.* 2nd ed. New York: Teachers College Press. See annotation, p. 61b.

Goforth, Frances S., and Carolyn V. Spillman. 1994. *Using Folk Literature in the Classroom: Encouraging Children to Read and Write.* Phoenix, AZ: Oryx Press. See annotation, p. 65b.

Huck, Charlotte S., Susan Hepler, and Janet Hickman. 1993. "Traditional Literature." In *Children's Literature in the Elementary School.* 5th ed. (pp. 251–307). Fort Worth, TX: Harcourt Brace.

> *Various types of folktales are discussed, such as cumulative tales and beast tales. Characteristics of folktales, including plot structures, characterization, style, themes, and motifs, are elaborated. Variations of popular folk and fairy tales from around the world are shared.*

Hurst, Carol Otis. November–December 1985. "The World of Once upon a Time." *Early Years/K–8,* pp. 26–31.

> Carol Hurst presents thirty-five wonderful activities to go along with fairy tales. Pick and choose what will work for you and your students.

Moss, Joy F. 1994. "Modern Fairy Tales and Traditional Literature: Revisions and Retellings." In *Using Literature in the Middle Grades: A Thematic Approach* (pp. 43–62). Norwood, MA: Christopher-Gordon. See annotation, p. 69b.

Moss, Joy F. 1990. *Focus on Literature: A Context for Literacy Learning.* Katonah, NY: Richard C. Owen.

> *This practical text connects theory and practice and offers in-depth literature units around the following focuses: transformation tales, Baba Yaga tales, devil tales, cat tales, magic object tales, bird tales, wish tales, horse tales, Cinderella tales. Each unit includes plans for daily sessions, meaningful literature extensions, and bibliographies of tales.*

Moss Joy F. 1984. *Focus Units in Literature. A Handbook for Elementary School Teachers.* Urbana, IL: National Council of Teachers of English.

> *"Folktale Patterns: A Focus Unit for Grades Three and Four," pp. 107–124, offers suggestions for connecting folktales from different countries. References and teaching ideas are presented for three patterns: the theft of magical objects, the use of superpowers by helpful characters, and stories where greedy characters wind up with little ("circle tales").*

Spritzer, Daune Rebecca. Fall 1988. "Integrating the Language Arts in Elementary Classroom Using Fairy Tales, Fables, and Traditional Literature." *Oregon English. Theme: Whole Language,* pp. 23–26. (Journal available for purchase through National Council of Teachers of English, Urbana, Illinois)

> *The author shares a workable four- to six-week unit on folktales with lots of thoughtful ideas and activities for the classroom teacher. Included are examples of questions to promote critical thinking.*

Trousdale, Ann. Fall 1989. "The True Bride: Perceptions of Beauty and Feminine Virtue in Folktales." *The New Advocate,* pp. 239–248.

> *The author notes variants of fairy tales in which the virtues of the female characters go beyond beauty. For example, in* Mufaro's Beautiful Daughters *by John Steptoe, the heroine emerges for her character, not her beauty. Other tales cited have truthfulness, generosity, and loyalty as virtues held above beauty. This is an important article for giving students balanced perspectives of heroines in fairy tales.*

What follows are eighteen instructional plans that have been used successfully in a heterogeneous fourth-grade class. An instructional plan may be used one day, several days, or as long as several weeks. You will find that certain plans will need to be repeated to allow enough time for a concept or activity to be understood and fully discussed.

Allowing about one hour and thirty minutes each day for the folk/fairy tale unit has worked well. This time includes following through on the instructional plan as well as sharing problems and successes. For example, students and teacher may take the time to respond to a written draft of an original fairy tale or share completed storymaps or fairy tales. Note that samples of students' work that have been included come from average students.

The following plans are meant to be used only as a guide. You will want to change the sequence to suit your class needs, to delete some activities, and to add others.

Instructional Plan One: Characteristics of Fairy Tales (whole class)

Brainstorm with the class the characteristics of familiar fairy tales. Have a student act as scribe and list them on chart paper. Post the chart where it is easily visible and accessible. The chart is revised throughout the unit as new insights appear.

Characteristics usually mentioned include:

1. Happens in the past—time period not defined
2. Usually has a happy ending
3. May involve the supernatural
4. Often has a clear conflict between good and evil
5. Often begins with "Once upon a time"
6. Often includes a task, which if completed, brings a reward
7. All have plots and problems
8. Often includes a magic object/person to protect or help the main character
9. Often have brave heroes who rescue a helpless maiden
10. Main character sometimes gets fooled
11. Usually has to do with royalty
12. May have a fairy godmother, fairies, elves, or a witch

Instructional Plan Two: Characteristics of Fairy Tales (independently)

From the classroom collection of fairy tales you gathered, have the students select a fairy tale to read independently. Instructions to students: "Read your fairy tale silently. As you are reading, take notes in your literature response log on the characteristics you find that make this a fairy tale. Use the characteristics we listed on our chart, as well as any we may have missed."

After students have individually read the books or worked in pairs—jotting down the characteristics they found in their literature response logs—meet in literature discussion groups. Students share their discoveries.

Instructional Plan Three: Characteristics of Fairy Tales

As a whole-class activity, revise the list of characteristics on the chart. Students then select a new book and follow procedures for Instructional Plan 2. Sharing can be whole class, in pairs, or in discussion groups.

Instructional Plan Four: Comparative Analysis of Fairy Tale Variants (ongoing activity, can be combined with other plans)

Over a period of several weeks, read to the students, or have available for them to read silently, as many versions of one fairy tale as you can locate. Students note some of the points of difference in their logs. *Cinderella,* which has many variants, is one tale that works well. Students' favorites have included:

Cinderella by Charles Perrault; Amy Ehrlick, reteller; illustrated by Susan Jeffers (Dial, 1985).

Cinder Edna by Ellen Jackson, illustrated by Kevin O'Malley (Lothrop, Lee and Shepard, 1994). See annotation, p. 145b.

Mufaro's Beautiful Daughters by John Steptoe (Lothrop, Lee and Shepard, 1987). See annotation, p. 132b.

Princess Furball by Charlotte Huck, illustrated by Anita Lobel (Greenwillow, 1989).

The Rough Face Girl by Rafe Martin, illustrated by David Shannon (Putnam, 1992). See annotation, p. 136b.

The Talking Eggs by Robert D. San Souci, illustrated by Jerry Pinkney (Dial, 1989). See Annotation, p. 127b.

Yeh Shen: A Cinderella Story from China by Ai-Ling Louie, illustrated by Ed Young (Putnam, 1982). See annotation, p. 138b.

A comprehensive listing of *Cinderella* variants is included in *Focus on Literature* by Joy Moss, pp. 183–185. Check with your librarian for other well-known tales with multiple variants.

Instructional Plan Five: Settings in Fairy Tales

As a whole class, discuss what a setting is. Note the settings in tales read so far, and ask the children to be prepared to describe the setting in the tale they read today. In their logs, students write a paragraph describing the setting of their tale. After the tales have been read silently and paragraphs written, students meet in literature discussion group(s) and focus on the settings in their tales.

Instructional Plan Six: Use of Storymapping Format (demonstration)

Read aloud a favorite fairy tale and demonstrate, with input from the students, how to construct a storymap. This can be done on the chalkboard, on the overhead projector, or on large chart paper. This activity is done whole class with teacher guidance that invites student participation. Each student fills in his own copy of the storymap, which is kept and used as a reference model for constructing other storymaps (see Figure A-2).

Storymapping Format

Title of Story

Author

Setting (where and when)

Characters (who)

Problem

Action: 1, 2, 3. . .(as many as needed)

Resolution (use key words from the story)

Instructional Plan Seven: Storymapping (practice phase; repeat this activity two or three times)

Pair the children within a literature discussion group. Assign them the task of reading a self-selected fairy tale with their partner and mapping it according to the format (see Figure A-3). This activity can also be done individually or as a small group.

Instructional Plan Eight: *Comparing/Contrasting Fairy Tales* (optional; depends on availability; check with your librarian)

Show a film or filmstrip of a folk or fairy tale. Then read the book to the class and compare main character, setting, illustrations, and outcomes.

Which was more exciting? Which let you sense what was going to happen next more clearly? Which used more descriptive language? What elements of the fairy tale were different?

Instructional Plan Nine: *Focusing on Magic*

As a whole class, the element of magic is discussed as it has occurred in fairy tales read up to this point. Every student then selects and reads a new fairy tale independently. The students take notes in their literature response logs on:

- What if the magic didn't work?
- Find the magic moment in the fairy tale and speculate on what would happen if the magic failed.

Students share their speculations in literature discussion groups.

Figure A-2   A Storymap Done Whole Class With Teacher Guidance

Lindsay Kathleen
Campbell

STORY MAPPING FORMAT

Title of Story   Hansel and Greatal By The Brothers Grimm

Setting (where and when)   Large Forest, witches house, long ago

Characters (who)   Hansel and Gretal and Woodcutter and witch

Problem   Getting away and back home

Action

1. stepmother kicking them out
2. Lost in woods (2 times)   6. Getting home
3. Captured by the witch
4. Deal with the witch
5. money / jewels

Resolution   (use key words from the story)

Jewels/stepmother gone/Kill Witch/
Get home

Note: Resolution will tell how the problem was solved.

Actions will be main happenings in the story.

Instructional Plan Ten: Dramatizing Fairy Tales

Since several fairy tales have been read by now, ask the children to name some that would be good for dramatization. List the tales on the board. Divide the children into small groups of four or five. Let each group select a tale from the list and prepare to act it out for the rest of the class. The groups should be instructed to keep the tales fairly simple. No costumes or scenery are necessary. Items on hand in the classroom can be used as props. After about thirty minutes, the students give their presentations. Students could use *Tales for Telling from Around the World* (Medlicott, 1992), which contains many tales to retell or dramatize.

Instructional Plan Eleven: Math Activity

Read aloud a version of *Little Red Riding Hood*. Then give the following homework assignment:

"How many miles is it to your grandmother's (or grandparents') house?"

The next day, have students push pins on a world map to show where grandmothers (or grandparents) live. Make a graph showing how many miles away most grandmothers live. This makes an interesting bulletin board.

Instructional Plan Twelve: Comparative Analysis of Fairy Tale Variants (**may take several days**)

Based on the many fairy tales students have now heard and read, brainstorm, whole class, the main categories that could be compared in the fairy tale variants. List the categories on the chalkboard. Some categories that fourth graders came up with for variants of *Cinderella*

Figure A-3   A Student's Storymap of The Girl Who Loved The Wind

STORY MAPPING FORMAT

Title of Story Screen of Frogs

Setting (where and when) Long ago Japan

Characters (who) Koji Frog

Problem Koji does not want to work

Action

1. He begins selling the fields, lakes and mountains for money.
2. He only has one house, a lake and a mountain left.
3. The begs him not to sell his land.

(as many as needed)
4. He sells all his posesions and keeps the land.

Resolution (use key words from the story)

He learned the value of work.

Note: Resolution will tell how the problem was solved.

        Actions will be main happenings in the story.

included: personalities of main character; qualities of Cinderella, stepmothers, or trouble-makers; why Cinderella was chosen as bride; helpers; ending.

In small groups of four or five have the students work together to make comparison charts. Students list the variants across the top of the chart. Each group chooses the categories it thinks are important to compare and lists them down the left side of the chart. See Figure A-4 for charts that resulted from two different groups. Each group then presents its findings to the entire class. Discussion with agreement and disagreement will result. Acting out favorite variants, for peers and other classes, can also follow this activity.

Instructional Plan Thirteen: Recognizing Different Points of View

This lesson will focus on recognizing a different point of view in fairy tales. Features of satire and parody can be included for older students. The teacher reads aloud *The True Story of the 3 Little Pigs* by A. Wolf as told to John Scieszka. This humorous tale convincingly presents a wolf's reasons for the misfortunes of the three pigs. Differences between this tale and the traditional tale elicit a lively discussion. Among other things, students note that point of view can make a difference in how a character is perceived.

Then ask the children to tell you the characteristics of a traditional prince and princess fairy tale. List them on the chalkboard. Next, read the nontraditional tale *The Paper Bag Princess* by Robert N. Munsch to the class. This is a facetious story of a modern-day princess who saves the prince and then decides he's not to her liking. (If you have multiple copies, students can read in pairs.) Following the reading, have the students answer the following question in their literature response logs: "What different points of view does the author present?"

Meet in response groups, or whole class, and share the contrasts between the traditional prince and princess tale and *The Paper Bag Princess*. See Figure A-5 for a chart that resulted from a whole-class discussion.

Use the book *The Girl Who Loved Caterpillars* (Merill, 1992), a telling of a young Japanese woman in twelfth-century Japan who resists social and family pressures as she befriends caterpillars and other socially unacceptable creatures. Have students discuss issues of independence and what the tale might have been like if the protagonist were male.

Instructional Plan Fourteen: Becoming Aware of the Role of Illustrations in Folk and Fairy Tales

Most notable fairy tales, such as *Moon Rope* (Ehlert, 1992) and *Raven: A Trickster Tale from the Pacific Northwest* (McDermott, 1993), have outstanding, vibrant illustrations. Discuss the role and impact of illustration in folk and fairy tales, the importance of art in different cultures, and compare illustration styles and techniques of different books. Also, use the "Author/Illustrator Books and Resources" on page 97b to share information about notable illustrators. Students can work in small groups to note characteristics and comparisons of illustrations in fairy tales. In preparation for writing their own fairy tales, they can begin to think about the role that illustration will play in their own tales.

Instructional Plan Fifteen: Developing a Good Lead for an Original Fairy Tale (may take several days)

Today students will concentrate on the way storytellers begin their stories. The teacher, or students working individually or in pairs, rereads just the first paragraph of several familiar fairy tales. Ask the students: "Which beginning makes you curious about what is going to happen? Why? Which beginning tells you the most about the story? What information does the author give in the first paragraph?"

Brainstorm a topic for the beginning of a fairy tale that the class could write about. Create

Figure A-4   Comparison Charts for "Cinderella" variants: Two Different Group Interpreta-tons

	Grimm's Cinderella	Perrault's Cinderella	Mufardy Beautiful Daughters	Princess Furball	Vasilisa The Beautiful
Personalities of Main Character	Clever Sometimes depressed Kind	nice / kind smart sensitive mostly happy	kind willing helpful giving generous	smart, kind clever, tricky,	beautiful kind loving sweet giving willing
Why Prince or King chooses her	She's beautiful kind - she's got nice clothes	she's pretty, has beautiful clothes, kind, considerate	helpful past test kind gentle willing beautiful	makes good soup beautiful giving	beautiful good weaver good helper cooperative
Helpers	Animals	fairy God mother	Nyoka and father	nurse	magic doll
~~Stepmothers Trouble-makers~~ Family History	Mother dies, replaced by step mother, step mother brings two step sisters	Mother dies God mother helps Cinderella Cinderella has two stepsisters	no mother loveable father mean, picky, greedy sister	mother died	mother dies father remarries leaves town mother gives Vas. a magic doll
Ending	Gorry happily	There's a wedding happily ever after	prove sister wrong Marriage Happy Ending	marriage happy	wedding happy ending "unedited"

	Grimm's Cinderella	Princess Furball	Mufaro's Beautiful Daughters	Tattercoats	Vasilisa The Beautiful
Personalities of Mischief-Makers	Stepsisters-greedy, spoiled, jealous Stepmother-jealous, evil	father- promises hand in marriage to an Oger.	Manyara-selfish selfcentered impolite, rude consided	Maids- inconsiderate grandfather- stubborn	Babayaga-1/2 + 1/2 stepsisters-jealous, rude, cruel, inconsiderate, selfish stepmother-self centered, self conceited
Qualities of Cinderella	kind and pretty extremly good	smart, kind, beautiful, genours	kind, genours, caring, beautiful	beautiful, sad, getting happier every day	beautiful, kind genours, tough
Why choose Cinderella as bride	because the shoe fit and beauty and The blood was running from the stepsisters feet	Food, Trickery + beauty,	Beautiful + kind to everyone.	He loved Tattercoats for her beauty	because she was beautiful and her very beautiful clothing
ending	doves-pecked out eyes of stepsisters. happily ever after for Cinderella	Happy ending for Furball	Happy ending for Nyasha	sadly ends for grandfather happily ends for Tattercoats	Vasalisa kept doll in pocket all the time stepsisters burnt to ashes
helpers	Birds	Nurse	Snake	goose Header geese	Doll "unedited"

several beginnings as a shared writing. Analyze each one. Which one would make you want to read on? Why? (Use the overhead projector or large chart paper so students can refer back to the shared writing.)

Have the children work in partners and write the beginning of a fairy tale or rewrite a new beginning for a favorite tale. Share these beginnings in a response-group format, having students and the teacher note what is well done and offering suggestions for improvements.

Instructional Plan Sixteen: Revising a Good Lead (whole class)

Using a student's fairy tale beginning (with the student's permission) on the overhead projector, revise for content and clarity as a whole class. Then have students work in pairs revising their fairy tale beginnings. Share in response groups.

Instructional Plan Seventeen: Storymapping an Original Fairy Tale

Have students storymap the fairy tales they have started writing. This will cause them to plan the characters, the problem, the action, and the resolution. To clarify their storymap, students can also draw a picture of the characters in the setting. This enables the students to be descriptive in their writing. Have a sharing time at the end of the period. This activity will take more than one period.

Instructional Plan Eighteen: Writing an Original Fairy Tale

When students have mapped out their fairy tales and conferenced with the teacher or peer group, they may begin writing their fairy tale. The tale will go through the writing process:

Figure A-5   Comparison Chart from Whole-Class Discussion

Comparing Traditional Tales with Princes and Princesses to The Paperbag Princess by Robert Munsch

Traditional Tale	*The Paperbag Princess*
Usual point of view	Different point of view
beautiful princess, beautifully dressed	beautiful, not well dressed (in paper bag)
helpless princess	independent princess, not helpless
kind prince	conceited prince
prince saves princess	princess saves prince
prince and princess get married	princess refuses to marry prince
not much humor	very humorous
evil person fought	evil force outwitted
ball, helping person	no ball, no helping person
happy ending	not happy about break-up, but happy to be
illustrations—clear, beautiful	separated from prince
begins "Once upon a time..."	illustrations—modern, humorous
ends "...happily ever after."	not usual beginning or ending words

Figures A-6 and A-7   Two Students' Mock Classified Ads

WaNT AD
WANTED. PRince MUST Be: HandioME,
Good WORKER, CaRing, INTelligeNT,
GooD MANNERED, Good, NaturaL,
GallaNT, GeNeROus, and MiNdful.
Most of all Rich and PoweRful.
REWaRd: PRincess NaMED PeTRoNella
IN MaRRiage. Beutiful, KiNd,
HeaRty, and GeNtle INtelligent,
Good NaturEd

rough draft, conference, revision, editing, final copy. This will take several weeks to bring to completion. Completed tales are shared and displayed in the classroom.

Optional Activities (allow student choice)

(For students who have completed fairy tales and/or for end of unit projects)

- *Math activity*   Write down the fairy tales read in class. Have children select their favorites. (Pass out a survey or interview classmates.) Graph the results on a large chart.
- *Diary*   Write a diary entry as if you were the fairy tale character after a major event has occurred, for example, the Beast after Beauty fails to return, Cinderella after the ball, Little Red Riding Hood after she meets the wolf in the woods.
- *Filmstrip*   Using a kit for filmstrips that contains blank film and markers, have students make a filmstrip of a fairy tale. Students also prepare an accompanying script, which they read when presenting the filmstrip to the class.
- *New fairy tale*   Create a new version of a well-known tale. Have students storymap the tale first, and note how this version will be different. Also encourage tales from different points of view. For example, students could choose to write *Little Red Riding Hood* from the wolf's point of view, *Beauty and the Beast* from the vantage point of the Beast, or *The Three Billy Goats Gruff* from the troll's point of view.
- *Newspaper*   Use a newspaper format to write headlines, articles, classified ads, and editorials about fairy tale characters. For example, an ad might be written looking for Cinderella's lost slipper; a headline might read: "Children Foil Witch and Reap Bounty"; an editorial might call for the arrest of the wolf after he has demolished two pigs' houses. Captions and illustrations could be included (see Figures A-6 through A-8).
- *Riddle Book*   Write riddles about characters from fairy tales and share them with other classes. Each page would have an illustration and a riddle, for example, a picture of a cat in hat and boots. The riddle might say, "He was a very clever cat. Who was he?" The back page would list the answers to the riddles. (The answer to the above riddle is Puss

Figure A-7

LOST

A slipper, a pure glass slipper. A very, small, pure glass slipper. With high heels and very narrow. It was lost at the ball on May 7, 1800. The prince at the castle is looking for it. REWARD: dance one dance, your choice with the prince. You should return the slipper to the castle immediately.

by Lindsay

from *Puss in Boots*.) These riddle books can be made clear and easy enough for first- or second-graders to enjoy.

- *Crossword puzzle*   Design a fairy tale crossword puzzle using words frequently used in fairy tales, such as: prince, princess, witch, Hansel, wolf, pigs, forest, stepmother, spell, magic (see Figure A-9).
- *Dramatization of point of view*   A small group of students plans a dramatization of *The Three Little Pigs* from the wolf's point of view, using and adapting the dialogue from the book *The True Story of the 3 Little Pigs* by John Scieszka. Before presenting the drama, the group reminds the audience of the traditional tale by recalling specific events in the familiar version. This dramatization could be presented to other classrooms.
- *Dialogue*   Two students write a conversation between two fairy characters. It can be taped, written in dramatic form, or read orally as Readers Theatre.
- *Game*   Keeping the theme of a familiar fairy tale, students enjoy designing original games with cards and directions. Students use tagboard and make colorful drawings of events and motifs from the fairy tale. This is an excellent activity for a pair of students. When the game is completed, the students put it to the test by having other students play it.
- *Crafts/arts*   Make a gift for a fairy tale character. The gift could be something the fairy tale character could use to get out of a difficult situation.
- *Fairy tale party*   Under the supervision of the teacher, plan a fairy tale party for another class to attend. The students design and send out invitations. Refreshments are planned, and volunteers bring them in. Students are asked to give presentations such as: the filmstrip, dramatization of the fairy tale books written by the students, and art projects completed. This party is held near the end of the unit (see Figure A-10).

Fairy Tales/Folktales

The tales listed here are just a sampling of the wonderful folk and fairy tales that exist. For additional titles and ways to use them, look for the many annotations of recommended folktales and fairy tales included in the grade-level literature lists in these "blue pages." Also, check with a librarian, and use the "Resources" on page 172b to locate other quality titles.

Figure A-8   A Student's Mock Newspaper Article

By Linnea
Loudmouth
Locust

Wolf's Honor?

Still waiting for his trial
Alexander T. trouble-maker Wolf continues
to plead guilty. His attorney,
Francine Slye Fox, said the following
"I plan to prove AL innocent. I
couldn't stand seeing him die in the
electric chair. He is to much of a
sly guy." With the new evidence,
including a trip to the doctors
office, Mr. Wolf just might be
released. Though I feel he is
lying, the examination proved that Mr.
Wolf indeed did have a cold, and
a search of his house proved
he was trying to bake a cake, and
he was out of sugar.
It is also true that house
A. and house B. are on the
ground in pieces. The plaintifs
attiorney, Rachel Trust-me Rabbit
commented, "It's all fake." Thats
what I think, Its all fake Mr.
Wolf should be condemned immeadiatly,

Anderson, Hans Christian. 1987. *The Snow Queen.* Illustrated by Bernadette Watts. New York: North-South Books.

Anderson, Hans Christian. 1981. *The Wild Swans.* Pictures by Susan Jeffers. Retold by Amy Ehrlich. New York: Dial.

Brown, Marcia. 1954. *Cinderella.* New York: Macmillan.

Cauley, Lorinda Bryan. 1986. *Puss in Boots.* New York: Harcourt Brace Jovanovich.

Demi. *The Magic Boat.* 1990. New York: Henry Holt.

Ehlert, Lois. 1992. *Moon Rope.* New York: Harcourt Brace Jovanovich.

Gipson, Morrell. 1984. *Rip Van Winkle.* New York: Doubleday.

Goble, Paul. 1993. *The Lost Children.* New York: Bradbury Press.

Grimm, The Brothers. 1986. *Grimm's Fairy Tales.* Illustrated by Richard Walz. Racine, WI: Western Publishing.

Figure A-8 *(Continued)*

before he kills any other
innocent pig, person, or peacock.
All pigs will live in terror untill
Mr. Wolf is condemned and put to
death.
After talking to the last little
pig, Mr. Patric spared Pig, I am
toatlly convinced the story fiom
the wolf's point of view is a
complete lie.
He knocked down the houses
trying to get at the pigs, buried his
sugar, and rigged it to make it look
like he was baking a cake.
The only thing that is
real is the cold Tough luck Mr.
Alexander T. Wolf.

By Marie Frisof

Grimm, The Brothers. 1981. *Hansel and Gretel.* Illustrated by Anthony Browne. New York: Knopf.

Grimm, The Brothers. 1980. *Hansel and Gretel.* Pictures by Susan Jeffers. New York: Dial.

Grimm, The Brothers. 1983. *Little Red Riding Hood.* Retold and illustrated by Trina Schart Hyman. New York: Holiday.

Grimm, The Brothers. 1982. *Rapunzel.* Retold by Barbara Rogasky. Illustrated by Trina Schart Hyman. New York: Holiday.

Grimm, The Brothers. 1983. *Rumpelstiltskin.* Illustrated by Donna Diamond. New York: Holiday.

Grimm, The Brothers. n.d. *Snow White and Rose Red.* Retold and illustrated by Bernadette Watts. New York: North-South Books.

Hamanaka, Sheila. 1993. *Screen of Frogs: An Old Tale.* New York: Orchard Books.

Haley, Gail. 1986. *Jack and the Bean Tree.* New York: Crown.

Haviland, Virginia. 1994. *Favorite Fairy Tales Told in England.* Illustrated by Maxie Chambliss. New York: Beech Tree. See annotation, p. 130b.

Hodges, Margaret. 1984. *Saint George and the Dragon.* Illustrated by Trina Schart Hyman. Boston: Little, Brown. See annotation, p. 141b.

Huck, Charlotte. 1989. *Princess Furball.* Illustrated by Anita Lobel. New York: Greenwillow.

Hyman, Trina Schart. 1977. *The Sleeping Beauty.* Boston: Little, Brown.

Littledale, Freya. 1986. *The Little Mermaid.* Illustrated by Daniel San Souci. New York: Scholastic.

Magnus, Erica. 1986. *The Boy and the Devil.* Minneapolis, MN: Carolrhoda Books.

Figure A-9   Fairy Tale Crossword Puzzle

Adam G.
Dina L.   Fairy Tale Crossword Puzzle

Down

1. One of the seven Dwarfs
3. A poison food that Snow White Ate
5. Cinderella lost her glass _____.
7. Jack sold his cow for some magic _____.
7. Rumple Stiltskin _____ straw into gold.

Across

2. A reptile, that was turned to a prince.
4. It ate Little Red Riding Hood.
6. The opposite of Beauty
7. Goldilocks went into this animals house
8. Mirror, Mirror, on the _____
10. Little Red Riding Hood Picked _____, for her Grandmother.

Mayer, Mercer. 1980. *East of the Sun and West of the Moon.* New York: Four Winds Press.

McDermott, Gerald. 1993. *Raven: A Trickster Tale from the Pacific Northwest.* New York: Harcourt Brace. See annotation, p. 132b.

Medlicott, Mary (ed.). 1992. *Tales for Telling from Around the World.* Illustrated by Sue Williams. New York: Kingfisher Books.

Merrill, Jean. 1992. *The Girl Who Loved Caterpillars: A Twelfth-Century Tale from Japan.* Illustrated by Floyd Cooper. New York: Philomel Books.

Mollel, Tololwa M. 1991. *An Orphan Boy: A Maasai Story.* Illustrated by Paul Morin. New York: Clarion.

Figure A-10   A Student's Welcome Note to a Fairy Tale Party

Letter From: Little Red Riding Hood

Welcome to the Fairy Tale Party. I have been looking forward to seeing you today! We will have some drinks and a snack for you to "munch/drink" during the play we set up for you, but be careful, the Big Bad Wolf will snatch your food if you don't keep an eye out for him!

Hope you enjoy the party!

Munsch, Robert. 1980. *The Paper Bag Princess*. Toronto: Annick Press.

Ransome, Arthur. 1968. *The Fool of the World and the Flying Ship*. New York: Farrar, Straus, & Giroux.

Rappaport, Doreen. 1991. *The Journey of Meng: A Chinese Legend*. Illustrated by Yan Ming-Yi. New York: Dial Books for Young Readers.

Scieszka, Jon. 1989. *The True Story of the 3 Little Pigs*. Illustrated by Lane Smith. New York: Viking Kestrel.

Steel, Flora Annie. 1976. *Tattercoats*. Illustrated by Diane Goode. New York: Bradbury.

Steptoe, John. 1987. *Mufaro's Beautiful Daughters*. New York: Lothrop, Lee, and Shepard. See annotation, p. 132b.

Whitney, Thomas. 1970. *Vasilisa the Beautiful*. Illustrated by Nonny Hogrogian. New York: Macmillan.

Yolen, Jane. 1987. *The Girl Who Loved the Wind*. Illustrated by Ed Young. New York: Crowell.

Appendix B: Teacher's Guide for Amos & Boris

TEACHER'S GUIDE
by Susan Hepler

AMOS & BORIS
by William Steig

SUMMARY

In this story, similar to "The Lion and the Mouse", a sea-going mouse falls off his boat and is helped by a whale. The mouse returns the favor later. Steig's elegant telling of the story is matched by his dramatic illustrations.

INITIATING ACTIVITIES

1. What can you tell about the story from looking at the cover and the title page?
2. Read the first page. How can you tell this story is going to be unusual? What do you notice about the words?

THINKING CRITICALLY

1. How did Boris the whale help Amos? How did Amos return the favor? Does this sound like any other story you know?
2. What kinds of things did Amos put in his boat before he set out? What use might he make of each of these things?
3. What happened when Boris "sounded"? What does it mean when a whale "sounds"?
4. Make a chart of interesting words or groups of words from the story. Beside each word or groups of words, put in your own idea of what they mean.
5. Why do you think Amos and Boris were sad to part? Why would they "never forget each other"?

READ SOME MORE!

Other stories of little and big animals helping each other are The Lion and The Rat, illustrated by Brian Wildsmith, and The Lion and The Mouse, illustrated by Ed Young. Other modern-day fables include Marcia Brown's Once a Mouse, Leo Lionni's Frederick, Arnold Lobel's Fables, and John Ciardi's John J. Plenty and Fiddler Dan.

H.P. Kopplemann Inc., P.O. Box 145, 140 Van Block Ave., Hartford, CT 06141-0145   203-549-6210   1-800-243-7724   IN CT 1-800-842-2165

DO IT YOURSELF

1 Make a display of the things Amos took along in the Rodent. Label each one and make a title for your display.

2 Make a mouse-sized model of the Rodent. Write a description of how you made the model or tell something about it.

3 Pretend that you are Amos telling your grandchildren about your wonderful adventure. Tell or write this story for them.

4 Write a newspaper article telling how "Whale Is Saved During Hurricane Yetta".

5 Paint a picture of your favorite part of the story. Write or tell about your picture.

6 Make a picture of another meeting Amos and Boris might have. Write or tell about your picture.

7 Keep a diary as Amos or Boris would have kept it and report each day's adventures.

by William Steig

Reprinted with permission of H.P. Kopplemann Inc., Hartford, CT.

186b

Appendix C: Teacher's Guide for Journey to Topaz

TEACHER'S GUIDE
by Susan Hepler,

JOURNEY TO TOPAZ
by Yoshiko Uchida

About the Story

Eleven-year-old Yuki Sakane and her family are evacuated to a Japanese internment camp at the beginning of the United States' war against Japan. This restrained story is based on the author's experiences during World War II and reflects the quiet dignity, courage, and loyalty with which Japanese-Americans dealt with this unjust treatment.

Initiating Activities

1. What can you predict about this story by looking at the front cover and the Contents? What feelings does the cover try to show?

2. Read the first paragraph of the Prologue aloud. What do you know about World War II? (Read aloud the whole Prologue before reading the story, or after finishing, depending on the level of students.)

3. Do you know any people now, or in times past, who have been forced to leave their homes and live in guarded camps? What feelings might these people have had?

Thinking Critically

Chapter 1: "Strangers at the Door" (Pages 1–9)

1. Who is in Yuki's family? What can you tell about them? How are they like families you know? How are they different?

2. Why does the FBI come to Yuki's house? What do they do there?

Chapters 2–3: "The Long Wait" and "A Lonely Christmas" (Pages 11–29)

3. Why does Mother serve tea to the FBI men? How do you think the FBI men feel about the Sakane family? Why do you think that?

4. Besides serving tea, what other Japanese customs does Mother keep?

5. What are Issei? Nissei?

6. What has happened to Father? Why do you think this has happened? Is Father guilty of any crime?

7. What is the "evacuation"? Who ordered it? Why? How does the Sakane family feel about this? How does Mr. Jamieson feel about this?

Chapter 4: "Ten Days to Pack" (Pages 31–39)

8. What things do Japanese-Americans have to give up or stop doing before they are to be evacuated?

9. What preparations do the Sakane family make before going to the evacuation camp? What do you think is hardest for each person to give up?

10. Do all Caucasian people feel that the Japanese-Americans are being treated fairly?

Chapters 5–6: "Inside the Barbed Wire" and "Home is a Horse Stall" (Pages 41–58)

11. How does the Sakane "apartment" compare with their former home?

12. What small things give the Sakane family comfort at Tanforan?

Chapters 7–8: "A New Friend" and "Ken Spoils a Party" (Pages 59–74)

13. If the Sakane family had made a list of their complaints about the situation at Tanforan, what things would be on that list?

14. Why is Chapter 8's title a good one? What does Ken's decision mean for Yuki and her mother?

Chapters 9–10: "A New Rumor" and "Goodbye, Tanforan" (Pages 75–91)

15. Why do you think Yuki is glad to be back in school? Have you ever felt that way?

16. Yuki and Emi play "Jan Ken Po." What game does this sound like? What do you call "zoris"?

17. What is Yuki trying to tell Ken when she gives him not a half but a whole candy bar?

18. Mr. Kurihara says America is making prisoners of its own citizens. But Mother has an answer for him (page 90) beginning, "Fear has made this country do something . . ." What do you think Mother means?

Chapters 11–12: "A Home in the Desert" and "Dust Storm" (Pages 93–109)

19. On a map of the western United States, locate and label: where Father is; the Sakanes' former home town; Tanforan; and the route to Topaz. The last two may take some detective work.

20. Is Topaz a better place than Tanforan? Why or why not?

21. What is a *trilobite*, the gift Yuki gave to Emi?

Chapters 13–15: "A Last Visit," "Tragedy at Dusk," and "Good News" (Pages 111–130)

22. How have Yuki's feelings changed toward Mr. Kurihara? How does he die? Why? How does the camp show their grief? What does Yuki do? Why?

23. What happy occurrences make Yuki feel a little more hopeful?

24. Why do you think Ken feels so distant from his family?

Chapters 16–17: "Another Goodbye" and "Hello, World" (Pages 131–149)

25. What are the arguments for Ken's joining the all-Nisei army unit? What are the arguments against it? What is Father's advice? What would you have done? Why?

26. Why does Mr. Toda feel so bad?

27. Why can the Sakane family go free in Utah but not in any West Coast state?

28. The Sakane family has many friends both in and out of camp. Which ones help them through the hard times? How? Who do you think helps the most? Why?

29. Do you think this experience may change Yuki? How?

187b

DO IT YOURSELF

1 Pretend you are a friend to Yuki, like Mimi or Mrs. Jamieson, and fix a box of things you'd send to her in Topaz to cheer her up. Make a table display and label your gifts.

2 Mimi gave Yuki a red-covered diary in which to keep her thoughts. Write four or five entries Yuki might have made during some of the difficult or happy times in the story. Don't forget details to make it interesting.

3 Look up "Japanese Internment Camps" in magazines from 1942. What else can you find out from these articles?

4 Write the letters Yuki would write to Mr. Toda or to Emi after she and her family settled in Salt Lake City. What do you imagine might happen next?

5 Invite a Japanese-American person into your classroom to talk about Japanese customs they still keep. Or locate someone who may know about internment camps and ask them to talk about them to the class.

6 Make a book of Japanese customs that were followed by the Sakane family, such as Dolls Festival Day, paperfolding, using certain words, serving tea, and so forth. Do some research on other Japanese customs and report your findings to the class using your informational book.

READ SOME MORE!
Journey Home is a sequel to this story, and The Eternal Spring of Mr. Ito by Sheila Garrigue tells of a Japanese-Canadian family's difficulty during this time. Yoshiko Uchida has also written many other books about the experiences of Japanese-Americans. An excellent informational book about the internment camps with many illustrations is Behind Barbed Wire by Daniel S. Davis.

Reprinted with permission of H. P. Kopplemann Inc., Hartford, CT.

Appendix D:
Using the Goldilocks Strategy to Choose Books*

Easy Books

Ask myself these questions. If I am answering yes, this book is probably an EASY book for me. I'll have fun reading it.

1. Have I read it lots of times before?
2. Do I understand the story?
3. Do I know (can I understand) almost every word?
4. Can I read it smoothly?

Just Right Books

Ask myself these questions. If I am answering yes, this book is probably a JUST RIGHT book for me. I'll give it a try.

1. Is this book new to me?
2. Do I understand what I've read so far?
3. Are there just a few words per page I don't know?
4. When I read are some places smooth and some choppy?
5. Can someone help me with this book? Who?

Hard Books

Ask myself these questions. If I am answering yes, this book is probably a HARD book for me. I'll spend a little time with it now. I'll give it another try later (perhaps in a couple of months).

1. Are there more than a few words on each page I don't know?
2. Am I confused about what is happening in this book? Do I feel bored?
3. When I read, does it sound pretty choppy?
4. Is everyone else busy and unable to help me?
5. Is there a way to get this book closer to a Just Right?

From "Lessons from Goldilocks: 'Somebody's Been Choosing My Books But I Can Make My Own Choices Now!'" by Marilyn M. Ohlhausen and Mary Jepsen. *The New Advocate*, Vol. 5, No. 1, Winter 1992, p. 36. Norwood, MA: Christopher-Gordon. Reprinted with permission of the authors.

* Students can also generate their own version of the Goldilocks Strategy. With teacher guidance, students brainstorm how good readers successfully choose books. The teacher transcribes students' thoughts onto a chart that is displayed in the classroom.

Appendix E: A Sliding Mask and a "Flag"

A Sliding Mask

I keep two sizes on hand, one to use with Big Books and the other for regular-size text on the overhead projector or in the small-group or one-to-one reading situation. The slide fits into the slot and is moved to mask, gradually expose, and highlight features of text. Below

(actual size)

4"

2"

1/4"

window ↑

1/4"

2"

slot ↙

5"

1"

slide ↑

Big book size: 6 1/2" x 2 1/2" (shown reduced)

3"

1/2"

1/2"

are two sizes that I use. I outline the windows with black magic marker to make the print stand out. Check the text size of your books to determine what sizes will work well for you. Construct with tagboard or file cards.

A "Flag"

I use tongue depressors and tagboard to construct flags of different sizes. I usually keep three sizes on hand. I tape or glue the rectangular size tagboard onto the tongue depressor. Experiment to get the sizes that work for you. The size of the flag determines how long a word you can highlight.

Use

With the overhead projector and screen, you can use a "flag" to call attention to a word. Place the flag on the screen behind you (not on the transparency on the overhead projector) directly over the particular word you want to highlight. Slowly and steadily move the flag away from the screen. The flag lifts the word off the screen and moves it onto the flag. The word is taken out of context so it can be studied or highlighted. Then the word goes back into context by moving the flag back onto the word on the screen. This is a dramatic visual technique that is easy and effective to use with students of all ages.

Appendix F:
Notes on Use of
the WEB
1993–1994

Organization of WEB

Books are organized and filed by type (see attached sheet, "Filing Locations"). The literature sign-out book has a location column for each book in the WEB that corresponds to the abbreviations listed under "Filing Locations." There are specific Animal, other Nonfiction, Biography, Poetry, "City Kids" (Rigby), Fairy Tale/Folk Tale Picture Books, and Audiotapes. There are also separate shelves for the Beverly Cleary, Bill Peet, and William Steig collections. All books are shelved in one layer. Check behind for additional copies of a title.

All fiction books are organized from floor to ceiling by grade level. Books are filed alphabetically by title. First-grade books are organized by level of difficulty. Each level is then filed alphabetically by title. For your reference there is a listing of these books by level in a separate reference book ("WEB Collection: Sorted by Location") in the WEB room. Big Books are also filed alphabetically by title, in large boxes next to the WEB. All second, third, and fourth grade core books are located in a cabinet in the hall outside the WEB room.

Notices of upcoming whole language workshops are posted on one wall.

Periodically, you may want to check in the file folders for each of the core books. The folders are continually being updated with additional information/activities about these books. They are housed on a top shelf in the WEB.

Our WEB room coordinator is Donna Jackson. She will be glad to have a meeting with all Mercer parent volunteers to train them on book repair or WEB organization.

Book Sign-Out and Return

All WEB books are listed alphabetically by title in the sign-out book and include notations for the recommended grade level, the number of books in the collection, and the shelving location of book. Note that the sign-out book also includes a separate reference listing of all books in these categories: Big Books, Biography, Bill Peet, Poetry, William Steig, Beverly Cleary, Animals, Nonfiction, City Kids, Fairy Tale/Folk Tale Picture Books, Science core Books, Audiotapes, and second, third, and fourth grade core books. There are also listings of books by difficulty level in the first-grade fiction area. The sign-out book also has a listing of new titles added during the year.

It is necessary that all books be signed out and signed in with your initials, number of copies taken, and the dates so teachers know where books are and so we can maintain an accurate record-keeping system. If you are signing out many titles at one time and need assistance recording the titles in our WEB sign-out book, please arrange for a parent volunteer from your room to help you. You may want to choose one parent volunteer to assist you all year with signing out, signing in, shelving, and repairing books. Please return books to their proper location and grade level. The books are marked for easy return. All first-grade fiction books are filed within the color-coded shelves. All the other books have the type of book marked in red ink on the inside upper right corner. Fiction books for grades two, three, and four will have that number on this corner. Please return them repaired and bound with rubber bands for easier storage. Be sure you return books in alphabetical order by the title. This includes all Big Books.

Also, note the list of core books per grade level is posted on one wall. Those titles may be used only at the designated grade level or higher grade level.

Each teacher is supposed to have a personal copy of each core book to use as a teacher's guide. See Dr. Stokes if you need any titles.

Classroom Procedures

Each book has a number and school stamp on the inside front cover. To ensure that students take responsibility for core books and WEB books, be sure to note the number of the book each student receives. Work out your own accountability system. Please take the time to talk with your students about taking responsibility for our books. For example, books should not be placed open on a desk face down, because it weakens the spine. Have your students use book marks.

Book Repairs

The care and handling of our books is a high priority and needs to be discussed with all students. You may want to invite an older student in to talk about this with younger students.

Your room representative will be responsible for recruiting a parent from your room to repair books monthly.

As best as we were able, most books were repaired in June and are in good shape. Core books that were cancelled have been replaced. In some cases, you will need to have students or parent volunteers repair the books before you use them. It is necessary that we all assume responsibility for book repair to ensure long life for our books. Please be sure books are repaired before you return them.

Book mending tape is available in the WEB room. Fourth graders, previously trained in book repair, can be used to demonstrate book repair to students in grades two and three. Some teachers have found that it works well to assign specific students to this ongoing task. Kindergarten and first-grade teachers may want to get some parent volunteers or upper-grade students to keep up with book repair. There are two book repair machines for your use and students can easily be taught to use them. These machines can be signed out through Regie.

Lost and Damaged Books

If a book is lost, encourage the student to purchase a replacement copy (it is tedious work to order and replace single copies). Otherwise, the student should be charged a $3.00 replacement fee for the lost book. There is a form to be used for this. A copy is attached. More are available in the WEB room.

Monies collected for lost books should be turned into the office along with the title of the lost book. Please keep a record of all books that have been lost and paid for (and give that list to Regie in June) so we know what books to replace.

Fines should be assessed for damaged books. Repair charges can range from $.25 to $1.00. The money will be used for book replacement and WEB supplies.

See Regie or Donna Jackson for any assistance/concerns/suggestions. We are better organized this year, due to everyone's input and cooperation.

WEB BOOKS

Date _____

Dear Parent,

Your child _____ has lost/damaged the following book(s):

Title   Author

_____

_____

_____

_____

_____

Please send in _____ for damage/replacement cost.

Comments:

_____

Classroom teacher

Appendix G: General Guidelines to Students for Submitting Stories, Poems, or Manuscripts to Publishers

- The writing should belong to you, the student. While adults may respond to the writing, ownership and authorship must remain with the student.
- Conference with your teacher and peers as you go through the authoring cycle. Allow plenty of time for thinking, creating, sharing, revising, and editing.
- Check to see that your material fits the format of the publication to which you are submitting. If unsure, write to the publisher with specific questions.
- Make as many of your changes as possible in the revising and editing stages prior to submitting your finished manuscript. In that way, the voice of the author can be completely respected.
- If you are interested in including illustrations, check with the publisher to see if illustrations are accepted. Be sure to acknowledge the illustrator if you are collaborating with another person in the process.
- Send only your best stories or manuscript.
- Submit to only one publisher at a time. Keep a copy of your submission with the name of the publisher and date sent.
- Acknowledgment of those who have helped you is recommended.
- Submissions should be typed, word processed, or in your very best handwriting.
- All manuscripts submitted should be copyrighted by the use of the "c" with a circle around it, the date, and the name of the author. It's also a good idea to seal the original in an envelope, mail it to the author's home address by registered mail, and keep it sealed, as proof of authorship.
- Enclose a self-addressed, stamped envelope for future correspondence.
- The publisher will notify you if the manuscript is accepted. While royalties are not usual, the publisher will discuss any business aspects with the author.
- The publishing time period varies with each book. Usually publication occurs within six months to eighteen months after a submission is received by the publisher. Just as the authoring cycle takes time, so does the publishing cycle. If a submission is accepted, any necessary conferencing will usually occur by telephone or letter.
- Don't be discouraged if you are rejected. Most writers receive multiple rejections before getting an acceptance.

Regie Routman gratefully acknowledges the input of children's publisher Billie White Price of Quality Publishing in Conway, South Carolina.

Appendix H:
Spelling
Interview

NAME: _____ Grade _____ Date _____

1. Are you a good speller? _____
   Why do you think so? _____
   _____
   _____

2. What makes someone a good speller? _____
   _____
   _____
   _____

3. What do you do when you don't know how to spell a word? _____
   _____
   _____
   _____

4. If someone is having trouble spelling a word how could you help that person? _____
   _____
   _____
   _____

5. Is it important to be a good speller? Why or why not? _____
   _____
   _____
   _____

Appendix 1

HAVE-A-GO

Copy Word	1st Attempt	2nd Attempt	Standard Spelling

Appendix J: Communicating with Parents

J1: Getting Parents Involved

GETTING PARENTS INVOLVED

Children who take pride in expressing their ideas in writing may become discouraged if parents criticize their approximations, particularly the use of temporary spellings. The more knowledgeable parents are about the writing process, the more supportive and enthusiastic they are likely to be about their children's work. The following letter may be copied or paraphrased to help parents better understand the writing process.

Dear Parents,

Some parents have been wondering why children in early primary grades are bringing home papers with temporary spellings that haven't been corrected.

Do you remember when your child learned to talk? She probably made many "mistakes" or approximations, in speech, and they didn't bother you much. You may have corrected a few, now and then, but mostly you included the child in the events of everyday life, encouraged the child to talk, and enjoyed the conversations. You probably knew, as parents do, that children learn to talk the way they learn to sit up and crawl and walk—they learn to talk by talking.

Learning to write works the same way. For example, early in the year, one child wrote:

Now this doesn't look like your writing any more than a child's early words sound like your speech. But it's a tremendous piece of work! First of all, and most important, this child knows that written language is supposed to mean something, and he knows exactly what it means:

> I was watching TV at my house. Then I saw a little mouse.

Just about every letter stands for one word in the story.

I	y	s		tv	a	m	H		D	i	s	a	l	m

I was (watching)   TV at my house.   Then I saw a little mouse.

Some developmental stages in writing come before this one, and others come after. From this sample we see that the child knows the following:

- print proceeds in a straight line from left to right across a page
- print is made up of letters

198b

- letters come in upper and lower case
- letters stand for sounds in the words he wants to write.

Later on the child wrote the following response to a story about two friends playing together:

I like the part (where) the blue and the yellow turn into green from (author's name)

The writing still doesn't look like yours, but it's closer.

Since writing the earlier sample, this child has learned that:

- written language is made up of words separated by spaces
- each word between spaces stands for one word in speech
- written words are made up of a number of different letters
- there are a number of letter/sound combinations in each word (both beginning and ending sounds are included here)
- when you "know" a word (The), you spell it the same way every time
- if you don't "know" a word, you can use what you do know about letters and sounds to say what you mean until you learn the dictionary spelling
- you self-correct your own writing when it doesn't look right to you, just as children self-correct their own speech
- punctuation is part of written language.

That's a lot to have learned, and the child has doubtless learned more that cannot be documented by looking at this one sample alone.

Teachers help children learn to write the way parents and families help them learn to talk. If we put all our energy into correcting temporary spellings, children get discouraged and lose a natural desire to write. They learn from heavy correction that meaning is less important than spelling the words right.

If we invite them to use their oral language in their writing, even though they can't spell all the words correctly, we free them to say what they mean. And, in fact, as the examples show, they learn a lot about writing in general, and spelling in particular, from the risks they take along the way. Children learn to write by writing, and we are most helpful to them when we appreciate and encourage their "best attempts."

Is there a time for teaching particular points of spelling, grammar, punctuation, and handwriting? Yes. Full group and individual conferences address such points as the need is noted in the children's own writing.

Is there a time when children correct their work and turn out finished copy? Yes—when publishing or 'going public.' In very early grades the children do the hard work—writing the stories—and we make the corrections. As children become more experienced, they begin to take responsibility for this work, too.

I hope this letter helps you to share some of your child's joy in writing, much as you share his/her pleasure in speaking.

    Sincerely,

Fall 1988 Newsletter, Whole Language Teachers Association, 16 Concord Road, Sudbury, MA 01776. Reproduced with permission.

J2: Ways to Help Your Child with Reading at Home

Setting the Atmosphere

Help your child find a quiet, comfortable place to read.

Have your child see you as a reading model.

Read aloud to your child. Reread favorite stories.

Read with your child.

Discuss the stories you read together.

Recognize the value of silent reading.

Keep reading time enjoyable and relaxed.

Responding to Errors in Reading

Based on the way most of us were taught to read, we have told the child to "sound it out" when he comes to an unknown word. While phonics is an important part of reading, reading for meaning is the primary goal. To produce independent readers who monitor and correct themselves as they read, the following prompts are recommended *before* saying "sound it out."

- Give your child wait time of 5 to 10 seconds. See what he attempts to do to help himself.
- "What would make sense there?"
- "What do you think that word could be?"
- "Use the picture to help you figure out what it could be."
- "Go back to the beginning and try that again."
- "Skip over it and read to the end of the sentence (or paragraph). Now what do you think it is?"
- "Put in a word that would make sense there."
- "You read that word before on another page. See if you can find it."
- "Look at how that word begins. Start it out and keep reading."
- Tell your child the word.

Most important, focus on what your child is doing well and attempting to do. Remain loving and supportive. When your child is having difficulty and trying to work out the trouble spots, comments such as the following are suggested:

- "Good for you. I like the way you tried to work that out."
- "That was a good try. Yes, that word would make sense there."
- "I like the way you looked at the picture to help yourself."
- "I like the way you went back to the beginning of the sentence and tried that again. That's what good readers do."
- "You are becoming a good reader. I'm proud of you."

Regie Routman, language arts resource teacher

J3: Letter to Parents Explaining Independent Reading Program

September 1994

Dear Parents,

W.E.B. (Wonderfully Exciting Books) is an important component of our reading program. The student self-selects books from our classroom, school, public, or home library for independent reading.

Your child and I will have frequent opportunities to discuss what has been read independently. The W. E. B. book will be used for reading at home and may also be used for independent reading during language arts time or during S. S. R. (Sustained Silent Reading). A record of your child's daily reading and a list of completed books will be kept in the classroom.

Your child's responsibility is to read for about thirty minutes each evening and to carry the book back and forth to school each day in a waterproof bag. Your child is also expected to take good care of this book. There will be a fine for damaged books or a replacement fee for lost or severely damaged books.

Over the school year, consistent daily reading will expose your child to various author's styles and will improve your child's fluency, vocabulary, comprehension, and writing. Our main goal is that your child will enjoy reading and choose to read for pleasure.

Please join with me in helping to create an environment where our children can enjoy books for a lifetime. Together we can build a community of readers.

Thank you for your help, support, and cooperation with our W. E. B. program.

Sincerely yours,

Please indicate that you have read this letter.

_____
(signature of parent or guardian)

J4₁ & J4₂: Explanation of Integrated Spelling Program

September 1994

Dear Parents,

The purpose of this letter is to introduce our spelling program to you. We support the philosophy that views spelling as an integral part of the total language arts program. We believe children develop spelling strategies through purposeful daily reading and writing. Therefore, your child will be creating personal spelling lists from daily writing, high-frequency words, and content-area words in the curriculum. Through research and our own teaching experiences, we have found that children are most interested in learning to spell words they need to use to communicate. We have also found that the more children read and write, the better they read, write, and spell.

We will emphasize three strategies in helping your child become a better speller:

- discovering and applying the rules and patterns
- proofreading
- using the dictionary and other resources

These are the same strategies adults use when trying to spell a word.

When your child asks you how to spell a word, here are some questions you can ask that may help him/her figure out the correct spelling:

Does it look right?

Can you try writing it another way?

How does the word start? How does it end?

Have you seen that word somewhere else? Can you find it for me?

What sounds do you hear?

After your child's attempts, verify the spelling by confirming the correct spelling or supplying it. Encourage your child to write the word as a whole, from memory, rather than copying it one letter at a time. Also use the attached sheet "Am I Becoming a Good Speller?", which your child has in his spelling folder, as a guide.

Keep in mind that the goal is not perfect spelling, which we as adults are still developing. The goal is to have children become more aware of spelling strategies and to be able to express themselves legibly, competently, and confidently when writing. Remember, there is no reason to learn to spell if you don't write; writing must come first.

Here are some suggested writing activities to promote writing at home:

notes to each other

greeting cards and invitations

lists for shopping, trips, gifts, parties

letters to grandparents, relatives, and friends

signs

posters

bumper stickers

recipes

songs

phone messages

post cards

puzzles
imaginative stories
jokes and riddles
cartoons
menus
map for a planned trip
diary of a trip
captions for photo pictures

We welcome your cooperation, participation, and questions concerning the spelling program. Please feel free to contact us.

Sincerely,
Elaine Weiner, second grade teacher
Linda Cooper, third grade teacher
Regie Routman, language arts resource teacher
Dr. Bernice Stokes, principal

J4₂

September 1993

Dear Families,

Your child will not be using a spelling book this year, but I will be teaching spelling! My goal is to move your child from invented spelling to conventional spelling through daily reading and writing activities and using many of the rules and patterns found in traditional spelling programs.

Each week your child will bring home 5 to 10 new words that she/he has chosen (sometimes with my help) to learn. Your child's weekly personal list is a combination of words chosen from journal entries, class themes, and high frequency words used in reading and writing. A few minutes each night will ensure success.

Please have your child bring in a name and address of a friend or relative that she would like to correspond with during the school year. This person will become your child's pen-pal.

Sincerely,

Loretta Martin

Loretta Martin

By Loretta Martin, grade 2 teacher

J5: *Parents as Allies in Children's Education*

Parents as Allies in Children's Education

"How can I help my children learn to read and write?"

Parents who ask this question can become valuable allies—all we need do is encourage them to take active roles in helping with their children's education. In particular, parents can be especially helpful in conveying to children the idea that there are good reasons for learning to read and write.

The following are some of the ideas my colleagues and I have suggested to parents in our community, ideas that they say have worked well for them and that they have enjoyed using:

1. Be a role model for reading

- Let your children see you reading different materials for different reasons and encourage them to do the same.
- Join a book club.
- Give you children books or magazine subscriptions as gifts.
- Visit the library on a regular basis.

2. Read to your children every day

- Find a quiet spot.
- Choose interesting material.
- Encourage your children to read to you, to each other and to other members of the family.

3. Provide opportunities for listening to audio tapes and for watching selected TV programs

- Encourage your children to listen to recordings by authors or storytellers.
- Make your own recordings of your children's favourite selections.
- Allow your children to select from the program guide appropriate TV programs for viewing. Their viewing time may constitute one full evening a week, or one or two programs each night. Ask for a written schedule showing times, channels and selected programs. (Make it a rule that they have to vary the times and/or channels.)

4. Provide opportunities for reading

- Collect simple recipes and allow your children time to do some cooking.
- Always leave lots of notes for your children. Place them on the fridge door or in their lunch boxes. Sometimes it's fun to leave notes about tasks and include promised rewards for tasks that are completed. An example might be: "Please clean your rooms when you get home from school. When you're finished we'll all go out to eat at the shopping centre this evening."
- Play board games that encourage reading or word play.

5. Be a Role model for writing

- Allow your children to see you writing every day for different reasons, business and pleasure.
- Be positive. Don't overemphasize errors in your children's grammar, punctuation or spelling.

6. Provide opportunities for writing

- Set up a writing corner. Have a good selection of materials available. Vary the paper (lined and unlined) by size, colour, texture and shape.
- Purchase blank books or make your own by sewing pages together. Wallpaper scraps make good covers.
- Encourage your children to share what they've written.
- Encourage your children to proofread what they've written.
- Provide an incentive for your children to write by typing out some of their writings. If possible, allow them to use a typewriter or word processor themselves.
- Encourage your children to keep a special diary for private writing where they can freely express feelings and opinions. Promise them you will respect their privacy.
- Keep a communal journal when travelling as a family so all the members can write about what they see and discover.
- Have your children assist you in writing out grocery lists. If your children come with you when you go shopping, have them check off items as you pick them out.

7. Encourage the writing of letters

- Encourage your children to write thank you notes for presents received.
- Encourage your children to write to grandparents and other relatives and friends.

8. Encourage Creativity

- Encourage your children to rewrite TV commercials—or make up new ones.
- Encourage your children to perform commercials or plays that they've written.
- Encourage your children to illustrate their writing—start a file of pictures, photos, illustrations and cartoons for your children to use in illustrating their writing. (Such a file can be a great tool in helping to motivate the reluctant writer.)

Above all, let your children know that reading and writing are meaningful activities. It's true that we learn to read and write for practical reasons, but it's also true that reading and writing are tremendous sources of enjoyment.

By Shary Rea, B. Ed. (elementary school teacher, Alberta, Canada). Reprinted by permission.

J6: Letter to Parents to Help Make Book Covers

SHAKER HEIGHTS CITY SCHOOL DISTRICT

MERCER SCHOOL
23325 Wimbledon Road
Shaker Heights, Ohio 44122
(216) 921-1400

BERNICE STOKES, Ph.D.   April 13
Principal

Dear Parents:

I am writing to you to request your help with an urgent need for the publishing program for the first and second grades. We have run out of book covers! A wonderful emergency! Our estimation is that the children in the school have used over 1500 covers since the beginning of school and most of those have been in the first and second grades. (Most book covers for the upper grades are made as part of a classroom project.)

I would like to ask for volunteers to help us with the covers. I will package for you the supplies and directions necessary to make 10 covers. All you will need to do is to provide glue and about one hour of your time. The covers can be returned in the manila envelope we send home with your supplies.

If you are interested in helping us please fill out the tear sheet below and return it to your classroom teacher.

Thank you for your help in making this important program a success.

Susan Long
Parent Volunteer Coordinator
Mercer School

- -

NAME _____

Classroom teacher _____

I will do _____ packet(s) of book covers.

Thank you.

Year of the Young Reader

J7: Request to Parents to Make Book Covers

BOOK-MAKING WORKSHOP

Wednesday, May 31
District Library Media Center
Woodbury School
9:30 A.M.—3:00 P.M.

This is a "drop in" workshop for kindergarten and first grade parents on making wallpaper book covers for the district's first grade publishing program.

Come when you can, for as long as you can, and learn the easy craft of book-cover making. We need to make hundreds of book covers to replenish our stock so that the Boulevard, Fernway, Lomond, Mercer, and Onaway Publishing Companies are ready to go next fall.

We plan to have as much fun as quilters at a quilting bee so please join us if you can.

—Marianne Sopko

J8: Communicating with Parents about the Reading-Writing Program

PARENTS NEWSLETTER

ONAWAY ELEMENTARY SCHOOL—GRADE 3

October 1993

My goals for this school year:

- to continue to promote a positive self image in each student;
- to foster a learning environment which focuses on cooperation and respect for others;
- to individualize educational approaches in order to meet your child's needs;
- to become a community of learners who communicate compassionately.

My thoughts on education:

- All learners must be respected.
- All students can learn.
- Focusing on the strengths must come first when looking at learners.
- The goal of education is independence.
- The learning process is highly valued and lifelong.
- The teacher is a facilitator and co-learner.
- Learners need to make choices and decisions about the curriculum.
- Collaboration builds communities of learners who support and learn from each other.

The Curriculum

I. COMPONENTS OF THE READING PROGRAM

A. Intensive Reading

1. Whole Class Reading
   Everyone is reading and discussing the same book. The students read in pairs, read silently, and I read to them.
2. Literature Response Groups
   Students engage in conversations about the core book in small groups. They keep a response log to respond to the book.
3. Specific Needs Groups
   Students are grouped according to specific needs, such as a strategy for reading or an enrichment book.
4. Read Aloud Daily to the Children.

B. Extensive Reading

1. WEB Program
   WEB stands for Wonderful Exciting Books. The goal of the program is to help the children become lifelong readers by providing them with quality literature and encouraging them to read. The students are required to read for at least 20 minutes each night.

They keep a record of the books they read in their WEB log. At the completion of a book, I interview the student about the book.

2. RAP

RAP stands for Reading Any Place. Each day the students and I read for 20 to 30 minutes silently. The goal of RAP is to educate their imaginations and grow as readers.

3. Reading with Younger Children

We read with a kindergarten class every Friday.

4. Literature Extension Activities

The students often do activities that extend the literature they read in reading group or that is read aloud to them daily. Some examples are:

- Readers Theatre
- Wanted Posters
- Book Sales
- Murals/Dioramas

II. COMPONENTS OF THE WRITING PROGRAM

A. Writing Workshop

The goal is to create a community in which writing matters because it's done for real reasons by real writers who ache with caring about their topic. The students write stories, research reports, letters, and class newspapers. The writing process is emphasized, including:

1. prewriting;
2. drafting;
3. revising;
4. editing;
5. publishing.

Conferencing is an important component of Writing Workshop. Each student is expected to publish at least one book per semester.

B. Poetry Workshop

The goal is to open up a world of feelings and give a voice to an experience of life. During this time we read, share and discuss poetry. We write poems using different styles of poetry in our writer's notebook. We also enjoy our "poet of the week" who reads a poem each morning to start our day.

III. SPELLING

Spelling is an integral part of the total language arts program. I believe children develop spelling strategies through purposeful daily reading and writing. Therefore, your child will be creating personal spelling lists from daily writing, high frequency words and content areas words from the curriculum.

I will emphasize three strategies in helping your child become a better speller:

1. Through discovery and application, we will identify rules and patterns.
2. We will use the skill of proofreading.
3. We will use the dictionary and other resources.

By Julie Beers, grade 3 teacher

J9: Communicating with Parents Through a Student Newspaper

Reading

In Miss Beers class we read
Stone Fox. Stone Fox is an Indian.
He won all of his races. Little Willy
just ran one race. He won $5,000.
Grandfather got better. We read
the book in reading groups. Miss
Beers put questions on the board,
and we answered the questions in
our reading log.

Article by
Joseph Simon
Jr. Editor

Hi. My name is Sarah VanAken,
your Onaway Times reporter. In
reading group we read Stone Fox.
Stone Fox was about a boy named
Little Willy and his grandfather and
how Willy fought to win the race
for the money to pay back the
taxes to keep the farm. After we
read the book, Mrs. Douglass' class
came and watched the movie with
us. After the movie we got into
groups and made a small Venn
diagram to show how the book and
the movie were the same and
different. We talked about things
only in the movie, things only in the
book, and things that were in both.
Then we put it all together and
made a big Venn diagram and that's
what we did for Stone Fox.

I.W.T. Stands for independent
work time. The teacher gave us
a folder and gave us some
sheets of paper for a homonym
book shaped like pears. Then we
write sentences. She gave us a
sheet of activities to work on too.
She gave us a poster to make. We
are drawing pictures and writing
sentences about Stone Fox.

Article by
Siquia Whitley

Reading Activity Rebat : A

* Hot Dog

Cover page, grade 3, Julie Beers's class.

J10: Letter to Parents Guiding Book Club Selection

Dear Parents,

Attached is the current Lucky Book Club order form. Lucky Book Club provides you with the opportunity to purchase good literature for your child at very reasonable prices. You are not obligated, however, to purchase anything.

If you do choose to take advantage of this opportunity, I would recommend the following books from this month's selections:

Please return the order form and your payment to school by _____. Make checks payable to Lucky Book Club.

Thanks.

Adapted from an idea developed by Nellie Edge.
For information on Book Clubs, see page 105b.

J11: Involving Parents in Evaluating Journal Writing

Dear Families,

Yes, it IS report card time again! Please read carefully the attached writing criteria which the class has developed. We discussed the characteristics of good first grade writing. The most important criteria, those that have to do with meaning, are listed first. The criteria which have to do with readability are of secondary importance and, therefore, are listed second.

Your child has brought his/her writing journal home this weekend. Please look through the journal and notice the progress he/she has made. Point out how his/her writing has improved since the beginning of first grade. Emphasize the positive. Please resist the urge to criticize.

On Monday, please return the student/adult comment sheet. Refer to the writing criteria to specifically note those elements of good first grade writing which your child is using.

Your input is very important. I appreciate this opportunity for you to celebrate your child's growth. Also, please be sure to remind your child to bring the journal back on Monday. Thank you.

Sincerely,

Peg Rimedio

What is good first grade writing? (Spring)

Developed by Room 5 students, 4/2/92

°°It makes sense.

°°The story is all about the same thing.

°°The writer is brave enough to write words the way they are said and spell them the way they sound.

°°The story tells a LOT about the subject.

°°The writer uses ALL the ideas in his/her head.

°°The writer changes the story to make it better.

°°The writing is original.

°°Ideas are written in the right order.

°° = About Meaning
    Most important

°There are spaces between words.

°The writer uses words for free.

°He/she uses some conventional spelling.

°He/she uses periods (.) at the end of sentences.

°He/she uses commas (,) to stop a little.

°He/she uses capital letters at the beginning of sentences, for names, days, and months, "I," names of states and countries, teams, etc.

°He/she skips spaces between lines.

° = About Readability
    Important

by Peg Rimedio

J12: Explanation about Spelling Development

April 26, 1994

Dear Families,

Your child has been very busy with reading, writing, and spelling this year. As a result of the numerous and varied reading and writing activities (along with instruction and study), your child's spelling has improved. As your child continues to read and write, to use spelling rules as well as the dictionary, his/her spelling will continue to improve.

Many of the students have reached a stage in their spelling development which has allowed them to learn and to apply spelling rules and strategies. The rules and strategies taught this year are beginning to make sense, although reminders and review are always in progress.

Attached is the core spelling list for the second grade and your child's latest spelling check. Those words missed have become the primary focus for your child's individual list for the remainder of the year. If all or only a few words are misspelled, your child will continue to pull words for his/her journal and theme words. If your child is an excellent speller, he/she will continue to receive instruction revolving around spelling rules and strategies and dictionary skills based on the child's needs.

Please use the list to reinforce your child's spelling progress. A few minutes each night will aid classroom instruction.

Thank you,

Loretta Martin

Loretta Martin

by Loretta Martin, grade 2 teacher

Appendix K: Do Nothing to Destroy the Joy

Do Nothing to Destroy the Joy

How often have you heard someone say, "Yes, I use literature in my classroom. I DO Whole Language"? But, the reality is that Whole Language is not just having a classroom full of books and it is not something we "do." Whole Language is not a method or a set collection of ideas and activities. It is a mindset . . . a philosophy of teaching; a belief system about how children learn. It is, among other things, a belief that learning is easiest when it is from whole to part, when it is in authentic contexts, and when it is purposeful for the learner . . . Whole Language is not static; it is a definition in process. It is a label for mutually supportive ideologies and conventions. Whole Language "thrives on the principle that literacy tasks should never be ends unto themselves; instead they should be means to other ends, such as learning, enjoyment, persuasion, and communication" (Pearson, 1989). And so, when teachers employ literature in their classrooms and believe themselves to be "Whole Language teachers," they give consideration to these tenets.

Upon entering a classroom, what is it that allows one to distinguish a Whole Language classroom from a more traditional environment? At first glance it may seem that the activity being carried out in both rooms is very similar . . . there are several books; children are reading to themselves or the teacher is reading to them. But, in reality, it is only on this very superficial level, like leaving the lid on the cookie jar or the envelope on the letter, that the resemblance exists. When one ventures further to remove the lid or the envelope and take a closer look within the children's environments, there are certain common characteristics to the activities that one sees in a Whole Language classroom which are often lacking in more traditional settings. Activities relating to literature in Whole Language classrooms are authentic learning experiences which focus on exploring, problem solving and questioning . . . they are not isolated skills taught out of context. Activities are meaningful to the learner as the child finds himself/herself engaged in purposeful learning; learning in which the child takes an active part and builds upon his/her prior experiences to make sense of the world. In a Whole Language classroom, children are allowed to make choices and encouraged to become risk takers.

If a teacher is reading to his children just to fill in time at the end of the day and leaves no time for reflection or discussion . . . that's not Whole Language. Or if there is time for discussion and the only questions the teacher asks are efferent whereby the teacher is simply pulling information from the text . . . the who, the what, the where . . . forgetting to include the aesthetic aspect . . . how did you feel? how did you think? why? that's not Whole Language. If the teacher plans a worksheet on critical thinking as a follow-up activity to a story that the children have read or listened to . . . that's not Whole Language. (Indeed, it is instead a contradiction to the words "critical thinking" themselves.) If a teacher has a list of words taken from the story that he expects the children to recite and memorize before he introduces them to the story . . . that's not Whole Language either. Yes, this teacher is using literature in his classroom but the activities designed around the literature have been contrived and elude an air of basalization.

I have heard Yvonne Siu-Runyan say, "How sad it would be if our students groaned when we presented literature to them because we didn't know how to use it effectively." A prime example of stabbing literature though the heart to let it die a quick death occurred in our own family.

My daughter, in grade 8, was presented with a new novel to read over the weekend. Her assignment was not to read the novel and reflect upon its power and beauty, nor was it to relate to a particular character or to question and wonder about some of the events which took place but instead it was as follows: "Read the entire 146 pages. While you are reading make a list of 100 words that you don't know the meaning of. Find the meanings in your dictionary." Needless to say, she hated the novel before she even began to read it . . . the enchantment that good literature brings was lost before it was even given a chance. Instead of sighing because the words before her elicited a deeply felt pleasure, she sighed in disgust and despair. Yes, my daughter, being the studious and conscientious young lady that she is, listed 100 words (she said that she knew what most of them meant anyway but she NEEDED 100 words) and returned to class on Monday mumbling under her breath about "the stupid book" she had to read. As the assignment was so arduous, many of her classmates had not completed it, and so the teacher decided to give them class time to work at it. My daughter's reward for having completed this bastardization of literature was to find 25 more words! I ask you, what would have been so sinful about reading the book for reading's sake! What would have been so wrong with happiness or laughter or fright or sadness as an outcome of reading this novel? This was NOT Whole Language!

But, on the other hand, if you enter a classroom and the teacher is reading a book to the children and you can sense by the tone of the teacher's voice and by the way he/she engages himself/herself in the print and helps the children interact with the text, that the literature yields a satisfaction that is true and lasting . . . this IS Whole Language. If before or during the reading the teacher gives the children opportunities to take risks by asking predictions, if he/she stops to ask, "How did that make you feel?", if the teacher helps children make sense of their world by helping see similarities to their own lives . . . this IS Whole Language. If after reading several of Mem Fox's books and expressing interest about the animals of Australia, these children engage in research and map reading . . . this IS Whole Language.

Dorothy Menosky in her wisdom says, "Do nothing that will destroy the joy!" How many teachers feel that as long as they are using literature vs. basal readers, they are "doing" Whole Language and profess to be "Whole Language teachers"? But nothing can be further from the truth. We must always be asking ourselves whether the activities our children engage in, in relation to literature, are purposeful and authentic. Are they functional? Do they encourage risk-taking? Do we, through our use of literature in the classroom invite children inside the cover of another book and another and another? We, as Whole Language teachers, must remember to tread softly so as not to "destroy the joy."

by Peterette M. Dolyniuk
Language Development Teacher
River East School Division #9
Winnipeg, Manitoba
Canada
Reprinted with permission of the author.

Pearson, P. David. 1989. "Commentary . . . Reading the Whole Language Movement." *Elementary School Journal* 90(2).

Appendix L: Questions to Think About in Choosing a Writing Topic

What do I keep thinking about?

What do I know a lot about?

What do I know how to do really well?

What is important to me?

What do I want to find out more about?

Who or what do I care a lot about?

Who is someone important to me that I want to write about?

What do I like to do?

What was an important time in my life?

If I think back to an earlier time, what do I remember?

What am I worried about?

What am I happy about?

What am I angry about?

Inspired by *Shoptalk* by Donald Murray, pages 79–80. Heinemann, 1990.

Appendix M: Teachers' Self Evaluation Observations About the Student as a Reader/Writer

M1: Observations About the Student as a Reader

- Chooses to read;
- Selects appropriate reading materials;
- Reads a variety of genres;
- Uses a variety of strategies to make sense of print:
    prediction
    semantics (sentence sense, pictures)
    syntax (grammar, punctuation, paragraphing)
    phonics
    self-correction
    prior knowledge
- Reads with fluency;
- Understands text;
- Actively participates in literature discussion groups:
    makes thoughtful comments
    listens attentively
    responds to peers
- Responds to literature:
    shares reading
    writes effective responses to literature
    completes literature-related activities
    keeps record of reading
- Requests appropriate help as needed;
- Utilizes resources;
- Puts forth best effort

M2: *Observations About the Student as a Writer*

- Chooses to write;
- Selects own writing topics;
- Writes in a variety of genres;
- Uses a variety of strategies to create meaningful writing:
    adherence to topic
    appropriate and interesting vocabulary
    logical development
    description and detail
    sentence and paragraph sense
    punctuation and capitalization
    standard spelling of high frequency words
    appropriate invented spelling
    awareness of audience
- Actively participates in writing conferences:
    listens attentively
    makes meaningful comments to peers
    considers suggestions for own writing
- Willing and able to revise writing;
- Proofreads and edits for meaning, mechanics, and spelling;
- Requests appropriate help as needed;
- Utilizes resources;
- Shares writing;
- Puts forth best effort

Appendix N: Self-Evaluation Forms

N1: Self-Evaluation: Reading

Name _____ Grade _____ Date _____

What is your favorite book that you've read?

Why is it your favorite?

How have you changed as a reader?

What do you want to do better as a reader?

N2: Self-Evaluation: Journal Writing

Name _____ Grade _____ Date _____

What is your best journal entry?

Why is it your best?

What are you doing now as a writer that you weren't doing before?

What do you want to do better as a writer?

N3: Self Evaluation: Literature Discussion

Self-Evaluation

_____ Discussion Group

Name _____   Date _____

Book/Topic _____

1. What did I do well today (and/or improve on) during group discussion?

2. What do I still need to improve on during group discussion?

N4: Self-Evaluation Form for Any Grade or Area

Name _____

Date _____

Subject _____

What I can do well	What I find hard

What I am doing better	What I am going to work on next

N5: Ways to Involve Students in Self-Evaluation

- Interviews/Attitude surveys
- Conferences
- Audiotapes
- Reflection logs
- Editing earlier writing samples
- Noting difficult words and questions when reading
- Rating books
- Self-evaluation forms
    literature discussion
    behavior
    group work
    academic areas
    strengths, weaknesses, goal setting
- Making choices
    books
    writing topics
    projects
- Rubrics
- Report cards
- Selecting work for portfolios

N6: Weekly Self-Evaluation

Weekly Evaluation

Name _____   Date _____

This week I learned

What was most important to me this week was

I did very well

I am confused about

I want to work on

Student signature _____

Teacher signature _____

Parent signature _____

N7: A Self-Evaluation Checklist for Teachers

Am I reading literature aloud to students every day?

Am I providing time and choice daily for students to read and write on self-selected books and topics?

Am I noticing and commenting on what students are doing well and are able to do?

Are students in my class excited about learning?

Am I a happy and effective reading and writing model for my students?

Am I taking the time to demonstrate and not just assigning?

Are my questions allowing for varied responses and interpretations?

Am I equally respectful of all students regardless of culture and background?

Are my expectations high for all students?

Do students know and understand how they will be evaluated or graded?

Are my responses to students, both orally and in writing, specific and helpful?

Am I using the "red pencil" sparingly, or not at all?

Are children in my classroom feeling successful, regardless of their abilities?

Do I provide regular opportunities for students to share and collaborate?

Is the work students are doing meaningful and purposeful?

Am I encouraging students to solve their own problems and take ownership of their learning?

Am I providing opportunities for students to reflect on their progress?

Are my evaluation procedures consistent with my philosophy and my teaching?

Am I communicating effectively with parents and administrators?

Appendix O:
Approaches to
Teaching Reading

Meaning-Centered Approach

Skills Approach

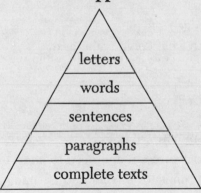

Appendix P:
Reading
Strategies for
Unknown Words

- Skip the difficult word.
  Read on to end of sentence or paragraph.
  Go back to the beginning of the sentence and try again.
- Read on. Reread inserting the beginning sound of the unknown word.
- Substitute a word that makes sense.
- Look for a known chunk or small word.
  Use finger to cover part of word.
- Read the word using only beginning and ending sounds.
  Read the word without the vowels.
- Look for picture cues.
- Link to prior knowledge.
- Predict and anticipate what could come next.
- Cross check.
  "Does it sound right?"
  "Does it make sense?"
  "Does it look right?"
- Self-correct and self-monitor.
- Write words you can't figure out and need to know on Post-Its.
- Read passage several times for fluency and meaning.

Use errors as an opportunity to problem solve.

by Regie Routman

Appendix Q: Authentic Assessment: Some Examples

- interviews/surveys
- anecdotal records
- reading records
- literature response logs
- journals
- learning logs
- self-evaluations
- writing samples
- audiotapes
- videotapes
- projects
- running records
- retellings

Index